MASKS MIMES AND
MIRACLES

By the Same Author

THE DEVELOPMENT OF THE THEATRE
A STUDY OF THEATRICAL ART FROM THE BEGINNINGS TO THE PRESENT DAY
With 271 illustrations in half-tone and line. Demy 4to, 248 pages.

BRITISH DRAMA
AN HISTORICAL SURVEY FROM THE BEGINNINGS TO THE PRESENT DAY
With 16 illustrations in half-tone and photogravure frontispiece.   Demy 8vo, 502 pages.

READINGS FROM BRITISH DRAMA
EXTRACTS FROM BRITISH AND IRISH PLAYS
Demy 8vo, 440 pages.

THE THEORY OF DRAMA
Demy 8vo, 262 pages.

A SCENE FROM A MIME IN THE SIXTH CENTURY

Ivory diptych of Anastasius, A.D. 517, now in the Victoria and Albert Museum (Inv. 368-1871). The upper illustration is a photograph of the relevant portion of the diptych as it exists to-day; the lower illustration shows it as it was before being broken. The latter is taken from A. Wilthemius, *Diptychon Leodiense ex consulari factum episcopale et in illud commentarius* (Lüttich, 1659); the former is a photograph by the Victoria and Albert Museum.

MASKS MIMES AND MIRACLES

STUDIES IN THE POPULAR THEATRE

BY

ALLARDYCE NICOLL M.A.

PROFESSOR OF ENGLISH LANGUAGE AND LITERATURE IN THE
UNIVERSITY OF LONDON
AUTHOR OF " THE DEVELOPMENT OF THE THEATRE " " BRITISH DRAMA "
" THE THEORY OF DRAMA " ETC.

WITH TWO HUNDRED AND TWENTY-SIX
ILLUSTRATIONS

COOPER SQUARE PUBLISHERS, INC.   •   NEW YORK

1963

PREFACE

THIS book is not intended to be a work of 'scholarship.' It aims at appealing to all interested in the theatre—not merely to those whose profession is scholarly research; and, while every endeavour has been made to render it as accurate and as comprehensive as possible, it does not profess to deal in exhaustive detail with any of the special aspects of its theme. The sub-title, *Studies in the Popular Theatre*, indicates its general scope. The subject, of course, has not remained entirely neglected in the past. Apart from writers of essays and books on individual problems and selected periods, such authors as Magnin in France and Dieterich and Reich in Germany have devoted wide surveys, not indeed to the whole of the field, but at any rate to considerable portions of it. A re-surveying of the extant materials and an attempt to provide a kind of perspective arrangement of the various items of evidence seemed, however, to be demanded for several reasons. In the first place, there is no work in English which essays in any way to deal with the subject, although this consideration in itself appears of minor importance compared with the others. Relatively little use has hitherto been made of the exceedingly important pictorial evidence provided by almost all the centuries covered in this book. Sporadic efforts, it is true, have been made in this direction, and many of the relevant illustrations have been collected for the classical and for the Renascent epochs respectively; but neither have all the most important documents in this kind been so utilized nor has any examination been devoted to these in their entirety, from the earliest pre-Periclean times to the seventeenth century. Apart from this, there does not seem to be any one work which definitely carries the survey (even without the assistance of pictorial evidence) from ancient Megara through medieval Rome to Renascent Mantua. Reich's valuable contribution, to which every writer on this subject must be deeply indebted, is devoted almost exclusively to the classical period and to that which immediately followed; Dieterich confines himself to a few special problems; and recent writers on the *commedia dell' arte* have been more eager to affirm or to deny classical influence, without fully investigating the subject, than to consider the problems impartially and at length.

The *commedia dell' arte* is that portion of the whole theme to the knowledge of which the most important additions have been made in recent years. The discovery of various collections of scenarii, the finding of fresh pictorial evidence, and the results of many other researches in Italian archives have given an entirely new orientation to our study of the improvising players and of their art. A history of the *commedia dell' arte*, of course, was far beyond the scope of this volume, and no suggestion of such is intended here. On the other hand, since there does not at present exist, even in Italian, a truly comprehensive survey of this theatrical type in which all the recent researches are used, and since the *commedia dell' arte* throws considerable light by analogy on earlier forms assumed by the popular theatre, it seemed necessary to cover the ground here in summary form. We still await both the exact and scholarly history of the improvised comedy and the critical study of its influence on English drama of the seventeenth century; such works would, of course, discuss in detail much that is here hurried over, and would stress certain aspects of which it was not within the scope of this book to treat. No doubt, too, a still further sifting of Italian archives would necessitate the reframing of theories concerning some of the companies and many of the individual players. All that was possible here was the utilization of as much of the recent contributions to the subject as could be obtained. While full reference is made to these, and while the results of such researches, where practicable, have been incorporated in the text, it must be emphasized that this book has not been written as a study of the Italian comedy, but is designed to investigate, in broad outline, the development of a certain popular dramatic tradition which seems to reach its culmination among the companies of Italian actors in the sixteenth and seventeenth centuries. The slightly greater space allotted to that comedy is due simply to the fact that for this period the records are richer and often more illuminating; by their aid we may form a mental picture of the organization of the troupes and of their art, and from these we may pass to shape for ourselves more concrete images of the similar theatrical organizations of earlier classical times. To this section on the *commedia dell' arte* has been added an appendix, manifestly summary in execution and not exhaustive. Its inclusion seemed to be rendered necessary because of the fact that, while lists of the titles of plays by classical mimographs such as Epicharmus, Pomponius, and Novius are easily come by in standard works of reference, no such work exists giving in convenient form the kindred information concerning the collections of scenarii and their contents. A full and detailed list of these scenarii, indicating the relationships of the various texts, is certainly much to be desired. It will be understood that the brief list of titles presented here is intended in no wise to take the place of such a *catalogue raisonné*, but is inserted merely for convenience, in order that an indication may be provided at least of the typical subject-matter of the improvised comedy, and that comparison may be made between it and the subject-matter indicated by titles and extant records or fragments of classical mimic drama.

Since this book was designed to appeal to the general reader as well as to those particularly interested in earlier theatrical history, the authorities quoted have for the most part been presented in translation, although generally the original has been added in a footnote. There are a few exceptions to this practice where translation would have meant loss of significance in the passages referred to.

In closing the preface I should wish to thank all those who have kindly given me permission to make use of pictorial material; indication of my indebtedness in this respect is provided below the various illustrations. My thanks are due also to the officials of the British Museum, the Victoria and Albert Museum, and the London Library, from whom I have received much assistance, as well as to those of many French, Austrian, and Italian libraries and museums, in particular the Musée du Grand Opéra, the Bibliothèque Nationale, and the Bibliothèque Sainte-Geneviève in Paris, the Studien-Bibliotek at Salzburg, the Kunsthistorisches Museum in Vienna, and the library of the Museo Civico in Venice. Professor Brunner, of Innsbruck, gave me much help in collecting some material in the Ferdinandeum; Professor V. N. Peretz courteously sent me from Russia a copy of his reprint of early Russian scenarii, published in Petrograd in 1917 and apparently unobtainable in this country; with great kindness my colleagues Mr J. R. Mozley and Professor Ernesto Grillo read the proofs of this volume. To all I extend my heartiest thanks for their assistance and helpful suggestions.

A. N.

EAST LONDON COLLEGE
June 1931

CONTENTS

PAGE

I. THE MIMES

(i) INTRODUCTORY
Secularism, Paganism, and Christianity, p. 18.
17

(ii) THE DORIAN MIME
The Comic Figures and their Costumes, p. 20. Mythological Burlesque and other Themes, p. 25. The Characters, p. 27. Animal Masks, p. 30. Dance and Song, p. 32. Acrobats and Jugglers, p. 35.
20

(iii) EPICHARMUS AND THE GREEK MIME
Epicharmus, p. 38. Herodas, p. 41. Theocritus and Sophron, p. 44. The Erotic Fragment, p. 45. An Athenian Terra-cotta, p. 46. The Mimic Fool, p. 47.
38

(iv) THE PHLYAKES
Rhinthon and Mythological Burlesque, p. 50. Herakles and Odysseus, p. 51. Zeus and other Mythological Figures, p. 54. Scenes of Daily Life, p. 58. The Typical Masks, p. 60. The Phlyax Stage, p. 63.
50

(v) THE ATELLANÆ
Origin and Style, p. 66. L. Pomponius Bononiensis and Novius, p. 68. The Stock Masks : (a) Bucco, p. 69 ; (b) Dossennus-Manducus, p. 70 ; (c) Maccus, p. 72 ; (d) Pappus, p. 73 ; (e) Cicirrus, p. 74. Connexions with the Mime, p. 75. Summary, p. 78.
65

II. THE HEYDAY OF MIMIC DRAMA

(i) THE NATURE OF THE MIME
Definitions of the Mime, p. 80.
80

(ii) THE MIMIC ACTORS
Terminology, p. 83. The Acrobats and Jugglers, p. 84. The Companies, p. 85. The Arch-mime and the Mimic Fool, p. 87. Costumes and Masks, p. 90. The Mimic Actress, p. 92. Individual Actors and Actresses, p. 94. The Methods of Performance, p. 99.
82

(iii) THE MIMIC PLAYS
Roman Mime-writers, p. 110. The Oxyrhynchus Mimes, p. 115. Adultery Mimes, p. 119. Christian Mimes and Others, p. 120. Mimic Obscenity, p. 123. Mimic Satire, p. 124. The Mimic Style, p. 126.
110

(iv) THE DECAY OF THE MIMIC DRAMA
129

(v) THE PANTOMIME
131

III. THE FATE OF THE MIMES IN THE DARK AGES

(i) THE TRACKS OF THE MIMES
The Church Councils and other Records, p. 136.
135

(ii) THE SECULAR DRAMA OF THE MIDDLE AGES
The Joculatores or Jongleurs, p. 151. The Terence Codices, p. 153. Dramatic Activities of the Jongleurs, p. 157. The Medieval Fool, p. 160. Records of the Mimi, p. 164. The " Elegiac Comedies," p. 169. Farces and Interludes, p. 171.
150

(iii) THE RELIGIOUS DRAMA OF THE MIDDLE AGES
Theories regarding the Medieval Religious Drama, p. 176. The Mystery Cycles, p. 178. The Comic Scenes, p. 179. The Medieval Devils, p. 187. The Actors, p. 192. The Medieval Stages, p. 194. The Mansions, p. 203. Scenic Effects, p. 206. Medieval Ideas of the Classical Stage, p. 208. The Drama in Byzantium, p. 209.
175

9

MASKS MIMES AND MIRACLES

PAGE

IV. THE COMMEDIA DELL' ARTE

(i) INTRODUCTORY 214

Theories regarding the Origin, *p.* 214.   The Meaning of the Term, *p.* 215.   *Uscite* and *Chiusette*, *p.* 218.   The *Lazzi*, *p.* 219.   The Mountebanks, *p.* 221.

(ii) THE SCENARIO 225

The Types of Scenarii, *p.* 227.   The Value of the Scenarii, *p.* 230.

(iii) THE STOCK TYPES : (1) THE ' SERIOUS ' PERSONS 233

The Innamorato, *p.* 234.   The Innamorata, *p.* 236.   The Servant-maid, or Fantesca, *p.* 242.

(iv) THE STOCK TYPES : (2) THE CAPITANO 246

(v) THE STOCK TYPES : (3) THE OLD MEN 253

Pantalone, *p.* 253.   The Dottore, *p.* 256.   Pasquariello, *p.* 260.   Cola, Cassandro, and Coviello, *p.* 261.

(vi) THE STOCK TYPES : (4) THE ZANNI 263

The Origin and Significance of the Word ' Zanni,' *p.* 263.   Arlecchino, *p.* 267.

(vii) THE STOCK TYPES : (5) BRIGHELLA, SCAPINO, MEZZETINO, AND SCARAMUCCIA 282

Brighella, *p.* 282.   Scapino, *p.* 285.   Mescolino and Mezzetino, *p.* 285.   Scaramuccia, *p.* 287.

(viii) THE STOCK TYPES : (6) PULCINELLA, PEDROLINO, AND OTHER ZANNI 290

Pulcinella, *p.* 290.   Pedrolino, *p.* 294.   Other Zanni, *p.* 295.

(ix) THE COMPANIES : (1) THE EARLY TROUPES 298

André, or Andrea, and Marcantonio, *p.* 299.   Soldino and Anton Maria, *p.* 300.   The Troupe of Alberto Ganassa, *p.* 301.

(x) THE COMPANIES : (2) THE GELOSI AND GELOSI-UNITI 303

(xi) THE COMPANIES : (3) THE CONFIDENTI 315

(xii) THE COMPANIES : (4) THE DESIOSI AND THE ACCESI 322

The Desiosi, *p.* 322.   The Accesi, *p.* 322.

(xiii) THE COMPANIES : (5) THE FEDELI 327

(xiv) THE COMPANIES : (6) THE LATER MANTUAN TROUPES AND THE TROUPES OF PARMA AND MODENA 335

(xv) THE COMPANIES : (7) THE ITALIAN COMEDIANS IN FRANCE 342

(xvi) CONCLUSION 346

APPENDIX : THE COMMEDIA DELL' ARTE 351

I. THE PARTS 351

II. THE ACTORS 359

III. THE SCENARII 377

INDEX 391

ILLUSTRATIONS

FIG.   PAGE

A Scene from a Mime in the Sixth Century   *Frontispiece*

1. Acrobats in Ancient Egypt   17
2. A Roman Mask representing an Old Man, and a Comic Mime Actor   19
3. A Dorian Mime Scene   21
4. A Dorian Mime Scene   21
5. The Return of Hephæstus to Olympus   22
6. Two Attic Comedians   22
7. A Comic Actor   23
8. Comic Actors preparing for their Parts   23
9. The Broth-makers   24
10. An Old Man and his Slave   25
11. Mask of an Old Woman   28
12. Mask of an Old Woman   28
13. Maison, the Megarean Cook   29
14. Mask of the Leading Slave   29
15. Set of Masks: Old Man, Fair Youth, Youth with Curly Hair, and Leading Slave   30
16. Actor with Peaked Beard   30
17. Processional Chorus of Mimic Animals   31
18. Processional Chorus of Mimic Horses   31
19. Animal-masked Actors in Athens   32
20. Bird-masked Actors in Athens   33
21. An Actor with the Head of a Rat   33
22. An Actor with an Animal Head   33
23. Mimic Dancers   34
24. Greek Acrobatic Dancer   35
25. An Ancient Acrobat   36
26. Acrobatic Dancer   37
27. Œdipus and the Sphinx   40
28. A Greek Mimic Actor   43
29. A Mimic Fool   45
30. Mimic Players at Athens   47
31. Mimic Fools   47
32. A Mimic Fool   48
33. A Mimic Fool   48

FIG.   PAGE

34. Mimic Fools — 48
35. A Mimic Fool — 49
36. A Mimic Fool — 49
37. Mask of the Bald-headed Fool — 49
38. Herakles and a Woman — 52
39. Herakles before Zeus — 52
40. Herakles and Apollo — 53
41. Odysseus and the Palladion — 54
42. Odysseus struggling for a Woman — 54
43. Zeus receiving a Visit — 55
44. The Birth of Helena — 55
45. Zeus visiting Alcmena — 56
46. Zeus visiting Alcmena — 57
47. The Death of Priam — 57
48. Hephæstus and Hera — 57
49. A Drunken Actor before Dionysus — 58
50. Cheiron and his Companions — 58
51. A Good Feast — 59
52. The Treasure Chest — 59
53. The Return from the Revel — 60
54. The Settling of the Rent — 60
55. Statuette of a Comic Actor — 61
56. A Phlyax Slave — 61
57. Preparations for a Feast — 62
58. A Comic Mask — 62
59. A Phlyax Fool — 63
60. A Mimic Fool — 63
61. Side-view of a Phlyax Slave — 64
62. Two Phlyax Clowns — 64
63. Herakles and Eurystheus — 65
64. A Phlyax Slave — 66
65. Bucco — 69
66. Manducus-Dossennus — 70
67. Manducus-Dossennus — 70
68, 69. Manducus-Dossennus or a Similar Type — 71
70. Maccus — 72
71. A Roman Comic Actor — 72
72. Pappus — 73
73. Pappus — 73
74. Pappus — 74

ILLUSTRATIONS

FIG.		PAGE
75.	Cock-crested Actors	74
76.	A Mime Scene, showing an Actor with an Ass's Head	75
77.	A Mime Actor	79
78.	The Mimus Calvus	82
79.	Circus Shows in the Third Century	86
80.	A Mimic Fool	88
81.	A Mimic Fool	88
82.	Hunchback and Fool	89
83.	"Divertimenti per li Regazzi," by D. Tiepolo	89
84.	The Small Comic Theatre at Pompeii	100
85.	The Tragic Theatre at Pompeii	100
86.	The Remodelled Greek Theatre at Segesta, Sicily	101
87.	The Stage Buildings of the Theatre at Taormina, Sicily	102
88.	The Geeek Theatre at Taormina, Sicily	103
89.	The Stage Buildings of the Theatre at Taormina, Sicily	104
90.	A Roman Frons Scænæ	105
91.	A Commedia dell' Arte Stage	107
92.	The Arena at Verona	108
93.	The Private Stage in the Casa degli Amorini Dorati at Pompeii	109
94.	Head of a Mimic Actor	109
95.	A Roman Comic Actor	128
96.	A Bald-headed Roman Comic Actor	130
97.	A Pantomimic Actor with his Masks	132
98.	A Roman Mask, probably of a Pantomimic Actor	134
99.	The Diptych of Anastasius, A.D. 517	143
100.	The Diptych of St Étienne of Bourges	144
101.	Medieval Actors	150
102.	Medieval Mimes	154
103.	Medieval Mimes	155
104.	A Scene from Terence	156
105.	A Scene from Terence's "Andria" (I, v)	156
106.	A Scene from Seneca's "Hercules furens"	157
107.	Eastern Mimi of the Middle Ages	159
108.	A Medieval Fool	161
109.	Medieval Fools	161
110.	Dancing Entertainers of the Middle Ages	162
111.	Dancing Entertainers of the Middle Ages	162
112.	Dancing Entertainers of the Middle Ages	162
113.	Dancing Entertainers of the Middle Ages	163
114.	Medieval Fools	164

FIG.

115. ANIMAL MASKS IN THE MIDDLE AGES
116. MEDIEVAL TUMBLERS
117. A PERFORMING BEAR IN THE MIDDLE AGES
118. PERFORMING HORSES IN THE MIDDLE AGES
119. PERFORMING MONKEYS IN THE MIDDLE AGES
120. TWELFTH-CENTURY PUPPETS
121. TWO MEDIEVAL PUPPET-SHOWS, OR PAGEANTS
122. THE SHEPHERDS OFFERING THEIR GIFTS
123. THE ADDER WITH A MAIDEN'S FACE
124. BELIAL
125. SEILENOS
126. THE DEVIL ASTAROTH
127. AN EARLY DEVIL'S COSTUME
128. A DEVIL'S MASK
129. DEVIL BELL
130. MEDIEVAL DEVILS' MASKS
131. THE VALENCIENNES MYSTERY PLAY
132. THE MARTYRDOM OF ST APOLLINE
133. PLANS OF THE MANSIONS IN (1) THE VALENCIENNES MYSTERY PLAY, (2) "ST APOLLINE," AND (3) "ST VINCENT"
134. PLAN OF THE MANSIONS IN THE EARLY FRENCH "RESURRECTION"
135. PLAN OF THE DONAUESCHINGEN PLAY
136. PLAN OF THE LUCERNE EASTER PLAY: SECOND DAY
137. RECONSTRUCTED SETTING OF RUOF'S WEINGARTENSPIEL
138. PLANS OF THE MANSIONS USED IN GERMAN MYSTERY PLAYS
139. THE ROUND, OR PLAN-AN-GUARE, AT PERRAN, CORNWALL
140. PLAN OF THE MANSIONS USED IN THE THREE PARTS OF THE "ORIGO MUNDI" IN CORNWALL
141. PLAN OF THE MANSIONS IN "ST MERIASEK" (FIRST DAY'S PLAY)
142. PLAN OF THE MANSIONS IN "THE CASTLE OF PERSEVERANCE"
143. "THE CONCEPTION" AS GIVEN AT VALENCIENNES
144. SCENE FROM "LA VENGEANCE DE NOTRE SEIGNEUR"
145. BELIAL AND THE DRAGON'S MOUTH
146. A MYSTERY PLAY AT BYZANTIUM
147. HERAKLES IN TURKEY
148. AN OPEN-AIR PERFORMANCE IN VENICE
149. MOUNTEBANKS IN THE PIAZZA SAN MARCO, VENICE
150. A FRENCH CHARLATAN STAGE, WITH THE FIGURES OF POLICHINELLE AND BRIGANTIN
151. PANTALONE AND ZANNI
152. THE INNAMORATO

ILLUSTRATIONS

FIG.		PAGE
153.	MEDAL STRUCK IN HONOUR OF ISABELLA ANDREINI	237
154.	ISABELLA ANDREINI	238
155.	ISABELLA ANDREINI AND HER TROUPE	239
156.	RICIULINA AND METZETIN (MEZZETINO)	243
157.	FRANCISCHINA AND GIAN FARINA	243
158.	FRANCISQUINA AND SIGNOR LEANDRO	244
159.	ARLECCHINA	244
160.	SMERALDINA	245
161.	THE CAPITANO, 1601	246
162.	THE CAPITANO	247
163.	CAPITAN SPACAMONTE AND GILLE LE NIAIS	248
164.	CAPITAINE FRACASSE, TURLUPIN, GROS GUILLAUME, AND GAULTIER GARGUILLE	249
165.	CAPITAN COCODRILLO	251
166.	CAPITAN MALA GAMBA AND CAPITAN BELLAVITA	252
167.	THE CAPITANO	252
168.	PANTALONE	253
169.	PANTALONE JEALOUS	254
170.	PANTALONE, THE COURTESAN, AND ZANNI	254
171.	PANTALONE, DOTTORE, AND ARLECCHINO	255
172.	PANTALONE	256
173.	A PUPPET FIGURE OF PANTALONE	256
174.	THE DOTTORE	259
175.	DOTTOR BALANZONI	259
176.	ANIELLO SOLDANO AS DOTTOR SPACCA STRUMMOLO	259
177.	BRINQUENAZILLE, FRANCATRIPPE, SCAPPIN, AND PASQUARIELLE	260
178.	COVIELLO SINGING	261
179.	EIGHTEENTH-CENTURY PUPPET-SHOW	262
180.	A COMMEDIA DELL' ARTE SCENE	264
181.	ZANNI	265
182.	LEATHER MASK OF A ZANNI	266
183.	LEATHER MASK OF A ZANNI	266
184.	COMMEDIA DELL' ARTE TYPES, 1572	270
185.	ARLECCHINO, 1601	271
186.	HARLEQUIN AND HORACIO, OR ORAZIO	272
187.	HARLEQUIN, ZANY CORNETO, AND PANTALON	272
188.	CHINA FIGURES REPRESENTING COMMEDIA DELL' ARTE CHARACTERS	273
189.	ARLEQUIN	274
190.	ARLECCHINO	274
191.	A PUPPET ARLECCHINO	274
192.	MARIONETTE THEATRE WITH FIGURES OF THE COMMEDIA DELL' ARTE	275

Still Philemon remained obdurate.

For a time confusion reigned. The poor deacon was hurriedly dragged into the presence of the prefect and asked why he had not selected some other man for whom nobody cared, and not this mime who was manifestly the joy of the whole city (*istum civitatis manifestam lætitiam*). So the storm raged, until at last, with heavy heart, Arianus ordered the persecution to begin. Three attendants started to lash the mime with whips, but when the people saw this being done they set up a great clamour and cried, " Do not kill our beloved one " (" *Noli cædere carum nostrum* "). Once more Arianus addressed himself to Philemon. " O Philemon," he cried, " spare yourself and make the offering. Look at the people, how grieved they are at the very thought of your death ! Consider how much greater will be their grief when they see you on the cross of torment. You will be the cause of universal lamentation. Hitherto perhaps you did not imagine yourself so beloved by the citizens, but now, thanks to the gods, you have a proof of that devotion you did not realize before. Gratify your friends now and make the offering. By doing so you will recall to these good folks, who have suffered so much to see you suffer, joy and merriment at this great festival which is approaching. Nay, if you recant I myself with all my court will go at once to the baths in honour of the occasion."

None of these words could move Philemon. Gravely he replied, " Good people of Antinoe, be not distressed at the blows I have received. I doubt not ye remember the time when I was a mime—how to my shame in the theatre blows were rained on me by my fellow-actors. You laughed at those comic blows then, but the angels wept. Now, therefore, it is just that your tears should not weigh against the joy which the angels feel at my salvation."

No further argument could be fruitful, and Philemon went joyously to his death, while the citizens of Antinoe mourned over him as if he had been a famous emperor. His constancy had made him a saint of the Catholic Church.[1]

Secularism, Paganism, and Christianity

This story of St Philemon, true or not, has more than an ephemeral significance. In many ways it is broadly symbolic, for it brings into close material connexion three of the most potent elements in the history of European civilization. Arianus stands for paganism, for belief in those old gods whose divine forms clothed in corporal raiment were born in ancient Greece. The deacon and the transformed Philemon stand for the force of Christianity, while the mimes themselves (typified in the earlier, joyous, care-free Philemon) represent a power and an ideal separate from both. That power and that ideal may be called secularism, the glad acceptance of life's brightness, the amused and untroubled realization that this world is nothing but a jest. Very definitely secular were the mimes in spirit. They based their work on life itself, and never looked beyond ; they ridiculed the legends of the old gods just as later they ridiculed the Christian rites ; but, as representing the force of secularism, they fared under Christianity far differently from the way in which they fared under paganism. The pagan spirit subordinated fanaticism and spiritual questing to ease and culture and beauty on this earth. A Venus Genetrix, even an Aphrodite Urania, brought to men no ideal beyond what could be realized in this life. With this spirit that of the mimes harmonized. Those who believed in the pagan gods could still laugh when these gods were reduced to ridiculous terms upon the stage. When, however, Christianity came to capture Western Europe a new mood entered in. Something of Oriental fervour, something of a severer gravity, drove the culture and the beauty and the ease away, so that the laughter of the mimes became ever

---

[1] This account of Philemon's death is based on the record of his martyrdom as given in Bollandus, *Acta Sanctorum* (Paris and Rome, 1856; March, vii, 751–754). See Hermann Reich, *Der Mimus : Ein litterar-entwickelungsgeschichtlicher Versuch* (Berlin, 1903), i, 85, 179–181.

fainter and more timorous. Christ on the cross is other than Apollo; the Virgin Mary, as seen by believers, is not a beautiful woman, like some old Grecian goddess, but an ideal of the mind. Thus the world of the spirit which Christianity reflects triumphed as secularism died; Rome the Eternal arose when Imperial Rome sank crumbling in devastation, a mass of vague and almost indistinguishable ruins.

Of the allied forces which in early times did battle with Christianity—paganism and secularism— the former necessarily perished. The old gods were powerless before that new God whose tortured face looked down from a rough-hewn cross and whose baby eyes, full of a precocious wisdom, gazed trustfully upward from the Herod-threatened cradle. But the spirit of secularism was not so easily crushed. Christianity makes appeal to the vision of a life beyond; the mimes, expressing secularism, frankly accept the world; and many even of those who embraced the new religion still tried to make the best of both. If a prayer in the chapel might perhaps add a stone to the celestial stairway, a good honest laugh in the theatre was at least a comforting, tangible, and immediate joy. Thus, while the spirit of secularism outwardly was vanquished, the vanquished did not entirely perish with the triumph of the victor. All through the Middle Ages the Feast of Fools, the Feast of the Ass, the Feast of the Boy Bishop, as well as those still more ancient *saturnalia* against which the Councils fulminated, testified to the power of this spirit, providing a kind of safety-valve for those repressed sentiments which otherwise might have broken their bonds more violently and destroyed thereby the material fabric (the Church Catholic) of the idea spiritual.

Fig. 2. A Roman Mask representing an Old Man, and a Comic Mime Actor
From Francisco Ficoroni, *Dissertatio de larvis scenicis et figuris comicis* (Roma, 1754), Plate VIII.

In life the secular spirit endured through ages of tumultuous barbarity and of mystical religion; but what of that which, in the year 287 of our era, was the typical expression of this secular spirit? In the late Middle Ages we find farces very similar to those Roman mimes of which the scattered relics alone remain to us. Very similar, too, are some of those pieces with which the actors of *commedia dell' arte* companies made merry the princes and the folk of the Renascence. Are we to count these as independent, reborn forms of the spirit secular, or have they indeed some direct connexion with the mimes of Imperial Rome? Is the martyrdom of St Philemon to be taken as symbolic of something further still? Did the fanaticism of Christianity take their profession away from all the old godless or pagan mimes, or did the passion of the people of Antinoe—of Rome, of Alexandria—preserve intact that merry posturing and that joyous scenic display at which the angels wept?

It is in an attempt to discover some form of answer to these questions that the present book has been written. The complete solution of the problems raised may be difficult or even impossible to come by, but careful analysis and judicious piecing together of the scattered evidence may perhaps enable us to form some conception of the development and fate of that mimic drama which was the delight of the folk, the typically professional form of theatrical entertainment and the very symbol of secularism in life. For our purposes we must move both backward and forward. Our survey begins before the days when Aristophanes ridiculed the Socratic doctrines in the great Theatre of Dionysus at Athens, and possibly it might be extended until, in a modern music-hall, under a searching limelight, it witnesses a low comedian presenting a mock sermon to a delighted audience.[1]

Our quest will be for the ancestors and the descendants of St Philemon, the delight of his city —*civitatis nostræ deliciæ.*

(ii) THE DORIAN MIME

In our search for origins the journey leads back inevitably to ancient Doria. Aristotle, than whom no authority could have greater value and importance, has given us a traditional record of his own day to the effect that the Dorians, particularly the citizens of Megara, had developed a form of comedy prior to the appearance of that dramatic type in Athens itself.[2] The cardinal facts as presented by Aristotle are these. Comedy arose in Megara during the period of its democracy : that is to say, after 581 B.C., when it drove out its tyrant, Theagenes. Epicharmus was writing " long before " (πολλῷ πρότερος) Chionides, who is known to have made his first appearance as a comic poet at Athens in 487 B.C. As Epicharmus was writing plays at the Court of Gelo in Syracuse from 485 to 478 B.C., it is likely that he had started his dramatic career in the Dorian Megara Hyblæa a number of years previous to his Syracusan *première.* The interest of this question for us lies in the facts that the Dorian and Sicilian comedies (thus linked together) are in reality small mimes, not choral dramas such as those of Aristophanes, that common features are to be traced in these plays of Epicharmus, the Old and New Comedy of Athens, and the productions of the Southern Italian Phlyakes (Φλύακες),[3] with the suggestion of a Dorian original for all, and that the comedy-mime type thus established descended naturally to the Roman mimic drama. The first step in our investigation, therefore, is to discover, if we may, what were the main elements in this Dorian, or Megarean, comedy.

THE COMIC FIGURES AND THEIR COSTUMES

At the very start pictorial evidence comes to our aid, in the form of a series of Corinthian vases which display comic figures of a peculiar sort.[4] Often these figures appear in pairs, dancing together, and all, or nearly all, have the same costumes, consisting of a tight-fitting vest, either

---

[1] The treatment of comic types is so extended in Max Bauer's recension of K. F. Flögel's *Geschichte des Grotesk-komischen* (Munich, 2 vols., 1914), while Reich is apt to see direct connexion between modern music-hall turns and Roman divertisements. In an article in *L'Acropole* (i, 4, October–December 1926) Alexander Philadelpheus compares the ancient Greek mimic dance with the modern cinema. While it is, of course, foolish to suggest that these and similar manifestations of the spirit of entertainment owe anything directly to the ancient mime, a true conception of the latter is to be gained only by a careful and appreciative estimate of the modern music-hall, circus, and ' picture-house.'

[2] The subject of Dorian comedy is, of course, dealt with incidentally in all works devoted to the subject of comic origins and in most of those devoted to the subject of the Greek theatre. Reich does not enter into this theme fully, but several monographs have been written on it. Opinions in these vary greatly as to the extent of the influence exerted by the Megarean comedy on the Attic literary type, but this is an aspect of the question which does not concern us here. Among the special works may be mentioned K. J. Grysar, *De Doriensium comœdia quæstiones* (Cologne, 1828) ; Ulrich von Wilamowitz-Moellendorff, *Die megarische Komödie* (*Hermes*, ix (1875), 319–341) ; J. A. Führ, *De mimis Græcorum* (Göttingen, 1860) ; W. Hörschelmann, *Der griechische Mimus* (*Baltische Monatsschrift*, Riga, xxxix (1892), 593–608) ; A. Körte, *Archäologische Studien zur alten Komödie* (*Jahrbuch des K. deutschen archäologischen Instituts*, viii (1893), 61–93) ; J. Poppelreuter, *De comœdiæ atticæ primordiis* (Berlin, 1893) ; Thaddæus Zieliński, *Die Gliederung der altattischen Komödie* (Leipzig, 1885) ; C. Hertling, *Quæstiones mimicæ* (Strassburg, 1899, pp. 31 f., " De primordiis artis mimicæ ") ; and E. Bethe, *Prolegomena zur Geschichte des Theaters im Altertum* (Leipzig, 1896). The subject is dealt with also in J. L. Klein, *Geschichte des Dramas* (Berlin, 1865–76), vol. ii, on Greek mime and Roman mime, and Edelstand du Méril, *Histoire de la comédie ancienne* (Paris, 1869, vol. i, on Greek mime, vol. ii, on Roman mime) ; Charles Magnin, *Les Origines du théâtre antique* (Paris, 1838, on both Greek and Roman mime). The relevant texts are carefully analysed and discussed in A. W. Pickard-Cambridge, *Dithyramb Tragedy and Comedy* (Oxford, 1927). The principal passages in Aristotle will be found in the *Poetics* (iii, 1448a, 30 f.) and in the *Nicomachean Ethics* (iv, 3).

[3] On these see *infra*, pp. 50–65.

[4] These are discussed in all works devoted to the Greek theatre and its actors. In particular see A. Körte, *Archäologische Studien zur alten Komödie* (*Jahrbuch des K. deutschen archäologischen Instituts*, viii (1893), 61–93) ; Heinz Schnabel, *Kordax : Archäologische Studien zur Geschichte eines antiken Tanzes und zum Ursprung der griechischen Komödie* (Munich, 1910) ; G. Loeschcke, *Korinthische Vase mit der Rückführung des Hephaistos* (*Mittheilungen des Kaiserlich deutschen archäologischen Instituts : Athenische Abtheilung*, xix (1894), 510–525).

plain-colour or ornamented with spots, and heavy padding, sometimes both behind and in front, sometimes only at the back. Many of them, although not all, are phallephoric, and one suspects that the majority are supposed to be wearing masks. Wine-jars figure freely in these vase-pictures, and scenes of orgy and theft seem often to be depicted. The nature of the characters represented is suggested in what is probably the best-known of the whole series, a vase now in the Louvre (Fig. 3), which contains a fairly definite clue to the identification of the persons. On the front side of this vase appear two groups of men. The chief actor in the first is a phallephoric character, armed with two sticks, who seems to be pursuing and checking a couple of slaves engaged in the theft of a wine-jar. The second group

Fig. 3. A DORIAN MIME SCENE

Early vase in the Louvre, Paris. From the *Jahrbuch des K. deutschen archäologischen Instituts*, viii (1893), 91.

includes a flute-player and a bearded figure who is dancing to his music. The interest of this particular vase, however, does not rest on the figures alone; more important still is the fact that at least three of the actors are indicated by name. The dancing man is labelled *ΕΥΝΟΣ* (Εὔνους, Eunous), one of the slaves *ΟΦΕΛΑΝΔΡΟΣ* (’Οφέλανδρος, Ophelandros), and the master *ΟΜΡΙΚΟΣ* (’Ομρικός, Omrikos). Now Eunous and Ophelandros appear elsewhere as the names of demons associated with Dionysus, while in the form Ombrikos (’Ομβρικός) the name Omrikos is given to Dionysus himself. We are accordingly justified in believing that these particular figures represented on this vase are definitely Dionysiac in character, and perhaps we might be allowed to go further and suggest that the many other similar but unlabelled characters to be found on the Corinthian vases also depict Dionysus and his attendants.[1]

Fig. 4. A DORIAN MIME SCENE

Corinthian vase in the Louvre. From M. Bieber, *Denkmäler zum Theaterwesen im Altertum* (Walter de Gruyter and Co., Berlin and Leipzig, 1920), Abb. 123*b*.

The question now arises concerning their dramatic significance. Many of the scenes might be nothing but imaginative conceptions of grotesque Dionysiac revelry or pictures of real-life festivity wholly unconnected with the theatre, but several indications are given to us that some at least of these vases do reproduce scenes of a theatrical kind. The particular vase which we have had under consideration suggests a farce in which Dionysus is robbed by his slaves, while on the other side (Fig. 4) appears a picture which might also be interpreted as theatrical, some scene showing the effects of a drunken orgy.

[1] On this vase see Georg Thiele in *Die Anfänge der griechischen Komödie* (*Neue Jahrbücher für das klassische Altertum*, v (1902), 413–416).

Mere supposition, however, is happily dismissed when we discover that the costume worn by the characters on these Corinthian vases was adopted, almost without alteration, by the actors in the

Fig. 5. THE RETURN OF HEPHÆSTUS TO OLYMPUS

Corinthian vase in National Museum, Athens. From *Mittheilungen des K. d. archäologischen Instituts: Athenische Abtheilung*, xix (1894), Taf. VIII.

Fig. 6. TWO ATTIC COMEDIANS

Terra-cotta in the Kunstgeschichtliches Museum, Würzburg University.

Photo Rudolf Hatzold

Athenian Old Comedy. That the costume itself was of great antiquity is proved by its appearance on a black-figured Corinthian amphora now in Athens (Fig. 5), which dates from the beginning of the sixth century B.C. The scene depicted here illustrates the return of Hephæstus to Olympus in order to free the imprisoned Hera. The persons, two of which wear the phallus, are costumed in the same manner as those on the other vase, and again represent Dionysiac demons, possibly suggested at least by dramatic performances of a burlesque nature. This costume, then, was already associated with Dionysus among the Dorian peoples at the beginning of the sixth century B.C. In Athens, however, all the early vases with Dionysiac subjects show the wine-god attended, not by these padded slaves, but by satyrs or sileni. There seems not the slightest doubt that in Athenian territory, before the advent of the Old Comedy, the satyr or the silenos was his inevitable companion, yet when we reach the time of the Old Comedy itself we find that the characters (and we must remember the close connexion between comedy and the satyric drama) all wear garments similar to those which have already been discussed. If we turn, for example, to the terra-cotta statuette group of two actors of the Old Comedy now in the Kunstgeschichtliches Museum at Würzburg University (Fig. 6), we find what is virtually a replica of the Corinthian costume. This particular example, which dates from the second half of the fifth century B.C., shows an old man and a slave, the former seemingly whispering some secret to the latter. The old man is clad in the long aristocratic garments of his day, but his stomach is padded as were the stomachs of the Dionysiac demons, while the slave has the short vest of earlier times, with a leather phallus and yellow tights. One other example may be taken, a fourth-century terra-cotta of a comic actor now in the Louvre (Fig. 7). Here the actor, wearing a large mask, is shown eagerly beating a cymbal. He sports a very short chiton, and his stomach is heavily padded. Below the edge of the chiton the phallus is apparent. That these figures do represent actors can remain not a moment in doubt; if other evidence is desired it can readily be found in the scene depicted on a fourth-century Attic vase discovered in the Crimea and now at Leningrad (Fig. 8). This shows in the centre three persons, one of whom is seated. All are heavily padded like the terra-cotta figures, and each holds his mask in his hand. The masks can indicate nothing but that these are actors preparing themselves for a theatrical performance.[1]

No further examples of the costumes used in the Old Comedy need here be given. One might, it is true, continue exemplifying these from scores of terra-cottas and vases, but this would do no more than stress their absolute regularity. We are faced, then, with the fact that, in spite of the association in Athenian imagination of Dionysus and the satyrs and sileni, the actors in the Old Comedy, itself an offshoot of Dionysiac merriment, adopted the padded costumes of the Peloponnesus. That they did so seems to prove definitely the existence of such costumes in early Dorian theatrical shows, and leads one to believe that the characters depicted on the Corinthian vases are not imaginative figures, but either pictures of actors in their *rôles* or else inspired by performances of such actors.

Still further than Athens may we trace this Dorian costume. Figures similar to the Corinthian are to be found in the so-called Kabeiroi vases of Thebes in Bœotia.[2] Undoubtedly

many of these must be imaginative in subject and in treatment, but one at least, a red-figured crater now in Athens, shows what appears to be a kind of mimic scene, and Dieterich[3] may not be far wrong when he styles the two figures *rechte und echte macci* (Fig. 9). In the middle stands a cauldron, which two men, probably intended to be masked, are apparently

Fig. 8. Comic Actors preparing for their Parts
Fourth-century Attic vase at Leningrad. From Roy C. Flickinger, *The Greek Theater and its Drama* (University of Chicago Press, 1918), Fig. 17.

[1] See, on this subject of costume, Max von Boehn, *Das Bühnenkostüm in Altertum, Mittelalter und Neuzeit* (Berlin, 1921), and H. Dierks, *Über das Kostüm der griechischen Schauspieler in der alten Komödie* (*Archäologische Zeitung*, xliii (1885), 31–51).

[2] In his treatment of this subject Pickard-Cambridge (pp. 261–270) follows A. Körte (*Neue Jahrbücher für das klassische Altertum*, xlvii (1921), 310–312; review of Bieber's book) in rejecting the Theban vases as non-theatrical. While they are clearly more fanciful than the others, several deserve to be included in any discussion of early burlesque types.

[3] Albrecht Dieterich, *Pulcinella : Pompejanische Wandbilder und römische Satyrspiele* (Leipzig, 1897), pp. 91–92. On this vase see A. Körte, *Eine böotische Vase mit burlesker Darstellung* (*Mittheilungen des K. deutschen archäologischen Instituts : Athenische Abtheilung*, xix (1894), 346–350); M. Collignon and L. Couve, *Catalogue des vases peints du Musée National d'Athènes* (Paris, 1904), No. 1927, p. 627; Margarete Bieber, *Die Denkmäler zum Theaterwesen im Altertum* (Berlin and Leipzig, 1920), Taf. LXXXVII, 1.

engaged in tending. A goose, straddling in on their left, seems to be interrupting the culinary operations. Both of the men have comic padding, both wear vests similar to those in the Corinthian vases, and both seem to have tights on their legs. These are companions at least of Omrikos and Ophelandros. Much more important, however, than the only doubtfully theatrical Theban scenes are those which depict incidents in plays of a kind which has already been briefly referred to—the South Italian mimic Phlyakes. Since it will be necessary to devote some considerable space to this form of dramatic art in a later section, attention must here be confined strictly to the costume of the players. For this purpose a single example may serve as typical. Perhaps the

Fig. 9. THE BROTH-MAKERS
Vase in the National Museum, Athens (No. 5115/1391). From M. Bieber, *Denkmäler zum Theaterwesen im Altertum*, Taf. LXXXVII, 1.

most characteristic is that on a vase found at Bitonto and now preserved in Bari (Fig. 10), where appears a pair of figures fundamentally identical with the Attic terra-cotta group (Fig. 6). Both characters are padded ; both have the short vest ; both are clad in tights ; and both openly display the ancient phallic symbol. Now, the Phlyakes mimic comedy has absolutely nothing to do directly with the comedy of Aristophanes at Athens, and there is not the slightest possibility that the actors' costumes shown here were taken over from the Old Comedy. Since, on the other hand, this Phlyax mime arose in the city of Tarentum, the centre of the Dorian colonies in Italy, it is positively certain that the actor types displayed on the Corinthian vases formed the original model for these later performers. This Phlyax entertainment, in turn, seems to have been the ancestor of the more purely Italic mimic drama, so that we have here not only a very definite link between the merrymaking characters in Dorian villages and the mimic actors of Rome, but also a further link in the chain of evidence which connects the Corinthian vase types with actual stage performers. In all probability the Phlyax comedy was only a slightly more fully developed form of the mime originated in Megara.

MYTHOLOGICAL BURLESQUE AND OTHER THEMES

Leaving aside the matter of costume, we have in those Corinthian vases still another point of connexion between the new mime and the old, with ramifications extending into the realm of Aristophanic comedy. If we are right in assuming that the Corinthian vases have a theatrical colouring, then we have there Dionysiac scenes treated in a burlesque spirit. It is therefore legitimate to suppose that in ancient Doric lands mythological travesty either originated or became exceedingly popular. The form this burlesque took called evidently for the dragging down of the divine legends to the level of ordinary life. Of prime importance is it to note that burlesque of divine or heroic legend has always been associated with all forms of the mimic drama. It appears in the fifth-century plays of Epicharmus;[1] it appears in the fourth-century farces of the Phlyax type;[2] later it embraced within its scope even the newer cult of Christianity.[3] Similar travesty, of course, is to be found in the Old Comedy of Athens, but already it has been indicated that that Attic drama seems to have been deeply influenced by the Dorian or Megarean comedies, while in the New Comedy and in its representative, the Terentian and Plautan comedy of Rome, this mythological element has to a large extent disappeared. The evidence at hand seems to indicate that, while the mime had no monopoly in this style, the farcical treatment of gods and religions, from the first days of the mimic drama to its latest, provided one of the main sources of plot, action, and character.

Fig. 10. AN OLD MAN AND HIS SLAVE
Phlyax vase at Bari. From M. Bieber, *Denkmäler zum Theaterwesen im Altertum*, Taf. LXXXV, 1.

Unfortunately, not very much of a certain kind is known about this original Doric mime. Our mental picture has to be based partly at least upon deductions and suppositions; only thus can we eke out the meagre records that remain. Among the more important of these records is an account given by Athenæus of a number of customs and entertainments associated with the Peloponnesus.[4] The first of these, given on the authority of Sosibius, who lived about the year 300 B.C., concerns the activities of a group in Lacedæmon whom he calls the *deikelistai* (δεικηλίσται). Already in the time of Sosibius their "comic sport" (κωμικῆς παιδιᾶς) was "an ancient custom" (τις τρόπος παλαιός), so that we have every reason to believe that its tradition passes back to a period anterior to the

[1] *Cf. infra*, pp. 38–41. Mythological burlesque, of course, was not confined to the mimes. It appeared in literary Greek comedy; for an interesting example see L. R. Farnell, *Plato comicus : frag. Phaon II. : A Parody of Attic Ritual (The Classical Quarterly*, xiv (1920), 139–146).
[2] *Cf. infra*, pp. 50–65. [3] *Cf. infra*, pp. 120–122.
[4] Athenæus, *Deipnosophistai*, xiv, 621d–622b (ed. G. Kaibel, Leipzig, 1925). These references are fully discussed by Pickard-Cambridge, and are touched on less fully by Reich. I omit here reference to the Spartan customs related by Plutarch in his life of Lycurgus (xvii). These seem to be merely boyish pranks.

25

development of comedy in Athens. Apparently in this comic sport there were characters who stole fruit and another who impersonated a doctor.[1] The account seems to suggest a mimic type of farce, and Athenæus himself states that the name *deikeliktai* meant ' those who get up plays,' or mime performers.[2] The word is associated with *deikela* (δείκηλα), which apparently signifies masks, characters in a play, or representations, and a later writer identifies *deikelon* and *deikeliktai* with ' actors ' in general.[3] The real technical significance of the word is interestingly exemplified by Plutarch in his life of Agesilaus, where an anecdote is given regarding a certain great tragic actor named Kallippides. Ignored by the monarch on one occasion, he exclaimed, " Do you not know me, O King ? " and Agesilaus, in order to insult him, replied, "Ah, yes, you are Kallippides the *deikeliktas* (or *deikeliktas*), are you not ? " To this story Plutarch adds the explanatory note that *deikeliktai* was a word which the Lacedæmonians applied to the mimes, a statement which is corroborated by Hesychius, who treats the two as one.[4] In view of this evidence, therefore, we may be permitted to believe that in Lacedæmon, probably with Sparta as a centre, there was a type of mimic farce in which actors, no doubt wearing masks—for the original meaning of *deikelon* seems to imply this—took a variety of parts, the most popular being fruit-thieves and comic doctors.

These, however, were not the only persons introduced into the mimic drama of ancient times, nor do the performances seem to have been all of one type. Besides the representations of the *deikeliktai*, Athenæus describes a number of others which, although evidently undramatic in the larger sense and introducing choral elements foreign to the true mime, may well have had an influence on, or a close connexion with, that type. Under the general form he recognizes as intimately allied species the activities of the *phallophoroi* (φαλλοφόροι) of Sicyon, the *autokabdaloi* (αὐτοκάβδαλοι) of an unmentioned district, the Phlyakes (φλύακες) of Italy, the *sophistai* (σοφισταί), the *ithuphalloi* (ἰθύφαλλοι), the Theban *ethelontai* (ἐθελονταί), and the Syracusan *iambistai* (ἰαμβισταί). Most of his information he appears to take from a writer of the second century B.C., Semus the Delian. In trying to interpret his words we must, of course, remember that both he and his authority may have been in error, but at the same time we must pay due attention to this direct statement that the *deikeliktai*, whom we know to have been mimes, the Italian Phlyakes, who certainly belonged to the mime tradition, and the others were all varieties of one common type. Unfortunately Athenæus' remarks are neither very informative nor conclusive. The *phallophoroi*, he declares, had flowers hanging in front of their soot-smeared faces and wore crowns of ivy and violets. As the name signifies ' phallus-bearing,' they were obviously adorned with that comic symbol. Entering the theatre, these ' actors ' chanted a hymn to Bacchus, and then proceeded to ridicule certain members of the audience. There is certainly not much here that seems dramatic, but the soot-smeared faces and the phallus have a certain significance.[5] The name *autokabdaloi* is derived from αὐτοκάβδαλος, which means ' unprepared,' ' not

---

[1] Apart from the theatrical ' doctors ' mentioned below, it is interesting to note the persistence of this type in folk custom. Leaving aside the ' St George ' plays of England and confining attention to Greece, we note the existence at Kissos of a festival of ' Maymen ' (Μαίηδες) in which appear a bride, an Arab, a janissary (γενίτσαρος), a doctor, an old woman, and a Μαιόπουλο; a doctor and two devils figure in a similar festival at Agyia below Mount Ossa. See A. J. B. Wace, *Mumming Plays in the Southern Balkans*, in the *Annual of the British School at Athens* (xix (1912–13), 248–265). *Cf.* also J. Witkowski, *Les Médecins au théâtre, de l'antiquité au xviiᵉ siècle* (Paris, 1905).

[2] His actual words are : ἐκαλοῦντο δ' οἱ μετιόντες τὴν τοιαύτην παιδιὰν παρὰ τοῖς Λάκωσι δεικηλίσται [οι δικηλισταί] ὡς ἄν τις σκευοποιοὺς εἴπῃ καὶ μιμητάς. Since the word σκευοποιός is used by Aristophanes to signify ' one who prepares actors for the performance ' (the modern ' producer '), the terms of Athenæus—σκευοποιούς and μιμητάς—clearly have a theatrical significance. On this see Pickard-Cambridge (p. 229).

[3] Eustathius in commenting on Homer declares categorically that the two words mean κωμικοί, or ' actors.' Hesychius relates *deikela* with *prosopa* (πρόσωπα), ' masks ' or ' characters ' in a play.

[4] *Agesilaus* (xxi): ἀλλὰ οὐ σύγε ἐσσὶ Καλλιππίδης ὁ δεικηλίκτας ; οὕτω δὲ Λακεδαιμόνιοι τοὺς μίμους καλοῦσι. (*Cf.* Plutarch, *Laconica apophthegmata*, ccxii, 38.) Hesychius avers that the δεικηλίσται were the μιμηταί [' mime actors '] παρὰ Λάκωσι. The point of Plutarch's anecdote is, of course, that the tragic actors regarded themselves as superior to their mimic brethren.

[5] Bethe (p. 54) thinks that the *phallophoroi* were Delians ; for this there is no proof. Reich (i, 277) identifies a figure in Furtwängler's *Die Sammlung Saburoff* (Taf. CXXVII) as one of these. Pickard-Cambridge (pp. 235–236) would reject the association by Athenæus of the *deikeliktai* and the *phallophoroi* on the ground that the latter were choral, but, in view of the scantiness of our information, it seems that such a rejection cannot be final.

planned out before,' or 'improvised';[1] and this name recalls to our minds the fact that much of mimic work in the theatre has been authorless. Improvisation seems to have been a characteristic of the early mime even as it was of its later counterpart, the *commedia dell' arte*. Concerning the *ithuphalloi*[2] we are told that they wore the masks of drunken men, with garlands on their brows. A white striped tunic with flowered sleeves and a long, fine garment styled a *tarantinon* (ταραντῖνον) formed their official stage costume. Regarding the activities of the *ethelontai* (a name that suggests non-professional festivity), the *sophistai*, and the *iambistai* we know practically nothing. The first may be connected with the Theban Kabeiroi vases,[3] but, as has been seen, this is by no means certain. It has been suggested, however, that of these various types of performers thus grouped under one generic form some were professional and some wholly amateur.[4] If this were so then the distinction between the *sophistai* and the *ethelontai* might be easily explained. With the former might be grouped the *deikelistai* and the Phlyakes; with the latter, the *ithuphalloi* and the *phallophoroi*. Whether this be a correct supposition or not, the probability is that in Athenæus' account we have to deal with both kinds of entertainments, and we must conclude that the later mime was indebted to each.

THE CHARACTERS

This rapid survey of the records concerning some primitive shows and ceremonials indicates the variety of forms which the Dorian mimic drama might assume, but the account of those actors who were comrades of the *deikelistai* has not added to our knowledge in regard to the characters by them presented before the public. We must therefore retrace our steps, returning to the thievish slave and the comic doctor of Lacedæmon. Again the evidence has to be gathered and pieced together from a diversity of sources. Among the more important passages is that well-known address to the audience at the beginning of Aristophanes' *Wasps*, put into the mouth of the slave Xanthias.[5] " Don't expect anything great and wonderful from us," says the Athenian author. " Don't look for merriment filched from Megara. We haven't got a couple of slaves here to scatter nuts from a basket among the spectators, nor have we Herakles defrauded of his dinner." To this passage a scholiast has added a line from a play by Eupolis referring to a " dull and wanton Megarean jest " (τὸ σκῶμμ' ἀσελγὲς καὶ Μεγαρικὸν καὶ σφόδρα ψυχρόν).[6] These lines agree with others quoted from Ecphantides, and with still others which, interpreting " Megarean laughter " (γέλως Μεγαρικός), explain that the Athenians laughed in mockery and disdain at these untimely and unbecoming jests.[7] From such passages, then, we can deduce the facts that the merriment of Megara was of a somewhat unpolished kind and that certain stock figures were associated in the minds of Aristophanes and his audience with that merriment. Clownish slaves and a buffoonish Herakles were evidently well-known figures, and these, we shall find, were retained both in the mimes of Epicharmus and in the later essays in that style presented in Roman theatres.

Mythological burlesque, burlesque of legends, comic thievish slaves and foolish doctors[8]—these seem definitely established as belonging to the Dorian farce. Still further may we go in our search. A variety of scattered references prove the presence in early Dorian folklore of characters named

---

[1] For a discussion regarding the exact significance see Pickard-Cambridge (p. 232). See also W. Christ, *Geschichte der griechischen Litteratur bis auf die Zeit Justinians* (Berlin, 1890), p. 239.

[2] For the Phlyakes see *infra*, pp. 50–65.   [3] See *supra*, pp. 23–24.

[4] This suggestion seems to have been made first by Georg Thiele in *Die Anfänge der griechischen Komödie* (*Neue Jahrbücher für das klassische Altertum*, v (1902), 410–412). See also Pickard-Cambridge.

[5] Ll. 56–60.

[6] This passage is repeated also in the scholia to Aristotle's *Nicomachean Ethics* (iv, 3), where it is attributed to Murtilos. The Ecphantides passage is also given in these scholia.

[7] For these passages see Reich, i, 504; Pickard-Cambridge, pp. 275–276; and W. Christ, p. 240.

[8] It is to be noted that a drug-dealer mentioned in a fragment of Theopompos is referred to as a native of Megara—φαρμακοπώλης Μεγαρικός (Theodorus Kock, *Comicorum atticorum fragmenta* (Leipzig, 1888, i, 733, fr. 2)).

Morychos (Μόρυχος), Momar (Μῶμαρ), and Marikas or Maricas (Μάρικας), and Reich[1] has suggested that all of these are to be connected etymologically with *moros* (μωρός), which is the common generic

Fig. 11. MASK OF AN
OLD WOMAN

Clay mask (sixth century B.C.) found at Sparta. From A. W. Pickard-Cambridge, *Dithyramb Tragedy and Comedy* (Oxford University Press, 1927), Fig. 19.

name for a mimic fool. These figures were no doubt in origin demonic powers, a supposition which is strengthened when we discover that beside them existed at least three female and corresponding figures named Mormo (Μορμώ), Akko or Acco ('Ακκώ), and Alphito ('Αλφιτώ), each of whom had such a significance. The first of these, clearly belonging to what we may call the *moros* group, is described by an early writer as a " terrifying mask " (προσωπεῖον ἐπίφοβον), and is placed by Lucian alongside chimeras and gorgons as calculated to terrify childish bosoms ; while Akko and Alphito are similarly referred to by Plutarch as creatures whom mothers use wherewith to frighten children. Reich has suggested that Akko represents the Sanskrit Akka (' Mother '), and that Alphito may gain her name from the Greek *alphiton* (ἄλφιτον, 'barley'), so being a 'corn-mother' or 'corn-goddess.' Whatever be the truth of these etymological deductions, it is certain that for Hesychius Mormo was a 'wandering demon' (Μορμόνας, πλάνητας δαίμονας). Mormo and her companions, then, were creatures designed to cause terror in children, and there is at least the possibility that they were stage figures as well as imaginative fantasies ; perhaps we should picture them as old, withered hags, with one fang-like tooth in an otherwise empty jaw. Happily for our present purpose, the British School at Athens has recently unearthed a number of clay replicas of masks buried in the sanctuary of Artemis Orthia at Sparta.[2] These masks, which date from the

beginning of the sixth century B.C., among other types, show an old woman, with heavily lined face and hideous jaws, having one or two solitary teeth peering between her ugly lips (Figs. 11 and 12). As Pickard-Cambridge, who was the first in England to draw attention to the dramatic value of these finds, has pointed out, the main characteristics of the masks are reproduced in some later masks of the New Comedy and agree perfectly with the relevant description of the old woman type as presented by Pollux. The mime, until its latest days, loved this witch-like old woman, a descendant of whom in the spirit is to be discovered in the Mome Helwis of medieval times, and here is some slight evidence, at least, to indicate that, as a stage figure, she was born in the Dorian farce.

Fig. 12. MASK OF AN
OLD WOMAN

Clay mask (sixth century B.C.) found at Sparta. From A. W. Pickard-Cambridge, *Dithyramb Tragedy and Comedy* (Oxford University Press, 1927), Fig. 21.

It seems highly probable, then, that the hag type crept into Athenian comedy from Sparta, and that the same type was preserved, in variant forms, during the later career of the mime. Nor does the indebtedness of both of these to Dorian originals cease at this point. Among the various comic masks described by Pollux there appears one who is called Maison (Μαίσων). Tradition is confusing in regard to the development of this character, but three ideas emerge from separate statements or suggestions presented by Athenæus, Aristophanes of Byzantium, and Hesychius.[3] These are as follows: (1) the name Maison is taken from *masasthai* (μασᾶσθαι, ' to clutch or seize greedily ') and signifies a glutton; (2) it is taken from the name of

[1] Reich, i, 504–509.
[2] A number of these were first reproduced by Pickard-Cambridge. On Mormo and the connexion of the word with μῖμος (' mime '), together with a series of (supposed) derivatives in modern tongues, see Leo Wiener, Μορμώ (*Romanische Forschungen*, xxxv (1916), 954–985).
[3] For this type see Carl Robert, *Die Masken der neueren attischen Komödie* (Halle, 1911), p. 76, and Pickard-Cambridge, pp. 275–279.

its inventor, a Megarean actor called Maison, who also invented a popular slave type, the 'leading slave' (θεράπων ἡγέμων); (3) it arose in Megara, and is associated with gluttony. Very probably the actor Maison here mentioned has been invented to explain the character, and if we thus dismiss this suggestion we are left with the statements that Megara was Maison's home, that he is a symbol of gluttony, and that with him developed the person of the 'leading slave.' Let us take the Maison type first. In addition to the information given above, we are told by Pollux that he was ruddy and bald-headed, while Festus adds that his regular profession was that of cook or sailor. One may agree with Robert that he is fairly easy to identify among the extant terra-cottas of a theatrical cast. A most interesting example comes from the Berlin Museum, the original provenance being in all probability Megara itself (Fig. 13). Here we are shown a good-natured, fat creature with raised eyebrows and head innocent of hair, save for a few locks at the sides. His face and arms are a ruddy brown. In his hands he bears a light-yellow basket containing a fish, which no doubt he is to cook for supper. Here, apparently, is a concrete picture of one of the favourite types in the Dorian farce as taken over by the Attic dramatists. Another of these types, as we have seen, is the 'leading slave.' This person, according to Pollux, had reddish hair arranged in the form of a *speira* (σπεῖρα), with bushy, raised eyebrows. He is described for us in the *Pseudolus*, where the title-person is called "a red-

Fig. 13. MAISON, THE MEGAREAN COOK

Terra-cotta in the Berlin Museum, No. 7042a. From M. Bieber, *Denkmäler zum Theaterwesen im Altertum*, Tafel LXXII, 1.

haired fellow, pot-bellied, with thick legs, somewhat dark in complexion, with a big head, sharp eyes, red mouth, and large feet." [1] The *speira*, as Robert has shown, seems the main characteristic of this figure, and the *speira*, from the evidence of early sculpture, was particularly associated with the Dorian peoples. It is almost certain that the masks shown in Figs. 14 and 15 represent this person.

Fig. 14. MASK OF THE LEADING SLAVE

Stone mask in the Museo Nazionale, Naples.

Photo Alinari

Proceeding from these two stage-figures, Maison and the 'leading slave,' whom tradition definitely associates with Megara, we may pause a moment to consider further implications raised in Pollux's account of comedy masks. In this account there are described two old men whose chief characteristic feature is a peaked beard. Now, this peaked-beard person must date back to the fifth century B.C., and, since peaked-beard types appear often in the scenes of the Phlyakes farce, itself taken directly to Italy by Dorian settlers, there is some reason to believe that we may have here also stage-figures originated in Megara.[2] There can be no question of certainty, but at least a possibility exists that we can now add one other character (*cf.* Fig. 16) to the gallery of types inspired by the Megarean farce.

It may be well now to stay for a moment in order to summarize briefly the main results which have emerged from this scattered evidence. Without, of course, being able to establish any

---

[1] " Rufus quidam, ventriosus, crassis suris, subniger, magno capite, acutis oculis, ore rubicundo, admodum magnis pedibus."
[2] See Robert, pp. 108–109.

Fig. 15. SET OF MASKS: OLD MAN, FAIR YOUTH, YOUTH WITH CURLY HAIR,
AND LEADING SLAVE
Marble relief in the Museo Vaticano, Naples.
Photo Moscioni

Fig. 16. ACTOR WITH
PEAKED BEARD
Terra-cotta in the British
Museum (Case K, c. 239).

absolutely definite facts, we may be permitted to believe that during the period immediately prior to the appearance of Attic comedy there developed in different centres inhabited by the Dorian peoples a type of mimic farce, rude in form, popular in its appeal, and ever eager for boisterous merriment. In this farce mythological and legendary burlesque must have formed a staple ingredient, and Herakles in particular must have been a favourite character. In addition to the person of Herakles, we may picture as stock types an old man with a pointed beard, an old, hag-like woman, a fool, a doctor, and at least two slaves, who on occasion may have acted as thieves. These must have been the outstanding persons in 'the Megarean drama' (τὸ δρᾶμα τὸ Μεγαρικόν),[1] which is the parent of the mime and may be one of the parents of Aristophanic comedy.

ANIMAL MASKS

Perhaps another element in this primitive farce may be distinguished, and here Aristophanes once more comes to our assistance. In *The Acharnians* a Megarean character mentions the changing of his daughters

[1] As such it seems regularly referred to in Athens, to distinguish it from the native 'comedy.'

into pigs, and refers to this as "a Megarean trick" (Μεγαρικά τις μαχανά). Now, while it is by no means certain that the Dorian comedy specialized in the introduction of animal figures, we have ample evidence to show that these animal figures, or characters assuming the features of animals,

were familiar in the mimes, just as they were familiar figures in Attic comedy. *The Wasps*, *The Birds*, and *The Frogs* of Aristophanes are the best-known examples from the sphere of literary drama, but these are only a few out of many; here may be mentioned *The Birds*, *The Insects* (ψῆνες), and *The Frogs*, by Magnes, *The Goats*, by Eupolis, *The Fish*, by Archippus, and *The Ants*, by

Fig. 17. Processional Chorus of Mimic Animals

Sixth-century vase in the Boston Museum. From Roy C. Flickinger, *The Greek Theater and its Drama* (University of Chicago Press, 1918), Fig. 16.

Plato. The chief persons in such plays were, of course, costumed in such a way as to suggest the creatures whose name gave the title to the play. Thus in *The Clouds*, according to a scholiast, the chorus wore masks with bird-like features. When Strepsiades ejaculates, "But these have noses!" (αὖται δέ γε ῥῖνας ἔχουσιν), it is explained that the actors wore large comic masks with enormous beaks.[1] In all probability these animal dramas developed naturally out of mimic dances such as are depicted for us in a number of early Attic vases. Four of these illustrations in particular aid us in creating

Fig. 18. Processional Chorus of Mimic Horses

Amphora in Berlin. From Roy C. Flickinger, *The Greek Theater and its Drama* (University of Chicago Press, 1918), Fig. 14.

a mental picture of the forms they assumed. Two, a black-figured vase in the Museum of Fine Arts at Boston (Fig. 17) and an amphora in Berlin (Fig. 18), show riding figures. In the latter the horsemen are shouting "Gee up!" (*EIOXEOXE*) to their steeds, which are men with horse-skins and long black tails. Another amphora in Berlin (Fig. 19) depicts a flute-player standing in front of two actors who are heavily wrapped in thick cloaks. Their faces are some-what rhinoceros-like, with turned-up noses and thick, pouting lips, but the red feathers on their heads and the tuft of red under their chins mark them out as cock types. The fourth

vase is a black-figured œnochoe in the British Museum (Fig. 20). Here two bird-clad figures dance in front of a flute-player. This, be it observed, is not an illustration of *The Birds* of Aristophanes, for the vase itself is at least seventy years older than that play, which made its first appearance in 414 B.C.[2] These are all examples from literary comedy and from primitive animal-dance cere-monies not directly connected with the mimic drama; they have been presented here because they may be useful in eking out our knowledge of animal representations, which certainly were popular, in the mime. Happily we need not rest solely on the early pictures seen on the Attic vases. Several

[1] Scholium to l. 344 : εἰσεληλθασι γὰρ οἱ τοῦ χοροῦ προσωπεῖα περικείμενοι, μεγάλας ἔχοντα ῥῖνας καὶ ἄλλως γελοῖα καὶ ἀσχήμονα.

[2] See particularly Cecil Smith, *Actors with Bird-masks on Vases* (*Journal of Hellenic Studies*, ii (1881), 309–314); and cf. H. Reich, *Der Mann mit dem Eselskopf* (*Jahrbuch der deutschen Shakespearegesellschaft*, xl(1904), 108–128). A. B. Cook in his *Animal Worship in the Mycenæan Age* (*Journal of Hellenic Studies*, xiv (1894), 81–169) discusses the stage significance of the animal types (pp. 163–164). See also *infra*, pp. 74–75.

later terra-cottas and bronzes, seemingly of theatrical origin, put before us human (no doubt mimic) actors wearing masks of animals. Two examples here may serve for many. The first (Fig. 21) shows a human figure wrapped in a long cloak, wearing what is unquestionably the mask of a rat's head. A similar mask, but in this case representing either an ass or a pig, appears on the second statuette, which also represents a cloaked actor who holds in his hands a large cymbal (Fig. 22). Of all the animal types, however, that of the cock seems to have proved the most successful. All through the course of the mimic drama it held its popularity, and it is not fanciful

Fig. 19. Animal-masked Actors in Athens
Sixth-century amphora in Berlin. From *The Journal of Hellenic Studies*, ii (1881), Plate XIV.

to see in the cockscomb of the medieval fool remnants of this character. " The cock," says one early writer on physiognomy, " which the Greeks call ἀλεκτρυών, is a stupid bird, insatiably libidinous, and inordinately proud of its appearance and voice," whereon he proceeds to give these characteristics to men whose physical appearance resembles this bird. One type of mimic fool assuredly rose out of such an interpretation, developing out of those mimic dances records of which are still preserved on ancient Attic vases.

DANCE AND SONG

The dance generally had much to do with the evolution of the mimic drama. Animal dances were one thing, but besides these there were many others, most of an indecent character, which may

Fig. 20. BIRD-MASKED ACTORS IN ATHENS

Sixth-century œnochoe in the British Museum.   From *The Journal of Hellenic Studies*, ii (1881), Plate XIV.

Fig. 21. AN ACTOR WITH THE HEAD OF A RAT

Bronze in the Bibliothèque Nationale, Paris (No. 3682).

Photo Giraudon

Fig. 22. AN ACTOR WITH AN ANIMAL HEAD

Terra-cotta from Myrina (third century B.C.), now in the Louvre.

Photo Giraudon

be grouped under the generic name of the *kordax* (κόρδαξ).[1]   Only incidentally has information been provided by antiquity concerning these, but we know that many were mimetic in character; " the dancers," says Aristotle, " imitate, by means of rhythmic movement, manners and passions and actions." [2]   It seems highly probable, also, that these mimetic dances were of several kinds, corresponding in tone to tragedy, comedy, and satyric drama.[3]   In any case, we may rest assured that such *orchestikoi* (ὀρχηστικοί), or dancers, as are depicted on a red-figured amphora at Corneto (Fig. 23) provided at least some of the merriment associated with the mime.   It is important, indeed, to remember that the mime, both in its earliest days and in its latest, was not merely an affair of spoken dialogue.   The music-hall comedian of to-day mixes dialogue (or monologue) with snatches of song, a few dance steps, and perhaps a little sleight-of-hand, and the modern representative of the ancient

[1] See Heinz Schnabel, *Kordax : Archäologische Studien zur Geschichte eines antiken Tanzes und zum Ursprung der griechischen Komödie* (Munich, 1910) ; F. Weege, *Der Tanz in der Antike* (Halle, 1926).

[2] καὶ γὰρ οὗτοι [the dancers] μιμοῦνται διὰ τῶν σχηματιζομένων ῥυθμῶν καὶ ἤθη καὶ πάθη καὶ πράξεις (*Poetics*, i, 6).

[3] On this see particularly J. Sommerbrodt, *De triplici pantomimorum genere*, in *Scænica* (Berlin, 1876), pp. 36–47.

C

mime-actor is precisely this music-hall comedian, who thus varies his methods of appeal to the audience, and who mingles lascivity with pathos, proverbial wisdom with personalities. Nor must the musical element in the mime be forgotten ; dance in drama obviously associates itself at once with music. The *mimodos* (μιμῳδός), the singer of mimes, was as important a person as the *mimus*, or speaker of mimes, himself ; rather might we say that the *mimus* and the *mimodos* were one and the same person ; for the mimic drama mingled together spoken and operatic features. Ancient authors, indeed, made attempts to classify the different forms which this operatic element might

Fig. 23. MIMIC DANCERS

Red-figured amphora at Corneto. From Heinz Schnabel, *Kordax: Archäologische Studien* (C. H. Beck'sche Verlagsbuchhandlung, Munich, 1910), Taf. I.

assume. The *magodia* (μαγῳδία), the *hilarodia* (ἱλαρῳδία), the *simodia* (σιμῳδία), and the *lysiodia* (λυσιῳδία) are four of these semi-distinct forms thus analysed.[1] The first and second of these seem to have been distinguished by their general atmosphere ; according to Athenæus, Aristoxenus thought that *hilarodia* was to be associated with tragedy and *magodia* with comedy. Concerning the latter, Athenæus informs us that it introduced as its chief characters women, gallants, and pandars, sometimes showing a drunk man at a feast approaching his mistress. In other words, the form of lyric mime which is known as *magodia* introduced precisely those intrigue themes which so pleased later spectators in the days of Imperial Rome.[2] The *hilarodia* was associated with tragedy only in the way of burlesque. " The *hilarodos*," says Festus,

" is the singer of lascivious and facetious ditties," [3] no doubt ' taking off ' the mouthing heroes of serious drama. Concerning *simodia* and *lysiodia* almost nothing is known. Some derive the names from a Simus of Magnesia and a certain Lysis, who, it is said, made the *magodia* and *hilarodia* ' literary,' and, in doing so, gave them their own names. Others prefer to go back to a mythic god Lysius (Λύσιος), who is supposed to be a kind of Dionysus, and to a Simus (Σῖμος), who is taken as a satyric figure.[4] Both, according to this interpretation, would be connected with the same worship of Dionysus which gave us regular tragedy and comedy. Whatever the truth, this is certain, that all these forms belong to one general type, the *mimodia* ; that the *mimodia*, as its name implies, is merely a type of lyric or operatic mime ; and that all these forms, together with dancing, were mentally classed together in antiquity—does not Plutarch thus combine the singers of *mimodia* and the terpsichorean artists (μιμῳδοῖς καὶ ὀρχησταῖς) ? [5] All had something very definite to do with the later history of the mime.

---

[1] On this subject see Dieterich, p. 30, and Reich, i, 234 and 532. The most important classical discussion of these forms appears in Athenæus, xiv, 620c–f, 621a–e. On this see E. Hiller, *Zu Athenæus* (*Rheinisches Museum*, xxx (1875), 68–78).
[2] See *infra*, pp. 119–120.
[3] " Hilarodos lascivi et delicati carminis cantator."—*De verborum significatu* (ed. W. M. Lindsay, Leipzig, 1913), p. 90.
[4] Reich holds to the former explanation ; Dieterich, quoting Usener's *Götternamen* (p. 355), believes in the divine origin.
[5] Plutarch, *Sulla*, ii.

34

ACROBATS AND JUGGLERS

So, too, had the acrobats and the jugglers.[1] As far back as the days of the *Iliad* we hear of the *kybisteter* (κυβιστητήρ), or 'tumbler.' The word is derived from κυβιστάω, 'I tumble headlong.'[2] That such acrobats, probably combining with their gambollings the activities of the *thaumatopoios* (θαυματοποιός), or 'conjurer' (from θαῦμα, 'a wonder or marvel'),[3] continued their entertainments in one unbroken line of tradition may hardly be denied, although, quite naturally, records of their profession are scarce. More must be said of their activities when we reach the period of Roman grandeur ; here are to be noted merely the antiquity of their art and the impress which that art made on the mimic drama. While, of course, these acrobats and jugglers were not confined to the Peloponnese, it is probable that through their initiative the professional performances of the mimes were inaugurated. The 'entertainers' were not beings kept apart from the actors. Two inscriptions at Delos mention a θαυματοποιὸς Κλευπάτρα (a juggler or acrobat named Cleopatra), along with four τραγῳδοί (tragic actors) and two κωμῳδοί (comic actors), while another θαυματοποιὸς Σέρδων or Κέρδων (a juggler named Serdon or Kerdon) occurs among another company of theatrical performers. The dates of the two inscriptions are 270 and 261 B.C. respectively.[4] This is late evidence, it is true, but the association of the three types of entertainers in all probability stretches far back to earlier centuries, and when Diodorus informs us that "Antiochus took delight in mimes and actors, indeed in all kinds of entertainers, and strove to learn their art,"[5] we must believe that there was but little distinction in his mind between one and another.

Fig. 24. GREEK ACROBATIC DANCER
Vase in the British Museum (F. 232).

This last quotation indicates well that the θαυματοποιός was by no means a person despised. In the days of Alexander many of these men were patronized by the great, and Athenæus saw fit, in his enormous collection of fact and anecdote, to signalize the names of some of the more famous in this profession—Eurykleides, whose statue was set up in the Athenian theatre alongside that of Æschylus ;[6] Theodorus, a juggler, a statue in honour of whom, with a conjurer's pebble in his hands, was raised by the people of Hestiæa and of Oreus ;[7] Xenophon, a θαυματοποιός, whose art was carried on by his pupil, Kratisthenes ;[8] Nymphodorus, another of the same art ; Skymnus of Tarentum ; Philistides of Syracuse ; and Herakleitus of Mitylene.[9] Some of their tricks are described for us. Kratisthenes could make fire burn spontaneously. Diopeithes, the Locrian, " attached bladders filled with wine and milk under his belt, then squeezed them and pretended to bring these liquids from his mouth."[10] Matreas, the πλάνος, or clown, of Alexandria, who was famous alike among

35

Grecians and Romans, " made up problems in burlesque of Aristotle's and propounded them in public : such as " Why does the sun descend and not dive ? " or " Why do sponges drink together but not get drunk ? " [1]

Further evidence regarding the association of mimes and jugglers is provided by this account, for alongside the θαυματοποιοί, Athenæus refers to Eudicus, a *gelotopoios* (γελωτοποιός), and to another who presented ' mimed dithyrambs.' [2] The word *gelotopoios* signifies literally ' he who arouses laughter,' and it may perhaps be taken as the equivalent of a buffoon. In form it reminds us of the now familiar *thaumatopoios*, but in sense it evidently had to do with regular dramatic performances. This Eudicus, Athenæus tells us, won his popularity for his skill in miming, particularly in imitating wrestlers and boxers (μιμούμενος παλαιστὰς καὶ πύκτας). Agathocles, according to Diodorus,[3] was both a *gelotopoios* and a mime, while Artemidorus speaks of " the mimes and all the buffoons " (μιμολόγοι δὲ καὶ ἄπαντες οἱ γελωτοποιοί). We shall no doubt be close to the truth, therefore, if we imagine the earliest professional entertainers as a motley group of jugglers and acrobats, gradually enlarging and enriching their repertory by taking over whatever elements in folk festival seemed to them likely to appeal to the populace, becoming figures of importance until there was but little distinction among the varied ranks of " cithara-players and chorus-singers, mimes and rope-dancers " (*citharistrias, choraulas, mimos, schoenobatas*), who are all spoken of together by Sidonius Apollinaris in his poem on the city of Narbo.[4]

Fig. 25. An Ancient
Acrobat

Bronze in the Bibliothèque
Nationale, Paris (No. 3674).
Photo Giraudon

Professionalism means much in the world of the theatre, and it is precisely this professional tone which is the element of greatest importance in the work of these entertainers, but even beyond that they aided in directing the mime along certain paths which it was to follow down to its latest days. Their acrobatic agility guaranteed that the mime should never become static. Their frank seeking for fun demanded that it should never be dull, never be fettered by religious prejudice or ceremonial. These professional entertainers, above all other things, stood for secularism and the right to laugh. They demanded, too, that the mime with which they came to associate themselves should be thoroughly true to life. They preserved the mime as a μίμησις βίου (' an imitation of life '), and such terms as βιολόγος (*biologos*, ' biologue ') and ἠθολόγος (*ethologos*, literally ' character-speaker ') became almost identical with the original μῖμος, or mime.[5] The fuller significance of this we shall discuss later when we come to analyse the meaning of the word ' mime ' itself ; here be it sufficient to note one particular effect of this μίμησις βίου. In classical Athenian comedy and tragedy no women came upon the stage ; the entire Dionysiac performance was a masculine affair. From very early times, on the other hand, we find mimic actresses alongside the mimic actors, and this introduction of actresses the mime almost certainly owed to the influence of the juggling and acrobatic troupe. Athenæus refers to θαυματουργοὶ γυναῖκες (' acrobatic women ') alongside the θαυματοποιοί, and these ' acrobatic women ' may be regarded as the far-off predecessors of the actress

[1] Athenæus, 19d. Ἐθαυμάζετο δὲ παρ' Ἕλλησι καὶ Ῥωμαίοις Ματρέας ὁ πλάνος ὁ Ἀλεξανδρεύς · ἐποίησε δ' οὗτος καὶ παρὰ τὰς Ἀριστοτέλους ἀπορίας καὶ ἀνεγίνωσκε δημοσίᾳ, διὰ τί ὁ ἥλιος δύνει μὲν κολυμβᾷ δ' οὔ, καὶ διὰ τί οἱ σπόγγοι συμπίνουσι μὲν συγκωθωνίζονται δ' οὔ. It is in this section also that Athenæus mentions the ἠθολόγος Noemon, the clowns (πλάνοι ἔνδοξοι) Cephisodorus and Pantaleon, the " philosophic dancer " (φιλόσοφος ὀρχηστής) named Memphis (20a–c). *Cf.* also the account (iv, 130c) of the γελωτοποιός Straton, who danced with his wife when she was over eighty years of age.

[2] *Id.*, 19f. Στράτων ὁ Ταραντῖνος ἐθαυμάζετο τοὺς διθυράμβους μιμούμενος.

[3] *Cf.* Grysar, p. 242.   [4] xxiii, 300–301; *cf.* Reich, i, 522.

[5] See Reich (i, 284), who notes that Cicero associates the mime and the *ethologos* (*De oratore*, II, lix, 242), and Magnin (143–144, 147–157).

of to-day. The professional atmosphere allowed of their appearance, just as the "imitation of life" demanded their presence.

This is a matter of major importance; of less apparent importance, but none the less of interest to anyone who would understand aright the development of the early stage, is the fact that with these acrobat-mimes of a professional sort the puppet-show began to assume a place of value. Already in the fifth century B.C. Xenophon introduces us to a mimic actor who supports himself with his little, cord-controlled figures.[1] Numerous authors of later date testify to the skill with which these marionettes were managed. With absolute freedom they bent their necks, moved their hands and arms, and rolled their eyes, so that one could have sworn they were alive.[2] So popular did they become that on one occasion the Athenians handed over the great theatre of Dionysus to a νευροσπάστης (neurospastes, 'puppet-showman') named Potheinos.[3] The puppets naturally took over certain themes which were more largely interpreted by breathing actors, and as a result a kind of double influence ensued, the puppets taking farces from the performers, the performers themselves sometimes viewing in the puppets methods of expression which might be employed on the stage. Most of what we know of the ancient marionettes comes from considerably later times, but we must not forget, in noting the influence of these later puppet figures, that they have an ancestry which carries us back to that period when the last landmarks of history become enveloped in the mists and vapours of the prehistoric era. Out of these mists step the puppet showmen, the acrobats, and the jugglers, and by their side we can just distinguish the comic and terrifying forms of the Dionysiac demons who were to enter into their bodies, never to be exorcised.

Fig. 26
ACROBATIC
DANCER

Hellenistic terracotta. From *La Revue archéologique*, Sér. V, xix (1924), 216.

Vague as are the references, scattered as are the authorities, we have thus seen reason to believe that, prior to the development of Attic drama, and independently of the works of Epicharmus, there was a widespread activity of a theatrical kind among the Dorian peoples. Aristotle knew of this, and other critics recognized, beside the tragic, comic, and satyric forms of drama, a fourth, which was the mime, and the mime, scorned as it may have been at times, found its own supporters. Plato, we are told, loved the little playlets of Sophron; indeed, some have said that his own dialogues owed not a trifle to mimic example. If Demosthenes referred slightingly to "the mimes of the jesters" (μίμους γελοίων) a scholiast could arise who, no doubt repeating ideas of an antiquity far greater than his own, explained that, as tragedy is an "imitation" (μίμησις) and comedy an "imitation," then the mimes, which spring from the μίμησις βίου itself, must be the very essence of this literary inspiration.[4] After all, what pleased Plato was not likely to be entirely scandalous, what Aristotle saw fit to mention in his *Poetics* was not likely to be lacking entirely in literary form. The acrobats may have indulged in mere gymnastics, but the acrobats in themselves are of no import; when they came to associate themselves with the mime, then their dancing and leaping and tumbling were subordinated to dramatic necessity. Wandering from city to city and from land to land, they carried afar those traditions which once had been naught but local folk-customs associated with the joyous worship of Dionysus.

[1] Ἀλλὰ μὰ Δί', ἔφη, οὐκ ἐπὶ τούτῳ μέγα φρονῶ. Ἀλλ' ἐπὶ τῷ μὴν; Ἐπὶ νὴ Δία τοῖς ἄφροσιν· οὗτοι γὰρ τὰ ἐμὰ νευρόσπαστα θεώμενοι τρέφουσί με (*Symposium*, iv, 55). *Cf.* Reich, i, 669. On experiments made with mechanical model stages and puppet-figures see *Les Théâtres d'automates en Grèce au* ie *siècle avant l'ère chrétienne d'après les* Ἀυτοματοποιῖκὰ *d'Héron d'Alexandrie*, by V. Prou (*Mémoires présentés par divers savants à l'Académie*, I, ix (1884), 117) and Wilhelm Schmidt, *Heron von Alexandria* (*Neue Jahrbücher für das klassische Altertum*, ii (1899), 242–252).
[2] *Cf.* Apuleius, *De mundo*, xxvi, 351 (ed. P. Thomas, Leipzig, 1908, iii, 164).
[3] Athenæus, i, 19e. The still standard work on the marionettes is the *Histoire des marionettes en Europe depuis l'antiquité jusqu'à nos jours* (Paris, 1862) of C. Magnin.
[4] *Cf.* Reich, i, 55.

the rustic as a type is familiar in Epicharmus,[1] and once more we seem to be on the track of the influence of the mime upon literary comedy. The schoolmaster of Herodas is the son of Epicharmus' doctor and the grandson of the doctor of the *deikelistai* ; he is cousin-german of Socrates as presented in *The Clouds*. The pandar is another character whose presence is to be traced both in mime and in comedy. As a *leno* he is familiar in Latin drama, but concerning his ancestry we can say nothing. In the hands of Herodas he appears a kind of burlesque ἀλαζών type.

It is certain that Herodas' work does not by any means indicate the full scope of the early Greek mime. No doubt he has made it more ' artistic,' and some at least of its aspects have been by him entirely neglected.[2] On the other hand, no amount of sophistication can take the true mime quality from these little plays. They are thoroughly in accord with the tradition which we have been trying to trace, and they agree equally well with the later developments of the mimic drama in Rome. Unfortunately, however, we know not how or even whether they were acted. Some scholars have denied to them any sort of stage performance, but this is by no means certain, and the consensus of opinion now favours the view that they were written for, and were given, some kind of theatrical performance. From an examination of *The Jealous Woman* Nairn would even go so far as to suggest that three separate ' sets ' must have accompanied the acting of that play. More probably, in this as in the other mimes, a plain background with two or more doors, or, in lieu of that, a curtain with two openings, served to give the illusion both of inner and outer action.

With the plays of Herodas we have entered into the Alexandrian epoch, a period that witnessed the flourishing of many by-forms of the mimic drama. It was in the third century B.C. that Theocritus wrote his highly finished pastoral poems, one of which at least is naught but a refined mime, while records remain of much similar work patronized by the Ptolemies. The activities of the Alexandrians were well known to the Romans, so that, especially when we take into account the Phlyakes of the fourth century B.C., we can say with definite assurance that here we have a perfectly clear tradition traceable from the days of Epicharmus on to the times when Rome began to assume material power, and, in assuming that power, developed spiritual and artistic tendencies of her own.

THEOCRITUS AND SOPHRON

Epicharmus and Herodas contribute most fully to our knowledge of the earlier Greek mimic drama, but additional information is to be gleaned also from a variety of sources. Some of these, it is true, carry us from the sphere of the popular to the sphere of the sophisticated, but all serve to round out the conception basically outlined in the work of those two authors. Perhaps Theocritus need not detain us long, for Theocritus is the most literary and sophisticate of all. Born in Syracuse about the year 310 B.C., he seems to have spent a wandering life, visiting the little island of Kos, which was Herodas' home, visiting Greece, and visiting Alexandria. Most of his poems are simple bucolic idylls, but one, the Ἀδωνιάζουσαι (*Adoniazousai, The Women at the Festival of Adonis*), we should have recognized, even without the notes of the scholiasts, as a little mimic drama on the lines of the similar pieces we have already discussed.[3] Gorgo and Praxinoe are the interlocutors here, with occasional interludes from an old woman and a man. The scheme and treatment is the same as in the cognate plays, idle prattle on the women's part giving an impression of lifelikeness and reality to the whole. Whether this particular example was intended for performance we cannot tell ; it belongs, at any rate, to the tradition the course of which we have been following.

---

[1] See *supra*, p. 38. On this subject consult the important essay of O. Ribbeck, *Agroikos, eine ethologische Studie* (*Abhandlungen der k. sächsischen Gesellschaft der Wissenschaften*, Phil.-hist. Klasse, x (1885)).

[2] It is highly probable that we have to deal here, not with real stage pieces, but with poems inspired by such.

[3] The Theocritus literature is vast, and no attempt need be made here to indicate even part of the critical studies. English readers may be referred to Jack Lindsay's rendering of the poems (*Theocritos: The Complete Poems Translated*, 1929). A sketch of the life and selections appear in A. Körte, *Hellenistic Poetry* (pp. 279–320).

44

EPICHARMUS AND THE GREEK MIME

Concerning the work of the other mimic writers of these times unfortunately little sure information has survived. Susarion of Icara is but a name [1]—perhaps not even that, for he may be only a myth. Sophron, certainly, had a real personality in the fifth century B.C., but all the evidence regarding him and his writings comes from late, mostly scholastic sources.[2] He too is said to have been a Syracusan : he wrote two kinds of mimes—μίμους ἀνδρείους (' masculine mimes ') and μίμους γυναικείους (' feminine mimes '). Among the types of the former are mentioned a messenger, some old men, and fishers ; among those of the latter sempstresses, a mother-in-law, and women attending the Isthmian games. We may hence conclude that the majority of Sophron's mimes belonged to the life-like Herodian type, with sharp topical touches and much proverbial wisdom.[3] Beyond this we can say no more ; shadowy he remains in the night of time. Even as shadowy stands Xenarchus, Sophron's son, who wrote at Syracuse under the tyrant Dionysius.[4] All else is dark save the fact that he used the mime for purposes of political satire. Just a trifle more is known of a certain Phormus, who was a contemporary of Epicharmus and an intimate companion of the Syracusan tyrant Gelo.[5] Suidas, in referring to Epicharmus, says that that writer " invented comedy in Syracuse at the same time as Phormus," and later describes the latter as " a Syracusan, a comic poet, the contemporary of Epicharmus, a personal friend of Gelo, the Sicilian tyrant, and tutor of his children. He wrote seven plays," the titles of which have been preserved. Four are evidently legendary in character—Ἄδμητος (*Admetos*), Ἀλκίνοος (*Alkinoos*), Ἰλίου πόρθησις (*The Sack of Troy*), and Περσεύς (*Perseus*) ; two have animal titles—Ἀλκύονες (*Alkuones, The Kingfishers*) and Ἵππος (*Hippos, The Horse*) ; while one has a delightfully intriguing name—Κηφεὺς ἢ κεφάλαια (*Kepheus,*[6] *or The Crowns*). Whether the style of Phormus resembled that of Epicharmus cannot be determined, but the probability is that there

Fig. 29. A MIMIC FOOL
Terra-cotta in the British Museum.

was some general affinity between them. The suggestion here of mythological burlesque is characteristic, while it is interesting to notice how, in his work, there is provided another link between the antique animal dance and the more famous animal plays of Aristophanes and other Attic comedians.

THE EROTIC FRAGMENT

It were little use here lingering over the records of such men as Deinolochus, son or rival of Epicharmus, who wrote fourteen plays in the Dorian dialect,[7] or speculating on the identity of that Neikias, of whom the fame is but fragmentarily preserved in an inscription at the base of a statue found in Eski-Zaghra.[8] More profitable is it to consider two other tangible relics of the Greek mime, one a fragment of manuscript and the other a terra-cotta. The former is the so-called

---

[1] See Pickard-Cambridge, pp. 280–282.

[2] See Reich, i, 78, 183 ; J. A. Nairn, p. xxiii ; W. Christ, p. 242 ; *Sophronis mimographi fragmenta* (*Museum criticum, or Cambridge Classical Researches* (Cambridge, 1826), ii, 340–358, 559–564) ; J. Botzon, *Sophroneorum mimorum reliquiæ* (Marienburg, 1867) ; G. Kaibel, *Sophron. fragm.* 166 (*Hermes*, xxxiv (1899), 319–320) ; Ulrich von Wilamowitz-Möllendorff, *Lesefrüchte* (*Hermes*, xxxiv (1899), 206–209).

[3] Concerning the latter Reich (i, 78) quotes an interesting passage from Demetrius (περὶ ἑρμηνείας, 156).

[4] See Reich, i, 183 ; W. Christ, p. 242.   [5] See Pickard-Cambridge, pp. 413–414.

[6] Kepheus was the father of many sons who took part with Herakles in an ill-fated expedition.

[7] Suidas is the main source of information here.

[8] See *Bulletin de correspondance hellénique* (v (1881), 130, No. 2) and the emendations of W. Dittenberger in *Ein griechischer Mimendichter und Mimenkünstler* (*Rheinisches Museum*, xxxvi (1881), 463). The statue was raised to Neikias " by decree of his fatherland " on account of " the delightful mimes which he wrote so wittily " (τερπνῶν τε με(ί)μων οὓς ἔγραψεν ἀστείως).

45

" Erotic Fragment " discovered on a slip of papyrus some few years ago.[1] It may be dated about the middle of the second century B.C. There is no dialogue here, but there is a very definite dramatic note, and, after all, one of the Herodas mimes was nothing but a grandiloquent speech. Everything points to the fact that this is a fragment from a work belonging to the mime tradition. A girl, betrayed by her lover, is speaking :

> We twain with one will and one heart were united
>   Beneath the connubial yoke,
> And Cypris herself, that fair goddess of loving,
>   Our sealèd affection bespoke.
>
> Pain seizes me when I remember the way
>   His kisses burned into my soul—
> He, the author of discord, who left me abandoned,
>   He that played such a treacherous *rôle* !
>
> Dear stars of the heaven, and pale queenly night,
>   My partner in passion and pain,
> Bring me now, willing slave, to his side, whom fair Cypris
>   And conquering Love lead again.[2]

Such is the style of the piece, reminding us of that passionate *Incantation* by Theocritus, with its picture of a deserted maiden slowly melting the wax image of her lover over the flickering flames, with its haunting refrain " Turn, magic wheel, and draw my Love to me." There is more than lyric quality in both ; a dramatic situation is prefigured, and perhaps there is to be found here more than a mere suggestion of the ' love-mime ' as developed in the Alexandrian period.

An Athenian Terra-cotta

Finally, we come to the terra-cotta, one of the most interesting records of the early mime which have been preserved. A number of years ago this object, a terra-cotta lamp, was discovered on the west side of the Acropolis at Athens (Fig. 30).[3] Archæologists are agreed that it belongs to the third century B.C., so that it is contemporary with some other manifestations of the mime which we have had under consideration. On the outside of the lamp three actor figures are standing in a group. That they are actors, and mime actors at that, is proved by an inscription on the side, which reads : *ΜΙΜΟΛΩΓΟΙ ΗΥΠΟΘΗΣΙΣ ΕΙΚΓΡΑ*—that is to say, μιμολόγοι, ὑπόθεσις Ἔκυρα, which, being expanded, will signify, ' Mime actors ; the theme [or the subject of the play], *Hecyra*.' The word μιμολόγοι (*mimologoi*) need not cause any trouble. Already indication has been made of the fact that there were many variants of the familiar μῖμος, or mimus.[4] Thus the word λογομῖμος (*logo-mimos*) is used to describe a certain Herodotus who flourished at the Court of Antiochus II in Syria in the third century B.C.,[5] while *mimologos* was so usual that a verb μιμολογέω (*mimologeo*) was formed from the substantive. The *mimologoi*, therefore, are nothing but the ordinary mimes. The word ὑπόθεσις (*hypothesis*) was regularly used to indicate a mimic plot, so that ' theme,' ' subject,' or ' title ' would all be reasonable renderings. This title, as is indicated, was *Hecyra*—one familiar to

[1] A good deal has been written on this. See particularly H. Weil, *Un Monologue grec récemment découvert* (*Revue des études grecques*, ix (1896), 169–174), B. P. Grenfell, *An Alexandrian Erotic Fragment and other Greek Papyri chiefly Ptolemaic* (Oxford, 1896). *Cf.* also H. Diels' review of Grenfell's book in *Deutsche Litteraturzeitung* (xvii (1896), col. 614–615) ; Otto Crusius, *Grenfells Erotic fragment und seine litterarische Stellung* (*Philologus*, lv (1896), 353–384) ; Erwin Rohde's review in *Philologische Wochenschrift* (xvi (1896), col. 1045–48) ; F. Leo, *Die plautinischen Cantica und die hellenistiche Lyrik* (*Abhandlungen der k. Gesellschaft der Wissenschaften zu Göttingen*, N.F., i, No. 7, 1897).

[2] Anonymous translation in A. Körte, *Hellenistic Poetry* (pp. 348–349). This is a very free rendering, but catches something of the spirit of the original. For a similar piece see H. J. M. Milne, *Catalogue of the Literary Papyri in the British Museum* (1927), pp. 39–40.

[3] See Carl Watzinger, *Mimologen* (*Mittheilungen des k. deutschen archäologischen Instituts : Athenische Abtheilung*, xxvi (1901), 1–8) ; Reich, i, 553–555 ; S. Sudhaus, *Der Mimus von Oxyrhynchos* (*Hermes*, xli (1906), 273–274) ; R. Herzog, *Zur Geschichte des Mimus* (*Philologus*, lxii (1903), 35–38).   [4] See *supra*, p. 34.   [5] *Cf.* Reich, i, 281–283. The reference is from Athenæus, 19*d*.

46

us through its use by Terence and through another recorded *Hecyra* by Apollodorus of Karystus. The lamp shows that the theme, centuries before Terence touched it, was popular in the hands of the mimes. The three figures themselves all display characteristic features. To the left is a long-haired, youthful-looking person clad in a long *himation* and carrying a roll in his hand. The central actor is more definitely comic in conception. Wearing a short *chiton* which reaches only to his knees, he stands between the other two characters as though he had been receiving a heavy lecture from them. He has a broad and slightly hooked nose, a glistening bald head, and long, exaggerated ears. To his left comes a second *himation*-clad figure, beardless but older than his companion.

In the three characters, then, we have an illustration of a scene from a mimic burlesque play, *Hecyra*. Two of the actors do not differ from the actors of regular comedy, but the middle figure of the slave is thoroughly and distinctively mime-like. The exaggerated and yet intensely ' realistic ' face—the union of ridiculous burlesque and naturalism—agrees with the impression we have formed of the early mimic drama. His ass-like ears will be referred to later ; here a word must be said of that glistening bald head. In reading of the Latin mime we are constantly meeting a character who is described as

Fig. 30. Mimic Players at Athens

Third-century terra-cotta lamp in the National Museum, Athens. From *Mittheilungen des k. deutschen archäologischen Instituts : Athenische Abtheilung*, xxvi (1901), Taf. I.

the μωρὸς φαλακρός, or *mimus calvus*—in other words, as " the bald-headed mime." This figure, we are told, at each festival creates great amusement among the spectators in the theatres. He is not, we are assured, a bald-head by nature, but laboriously makes himself so by art, " going to the barbers' shops several times each day " (βαδίζων ἐπὶ τὰ κουρεῖα τῆς ἡμέρας πολλάκις).[1] Of him there will be much to say in later sections of this book. The Athenian lamp proves that already in the third century B.C. he had an important independent existence.

The Mimic Fool

That the theatrical figure thus delineated was not unique is proved by a number of other terra-cottas which show fundamentally the same features at varying dates.[2] Two of these bald-headed fools are grouped together in a small statuette, probably of Egyptian origin and now preserved at Hildesheim (Fig. 31). The short *chitons*, the shaved heads, the broad noses, and the full lips at once establish immediate identity with the type discovered in Athens. If, as seems likely, the mimes of Fig. 31 represent figures popular on the Alexandrian stage, then we have proof of the direct retention in

Fig. 31. Mimic Fools

Terra-cotta in the Pelizacus Museum, Hildesheim. From M. Bieber, *Denkmäler zum Theaterwesen im Altertum*, Taf. CVIII, 5.

---

[1] See the description of Synesius quoted by Reich, i, 831.

[2] It is, of course, sometimes difficult to determine when these ' grotesques ' are truly theatrical ; many must have had a magical significance, being used to ward off the evil eye. See A. J. B. Wace in the *Annual of the British School at Athens* (ix (1902–3), 241, and x (1903–4), 103–114); and A. H. S. Yeames in the *Annual of the British School at Rome* (iv (1907), 279–282).

Egypt of theatrical personages known in third-century Athens and probably passing back in tradition to the sixth century B.C. Fundamentally the same character is shown in Fig. 32,[1] although this particular example leads toward a still further development of the bald-headed person which we shall have to discuss in dealing with the Atellan farces.[2] A side-view of the figure is presented here, and note should be made of the short *chiton*, the hooked nose, the long ears, and the phallus.

Fig. 32. A MIMIC FOOL
Bronze (probably Greek) now in the Metropolitan Museum of Art, New York.
Photo Metropolitan Museum

At the back of the head is a small indentation which seems to have been made for the insertion of polished silver, the better to convey the impression of baldness. Another example of this μωρὸς φαλακρός is given in Fig. 33. Bald head, large ears, broad nose, full lips, and staring eyes are common to this, as to the others. The original terra-cotta is coloured yellow with dabs of a darkish red; it may be that, for effect, the μωρὸς φαλακρός occasionally, if not habitually, painted his face. Similar types are to be discovered in a number of other terra-cottas scattered throughout the larger archæological museums; the people of Greece and Rome truly loved to reproduce the features of their favourite laughter-makers. For the sake of comparison, it may be profitable here to add three or four other examples from originals in the British Museum. The first two of these (Fig. 34) are certainly not identical, but they show

Fig. 34. MIMIC FOOLS
Terra-cotta statuettes in the British Museum (1907-5-18-8 and 1907-5-18-9).

---

[1] This piece has an interesting history. It was reproduced, not altogether exactly, by Ficoroni in 1754 (*De larvis scenicis*, Pl. IX, 2) and then apparently disappeared. It has now turned up in America. See G. M. A. Richter, *Grotesques and the Mime* (*American Journal of Archæology*, II, xvii (1913), 149).

[2] Cf. *infra*, pp. 87–88, and see also V. de Amicis, *L'Imitazione latina nella commedia italiana* (Florence, 1897), pp. 22–25.

sufficient resemblance one to another to warrant the assumption that they are variants of the same type. The one on the left is gesticulating with his right hand, while the other holds a short crooked stick resembling a phallic symbol. Both have bald heads and large ears, and both wear short garments caught by a belt at the waist. The character shown in Fig. 35, on the other hand, is naked. He has the same facial characteristics as the others, so that we must believe that he too is a mimic fool. With an air of gauche triumph he comes dancing upon the stage, holding some object (perhaps a purse) in his left hand, as if he were crying, "Ha! I have it!" To complete the picture one other example is here presented (Fig. 36). By a comparison of one with another perhaps some general conception may be gained of the common features of the type and of the varying individual forms it assumed.

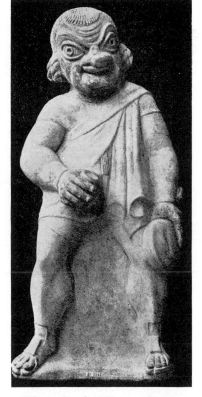

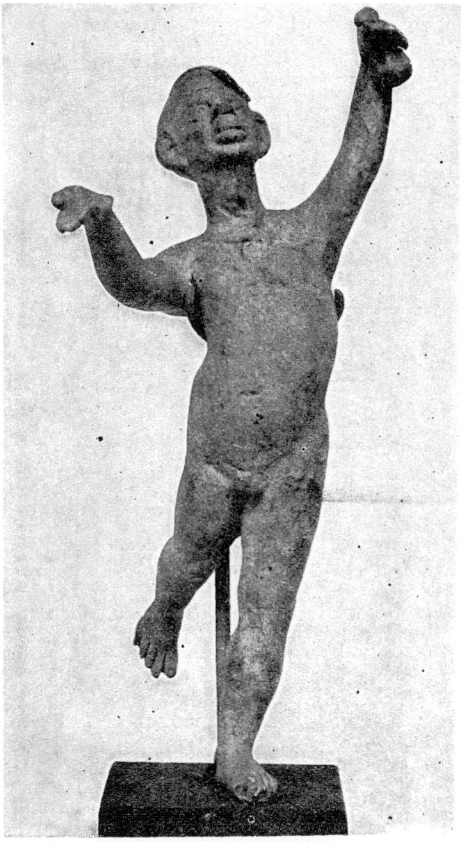

Fig. 35. A Mimic Fool
Terra-cotta statuette in the British Museum (1907-5-18-10).

Fig. 36. A Mimic Fool
Terra-cotta statuette in the British Museum (Case D, 234).

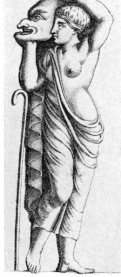

Fig. 37. Mask of the Bald-headed Fool
From Francisco Ficoroni, *Dissertatio de larvis scenicis* (Rome, 1754), Plate XXXXIV.

This final discussion concerning pictorial illustration will emphasize for us the necessity of thinking of the mime always in terms of the theatre. Literature, from the days of Epicharmus onward, may have entered in to add refinement to popular strength, but the popular strength, itself rooted to the stage, remained to the end its greatest and most powerful element. Above have been mentioned some records of actual entertainers who won special fame for themselves, and these records must be taken only as symbolic of many others. Already at an early date the mimes had become something more than the rude purveyors of vulgar merriment. Their appeal was universal; they were the companions of kings as well as the idols of the populace. The mimic actresses too soon came to assume those lofty airs and graces which were but the result of general flattery and common attention. A certain Myrtion, we are told, one of the most popular players of her time, was beloved of Ptolemæus Philadelphus (283–247 B.C.); with mention of her name this section may close, for

Athenæus, in citing her, unconsciously provides another link binding the new with the old. " One of the players," he describes her—μία τῶν δεικτηριάδων—and this word that he employs (δεικτηριάς, *deikterias*) recalls the fact that among the most primitive records of Dorian comedy was that which described the representations of the *deikelistai*. *Deikterias* and *deikelistes* have obviously something in common; as a name for a special type of mimic player the former seems to have an ancestry, to the antiquity of which we can place no bounds.

(iv) THE PHLYAKES

The trail now carries us northward. Hitherto the journey was to the south and the east, from the ancient Peloponnesus to Syracuse and Alexandria; now it moves upward into Italy itself. The Dorian settlers had not confined themselves to the shores of Sicily; onward they sailed to the Italian peninsula, leaving lovely traces of their wanderings at Pæstum and elsewhere, bringing with them from their homeland memories of native art and of native entertainment. It was here, in Southern Italy, among the Greek colonies, that the Φλύαξ (Phlyax) or Φλύακες (Phlyakes) flourished, the names being applied indiscriminately to plays and to players. On this dramatic form, because it is a bridge between Megara and Rome, our attention must now be concentrated.[1]

RHINTHON AND MYTHOLOGICAL BURLESQUE

That the Phlyax comedy was recognized generally by contemporaries as a kind of mime can be fully substantiated. Thus Athenæus, besides ranking the Phlyax with other forms of mimic drama,[2] refers to a certain Kleon, who flourished in the third century B.C., as " the best maskless actor among the Italian mimes " (τῶν Ἰταλικῶν μίμων ἄριστος ... αὐτοπρόσωπος ὑποκριτής), and as ' Italian mimes ' the Phlyax was known to later historians. Additional proof of identification is found in the facts that the word κίναιδος (*kinaidos*) was sometimes applied to the mime because of its occasionally obscene characteristics and that Suidas describes Sotades as a writer of Phlyakes or *kinaidous* (ἔγραψε φλύακας ἢ κιναίδους).[3] Little has been said by ancient commentators concerning the authors of these plays, for in all probability most of the Phlyax farce was made up of improvisation. Immediately after mentioning Kleon, Athenæus refers to another actor named Nymphodoros, who excelled in " the memorized mime " (ἐν τῷ μνημονευομένῳ μίμῳ), and the qualifying phrase serves to emphasize once more the necessity of regarding the whole field of the mime as essentially the actor's and not the dramatist's comedy. It is this that helps to keep the two kinds of play distinct, for, whereas comedy in the hands of an Aristophanes, a Menander, or a Terence tended to impose literature on the theatre, the mime nearly always compelled the ' poet ' to take a subordinate place. When the author as such intruded into the actor's field he succeeded only in destroying all about him. This seems to have been the fate of the Phlyax. One chief author in this kind has been remembered, a

---

[1] The Phlyakes farce is discussed in all works dealing with the Greek stage, but the emphasis is usually laid either on theatrical antiquities or on connexions with the literary drama. J. Sommerbrodt has an essay *De Phlyacographis græcis* (Breslau, 1875); see also Georg Thiele, *Die Anfänge der griechischen Komödie* (*Neue Jahrbücher für das klassische Altertum*, v (1902), 417–418). The standard work on the pictorial illustrations is that of H. Heydemann, *Die Phlyakendarstellungen auf bemalten Vasen* (*Jahrbuch des K. deutschen archäologischen Instituts*, i (1886), 260–313); additional information and criticism of his essay may be found in V. Macchioro, *Per la Storia della ceramografia italioia* (*Mitthei ungen des K. deutschen archäologischen Instituts in Rom*, xxvi (1911), 187–213); G. Patroni, *Questioni vascolari* (*Rendiconti della reale Accademia dei Lincei*, xxi (1913), 549–606); C. Picard in *Bulletin de correspondance hellénique* (xxxv (1911), 177–230); O. Jahn, *Beschreibung der Vasensammlung König Ludwigs in der Pinakothek zu München* (Munich, 1854); Adolf Furtwängler and Carl Reichhold, *Griechische Vasenmalerei* (Munich, 1900), iii, 178; and Bieber. On the different styles of workmanship in the vases see H. B. Walters, *Catalogue of the Greek and Etruscan Vases in the British Museum* (1896), iv, 15–21. E. Bethe in *Prolegomena* (Leipzig, 1896) (pp. 278–292) discusses the stage of the Phlyakes at some length, and P. Hartwig deals with the subject in *Œdipus vor der Sphinx* (*Philologus*, lvi (1897), 1–4).

[2] See *supra*, p. 26.   [3] Suidas, *s.v.* Σωτάδης.

certain Rhinthon of Tarentum,[1] who, writing Phlyax comedy, turned " tragedy into burlesque " ($\tau\grave{\alpha}$ $\tau\rho\alpha\gamma\iota\kappa\grave{\alpha}$ $\mu\epsilon\tau\alpha\rho\rho\upsilon\theta\mu\acute{\iota}\zeta\omega\nu$ $\grave{\epsilon}s$ $\tau\grave{o}$ $\gamma\epsilon\lambda o\hat{\iota}o\nu$).[2] The form in which he specialized, the so-called $\acute{\iota}\lambda\alpha\rho o\tau\rho\alpha\gamma\omega\delta\acute{\iota}\alpha$ (hilarotragodia, ' joyous tragedy ') was, however, no new form ; it is simply the mythological burlesque of earlier times ; and consequently we must believe that all Rhinthon did was to make it ' literary.' Now, the Phlyax comedy certainly existed as far back as the year 350 B.C., for the Assteas vases, showing scenes in that comedy, must be dated about the middle of the fourth century.[3] Rhinthon himself seems to have lived during the reigns of the first two Ptolemies—that is to say, about the end of the fourth century B.C.—and it is immediately after this that all trace of the Phlyax is lost. Rhinthon was not the father of the Phlyax ; he was maybe only the physician who administered to it a final and fatal dose of ' literarity.' [4]

As the references to Rhinthon show, the favourite theme of the Phlyax was mythological burlesque, and luckily we possess ample pictorial evidence to prove how this mythological burlesque was put upon the stage. The evidence in this kind, moreover, shows conclusively that ridicule of tragic subjects by no means furnished all the material of the ' Italian mime,' but that it, like the mimes elsewhere, introduced freely scenes of common daily life. Our information on these matters comes from the happy chance that a number of vase-makers, among whom one—Assteas—is known by name,[5] thought fit to decorate their work with scenes culled from the popular stage of their time, apparently reproducing those scenes with as much fidelity as the limitations of their art permitted. Many details in the Phlyax vases convince us that we are entirely justified in believing that they present more or less exactly the material stage characters and settings of the fourth century B.C. So important in every respect is the evidence thus given that considerable space must be devoted here to a general analysis of the subjects depicted and to a particular examination of some selected examples.

Herakles and Odysseus

At the very start we note an interesting, significant fact. In the mimes of Epicharmus both Herakles and Odysseus had been popular figures ; among the Phlyax vases many scenes clearly introduce these two characters as comic heroes. For the former Fig. 38 may be regarded as typical. Herakles, instantly recognizable by his skin covering, has been following a veiled woman, and, on her turning to reveal her face, is startled by her appearance. To his left stands an old man or woman, and to his right a slave looks on with trembling distress. Other vases show Herakles in a variety of situations. In one he is to be seen coming to the throne of Eurystheus, bearing with him a couple of cages which contain the Kerkopes, or men-monkeys, which he has caught.[6] Yet again he is depicted battering against a door with his club, while his servant, named Xanthias, seated upon a horse, keeps guard behind.[7] In Fig. 39 he is shown before Zeus. Old Iolaos to the right pours water on the altar, while the impudent hero, holding a tray with one hand, puts a sweet titbit into his mouth with the other. Zeus on his throne is shaking with impotent rage. With Apollo he appears in Fig. 40. An entertaining scene is this. Herakles and Iolaos have come to Delphi, and the poor wretched Apollo has sought for safety on the roof of his own temple. Iolaos stands on one side with right hand upraised, while Herakles, trying to put an ingratiating smile on his

---

[1] Although another authority says he was of Syracuse.
[2] W. Teuffel, Studien zu den römischen Komikern (Rheinisches Museum, viii (1853), 25–50), suggests that Plautus' Amphitruo is modelled on the fabula Rhinthonica (Rhinthon type of play) ; this is discussed and criticized by J. Vahlen, Plautus und die fabula Rhinthonica (Rheinisches Museum, xvi (1861), 472–476). For the fragments see Kaibel ; O. Crusius, Ein vergessenes Fragment des Rhinthon (Rheinisches Museum, xlv (1890), 265–272). On the burlesque in Greek drama consult P. Thomas, De la Parodie dramatique chez les grecs (Mons, 1873).
[3] Cf. Pickard-Cambridge, pp. 268–269.
[4] On Rhinthon see the charming little epigram presented in the Anthologia Palatina (vii, 414 ; ed. H. Stadtmüller, Leipzig, 1899, ii, 281).
[5] One vase (in the British Museum) preserves the name of a second artist, Python.
[6] Heydemann, p. 280, N (not O, as it is wrongly lettered) ; Bieber, Fig. 127. See Fig. 63.
[7] Heydemann, p. 283, R ; Bieber, Taf. LXXX, 1.

Fig. 38. Herakles and a Woman

Phlyax vase found at Lentini (Leontinoi), now in the Palazzo Pubblico, Lentini. From *Mittheilungen des k. deutschen archäologischen Instituts. Römische Abtheilung*, xv (1900), Taf. VI.

Fig. 39. Herakles before Zeus

Phlyax vase found at Ruvo, now in the Hermitage, Leningrad. From M. Bieber, *Denkmäler zum Theaterwesen im Altertum*, Taf. LXXVII.

ugly face, balances himself on the holy tripod and attempts to catch Apollo by tempting him with a basket of fruit.   His club he holds ready in his right hand.

None of the dialogue has been preserved, but these illustrations can arouse the imagination to depict the Herakles scenes, scenes perhaps not unlike that which Athenæus [1] records from a play called Λίνος (*Linos*), by Alexis, a writer of the so-called Middle Comedy. This play introduces Herakles bidden to select a book from which to read.   The hero takes a work on cookery, and the scene continues :

FIG. 40.   HERAKLES AND APOLLO

Phlyax vase in the Hermitage, Leningrad.   From M. Bieber, *Denkmäler zum Theaterwesen im Altertum*, Taf. LXXIX.

LINOS. Come on and select whatever book you wish.   Take time and look at all the titles with care ; then, at your leisure, you can read.   You'll find Orpheus there, Hesiod, tragedies, Chœirilus, Homer, Epicharmus, all sorts of histories.   By your choice your very nature will be revealed.

[*Herakles glances at the books and chooses one.*

HERAKLES. Here we are ; I'll select this one.

LINOS. Well, tell me what it is.

HERAKLES. A cookery-book, according to the title.

LINOS. Ah ! you are a wise man, that's clear ; for, disregarding those other works, you choose the essay of Simus.

HERAKLES. Simus ?   Who's he ?

LINOS. A very clever man.   Just at present he's much occupied with tragedy : among the whole bunch of actors he's by far the finest cook, as those deem who hire him, but among the whole bunch of cooks he's the worst actor, as those deem who have to see him act. . . .

[*Herakles drags back the conversation to the subject of eating.*

LINOS. You are a greedy individual !

HERAKLES. Go on ; say whatever you like about me.   I tell you, I *am* hungry ! [2]

[1] iv, 164*b, c, d*.

[2]
                  βιβλίον
ἐντεῦθεν ὅ τι βούλει προσελθὼν γὰρ λαβέ ·
ἔπειτ' ἀναγνώσει πάνυ γε διασκοπῶν
ἀπὸ τῶν ἐπιγραμμάτων ἀτρέμα τε καὶ σχολῇ.
'Ορφεὺς ἔνεστιν, 'Ησίοδος, τραγῳδίαι,
Χοιρίλος, "Ομηρος, 'Επίχαρμος, συγγράμματα
παντοδαπά.   δηλώσεις γὰρ οὕτω τὴν φύσιν
ἐπὶ τί μάλισθ' ὥρμηκε.   HP. τουτὶ λαμβάνω.
ΛΙΝ. δεῖξον τί ἐστι πρῶτον.   HP. ὀψαρτυσιά,
ὥς φησι τοὐπίγραμμα.   ΛΙΝ. Φιλόσοφός τις εἶ,
εὔδηλον, ὃς παρεὶς τοσαῦτα γράμματα
Σίμου τέχνην ἔλαβες.   HP. ὁ Σῖμος δ' ἐστι τίς ;
ΛΙΝ. μάλ' εὐφυὴς ἄνθρωπος.   ἐπὶ τραγῳδίαν
ὥρμηκε νῦν καὶ τῶν μὲν ὑποκριτῶν πολὺ
κράτιστός ἐστιν ὀψοποιός, ὡς δοκεῖ
τοῖς χρωμένοις, τῶν δ' ὀψοποιῶν ὑποκριτὴς
[κάκιστός ἐστι τοῖς θεωμένοις] . . .
ΛΙΝ. βούλιμός ἐσθ' ἄνθρωπος.   HP. ὅτι βούλει λέγε ·
πεινῶ γάρ, εὖ τοῦτ' ἴσθι.

The other popular figure of the Syracusan mime, Odysseus, certainly appears on at least one vase (Fig. 41), which illustrates the rape of the palladion. Odysseus, draped in a mantle, holds a sword in his right hand. On his head is a white *pilos*, or peaked hat, of which more must be said hereafter. Behind him comes Diomedes with a shield on his back. The palladion, in white and yellow, bears a helmet and a shield. Still another vase (Fig. 42) looks as if it depicted an Odysseus scene. A man with the same *pilos* and a younger, dark-haired companion are seizing a woman who crouches between them on the ground. Odysseus —for the first man seems to be he—brandishes his short sword in the air.

Fig. 41. ODYSSEUS AND THE PALLADION
Phlyax vase in the British Museum (F. 366).

ZEUS AND OTHER MYTHOLOGICAL FIGURES

Herakles and Odysseus, however, are not the only heroes of the Phlyax burlesque. Zeus appears frequently in person. Fig. 43 shows this god seated on a throne, with the symbol of his power, the eagle, in his left hand. He is looking,

with some perturbation, at a man with the Odysseus *pilos* who is approaching him by means of a flight of steps. On the ground below stands a slave, bearing sack, basket, and staff. In another vase (Fig. 44) the same god is shown in the act of breaking Leda's egg with a huge hammer. Out of the egg, like the Newly Born in *Back to Methuselah*, Helena makes her appearance, while Leda herself looks in at a door, and a slave on the other side warns the god to be careful in the wielding of the axe. A thoroughly typical scene is this, and fully instinct with

Fig. 42. ODYSSEUS STRUGGLING FOR A WOMAN
Phlyax vase at Jatta (No. 901). From M. Bieber, *Denkmäler zum Theaterwesen im Altertum*, Taf. LXXXIV, 2.

life. Equally vivid in its own way is the vase-picture (Fig. 45) which depicts the god, bearing a ladder, approaching a window at which appears the head of one of his mistresses, probably Alcmena. This woman has flowing hair caught in a golden net and bound with a pearl-ornamented purple bandeau. At the side of the window is Hermes, holding a lamp in his right hand. He is

54

Fig. 43. ZEUS RECEIVING A VISIT

Phlyax vase found at Bari. From M. Bieber, *Denkmäler zum Theaterwesen im Altertum*, Taf. LXXVIII.

dressed in a yellow chlamys with violet lining and the *petasos* on his head is yellow, trimmed with red. A scene very similar to this, and possibly intended to represent the same characters, appears on a bell-crater preserved in the British Museum (Fig. 46), where Alcmena wears a purple-ornamented *chiton*, and Zeus, mounting the ladder, holds up four apples, evidently as a kind of offering.

Mythological and legendary subjects come upon us, as we study these vases, in admirable confusion. A fragment of a vase by Assteas shows a woman, armed with spear and shield, standing on a pedestal. She is Athena Promachos. A hook-nosed and dark-haired hero clasps her knees, while he is seized from behind by a woman who is marked on the vase as Cassandra. The hero, therefore, is Ajax. An old, hag-like woman to the right (marked *IHPNA*, 'priestess') recalls the other, more antique old woman of the Dorian mime.[1] Still another depicts the death of Priam. Seated upon an altar, he shrinks back from

Fig. 44. THE BIRTH OF HELENA

Phlyax vase found at Bari. From M. Bieber, *Denkmäler zum Theaterwesen im Altertum*, Taf. LXXX.

[1] Bieber, Fig. 129; Ettore Gabrici in *Ausonia*, v (1911), Pl. III (*Frammento inedito di un vaso di Assteas*, pp. 56–68).

55

Neoptolemus, who pursues him with upraised sword (Fig. 47). One of the most famous vases of this type has for its subject the struggle of Hephæstus and Ares over Hera (Fig. 48). On the imprisoning chair sits the goddess, marked by the painter as Hera (*IHPA*). To her right is Hephæstus (labelled by the painter as *ΔAIΔAΛOΣ*, Daidalos), wearing a fez-like cap. To her left is Ares (called here *ENEYAΛIOΣ*, Eneualios), clad in a helmet with two long feathers and bearing, like Hephæstus,

Fig. 45. Zeus visiting Alcmena

Phlyax vase in the Vatican. From M. Bieber, *Denkmäler zum Theaterwesen im Altertum*, Taf. LXXVI.

a shield and a lance. On still another vase appears a representation of an Antigone theme; Antigone's old servant, clad in her clothes, stands before Creon and one of his guards.[1] Another yet seems to show, in an actor who rides on a (property?) fish, that Taras who was the native hero of the home of the Phlyax—Tarentum.[2]

Among these mythological scenes episodes of a Dionysiac character figure freely. Bacchic revels of one kind or another appear on several vases, and there are some in which portions of the Dionysus legend are to be traced. Thus the god appears along with Ariadne in one example,[3] and in others along with actors the correct identification of whom presents difficulty. Bearing a

[1] Heydemann, p. 303*t*; Bieber, Fig. 130.
[2] Heydemann, p. 307β; A. Reinach, *Répertoire des vases peintes* (Paris, 1909), ii, 332; Bieber, Fig. 131.   [3] Heydemann, p. 274, E.

thyrsus he steps behind a comic flute-player, stump-nosed and big-mouthed;[1] leaning on a stick, he holds out a couple of apples to an unnamed actor (Fig. 49); or at an altar he stands with a similar person.[2] Cognate legends too occur here. In one (Fig. 50) appear no less than six figures. At the top of a short flight of steps stands a bald-headed comic actor who has just laid down his sack and *pilos* in order to assist an old man to ascend. This actor is marked ... *VΘIAΣ*, which certainly is to be interpreted as *ΞΑΝΘΙΑΣ*, or Xanthias. The old man also is named; he is *XIPΩN*, the centaur Cheiron. Perhaps the white-haired character pushing him from behind is intended to be a second centaur. A youth (possibly Achilles), clad in long, solemn garments, is gravely looking on, while above two women marked *NY...AI* (*Nύ[μφ]αι*) are watching the scene; they are the Nymphs. As in so many of these vases, all is life, all is merriment. The figures depicted almost serve to recall the actual laughter which must have echoed once in theatres long since crumbled to dust, must have been echoing in that theatre of Tarentum when, in the year 302 B.C., the audience were startled from burlesque to reality on seeing the Roman fleet slowly sailing into their harbour.[3] That the centaur-farce inspiring the artist to paint this vase was not unique is proved by another scene, which shows a comic black-haired slave standing in front of a

Fig. 46. ZEUS VISITING ALCMENA
Phlyax vase in the British Museum (F. 150).

Fig. 48. HEPHÆSTUS AND HERA
Crater found at Bari, now in the British Museum (F. 269). From the British Museum *Guide to Greek and Roman Life.*

Fig. 47. THE DEATH OF PRIAM
Vase found at Naples, now in Berlin Museum (3045). From the *Jahrbuch des k. deutschen archäologischen Instituts,* xxvi (1911), Fig. 28.

---

[1] Heydemann, pp. 277–278, L. [2] *Id.,* p. 298*l.*
[3] Dio Cassius says that the people of Tarentum were witnessing a Phlyax comedy on this occasion (*Cassii Dionis Cocceiani historiarum romanarvm quæ supersunt,* ed. U. P. Boissevain (Berlin, 1895), fr. 39, 5; i, 114).

Fig. 49. A Drunken Actor before Dionysus
Phlyax vase in the British Museum (F. 183).

centaur who holds an amphora in his hands.[1] Noting these and the Dionysiac subjects, it is important to remember the occurrence of Dionysus matter among the mimes of Epicharmus, as well as the presence, in *Herakles among the Centaurs*, of a play in which centaurs made their appearance. It is just possible that the black-haired actor shown in the vase last mentioned may be the Pholus referred to by the Syracusan author.

SCENES OF DAILY LIFE

Besides these illustrations of scenes which we can definitely say belonged to the sphere of mythological burlesque, there are many others which seem to depict scenes from plays of ordinary life. Some of these, it is true, may likewise deal with legendary matter; but several at least cannot be placed in the same category as the others. Such, for example, is the little sketch of an old man looking back with some considerable misgiving at his slave, who holds a casket in his left hand (Fig. 10). Such, too, is that which shows a character marked *ΦΙΛΟΤΙΜΙΔΗΣ* ('Mr Desirous-of-Honour') sharing a meal with a woman, *ΧΑΡΙΣ* ('Miss Grace'), while a slave, *ΞΑΝΘΙΑΣ* (Xanthias) gazes moodily on them from the background (Fig. 51). It is positively certain, from the names of the characters, that we are here well outside the sphere of mythology. This particular example may be compared with another by the master Assteas, which shows a rude scene of action (Fig. 52). The centre of the

Fig. 50. Cheiron and his Companions
Phlyax vase found in Apulia, now in the British Museum (F. 151).
[1] Heydemann, p. 304, W.

58

Fig. 51. A GOOD FEAST

Phlyax vase found at Ruvo.   From M. Bieber, *Denkmäler zum Theaterwesen im Altertum*, Abb. 132.

stage is occupied by a chest presumably containing treasure.   On it is lying an old man named
ΧΑΡΙΝΟΣ (Charinos).   Evidently he wishes to preserve his gold, and is resisting the efforts
of two other men, named *ΕΥΜΝΕΣΤΟΣ* (Eumnestos) and *ΚΟΣΙΛΟΣ* (Kosilos), to drag him

off.   At the extreme right stands a fourth,
possibly the slave of the old man, who is called
ΚΑΡΙΟΝ (Karion).   From the names it seems
clear that this is a ' realistic ' scene, and not
one of legendary personages.

It would be impossible in the scope of
this section to present even a moderate percentage of the many scenes which are to be
found depicted on these vases.   In every one
there is movement, vigour, and rude comic
force.   Scenes of eating are common; scenes
of theft—mostly theft of wine or food—
occur as frequently.   Intrigue episodes, similar to that in which Zeus and Alcmena appear,
are represented here, and often do old men
receive a severe lecture from their better
halves.[1]   Many vases reproduce situations

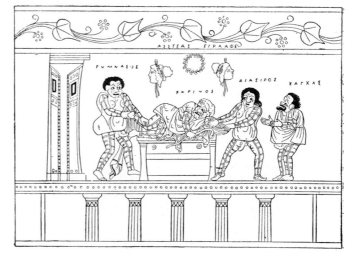

Fig. 52.   THE TREASURE CHEST

Phlyax vase found at Nola, now in Berlin.   From Baumeister, *Denkmäler des klassischen Alterthums* (1888), iii, No. 1830.

[1] Heydemann, p. 286, V.

59

familiar in the sphere of regular comedy; as in Menander or Terence an old man takes his drunken son to task after he has returned from a midnight revel (Fig. 53). To ordinary life too belongs that vase which clearly illustrates a play which might have been called *The Settling of the Rent* (Fig. 54). To the right sits a woman with a stilus in her right hand and an 'account book' in her left. Before her stands a man with a similar account book. He is lecturing severely a wretched peasant, who raises pleading hands and seems about to burst into tears.

THE TYPICAL MASKS

The subjects of these scenes are obviously of prime importance, and, as we have seen, the situations depicted are precisely those with which we have become familiar in the ancient Dorian mime. The Phlyax is simply a particular form taken by the vast dramatic movement which, arising in or around Megara, spread southward to Egypt and westward to Italy, retaining always its old interests—depiction of real life and a determination to allow no mystic thoughts to interfere with its profound secularism. The subjects, however, by no means furnish all that is of interest in the Phlyax vases. The characters

Fig. 53. THE RETURN FROM THE REVEL
Phlyax vase found at Capua, now in the British Museum
(F. 189).

too have their own importance. Among these we can distinguish a number of what are evidently stock types. There is the regular old man, of whom there seem to be three main varieties. The first has a snub nose and clean-shaven protruding chin as in Fig. 43; the second has a hooked nose, a bald patch in the centre of his head, and a straggling white beard (see Fig. 10); while the third is more 'ordinary' or realistic in features, like the Philotimides of Fig. 51. God-like figures, such as Zeus, and common mortals seem to have been played in the same mask, and Odysseus (Figs. 41 and 42), save for his *pilos*, is simply one of the old men. Of the middle-aged characters Herakles and Apollo may be taken as representative of two types. The former is dark-haired, and sports a kind of black stubbly beard and moustache. His nose is broad and hooked, while some illustrations show him with a row of wicked-looking teeth (Figs. 38, 39, and 40). The latter (Fig. 40) is also distinctive, wearing a mask which bears individual features. A

Fig. 54. THE SETTLING OF THE RENT
Phlyax vase found at Ruvo, now in the Hermitage, Leningrad.

worried, foolish expression is cast over it, and its reappearance in non-mythological scenes makes us believe that it was a stock-mask of a kind similar to that of Herakles. Two or three slave types are likewise to be distinguished. One has a stump nose, a wrinkled brow, an open mouth, and dark hair (Fig. 44 ; the Daidalos of Fig. 48 has the same mask). Along with this goes another type, in which the centre of the head is bald and the mouth is abnormally broad (Figs. 50 and 51). As in both these vases this slave is called Xanthias, we may be justified in believing that the name was regularly used for this stock type. Perhaps when he appeared upon the stage he was not unlike the statuette of a comic actor (Fig. 55) which, although it does not in any wise belong to the Phlyax tradition, may be utilized here for purposes of comparison and for the un-doubted interest it possesses in showing us the actor himself beneath his mask. The third Phlyax slave type is very similar to the second, having also an extraordinarily wide mouth, but differing from the other in having lighter hair on the temples and not such apparent baldness on the top (Fig. 38). It may very well be that a statuette found in the island of Ortygia and now in the Syracuse Museum (Fig. 56) is of this special variety ; it seems, at any rate, to have something to do with the Phlyax type. Still a fourth slave is suggested in another vase (Fig. 57), where we see two men, one of the black ' Herakles ' type, and the second a bald-head, with one eyebrow raised, as, we are told by Pollux, were raised the eyebrows of some ordinary comic masks. Again for purposes of comparison may be presented here a Hellenistic mask of a comic actor which shows clearly enough the effect of these asymmetrical brows (Fig. 58). The Phlyax vase which introduces this character seems to show a scene in which two slaves are triumphantly carrying off some ' goodies ' to a feast.

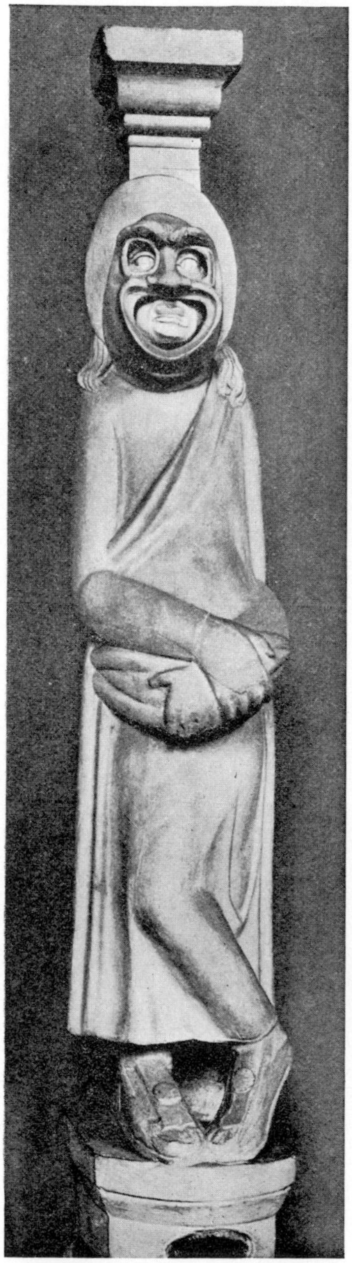

Fig. 56. A PHLYAX SLAVE

Terra-cotta statuette found at Ortygia, now in the Syracuse Museum, No. 1522. From M. Bieber, *Denkmäler zum Theater-wesen im Altertum*, Taf. LXXV, 5.

An analysis of the women's masks may be omitted here, but atten-tion must still be drawn to a pair of remaining types among the masculine figures. One of these is that represented by the peasant of Fig. 54. White-haired, this character has a peculiar under-jaw which protrudes mightily and then curves sharply upward. Already we have found the rustic as a stock type in Epicharmus ; here without a doubt we are presented with his physical appearance. Particularly interesting for comparative purposes is the vase which depicts the death of Priam (Fig. 47), for the monarch there has precisely the same mask as the unfortunate peasant. In such wise, of course,

Fig. 55. STATUETTE OF A COMIC ACTOR

Statuette found at Tralles, in Asia Minor, now in the Museum at Constantinople.

Photo Giraudon

did the Phlyakes succeed in burlesquing the legendary tales which had been treated majestically by the tragic poets. Finally, one other vase must be particularly noted (Fig. 59). This depicts an actor holding a long crook in his hand. He is an old man with raised eyebrows, and perhaps not fundamentally different from the other old men we have been considering. That which is interesting in this vase is the suggestion of a kind of cap with two peaks not unlike later fool's caps. Moreover, to the right of the picture is painted a bird. Seemingly it has something to do with the actor figure; is it too much to hazard the suggestion that the man is wearing a 'cock-cap'? Nothing can be said for certain, but when we compare this figure with the engraving of a terracotta reproduced by Ficoroni (Fig. 60), and when we compare both with the fool's cap and its cockscomb in the Middle Ages, we have at least to ask ourselves whether we are not in touch with a tradition which extends over many centuries. But this question too will occupy our attention later.[1]

Fig. 57. PREPARATIONS FOR A FEAST

Phlyax vase in the Hermitage, Leningrad. From M. Bieber, *Denkmäler zum Theaterwesen im Altertum*, Taf. LXXXVI, 2.

The costume of the characters has almost equal interest. Among the men there are two main types of dressing to be noted. In both the actors wear plain-coloured or striped tights (the Greek ἀναξυρίδες, *anaxurides*) fitting closely to the legs. Sometimes they have flat shoes, but more commonly their feet are bare. The distinction between the two types is that the first have a thin body-covering of a flesh colour, obviously simulating nakedness, while the second wear a short *chiton*, generally with a coloured border at the bottom. Most of the actors, whether clad in the one costume or in the other, have heavy padding (σωμάτιον, *somation*) of a comic kind, and practically all exhibit a large phallus. When we compare these costumes with the earlier Dorian stage dress or with that of the Attic comedy (see Figs. 3, 4, 5, 6, 7, and 8) no doubt can remain in our minds as to their substantial identity or relationship. The direct line of tradition is to be traced not only in subject and character, but in dress as well. At the same time this comic costume is not the only one presented on these vases. Occasionally, as in Fig. 43, a divine person such as Zeus is accoutred in a richer mantle; Apollo in Fig. 40 is similarly clad. This, however, is not of vital importance. Greater significance attaches to the fact that in the right-hand person in Fig. 50 we see a

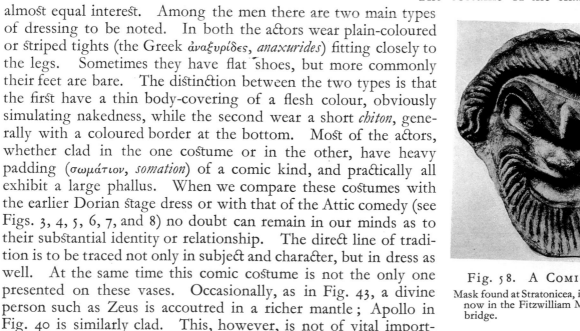

Fig. 58. A COMIC MASK

Mask found at Stratonicea, in Asia Minor, now in the Fitzwilliam Museum, Cambridge.

[1] See *infra*, pp. 160–162.

character who is by no means comically portrayed. Who this person is does not matter in the least. The point of value is that alongside the comic figures the Phlyax farce could introduce types of an 'ordinary' kind, and in considering the evidence of the vases it would seem that we must make allowance for the fact that the artists, in depicting their scenes, would naturally select the most comic, because the most vitally interesting, characters. In all probability, the typical mythological burlesque, or *hilarotragodia*, consisted of a play in which appeared four or five stock comic masks moving beside a number of persons treated in a more or less serious way. The contrast, one believes, may well have provided greater merriment than the isolated presentation of comic types alone ever could have done.

THE PHLYAX STAGE

As a final subject of interest comes the form of stage illustrated in these South Italian vases. Up to this point we have had no guide as to the methods of performance used by the mimes; now we meet with a wealth of valuable illustrative material. Not all the vases give indication of the stages employed, but from those which do we can differentiate several variant forms; and the very fact that the forms are different leads us to trust the more in the realism of the delineation. The most primitive type is shown in Figs. 10 and 54. In the latter three plain posts support a not very level or regularly hewn platform on which the characters are standing.

Fig. 59. A Phlyax Fool

Vase found at Pæstum, now in the Museo Nazionale, Naples. From H. Heydemann, *Die Phlyakendarstellungen auf bemalten Vasen* (*Jahrbuch des k. deutschen archäologischen Instituts*, i (1886), 274, F).

Fig. 60. A Mimic Fool

Roman terra-cotta. From F. Ficoroni, *Dissertatio de larvis scenicis et figuris comicis antiquorum romanorum* (Rome, 1754), Pl. LXXII, 2.

These posts are clear of one another, leaving a space underneath the platform. The same posts appear in Fig. 44, but are now partly covered by a piece of drapery roughly suspended by a set of nails below the stage. We cannot be sure whether the truncated posts of Fig. 42 are intended by the artist to be cut off by some drapery or not. In still other designs the posts have either disappeared or are joined up by panels, apparently of wood, bearing ornamental patterns. Fig. 48 thus shows two formal wing-like decorations, while another has six lines of vertical ornament. Perhaps we may regard all these as one type, consisting of a plain platform and unadorned posts, and sometimes introducing lower embellishments in the form of curtains or painted panels (the Greek πίνακες, *pinakes*). With Fig. 43, however, we reach a different model, for here, although the rough-hewn platform boards and curtains are still indicated, these boards are now supported on two Ionic columns. Columns are likewise indicated in Fig. 51, while five formal columns and a highly finished platform appear in Fig. 52. In several of these sketches steps from the stage to the ground are indicated, and it may be suggested that these steps could be of general utility. Flights of four steps appear in Figs. 43 and 50, and flights of seven steps in Figs. 38 and 48. It is to be observed that in Fig. 43 these steps are at the side of the stage, instead of at the front; this seems to indicate that they were not permanent structures, but could be moved at will.

Passing beyond the stage-platform itself, we notice in several of the vase paintings indications of a background for the actors, or what the Romans called a *frons scænæ*. In Fig. 38 there are two Ionic columns set at the very rear, and these support a decorative architrave. More commonly, however, the vases give the impression of a back wall broken by a door, or by doors, and having a window some ten or twelve feet above the stage level. Fig. 44 shows this door, through which Leda is peeping, and the small window is to be seen immediately above the shattered egg. In Fig. 51 a door is similarly placed, and fundamentally the same door is apparent in Fig. 52. It is significant that all of these are placed on the right-hand side of the stage (from the point of view of the actor). That the window was used for dramatic purposes is proved by Figs. 45 and 46, and perhaps by Fig. 50. We get the impression, therefore, of a back wall, containing a door and a window, and perhaps simulating the outside of a house. Two vases tell us something more. In Fig. 61 the artist has attempted to depict a cross-section (as it were) of the stage. The door is thus seen from the side instead of from the front. Over the thres-hold a man is stepping and lead-

Fig. 61. SIDE-VIEW OF A PHLYAX STAGE

Vase in the British Museum (F. 124). From H. Heydemann, *Die Phlyakendarstellungen auf bemalten Vasen* (*Jahrbuch des k. deutschen archäologischen Instituts*, i (1886), 293 d).

ing out a woman with his right hand. A similar effect is provided in Fig. 50. The steps rest against the edge of the platform seen from the side. Behind is a back wall surmounted by a sloping roof which would just cover the actual playing place. Perhaps we should assume the existence of this roof in all the Phlyax stages.

Here we have a 'formal setting.' There is no indication of change of scenery, but we do possess evidence of the use of what may be called scenic properties. Altars appear frequently, and many important characters are seated on thrones. In Fig. 40, moreover, occurs a tripod, and Apollo is seated on the top of a wooden structure which is obviously intended to be the temple at Delphi. Noticeable, too, is the laurel-bush in Fig. 38. This laurel-bush is represented in several vases not reproduced here, and its presence in these would

Fig. 62. TWO PHLYAX CLOWNS

Vase now lost, once in Hamilton collection. From H. Heydemann, *Die Phlyakendarstellungen auf bemalten Vasen* (*Jahrbuch des k. deutschen archäologischen Instituts*, i (1886), p. 307, γ).

seem to suggest that when the scene was supposed to take place in a grove a single bush was sufficient to create in the minds of the audience the imaginative illusion of the theatre.[1]

In discussing this subject, one would have wished to present the entire iconography of the Phlyax

---

[1] Although, of course, in Greek pictorial art tradition permitted the introduction of a simplified conventionalism. The Phlyakes vases, on the other hand, are sufficiently 'realistic' to allow of the above deduction.

characters, for every scene is full of life, laughter sparkles from each painted line. Space, however, must be reserved for other things, and possibly sufficient examples have been presented here to indicate the value of this material. Here we have something tangible. Here the joyous mime appears before us in concrete forms. That the Phlyax was not an independent growth seems proved, but as a dramatic type we hear no more of it after 300 B.C. Now we must move away from the Greek spheres to the sphere of native Italian activities, and, in doing so, we must ask ourselves whether this may not have been the end. The Phlyax certainly perished, and new Italic forms are to be traced in the following centuries ; are the two not really distinct ? Is it possible that there should be any direct connexion between the one and the other ? With this question in our minds, we may pass to the realm of the *fabula Atellana*, the apparently indigenous farce of Atella (the modern Aversa) which came to have such an influence on the Roman stage and which must form a starting-point for any consideration of the Roman mime.

Fig. 63. HERAKLES AND EURYSTHEUS
Vase found at Camarina, formerly in the Museo Biscari, Catania. From P. Duchartre,
The Italian Comedy (1929), p. 28.

(v) THE ATELLANÆ

Happily a connecting-link between the Greek and the Oscan-Roman is provided for us at once by one of the Phlyax vases themselves. This particular vase (Fig. 64) shows us a comic actor characteristically enough leaning against the pedestal of a statue of Herakles. He differs in no essential respect from the other figures depicted in the illustrations of this comedy-farce, and, like some of the others, he has his name set down on the vase by the painter.[1] Instead, however, of bearing a Greek name in Greek characters, this actor is marked in (inverted) Roman letters with what is apparently an Oscan form of a Greek slave-name already familiar to us. The "Santia" on the vase can be nothing but such an Oscan variant of that Xanthias whom we have already met in two vase illustrations, and its appearance here indicates conclusively that the original Dorian type of farce thus interpreted by the Phlyakes was, some time in the fourth century B.C., exerting an influence upon native Oscans and perhaps was being played, not in the Greek tongue, but in that of the Italian peninsula. How far the link thus established is substantiated by other evidence it will now be our business to discover.

[1] On this vase see Dieterich, p. 83.

E

The study of the *fabula Atellana*, or Atellan farce, differs from that of the Phlyax in that, whereas information regarding the latter was to be gained almost entirely from illustrative material, information regarding the former is to be derived almost wholly from literary references. It will therefore be necessary to set our imaginations at work in an effort to visualize those actors of the Atellanæ, to make concrete pictures of the records scattered throughout early Latin literature.[1]

Fig. 64. A Phlyax Slave
Phlyax vase in the British Museum (F. 233).

Origin and Style

Diomedes describes the Atellan farce as the third type of Latin ' comedy,' and remarks that " since these plays were developed in the Oscan city of Atella, they were styled Atellanæ ; in theme, in language, and in comic style they were akin to the Greek satyric drama." [2] There was, however, in his opinion, this difference between the two, that whereas in the satyric drama there appeared only satyrs or comic persons akin to satyrs, in the Atellanæ were introduced " Oscan types, such as Maccus." This statement of connexion between the *fabula Atellana* and the satyr-play is corroborated by the remark of another writer who, in referring to the latter, declared that " we [*i.e.*, the Romans] possess this type of drama in our Atellanæ." [3] At first sight it would appear as if statements such as these were to put aside entirely the possibility of any connexion between the Atellanæ and the earlier mime ; but, in reading these assertions by literary historians, we have to remember that the formal classification of literature has to be taken into account. The three main forms of Attic drama (apart from the mime) were tragedy, comedy, and the satyr play. The Romans developed tragedy and comedy directly from Greek models, but, save for a few isolated experiments, the purely Dionysian representation was unknown. There may, accordingly, have been a tendency on the part of historians to seek for the type in any kind of native drama which could not be placed in the ordinary tragic or comic category. If such a search were made then assuredly choice would fall on the Atellan farce. Its laughter-moving qualities, its mythological burlesque, would entitle it to this place ; indeed, there may have been a further reason for the critical identification. As we

[1] The most important references to the *fabula Atellana* are collected in Martin Schanz, *Geschichte der römischen Litteratur* (in *Handbuch der klassischen Altertums-Wissenschaft*, Munich, 1909). See also Aemil Schippke, *De spectaculis etruscis* (Breslau, 1881); E. Munk, *De fabulis Atellanis* (Leipzig, 1840) and *De L. Pomponio Bononiensi Atellanarum poeta* (Glogau, 1826); F. Marx, *Atellanæ fabulæ* (in Pauly-Wissowa, *Realencyklopädie*, Stuttgart, 1896, vol. ii); R. Maffei, *Le favole Atellanæ* (Forti, 1892) ; F. Graziani, *I personaggi dell' Atellana* (*Rivista di filologia*, xxiv (1896), 4); K. Sittl, *I personaggi dell' Atellana* (*Rivista di storia antica e scienze affini*, i (1895), 3); E. Lattes, *I documenti epigrafici della signoria etrusca in Campania e i nomi delle maschere atellane* (*Rivista di storia antica*, ii (1896), 2); T. Zieliński, *Quæstiones Comicæ* (Leipzig, 1887); I. Hilberg, *Tiberius-Pappus und Atellana* (*Wiener Studien*, xiii (1891), 167–168). Gustave Michaut gives an entertaining account of the Atellanæ and the mime in *Sur les Trétaux latins* (Paris, 1912; on the *exodium*, pp. 74–85; on the *fabula Atellana*, pp. 225–275; on the mime, pp. 280–346). Reich and Dieterich both treat the subject in passing. J. J. Hartmann, *De Atellana Fabula* (*Mnemosyne*, l (1922), 3) tries to prove that the extant fragments belong to a literary, and not to a popular, tradition. René Pichon, *Quelques textes relatifs à l'histoire de l'Atellane* (*Revue de philologie*, xxxvii (1913), 254–257) discusses the relevant passages, quoted below, from Livy, Cicero, and Suetonius.
[2] Diomedes, *Artis grammaticæ libri III* (in H. Keil, *Grammatici latini*, Leipzig, 1857; i, 489–490). [3] Dieterich, p. 111.

have seen, it seems probable that there is a real connexion between the Phlyakes and the Atellanæ; the Phlyakes we know introduced Dionysus and his legends; so that there is the possibility at least that such legends were carried over from the Greek to the Oscan farce. Whether this is so or not, however, it behoves us, before we try to deduce implications from Diomedes' statement, to study the manifestations of the Atellanæ as these are presented to us by other authorities.

Classic authors have provided two theories regarding the origin of the *fabula Atellana*. According to some, such as Livy and Diomedes, this type of farce arose in Atella; that is to say, it was originally acted by Oscan performers before purely Oscan audiences, and was only later carried over to Rome and there Latinized. The same opinion seems to have been held by Strabo, who describes the Atellanæ as a purely Oscan affair.[1] There is, on the other hand, the theory, warmly patronized in modern times by Mommsen, that the Atellanæ were entirely Roman in origin and were the result of the cultured Roman's laughter at the gauche follies of uncivilized Atella. " The true home of this kind of drama," Mommsen declares, " is Latium; its imaginative setting is the Latinized Oscan territories; with the Oscan nation itself it has nothing whatsoever to do." [2] Against this suggestion it may be urged that the bulk of the earlier evidence is against it, and that many passages may be cited from classic authors to show that Atella was by no means a symbol in Rome of folly and barbarism. It is impossible to make any definite statement, but we may certainly believe with a degree of confidence that Atella was the home of the farce which goes by its name, and not merely the butt for the wit of Roman poets. The probable home of the Atellanæ, then, is Atella itself, a locality not overfar removed from those Greek settlements amid which the Phlyakes flourished.

Most of what is known concerning this *fabula Atellana* is related to the fortunes of the type after it had become popular in Rome itself; but there is no reason to suppose that any radical alterations had been made there either in its structure or in its tone. The plays evidently were very short. Fronto calls them *Atellaniolæ* ('little Atellan farces'),[3] and, in noting the word, we recall the little mimes of Herodas, and we remember that there is the best authority for believing that the mimes of Epicharmus were considerably shorter than any ' literary ' comedies. From a reference in Juvenal,[4] when, speaking of the actor Urbicus, he says that he " moves laughter by Autonoe's actions in an Atellan *exodium*," we must suppose that frequently they were presented, not as the chief dramatic farce, but at the end of lengthier entertainments; for *exodium* practically means ' after-piece.' This agrees with a much later statement by Johannes Laurentius Lydus (born *c.* 490 A.D.) to the effect that " the Atellan play belongs to those who are called *exodiarii* " ('Ατελλάνη δέ ἐστιν ἡ τῶν λεγομένων ἐξωδιαρίων).[5]

The question now arises as to the subject-matter and the characters of these *Atellaniolæ*. Already we have seen that Diomedes cites Maccus as a typical Oscan type as introduced at Atella, and we have a good deal of evidence regarding not only Maccus himself, but other ' Oscan ' comic figures who were his companions on the stage. These for the moment we may leave. Their presence is certain; but we must ask ourselves this question : Were these Oscan types the only characters introduced into the *fabula Atellana*? Fortunately a good deal of information has been preserved on this subject, so that we can find an answer more or less definite. A start may be made with that passage from Juvenal already cited in which we are told how Urbicus raised laughter in the theatre with his mimic presentation of Autonoe. Autonoe is a legendary character, and consequently we realize that we are here still in the sphere of burlesque; it is precisely this burlesque which aids us in interpreting that reference to the ' satyric ' style which has been discussed above. In a note on

---

[1] See, in particular, Livy, *Ab urbe condita*, VII, ii, 12.   [2] Th. Mommsen, *Römische Geschichte* (Berlin, 1884–94), ii, 438.
[3] *Ad M. Caes.*, ii, 10 (ed. Naber, p. 34).   [4] *Sat.*, vi, 67–72.
[5] *De magistratibus* (ed. Ricardus Wünsch, Leipzig, 1903), i, 40. *Cf.* Grysar, p. 239.

the type we inevitably recall the fact that references to eating are common in Epicharmus, that food figures largely in the Phlyax scenes, and that the ancient character of Maison seems to have gained its name from the guzzling propensities of its owner. While it is, of course, impossible to be certain, one may not be far wrong in seeing this Atellan type in some of the strange grotesques figured in Ficoroni's collection (Fig. 65).

(b) DOSSENNUS-MANDUCUS

Fig. 66. MANDUCUS-DOSSENNUS

Bronze found near Cologne, now in the Cologne Museum (No. 3851). From M. Bieber, *Denkmäler zum Theaterwesen im Altertum*, Taf. CVIII, 1.

The second stock type, Dossennus, gave the title to one of the plays of Novius (*Duo Dossenni, The Two Dossennuses*), and various authors have left us information on his appearance and nature. In the first place, it must be noted that he had an *alias*—Manducus. Says Varro, "The word *mandier* comes from *mandendo*, whence *manducari* ['to be chewed']; thus in the Atellanæ Dossennus is called Manducus." [1] Manducus, then, has something to do with eating or being eaten. The other word, Dossennus, is easily explained. It comes directly from the Latin *dorsum*, and signifies 'humpbacked.' Now, among the satires of Juvenal [2] there is an entertaining account of the performance of an *exodium* in the theatre when the sight of one of the characters terrifies a peasant child in its mother's lap. That this character was Manducus is suggested by a passage in the *Rudens* of Plautus. [3] "What," says Labrax, "if somehow or other I hire myself out to the theatre as Manducus." "Why?" asks Charmides. "Because," answers Labrax, "my teeth are clashing together so loudly." Putting all these things together, we shall probably be justified in picturing for ourselves a rather terrifying humpbacked creature who displays a row of large teeth in a, no doubt, exaggerated jaw; nor should we have much difficulty in identifying some extant theatre masks with this figure. Several examples have been preserved of a type which has a long hooked nose sharply carried upward at the nostrils and a wide, grinning mouth with a row of protruding teeth. One of these (Fig. 66), besides the hawk-nose and the grinning mouth, shows a large wart on the brow. It is important to note that specimens of masks similar to this have been discovered in localities as far apart as Germany and Holland (Cologne, Worms, Utrecht), Southern Italy (Tarentum), and Crete. [4] A cognate mask, lacking the wart, is shown in Fig. 67. Comparing these two, one realizes that they have many features in common, even while recognizing that they are by no means identical. This leads one to presume that there were in all probability many variants of the Dossennus-Manducus mask, just as there were variants of Pulcinella and Arlecchino masks in the seventeenth century. If that be so, then quite possibly the 'mimic fool' shown in Fig. 32 may also be connected with, or may even definitely represent, the same Atellan figure. He is to be recognized also in a highly

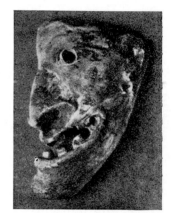

Fig. 67. MANDUCUS-DOSSENNUS

Terra-cotta found near Cologne, now in the Provinzialmuseum, Bonn (No. 2877). From M. Bieber, *Denkmäler zum Theaterwesen im Altertum*, Taf. CVIII, 2.

[1] Varro, *De lingua latina*, vii, 95M.

[2] iii, 173–179. K. Sittl (*loc. cit.*, p. 30) is doubtful concerning the *dorsum* origin. He points out that Dossennus is a real surname (*cf. Corpus inscriptionum Latinorum*—cited hereafter as *C.I.L.*—i, 430; v, 2256), and suggests that the stage type came from a living person.

[3] II, vi, 51.   [4] See Bieber, pp. 174–175.

important terra-cotta statuette which is now preserved in the Louvre (Figs. 68 and 69). This shows a corpulent man clad in a short garment belted at the waist. Over this is cast a cloak which has a buckle at the right shoulder. His head is completely bald, and the most noticeable feature in his face is an enormous nose, on which is to be seen a large wart. Clearly, in discussing the later Italian character of Pulcinella, we must refer back to this person; at present we may simply accept him as an example of the kind of comic exaggeration in which the *fabula Atellana* rejoiced.[1] Beyond the

Figs. 68, 69. MANDUCUS-DOSSENNUS OR A SIMILAR TYPE
Terra-cotta found in Italy, now in the Louvre, Paris (No. 607).
Photo Giraudon

appearance of Dossennus, a few more things are known of him. A sharp saying of his is recorded in a fragment from the *Philosophia* of Pomponius, and this, put alongside the epitaph mentioned in Seneca's letters—" Stranger, stay and learn the wisdom of Dossennus "[2]—makes us believe that he was noted for a mordant wit. In this connexion we have to remember that the mimic fool, with whom Dossennus has undoubtedly something in common, was not merely an idiot. 'Fool's wit' has always been proverbial, and Dossennus no doubt inherited a sharp tongue from his predecessors. This Dossennus probably appeared in a variety of *rôles*. Horace[3] places him among the parasites, and this is borne out by a fragment from the *Campani* of Pomponius from which it appears that there he was presented as obtaining his food at the public's expense. Another fragment suggests that at times he could take the part of a schoolmaster. We shall probably be

[1] Duchartre, *The Italian Comedy* (translated by Randolph T. Weaver; London, 1929) (pp. 208–209), has an entertaining but wholly imaginative passage on the Atellan origin of Pulcinella. Not only, however, are his analyses of the characteristics of the Atellan types based merely on his imagination, but all he says of the person Maccus seems to belong to Manducus. It was the latter who was hunchbacked, not the former.

[2] Seneca, *Epist.*, 89, 7.   [3] *Epist.*, II, i, 170–173.

correct in regarding him as the child both of the ἀλαζών type of early drama and of the mimic fool, combining in himself something of the nature of each.

(c) MACCUS

From Dossennus-Manducus we pass to Maccus. This character, as has been noted, was regarded by Diomedes as one of the most typical of the 'Oscan' masks. The name itself seems Greek in origin. μακκοᾶν (*makkoan*) means ' to be stupid ';[1] the sense is preserved till the present day in the Sardinian and Sicilian *maccu*, which signifies a 'booby.' Other derivations have been suggested, such as μακκώνω ('to become livid by thrashing') and the *macco* of Lucilius, which means 'corn.'

Fig. 70. MACCUS

Terra-cotta in the Provinzial-museum, Bonn. From M. Bieber, *Denkmäler zum Theaterwesen im Altertum*, Taf. CVIII, 3.

Fig. 71. A ROMAN COMIC ACTOR

From Francisco Ficoroni, *Dissertatio de larvis scenicis* (Roma, 1754), Plate XXIX.

If the last-mentioned were correct, then, as Dieterich thinks, there might be some connexion between Maccus and the modern Italian *macaroni*. "Macaroni," says Theofilo Folengo in the preface (1521) to his poems, "is a kind of food made of meal, cheese, and butter—gross, rude, and rustic," and the suggestion is made that we have here a transference of a word from a character to what is associated with him—in other terms, that the person of Maccus represented a stupid, blundering rustic with a taste for stodgy food. Even in old Attic days the peasant was noted for his munching propensities (ἀγροῖκος . . . κυαμοτρώξ, as Aristophanes describes him[2]), and the comic figures on the Theban vase shown in Fig. 9 are busily engaged in cooking some kind of mealy mess. While, however, gluttony does indeed seem to be one of the main qualities of Maccus, it is highly probable that, through a Greek Μακκώ (Makko) or Μακκός (Makkos), his name is derived from μακκοᾶν; if he is a glutton he is also a fool. As a representative of stupidity he is singled out with Bucco in the *Apologia* of Apuleius[3] (*macci . . . et buccones*); while in *Maccus exul* (*Maccus an Exile*) a fragment of text preserves these typical lines : " On the lintel I often cracked my wretched head ; on the threshold I stubbed my toes. "[4] His awkwardness clearly was made use of in the theatre. Concerning his appearance, unfortunately, we know nothing for certain. It is just possible that he is the representative in this form of drama of the more stupid *mimus calvus*, or bald-headed fool ; perhaps in Fig. 70 is to be found his portrait. This illustration shows a little man drawing his mantle around him. His face is foolish enough, and likewise bears a certain general resemblance to the other bald-headed fools whom we have met in other spheres. We cannot, however, be sure, and Maccus' features might as readily be sought for in that design reproduced in Ficoroni's volume which shows an almost "naked" figure whose plump face expresses rustic stupidity and heavy, if not over-refined, feeding. Like Dossennus, Maccus seems to have appeared in a variety of *rôles*.

---

[1] On this name see E. Bethe, *Prolegomena* (Leipzig, 1896), pp. 296–299; Dieterich, pp. 85–86, 235–236; Scherillo, *La Commedia dell' arte* (Florence, 1897), pp. 52–56; Flögel, *Grotesk-Komik* (1914), pp. 25–26; L. Stoppato, *La Commedia popolare in Italia* (Padua, 1887), pp. 51–55. F. Graziani (p. 390) refers to the dialect word μακ(κ)ύμενος still in use. K. Sittl (p. 28) draws attention to the fact that Maccus too was a personal name (*cf. C.I.L.*, vi, 1056, 1081 ; vi, 2437 ; x, 8148), but suggests that as all the Mac- (μακ-) roots signify stupid greed this was Maccus' chief quality.

[2] *The Knights*, l. 41.   [3] *Apologia*, lxxxi (ed. H. E. Butler and A. S. Owen, Oxford, 1914).

[4] Another fragment from *Maccus miles* indicates his gluttony.

In the list of Pomponius' plays we get *Macci gemini* (*The Maccus Twins*), *Macci priores* (*The Foremost Macci*), *Maccus miles* (*Maccus a Soldier*), *Maccus sequester* (*Maccus an Umpire*), and *Maccus virgo* (*Maccus a Maid*), while the Novius list, besides a simple *Maccus*, provides us with a *Maccus copo* (*Maccus an Innkeeper*) and a *Maccus exul* (*Maccus an Exile*). Before leaving this evidently popular type it may be well to refer, even for a moment, to his later fortunes. If it be true that the macaronic poetry ultimately derives from him, then Maccus preserved his existence, if only in shadowy forms, up to the period of the Renascence. In this connexion Dieterich and others[1] have adduced some interesting, if slight and inconclusive, evidence. In the first place, a Buffalmacco or Macco appears in a comic *rôle* in early fifteenth-century fiction,[2] and, in the second, a transcriber of Apuleius in the eleventh century, instead of following the original *macci et buccones*, has altered his text to read *macchi et buccones*. The latter fragment of evidence may suggest that the unknown transcriber was familiar with the type in his own day and accordingly altered the spelling to make it accord with the plural of the name Maccus or Macco. The evidence is flimsy in the extreme, but it must be weighed carefully along with the other evidence for the continuance of the mimic figures.

Fig. 72. PAPPUS
From Francisco Ficoroni, *Dissertatio de larvis scenicis* (Roma, 1754), Plate XIII.

(d) PAPPUS

We reach, ultimately, the last of the four stock characters mentioned in antiquity as belonging to the *fabula Atellana*. His name occurs in no less than five titles of plays by Pomponius and Novius — *Pappus agricola* (*Pappus a Farmer*), *Pappus præteritus* (*Pappus Shown Out*), *Hirnea Pappi* (*Pappus' Hunchback*), *Sponsa Pappi* (*Pappus' Marriage*), all by Pomponius, and another *Pappus præteritus* by Novius. Varro[3] declares that this old man was also called by the Oscan name of *Casnar*.[4] The word Pappus itself clearly comes from the Greek πάππος (*pappos*), and as clearly his is the part of the old man ('Papa'), stupid and wandering in his mind, who is gulled by his more youthful companions. He is, of course, nothing but the old man of the earlier mimes translated into Oscan and Roman surroundings. The identification of his portrait does not seem to be over-difficult. In Ficoroni's collection two illustrations seem to portray him. The first of these (Fig. 72) shows an aged man with bald head and straggling square beard, dressed in a short tunic. In Fig. 73 appears the same type, but this time clad in longer garments and bearing a crook in his right hand. Could this be *Pappus agricola* himself? One other illustration may be given here—that of a small terra-cotta in the British

Fig. 73. PAPPUS
From Francisco Ficoroni, *Dissertatio de larvis scenicis* (Roma, 1754), Plate XXXII.

[1] *Cf.* Dieterich, pp. 235–236.

[2] It is certainly peculiar that Buffalmacco in the *Decamerone* (viii, 9) dresses himself in a rough cloak and has a mask " of a devil . . . furnished with horns." On these devils' masks and their features see *infra*, pp. 190–192.

[3] *De lingua latina*, vii, 29.   [4] On Pappus see Dieterich, pp. 86–87; Stoppato, p. 53; K. Sittl, p. 31.

Museum (Fig. 74). The features are the same as those of the others, and the good-humoured foolishness stamped on his face well agrees with what else we know of this stage person.

(e) Cicirrus

These four figures are the Atellan stock types which were recorded by ancient historians and grammarians. Possibly they all appeared in most of the little farces, forming a definitely comic quartette in dramas of otherwise legendary or realistic theme. Old Pappus, malicious Dossennus, greedy Maccus, and Bucco, stupid and talkative, must have raised much merriment in Atella and in Rome. To this quartette, however, modern scholarship is inclined to add a fifth. The credit of his discovery is due to a brilliant conjecture of Dieterich.[1] This scholar noted that, when Mæcenas, Vergil, and Horace [2] were the guests of Cocceius in his villa at Candium, a couple of entertainers entered to amuse the company. One was named Sarmentus, and the other, an Oscan, was called Messius Cicirrus. These two men indulged in some buffoonery, in which was introduced at least the semblance of an animal mime. Passing further, Dieterich noted that a scholiast (Hesychius) had identified Cicirrus (in the Greek form, κίκιρρος) with a cock (in the Greek, ἀλεκτρυών), and as a result he has suggested that here we have another Oscan comic figure—the 'cock type.' At once our minds go back to those Attic animal figures centuries distant (Figs. 17-22), and we remember the formal significance which writers on

Fig. 74. Pappus
Terra-cotta found at Capua,
now in the British Museum.
Photo Fleming

physiognomy had given to men with bird-like features. We recall, too, the bird on the Phlyakes vase (Fig. 59) and the peculiar fool's hat of the actor depicted there. That the Oscan mimes dealt at times with animal stories seems suggested by the occurrence of animal titles in the plays of Pomponius and Novius; it is assuredly interesting to notice, in view of Pomponius' *Asina* (*The Female Ass*) and of Novius' *Asinus* (*The Male Ass*), that there has been preserved from antiquity an illustration of what seems to be a genuine ass-mime, most probably of the Atellan type. This illustration, which appears on a jar recently discovered at Pasqui (Fig. 76), shows an ass-headed actor turning round to look at a second figure pursuing

Fig. 75. Cock-crested Actors
Design on Greek vase, now apparently lost. From William Tischbein, *Collection of Engravings from Ancient Vases of Greek Workmanship . . . now in the Possession of Sir William Hamilton* (Naples, 1795), ii, Plate 57.

[1] Dieterich, pp. 94–95.   [2] Horace, *Sat.*, I, v, 52–60.

him from behind.[1]   An animal scene of a mimic type is unquestionably indicated here, and, relating this to the Horatian Cicirrus, we may not be far wrong in assuming that themes of a similar kind played at least some part in Atellan merriment.

CONNEXIONS WITH THE MIME

In thus discussing the animal types of the Atellanæ, it is important to note that, while, as among the Phlyakes, there could be ' maskless ' actors, the main comic characters normally wore masks on their faces.   This wearing of masks was also in practice among the earlier Greek mimes, although

Fig. 76. A MIME SCENE, SHOWING AN ACTOR WITH AN
ASS'S HEAD

Bronze relief (first century A.D.) found at Pasqui.   From *Neue Jahrbücher*,
xiii, 1 (1904), 711.

in the Roman mime the human face more generally seems to have been used for comic effect.   In many respects the Atellanæ are thus bound to earlier traditions.   It is, of course, impossible to state dogmatically that these farces were derived directly from such play forms as were indulged in by the Phlyakes, but even in this rapid survey there have been observed many elements which the two appear to have in common.   The connexion, indeed, contrary to our expectations, extends as far as the language.   This is proved by an incident related in Suetonius' *Life of Nero*.[2]   One day the Emperor was in the theatre, and a certain "Datus, player of Atellan farce," commenced singing, in Greek, ὑγίαινε πάτερ, ὑγίαινε μῆτερ, thus referring, as Suetonius says, to the deaths of Claudius and Agrippa.   For his indiscretion the actor was banished.   This record tells us of four things—first, of the use of Greek in the *fabula Atellana*; secondly, of the introduction of music there ; thirdly, of the privilege of improvisation, or at any rate of gagging; and, fourthly, of its at least occasional satiric tendency in so far as politics were concerned.   We shall have occasion to discuss these points in the following pages; be it noted here that not even the bar of a different language kept the Phlyakes and the Atellanæ apart.   The more we study the two together, indeed, the more is it borne in upon us that,

[1] On this ass-mime and on the ass-theme in drama see H. Reich, *Der Mann mit dem Eselskopf* (*Shakespeare-Jahrbuch*, xl (1904), 108–128), and *Der König mit der Dornenkrone* (*Neue Jahrbücher für das klassische Altertum*, xiii (1904), 711–714).
[2] xxxix, 3. René Pichon (*loc. cit.*, p. 255) thinks, however, that there is reference here only to the occasional introduction of Greek terms.

if the Oscan be not derived from the Greek, at least the two belong to one general style of theatrical representation. The very Phlyax scenes themselves seem to agree with the Atellan figures. Fig. 40 is for this purpose characteristic. Herakles has the teeth and fearsome appearance of a Dossennus-Manducus (although it is highly improbable that the one corresponds exactly with the other), Apollo on the temple-roof bears the foolish visage of a Maccus, Iolaos by the altar is of a Bucco countenance, while, to make the quartette complete, an old man's mask at the left-hand side provides us with a Pappus. It is more than probable that the fully established Phlyakes mime, if it did not originate, at least deeply influenced the Oscan mime of Atella.

Evidence of connexion between the new and the old does not cease when we pass on to consider the stylistic and other qualities of the Atellan farce. So far we have observed as typical subject-matter of this kind the mythological burlesque, the debate, the animal theme, and the scenes of ordinary life—most of them reminiscent of Epicharmus and of Herodas. It was suggested above that political satire also intruded. The words that Datus sang before Nero were sufficiently bold, and brought their punishment with them. This political element in the Atellanæ is referred to several times in classic literature. Thus on one occasion Galba, who had lost the favour of his people, came to the theatre, and the performers in an Atellan farce struck up a well-known song (*notissimum canticum*) containing the lines, " Onesimus comes from his villa." Immediately all the spectators, with one accord, took up the remaining lines and roared out the chorus several times.[1] Some of these bold spirits escaped punishment ; some, like Datus, were banished ; for some was reserved a heavier fate. Caligula went so far as to burn the writer of an Atellan farce (*Atellanæ poetam*) in the middle of an amphitheatre because of a line of an ambiguous nature (*ob ambigui ioci versiculum*).[2] Similar records are found in the days of Tiberius. A remark about " an old he-goat " in an Atellan after-piece (*in Atellanico exodio*) was loudly applauded at the time when the Emperor was making himself obnoxious by his excesses ;[3] and so mordant did the satire become that, in A.D. 22, Tiberius found himself compelled to bring an order of suppression before the senate.[4] This political element is in entire accord with all we know of the earlier mime. Bold remarks of Epicharmus have been recorded, and political satire of a similar kind is associated with the mimic work of Sophron, Herodas, Theocritus, and Sotades. In later times, as we shall find, the old style was continued, for the mime, whatever name it assumed, stood forth always as the champion of the people. Was not Philemon the darling of the populace ?

Like the Dorian mime, the Atellanæ were condemned by some superior people as being obscene. We do not know whether the actors were phallephoric or not; the probability is that they were. A main feature of the performances was the so-called *tricæ*, and these certainly must often have been of an indelicate nature. The word *tricæ*, which is connected with the verb *intricare* and the modern 'intrigue,' seems to be derived from the Greek θρίξ (*thrix*), and is the equivalent at once of what we should call ' episodes ' and of that characteristic element in *commedia dell' arte* performances to which was given the name of *lazzi*.[5] These *tricæ* are stock intrigues, situations, or scenes of action, but of their real nature we know nothing. Only, from a comparison with the earlier and later mime, we may imagine that they introduced many episodes from real life, exaggerated and satirically treated, which did not always display the very best of refined taste.

With the *tricæ* were associated various stylistic features. On occasion the authors of the Atellanæ could be polished and delicate. Julius Victor declared that " the old comedies—*togatæ, tabernariæ,* Atellanæ, and mimes—bring a good deal of eloquence to our tongue." This polish and " eloquence " was probably associated most with the mock serious discourse on trivial subjects. M. C. Fronto

---

[1] Suetonius, *Galba*, xiii.
[2] Suetonius, *Caligula*, xxvii.
[3] Suetonius, *Tiberius*, xlv. *Cf.* Isidor Hilberg, *Tiberius-Pappus und Atellana* (*Wiener Studien*, xiii (1891), 167–169).
[4] Tacitus, *Annales*, iv, 14. *Cf.* Reich, i, 189–192.
[5] See Dieterich, p. 98.

thus proposes in one of his letters to write a eulogy on smoke and dirt.[1] But, he says, the treatment of such a subject demands a special art, and " nothing in Latin exists of this kind sufficient for the purpose except what appears in comedies or Atellan farces. He who intends to deal with matters in this way will seek out numerous ideas, will mass them together and join them subtly one to another." Reading these words, one thinks of a Charles Lamb type of humour. Polish and eloquence, however, were not the main characteristics of this form ; that which marked out the Atellan style above all other things was a mixture of wit and rustic gaucherie. " You will get delicate phrases from comedy," says Fronto, " elegant words from the *fabula togata*, and witty, clever things from the Atellanæ " (*ex Atellanis lepidas et facetas*).[2] The same author speaks of the " rustic, facetious, and ridiculous words " used in this form of mime (*verbis rusticanis et iocularibus ac ridiculariis*).[3] Much of the wit must have been of the punning variety. One such example occurs in the *Auctoratus* of Pomponius—*occidit taurum toruiter, me amore sauciavit*—which may be rendered : " He killed the bull in a 'bould' manner; he wounded me with love." It is interesting to note that such puns were equally beloved in the days of Epicharmus. An extant fragment by that writer thus rings the changes on the words γ'ἔρανον (' the meal ') and γέρανον (' the crane '). The words of the Atellanæ, as we have seen, were not only "facetious," they were rustic; and this statement of Fronto's is corroborated by many others. Pomponius, we are told, was " quick in wit and rude in word," [4] and Varro refers to the rustic types introduced into these farces.[5]

The Atellan farces soon became popular in Rome, appealing both to amateur and to professional performers. The city youths, according to Livy, amused themselves by bringing before the public either these Oscan plays or others of a like character ; [6] Tiberius himself, according to Suetonius, acted in Atellanæ.[7] The professional performances seem to have been given either in the theatres or at banquets, in both instances no doubt without elaborate scenery. It was in a theatre that the simple peasant child was terrified by the mask of Manducus, and Tiberius, Nero, and Galba were all ridiculed by the actors of this kind of farce in the playhouses before an audience. On the other hand, with a variety of other entertainments, it was included in princely revelry. Hadrian, according to Ælius Spartianus, " often brought forward at his banquets tragedies, comedies, Atellanæ, harp-players, readers, and poets, just as suited the occasion." [8] Unquestionably at these banquets the performers must have given their shows either on a raised *daïs* or on the stage of one of those strangely modern private theatres which are represented now by the magnificent example in the Casa degli Amorini Dorati at Pompeii (Fig. 93). Properties, as in the Phlyakes, were no doubt used freely to suggest locality, but the task of raising imaginative illusion in the audience must have been left mainly to the players. What their precise accoutrements were we do not know, but probably the utensils and weapons they carried were similar to those shown in the Phlyakes vases. One reference, however, points to something that we have not met before. A fragment from the *Phœnissæ* of Novius contains the line : " To arms ! I'm going to kill you now with my cudgel of straw " (*Sume arma, iam te occidam clava scirpea*). This certainly is peculiar, and causes our minds to leap ahead over centuries to the time when a Pagliazzo, or Pagliaccio, or Pagliacci, who bears a name which literally means ' chopped straw,' was to be a popular figure. Perhaps in doing this we are over-adventurous and over-credulous, but the fact remains that some one is to " kill " another with " a cudgel of straw "—Harlequin's blunt baton and Pagliacci's name fifteen centuries before their time. Maybe that cudgel of straw is illustrated in one of Ficoroni's engravings (Fig. 2).

What precisely happened to the *fabula Atellana* we do not know. In 55 B.C. Cicero [9] was writing

[1] Ed. Naber ; p. 211.   [2] Ed. Naber ; p. 105.   [3] Ed. Naber ; p. 62.
[4] Velleius Paterculus, *Historia romana*, ii, 9 (ed. J. C. K. Krausius, London, 1822, p. 88).
[5] *De lingua latina*, vii, 84 (ed. C. O. Müller, Leipzig, 1833, p. 152).   [6] Livy, *Ab urbe condita*, VII, ii, 11.
[7] Suetonius, *Tiberius*, xlv.   [8] Ælius Spartianus, *De vita Hadriani* (ed. Peter, i, 28).
[9] *Ad fam.*, ix, 16.

to a friend and saying that the Atella was a thing of the past, that its place was being taken by the mime ; yet the Atellanæ are still seen flourishing in the first century A.D.—150 years later. The probability is that its death was slow. The more elaborate mimic drama no doubt came to supplant it in popular favour, but we need not suppose that, either in its pure form or in direct influence, it completely disappeared. Itself a child of the Greek mime, it came to mould the mime of Rome. As a living form and still familiar as an after-piece, the 'Ἀτελλάνη (Atellane) is known to Lydus in the sixth century A.D., and it is not entirely fanciful, as some modern scholar-sceptics suppose, to trace the influence of the Atellanæ down to the period of the Renascence. That the mime outvied it in popular favour cannot be denied, but it may well have retained its hold upon audiences in rural districts. The nearest we can come during the later age to the spirit of the Atellanæ is in the *Balli di Sfessania* as delineated by Callot, and these seem somehow or another to be connected, partly at least, with those rustic and originally pagan festivals which the medieval Church never quite succeeded in suppressing.

SUMMARY

With the Atellanæ we have passed completely into the world of Rome, for, as even those few representative notices which have been summarized above go to show, the Oscan mime drama became one of the most popular divertisements there both among the aristocracy and among the plebeians. Before proceeding further with the Latin stage it may be well to pause for a moment in order to summarize and to tabulate our results. The types of drama which we have been considering are all bound together by one common tie—each one, although it may influence literary comedy, is distinct from that form of theatrical expression. All make free use of every means offered by the stage. Music, dancing, and acrobatics mingle with regular dialogue. The dramatic poet for the most part remains in the background ; much of the mimic activity is purely improvisational. All keep strictly to life. There may be exaggeration, but there is no artificiality. The gods are brought from the high paths of Olympus to walk common streets along with grotesquely conceived characters of the day. The bombastic and grandiloquent language of tragedy is dragged from its tottering throne and mocked at. Naturally, this being so, all these forms of drama are unconfined in scope ; they sweep not only over the whole of human life, but, in their secular tendencies and in their general appeal, embrace along with these all the creations of myth, all the abstract figures of the popular imagination. Death is here a companion of a Peasant, and Jove talks freely to a Clown. The fact that, in spite of this breadth of interest, we can yet trace certain definite comic characters in all these forms of theatrical representation serves the more to emphasize their communion one with another. The early *deikelistai* have their fruit-stealing slaves and doctors. Megarean comedy had its comic slaves, and there Herakles was cheated of his dinner ; some kinds of Dorian drama had both mimic fools and hag-like old women. These hag-like old women and corresponding old men have their features preserved in early Spartan masks. The fat, gluttonly Maison may also belong to this age, and here too we find suggestions of animal masquerade. In Epicharmus Herakles reappears along with a rustic, a parasite, and a wise man (a doctor). Herodas preserves the wise man as a schoolmaster and the hag-like old woman as a bawd. The Athenian lamp presents the person of the bald-headed fool. Herakles reappears among the Phlyakes, as do thievish slaves, old men, rustics, and fools. The Atellanæ in their turn give to us their stock types—fat, talkative fool, malicious character, stupid, greedy fool (rustic), old man, and cock type, recalling several previous examples. The correspondence of these figures is truly remarkable, and, when we take into account the fact that there is evidence for the influence of the Dorian drama upon Attic comedy, as remarkable is the appearance of similar types in the plays of Aristophanes and of those later dramatists who patronized the ' new ' style in comedy.

78

There seems here ample material on which to base the theory that from the days of ancient Megara to those of Republican Rome there existed a very clear and definite theatrical tradition of a 'popular' sort. The literary drama continues its own career, but here is essentially the actors' theatre of antiquity—a thing passed down from generation to generation, changing its name and its medium, but preserving fundamentally the outlines which had been established in dim days before history began, just as, in our own times, the itinerant puppet-player and the essentially popular clown have retained something of that tradition which was fully established in Renascence Europe by the *commedia dell' arte*.

Fig. 77. A MIME ACTOR

Roman lamp. From Pietro Santi Bartoli, *Le Antiche lucerne sepolcrali figurate raccolte dalle cave sotterranee e grotte di Roma* (Roma, 1691), i, Plate 34.

II

THE HEYDAY OF MIMIC DRAMA

(i) THE NATURE OF THE MIME

THE Atellanæ, as we have seen, succumbed before the encroaching power of the pure mime. That all was not lost we have every reason to believe, and even after some centuries had driven memories of the *fabula Atellana* from the heads of cultured men and women the ghosts of Bucco and Dossennus no doubt lingered on the stages of which once they had been kings. We shall have, in later discussions, frequent occasion to refer to them and to find in their efforts the remote original of many later forms.[1] Unquestionably those who believe that this type of play utterly perished have overlooked some important evidence from the period of the Dark Ages.

DEFINITIONS OF THE MIME

Before we proceed further it would be well to pause for a moment in order to consider the significance which was regularly attached by antiquity to the term *mimus*. In other words, we must attempt to discover some kind of definition, or at any rate some kind of general analysis of that type of theatrical expression the fortunes of which we have been engaged in tracing. That there was at one and the same time a confusion and an association between the terms 'mime' and 'comedy' is evident from many references both early and late. "Comedies and mimes" are mentioned together by Quintilian;[2] "comedies, Atellanæ, and mimes" by Arnobius.[3] The first thing which we must do is to make as clear a distinction as we may between the one and the other; but before we reach this stage we must note that the word *mimus*,[4] or 'mime,' could be applied either to an actor or to a play. "As a mime I return home" (*Domum revertar mimus*) is a phrase from a famous prologue by Laberius,[5] and the sense given here is repeated in many another passage. Ovid thus speaks of "the mimes with their indelicate entertainments."[6] In later times the name of the mimic actor tended to change; *actor mimicus* and even *histrio* were the more usual appellations. On the other hand, when Herodian speaks of "the performers of mimes" (μίμων ὑποκριταί)[7] or when Aristotle first mentions the mimes of Sophron (Σώφρονος μίμους), the sense is clearly either

---

[1] Reich is inclined to deny that the Atellanæ had any direct influence on the later mime, but he seems to leave unexamined the possibility of (1) indirect, 'second-hand' influence, and (2) the influence of degraded forms of the *fabula Atellana*. These may certainly have persisted in spite of the popularity of the pure mimes and pantomimes. [2] IV, ii, 53. [3] vii, 33.

[4] The standard work on the whole subject of the Roman mime is, of course, that of Reich. On pp. 6–11 he gives a survey of the critical literature up to the time (1903) when his work appeared. To the works cited there may be added E. Nöldechen, *Tertullian und das Theater* (*Zeitschrift für Kirchengeschichte*, xv (1895), 161–203); and some reviews or criticisms of Reich's own work (*e.g.*, A. Körte in *Neue Jahrbücher für das klassischen Altertum*, xi (1903), p. 537; S. Sudhaus, *Der Mimus von Oxyrhynchos* (*Hermes*, xli (1906), 247–277); C. Formichi, in *Atene e Roma*, viii (1905), 311, 386; R. Herzog, in *Berliner philologische Wochenschrift*, xxiv (1904), 1089–1099). Reich has a summary of his main thesis in the *Deutsche Litteraturzeitung*, No. 2679, and an essay on a special problem, *Der König mit der Dornenkrone*, in *Neue Jahrbücher für das klassischen Altertum*, xiii (1904), 705–733. There is not much of value in two early dissertations not cited by Reich—J. Weaver, *The History of the Mimes and Pantomimes* (1728), and Boulanger de Rivery, *Recherches historiques et critiques sur quelques anciens spectacles et particulièrement sur les mimes et pantomimes* (Paris, 1751). In spite of the encyclopædic nature of Reich's work, the earlier study of Grysar is still of considerable value, although, of course, it is in places very much out of date.

[5] See *infra*, p. 111. [6] *Tristia*, II, 497–498.

[7] V, vii (*Herodiani historiarum libri octo*, ed. I. Bekker, Berlin, 1826, p. 115).

that of a performance or of a play ; and it is this latter which, in the first instance, we must attempt to define.

For this purpose we may glance at such definitions as have been left to us. The simplest make the bare statement that the mimes ' mimic ' life. " They are called mimes in Greek," says Isidore of Seville, " because they are imitations [or imitators] of human affairs " (*rerum humanarum . . . imitationes* [*imitatores*]).[1] Other definitions are more elaborate, as that of Diomedes :

> The mime is an imitation and irreverent [*i.e.*, secular] expression of some dialogue, or the lascivious imitation of indelicate deeds and words ; it is thus defined by the Greeks : " The mime is an imitation of life (μίμησις βίου).". . . The word ' mime ' comes from μιμεῖσθαι (' to imitate ') as if it had a monopoly of imitation, although other forms of literature are based on this. It alone, however, was granted this common quality as a privilege, just as the man who makes verse is called a poet (ποιητής, literally ' a maker ') while artists, who also make something, are not called poets.[2]

The Greek passage which Diomedes quotes is from an unknown author, although, as has been suggested, Theophrastus may originally have been responsible for it. We are not concerned, however, with any identification of authorship ; what we are concerned with is the implications of this definition. Here the mime is regarded as the imitative art *par excellence*, while its " indelicate " characteristics and its " irreverent " tone are duly stressed. When we remember the phallic actors and the mythological burlesque we understand the qualities to which Diomedes was referring. In other words, the mime is the pure example in dramatic art of Aristotle's theory of *mimesis*, or imitation. It takes the whole of life for its province, and, like nature itself, has naught to do with either morality or religion. Utterly rational in tone, it stands forward as the chief exponent of secularism in the theatre. In this capacity it rejects nothing ; its mission is to imitate life, and life, good or bad, virtuous or vicious, it puts upon the stage, having no thoughts of moral distinctions, having no outer control beyond the force of nature itself. According to Aristotle, tragedy " imitates " men as better than they are ; it selects from life some " worthy or illustrious and perfect action," for the purpose of arousing certain high emotions in the minds of an audience. Comedy, on the other hand, " imitates " men as worse than they are for the purpose of making ridiculous certain errors or vices. The mime stands apart from both in its completely unmoral and undidactic attitude toward life.

It is perfectly obvious that such an unmoral (or secular) attitude may be appreciated in two ways. We may accept the mime as it is, and thereby appreciate its tone and aim ; or we may regard it from a falsely moral standpoint and condemn it because it does not pretend to moral elevation. Many other definitions of, and references to, the Roman mime are confused and obscured by this latter attitude. " After the time of the New Comedy in Greece," declares Euanthius, " the Romans introduced many kinds of drama such as . . . the mimes based on the imitation of base things and of worthless characters [*vilium rerum ac levium personarum*]." [3] " Among the other qualities of Terence," says the same critic, " this is noteworthy, that his plays are of such a character that they neither rise to tragic heights nor sink to the baseness of the mime [*ad mimicam vilitatem*]." Others note the association of the mime with jugglers and acrobats. " Alexandria we had heard of," says Cicero, " now we know it. There we find all the race of jugglers ; there, I say, we find all their tricks ; yea, all the themes of the mimes are based on them." [4]

We must, of course, admit that the mime, in taking life as its province, introduced unmorally the bad with the good. It made no fundamental selection. We have to admit, likewise, that there must have been mimes and mimes ; that some of the performers in these pieces were of the

---

[1] *Etymologiarum sive originum*, xviii, 49.
[2] *Artis grammaticæ libri III* (in H. Keil, *ed. cit.*, i, 491).
[3] *Fragmenta de comœdia* (ed. Wessner, i, 21).
[4] *Pro. C. Rabirio Postumo*, xii, 35.

lowest possible kind and that in many instances vulgarity was exploited for its own sake. But when these admissions are made there yet remains much more to be said. The mime in essence was the very incarnation, the first ideal of that *mimesis* on which is based the whole of the peripatetic literary theory ; and in later days the mimes were admired, not only by degenerate aristocrats of a debased Court, but by the most serious of Roman thinkers. The importance of the mime is stressed by Marcus Aurelius when he puts it alongside of such universal catastrophes as war, of such predominating human passions as fear, of such physical banes as illness and disease.[1] He is condemning, but his very condemnation is a glory to the form. There were, too, philosophers who saw in the mime something more than a mere entertainment. Seneca, in his *Moral Epistles*, speaks of " this mime of mortal life [*hic humanæ vitæ mimus*], in which we are apportioned *rôles* which we misinterpret." [2] The same idea was expressed by the Emperor Augustus. " On the last day of his life," writes Suetonius,[3]

> he asked those friends of his who had been admitted to his chamber whether they thought he had acted the mime of life in a fitting manner. Then he added these words :
>
> > Since well I've played my part, all clap your hands,
> > And from the stage dismiss me with applause.

The idea contained in these two passages unquestionably gives us a higher conception of the mimic drama. Dying emperors can think of it in their last hours, and grave philosophers use it in their disquisitions upon life. It is this conception which we must bear in our minds as we endeavour to understand the growth and development of the type. We must not be misled by hasty generalizations concerning mimic obscenity ; that alone could not have induced the serious Seneca to adduce, for his philosophic purpose, *hic humanæ vitæ mimus*.[4]

---

[1] x, 9. [2] *Epistulæ morales*, xi, 1 (ed. F. Haase, Leipzig, 1853; iii, 205).

[3] *Divus Augustus*, xcix. On this see Otto Hirschfeld, *Augustus und sein Mimus vitæ* (*Wiener Studien*, v (1883), 116–119) and Ulrich von Wilamowitz-Moellendorff, *Res gestæ Divi Augusti* (*Hermes*, xxi (1886), 626–627).

[4] Within the spheres of dramatic representation and of literary form, of course, the word *mimus* and its various derivatives could have different significations. The ' mimes ' or ' mimiambs ' of Theocritus and Herodas obviously were other things than the popular mimic dramas represented in the Oxyrhynchus finds. While the latter seem to have been dramas demanding the participation of a large company of actors, the former were short playlets calling for the presence of at the most three or four performers. Besides these, there were the ' mimes ' which were recited by one person only, who interpreted the various parts by the use of suitable gesticulation and change of voice. The skill of such entertainers is indicated by the verses in honour of Vitalis (see *infra*, p. 95). It is to be remembered that men of this type were popular in classic days and that their activities were similar to those of many of the medieval *jongleurs*.

Fig. 78. The
Mimus Calvus

From Francisco Ficoroni,
Dissertatio de larvis scenicis (Roma, 1754), Plate
XXVI.

(ii) THE MIMIC ACTORS

Having thus established, as it were, the fundamental basis of the mime as an artistic form, we may proceed to consider the particular manifestations of this form, and perhaps our survey will be made the easier if first of all we attempt a survey of the activities of the mimic actors and of their methods of performance.

TERMINOLOGY

The mimic actor, as we have seen, was originally called a *mimus*, or a mime, and in earlier times there seems to have been a strict differentiation between the *histrio*, or actor of tragedy and comedy, and the *mimus*, who confined himself to the mimic form. Gradually, however, this distinction disappeared. The mime rapidly came to take the principal place among Roman entertainments, and as a consequence its performers came to be called by the same name as the others—*histriones*; or, rather, the word *histriones* came to be used as a generic term for every kind of actor.[1] "The wagons," says Trebellius, "went in rich procession bearing the mimes and all the crowd of actors [*omni genere histrionum*]."[2] It was mimes whom Verus brought from Syria, but Julius Capitolinus in his life of that emperor calls them *histriones*.[3]

The word *mimus*, however, is not used by itself. Apart from the obvious synonyms such as *actor mimi* ('performer of a mime') and *actor mimicus* or *mimarius* ('mimic actor'), we find a variety of terms used to designate the entertainers of the mimic stage, and, as these serve to indicate certain characteristics of the mime itself, we may devote some space here to their consideration. In earlier times the word *saltator* (literally 'dancer' or 'acrobat') is often used to indicate a mime actor, and this use is continued on to medieval times. Cicero thus draws a distinction between the "action of the actor" (*histrionis actio*) and the "movement of the *saltator*" (*saltatoris motus*). Festus in A.D. 211 speaks of a "mime who dances to the sound of the flute,"[4] while an inscription has the phrase, "among the dancing mimes" (*in mimis saltantibus*).[5] The employment of this word *saltator* reminds us that the Dorian mime may well in origin have been merely a mimic dance, and that the terpsichorean element endured to its very latest days. Dancing figures are shown on a Greek vase (Fig. 23), and dancing figures reappear among the Phlyax farces (Fig. 62); the Roman mimes made as much use as their predecessors of the dance, and with the dance they unquestionably introduced a good deal of acrobatic movement. Exaggerated gesture was freely employed by them. "The orator," declares Quintilian, "should not copy those distorted grimaces and gestures which we are accustomed to laugh at in the mimes."[6] This element of dancing, acrobatic movement, and gesture is something that must be fully borne in mind while discussing the mime, and, as we shall see, it is still further stressed in various subsidiary names given to the mimes or to those associated with them.

Among all these names none is commoner than that of *planus* or *planipes*, and often this is associated with the other term, *saltator*. Festus speaks of *mimi planipedes*,[7] and Diomedes uses the word for the mime drama itself; "the fourth type [of comedy]," he says, "is the *planipedia*, of which the Greek name is *mimus*."[8] *Planus* itself means 'plain' or 'flat,' and *planipes* means 'with bare feet,' the obvious implication being that the mimic actor was distinguished from the other actors through the fact that he did not wear either the *cothurnus* of tragedy or the *soccus* of

[1] On this question see Grysar, p. 320.
[2] Trebellius, *Gallieni duo*, viii.
[3] *Verus*, viii.
[4] *Cf.* Reich, i, 57.
[5] *C.I.L.*, VI, ii, 10118.
[6] Quintilian, VI, iii, 29. *Cf.* Grysar, p. 265; Reich, i, 75.
[7] *Pauli excerpta*, ed. W. M. Lindsay (Leipzig, 1913), p. 342.
[8] *Artis grammaticæ libri III* (in H. Keil, i, 490). *Cf.* Grysar, p. 248.

comedy. He was barefooted in order to leave him greater ease of movement. The distinction between the two types of actors is well brought out in Seneca's admiring exclamation regarding the mimes of Publilius : " How many things Publilius says which are fit for tragedy [*cothurnatis dicenda sunt*] rather than for the mime [*non excalceatis*]." [1] Diomedes, after making the remark cited above, continues similarly to expand his statement of fact. The *planipedia* is the drama of the mimic type. " This is called *planipes* in Latin," he explains, " because the actors come before the proscenium with ' flat ' feet—that is to say, naked feet—not like the tragic actors with the *cothurnus* or like the comic actors with the *soccus*." The fact that Diomedes, in thus discussing the significance of the word *planipes*, seems to make a distinction between that dramatic form and the *mimus* itself does not in any way indicate a distinction between the two. Certainly, at the beginning of his discussion he remarks that " there are many kinds of comedy—the *palliata*, *togata*, *tabernaria*, Atellana, *mimus*, Rhinthonica,[2] and the *planipedia*," thus presenting the same formal division given by Johannes Lydus,[3] but he distinctly connects the *planipes* with the *mimus*, and, if making any difference at all, is merely thinking of the Roman form of mime as distinct from the Greek. The first explanation of *planipes* presented by Diomedes is that usually accepted in antiquity, but he himself puts forward a second, and other writers have mentioned a third. Perhaps, says Diomedes, the word *planipes* is used " because formerly the mimic actors used to perform not on the stage itself, but on the ' plain ' or level of the orchestra [*in plano orchestræ*]." Donatus provides the third suggestion. This type of comedy, he imagines, " was called *planipedia* on account of the baseness of its themes and the worthlessness of its actors." [4] No doubt the last-mentioned explanations are of a ' literary ' kind, devised to explain the use of a word from theory, although each, whatever its worth, had considerable influence on the later developments of the theatre. We may accept more surely the first suggestion. The *planipes* was a performer who wore no stage shoes, in order to be free in movement. Gellius speaks of the " dancing mimic " (*planipes saltans*),[5] while a fragment from a comedy by one Atta (died 77 B.C.) refers to the " frisking about " of a *planipes* (*exultat planipes*).[6]

THE ACROBATS AND JUGGLERS

To the *mimus* proper are attached a mighty company of lesser entertainers, many of whom must have provided amusement and interest during the performance of the mimic drama. These too have to be taken into consideration ere we pass further in our survey. In one of his satires Horace speaks of " the colleges of Syrian flute-players, quacks, beggars, mimic actresses, parasites, and all their kind." [7] The reference seems to be mainly to wandering entertainers who, like the charlatans of the Renascence, mingled profitable sale of cheap drugs with little, farce-like shows. These men and women were, of course, closely allied to the acrobats of ancient Greece, and belonged, like those, to many different yet allied categories.[8] Among the most popular of these seem to have been the *funambuli* or *neurobatæ*, who performed on thick or thin ropes, and who, according to Suetonius, were first introduced to the regular theatres by the Emperor Galba.[9]

---

[1] *Excalceatis* means literally ' bootless,' and is simply a synonym for *planipes*. Seneca, *Epistolæ*, viii, 8. For the πλάνος, or *planus*, in Greek see Athenæus, xiv, 615*e–f* and 616*a–b*.

[2] That is to say, the Phlyax ; see *supra*, p. 51.   [3] Lydus, *De magistratibus*, i, 40.

[4] *Excerpta de comœdia* (ed. P. Wessner, Leipzig, 1902, i, 26). He goes on to elaborate this by saying that the word *planipes* is used " because the type of play does not deal with the affairs of people dwelling in towers and large rooms, but of those in ' plain ' and humble places."

[5] *Noctes atticæ*, I, xi, 12.   [6] T. Quinctius Atta, fr. 1 (O. Ribbeck, p. 188).

[7] *Sat.*, I, ii, 1–2 :

> " Ambubaiarum collegia, pharmacopolæ,
> Mendici, mimæ, balatrones, hoc genus omne."

[8] See Reich, i, 510–517, and H. Blümner, *Fahrendes Volk im Altertum* (*loc. cit*). Grysar (p. 316) also deals with this subject.

[9] *Galba*, vi.

THE MIMIC ACTORS

Sometimes these men were called *schœnobatæ* (σχοινοβάται), sometimes *oribatæ*. Perhaps some distinction was made in accordance with their ' turns.' Allied to them come the *petauristæ*, so called from the *petaurum* (πέταυρον or πέτερον), or trapeze, on which they exhibited their acrobatic skill. Petronius [1] describes a show given by these people in which a boy is bidden to do tricks at the top of a ladder, while another account by Claudian would seem to suggest that they included firework displays in their repertoire. [2] Already the Greek ancestors of the *prestigiatores*, or jugglers, have been mentioned. [3] Of these there were several kinds. Some specialized in fire-spitting and in sword-swallowing ; the *pilarii* juggled with balls, the *ventilatores* with daggers. There, too, came the stilt-walkers, called *grallatores* (or, in Greek, καλοβάται, κωλοβαθρισταί, from the stilts, κᾶλα, κωλόβαθρα). All of these, with the *derisores* and *scurræ* (buffoons), provided ample amusement both in the palaces of the nobles and in the theatres of the people, presenting their " scenic marvels " (*miracula in scænis*). [4] Some idea of the varied nature of their entertainments may be gained from a description of a show given by the Emperor Carinus in the third century A.D. [5] Rope-dancers wearing the tragic *cothurnus* seemed to hang in the air ; an animal-trainer performed with a bear, and other bears " acted a mime " (*ursos mimum agentes*) ; a hundred trumpeters sounded their instruments at one time ; there were hundreds of flute-players and thousands of pantomimes and acrobats ; while a firework " machine " succeeded in destroying the scenic buildings of the theatre. In the midst of these the ordinary mimes performed their shows. We notice how persistent was the old association between the mimic actor proper and the descendants of the ancient *thaumatopoios*.

Important for our purposes is the fact that each of these types of entertainers had its feminine counterpart. Beside the *mimi* acted those *mimæ* to whom Horace refers. The position of the *mimæ* we shall have to consider in greater detail in a later section. It is sufficient here to remark that the mimic actress could appear as a dancer and as a gesticulator in precisely the same way as her male companions. The actresses won as great fame as the actors ; was it not a mimic actress who, in later days, rose from the theatre in which she had been reared to occupy the proudest throne in Christendom ? Theodora, Empress of the Eastern Empire, was in her youth a *mima*.

THE COMPANIES

Before discussing the question of the position in art or in social life of the mimic actress, however, it will be advisable to see what evidence we have regarding the companies of which they formed a part and regarding the characteristics of individual performers. The body of actors was generally styled a ' college ' or a ' commune.' *Commune mimorum* occurs in one inscription, and *grex* (literally ' flock '), *corpus* (' body '), and *collegium* are all to be found in other authorities. [6] The number of actors in these companies certainly varied, but we must be prepared to recognize the presence, beside smaller troupes, of vast acting organizations counting their members by scores. The mimic drama found at Oxyrhynchus includes seven principal characters, with, in addition, a number of attendants, barbarian guards, and Amazons. Clearly a production of the play would call for not less than twenty people, even if the modern practice of ' doubling ' were allowed. Similarly the Christian mimes described in some accounts of the martyrs include among the characters a hero, a friend, a judge and his attendants, a bishop and his acolytes, with an indeterminate number of subsidiary persons representing soldiers, guards, neighbours, and Christians. Clearly we have here something different in scope from the mimes of Herodas, and happily an inscription of A.D. 169 exists to confirm our surmises. [7] This inscription was raised at Bovillæ in honour of the mime-director called L. Acilius Pomtinus Eutyches. It is of interest partly because

---

[1] *Satyricon*, liii.   [2] xvii, 326.   [3] See *supra*, p. 35–37.   [4] Quintilian, *Institutio oratoriæ*, X, vii, 11.
[5] Vopiscus, *Carinus*, xix.   [6] See Grysar, p. 269.   [7] *C.I.L.*, xiv, 2408.

it indicates the esteem in which a great actor was held, but mainly because of the fact that after the inscriptional praise of Eutyches comes a list of his company. This contains no less than sixty names. Reading this, we realize that we are working here with a sphere of theatrical art as free and as broadly organized as any developments of modern times.

At the head of this body of sixty persons was Eutyches, and his title is given in the inscription. It is that of *archimimus*, or arch-mime, varied in another inscription as *magister mimariorum*—master

Fig. 79. CIRCUS SHOWS IN THE THIRD CENTURY
Relief found in Bulgaria. From the *Bulletin de l'institut archéologique bulgare* (Sofia), I (1921–22), Plate IV.

or director of the mimes. He is the *maestro* of the company. Besides Eutyches, we know the names of one or two of these long-forgotten but once famous theatrical directors of the past. Sorix the arch-mime (ὁ ἀρχιμῖμος) had, according to Plutarch, a considerable influence upon Sulla. Favor held a similar position in the time of Vespasian. As late as the fifth century A.D. we hear of an arch-mime, one Masculas, who lived under the Vandal king Geiserich. This man was a Catholic Christian, and owes the mention of his name by historians to the fact that, under the Arian persecutions by the Vandals, he remained steadfast to his faith and suffered martyrdom in the year 486. "I cannot omit in this account," says Bishop Victor grudgingly, "the name of the arch-mime, Masculas," evidently feeling that it was not quite correct that an actor should be so staunch

86

a Catholic, but that his firmness deserved some recognition. Among the records of these arch-mimes none, however, is more pathetic than that concerning a certain Doctus as narrated by Seneca. " Doctus the arch-mime," he says, " now an old, decrepit man, has lately been acting daily in the Capitol as if he thought that the gods would look with pleasure on that which men had forsaken." [1]

So modern is this world in which we are treading that we find not only the actor-manager, but the actress-manager. There are *archimimæ* beside the *archimimi*. One inscription records the death of an Arete who managed her own company, and another that of a sister-manager, Claudia Hermione.[2]

The Arch-mime and the Mimic Fool

The arch-mime was distinctly the head of his, or her, troupe. Possibly in many instances he was also the chief actor, but this need not necessarily be so. Thus, if we are justified in identifying the C. Norbanus Sorix of an inscription with the Sorix mentioned by Plutarch, it would appear that that arch-mime took secondary parts. On the other hand, this reference to secondary parts does not imply that the *rôles* were secondary in the sense of inferior or of lesser importance. Two records prove to us the true nature of this part. One is derived from the account of the martyrdom at Rome of a certain Genesius on August 25 in the year 303. This Genesius was a " secondary mime " (μῖμος δεύτερος), and the narrator of his death tells us that he was a μωρός, or fool, the theatrical type whom the Romans called *stupidus*. Happily, Horace provides us with information concerning the meaning of the word ' secondary ' itself. Speaking of a contemporary in one of his epistles,[3] the poet says that he repeats the words of others and catches the phrases as they fall, even as a schoolboy repeats the words dictated to him by a stern master or a mime in secondary parts repeats what has gone before. The secondary mime, therefore, is the fool who apes the first mime, acting precisely as the modern circus clown. The strong man lifts the 500-lb. weight, and the clown has to make ridiculous attempts to do the same; the acrobat makes his somersaults, and the clown has to tumble down in his efforts to imitate his actions. This secondary mime, as we have seen, was also named the *stupidus* (' foolish person '), and on this word too we have been left some information. As describing an actor's *rôle* it appears in an inscription which records the death of " Aurelius Eutyches, *stupidus* of the city troupe " (*stupidus gregis urbani*).[4] That this type was none other than the ancient μωρὸς φαλακρός, or bald-headed fool,[5] seems proved when we read Nonius' explanation of the word *calvitur* (' he is deceived '). " *Calvitur*," he explains, " means ' he is deceived '; it is derived from the *calvis mimicis* [' bald-headed mimes '] because they are deceived by all." [6] This reference to the bald-headed fool at once carries us to familiar ground, and we recognize here the portrait of a well-known figure. The shaved heads (*vertice raso*) which Juvenal [7] describes are an ancient comic device, and as we pass onward over the centuries that shaved head of the mimic fool persists. The fool's gleaming baldness much offended the worthy Chrysostom. He describes how such an one " cuts off his hair with a razor " (ξυρῷ τὰς τρίχας περιαιρῶν), and throws his passionate scorn upon his actions.[8] The words of Synesius have already been quoted,[9] and Gregory of Nazianzus repeats the same description regarding hair and razors.[10] We have quite clearly here one of the principal and one of the most popular of mimic types, and once more we are led to think of that circus clown with his large, glistening, bald-headed

[1] Seneca, *Fragmenta*, xii, 36 (ed. F. Haase, Leipzig, 1853, iii, 426).   [2] *C.I.L.*, VI, ii, 10107 and 10106.
[3] *Epist.*, I, xviii, 12–14 ; *cf.* Grysar, p. 267, and also Cicero, *Divinatio in Q. Cæcilium*, xv, 48.
[4] I. C. Orelli, *Inscriptionum latinarum selectarum amplissima collectio* (Turici, 1828), No. 2645 (i, 462).
[5] On this see Reich, i, 23, 470, 578.
[6] Nonius Marcellus, *De conpendiosa doctrina*, ed. W. M. Lindsay (Leipzig, 1903), i, 10.   [7] *Sat.*, v, 170–173.
[8] Chrysostom, *Spuria de pænitentia* (J. P. Migne, *Patrologia cursus completus*, Series Græca, lix, col. 760).
[9] See Reich, i, 831–832 ; Flögel, *Geschichte der Hofnarren* (Liegnitz, 1789), p. 52.
[10] II, ii, carm. viii, 85–86 (J. P. Migne, *op. cit.*, Series Græca, xxxvii, col. 1582).

dome. Nor does the likeness end there. Gregory of Nazianzus in describing the theatre—
"wanton home of deformity" (ἀσελγὲς αἰσχρότητος ἐργαστήριον), he calls it—speaks of these mimic fools as "used to knuckles" (κονδύλοις εἰθισμένοι), while Chrysostom refers to their "slapping one another," and tells how the mimic fool "is slapped at the public expense" (δημοσίᾳ ῥαπίζεται). At once we move back to Martial's description of a mimic scene in which one character makes the "base ears" of a fool ring with a blow.[1] When we remember, too, that straw bludgeon used in an Atellan play we do not wonder that this mimic fool is called *alapus*—"one who receives *alapas* ['blows'] as his mede" (*qui propter mercedem alapas potitur*).[2] And the modern circus clown? Is not he just such a character? Is not the title of Andreiev's circus play *He Who Gets Slapped*? Thus does the theatre of to-day sweep back with a rush of fond and tender, yet unconscious, memory to the distant but ever-living theatre of the past.

Fig. 80. A Mimic
Fool
Roman bronze in the Bibliothèque
Nationale, Paris (No. 968).
Photo Giraudon

One other thing we know about this fool, this *stupidus*, this μωρὸς φαλακρός. Dieterich, by a careful examination of much scattered evidence, has been able to show that his habitual headgear was a long-pointed hat.[3] From an early glossary we learn that because of this he was styled *apiciosus*, which means that the hat he wore was formed in the shape of an apex, rising to a point at the end. At once we remember that in the Phlyakes vases Odysseus regularly appeared with a *pilos*, a hat of very similar form, and we are led to believe that once more we have in this article of attire still another relic of the ancient mime of Greece. The mimic fool and his cone-hat appears on a painted grave relief at Corneto. Brizio describes this figure as bearing on his head a long, cone-shaped hat, divided vertically by strips of material. His dress is multi-coloured, resembling in its way the patchwork costume of the later Harlequin.[4] This cap is indicated in the statuettes illustrated in Figs. 80, 81, and 82, and other examples have already been given. The conical headgear of eighteenth-century Policinelli as depicted by Tiepolo (Fig. 83), and the schoolboy's familiar dunce's cap can at once be brought into association with this article in the costume of the Roman mime.

Another name for the fool was *sannio*. Says Nonius: "The *sanniones* derive their title from *sannæ* ['grimaces']. They are foolish in speech, in manners, and in action. The Greeks called them *moroi* [μωροί, 'fools']."[5] A considerable number of references exist to these *sanniones*, and at the very start it

Fig. 81. A Mimic Fool
Roman bronze in the Bibliothèque Nationale,
Paris (No. 967).
Photo Giraudon

---

[1] See *infra*, p. 108. [2] Reich, i, 448.
[3] Dieterich, pp. 153–181; Reich, i, 448, 579. See also W. Helbig, *Über den Pileus der alten Italiker* (*Sitzungsberichte der k. Akademie der Wissenschaften, München*, Philosoph.-philolog. Klasse, 1880, 487–554).
[4] E. Brizio, *Tombe dipinte di Corneto* (*Bullettino dell' Instituto di corrispondenza archeologica per l' anno 1873*, Rome, 1873, pp. 75–76).
[5] Nonius Marcellus, *De proprietate sermonum, ed. cit.*, i, 81.

has to be noted that the word itself provides another link between the mime and earlier forms of mimic drama. The title of one of Novius' Atellan farces was *Sanniones*, so that we have reason to believe that both character and name extend back beyond the days of the Roman mime proper. The connexion with *sanna*, 'a grimace,' is likewise important, for this serves again to emphasize the physical vitality of the mimic drama. Cicero, in speaking of the ideal qualities of an orator, has occasion to refer to the type. "It must be noted," he declares, "that all ridiculous things are not witty. What can be more ridiculous than *sannio* ? He arouses laughter by his face, his aspect, his manners, his voice, his very body itself." [1] In other words, *sannio's* body acts as well as his face ; physically, as well as by words, he succeeds in expressing his folly to the audience. No greater praise of comic acting could have been given than an account by Diodorus of the performance of the famous Roman mime, Latinus. This man, he says, was a "comic - sannio" (Σαννίων γελωτοποιός), gifted with every

Fig. 82. HUNCHBACK AND FOOL

(1) Phallephoric bald-headed hunchback; bronze figure in the Kunsthistorisches Museum, Vienna (Antikensammlung, Inv. VI, 169). (2) Fool type with peaked hat ; figure in the Kunsthistorisches Museum, Vienna (Antikensammlung, Inv. V, 1521).

Photos Paul Frankenstein and Kunsthistorisches Museum

charm for raising laughter. He not only caused amusement in the theatre by his words, but even aroused merriment when he stood silent. A movement of his body would set all the audience a-smiling. *Sannio* we shall meet with later ; we need say no more of him at this point. On the other hand, we must note that the suggestion has been made that we can trace his name even beyond the time of the *fabula Atellana*. Dieterich [2] has observed that Hesychius cites the word σάνναρος (*sannaros*) as the name of a fool (μωρός) in the Phlyax *Tarantinos* of Rhinthon, while similar forms occur elsewhere. Thus Eustathius in a glossarial note refers to the word σάννας (*sannas*) in a comedy of Kratinus. This, he

Fig. 83. "DIVERTIMENTI PER LI REGAZZI," BY D. TIEPOLO

Painting in the collection of V. Rosenthal. From Constant Mic, *La Commedia dell' arte* (Éditions de la Pléiade, Paris, 1927), p. 55.

declares, does not indicate merely the mildly foolish, but the regular μωρός, or fool, and suggests

---

[1] *De oratore*, II, lxi, 251.

[2] Dieterich, p. 236.

that it may be derived from a popular word τζαννόν (*tzannon*), which peasants applied to barbaric Asiatics whom they thought uncultured and rude. Perhaps this is going too far, but, whatever the origin of his name, *sannio* was assuredly one of the most popular of all mimic types in the days of Imperial Rome.

Concerning his companions we know less. The parasite and flatterer must have been a familiar figure, as in olden days. Thus Seneca, in warning his brother against the evils of flattery, makes direct reference to the mimic stage,[1] while suggestions of the character are preserved elsewhere. A third type seems to have been named Ardalio, but our picture of this man is somewhat vague and perhaps has been wrongly drawn in the past. Reich [2] is inclined to regard him merely as a later variant of *sannio*, but the qualities of the two seem, from our scattered references, to be distinct. This Ardalio is heard of both early and late. A mime bearing that name (perhaps taken from the part he played) was martyred in the fourth century A.D., but Martial's references prove that he was known long before that date. In the latter he is presented as a troublesome old idler, evidently the man who thinks he knows everything, the born intermeddler with the affairs of others. Other qualities are suggested in a series of later glosses. *Ardalio* πολυπράγμων ('Ardalio, a busybody') corroborates Martial's account, but *Ardalio glutto vorax manducus* ('Ardalio, a glutton, voracious, a Manducus') provides us with something more, while in other glosses he is described as " malignantly subtle " (*argutus cum malignitate*). Reich seems to be wrong in connecting this figure with the Atellan Maccus ; it is Manducus whom he represents, and, if we think of his qualities as described in these excerpts, we have what would be an excellent comic portrait of Herakles, maliciously clever, gluttonous, and interfering with the affairs of others.[3]

Costumes and Masks

These characters, as well as the others whom we shall discuss in connexion with the mime dramas, must have appeared in many different costumes and playing many different parts. Just as of old the tottering, white-bearded ancient could step on the stage either as an ordinary father or as Zeus, King of the Gods ; just as in later days Harlequin could amuse an audience in his own person or don rich robes and be an Emperor of the Moon ; so in the mime drama the fool, the parasite, and Ardalio might figure in many diverse scenes. One of the most interesting records in this connexion is in an account by Philo of the Jewish persecutions under the Emperor Caligula in Alexandria.[4] In the midst of the popular excitement the crowd took a wretched fool from among their number, put on his head a paper crown, and gave him a papyrus roll as a sceptre. These insignia of royalty, we are told, he assumed as if all this had been a theatrical mime (ὡς ἐν θεατρικοῖς μίμοις), while youths with rods on their shoulders stood round him " like mimic guards " (μιμούμενοι δορυφόρους). The element of burlesque here, the fool as king, the paper crown, the mock guards—all serve to call up a mental picture of a typical mimic play.[5]

The costumes of the actors must have varied with the plays in which they appeared, but of some characteristic features we have extant record.[6] The fool's cone-like hat has already been

---

[1] *Naturalium quæstionum libri VIII*, iv, præfatio 12 (ed. A. Gercke, Leipzig, 1907, p. 141).

[2] *Cf.* Reich, i, 32–38, 445–455.

[3] There is no real authority for Reich's theories that Ardalio was created by Philistion and that he took the place of the earlier *sannio*. We do not know whence he came, and he seems a character distinct from the *sannio*. The latter represents Bucco, the former Manducus. Pertinent, however, is the stress laid on the introduction of the foolish sailor called Ardalio in *Apollonius of Tyre*. There must have been considerable links of connexion between the Greek romance and the mimic drama.

[4] Reich, i, 576.

[5] H. Reich, *Der König mit der Dornenkrone* (*Neue Jahrbücher für das klassische Altertum*, xiii (1904), 705–733), connects this with the comic barbarian king of the Oxyrhynchus mime, and suggests that there is some reference to mimic burlesque in the Biblical crown of thorns.

[6] On this subject see Reich, i, 580.

discussed, but this does not seem to have been his only distinguishing article of attire. In the painting which is described by Brizio the fool's costume is depicted in two colours, and these are to be regarded rather as typically representative than as faithfully reproducing actual forms. Apuleius, after citing the *syrma*, or flowing robe, of tragedy and the *crocota*, or saffron robe, of comedy, makes a reference to this garment which he styles the *mimi centunculus*.[1] This *centunculus* was a cloak or other garment, either of patchwork or of mixed colourings—the Harlequin dress of the days of Rome. Another article of attire is suggested in a remark made by Seneca in which he describes the way in which a person appeared with a cloak covering his head and wrapped round both his ears, "just like fugitive gods in a mime."[2] This may be merely a general reference to mythical intrigues in the mimic drama, but its exact parallel would seem to indicate some well-known comic costume. Of another dress do ancient records give information. Frequently the mimic actors and actresses made use of the *recinium*, or *ricinium*, otherwise known as the *mafurtium*, which was originally 'a short cloak for women' (*palleolum femineum breve*);[3] from its employment the mimic drama itself was occasionally styled the *fabula riciniata*. This dress was evidently used often for disguise and no doubt especially for burlesque disguise. Thus Arnobius refers, as a common thing, to the "*riciniatus* and bearded Jupiter,"[4] a reference which recalls that Senecan reference to a special headgear worn by "fugitive gods" of the mimic stage. Perhaps here Seneca was merely thinking of the *ricinium*.[5]

That many of the comic characters who appeared in the mimic drama retained the ancient phallus is attested by many a classical reference. A scholiast, commenting on Juvenal, refers to the phallus, "such as they have in the mimes,"[6] while a gloss describes the *struthem* as the name given in mimes to this indelicate symbol, tracing the word back to the Greek *struthos*, a word for 'sparrow.' In picturing a mimic performance we must assume that often, if not always, the characters appeared with this symbol, and that the phallus was indeed τὸ αἰδοῖον τῶν μιμολόγων—the thing of shame which the mimes reverenced.

The subject of the mask in the mimic drama is one fraught with peculiar difficulty. Masks, as we have seen, had been associated with the early Dorian representations, and, although actors might appear without them, masks were used both in the Phlyakes and in the Atellanæ. The statement is usually made that in the days of the Roman mime these masks were not employed, but such an assertion seems to demand qualification. It is certainly true that there are some references to the painting of their faces by the mimic actors, and we must believe that sometimes at least the performers appeared before their audiences without the disguise of masks; but it is difficult to conceive that the practice of the Phlyax and Atellan performers should have been completely forgotten or abandoned. Moreover, the use of masks persisted into the Middle Ages, and, as the mime was by far the most popular of Roman entertainments, it is reasonable to suppose that it was through these plays that the knowledge was passed down to succeeding generations. Since the *sannio* was a 'grimacer' he presumably did not don this disguise, and probably it was he who most indulged in those multicoloured face-paints which are mentioned by contemporaries. There is not, however, so far as I am aware, a single statement made by an earlier writer which stamps the whole mime drama as maskless; it seems probable that some parts at least required the use of exaggerated and comic masks. If there exists no proof of this, at least no positive assurance is given us that the supposition is wrong.[7]

---

[1] Apuleius, *Apologia*, xiii; *cf*. Grysar, p. 270.　　　　　[2] *Epistolæ*, cxiv, 6.
[3] Nonius Marcellus, ed. L. Müller (Leipzig, 1888), 542 M, ii, 210.
[4] *Adversus gentes*, vi, 25 (in J. P. Migne, *op. cit.*, Series Latina, v, col. 1213).
[5] See Grysar, p. 270; Reich, i, 799.　　　　　[6] *Cf*. Reich, i, 258.
[7] Grysar (p. 270) and Reich (i, 527–528) both assert that the Roman mimic actors wore no masks.

festival and rejoicing. And indeed, in our own times, a famous actress does not travel like the members of a fourth-rate provincial company or a minor music-hall troupe. It appears probable that the lower type of buffoon was given a technical name, *scurra*, from which our ' scurrilous ' is derived. The *scurra mimicus* was evidently a well-known figure, and would seem to have indulged in jesting of a ' music-hall ' nature. " Suddenly he drops his head on his breast," Phædrus tells us, " and makes his voice sound like that of a sucking-pig." [1] No doubt among the *scurræ* physical peculiarities were more stressed than among the better-class mimes, and the *hirnea*, or humpback, which belonged to Dossennus of the Atellanæ and was passed on as a legacy to the mimic stage, was exaggerated to undue lengths. Julius Victorinus thus speaks of the roughness of certain forms of art indulged in by the *scurræ* ; " many," he says, " when they want to be witty, copy not only the language, but the gestures and the dialects of the *scurræ*, thus being neither what they ought to be nor what they profess to imitate." Even among the mimes of the higher sort, those whom some called ethologues, the outlines were coarser than could be permitted, for example, to the orator. " If the imitation be excessive," Cicero warns his readers, " it will resemble that of mimes and ethologues." [2] Evidently the ordinary *iocus mimicus* was of a broad quality, and, recognizing this, we may form some vague idea of the *scurra's* jests.

By no means all of these actors and actresses were Roman or even Italian by birth. Several seem to have come from Greece, and still more from Syria and the Farther East. There are various accounts of the mimic activity in those lands, and the Syrian monarchs both favoured individual mimes and themselves appeared in a like capacity. Antiochus II counted among his greatest friends a ' logomime' (λογόμιμος), Herodotus, and a tragic actor, Archelaus, while his successor, Antiochus IV, at a feast held in A.D. 168, " appeared all dressed up among the mimes and placed himself in their midst as if he were one of them," dancing and acting " along with the jesters " (μετὰ τῶν γελωτοποιῶν).[3] As a consequence the Roman Emperor Verus on returning from Syria could bring with him a number of actors, " as proudly as though he were bringing kings to a triumph." [4] Among those brought on this occasion was a famous Paris and an Agrippus with a host of " harpers, trumpeters, actors, mimic jesters, and jugglers " (*fidicinas et tibicines et histriones scurrasque mimarios et præstigiatores*). The historian (Capitolinus) adds that these flourished luxuriantly in Syria and in Alexandria, and that Verus' campaign seemed rather " a histrionic than a Parthian war." The Syrian mimes remained famous up to at least the sixth century A.D.

Individual Actors and Actresses

The names and achievements of some of these mimic actors have been recorded, and much of the information which has been left concerning them aids us in picturing both their art and the conditions in which they lived. Agrippus, brought by Verus from Syria, has been noted above. His real name was Agrippus Memphius, but Verus renamed him Apolaustus—' the Enjoyable,' and after his manumission he appeared in more lordly style as L. Ælius Aurelius Apolaustus Memphius. Like some other mimes, he witnessed the changing fortunes of life under princes, for in A.D. 189 he was put to death by the Emperor Commodus.[5] Concerning Aliturus, a mimologue beloved of Nero, we know nothing,[6] and of Ardalio we learn no more than that in some Eastern city he was martyred on April 14, A.D. 298.[7] Another Christian mime, but one who seems to have ended his life in holy retirement, was a certain Babylas.[8] Still another, Cardamas

---

[1] *Fabularum æsopiarum*, Liber V, v, 8–16. [2] *De oratore*, II, lix, 242.
[3] This indicates the improvisatorial nature of the mimic shows, at least in Syria. See Reich i, 193–194 ; [Grysar, p. 306 ; both quoting from Athenæus, v, 195.
[4] Capitolinus, *Verus*, viii, 7. [5] Capitolinus, *Verus*, viii, 10 ; Lampridius, *Commodus*, vii, 2.
[6] Josephus Flavius, *Vita*, iii (*Opera*, ed. B. Niese, Berlin, 1880, iv, 324). [7] *Cf.* Reich, i, 85. [8] *Cf.* Reich, i, 777.

by name, likewise abandoned his profession and adopted that of an exorcist. He had, says one of Augustine's followers, Paulinus of Nola, given up the foolish levity of a mimic's name and assumed the reverent gravity of an exorcist's.[1] Among other Christian martyrs besides Ardalio we hear of a Gelasinus, who was put to death in Heliopolis in Phœnicia on February 27, 297; a Genesius, similarly killed in Rome on August 25, 303; Porphyrius, who met his end at Cæsarea in Cappadocia on November 4, 275; a second Porphyrius, who died at Constantinople on September 15, 362; and that Philemon whose story has already been told, and who perished for his faith on March 8, 284, in the city of Antinoe in Egypt.[2] Most of these mimic names are no more than names for us—the Carus cited by a Juvenalian scholiast;[3] the Cassius mentioned by Tacitus;[4] the Corinthus who acted with Thymele;[5] the Diogenes, "mimelos" (μιμηλός), "who wrote incredible things," according to Epiphanius;[6] the ethologue Dionysius, whose name appears in an inscription;[7] the Herakleides who was a "biologue man" (βιολόγος φώς); the uncertain Hippias; the Isidorus, father of Tertia; the C. Manneius Coranus who is recorded in an inscription;[8] the Phædrus, a mime, or mimograph, mentioned by Martial;[9] the Antonine Phœbus;[10] the Tutor, "an old mime, laughed at by the town," referred to by Cicero;[11] and the Valens whose name has been preserved by Tacitus.[12] That these men lived we know; that their art was esteemed by contemporaries is testified by the recording of their names; but how they acted, what *rôles* they took, what was their appearance, we have no means now of informing ourselves. Even the dry relics of their craft are perished. There are only one or two concerning whom we have more information. The "true mimic actor," Latinus, is described by both Juvenal and Martial, and from their words we can make out the plot of at least one of the plays in which he appeared.[13] Clearly he flourished in the age of Domitian, so that the scandal narrated by the Juvenalian scholiast to the effect that he was accused of adultery with Messalina, Nero's wife, cannot be true. Perhaps the tale arose out of the fact that in the play which has been recorded by Juvenal Latinus' part was that of a lover. There is a brief account of the art of Protogenes in an inscription recording his death, but hardly sufficient to prove a basis for any theory.[14] A long epitaph exists, too, for the mime Vitalis, although we do not know in what precise age he lived.[15] At least some idea of his style may be gained from these verses, which may thus be paraphrased:

> What shall I do to thee, Death, that thou wilt not let us alone?
> No jests can gratify thee, no joy can come near thy throne.
> Here in this town I won fame; here a rich house I had;
> And here applause was showered on me, for I made the people glad.
> Always I laughed, for I thought, "If we cannot laugh and sing,
> What use is this silly old world, tired with its wandering?"
> I calmed every raging heart that was fiercely burning for wrong;
> Grief that was bitter with tears would smile when I sauntered along;
> And fear that was pallid and chill would vanish away when I came;
> For each hour spent with me was a joy—hearts leaped with delight at my name.
> In gesture and word—yea, even when I was talking with serious art,
> Joy came on the stage with me, I brightened each weary heart.

[1] *Cf.* Reich, i, 776.   [2] *Cf.* Reich, i, 85.
[3] Schol. to Juvenal, i, 36 (ed. J. E. B. Mayor, Cambridge, 1853, p. 8), and *In D. Ivnii Ivvenalis satiras commentarii vetvsti* (Hamburg, 1823), p. 25.
[4] Tacitus, *Annales*, i, 73.   [5] *Cf. infra*, p. 119.
[6] *Cf.* Grysar, p. 314.   [7] I. C. Orelli, *op. cit.*, No. 2616 (ii, 458).
[8] A. F. Gori, *Inscriptiones antiquæ græcæ et romanæ in Etrvriæ vrbibus* (Florentiæ, 1734), ii, 178, No. 172.
[9] *Epigr.* III, xx, 5.   [10] *Cf.* Grysar, p. 315.
[11] *De oratore*, II, lxiv, 259. It may be that *mimus* is here used for a play, and that *Tutor* is a title of a farce, and not the name of an actor.
[12] *Historiarum libri qui supersunt*, ed. W. A. Spooner (1891), iii, 62, p. 335.
[13] Juvenal, *Sat.*, i, 35, vi, 44; Martial, *Epigr.*, i, 55, iii, 86, ix, 28; and *cf.* Grysar, pp. 245, 253-254.   [14] *C.I.L.*, i, 1297.
[15] *Cf.* Grysar, pp. 313-314. This actor may be of medieval date; indeed, he is generally believed to have lived in the ninth century; *cf.* J. P. Jacobsen, *La Comédie en France au moyen-âge* (*Revue de philologie française et de littérature*, xxiii (1909), 85).

MASKS MIMES AND MIRACLES

When I spoke I so changed my face, my habit so altered, and tone,
Men thought that many were there where I stood all alone.
How oft did they laugh to see, as I mimicked a dainty wife,
My gestures so womanly quaint, the shy blush done to the life!
O Death, thou hast slain more than me, for when me you carried away
You carried a thousand off on this bitter, predestinate day.
I, to whom life was dear, am mournful now and sad :
O Strangers, who read these lines, pray that my path be glad.
" What joy, Vitalis, you gave ! "—this you must utter in prayer—
" Where'er you may go from this earth, may joyousness meet you there ! "

More information is given us concerning the mimic actresses. A pleasant little poem by Antipater of Sidon describes the charms of a certain Antiodemis, a mimode, or lysiode (what we should perhaps call now an operatic star), who came to Italy from Greece in the second century B.C. With her " mild charm " (μαλθακίνη χάριτι) she seems to have captured the heart of the poet, and of others.[1] A lofty-minded Arbuscula is recorded both by Cicero and by Horace.[2] The former tells a friend who had been asking about her that " she was pleasing greatly," and describes the performances in which she was appearing as " magnificent and delightful," while the latter presents what purports to be a statement of her own. Once she was unsuccessful and was hissed off the stage ; proudly she declared that she cared not so long as the nobles welcomed her art. " ' It is sufficient for me if I am applauded by the knights,' " quotes Horace, " as the bold Arbuscula said in disdain of the rest when she was hissed from the stage." This was in the middle of the first century B.C. About the time of Antiodemis lived another famous actress, one Julia Bassilla, of whom at least one, perhaps two, inscriptional records remain. In 1805 there was found at Aquileia a tomb which presented her bust as well as a verse epitaph. In this we are told that the mimic actor, Herakleides, caused the stele to be raised in her honour. He declares that she, a kind of tenth muse, had been the dream of many states and of many cities. Of varied excellence in mime, in ballet, and in play, she was a mistress of her art and had obtained honour everywhere. Now this " musical body " of hers lay sleeping in the earth. The stele ends, " These things are said to you by your colleagues. Farewell, Bassilla. Naught is immortal." [3] This Bassilla, then, had won fame in many lands, had been, as it were, an international star ; and in this connexion it is very tempting to believe with Grysar [4] that to her refers a second inscription from the lovely city-state of Taormina in Sicily. The second stele is short, but its spontaneousness and its very conciseness are appealing :

The Council and People of the radiant city of Taormina have erected this stele in honour of the most radiant Julia Bassilla, eminent for her art, her virtue, and her wisdom.

Passing down the centuries, we come upon another once famous actress, one Cytheris, who, unlike Bassilla, preferred to leave her art for the luxuries of a lover's home. Originally named Volumnia, she appears to have been first taken from the stage by Volumnius Eutrapelus, the magnificence of whose Roman residence was common talk.[5] On one occasion Cicero went to dine at his house and found the fair Cytheris reclining at his feet. Later she became the mistress of no less a person than the triumvir Antony. Again Cicero describes the scene :

Laurel-crowned lictors marched in front, among whom, in an open litter, the mimic actress was borne. From the cities the worthy officials had to come . . . and greet her.

[1] Cf. Reich, i, 167–168.
[2] Cicero, Epist. ad Atticum, iv, 15 ; Horace, Sat., I, x, 76–77.
[3] Corpus inscriptionum Græcæ Siciliæ, 2342.
[4] Grysar, pp. 284–286 ; Reich, i, 157. The second inscription is in C.I.G., 1091. The text reads the name as Ἰαλλίαν Βάσιλλ[αν] or Βασσιανῆ[ν].
[5] Cf. Grysar, pp. 286–290, and authorities cited there.

The following year (48 B.C.) the susceptible Antony fought at Actium, but hurried back in order to join his mistress at Brundisium.   Scornfully Cicero addressed him :

> To Brundisium you came, to the embraces of your little mime [*tuæ mimulæ*].   If you were not ashamed before the townsfolk, were you not ashamed before your own veterans ?   For what soldier was there who did not see her in Brundisium ? . . . The same march back through Italy to meet the same pleasing actress.

Not that Antony confined himself to the attentions of Cytheris.   Plutarch informs us that his " house was full of mimes and jugglers and drunken parasites," and among these the *mimæ* seem to have figured.

We can imagine that these actresses must have earned enormous incomes, and we are not, as a consequence, surprised when we are told that a certain Dionysia, the *gesticularia* and *saltatricula*, gained at least 200,000 sesterces annually.[1]   If some led the lives of a Cytheris, others were praised as Bassilla was by the townspeople of Taormina.   Eucharis is described on her tombstone as " learned and erudite," and the praise is echoed elsewhere.[2]   It is not known what *privata mima* means in the inscription found at Verona recording the death of a certain Luria ;[3] possibly it signifies that she belonged to a company kept by a wealthy noble.   An Origo is recorded by Horace as being beloved by Marsæus,[4] and a Tertia, daughter of Isidorus, who had been forcibly carried off from Rhodes, is mentioned by Cicero in his Verrine speeches.[5]   Horace tells us that Marsæus, " that lover of Origo," gave his patrimony, his very household gods, to the mime, whereby " his fame lost more than his estate," while Tertia seems to have caused a similar contemporary scandal.   Concerning Thymele, a mime and pantomime, we get some information from Martial and Juvenal.[6]   One of her chief parts seems to have been that of the *zelotypus*, the jealous woman, a *rôle* that recalls the character of the jealous woman in Herodas.   It would appear that she was noted for the risquéness of her performances.   In this connexion she had little to learn from any-one, save perhaps from Bathyllus when he presented his pantomime of Leda and the swan.

We may conclude this rapid survey of those mimic actresses who are known to us by dwelling a moment on two of the most famous of all, Pelagia and Theodora.   The former, " the chief of the mimes in Antioch " (*prima mimarum Antiochiæ*), an actress and a dancer,[7] seems to have won un-bounded fame in her own day.   Perhaps because of her beauty, perhaps because of her riches, she was even better known as Μαργαριτώ, ' the Pearl,' than as Pelagia.   Symeon Metaphrastes is lavish in his description of her adornments and retinue :

> Pelagia passed by, richly clad as usual in robe and cloak.   She was seated on a litter, and a great crowd escorted her.   The gleam of her gems and pearls cast a coloured tinge on the air surrounding her, which, too, was scented with the odour of the unguents she used. . . . As she went numbers of personal atten-dants followed and preceded her.

She was, no doubt, typical of many a contemporary star, but of the others we do not hear.   Pelagia is known to us only through the lucky chance that her pearl-glittering and sweet-scented way met that of a certain Bishop Nonnus, who succeeded in piercing below the lovely form to the heart within and in making her a Christian.   Her name was later sung by pious men and women, not as a mime, but as a saint of the Church.   Her begemmed robes were exchanged for the drab raiment of a holy devotee.

This was in the fifth century A.D.   A century later in Byzantium there was a trio of sisters who had none too good a name in theatrical circles.   The eldest was named Comito, the second

---

[1] Cicero, *Pro Roscio comædo*, viii, 23.   [2] *C.I.L.*, VI, ii, 10096.
[3] *C.I.L.*, VI, ii, 10111.   Another *mima*, by name Thalassia, is recorded in the same work—VI, ii, 10112.
[4] *Sat.*, I, ii, 55.   [5] *In C. Verrem III*, xxxiv, 78.   [6] See *supra*, p. 95.
[7] She was called πρώτη τῶν πρωτοχορεστριῶν.   See Reich, i, 101-103.

G

Theodora, and the youngest Anastasia.[1] Daughters of the royal supervisor of the theatre, they no doubt grew up in familiarity with the mimes, and when their father died they naturally turned to the stage as a source of living. Theodora and Comito rapidly became famous for their beauty, and, like many actresses of the time, they both appear to have been of somewhat easy virtue. Perhaps the attacks later made on Theodora are exaggerated; it is, at any rate, doubtful whether, after an extensive tour in the East, she descended to an existence spent in a miserable brothel; but that some truth lies in the scandalous reports of gossipy or prejudiced historians would seem to be established. Theodora, however, was no ordinary courtesan. That she shone in her art is attested by Procopius, although he qualifies his praise by referring to her indelicate style and licentious mimicry:

> She entered with the mimes into the full life of the stage and shared their activities with them. Very clever and witty she was, and she gained great fame from her skill in her adopted profession. But as a woman she had no sense of shame. No one ever saw her blushing.

It is not, however, her art or her obscenity which made Theodora famous. Attracting the eyes of the great emperor Justinian, she became first his ἐρωμένη, or mistress, then was raised to patrician rank, and ended by becoming his empress. Whatever evil had existed in her earlier life evidently was not sufficient to kill in her a native grace and breadth of spirit. In spite of calumnious tongues, she proved an excellent queen to Justinian, aided him in his difficult policies, and carried on an able government after his death. Here truly was the first and the most glorious of all those marriages into the aristocracy which appear to be so modern, so much a symbol of the stage conditions of to-day. In ancient Byzantium a mimic actress could become the mistress and queen of the land she lived in.

It must be remembered that, although certain mimes may have been despised, the members of the acting profession in classical times might on occasion rise to the highest positions in the State, and that likewise on occasion nobles and kings would follow the practice of the Syrian Antiochus and appear alongside the professionals. It was Domitius who forced Roman knights and matrons to go upon the stage for the purpose of acting a mime.[2] "When an emperor has taken to harp-playing," says Juvenal satirically, "it isn't so very strange that nobles should act in a mime,"[3] referring thus to Nero, who seems to have taken a particular pleasure in seeing the Roman matrons and the old men of State making their public appearance at the Juvenales.[4] On occasion the emperors themselves took parts to act, but such a practice seems to have associated itself more with the wordless art of the pantomime.

Concerning the question of State control and support of the mimes we unfortunately know little. Some of the actors were mere wandering vagabonds; others, like Philemon, were associated with a town; others, like Bassilla, seem to have been touring international stars. A band of Court players, however, is suggested in the *Life of Hadrian* by Ælius Spartianus. Hadrian, he says, "presented plays of all kinds in the old manner on the stage and sent his Court actors to perform in public [*histriones aulicos publicavit*]."[5] In this connexion it is interesting to notice that in later periods there seems to have been a regular official, called a *tribunus voluptatum*, established in several cities, and that that official had control of the stage.[6] Theodora's father was overseer of the playhouse at Byzantium, where the post seems to have borne the title of ἄρχων τῆς θυμέλης (literally, 'leader of the stage'), while the *tribunus voluptatum* is recorded in Italy under Theodoric (fifth century A.D.) and at Carthage in the sixth century A.D.

Whatever position the individual mimes held, there appears to have been ample opportunity

---

[1] See Grysar, pp. 310–313. [2] Suetonius, *Nero*, iv. [3] *Sat.*, viii, 198–199. [4] Suetonius, *Nero*, xi.
[5] *Hadrian*, xix. [6] See Sir E. K. Chambers, *The Mediæval Stage* (Oxford, 1903), ii, 229.

for the amassing of money. When Nero gave 2200 million sesterces for shows some at least found its way into the hands of the mimic performers, and a Dionysia knew of other means of securing wealth. "The mimes and actors," says Chrysostom, "go about on their horses, and have their servants running in front of them"; thus was Pelagia escorted. The complaints go on until the mimes apparently vanish from sight in the Dark Ages. The scholars of Byzantium grumbled as some modern scholars have been known to do at the large sums acquired by those connected with the theatres. One of these, who was also a poet, Prodromos by name, satirically counselled the banishing of Aristotle and Plato. In his stanzas ἐπὶ τῇ ἀτιμίᾳ τοῦ λόγου (*The Contempt of Learning*) his words grow bitter when he thinks of the unfairness of it all :

> Let wisdom and books go hang,
>   And all this endless care.
> Stand by the actor's side
>   Or sit in the jester's chair.
> Spend all your time with the mimes—
>   Play with their childish toys—
> Nothing is honoured now
>   But jesting and laughter and noise.
> Let wisdom's erstwhile noble rage
> Be ceded to the mimic stage.[1]

The same testimony is given, from a different point of view, by that almost solitary defendant of the mimes, the bold Choricius. "Everywhere the mimes gain fame," he says. "Rightly they get wealth from their art. They revel in their rich clothing, their store of gold, their silvery attire, and their retinues of servants."[2] In spite of Christian opposition, it is certain that many of them won important and distinguished positions in the social life of their time centuries after that period when "the most radiant" Bassilla charmed the citizens of the "radiant," mountain-set city of Taormina.

THE METHODS OF PERFORMANCE

In classical times these mimes made their appearance normally at the end of other shows or in the midst of these, their plays being either after-pieces or *intermezzi*. In other words, the mimic drama came to take the place that had been occupied in former years by the *fabula Atellana*; it played the part of an *exodium*, and the performer was often called an *exodiarius*. "The *exodiarius*," says the ever-useful scholiast to Juvenal,

> came on the stage in ancient times at the end of the play. He uttered witty speeches in order to relieve a little the tears and the sadness resultant upon tragic action by the merriness of his performance.[3]

When Cicero, in writing to Pætus in 46 B.C., came to the last point he wished to raise he likened his semi-postscript to a mime, noting that the mime had taken the position of after-piece once occupied by the Atellana.[4] Festus informs us that these mimes were also employed for a different purpose. They used, he declared,

> to come forth in the orchestra and perform with obscene gestures while the scenes of the play were being prepared on the stage itself.[5]

Donatus gives much the same account, with particular reference to a special adjunct of the theatre.[6] After speaking of the large woven *aulæum*, or curtain, used for regular plays he mentions the *siparium*,

---

[1] *Cf.* Reich, i, 162–163.　　[2] See *infra*, p. 142.　　[3] *Schol. ad Juv.*, iii, 175 (ed. J. E. B. Mayor, Cambridge, 1853, p. 62).
[4] See *supra*, p. 67.　　[5] Festus, *Fragmenta*, ed. W. M. Lindsay (Leipzig, 1913), p. 436.
[6] *Excerpta de comœdia*, viii, 8 (ed. P. Wessner, Leipzig, 1902, i, 30).

Fig. 84. THE SMALL COMIC THEATRE AT POMPEII
Photo Trampetti

Fig. 85. THE TRAGIC THEATRE AT POMPEII

which was the curtain for the mimes; this, he says, was put up " while the scenes of the plays were being changed" (*dum fabularum actus commutantur*). From this *embolium*, or interlude, the mimic actors were sometimes named *emboliarius* and *emboliaria*.

The *siparium*, or curtain, which has been mentioned here, possesses some significance, and, in view of this significance, it may be worth while pausing for a moment to take a rapid glance at some main features of the Roman stage. It is not necessary, of course, to discuss the relationship between the ancient Greek and the later Roman playhouses, but some attention may be devoted

Fig. 86. THE REMODELLED GREEK THEATRE AT SEGESTA, SICILY
Photo Alinari

to special aspects of the latter. In general, we may say that the typical Roman theatre is based on the principle of a semicircular auditorium with a long, narrow stage backed by a proscenium wall, or *frons scenæ*. These theatres of the Roman or Græco-Roman type are to be found in many towns; illustration from a selected few will serve our purposes here. The arrangement of a typical auditorium is well seen in the two playhouses at Pompeii (Figs. 84 and 85). In the latter, the so-called Tragic Theatre, there will be noted, first, the foundations of the stage, with a familiar arrangement of recesses or niches, and, secondly, the lofty surrounding wall which sweeps round the upper tier of the auditorium seats. Many ancient Greek theatres were later remodelled to accord with the semicircular proportions of the Roman playhouse, and these may also be taken as typical. At Segesta there is such a building which must have been remodelled in later times (Fig. 86). The semicircular orchestra is well shown here with the remnants of the ancient stage wall and *paraskenia* (seen where the two men are standing), while the bases are revealed for pillars designed to support either a Roman stage or one intended for Phlyax performances.   If we imagine

Fig. 87. THE STAGE BUILDINGS OF THE THEATRE AT TAORMINA, SICILY
Photo Crupi

these pillars rising to support a wooden platform we can certainly picture such a representation as the vase-painters have left for us.   Since Taormina has been mentioned in connexion with the mime Bassilla, the theatre there may be used as a final example.   Here (Figs. 87 to 89) the orchestra

102

is again a perfect semicircle, with a radius of 87 feet, but this must have been remodelled from the original, greater than semicircle Hellenistic form. This orchestra is separated from the *cavea*, or auditorium, by two walls, each some 3 or 4 feet high and separated 5½ feet from one another. From the farthest of these the *cavea* rises in a steep slope extending for another 87 feet. As in Pompeii, the last tier of seats ends in a wall 10 feet high. The auditorium is divided by passage-ways into nine sections, or *cunei*, and to each of these passage-ways corresponds an opening in the upper wall. Thus there are really nine sections of wall, each about 60 feet long, indented with

Fig. 88. THE GREEK THEATRE AT TAORMINA, SICILY
Photo Crupi

four niches (no doubt once containing statues) and surmounted by five Corinthian columns. Beyond this is a high, semicircular wall, rising 20 feet and forming a corridor once vaulted; a second corridor is formed still farther outward by a row of tall columns. These corridors are 10 feet wide. In its complete state the auditorium must thus have presented a vast and imposing appearance. The stage buildings, which are equally imposing, have here been well preserved. The stage itself seems to have been some 7 feet above the orchestra level; it is 9 feet deep, with a rise of 6 feet to the level which contains the columns, and this in turn recedes another 9 feet. The total width of the stage is 132 feet. The back wall, or *frons scænæ*, which is 20 feet high, is broken by one large central doorway and by two smaller doorways at the sides, the latter being 10 feet wide. The two central sections of back wall thus formed have three large niches, and are faced by Corinthian columns of a height of 15 feet. Toward the top of the wall is a series of small niches, and seemingly the whole was surmounted by a row of columns with an architrave.

103

Behind the stage proper, and rising to its level, comes a vaulted passage-way extending the entire length of the theatre; this is 15 feet wide. At each side are two enormous halls (representing the original *paraskenia*).[1] The length of these is 57 feet. There are entrance doors from the rear, and openings which lead respectively to a platform running toward the stage and to a secondary room which connects by way of the *vomitoria*, or main entrances, to the auditorium and orchestra. The door leading to the stage is 12 feet wide, and that leading to the orchestra is 16 feet. Stair-

Fig. 89. THE STAGE BUILDINGS OF THE THEATRE AT TAORMINA, SICILY
Photo Crupi

cases carry one to an upper floor, which in turn has a door leading to the *cavea*. The walls of these *paraskenia* rooms are 5 feet thick.

The detailed description given here of the proportions of this theatre at Taormina has been presented in order to provide some idea of the main features and of the grandiose conception of a Roman or Græco-Roman playhouse. The fundamental features of the stage consist in a back wall, or *scænæ frons*, broken usually by three doors and generally having two rectangularly set side-openings, a long, narrow stage some 6 to 8 feet above the orchestra level, and side rooms of an imposing grandeur. A variant *frons scænæ* is shown in an interesting model relief, now in the Museo Nazionale, Rome (Fig. 90), in which there is a large central door and two side doors, each with double shutters. Four additional columned openings seemingly contain square niches. In

---

[1] A. Héron de Villefosse (in *Bulletin de la Société des Antiquaires de France*, 1916, pp. 235–237), quoting an inscription at Dugga, proves that the technical name of these halls was *basilicæ*.

many Roman theatres a roof, such as that shown in the Phlyakes stage (Fig. 50), extended over the acting platform, while in some awnings appear to have been spread over the whole of the auditorium. Within the enclosed space perfumes were used to keep the air cool. "If I were to question," says Horace, "whether a play of Atta's succeeds or not amid the saffron and the flowers . . .," thus making reference to the prevailing custom.[1]

The theatres, of course, were used for a variety of purposes. Gladiatorial fights and mimic sea-spectacles were perhaps in later years as common as plays. Queer things were seen there. The Emperor Claudius, so Suetonius informs us, had private combats of carpenters and stage-hands "when a piece of stage-machinery [*automatum vel pegma*] had not worked very well."[2] In the

Fig. 90. A Roman Frons Scænæ

Terra-cotta relief in the Museo Nazionale, Rome. From M. Bieber, *Denkmäler zum Theaterwesen im Altertum*, Taf. XL, 1.

fourth century A.D. a poet describes the removing of the weights, the descent of the great pageant-machine, the play of lights upon the stage, the fictional burning of the scenic towers. The means at the hands of the machinists must have been many. Already the Greek stage had invented a number of such devices, and the old methods were carried over to Rome, and were added to by the development of others of a startling and spectacular character. With its curtain, or *aulæum*, with its machines and with its painted scenery, the Roman stage was not so very far distant from our own. The question, however, must arise : how far did the mime actors make use of these effects which we know were used for other plays and for spectacular shows ? It is the mime which we are particularly considering, and at the moment the Roman stage has interest for us only in so far as it concerns their activities.

For this purpose we must return to that from which we set out, the *siparium*, and, by analysing the references to this, we must endeavour to make a mental picture of the settings usually forming the background for the mimes. We have already seen that two authorities describe these entertainers as performing in the orchestra either immediately after or in the midst of plays and that they associate the *siparium* directly with the mimic representations. The *siparium* is used by Seneca as the opposite of the *cothurnus*, in the sense that one was lighter drama and the other

---

[1] *Epist.*, II, i, 79–80. [2] Suetonius, *Claudius*, xxxiv.

MASKS MIMES AND MIRACLES

serious.[1] *Post siparium* seems to be used by Cicero as signifying " out of sight of the audience," [2] and Juvenal reverts to Seneca's use of the word when he accuses a contemporary, Damasippus, of having " hired himself to the *siparium*," or the mimes.[3] On this passage a scholiast has appended a note : " The *siparium* is the curtain which conceals the mimes before they come upon the stage. It is the door (*ostium*) of the mimes." This corresponds with Donatus' *mimicum velum*. The use to which the *mimicum velum* was put is suggested by an account of the attempted rebellion of Petronius in A.D. 365. This general, we are told, white as a ghost and clad in the insignia of royalty, entered suddenly in front of his soldiers. So sudden, indeed, was his appearance, and so startling, that one would have imagined oneself in the theatre witnessing the sudden entry of characters in a mime.

From these records it would appear that the *siparium* was a back-curtain, not one, like the *aulæum*, set in front of the acting platform.[4] It is the ' door ' or ' entrance ' for the players, and concealed the regular tragic or comic scenery behind. The question arises, however, as to its precise position. As we have seen, Diomedes explains the use of the words *planus* and *planipes* by saying that once the mimic performers acted, not on the stage (*in suggestu scænæ*), but on the orchestra level (*in plano orchestræ*). This statement is corroborated by Festus, who explains that the orchestra was not used by the regular actors, but " by those who are now called *planipedes*." That originally these mimes performed on a rude platform erected in the midst of the orchestra immediately in front of the permanent theatre stage would seem to be highly probable, and if this were so, then the *siparium* would be that piece of cloth attached to a frame which is to be seen in many illustrations of early *commedia dell' arte* and mountebank troupes. Perhaps the engraving reproduced in Fig. 91 will give some idea of this primitive platform. It is at least possible that when Cicero speaks of the curtain (*aulæum*) being removed at the end of a mimic drama he is not so much thinking of this curtain as marking the end of the mime as of its utilization to mark the beginning of the regular play to follow. The mimes have finished their *embolium*. All is prepared for the next act of the tragedy or comedy. The *siparium* is removed from the orchestra, and the *aulæum* is lowered. While, therefore, we may accept Donatus' derivation of *planipedes* from the fact that the mimic actors " went in bare feet [or flat-soled] on stage and platform," we may believe that their original performances in the theatres were confined to the orchestra.

Gradually, however, the mimes drove out not merely the hitherto popular *fabula Atellana*, but regular comedy and tragedy as well. They therefore became masters of the playhouse and ascended from their rude platform to the stage itself. The stage (*scæna*), we are told by Suetonius, was covered with blood during the representation of a certain mime ; [5] Donatus, in the passage quoted above, speaks of the mimes acting both on stage (*scæna*) and platform (*pulpitum*) ; while the use of the word " once " (*olim*) is to be noted in those references which place the mimes in the orchestra. The mime unquestionably came to stand by itself, and if we cannot accept the Suetonian survey of theatrical history as presented by Diomedes we must agree that his facts are more or less correct.[6] In effect he says that in earlier times regular comedy held the stage, such other elements (song, dance, and pantomime) as were required being kept subsidiary to the play. At various

---

[1] Tertullian's phrase *trans siparium cothurnatio est*, as applied to a mime, similarly means comic or mimic treatment of a tragic theme—that is to say, a tragic burlesque (*Adversus Valentinianos*, xiii; J. P. Migne, *op. cit.*, Series Latina, ii, col. 563).

[2] *De provinciis consularibus*, xv, 14.   [3] *Sat.*, viii, 186.

[4] How it was controlled in unknown. The *aulæum* did not fall, like the curtain in modern theatres, but rose from a recess in front of the stage. The apparatus for moving it is seen well in the theatre at Merida, in Spain, where small square conduits run along the length of the stage front, evidently for the purpose of retaining the curtain supports (see J. R. Mélida, *El teatro romano de Mérida* (Madrid, 1915), and R. Lautier in *Comptes rendus de l' Académie des Inscriptions et Belles-Lettres* (1915), pp. 164–174). Similar supports have been found in other playhouses, such as Timgad and Orange (*cf.* J. Formigé in *Comptes rendus* (1916), pp. 455–458). The *siparium* may have been similarly set in place; more probably it was supported on movable framework screens.

[5] Suetonius, *Caligula*, lvii.   [6] *Artis grammaticæ libri III* (in H. Keil, *ed. cit.*, i, 491–492).

times, however, there appeared individual entertainers who were specially skilled in their respective arts and who would not subordinate themselves to the main body of (perhaps less talented) actors. These, as a consequence, tended to set up for themselves, and so comedy and the play as a whole perished. If we put this historical sequence in the form that talented mimic actors came to appeal more than dull dramatic actors, we shall probably come fairly near the truth.

It is hardly likely that these mimes, when they once seized control of the playhouses, would forgo all the aids which the theatre had to offer them. No doubt the idea of the early *siparium* background was retained to the very end, but we have to believe that machine devices, spectacular effects, and all the many similar theatrical appurtenances would be brought into their service. As the extant accounts of mimes indicate, however, the mime to its latest days retained absolute freedom in regard to setting and scenes. This aspect will be discussed in greater detail in a later

section. Here we must observe that, for the most part, the mimic actors seem to have relied on their words, their actions, and a few properties to create imaginative illusion of place on the stage ; adding to these on occasion free use of the conventions on which the representations of classical comedy and tragedy were based. It is well known that, both among the Greeks and the Romans, the doors or entrances to the stage had all specific significations, practically providing a symbolic multiple setting. It seems highly probable that this imaginative significance of the entrances would be seized upon by the mimic performers, and we may believe that they combined the two conventions into one—sometimes making the openings in their *siparium* stand for individual ' houses ' or localities and sometimes standing on the unlocalized platform and giving to that, as occasion required, a local habitation and a name.

Fig. 91. A Commedia dell' Arte Stage

Print of 1630. From P. L. Duchartre, *The Italian Comedy*, p. 64.

The mimes seem to have presented fairly regular performances in the theatres, but naturally their activities were mostly associated with the various festivals celebrated in cities east and west. It must not, however, be assumed that the greater exponents of this art—a Latinus, a Bassilla, a Pelagia—were those whose indecent gestures and attire made notorious the festivities at the Floralia. The Floralia games, held on April 28, and established, according to tradition, in the year 238 B.C., became the annual celebration of obscenity. Here the *scæna levis* (' light stage '), as Ovid [1] informs us, had its home ; here no serious thoughts could intrude ; and here occurred those shameless denudings of women which startled contemporaries have recorded. It must have been, however, only the lesser actresses, if, indeed, actresses at all, who appeared on the stage at this festival. As we have seen, the scholiast to Juvenal mentions only *meretrices nudatis corporibus* (' naked courtesans ') there, while Lactantius significantly remarks that these courtesans took the place of the mimic actresses (*meretrices quæ tunc mimarum funguntur officio*).[2] It is certainly true that, in his familiar account of the manner in which the Younger Cato left the theatre at the Floralia, "in order that his presence might not hinder the customary spectacle," Valerius Maximus speaks of the nakedness of the *mima*,[3] but in all probability we have to take that word in a very general and a very loose sense.

Not only the theatres were used for the performance of the mimes. Their shows must have frequently been witnessed in the midst of Roman amphitheatres ; Choricius records their presence

---

[1] *Fasti*, v, 291–308. [2] See *supra*, p. 92. [3] See *supra*, p. 92.

in the recently excavated circus or hippodrome at Constantinople.[1]   We can imagine them setting up their platform-stage in the midst of the vast arena and performing there against the background of their movable *siparium*.   More important still, private houses often welcomed them.   We have already met that *privata mima* mentioned in an inscription, and possibly she, like others, belonged to troupes maintained by wealthy nobles.   Some of these 'private' mimes may have been more in the nature of Court fools than of regular entertainers.   Perhaps it was one of these who is referred to in the pious tale of *Xanthippe and Polyxena*.[2]   " And behold ! " says the writer, " the devil came

Fig. 92. THE ARENA AT VERONA
Photo " Grafia "

to the staircase in the likeness of a mime."   Xanthippe, being a wise lady, saw that he was not really of the household, penetrated his disguise, and duly drove him off.   This suggests that the particular mime referred to was a regular member of the establishment, but, in addition to those who were thus associated with one particular family, the public actors themselves were frequently to be found providing entertainments in private houses.   Augustus, so Suetonius informs us, engaged for his dinner-parties " musicians and actors or wandering players from the circus [*triviales ex circo ludios*]," [3] while Johannes Chrysostom was obviously referring to a regular custom when he warned contemporaries that if one admitted mimes to one's house one was welcoming naught but devils.[4]   Ample evidence exists to show the popularity in Roman times of the *moriones*, or house fools.   There was a regular fool-market (*forum morionum*) in Rome,[5] and these men, as Martial describes them, " with pointed head and long ears that moved like those of asses," [6] must have acted now merely as independent after-dinner entertainers like the jesters of the Middle Ages, now

[1] *Cf.* Reich, i, 153.
[2] *Texts and Studies contributory to Biblical Literature* (Cambridge, 1893), II, iii, 73 (*Apocrypha anecdota*, ed. M. R. James).
[3] Suetonius, *Augustus*, lxxiv.   [4] See Reich, i, 151.
[5] See Flögel, *Geschichte der Hofnarren* (Liegnitz, 1789), p. 159.   [6] vi, 39.

along with others in regular little mime plays of a private kind. There was probably little difference between the *moriones* and the *sanniones*.

Fig. 93. THE PRIVATE STAGE IN THE CASA DEGLI AMORINI DORATI AT POMPEII

Most of the private performances must have been given in ordinary rooms, but sometimes special structures seem to have been built for domestic representation. The little theatre in the Casa degli Amorini Dorati at Pompeii (Fig. 93) has a central court surrounded by reliefs of theatrical scenes and masks, while at one end there is a regular stage framed by what we should now call proscenium pillars. Here, no doubt, were witnessed on festive occasions performances by the mimes who were delighting the ruder populace in one of the two playhouses belonging to the city.[1]

This general survey of the acting conditions amid which the mime flourished may be closed with a reiteration of the necessity of remembering the 'variety' conditions of the Roman stage. Augustus had his musicians, his actors, and his circus players at the palace feasts; a list of payments for theatrical entertainments preserved in an Oxyrhynchus papyrus of the second century A.D. records a mime, an Homeric rhapsodist (ὁμηρίστης), a body of musicians, and a dancer (ὀρχηστής), all appearing on one and the same occasion.[2] The mimic drama, as a form of play-house art, embraced nearly all within its scope. It was musical and terpsichorean as well as dramatic; it made free use of jugglers, acrobats, and wonder-makers; this it did precisely because it was the mime, the art-form which took all life as its province.

Fig. 94. HEAD OF A MIMIC ACTOR

From Francisco Ficoroni, *Dissertatio de larvis scenicis* (Roma, 1754), Plate LXXXII.

---

[1] For a description of the private theatre in Domitian's villa at Albano see G. Lugli in *Studi Romani*, ii (1914), 21–52.
[2] *Oxyrhynchus Papyri* (1903), iii, 254–255.

(iii) THE MIMIC PLAYS

It has been suggested above that most forms of mimic drama were often improvisatorial, and we must believe that, even when we come to the work of individual authors, the effect of the particular performances must have depended more on the activities and skill of the actors than upon any spoken dialogue. Nevertheless, the names of many mime authors have been recorded, and several seem to have been regarded with profound respect by contemporaries. This author was usually called the *mimi* (or *mimorum*) *scriptor* or else the *mimographus*. Laberius is mentioned under the former title, Lentulus under the latter. Most of these men, like the actors who interpreted their words, are nothing now but names, and need hardly occupy much of our attention here. Accius was an amateur writer, according to Martial,[1] who also mentions an Attalus. Æsopus is recorded with Philistion by Ammianus Marcellinus. Suetonius cites Luc. Crassitius as an *adiutor mimographorum* (' collaborator of the mimic authors '), while a certain Cneus Matius won fame for his *mimiamboi*. A Nucula " invented mimes," according to Cicero. In Spain, at Tarraco, a *mimographus* called Æmilius Severianus erected a stone dedicated to a pagan god, thus preserving his name for posterity.[2] Of these men we know nothing more. There remain, however, a scant seven concerning whom additional information is extant—Catullus, Helvidius Priscus, Laberius, Lentulus, Marullus, Philistion, and Publilius Syrus. Since much of this information is characteristic not only of the individual authors, but of the mime in general, it must be our business now to consider at least its more important items.

ROMAN MIME-WRITERS

Q. Lutatius Catullus appears to have lived during the reign of Tiberius, Claudius, or Nero. Luckily the names of three of his mimes are known, and the subject-matter of two of these can be, more or less, reconstructed. The first is the *Phasma* (in Greek Φάσμα, *The Ghost*), recorded by Juvenal.[3] The poet is dealing satirically with the glutton Damasippus, who, through his extravagance, has dissipated his estate. Nothing has now remained to him except his voice, and that he has hired out to the mimes. " Your money done," he cries, " you've hired your voice, Damasippus, to the mimes, and there you've acted a noisy part in Catullus' *Phasma*." No real evidence exists for a reconstruction of this play, but we may assume that it was a spirit drama ; a scholiast tells us that Damasippus played, not the chief part, but that of a herald whose raucous tones Juvenal has celebrated with his " noisy " (*clamosum*).[4] The second mime by Catullus may have been called the *Servus fugitivus* (*The Fugitive Slave*). Juvenal calls it the *Fugitivus scurra* (*The Fugitive Jester*), but a scholiast informs us that " this is a mime in which the fugitive slave distracts his master." [5] The third is by far the most important. The main source of our information is, once more, the satirist Juvenal, although he does not this time indicate the author. All he says is : " The nimble Lentulus (a mimic actor) performed the part of Laureolus well, worthy, in my opinion, of a genuine cross." [6] This remark, by itself, would not be of great use to us, but happily others besides Juvenal have recorded this play. Tertullian distinctly states that it was by Catullus,[7]

---

[1] On most of these see Grysar, pp. 314-315.
[2] *C.I.L.*, ii, 4092 ; *cf*. E. Hübner, *Inscriptiones Hispaniæ Latinæ* (Berlin, 1864), p. 4092.   [3] See Grysar, p. 255 ; Reich, i, 148.
[4] It is to be noted that *Phasma* is the title of a comedy by Menander. Some scholars, notably Bethe and Ziegler, have supposed that this of Catullus was a mimic rendering of the (now lost) literary play. There is no authority for this supposition. The word *clamosum*, it may be observed, might be applied to the piece as a whole.
[5] Juvenal, xiii, 110, and scholia (ed. J. E. B. Mayor, Cambridge, 1853, p. 361).   [6] Juvenal, viii, 187-188.
[7] *Adversus Valentinianos*, xiv (J. P. Migne, *op. cit.*, Series Latina, ii, col. 565).

attribute any to this autho
occasion to point out that t

The rest of your licenti
at the farces of the Lentul
tricks of the mimes or at
[*masculum Lunam*], a torment
Herculeses are treated ridicu
Sun-god [*Sol*] mourns over
disdainful shepherd and yo
notorious fellow; an impu
do you not think that their

Now, while Tertullian doe
quite clearly it is this kind
move here obviously in t
remind us of an infinitely m
One of these plays, howe
suggestion regarding the "
burlesque of the ordinary
that Josephus narrates an i
Tertullian title. Briefly it i
but she is icy cold. There
regularly the temple of Isi:
is told that the god Anubis
herself to him in the templ
meets her there. The che
who crucifies the priests an
beloved by the mimes, and

Another mime-writer,
Julius Capitolinus, speaks
and Lentulus as one of tl
sayings, however, all his w
about whose work consid
as recorded by Hieronym
References to his name are
of merry Philistion." [6] H
during the second centur
Ammianus Marcellinus s
Susanna to " a mime by
and Pyrrha—the same the
His fame passes on. In t
seventh by Maximus, in t
by Tzetzes. A few facts,
no information, or at best
hearing that Menander ha
interest, however, arise fr

[1] *Apologeticus*, xv.
[4] *Apologia adversus libros Rufini*, x
[5] Reich, i, 426; Grysar, p. 303.
H

Lentulus (whom many scholars have assumed to be its author) being merely the chief actor. The scholiast has seen fit to give a long note on his master's lines :

> In this mime they pretend to crucify Laureolus. Juvenal intends to say that Lentulus is worthy of a true cross, because his very skill in the performance makes him so much more villainous. This Lentulus was a brilliant actor, and took the part in this mime of a slave who was, in pretence, crucified on the stage.

Josephus [1] knew of the play. It was a mime, he says, in which a robber-leader is captured and crucified; "there was a great deal of artificial blood," he adds, "which flowed down the cross." This last remark is corroborated by Suetonius; he too describes the scene of crucifixion, and declares that then " the stage ran with blood." [2] On some occasions, however, fiction passed into reality. The part of the robber-leader was taken by some criminal already condemned to death, and the crucifixion at the end of the play made the stage run, not with artificial blood, but with the true blood of the tortured wretch. "A Laureolus hanging on no false cross" is Martial's terse and significant summary of the scene. [3]

With these pieces of scattered evidence before us, we can build up a reconstructed theme for this mime. Laureolus (acted most brilliantly by Lentulus) is a slave who runs away from the house of his master and becomes the head of a band of robbers. No doubt there is presented some record of his villainies, and we must presume a scene where he is captured and another where he is finally condemned to death. The last scene of crucifixion is carried out with a considerable amount of stage realism. Such must have been the main subject of this mime, demanding the presence of a considerable number of characters and operating in as free a theatrical convention as the romantic *Die Räuber* of Schiller.

Regarding Helvidius Priscus the Younger we hear only from Suetonius. Domitian, this author states, caused the mimograph to be put to death because he thought he saw an allusion to his own divorce in a mimic after-piece called *Paris and Œnone*. [4] The treatment of the play is not known, but the bare record indicates three features of mimic drama—its use as an after-piece, its satirical tendency, and its subjects taken from mythology and brought down to the conditions of the day.

Much more information has been preserved on the life and works of Decimus Laberius, a Roman knight who became one of the most famous mimographs of his age. [5] Laberius seems to have been born in 106 B.C.—at any rate, on the occasion of his famous artistic combat with Syrus in 46 B.C. he describes himself as sixty years of age. His death occurred in 43 B.C. That which evidently appealed to contemporaries the most was his style and his biting wit. Marcus Fronto praises him beside Plautus, Nævius, and Accius for his skill in the use of words, and thinks that " wit-bolts " or " wit-flashes " (*dictabolaria*) would better express some of his sentences than the more ordinary word, " witty sayings " (*dicteria*). [6] Evidently part of this wit came from the use of strange words or of ordinary words in strange collocations. Gellius was inclined to wonder whether many of these were truly Latin, and considered that he had admitted too much " ignobleness and baseness " into the Roman tongue. [7] One example is cited by Fronto—" Your love grows as quickly as an onion (*porrus*) and as strongly as a palm " [8]—while a specimen of his satiric wit is recorded by Macrobius. [9] It is true that Horace would not recognize his works as " pretty

---

[1] *Antiquitates*, xix, 13 (ed. B. Niese, Berlin, 1880, iv, 213).   [2] *Caligula*, lvii.
[3] *De spectaculis*, vii. *Non falsa pendens in cruce Laureolus.* See also C. Magnin, p. 517.   [4] Suetonius, *Domitianus*, x, 4.
[5] The main facts are summarized in Schanz. See also Grysar, pp. 290–296, Reich, G. Malagoli, *Cavaliere e mimo* (*Atene e Roma*, viii (1905), col. 188–197), and additional notes by C. M. Patrono, *Ancora del " Prologo " di Decimo Laberio* (*id.*, x (1908), cols. 95–96).
[6] Ed. Naber, pp. 61, 155.   [7] Gellius, *Noctes atticæ*, xvi, 7, and xix, 13.
[8] Ed. Naber, p. 30. For these and other fragments see O. Ribbeck, *Comicorum Romanorum fragmenta* (Leipzig, 1898).
[9] *Sat.*, II, vi, 5.

III

poems " (*pulchra*
sides there is prais

Nothing of hi
plays from his pe
Atellana. A few
named play by Pl
seem to have dealt
Such are *Augur* (
Youth), *Fullo* (*The*
Natal (*The Birthd*
as typical. Two
(*The Gauls*)—whi
pretation. *Aries*
caldæ (*Hot Water*
Lake of Avernus),

Unfortunately
sufficient to enab
these fragments,
that he too lovec
dropped again ra
stingy old miser
But of the plot,
indeed, comes fr
occurred when t
follows.[2] Publi
Having risen in
him. At this p
by blandishmen
prologue which

Necessity, v
has captured m
could have infl
return home as
sepulchre, I be

Then, appearing
but uttered such
given to his op

Already we
Lentulus whose
been a differen
Tertullian, alth
of his life and
perhaps there i

[1] *Sat.*, I, x, 5–6.
[2] See Schanz; Gr
Museum, xxxix (1884)
[3] The above is m
[4] One of his lines

112

called variously Σύγκρισις Μενάνδρου καὶ Φιλιστίωνος (*A Comparison of Menander and Philistion*), Γνῶμαι Μενάνδρου καὶ Φιλιστίωνος (*Maxims of Menander and Philistion*), and Μενάνδρου καὶ Φιλιστίωνος διάλεκτος (*A Discussion of Menander and Philistion*). The interest of these lies in the facts that Philistion was evidently considered of sufficient importance to be compared with Menander and that his " maxims " entitled him to serious consideration by men of scholarly mind. Indeed, Marcus Diaconus has spoken of " the sayings of the mime Philistion, of Hesiod, and of other philosophers "; clearly *A Comparison*, the *Maxims*, *A Discussion*, and this reference prove that his work was regarded by antiquity as something more than a mere jest. The philosophy of Philistion, on the other hand, must have been of the true mimic kind; its strength must have lain in its laughter; and it is here that we come to the second matter of supreme interest. In his account of Philistion the chronicler Suidas declared that " he wrote a *Philogelos* (Φιλογέλως[1])." A definitely ascribed *Philogelos* is not extant, but libraries at Paris, Munich, and Vienna preserve manuscripts of a work entitled Φιλογέλως ἐκ τῶν Ἱεροκλέους καὶ Φιλαγρίου γραμματίκων.[2] It is to be observed that this is not described as a *Philogelos* by Hierokles and Philagrios, but as a *Philogelos from the Collections of* [ἐκ] *the Grammarians Hierokles and Philagrios*; and as a consequence, taking into consideration the character of the work, we may believe that here we have the volume mentioned by Suidas. The little collection is full of such scenes as might have appeared in the mime, and the characters introduced are true mimic types. One of the figures who appear most frequently is a *scholasticus*, a scholar or doctor, a person who at once reminds us of the learned doctor of earlier days and of the blundering *dottore* in the *commedia dell' arte*. He is depicted here as a stupid fool when matters of reality are to be considered. In one anecdote or scene he is asked to buy two young slaves, fifteen years old. His reply is that if he cannot get two of fifteen years old he'll buy one of thirty years. On another occasion he engages to tutor his ass to do without eating. The poor ass dies, and the *scholasticus* tells all and sundry that a great sorrow has befallen him—just when the ass had learned its lesson it passed away. Once he took it into his head that he would like to know whether he looked pleasant when sleeping, so he took a mirror, set it up before him, and closed his eyes. Walking down the street, he happened to see his doctor approaching. In order to avoid him, he dodged into a house, telling the astonished inmate that he hadn't been ill so long that he felt embarrassed when he met the doctor. Another day he was taking a stroll. A friend met him. " Funnily enough," said the latter, " I met you last night in a dream." " Did you ? " answered the *scholasticus*. " I've forgotten all about it. I must have been preoccupied with my own thoughts when you spoke to me last night." The regular mimic types appear in these anecdotes—the Bawd, the Slave, the Sailor, even the Bald-headed Fool. A characteristic story tells of the last. A barber accompanies the *scholasticus* and the bald-head on a journey. When they stop at night they agree that each shall wake and keep guard in turn. Lots are drawn; the barber is fated to hold the first watch and the *scholasticus* the second. The barber, however, is a merry man, and during his watch he shaves the head of the sleeping scholar. Then he wakes him. The *scholasticus* stretches himself and rubs his head. Finding himself without hair, he exclaims, " Oh ! that fool of a barber; he has wakened the bald-head instead of me ! " Surely here we have a true scene of a mime, with characters from real life—the Barber and the Scholar—and the ancient Bald-headed Fool, the μωρὸς φαλακρός.

It is highly probable that Philistion wrote only in Greek, but he was famous in Rome, and we shall not be far wrong if we consider his position there as somewhat similar to that occupied in sixteenth-century Paris by Arlecchino and the *comédiens italiens*.

[1] Literally, ' lover of laughter.'
[2] The identification of these with Philistion's work is due to Reich (i, 455). See also the chapter on a Syrian *Philogelos* in Josef Horovitz, *Spuren griechischer Mimen im Orient* (Berlin, 1905), pp. 55–76.

114

THE MIMIC PLAYS

The last mimograph whom we have to consider is the opponent of Laberius, Publilius Syrus. His name, as Macrobius informs us, was derived from his race; by birth he was a Syrian, most probably from Antioch.[1]   Apparently he had been brought thence to Rome as a slave; early he distinguished himself by his wit and grace, was freed and educated.   By 43 B.C. he was the leading mimograph in the Imperial city.   His successful contest with Laberius has already been described. Cicero admired his work, and Petronius could compare him with that great orator.   None of his plays are extant, but two titles of his have been recorded.   One of these seems to have been *Putatores* (*The Tree-cutters*)—a 'profession' name—and the other, which is given in variant forms, was probably *Murmurcones*, or *The Grumblers*.   The chief record of his activities, however, rests in the *Publilii Syri mimi sententiæ*, the *Maxims of Publilius Syrus, the Mime*.   These are to be found in several manuscripts, a few of which attribute the remarks to Seneca.   Their wit, their proverbial wisdom, and their incisiveness appealed to contemporaries.   Syrus was noted for his sharp sayings.   One example will suffice.   A certain Mucius was noted for his malevolent disposition, and one day, when Publilius saw him looking sadder than usual, "It seems," he said, "that either something unfortunate has befallen Mucius or somebody else has had a stroke of luck."   The same quality of biting and incisive wit appears in the *Sententiæ*, and it was this quality which made them appeal to all—to philosophers, to scholars, and to grammarians.   The elder Seneca thought that many of his maxims were better than anything which could be found elsewhere in similar kinds of literature, singling out such phrases as "The miser lacks what he has, quite as much as what he has not," and "O life! long in misery, short in happiness," among many other "most eloquent verses" (*plurimos versus . . . disertissimos*).[2]   Cassius Severus, we are told, was a "hearty admirer of Publilius" (*summus Publilii amator*); indeed, it is with him that Seneca agrees in praising the mimograph.   Many seem to have echoed the sentiments expressed in the following note of admiration :

How many most eloquent verses are to be discovered among the mimes !   How many things said by Publilius are fitted, not for the mimic stage, but for that of tragedy ! [3]

THE OXYRHYNCHUS MIMES

With this praise we may turn from Syrus and the mimographs.   In surveying their work we have found that the theme of one play, the *Laureolus*, can be reconstructed, that the theme of another, the *Lover Anubis*, may at least be conjectured, while the titles indicate the free use of mythological matter and of matter taken from common life.   It must now be our task to examine the records of other anonymous mimes which evidently proved popular.   Happily, the wonderful finds at Oxyrhynchus have provided us with something definite on which to form a conception of the mimic play.   Among the papyrus rolls found there appear two dramatic pieces, clearly of the type patronized by the mimes.[4]   Both have an overwhelming interest.   The first is a fantastic story, with a theme akin to the Greek romances, which reminds us of a Beaumont and Fletcher tragi-comedy.   The characters are marked by symbols, but the text enables us to identify them.

[1] The literature on Syrus is large.   In addition to Reich and Grysar see Eduard Wölfflin, *Der Mimograph Publilius Syrus* (*Philologus*, xxii (1864), 437–468); W. Meyer, *Die Sammlungen der Spruchverse des Publilius Syrus* (Leipzig, 1877); M. Manitius, *Die Dresdener Handschrift des Publilius Syrus* (*Hermes*, xli (1906), 293).   There are many editions of the *Sententiæ*; that consulted here is the recension by M. A. Spengel (Leipzig, 1874).   *Cf.* also A. Nauck, *Bemerkungen zu den Sprüchen Publilius Syrus* (*Mélanges gréco-romains tirés du Bulletin de l'Académie impériale des sciences de St-Pétersbourg*, III, ii (1872), 187–206).   [2] *Controversiæ*, VII, iii, 8.   [3] Seneca, *Epist.*, viii.
[4] These were originally printed in B. P. Grenfell and A. S. Hunt, *The Oxyrhynchus Papyri* (Egypt Exploration Fund, vol. iii, 1903).   See B. Warnecke, *Zum Plautinischen Rudens* (*Philologische Wochenschrift*, xliv (1924), cols. 498–502), for the connexion between these and *Rudens*. Reich's essay of 1904 cited above discusses the new finds; *cf.* also E. Romagnoli, review of Reich and of the text of the Oxyrhynchus mime in *Rivista d'Italia*, vii (1904), 493–499, and R. Stumpfl, *Schauspielmasken des Mittelalters und der Renaissancezeit* (*Schriften der Gesellschaft für Theatergeschichte*, xli (1931)).

The chief part was that of " A," who is named in the dialogue as Charition, evidently a young Greek girl. She is clearly in a position of danger in some barbarian country. It seems probable that the king of this land (indicated in the manuscript as βασ—bas—for βασιλεύς—basileus, 'a king') is in love with her, and that she has dedicated herself to some goddess in order to secure herself from his advances. The position would be not dissimilar to that presented in *Iphigenia in Tauris*.[1] Evidently her brother (marked " Γ ") has prepared a rescue-party, or, at any rate, is engineering her escape. With him are the 'funny man' (marked " B "), the captain of his ship (marked " Δ "), and a person who is his friend (marked " ϛ "). Besides these there are two individualized barbarians (marked " Z " and " ϛ ") and a woman (marked Γυν—gun—for Γυνή—Gune) A frequently occurring speech-heading (Κοι, koi) has been plausibly explained as meaning κοινῇ (koine), 'all together.' Throughout the text, it may be observed, there are abbreviated signs, the commonest of which is a figure like ⊉ which may be interpreted as a sign for music, possibly a contraction of τυμπανισμός, 'drums.' The first thirty-seven lines [2] of this piece are in a purely fragmentary condition, but following this there are several sections which are intelligible, and these, since this is one of the surest records we possess of early mimic activity, may here be roughly paraphrased. It should be observed that the barbarians are made deliberately to speak a strange language of their own (probably imaginative), and that with the Fool (" B ") is associated a word, πορδή (porde), which once at least he uses as the name of a goddess (κυρία Πορδή). In all probability it is employed as a kind of stage direction implying some comic business of a vulgar sort, for it signifies sudden flatulence. To avoid offending susceptibility I have rendered it here simply as " The Fool trembles." This, then, is the fragment of the mime :

> SCENE : *The precincts of a temple.* CHARITION *is standing with the* FOOL. *There is a noise of shouting without, and the* FRIEND *dashes in.*
>
> THE FRIEND. Lady Charition ! Rejoice ! I have escaped !
> CHARITION. Great are the gods !
> THE FOOL. What gods, fool ? The goddess Porde——
> CHARITION. Peace, slave !
> THE FRIEND. Wait here for me ; I'll go and get the ship brought to anchor.
> CHARITION. Go then. For see ! here are their women come from the hunting.
>   [*A crowd of* BARBARIAN WOMEN *suddenly make their appearance.*
> THE FOOL. Ow ! what enormous bows they have !
>   [*The* WOMEN *surround the* FOOL *and aim their arrows at him. He crouches down.*
> A WOMAN. Kraunou !
> ANOTHER WOMAN. Lalle.
> ANOTHER WOMAN. Laitalianta lalle.
> ANOTHER WOMAN. Kotakos anab iosara.
> THE FOOL [*trembling*]. Go-oo-od day !
> ALL. Laspathia !   [*They draw their bowstrings.*
> THE FOOL [*to* CHARITION]. O lady ! help !   [CHARITION *advances, and they move aside.*
> CHARITION [*in a commanding tone*]. Alemaka !
> ALL. Alemaka !
> THE FOOL. By Athena ! what an escape ! [3]
> CHARITION. Idiot ! they were on the point of shooting you as an enemy.
> THE FOOL. Everything goes wrong with me. Won't you come along to the river Psoleichos ?
> CHARITION. As you please.   [*Drums beat without. The* FOOL *trembles violently.*
> ALL. Minei !
>   [*At this moment the* FRIEND *returns ; he walks over to* CHARITION *and whispers to her excitedly.*

---

[1] Of which, perhaps, this is a burlesque.

[2] It will be understood that the reference is here to the lines which have been preserved. No doubt there were many scenes in the original text which are now completely lost. In this adapted version I have been aided by the translation in Grenfell and Hunt (iii, 52–54).

[3] The original is hopelessly corrupt here.

116

THE FRIEND. Lady Charition, I see there's a wind rising; it will enable us to escape over the Indian Ocean. Go in and get your things. If you can, fetch out one of the offerings to the goddess.

CHARITION. Be wiser, my friend. Those who seek for safety themselves ought not to mingle sacrilege with their petitions to the gods. How can the gods listen to men who would secure favour with sin?

THE FOOL. There's no question of *your* getting it. I'll bring it out.

THE FRIEND [*to* CHARITION]. Then get your own things.

CHARITION. I have no need even of them. Only my father's face do I crave to see.

THE FRIEND. Go in, then. [*To the* FOOL] See and give them strong wine: here they come.

Some time elapses between this scene and the next. In the latter the Fool is seen watching the Barbarian Women go off to bathe in the river Psoleichos while the Brother, Charition, and the Friend are making ready to escape. Charition is repeating the Friend's orders that the Barbarians should be plied with strong drink, and the Fool is butting in with his objections.

THE FOOL. But what if they don't want to drink it neat?

THE BROTHER. Fool, in this land wine cannot be bought. Thus, if they once get a hold of it, they'll swallow it neat without realizing what they're doing.

THE FOOL. I'll give it them down to the dregs.

THE BROTHER. Here they come after their bath.

[*Drums announce the entry of the* KING *and his barbarian guards.*[1]

THE KING. Brathis!

ALL. Brathis!

THE FOOL. What are they saying?

THE BROTHER. They're saying we should draw lots for the shares.

THE FOOL. Come on then.[1]   [*Music without.*

THE KING. Stouke pairo mello koroke.

THE FOOL. Away! Accursed wretch!

THE KING. Brathie! [*The music sounds again.*] Bere konzei damun petrekio paktei kortames bere ialero depomenzi petrekio damut kinze paxei zebes lolo bia bradis kottos.

THE GUARDS. Kottos!

THE FOOL. May " kottos " kick you on the shins!

THE KING. Zopit!   [*Drums are heard.*

THE FOOL. What's that they're saying?

THE BROTHER. Give them something to drink. Quick!

THE FOOL [*to the* BROTHER]. Do you, then, fear to speak? [*Turning to the* KING] Hail, thou on whom Fortune smiles!

THE KING. Zeison kormos ede.   [*The drums beat.*

THE FOOL. Ah! not if I know it!

THE BROTHER. It is too weak. Put in more wine.   [*Loud music sounds.*

ONE OF THE BARBARIANS. Skalma kata bapteira goummi.

ANOTHER BARBARIAN. Tougoummi nekelekethro.

THE FIRST BARBARIAN. Eitou belle trachouptera goummi.

THE FOOL. Ah! none of your beastliness. I say! Stop!

[*The drums beat. Rapidly the* KING *and his courtiers become intoxicated by the wine. They talk excitedly together.*

THE FOOL. Oh! what are you doing?

THE SECOND BARBARIAN. Trachounter mana.

THE FIRST BARBARIAN. Boulliti kaloumbai platagoulda.

THE FOOL [*imitating them*]. Apuleu kasar.   [*The drums beat.*

THE KING. Chorbonor bothorba . . . toumio naxizdespit platagoulda bi . . . sesorachis. [*The drums beat.*] Ouamesa resum psaradara ei ia da.

[*There is a confused conversation among the* BARBARIANS, *until the* KING *suddenly starts dancing*

---

[1] A portion of the manuscript is here too mutilated to be read.

THE KING [*singing drunkenly in Greek*]. O Lady Moon, a barb'rous dance and endless do I lead, advancing here with measure wild and rude, barbaric pace. O Indian chiefs, bid the holy drum strike up with Seric ditties. [*There is much drumming and beating of cymbals.*

ALL. [*shouting*]. Orkis!

THE FOOL. What's that they're saying now?

THE BROTHER. Dance, he says.

THE FOOL. And all as if they were real human beings!

[*The drums beat. Gradually the* BARBARIANS *sink intoxicated to the ground. As the* KING *falls the Greeks fall upon him.*

THE BROTHER. Get him down! Tie him up with the priests' girdles!

[*Loud music sounds. The finale.*

THE FOOL. They're all sodden now with drink.

THE BROTHER. Excellent! Charition, come on; this way.

CHARITION. Come on, brother. Quick. Have all preparations been made?

THE BROTHER. Yes, all. The boat is down there at anchor. What are you waiting for? Ho, boatman! bring in the boat, I say.

THE CAPTAIN. He'd better wait till I, as captain, give him his orders.

THE FOOL. Talking again, you booby? We'd better leave him out to kiss his ship's bottom.

[*A boat appears at the side of the stage, and all get hastily on board.*

THE BROTHER. All on board?

ALL. Aboard.

CHARITION. O unhappy me! A mighty trembling seizes on my body. Cast thy light on me, Lady Goddess; save thy handmaid!

Obviously we have here only the end of an exciting drama of adventure; the rest (the capture or shipwreck of Charition and the setting sail of her brother) our imaginations must supply. Enough, however, is given to us to show that we are in the presence of as 'romantic' a type of theatrical art as could well be found. Presumably the unity of place was broken in the original play. The plot is tragi-comic in the extreme, and calls for the presence of at least seven principal characters without counting the Barbarian guards and the women warriors. The company which presented the play clearly included also a number of musicians. In all, how near we are to the Elizabethan stage!

When we consider those mimes the subjects of which can be reconstructed we may hazard the guess that three chief types were popular. This Oxyrhynchus mime, to which we may give the Fletcherian title of *The Sea Voyage*, and the *Laureolus* of Catullus are alike in containing a good deal of what we are accustomed to call romantic incident. They are thus distinguished from the more 'ordinary' mimes of real life such as are presented in the little plays of Herodas and from the dramas which introduce either mythological burlesque or burlesque of religious ceremonies. The second type mentioned here is also represented in the Oxyrhynchus papyrus, and, peculiarly enough, in this particular example we have a variant form of that Herodas mime which has already been discussed.[1] The chief character in the Oxyrhynchus playlet is, as in the mime of Herodas, a woman of the ζηλότυπος nature. At the beginning we must suppose a lost scene in which this woman speaks of an old man, her husband, and tells of the love she bears to a slave in her house, Æsopus by name. Then we come to Scene 1. Here the love-infuriated mistress gives vent to a wild and temperamental outburst. Æsopus has disdained her and rejected her advances. She rages violently. " Fetch me the whips " (φέρε τὰς μάστιγας), she cries as she stands threatening the wretched man. The slave commanded to carry out this punishment evidently refuses, and she turns to another, whom she names Malacus. He too hesitates. From the following words of

---

[1] The best analysis of this mime seems to be that of S. Sudhaus, *Der Mimus von Oxyrhynchos* (*Hermes*, xli (1906), 247–277). It has, of course, been dealt with in all editions and studies of Herodas published after its discovery. I follow here the six-scene division suggested by Sudhaus.

the mistress it seems that Æsopus and a female slave, Apollonia, are in love with one another, a fact which largely explains her jealous outbursts. The scene ends with the errant Æsopus and Apollonia being sentenced to death. The second scene opens after a lapse of time. The two slaves, Malacus and Spinther, commissioned to execute the lovers return to the house and explain that, while they were on their way to carry out their mistress' commands, there suddenly appeared a marvellous, godlike vision, through means of which Æsopus and Apollonia escaped. In the meantime a noise sounds within the house. The woman hears it, and at length Apollonia is discovered; at once she is ordered to be handed over to the guards that she may be manacled, and strict commands are given that Æsopus must be tracked down and slain. Thus ends the second scene; in the third a new intrigue begins. The two slaves bring on to the stage a bier on which lies the body of Æsopus, apparently lifeless. At first the mistress is taken in, but, glancing at the two slaves, she is struck by the looks on their faces. " Spinther," she asks, " why are your eyes so bright ? " (πόθεν σου ὁ ὀφθαλμὸς ἡμέρωται;). From this moment the action becomes somewhat complicated, but apparently the idea enters into the mind of the mistress that she will poison her husband. A parasite is called in, and, seemingly through his device, a sleeping draught is substituted for the poison which the criminal wished to mix with the wine—just such a sleeping draught as was given to the wonderful dog whose skill in playing has been recorded by Plutarch.[1] All, of course, ends well, and no doubt Æsopus and Apollonia are sent off to live happily ever after.[2]

Typical characters are here once more apparent—the jealous woman, the slaves, the old man, and the parasite—there is, indeed, no essential difference between these figures and those which had already been animated, centuries before, by such writers as Herodas. It seems that we are in the presence here of a relic of theatrical art which belongs to the tradition that carries us back to Hellenistic realms and to classical Greece.

ADULTERY MIMES

Unhappily, these are the solitary fragments of mimic workmanship which the Oxyrhynchus finds have revealed, and even these, of course, are not strictly Roman. As we have seen, however, the playing of Greek mimes was common in the Empire, and there was, in all probability, little difference between these two pieces which have been under our consideration and the work of native Latin mimographs. The Oxyrhynchus manuscripts, in any case, date from the second century A.D., and chronologically belong to this period in the development of the mimic stage. That the themes were not unique is proved immediately when we compare the second drama (that of the jealous woman) with the example of an adultery mime mentioned by Juvenal.[3] Juvenal's description, it is true, is somewhat condensed, but we can make out from his lines that in this unnamed adultery mime there was a stupid old jealous husband, apparently performed by the actor Corinthus, and also his young wife, a part taken by the actress Thymele—*zelotypus Thymeles*, *stupidi collega Corinthi* ('the jealous husband of Thymele and colleague of the fool Corinthus'). Thymele is in love with a youth, a part taken by the famous actor Latinus, and apparently, during a scene of passion, the entry of a third person, probably a parasite, disturbs the lovers. Latinus is hurried into a chest, but, this unwanted visitor staying too long, he is in danger of smothering,

---

[1] See *infra*, p. 120.

[2] Nearly all this story is told through the words of the mistress herself. One may well wonder whether perhaps the papyrus which has come down to us is not incomplete, preserving only a main *rôle* in what may have been a much more fully developed mimic drama. On the other hand, many mimic actors (such as Vitalis) may have recited dramatic compositions almost unaided, with suitable alterations in the inflexion of their voices.

[3] *Sat.*, viii, 196–197.

burlesqued. The priest cries, " May he be baptized in the name of the Father, the Son, and the Holy Ghost ! " and all go through extraordinary antics in an appeal to the audience. Then comes a further scene in which the baptized Christian is accused before a magistrate. It is here that the martyrdom commences, for these mimes appear in the *Acta sanctorum* because of the fact that they felt themselves seized by some divine power and, throwing off their pretended characters, spoke loudly to the assembled populace, crying : " I truly am a Christian." They were those who, in Theodoret's words,[1]

> came upon the stage and suddenly entered into the ranks of the martyrs, gaining the victory and seizing the crown ; who by the attestation of their faith cast terror into the breasts of the devils whose slaves they had formerly been.

It is obvious that in these plays we have to do with dramas of a mimic kind which, like the dog mime described by Plutarch, " demanded the presence of many actors." The fool is there as the hero ; there is his friend, and there are the neighbours ; while, apart from the Roman soldiers and the magistrates required in the last scene, there are, in the words of the original account of the martyrdom of Porphyrius, " the bishops, the priests, the deacons, and the rest of that gang presented by the actors." [2] This anti-Christian mime is in no wise different from the earlier burlesques of pagan belief and of pagan ceremonial, examples of which have already been cited in the section devoted to the mimographs. That mythological material was excessively popular is proved, not only by the titles of plays there recorded, but by many other references to similar productions. Suetonius, writing of the times of the Emperor Domitian, mentions a *Paris and Œnone* by Helvidius Priscus.[3] Arnobius noted the furore for these pieces :

> The persons of the most holy gods are brought upon the stage by ludicrous mimes and jesters. In order to arouse the laughter and ridicule of the empty-headed spectators, these gods are treated in a spirit of burlesque buffoonery. The people stand up and cheer ; all the *caveæ* resound with clapping and applause.[4]

The burlesque of the pagan gods extended well into the period of Christianity. " They put on the stage," complains St Cyprian,

> the wanton Venus, the adulterer Mars, and Jove, that old wretch, prince of the realm of love not less on account of his own vices than on account of his position. They show him majestic with his thunderbolts, or made white with the feathers of a swan or descending in a golden shower.[5]

Venus and Adonis, Mars and Venus, Leda and the Swan,[6] *The Tower of Danaë*—these must have been familiar titles in St Cyprian's time. Tertullian has the same testimony.[7] Already, as we have seen, he mentions a *Lover Anubis,* a *Man-moon,* a *Diana.* Elsewhere he tells us of a Saturn play, an Isis play, and a play of Liber, the god of wine.[8] The second of this trio is cited also by Prudentius, who refers to an *Isis and Osiris*—" the mimic and jesting solemnities with their bald-headed fools." [9] A *Kinyras and Myrrha* occurs in Josephus,[10] while Augustine waxes wrath concerning the pagan follies of the stage. " In the theatres," he cries,

> the spectators may behold some counterfeit god Jove, committing adultery and hurling his thunderbolts at one and the same time ; there they show you this same Jove having Juno as his sister and his wife.[11]

---

[1] Ἑλληνικῶν θεραπευτικὴ παθημάτων, viii (J. P. Migne, *op. cit.*, Series Græca, lxxxiii, col. 1032–1033) : Ἀκούω δὲ ἔγωγέ τινας καὶ τῇ σκηνῇ ξυντραφέντας καὶ ἐξαπίνης τοῖς ἀγωνισταῖς ξυνταχθέντας, καὶ ἀξιονίκους γεγενημένους, καὶ τῶν στεφάνων τετυχηκότας, καὶ μετὰ τὴν ἀνάρρησιν σφόδρα δεδιττομένους τοὺς δαίμονας, οἷς ἦσαν ὑποχείριοι πάλαι.

[2] καὶ δὴ καταστήσαντες ἐπισκόπους καὶ πρεσβυτέρους, διακόνους καὶ τὰ λοιπὰ τάγματα οἱ θυμελικοί.

[3] *Domitianus,* x.   [4] *Adversus gentes,* iv, 36 (in J. P. Migne, *op. cit.*, Series Latina, v, col. 1074).

[5] *Epist.*, i, *ad Donatum,* viii (in J. P. Migne, *op. cit.*, Series Latina, iv, col. 211).

[6] This is the *cycnus stuprator* which *peccat inter pulpita* mentioned by Prudentius. See Grysar, p. 253.

[7] See *supra*, p. 113.   [8] Tertullian, *De spectaculis,* xxiii.

[9] *Contra Symmachium,* i, ll. 630–631 (in J. P. Migne, *op. cit.*, Series Latina, lx, col. 172).

[10] Josephus, *Antiquitates,* xix, 94 (*ed. cit.* iv, 226).

[11] *Ad catechumenos, de symbolo,* ii, 4 (J. P. Migne, *op. cit.*, Series Latina, xl, col. 639).

THE MIMIC PLAYS

In another section he reverts to the subject and cites a *Saturnus senex* (*Old Saturn*) and an *Apollo ephebus* (*Young Apollo*) as familiar themes. Note may be taken, too, of the reference in Choricius to the στρατηγὸν τῶν Τρώων, 'the leader of the Trojans,' who was Hector, and the στρατηγὸν τῶν Μυρμιδόνων, 'the leader of the Myrmidons,' who was Achilles, as mimic types in the sixth century A.D.[1] We may rest assured that practically everything in ancient mythology which might provide material for a jest was fully treated by the exponents of the mimic stage.

MIMIC OBSCENITY

One of the main objections which the Christian apologists had toward the mimic theatre was that there themes of adultery—as instanced in the stories of Venus, Mars, and Jove—were unduly popular. Two 'real-life' adultery mimes have already been described, and these, taken with the examples of the mythological type, undoubtedly prove that a good deal of attention was paid to this subject by the actors. Nor, once more, do we need to base our judgments only on chance-preserved titles. Contemporary literature is full of statements and complaints in this regard, and, still further, there are suggestions that the scenes of adultery were not always carried out on the stage as mere fiction. This accusation is certainly made by Lactantius[2] and by Minucius Felix.[3] Donatus, commenting on Vergil's *Æneid*,[4] says that " the mimes give pleasure only by dishonest themes of adultery " (*mimi solis inhonestis et adulteris placent*). " The subjects of the mimes," declares Valerius Maximus,[5] " are for the most part scenes of debauchery," and on account of this the citizens of Massilia at one period banned the mimes from the stage. Ælius Lampridius in his life of the Emperor Heliogabalus takes up the tale of Lactantius.[6] That monarch, he affirms, ordered that " in mimic adultery plays those things which should be done in fiction were to be carried out in reality." Chrysostom has much to say on this subject and refers us to some mimes in which mothers-in-law seem to have figured.[7] This reference is borne out by an extant fragment of the *Belonistria* of Laberius, in which evidently a mother-in-law fell in love with her own son-in-law.

The whole attack on mimic adulteries is bound up with the larger attack on mimic obscenity in general. An old gloss defines *exodiarius*, 'player of after-pieces,' as *turpitudo delectabilis*, 'delightful obscenity.'[8] The "mimic licence" (*mimica licentia*) is mentioned by Martial;[9] the "mimic's obscenity" (*planipedis impudica*) by Macrobius;[10] and the "obscenity put on the stage by the mimes" (*mimos obscœna iocantes*) by Ovid.[11] St Cyprian rages at the "scurrilous jests, the base parasites, the very toga-clad family men themselves, sometimes foolish, sometimes obscene, stupid in all things, shameless in all things."[12] "Fly from the shameless actresses," Chrysostom[13] cries to his contemporaries, "who utter vicious sentiments on the stage, who act more vicious scenes."

The testimony is manifold, and must as a consequence be taken fully into account. On the other hand, this matter requires to be very carefully considered, for we must not accept uncritically all that contemporary Jeremy Colliers had to say. We must not condemn the mimes unheard. At the very start we may admit once more that the actual records of mimic plays which have been preserved show that adultery themes were among the most popular, but this in itself is nothing. More serious is the accusation regarding the transformance of mimic into real obscenities. Here we must pause. That indelicate scenes (to use no stronger a term) were witnessed in many a Roman emperor's Court goes without saying, and that mimes had their share in these indelicacies seems

---

[1] *Cf.* Reich, i, 240.
[2] *Divinæ institutiones*, Epitome vi, 20.
[3] *Octavius*, xxxvii.
[4] v, 65 (ed. H. Georgii, Leipzig, 1905, i, 433).
[5] *Factorum dictorumque memorabilium libri novem*, II, vi, 7 (ed. J. Kapp, London, i, 274).
[6] xxv, 4.
[7] *Cf.* Reich, i, 120.
[8] See Angelo Mai, *Classicorum auctorum e Vaticanis codicibus editorum tom. VI* (Rome, 1834), vi, 561.
[9] *Sat.*, iii, 86.
[10] *Sat.*, II, i, 9.
[11] *Tristia*, ii, 497.
[12] *De spectaculis*, vi.
[13] *Hom. I in Iob.*, vi (J. P. Migne, *op. cit.*, Series Græca, lix, col. 28); cf. *Hom. VI in Matthæum*, vi (*id.*, lvii, col. 71–72).

highly probable ; but that such scenes as are described were habitually indulged in by mimic actors on the public stage appears utterly improbable. We may treat this as we treated the question of mimic nakedness. In discussing these adultery themes too we must bear in mind that the mime was in essence an imitation of life. Adultery occurs in life, and accordingly it takes its place within the mimic repertory. Some contemporaries were wise enough to realize this fact. " Truly now," says Seneca,[1]

> I think the mimes fail in reproaching the rankness of this age. Verily they omit much more than they put on the stage. Such a heap of incredible vices is to be found in this age of ours that the mimes may even be accused of negligence.

This, truly, is a wise man speaking. Without putting forward that ridiculous plea of moral aim which was bandied about so far as comedy was concerned during the period of the Renascence and of the Restoration, we must recognize that in laughter there is a definite social force. The satirical laughter of the mimes fell on everything ridiculous—on the old pagan gods, on church ceremonial, on theological controversy, on the dull stupidity of a browbeaten husband. The mimic obscenity was only the satirical presentation of the obscenity of life. Another wise man who saw this clearly was Choricius. The mime, he realized, is an imitation of life, and virtually he asks us whether we could in reason deny the mimes the right to draw from life such characters as they cared—"the monarch, the household slaves, the innkeepers, the sausage-dealers, the cooks, the hosts and their guests, the notaries, the babbling children, the young lover, the angry rival, and the man who endeavours to soothe his anger." [2]

Still another thing may be said. Not all the mimes, as our survey has revealed, were of an indelicate nature. " Many of the mimes," says Choricius, " which are put upon the stage do not lack dignity from beginning to end," and this judgment is borne out by our examination of extant records. At the same time different eyes see differently. Nathaniel Hawthorne could not endure Rome because of the many statues of nude men he saw there, and the Fathers of the Church rarely remembered that to the pure all things are pure. Their asceticism had made them hard, and a kind of perverted anti-sexuality dominated their minds. The result was that they would probably have found many things to grumble at even in the innocuous *Sea Voyage* of the Oxyrhynchus papyrus. That romantic stories of this kind (usually with a main love theme) were popular we have every reason to believe. M. C. Fronto mentions a " theme celebrated among the players, where a young girl stands in a tower at night with a lighted torch, waiting for her youthful lover who swims to her over the sea." [3] This story—most probably that of Hero and Leander—was " celebrated " in Fronto's day (c. A.D. 145–147), and similar tales must have been freely exploited on to the sixth century, grave theologians finding as much to attack in them as Puritan pamphleteers found in Elizabethan drama.

Mimic Satire

In dealing with this accusation of obscenity one other kindred aspect of the mime has been alluded to—its frequent satirical tendency. " This must be held," declares Euanthius, " that the mimes are called mimes from their continual imitation of base affairs and of light characters." [4] These mimic actors set out with no moral purpose, but they were decidedly eager to take advantage of anything in life which, because of its baseness, its meanness, or its triviality, provided that laughter-provoking contrast between man's mind and the fettering restrictions of his body, and, moreover, they were ever ready to stand forward, like the mimes of old, as the secular exponents of popular feeling. Emperors might flatter and feed them, but they never lost sight of the follies

---

[1] *Dialogorum libri XII*, xii, 8, " De brevitate vitæ " (ed. E. Hermes, Leipzig, 1905, I, i, 297).
[2] See Reich, i, 214.   [3] Ed. Naber, p. 50. *Cf.* C. Magnin, p. 440.   [4] Quoted in Grysar, p. 250.

to be found in a royal Court. Royally welcomed, they retained to the end their sense of humour. Anything out of the common appealed to them. When Trebatius prolonged his stay in the provinces for overlong Cicero wrote to advise his return, declaring that, should he not soon come back to Rome, he feared that Laberius or another might bring him on the mimic stage as " the British lawyer." [1] Occasionally actions for libel were taken, but, although a mime who had brought the poet Accius on the stage was condemned,[2] another, who had similarly treated the poet Lucilius, escaped punishment. Most men accepted freely the gibes of the mimes ; the Emperor Verus thus took delight in the actors, although many things were said by them against him.[3]

The records of satirical reference by Marullus and Laberius have already been quoted, and these may be taken as representative of many others. The mimes flinched not before Imperial powers, for nothing to them was sacred. An account of a theatre scene in the reign of Maximinus the Elder (A.D. 235–238), as narrated by Julius Capitolinus, is thoroughly typical, and may be given in the words of the historian : [4]

> In the end, because of his strength in body and mind, he [*i.e.*, the Emperor Maximinus] came to regard himself as immortal. A certain mime is reported to have uttered these Greek verses in the theatre when he was present :
>
>> He who cannot be killed by one is slain by many.
>> The elephant is huge, but he can be killed ;
>> The lion is strong, but he can be killed ;
>> The tiger is strong, but he can be killed.
>> Beware of many if you fear not individuals.
>
> But when the Emperor asked his friends what the mimic fool had said they replied that he had sung only some ancient verses against harsh men ; and the Emperor, being a Thracian and a barbarian, believed them.

The scene is so simply and vividly described that we can almost imagine ourselves present at the Marcellus Theatre on that day two thousand years ago. Everything of contemporary interest came on the stage. When the scandalous affair of Marcus Aurelius' wife came to men's ears the mimes promptly seized on it.[5] Once, when the Emperor was seated in the auditorium, a *stupidus* (mimic fool) asked a servant to tell him the name of an adulterer. The slave thrice repeated the word " Tullus " (*ter diceret Tullus*). When the *stupidus* questioned him further he replied, " I've just told you thrice, Tullus " (*Iam tibi dixi ter, Tullus*), thus punning on the *ter, Tullus* which means ' thrice, Tullus,' and the proper name of the contemporary culprit, Tertullus. The pun seems to have been loved for these innuendoes ; at least, a similar scene is recorded by Suetonius in his life of Augustus.[6] In allusion to some contemporary matters a mime uttered the words, *Videsne, ut cinædus orbem digito temperat*, which, according to the senses of *orbem* (' drum' or ' world ') and of *temperat* (' beats ' or ' sways '), may mean, ' Don't you see how a dancer beats a drum with his finger ? ' or ' Don't you see how a dancer rules the world with his finger ? ' Sometimes, of course, as in earlier days, punishment was freely meted out to the more daring spirits. When some mimes alluded to Commodus' vices [7] " he banished them so promptly that they did not appear again upon the stage." Sometimes, too, the allusions were complimentary, as in a scene recounted by Suetonius.[8] On one occasion Augustus was witnessing some theatrical performances

> when a mime uttered the words, " O lord, just and good ! " Whereupon all the spectators, as if the words applied to him [*i.e.*, the Emperor], cheered and applauded until he, with hand and countenance, stilled their clamour. On the day following he censured the demonstration in a severe edict.

[1] *Epist. ad fam.*, vii, 11.
[2] *Cf.* Grysar, p. 240.
[3] Capitolinus, *Verus*, vii, 4.
[4] *Maximini duo*, ix, 3–5.
[5] Julius Capitolinus, *Marcus Antoninus*, xxix, 2.
[6] *Augustus*, lxviii.
[7] Ælius Lampridius, *Commodus*, iii, 4.
[8] *Augustus*, liii.

Nor was this tendency and function of the mimes killed in later days. In sixth-century Byzantine realms, as Choricius informs us, " the mimes were in the position to ridicule injustice with impunity." [1] They had thus retained as a precious heritage from ancient times the satiric right to chide and criticize. By all they were regarded as the censurers of folly in action and in idea, so that when Minucius Felix combated the conceptions of Pythagoras he could declare that these were worthy, " not of the study of a serious philosopher, but of the ridicule of the mimes." [2]

THE MIMIC STYLE

This, however, was only one of its moods or styles. The freedom of the mimic drama is something which cannot be over-emphasized. Basing their art upon an " imitation of life," the mimes retained perfect liberty to interpret life according to its widest significance. The mythological element testifies to this, and we must endeavour, in the forming of our mental picture, to take into due account the fantastic element which met with the realistic. The mimes were sometimes called *paradoxi* (literally, ' strange beings '), and the mimic art was an art of hallucination (*mimus hallucinatur*, according to Apuleius).[3] They could introduce the most startling contrasts, presenting a character as one moment poor, another rich (Cicero's *persona de mimo modo egens, repente dives*).[4] It was no doubt in mimic dramas of this sort that there appeared those conversations between Euripides and Menander or between Socrates and Epicurus to which Cicero, on the authority of St Jerome (Hieronymus),[5] made reference. These men, he says, " we know were separated, not only by years, but by centuries. Yet what applause and cheering the scenes arouse in the theatre ! " Disgusted as academicians might be, the fact remains that in this very freedom lay the strength and freshness of the mimes. As Quintilian saw when he was writing to budding orators and telling them how on occasion even incredible things may be made real, the mimes above all had the power of making the impossible into the credible.[6]

Much of this power seems to have come from the polish of style, the native wit, and the scintillating dialogue in which the mimes revelled. They sought not for pure beauty, although verse forms might frequently intrude into their scenes ; [7] their goal was the refinement of ordinary witty prose and simple measures. Grammarians found that these plays could serve as models of style alongside of the *fabulæ togatæ* and the *comediæ veteres* (the Terentian comedies and the old comedies), while Seneca, as we have seen, waxed enthusiastic over the polish of phrase to be found in the work of Publilius. Some few accounts remain of the most typical methods of these mimic entertainers, and from those few a general conception may be formed of the whole. Puns—exemplified in the Tertullus episode—were popular in Rome as they were in the days of Epicharmus and Rhinthon. M. C. Fronto [8] cites, in his own words, a passage from a play of Laberius in which that mimograph speaks of " the charms of love being the harms of love, and its foison of gifts being poison," thus playing on the words *delenimenta* [9] and *deliramenta*, *beneficia* and *veneficia*. Viewing this propensity for puns, we may say that the general aim of the mimes was to employ words in such a manner as to produce an impression of the strange and the unexpected. The mimic jest, or ἦθος, must largely have depended upon this and upon the kindred use of uncouth or slang

---

[1] See Reich, i, 191.   [2] *Octavius*, xxxiv.   [3] *Cf.* Reich, i, 593–595.

[4] *In M. Antonium oratio Philippica*, II, xxvii, 65. Compare the reference to *omnes fallaciæ* cited above, p. 81.

[5] *Epistolæ*, lii, 8 (in J. P. Migne, *op. cit.*, Series Latina, xxii, 534). *Cf.* Isidore Hilberg, *Ein verkanntes Bruchstück von Ciceros Rede pro Q. Gallio* (*Wiener Studien*, xxvii (1905), 93–94), and E. Hauler, *Die in Ciceros Galliana erwähnten convivia poetarum ac philosophorum und ihr Verfasser* (*id.*, 95–105). The suggestion is made that Syrus may be referred to.

[6] *Institutio oratoria*, iv, 53.

[7] Dio Chrysostom refers to the use both of ἐμμέτρους and ἀμέτρους in the mimes of his day. See Reich, i, 569–570.

[8] Ed. Naber, p. 17.

[9] This seems to be the word intended, although the manuscript reads *deliberamenta*. Fronto's remark is to be dated A.D. 144 or 145.

terms. Cicero warned his oratorical readers to avoid the " scurrilous or mimic joke " (*scurrilis iocus . . . aut mimicus*),[1] partly, no doubt, because of the way in which words were there utilized, partly, perhaps, because many mimic jests were risky jests. The *risus mimicus* (' the mimic laughter ') was a recognized style. Quintilian [2] thought little of it, deeming it " a light thing, aroused generally by buffoons, mimes, and brainless characters." Some would make this *risus mimicus* a distinction between the impression of comedy and that of the mime ; at a mime you laugh, at a comedy you feel smiling pleasure ; the mimic drama is in no wise artistic, it only rouses a crowd by its laughter. But the arousing of laughter in itself is no mean thing, and when " all the theatre resounded with the mimic merriment," as Petronius [3] declares, some considerable art must have been required to evoke the mood and appeal to the audience. As Seneca's remark proves, the mimes did not rely entirely upon scurrility and obscene allusions.

For an understanding of those strange words in which the mimes delighted, and through which much of the *risus mimicus* was aroused, we can do no better than turn to the pages of Gellius' *Noctes atticæ*, where, in proof of his contention that Laberius was overfree in the use and coining of words, he provides a long list of concrete examples such as *mendicimonium* (' beggarship '), *mœchimonium* (' co-respondentism '), or *adulterionem adulteritatemque* (' adulterment ').[4] Through such words came largely the *mimicæ ineptiæ* (' mimic absurdities ') which have been singled out by many classical authors as one of the chief qualities of this dramatic form. These *mimicæ ineptiæ*, however, were also associated closely with the fool's wit so freely mixed with subject-matter of other kinds. " He gave expression to a foolish thought [*fatuam sententiam*] of a mimic kind," says Seneca,[5] thus, as it were, defining the *ineptiæ*, which Cicero, because they were light and belonging to the mimes (*levius et . . . mimicum*), thought for the most part unfitting for an orator to employ.[6] Yet, he added, even in the sphere of oratory they might have some utility, when the speaker could give, as it were, a witty impression of stupidity. These *subabsurda* (' foolish remarks '), he declares, " are suitable not only for the mimes, but also to a certain extent for us rhetoricians." [7]

Not much is known of the actual structure of the mimic dramas themselves ; probably that structure was as free as the life they imitated. One or two things, however, have been recorded in this connexion. Isidorus declares that " the mimes had an actor [or author] who announced the subject before they started to play." [8] This may, perhaps, indicate an announcement in the style of the modern circus-booth, but more probably it refers to a genuine prologue. If this be so, then the prologue which Laberius recited before Julius Cæsar was nothing but a personal application of a form which not only was well known already, but was an essential portion of a mimic performance. Above it has been mentioned that both prose and verse could appear in the typically Roman mime. This statement may here require some minor qualification. We shall gain a truer conception of the mime if we imagine it to be of the style of an eighteenth-century ballad opera, with ordinary prose or verse dialogue breaking at times into aria. Quite apart from literary experiments in the form known as *mimiamboi*,[9] the ordinary mime made free use of song. In Greek verses sung to music the actors ridiculed or alluded equivocally to contemporary affairs, and the *canticum* (' song ') was a recognized part of the mimic drama.[10] Gellius mentions the singer with his verse measures alongside the dancing *planipes*,[11] and Chrysostom describes the action of a mime who sang an ᾠδὴ πορνική (' indecent song ').[12] One other quality of this mimic drama is suggested to us in

---

[1] *De oratore*, II, lix, 239   [2] *Institutio oratoria*, vi, 3.   [3] *Satyricon*, xix.
[4] xvi, 7.   [5] *Controversiæ*, VII, v, 15.   [6] *De oratore*, II, lxviii, 274.
[7] *Id.*, II, lxvii.   [8] *Etymologiarum sive originum*, xviii, 49.
[9] On this word there is a good discussion by A. Hümer, *Gibt es einen Vers μιμίαμβος?* (*Wiener Studien*, xxvi (1904), 33–42). See also the various editions of Herodas.
[10] See Grysar, p. 258.   [11] *Noctes atticæ*, i, 11.
[12] *Contra ludos*, ii (J. P. Migne, *op. cit.*, Series Græca, vi, col. 267).

a phrase of Cicero's. Discussing the story put forward by Clodia, he endeavours to show not merely that this is a tissue of fiction, but that it has no real conclusion. " Its conclusion," he cries,

is not like that of an ordinary play; it is like the conclusion of a mime [*mimi ergo est iam exitus, non fabulæ*], in which, when no end can be found, the actor escapes from the hands of those who are holding him; the signal is given for the end of the piece, and the curtain rises for the next play.[1]

In all probability the mimes had no such exact structural forms as appeared in comedy or in tragedy. No rules fettered the mimographs, and the actors were free to express themselves as they cared. The only thing which dominated the mimes was the desire to please; for one hour, for two hours, they jested merrily and uttered their lines of proverbial wisdom, and then, just as life shuts itself off from the eyes of the individual spectator, so they, having played their appointed space, with a final jest rang up the curtain on the new piece—the comedy or the tragedy—which was to follow their representation.

The whole production seems to have been called an hypothesis (ὑπόθεσις), which practically translates that Latin word *argumentum* (literally, ' argument ') which Quintilian treats as a synonym for *fabula*, or play.[2] There is, however, some difficulty in interpreting aright the classical use of this ὑπόθεσις along with that of another word παίγνιον (*paignion*). The former, some have thought,

Fig. 95. A Roman Comic Actor

From Francisco Ficoroni, *Dissertatio de larvis scenicis et figuris comicis antiquorum romanorum* (Roma, 1754), Plate LXXXIII.

indicates the fully developed Roman mime, while the παίγνιον represents the Greek mimic drama of Dorian days.[3] The *locus classicus* for these two terms appears in Plutarch, where he separates the one from the other by the fact that the ὑπόθεσις is of considerable length and introduces many characters, while the παίγνιον is " full of absurdities and babbling " (πολλῆς γέμοντα βωμολοχίας καὶ σπερμολογίας).[4] No doubt the sense of παίγνιον changed with the passing of the years, for Choricius styles those mimic dramas of the sixth century, for which he has such an admiration, naught but παίγνια;[5] but in the time of Plutarch it seems probable that it had an invidious significance. This reminds us once more of the fact that there were mimes and mimes, as well as mimic actors and mimic actors. Some, like those which have been fully described for us, were of the ὑπόθεσις class, fairly lengthy dramas worthy of being put alongside Terentian comedy and interpreted by performers who gained wealth and fame and were social forces in their own times. Not all the mimic productions, however, were of this sort; the lesser existed by the side of the greater; and street mimes no doubt presented their vulgar παίγνια in the same years as the major actors charmed audiences with their more elaborate representations. This distinction between the two forms is an important one, and was not, of course, peculiar to classic times. In the age of the Renascence none were severer critics of rude ' popular ' companies than members of important *commedia dell' arte* troupes who cherished the dignity and the art of their profession. In the seventeenth century as in the first century unthinking, careless, and indelicate

performers were often confused with the others by general opponents of the theatre, causing thus bitter sentiments in the breasts of those to whom the true theatre and the genuine mimic art were dear.

[1] *Pro Cælio*, lxv.
[4] *Symposiacon*, vii, 8.
[2] See Grysar, p. 256.
[5] Reich, i, 418.
[3] See Reich, i, 420–421, commenting on Grysar, p. 240.

128

(iv) THE DECAY OF THE MIMIC DRAMA

Concerning the popularity of the mime and the distinguished patronage bestowed on members of the profession plentiful evidence has been afforded us. Throughout the records of Imperial Rome there are scattered references to these players, indicating how, in ways wise and in ways foolish, the various potentates welcomed and encouraged the activities of the players. Sometimes, of course, these records display merely the extra-professional charms exerted by the *mimæ*. Thus L. Messala, Consul and Governor of Achaia, is reported to have given " his patrimony to the actors, . . . presenting his own mother's robe to a mimic actress and his own father's cloak to a mimic actor."[1] Diogenes the Epicurean had been similarly attracted by a *mima*, and when Alexander presented him with a purple gown and a golden diadem he gave them both to her.[2] The house of the triumvir Mark Antony was " full of mimes and entertainers " (οἰκίαν μεστὴν μίμων καὶ θαυματοποιῶν), and he often, according to Cicero, spent his time with the actresses.[3] Verres was similarly attracted by the charms of Tertia, daughter of the mime Isidorus,[4] and Marsæus was infatuated by a certain Origo.[5]

Earlier and later records, however, both show that the attractions were not only of this kind. The mimes were esteemed for their skill as well as for their beauty, and there is a long tradition in the patronizing of their art. Julius Cæsar caused some splendid spectacles of diverse kinds to be produced in the theatres,[6] in spite of the fact that he must have been aware that his soldiers returning from their triumphs in Gaul were singing songs which likened the hero to the bald-headed gallant in the mimic dramas—" Citizens, take care of your wives, for we're bringing back with us the bald-headed gallant."[7] It was in his time, as we have seen, that the Roman knight Decimus Laberius came upon the stage. Octavianus, Augustus Cæsar, caused actors to perform in diverse centres and on many stages, bringing forward Greek plays as well as Latin.[8] His successor, Tiberius, it is true, showed no such love of the theatres ; he produced no spectacles and cut off the largess given to the actors ;[9] but Caligula assiduously brought forward scenic displays of every imaginable kind,[10] and his example was followed by Nero. " He brought out," says Suetonius,[11]

many diverse spectacles, *iuvenales*, circus-shows, and stage plays. . . . At the plays which he gave on behalf of the eternity of the Empire—called by his order *Ludi maximi*—the parts were taken by men and women of both the orders.

The presence of women indicates mimic dramas. Domitian, in spite of the fact that at times he gave " stage plays " (*scænicos ludos*) in public, saw fit to issue a decree limiting the activities of actors to private houses (a decree which shows the importance of the domestic stage),[12] while Marcus Aurelius " limited the largess to be given to the players."[13] This limitation, however, was only temporary. When we come to the second century we find in Commodus (*d.* A.D. 193) an emperor who was a complete enthusiast for all things theatrical. " He was expert," says the historian Ælius Lampridius,[14] " in those arts which do not befit a monarch ; . . . he danced, he sang, he whistled, and showed himself a perfect buffoon [*scurra*] and gladiator." " Jesters and actors of the most shameful kind," declares Herodian,[15] had him in their power, while another historian records that he divided much of his property among the mimes and the dancers, winning thereby

---

[1] *Cf.* Reich, i, 160.
[2] Athenæus, 211*a–d*.
[3] *In M. Antoninum oratio Philippica*, XIII, xi, 24 ; Plutarch, *Antonius*, xxi.
[4] See Reich, i, 164.
[5] Horace, *Sat.*, I, ii, 55–59.
[6] Suetonius, *Divus Julius*, x and xxxix.
[7] *Id.*, li.
[8] Suetonius, *Divus Augustus*, xliii and xlv.
[9] Suetonius, *Tiberius*, xxxiv and xlvii.
[10] Suetonius, *Caligula*, xviii.
[11] *Nero*, xi.
[12] Suetonius, *Domitianus*, vii.
[13] Julius Capitolinus, *Marcus Antoninus*, xi, 4.
[14] i, 8.
[15] *Historiarum libri octo* (ed. I. Bekker, Berlin, 1826), I, xiii, 8.

fame among the scene-adoring citizens of Antiochia.[1] Money was also freely given to actors by the Emperor Heliogabalus (d. 222). For charioteers, comic actors, and mimes he pledged his royal credit, and he caused many spectacles to be produced; laughter he loved, and often, says Ælius Lampridius, his roar of merriment drowned all other sounds in the public theatre.[2] A reign of parsimony ensued with Alexander Severus, who never had stage-shows at his banquets and who, when he attended the theatres, gave largess in the most niggardly manner.[3] "He never gave the actors gold or silver; barely did he deal out pence to them," his historian informs us, yet the fact that "he brought forward fools and pantomimes [*moriones . . . et pantomimos*] in public" shows that the people would not permit even a niggardly emperor to deny them their entertainment. Perhaps the record testifies, too, to the existence of Court jesters at this time; the *moriones et pantomimos* seem to have been men connected with the Court whom Alexander, possibly in order to save money, commanded to perform before the populace. Gordian the Elder (d. 238) had no such scruples as his predecessor. In all the chief cities of Campania, Etruria, and Picenum he caused stage plays to be produced at his own expense.[4] Aurelian (d. 275), an emperor whom none accused of degenerate ways, "took a strange delight in the mimes" (*miro modo mimis delectabatur*),[5] while of Carinus (d. 285) Flavius Vopiscus declares that "he filled his palace with mimes, courtesans,[6] pantomimes, singers, and bawds [*lenones*]." It was he who showed "bears acting a mime [*ursos mimum agentes*]; he gathered mimes together from all quarters" and gave "gold and silver, with presents of silk raiment, to Greek artists, wrestlers, actors, and musicians." Two peculiar accounts testify to the position of the mimes in the days of the Emperor Julian (d. 363). In his war with the Persians this monarch made the Plain of Ktesiphon, the "orchestra of war," into a "Dionysian stage" by having performed there some entertainments for his soldiers.[7] It was in the reign of this emperor that Porphyrius was martyred, and it is recorded that at a festival Julian commanded the mimes "to ridicule and make sport of the Christian religion."[8] This was in the year 362, but that Julian was not by any means the first to encourage this mimic ridicule of Christianity is proved by the earlier martyrdoms of another Porphyrius (d. A.D. 275), of Gelasinus (d. 279), and of Ardalio (d. 298).

Fig. 96. A Bald-
headed Roman
Comic Actor

From Francisco Ficoroni,
*Dissertatio de larvis
scenicis* (Roma, 1754),
Plate XX.

We are now in the period when Christianity, if still ridiculed, is rapidly coming to be the force in social life which dominates all others. Mimes who turn to the new religion are still martyred, and the mimic plays still sport with the ceremonies of the Church; but the day of reckoning is not far distant. In the year 436 the Roman legions were being hurried back from Britain and Gaul in order to take their stand in defending the Roman confines against the invasions of the Goths and the Vandals, and the Christian priests were almost welcoming the incursion of rude barbarian forces into a land where they could see naught but degeneration. It must be our task to see how far the spirit of cultured secularism—the mimic drama—endured under the onslaughts of barbarian brutality and of ascetic repression. We have seen enough to know that, without a shadow of doubt, this mimic drama was as strong at the end of the fourth century as it had been at the beginning of the first, and we have seen reason to believe that the line of tradition is complete and intact from the time when, in the sixth century B.C., we first meet historic record of the Dorian comedy. The question which we have to

---

[1] Malalas, *Chronographia*, 285–286 (J. P. Migne, *op. cit.*, Series Græca, xcvii, col. 430–432).
[2] *Antoninus Elagabalus*, xxii, 3; xxxii, 7.
[3] Ælius Lampridius, *Severus Alexander*, xxxiii, 3; xxxiv, 2; xxxvii, 1; xli, 5.
[4] Julius Capitolinus, *Gordiani tres*, iv, 6.   [5] Flavius Vopiscus, *Aurelianus*, l.
[6] Possibly this word is used for the mimic actresses. See *Carinus*, xix.
[7] *Eunapii fragmenta*, xxii (in *Historici græci minores*, ed. L. Dindorf, Leipzig, 1870, i, 226).
[8] *Cf.* Reich, i, 200.

bear in our minds is this : Did the mimic drama, after the triumph of barbarianism and Christianity, slowly die a natural death, leaving some of the intermediate centuries truly dark in so far as the theatre was concerned, or can we trace, if even ever so slightly, the footsteps of the barefooted and bald-headed mimes as they tread the weary road which, unlike the roads of ancient times, leads far from Rome ? [1]

(v) THE PANTOMIME

Before any answer to this question can be attempted it will be necessary to cast a brief glance at another type of Roman ' drama,' the *pantomimus*, or pantomime, which, itself (as its name implies) a child of the mime, came to rival its parent in popularity. Since, however, the pantomime, as a form of theatrical art, affects our argument only in certain respects, it will not be necessary here to attempt anything in the nature of a broad and detailed survey. Only the characteristic features of the type require to be discussed.[2]

The pantomime, of course, is the art of interpretative dancing. The Greeks commonly used the word ὀρχηστής (*orchestes*, ' dancer ') to designate the actor in this kind of drama, and ὀρχηστής continues to be employed through many centuries, particularly by the inheritors of the Greek tradition in Byzantium. In Rome, however, the performers were more commonly styled *pantomimi* from the rarer Greek παντόμιμος, or, even more frequently, they were called simply *saltatores* (' dancers '). Thus a certain P. Rusticellius is designated in an inscription simply as *saltator*,[3] while the phrase *saltare tragœdiam* (' to dance a tragedy ') was a synonym for ' to act a pantomime.' This dancing naturally was accompanied by music, and it seems highly probable that the dancing figure or figures had as assistants either a singer or a chorus, who outlined in chanted form the development of the pantomimic plot. In any case, the word *canticum*, or song, is frequently met with, and we are distinctly told by Macrobius that Hylas, a famous pantomimic actor, " danced a song " (*quum canticum saltaret Hylas*).[4] A picture of such a performance is drawn by Cassiodorus when he mentions the applause greeting the appearance of the chief of the pantomimes ; " well-trained and harmonious choruses, accompanied by diverse instruments, assist him in his art " (*assistant consoni chori diversis organis eruditi*).[5] *Cantare tragœdiam* (' to sing a tragedy '), therefore, comes to mean the same as *saltare tragœdiam*.

Concerning the true nature of the pantomime no ancient authority has left any certain statement. When Cassiodorus [6] says that " the name *pantomimus* is derived from the manifold imitation " indulged in by this art he fails to make any clear distinction between the pantomime and the mime, and a similar failure is to be found in the relevant section of Diomedes' work on Latin grammar.[7] It seems highly probable, however, that normally (although not necessarily always) the pantomime was distinguished from other forms of theatrical art by the fact that one individual actor took a variety of *rôles* in a single play. Masks certainly were worn by the performers, and apparently these masks were often changed, in order to mark off different characters. These pantomimic masks were distinguished from the ordinary theatrical masks by having no mouth openings. " With closed mouth," says Cassiodorus,[8] " the pantomimic actor speaks with his

---

[1] We are, of course, concerned here neither with attempts made to discover mimic influence on non-dramatic classical literature, such as those of Reich (i, 296–416) regarding Plato, and K. Preston (*Some Sources of Comic Effect in Petronius*, in *Classical Philology*, x (1915), 3) regarding Petronius, nor with those made to discern similar influence on medieval *fabliaux*. In this discussion I have kept strictly to theatrical forms.

[2] The best study of the Roman pantomime is that by C. J. Grysar, *Über die Pantomimen der Römer* (*Rheinisches Museum*, ii (1834), 30–80). Many of the works on the mime deal also with this subject. *Cf.* C. Magnin, pp. 468–516.

[3] I. C. Orelli, No. 2641 (i, 461).

[4] Macrobius, *Sat.*, II, vii, 13.

[5] Cassiodorus, iv, 51 (*Opera*, ed. J. Garetii, Venice, 1729, i, 73).

[6] iv, 51 (*ed. cit.*, i, 73).

[7] *Artis grammaticæ libri III* (in H. Keil, *ed. cit.*, i, 492).

[8] Cassiodorus, i, 20 (*ed. cit.*, i, 11).

hands. By gesture he conveys what hardly could have been rendered by word of mouth or written text." Contemporaries raved over the art of these performers. The famous Pylades, according to an inscription, was "held in honour by the greatest cities of Italy ";[1] laurel-crowning of well-known actors was common; factions were formed in favour of this man or that. Suetonius refers to the *seditiones pantomimorum* (' dissensions over the pantomimes ') in Nero's time,[2] and tells how these were alternately favoured and condemned by the Emperor. On one occasion the *pantomimorum factiones* were banished; on others

Fig. 97. A PANTOMIMIC ACTOR WITH HIS MASKS
Ivory relief in Berlin. From M. Bieber, *Denkmäler zum Theaterwesen im Altertum*, Taf. LXIII, 2.

even in the broad light of day he would be carried in his chair to the theatre, and there would watch the brawls of the pantomimes from the top of the proscenium and urge them on. When they came to blows and threw stones and broken benches at one another he himself would throw many missiles at the crowd beneath.

Hardly dignified, perhaps, but testifying to the enthusiasm which the pantomimic performers aroused. That enthusiasm was also expressed in written form. " The most loquacious hands, the speaking fingers, the clamorous silence" (*loquacissimæ manus, linguosi digiti, silentium clamosum*) of these men were admired and praised.[3] " A marvellous art it is," declares a writer in the *Latin Anthology*, " which makes the limbs speak when the tongue is silent!" (*Mirabilis ars est, quæ facit articulos ore silente loqui!*).[4]

While undoubtedly, as has been noted above, one performer took many parts by means of changed masks and raiment, it can hardly be believed that every pantomimic show was thus presented. The phrases *maximum pantomimorum* (' chief of the pantomimes '), which appears on an inscription raised by L. Sorredus Valerianus,[5] and the *grex Romanus pantomimorum* (' Roman pantomimic company '), which erected a stone in honour of Pylades,[6] may, it is true, refer only to groups of performers who served as a kind of chorus; but we may believe that on many occasions more than one actor appeared in the pantomimic ballet. In other words, the pantomime must often have assumed the form of the operatic dance show which is associated in the minds of moderns with the Russian Ballet.

A certain amount of information has been preserved regarding the more famous exponents

---

[1] I. C. Orelli, No. 2629 (i, 460).   [2] Suetonius, *Nero*, xxvi.   [3] Cassiodorus, iv, 51.
[4] Grysar, *loc. cit.*, p. 39.   [5] I. C. Orelli, No. 2637 (i, 461).   [6] I. C. Orelli, No. 2629 (i, 460).

of this art in Roman times, and, as this information has more than a particular significance, some of it may be briefly summarized here. Pylades and Bathyllus are generally credited with having introduced the fuller form of pantomimic display in the time of Augustus.[1] This, of course, does not mean that the dance was unknown in earlier periods, but simply that the elaborate type of ballet opera was developed in their time. Bathyllus, who is said by Athenæus to have been an Alexandrian, may have been a freedman of Mæcenas.[2] " Tender Bathyllus " he was called by Juvenal,[3] who added that, when he danced in *Leda and the Swan*, he was about the only one who could teach anything to the fairly sophisticated mimic actress Thymele. A memorial to him is engraved in Ficoroni's *De larvis scenicis*.[4] Another inscription, already cited, gives us some information regarding Pylades. This, dedicated to his honour by his companions, declares that he was the " best of his time " (*sui temporis primus*) in a pantomime called *Troades* and in another called *Iona*. One of his pupils, Hylas, seems to have won fame, but of him we learn nothing but the uninteresting fact that he was publicly whipped in the court of Augustus' palace.[5] Two performers of the name of Paris likewise shared in honour and disgrace. The older and less important was a freedman of the elder Domitia, the aunt of Nero. In spite of the fact that at one time he was a favourite of the Emperor, an ignominious death came to him in A.D. 67. The second lived under Domitian, whose favourite he was. " Ornament of the Roman stage " (*Romani decus theatri*), Martial[6] calls him; but, ornament or not, he was executed by his emperor friend twenty years after the earlier Paris.

So far as the extant records go, it would seem that the most popular pantomimic themes were those taken from myth and legend. A *Leda and the Swan* has already been mentioned, together with a *Troades* and an *Iona*. Various authors and other authorities prove that these were not isolated examples. Lucian,[7] in his famous work on dancing, mentions ballets which dealt with Rhodope, Parthenope, and Phædra. Both Arnobius[8] and Juvenal refer to the popularity of the Leda theme, and the former adds as additional subjects Europa, Danaë, Ganymede, Atys, and Adonis. A Hercules ballet and another on Œdipus are mentioned by Macrobius.[9] Josephus cites the theme of the unnatural love of Myrra for her father Kinyras as that of an ὀρχηστὴς δρᾶμα (' pantomimic drama ').[10] An *Acteon*,[11] according to Varro, appeared either as a mime or as a pantomime. Virgil's Turnus was adapted for ballet action, as Suetonius[12] informs us, while Juvenal records that the younger Paris appeared as Agave. It seems probable, indeed, that the whole sphere of myth and legend was put under contribution by the actors and by the writers of the orchestral *canticum*. It is to be noted that the mime and the pantomime had thus many themes in common; indeed, often we cannot tell whether a particular author, such as Augustine, is referring to the one or to the other; but it seems probable that, whereas the mimic treatment must have been almost always of a burlesque kind, the pantomimic treatment was almost always serious. Lucian thus draws attention to the connexion between tragedy and the pantomime. " The themes [αἱ δὲ ὑποθέσεις] of both are alike," he says,[13]

and the pantomimic actors do not differ from the tragic actors save that the former are more versatile, more subtle and skilled in presenting an infinite number of changes.

If this was so they did not escape the accusation of obscenity. Such themes as those of *Leda and the Swan* caused much scandal, and perhaps were rendered the more obnoxious in ' tragic ' pantomimic treatment than they had been in the hands of the joyous, irrepressible

---

[1] Grysar, *loc. cit.*, p. 30.   [2] Athenæus, i, 20*f*.   [3] *Sat.*, vi, 63–65.

[4] F. Ficoroni, *Dissertatio de larvis scenicis* (Romæ, 1754; second edition), Plate V, and *cf.* pp. 18–20.

[5] Suetonius, *Divus Augustus*, xlv.   [6] See Grysar, *loc. cit.*, p. 77.

[7] Περὶ ὀρχήσεως, ii (ed. C. Iacobitz, Leipzig, 1887, ii, 144).

[8] *Adversus gentes*, xxxiii (in J. P. Migne, *op. cit.*, Series Latina, v, cols. 1265–66).   [9] *Sat.*, II, vii, 15–16.

[10] xix, 94 (*ed. cit.*, iv, 226).   [11] *Menippearvm reliqviæ* (ed. F. Bücheler, Berlin), 1882, p. 216.

[12] *Nero*, liv.   [13] Περὶ ὀρχήσεως, xxxi (*ed. cit.*, ii, 154).

heathens in honour of any idol is resorted to in a public show by faithful Christians, and the heathen idolatry is maintained, and the true and divine religion is trampled upon in contempt of God?

It was largely against these erring Christians that the writings of the Fathers of the Church were directed. From east to west, in Constantinople, in Antiochia, in Alexandria, in Rome, the mimic drama flourished, uniting together old pagans and new Christians in the one common enjoyment of pure secularism. Dio Chrysostom[1] records the activities of the μῖμοί τ' ὀρχησταί ('mimes and dancers') at Alexandria alongside the swift charioteers. Ammianus Marcellinus[2] notes the rapt attention paid to the mimes at Antiochus in the time of the Emperor Gallienus (fl. 253–268). A monarch had to gather together flute-players and mimes and cithara-players and entertainers of all kinds, thought Dio Chrysostom, if he intended to amuse the people well and skilfully. Even the Atellanæ persisted. Tertullian[3] in the third century mentions an *atellanus gesticulator*, while of an attempt made by a deacon named Sabianus to run away with a nun St Jerome (Hieronymus) (d. 420)[4] declared that his crime was such as could not have been conceived by a mime, could not have been presented by a *scurra*, or buffoon, could not have been acted by an Atellan player (*Atellanus*). The popular interest in *mimis theatralibus* is attested likewise by a reference in a tractate by St Hilary[5] (d. 366), who was Bishop of Poitiers.

The severer Christians, of course, persisted in their attacks. Accounts of at least three brave fanatics who met their deaths by rising from the theatre benches to preach against the scenic spectacles have been preserved,[6] and the early Fathers have many fulminations against the iniquities of the stage. "What noise!" cries Chrysostom (d. 407) in his sermon on Matthew,[7]

> What tumult! What satanic clamour! What diabolic dress! Here comes a youth, with hair combed back, who makes himself effeminate in look, in manner, in dress—aye, in everything takes on the shape and guise of a tender girl. Here comes an old man with his hair all shaved, who has cast off shame with his hair, and who stands there to receive slaps on the face and who is prepared for all that is said and done. And the women too! With uncovered heads, all shame lost, they stand talking to the people, aiming at unchastity, arousing the minds of the spectators to wantonness and obscenity. For these wanton words, these ridiculous manners, these foolish tonsures, these ways of walking, these dresses, these voices, that softness of limb, that winking of the eyes, these pipes and flutes, these dramas and arguments—aye, all are full of utter wantonness. Here are to be seen naught but fornication, adultery, courtesan women, men pretending to be women, and soft-limbed boys.

It would be exceedingly difficult to say more; but the very strength and vigour of Chrysostom's attack is a reflex of the power possessed by the mime. Varied were the methods adopted by Chrysostom and his companions to dissuade people from the theatres. "Truly," exclaims this Father,[8]

> Truly it is not for us to pass our time in laughter, in light entertainment, in trivial delights; that is good only for the stage-players, for the indelicate actresses, above all for the parasites and flatterers, . . . for those who execute the will of the devil.

This emphasis on the devil's business was not Chrysostom's own. Tertullian[9] had called the theatre "the home of Venus and Liber," while Cyprian[10] had discovered that all theatrical affairs

---

[1] See Reich, i, 145.

[2] xxiii, 5, 3 (*Ammiani Marcellini rerum gestarum libri qui supersunt*, ed. V. Gardthausen, Leipzig, 1875).

[3] *De spectaculis*, xvii.   [4] *Epist.*, cxlvii (J. P. Migne, *op. cit.*, Series Latina, xxii, col. 1199).

[5] *De trinitate*, xxxix (J. P. Migne, *op. cit.*, Series Latina, x, col. 232). Salvianus in his *De gubernatione Dei* (vi, 4; J. P. Migne, *op. cit.*, Series Latina, liii, col. 112) speaks of the "thousands of Christians" who attended the theatres in his time, and St John Chrysostom found occasion to censure even old men of the Church who, by going to see plays, corrupted the young (*In epistolam ad Hebræos* (J. P. Migne, *op. cit.*, Series Græca, lxiii, col. 65).

[6] See Reich, i, 96.   [7] *Hom. VI in Matt.*, xxxvii and xxxviii.

[8] *Hom. VI in Matt.* (J. P. Migne, *op. cit.*, Series Græca, lvii, col. 71).   [9] *De spectaculis*, x.   [10] *De spectaculis*, iv.

had been established by demons, and not by God. All this was but an attempt to discredit the theatre in the eyes of Christians and a result of pent-up hatred. Everything said and done on the stage was satanic, and the songs in the theatre were but the charms of the Prince of Darkness. The general attitude taken by these early writers may indeed be excellently, and not unamusingly, summed up from the entry under " Devils " in the index to Prynne's *Histriomastix*, where the words of the Fathers are analysed and tabulated :

> *Devils* and *Devill-Idols* the inventors, the fomentors of Stage-playes, and Dancing which were appropriated to their solemne honour and worship, their Festivals being spent in Playes and Dancing, which they exacted from their worshippers. . . . [Devils] have Stage-playes in Hell every Lords-day-night. . . . The inventors of no good things, and the enemies of mankinde. . . . Claime Playes, Play-haunters, and Play-houses as their owne, . . . honoured oft-times in stead of Christ. . . . The onely gainers by Stage-playes.

Thus did Tertullian and Chrysostom speak.[1]

It were needless here to emphasize further the bitterness of these attacks. They all take the same form. " What am I to say," asks Lactantius [2] (*d. c.* 330) rhetorically,

> What am I to say of the mimes who sustain the habits of corruption, who exhibit adulteries while they act in pretence and so lead from fiction to fact ? What do youths and maidens do, when they see that these things, done shamelessly and openly, are watched by all ?

As we have seen, there is considerable authority for the belief that such accusations, and others similar to these, were not completely justified in fact. It is probable that a good deal of exaggeration is due to a burning zeal and a fanatical hate.

These early centuries, however, provide us with something other than mere vituperation of the mimes by Christian apologists, something more than mere open or shamefaced attendances at mimic performances by laymen or clerics. One of the most famous of all the early sects within the early Church was that called Arianism, after its founder, Arius of Alexandria (*d.* 336). In 325 Arianism was formally condemned by the orthodox, but it endured under the favour of emperors such as Constantine II and was spread widely by its most devoted adherents, the Goths and the Vandals. Among its early critics none was more formidable than Athanasius, elected Bishop of Alexandria in 326, whose creed—or a creed called by his name—has been preserved, in a vital form, down to the present day. Now, in the controversy between Athanasius and Arius the word ' mime ' is of frequent occurrence ; evidently some kinship between the ceremonial desired by the heretic and the entertainments given by the other was perceptible to contemporaries. Clearly the Arians were prepared to make their services more popular by utilizing the gesticulation and the changing inflexions of the mime. " They show themselves," says Chrysostom,[3]

> no better than madmen, agitating and moving their bodies, uttering strange sounds, engaging in customs foreign to the things of the Spirit. They introduce the habits of mimes and dancers into sacred places. Their minds are darkened by what they have heard and seen in the theatres. They confuse theatrical action with the ceremonials of the Church.

When we hear Athanasius accusing his opponent of following the model " of the Egyptian Sotades," [4] the mimograph, when we hear that the Arian liturgies are styled " stage books " (θυμελικὰς βίβλους), and when we hear a prominent Arian described as " the leader of the Arian

---

[1] On this subject see J. B. Eriau, pp. 58–63.

[2] *De vero cultu* (in J. P. Migne, *op. cit.*, Series Latina, vi, col. 710–711). *Cf. The Works of Lactantius* (*Ante-Nicene Christian Library*, vol. xxi, Edinburgh, 1871), p. 408.

[3] *Cf.* Reich, i, 135.   [4] *De synodis*, xv (J. P. Migne, *op. cit.*, Series Græca, xxvi, col. 705).

stage ballet " (πρωτοστάτην τῆς ᾿Αρείου θυμελικῆς ὀρχήστρας) [1] we realize that here we are in the midst of a religious movement which is attempting to counter the activities of the mimes by introducing some of their characteristic methods of appeal into the Church services. Gesticulation, variety of vocal tone, and, later, music came to be used for this purpose. Gregory of Nazianzus was said to have followed the model of " the Syracusan Sophron," [2] just as Arius had been accused of following Sotades. The mimic *canticum*, in his hands, was made holy, and the more strictly orthodox were amazed and dismayed at seeing this attempt to use the forces of evil (the diabolic theatre) in the cause of good (the kingdom of the Spirit). Although a discussion concerning the sources of religious drama must be left to a later section, it must be noted here that these records of theatrical Arianism are of prime importance. They indicate clearly how a certain section of the Church endeavoured to rival the mimes, and, as it were, to beat them on their own ground. Already in the fourth century A.D., if not before, men had considered the possibilities of a religious theatre.

When we pass from the fourth to the fifth century we find the Church Councils quite as active in their decrees and prohibitions. In 401 three canons were issued at the fifth Council of Carthage [3] —each one characteristic. The first provided that any of the clergy who should take delight in obscene jests, or who should dance and sing at feasts, should suffer some small degradation in rank. It is to be noted that the punishment is by no means severe. The second advised new converts to abstain from attending the theatres (again mildly expressed), while the third threatened excommunication for those who abandoned a Church service on any feast-day in favour of the scenic spectacles. The African Council of 408 offered baptism to those stage-players (*scenicis atque histrionibus*) who renounced their professions, and advised that theatrical shows (*spectacula theatrorum*) should be given up on Sundays. It is noticeable that this canon draws attention to the popularity of the stage. " In Easter week," it runs, " the people flock much more willingly to the circus than to the church." Eleven years later was held the seventh Council of Carthage,[4] where once more the " infamy " of the *histriones* is emphasized. The second synod of Arras [5] in 452 decided that actors who were of the faithful must abandon Communion while they were engaged in acting.

From the words of the assembled bishops themselves it is quite plain that, in the African East at any rate, the love of the theatrical show endured unchecked. The *histriones* still ply their trade, and the phrasing of many canons is petitionary rather than commanding. Other sources of information corroborate these assumptions. Characteristic are the confessions of St Augustine (354–430). Like most young men of his period, the future saint in his early years at Carthage adored the theatre. " The scenic spectacles," he mournfully admits,[6]

enraptured me. In my time I had a violent passion for these spectacles, which were full of the images of my miseries and of the amorous flames of fire which devoured me.

And he tells of the tears he once shed at the misfortunes of the stage lovers, and shows that some men " were more easily pleased by a pantomime than by God." [7] The whole of St Augustine's writings are starred by retrospective references to the theatre, thus proving how deeply the stage had once influenced his mind, and even he could echo that sentiment of a long-dead Roman emperor and declare that " we too are acting in life this mime of ours." [8] The old attacks go on, Neilos, or Nilus, a pupil of Chrysostom, carrying on his master's work, singling out as the object of his

---

[1] Reich, i, 135.　　　　　　　[2] See Reich, i, 137.　　　　　　[3] Canons iv, v, vii; J. D. Mansi, iii, 888.
[4] Canon ii; J. D. Mansi, iv, 437.　　　[5] Douhet, col. 18.
[6] *Confessiones*, iii, 2–3 (in J. P. Migne, *op. cit.*, Series Latina, xxxii, col. 683).
[7] *In Psalm xxxii ; Sermo i* (J. P. Migne, *op. cit.*, Series Latina, xxxvi, 277).
[8] *In Psalm cxxvii ; enarratio* (in J. P. Migne, *op. cit.*, Series Latina, xxxvii, col. 1686).

principal attack a certain Nikotychos, who had patronized the mimes.   None of his remarks need be quoted here, for the tone he adopts is as that of the others : [1]

> The face of woman is a poisoned dart which wounds and festers the soul. . . . He who desires to avoid these wounds must avoid going to public spectacles, for it is wiser to remain at home than fall into the hands of the enemy while you think to honour these celebrations.

There is naught different here.   There is the same bitterness, the same indirect proof of the continued popularity of the mimes and of theatrical shows, the same evidence of the enthusiasm for the " foolish words of Philistion " (τὰς μὲν μωρολογίας Φιλιστίωνος).   It may be that, as some writers have thought, the mime in this period was decaying as an artistic form, but the proofs brought forward hardly serve to establish any essential distinction between the mimes of the later and those of the earlier times.   When Gregory of Nazianzus speaks of the ῥαπίσματα τῶν μίμων (' the blows of the mimes ') [2] he is only referring to the *alapas* which classical authorities had noted centuries before his period, and the accusations of obscenity, besides being no doubt exaggerated, vary in character not at all from the similar accusations in previous ages.   Aristophanes in ancient Athens had professed to find the Dorian comedy, from which he took many of his ideas, coarse and uninteresting.   Babylas, Cardamas, and Masculas [3] seem to have been in no way different from the mimes and arch-mimes of earlier years.   The last-mentioned was martyred under the Vandal persecutions of King Geiserich in the year 486, but this fact must not lead us to suppose that the barbarian monarchs did not countenance the theatre.   It is true that Salvianus of Marseilles in his *De gubernatione Dei* (439–451),[4] in testifying to the enthusiasm for the mime at Marseilles and at Rome, thinks the barbarians in some ways superior to the Romans in that the former had no scenic displays, but there is plentiful evidence to show that, if they came with no theatrical art, the barbarians soon adopted southern and eastern practices.   In later years Theodoric the Great thought that the best way of accustoming the Romans to the rule of a Teutonic king was to encourage the mimes,[5] while in this period the Emperor Theodosius freely patronized the stage.   The μῖμοι and the ὀρχησταί appear to have won from him considerable favour.

Before leaving the fifth century there are two other matters which may be noted in connexion with the links binding the ancient and the later mime together.   The first concerns the person of *sannio*, who, as we have seen, was one of the familiar figures in the Roman mime of the first century B.C.   Perhaps we might have expected him to disappear, yet his name occurs in a piece of religious controversy about A.D. 431.   A certain Julianus, Bishop of Eclanum, had adopted some unorthodox ideas concerning the subject of original sin, and Marius Mercator, a pupil of St Augustine, proceeded to attack his heresy.[6]   He bids the unhappy man blush for the " mimic obscenity " of which he has been guilty, declares that he may well be likened by the populace to Philistion, Lentulus, and Marullus, and wonders what *sannio* could have dared with the licence of professed depravity to bring these things before the public.   Evidently Sannio was still a character well known on the mimic stage.   The second matter of interest concerns the use of the phallus, and here incontestable fifth- or sixth-century proof is forthcoming from a scholiast's comments on Gregory of Nazianzus.   Gregory himself lived at the end of the fourth century, so that at the earliest we have to reckon here with an account of the following age.[7]   Speaking of the phallus, this scholiast makes the usual remark that it was an indelicate and shameful symbol, adding, however, the significant words that " the mimes now " (νῦν οἱ μῖμοι) wear a similar appendage of leather " which they call a φαλητάριον, or *phaletarion*."   The importance of this note cannot be over-emphasized,

[1] See Reich, i, 204.   [2] *Cf.* Reich, i, 125.   [3] For these see *supra*, p. 94.
[4] J. P. Migne, *op. cit.*, Series Latina, liii, col. 112.
[5] For his *tribunus voluptatum* see *supra*, p. 98.   *Cf.* Reich, i, 143.   [6] Reich, i, 475.
[7] Reich, i, 502; J. P. Migne, *op. cit.*, Series Græca, xxxvi, cols. 1047-48

for it shows that we are still dealing with a form of comic drama the roots of which are to be traced to furthest antiquity.

Precisely the same conditions are operative in the sixth century. The Council of Agde (*Concilium Agathense*) [1] in 506 prohibited priests, deacons, and sub-deacons from attending the *spectacula* at feasts and marriages, and likewise had some hard things to say of buffoons, who were thus still flourishing. This was the age of Theodoric the Great, who, as we have seen, patronized the theatres from political motives. Through his Minister, Cassiodorus, this monarch reconstructed the playhouse at Rome.[2] There were performed tragedies and comedies and pantomimes, and although the mime is spoken of in somewhat derogatory tones, Cassiodorus evidently realizes its importance and genuine artistic quality. Even the old tag of μῖμος ὁ βίος ('the mime of life') could be quoted by a Bishop Fulgens about 530,[3] and a Choricius could come forward with a lengthy and reasoned defence of the whole mimic stage. This sixth-century defence of Choricius is one of the most valuable documents on this subject which we possess, and all who would penetrate more deeply than is possible here into the fortunes of the stage immediately after the fall of Rome have of necessity to read every line of it with care and comment.[4] Point by point Choricius argues with Chrysostom and the Christian apologists. He shows that some mimic actors may be despicable, but such, he deems, are not true mimes and should not be taken into account. He denies that an actor who assumes a certain part should be identified morally with that part. He rejects the theory that laughter in itself is evil. The world and work will go all the merrier for a little amusement and entertainment. Man is distinguished from the brutes by this god-given quality, and we should thank the good Dionysus for having brought it to us, instead of treating him as an ally of Satan. Certainly, agrees Choricius, there are things in the mime of which serious thinkers may not approve, but these are only part of the whole, and it is illogical to treat the part as if it were the whole. Some characters shave their heads and get knocked about, but all the mimic actors are not fools; the majority have long hair and occupy dignified *rôles*. There is adultery in the mimic drama, but then there is adultery in Homer and Æschylus (perhaps he would have added, had he dared, in the Bible also), but we do not condemn Homer and Æschylus because of individual episodes. " Of what," he asks,

> Of what indeed can the mimes be accused—unless you charge them with the crime of not imitating the better only ? And how could they be worthy of the name ' mime,' which is theirs because of their portrayal of life, if they were to delineate some parts of life and to neglect others ? . . . Instead of blaming the mimes, blame those who do commit the evil actions which are themselves the basis of the miming, or imitation of evil. When we thus reflect on the matter we see that the actors are not guilty of any crime.

This defence of the mimic drama as an " imitation of life " is the cardinal tenet to which Choricius holds, and from his words we see clearly that in his time the mimic actors were providing precisely the same dramatic fare as had been provided by their predecessors. They had certainly not sunk into being mere acrobatic entertainers ; their scope of imitation was still broad as life itself.

Choricius, of course, is speaking of Northern Africa, and it is impossible to generalize from his remarks for the whole of the two Empires, but other indications prove to us that the mimes still flourished in many centres. Procopius and Joannes Malalas,[5] it is true, state that Justinian (527–565) closed τὰ θέατρα (' the theatres ') in Constantinople, but, if this action were indeed taken by him, those theatres must soon have been reopened. As we shall see, there is mention of Byzantine performances before the public in the middle and end of the following century, while Justinian was responsible for a series of important edicts concerning the position of the actor and actress.

---

[1] Canon lxx ; Douhet, col. 18.   [2] See Reich, i, 144.   [3] See Reich, i, 770.
[4] A full account and many quotations are given in Reich (i, 204-222). The text is edited by Charles Graux, *Chorikios Éloge du Duc Aratios et du Gouverneur Stephanos*, in *Revue de philologie*, N.S., i (1877), 55–84.
[5] Reich, i, 133-135.

Theodosius in his famous *Codex* (435) had had much to say concerning the stage and its professionals, defining, so far as lay in his power, their position in social life, acknowledging their importance but relegating them to a position of a somewhat ignominious kind. These edicts were,

to a certain extent, modified under the hand of Justinian, who, as the husband of Theodora, had every reason to ameliorate the position of her erstwhile sisters. His most important modification of the existing laws consisted in the permission granted to a nobleman to marry, if he willed, a *scenica*, provided that she abandoned her profession. Such a law proves conclusively that in the sixth century, in Byzantium, the mimes and their companions, the other entertainers, were continuing their activities almost as fervently as their predecessors had done five hundred years before.

Something of their *répertoire* is hinted at in a record dating from the second half of the century.[1] About that time the Syrian Bishop Johannes of Ephesus, walking in the streets, once encountered a beautiful youth clad in mimic dress (the reference to a particular costume is important), accompanied by a lovely girl, his mimic companion. The record, which goes on to tell of a wondrous miracle, informs us that these mimes were in the habit of bringing Christian clerics and all the world to ridicule, the reference evidently applying to the anti-

Fig. 99. THE DIPTYCH OF ANASTASIUS, A.D. 517
Ivory in the Bibliothèque Nationale, Paris.
Photo Giraudon

Christian farces such as those which have already been discussed. When these anti-Christian farces vanished we cannot tell; here we have proof of their continued popularity about the year 575.

Finally, one may note two important pieces of pictorial evidence happily subsisting from this period. In the Bibliothèque Nationale there is preserved an ivory diptych, the so-called Diptychon Bituricense, or Diptyque d'Anastasius, dated 517 (Fig. 99).[2] This ivory, which is in two parts, shows, below the seated figures, a number of scenes from the amphitheatre. On the right the semicircle obviously is intended to suggest such an amphitheatre, and the heads of a few

---

[1] See Josef Horovitz, *Spuren griechischer Mimen im Orient* (Berlin, 1905), pp. 38–39.
[2] On these diptychs see Richard Delbrueck, *Die Consulardiptychen* (Berlin, 1929).

143

spectators are depicted at each side. This right-hand picture is devoted to animals. Two men rush about with ropes, and a horseman is riding furiously across the arena. Below we see the

Fig. 100. The Diptych of St Étienne of Bourges
Ivory in the Bibliothèque Nationale, Paris.
Photo Giraudon

animals released from their cages and pursuing either Christians or their tormentors. The picture to the left continues with the sports of the amphitheatre. A couple of grooms lead on two prancing racehorses, while beneath some actors give a mimic show. In all there are seven performers. The three to the right are clad in tragic costume with high *onkos*, and one of the others (second to the left) may also be a 'tragic' figure. The remaining persons, however, are truly comic. All three seem to have shaved heads, and perhaps two of them are receiving those *alapas* about which the Fathers of the Church said so much. In all probability we are witnessing here the performance of a mimic burlesque, maybe, as has been thought, a burlesque of the healing of the blind. The 'tragic' figures can hardly be taking part in the performance of a true tragedy, for we have every reason to believe that tragedy completely disappeared when the elaborate pantomime was established. The mixture of tragic and comic figures suggests a travesty along the time-honoured lines of antiquity. The second diptych, also associated with Anastasius, is preserved in the Victoria and Albert Museum (see frontispiece).[1] Unfortunately part of this is now destroyed, although an early engraving presents its main features. Here mimic players very similar to those in the first scene make their appearance. They are bald-headed and clearly engaged in some farcical episode of popular

merriment; the big crab hanging on to the nose of the central player testifies to the rude laughter-raising qualities of the piece in which they are performing. Taken together, the

---

[1] At least, the more important portion is preserved there. Part is in Berlin. On this diptych see A. Wilthemius, *Diptychon Leodiense ex consulari factum episcopale et in illud commentarius* (Lüttich, 1659).

two pictures offer conclusive testimony regarding the continued vitality of the profane or secular drama in the sixth century, and the links between that drama and the more ancient mime are fully evident. One other diptych, of less interest certainly, may be given here as a kind of additional proof that the drama as such was not forgotten in this epoch (Fig. 100). Among the Muses stands Melpomene, with a true tragic mask; the familiar theme of Leda is shown to the right of the first row of figures; while a group of persons below are evidently engaged in some form of Dionysiac merriment, apparently of a dramatic kind. It is impossible to say, but, from the liveliness of the scene and the variety in the portraiture, one might hazard the suggestion that this Bacchic picture is definitely connected with the theatre.

The attacks on *spectacula* continue unabated in the seventh century. King Sisebuto, or Sisebert, of Spain (612–621), writing to Eusebius, Bishop of Barcelona, lamented the popularity of " theatrical shows " (*ludis theatriis*).[1] Dancing and singing at feasts are referred to in many other seventh-century canons, and when, in 610, the Bishop of Bracara collected together the chief canons of the Greek Synods he inserted one which declared that

> it is not lawful for priests or the clergy to witness any *spectacula* at marriages or feasts; they ought to rise and go from thence before these *spectacula* are introduced.[2]

More important for our purposes are the canons of the Concilium Trullanum held at Constantinople in 692.[3] This was one of the most important of such gatherings in early times, and the wording of their judgments can leave no doubt in our minds as to the existence and popularity of the mimes. The bishops gathered in conclave decided (Canon li) " utterly to prohibit those who are called mimes, together with their theatres " (τοὺς λεγομένους μίμους καὶ τὰ τούτων θέατρα). Continuing, they condemn " the dancing on the stage " (τὰς ἐπὶ σκηνῶν ὀρχήσεις), and threaten deposition for a priest, excommunication for a layman, who dares to disobey. In Canon lxi they extended their veto to " those who carry about bears ";[4] in Canon lxii they attacked the pagan festival of the Kalends and decreed that " no one shall put on comic, satyric, or tragic masks."[5] Canon lxvi has bitter things to say of those who abandon the church on holy days for " public shows," while theatres are cited again in Canon lxxi. The old names given to the mimic plays are continued here. Thus, in Canon xxiv, all priests and monks are forbidden to attend the race-course and the performance of " stage-*paignia* " (θυμελικῶν παιγνίων). There can be no doubt that in the last decades of the seventh century at Constantinople there was a very fully developed and popular mimic drama which was presented both in the theatres and at private houses, which had ramifications into the fields of the vulgar festivals (originally, and still largely, pagan), and which even yet retained sufficient connexion with classic days to employ comic, satyric, and tragic masks. As we shall see, even the thundering prohibitions of the Eastern bishops failed to kill this thing beloved of the people.

It is in the seventh century that we begin to hear more of the theatrical activities in the extreme West. No doubt the mimes had continued flourishing in the old Roman provinces, but sure information concerning their activities is not forthcoming until this period. Happily, we are not left now in any considerable doubt. Testimony as to the existence in Spain of these mimic actors is provided by the famous Isidore of Seville, whose *Originum sive etymologiarum libri xx* is a regular mine of information concerning seventh-century terminology. It has been pointed out that, in his sections devoted to the theatre, most of Isidore's descriptions are in the past tense, whereas

---

[1] Henrique Florez, *España sagrada* (Madrid, 1754–79), vii, 317. Chambers (i, 21), quoting from a different source, suggests that this refers merely to a bull-fight.

[2] lx; D'Ancona, i, 52. [3] J. D. Mansi, xi, 943–975.

[4] This may refer to the use of amulets of animal skin.

[5] Here, too, were condemned the *Bota* (feasts in honour of Pan) and the *Brumalia* (feasts in honour of Bacchus).

when he comes to the subject of actors and mimes he freely employs the present. He starts off with a present-tense definition of a theatre as a whole : [1] " The theatre is that which includes the stage ; it has a semicircular auditorium in which spectators stand." But when he comes to discuss the stage itself his glance is retrospective :

> The stage [*scena*] was a place under the theatre constructed like a house with a platform ; this platform was called the orchestra, and there the comic and tragic actors chanted and the *histriones* and *mimi* danced. The name *scena* comes from the Greek ; it was so called because it was built like a house.

Immediately, however, we reach the *histriones* and the *mimi* we are on firmer ground. " The *histriones* are those who put on feminine garments and act as shameless women," while " The *mimi* get their name from the Greek because they are imitators of human life."

It seems highly probable from these definitions that, while Isidore knew of theatres only as disused buildings, he was personally acquainted with the activities of the *histriones* and the *mimi*. It is noticeable, also, that in another section of his work Isidore distinctly refers to mimic obscenity as a thing with which the Christians of his time should have naught to do. All this goes to prove that acting of a kind was being continued in his time, with performers who had carried over from classic days the old tradition of mimic impersonation with its ' imitation ' of life and its secular tendencies.

Before we leave this century one other glance may be cast back from Seville to Constantinople. A little tale is told by Bishop Leontius, of Neapolis, in his life of a certain monk, Symeon Salos,[2] who must have lived in the reigns of Justinian and Maurice. The episode described is therefore of the mid-seventh century. Its exact details need not concern us here ; sufficient for our purposes is it to know that this Symeon became filled with a desire of converting a certain man named Psephas. Now, this Psephas was an ordinary actor, and, in introducing his account of Symeon's action, Bishop Leontius commences by remarking that " the mimes were playing in the theatre " (Ἐθεάτριζόν ποτε μῖμοι εἰς τὸ θέατρον). Leontius was a contemporary of Symeon's ; no one should have known better than he whether it was a familiar sight to see performances in the Constantinople play-houses.

That the theatres were not closed completely, and that the mimes continued their activities after the promulgation of the Trullan canons,[3] seems fairly conclusively proved by the various comments made on them by the priests Balsamon and Zonaras.[4] The latter, in discussing " the actors and mimes " (τοὺς σκηνικοὺς καὶ μίμους), remarks that " the Fathers of old used to think that these should be prohibited," as if a different attitude was taken by the Church of his day, while Balsamon adds many notes which seem to indicate the continued existence of the mimes in after years. " The actors," he declares, " put on [5] many kinds of masks and mock freely the monks and priests " ; clearly the old anti-Christian mime persists, even when the Church has gained full control and excommunication is used as a punishment.

Naturally, the Councils are not silent. Pope Zachary's Synodus Francica in 742 speaks of pagan festivals among the people.[6] Entertainments, horse-races, and indecent amusement at feasts are grouped together in the second Council of Cloveshow in Mercia (747),[7] while the Synod of Nicæa of 787 expressly denied the righteousness of an actor's life. The *scenici* are here evidently as great a source of alarm to the worthy bishops as they were to their predecessors.

Nor were there lacking followers of Chrysostom and Tertullian. St John of Damascus (eighth century), whom some make the author of a lost religious play,[8] testifies to the popularity of *spectacula*

---

[1] See Migne, *op. cit.*, Series Latina, lxxxii.   [2] See Reich, i, 684–685.
[3] See *supra*, p. 145.   [4] Reich, i, 134–135.
[5] The present tense is to be observed : οἱ δὲ σκηνικοὶ παντοῖα πρόσωπα ὑποδύονται καὶ ἀδεῶς τοὺς μονάχους ἐμπαίζουσι καὶ τοὺς κληρικούς.
[6] Douhet, col. 19.   [7] Canon xvi. Douhet, col. 20.   [8] See *infra*, p. 210.

in his time. " There are some towns," he declares, " which feast their eyes on diverse scenic shows from morn till night." He speaks of their obscenity and their licentiousness, contrasting with them the solemn spectacle of the Mass. As for the " comedies " of the secular players they are naught but " pomps of the devil," and to the devil's voice the spectators listen when they sit in front of the mimes. From St John's words it is easy to see that he might have considered the making of religious plays as a rival attraction, and certainly a contemporary of his, Stephanos the Sabbaite, composed in Greek, about the year 790, a kind of sacred play called *The Death of Christ* ('Ο θάνατος τοῦ Χριστοῦ).[1]

There seems, indeed, to have arisen in Constantinople about this time a marked enthusiasm for some form of religious drama. Ignatius, deacon in Constantinople and later Metropolitan of Nicæa, appears to have been actively engaged about this time in encouraging these efforts,[2] and a century later, according to recent opinion, appeared the famous Χριστὸς πάσχων (*Christ's Suffering*),[3] possibly not a work unique but merely one of a group of similar experiments. Probably a deliberate attempt was being made to rival the attractions of the secular theatre, which apparently was still flourishing both in the East and in the West. In the year 791 Alcuin[4] was writing to a friend and warning him that " the man who brings actors and mimes and dancers [*histriones et mimos et salta-tores*] to his house knows not what a bevy of unclean spirits follow them." A few years later, at the beginning of the ninth century, Leidradus[5] was speaking of the " poet's song, together with the witticisms and verses of comedies and mimes " (*comœdiarum mimorumque urbanitatibus et strophis*). At the same period, in 813, the Synodus Turonensis (Tours)[6] decided that the clergy should abstain from any temptations of eye or ear, and as a consequence ought to fly from " the obscenity of the players and the scurrilities of debased jesting " (*histrionum quoque turpium et obscænorum insolentias jocorum*[7]). Almost the same words (*histrionum sive scurronum et turpium seu obscænorum jocorum insolentiam*) are used by the Synodus Cabilonensis, held the same year. Indeed, the year 813 is particularly rich in notices of this kind, for at the same period was held the Concilium Moguntiacum (Mayence),[8] in which a canon was promulgated, forbidding priests and monks to associate themselves with secular affairs. Among these secular affairs (*negotiis secularibus*) there is cited the profession of the " jester " (*turpis verbi vel facti joculatorem esse*).[9] Especially interesting is a notice in the canons put forward by the Concilium Aquigranense (Aix-la-Chapelle),[10] held three years later, in 816. This declares " that priests and clergy should not be present at any shows given *on the stage* [*in scenis*] or at marriage-feasts; but that, when the actors come in, they should rise and go out." It is important to notice that, in 816, we are still in the midst of a dramatic activity which is not wholly reduced to ' domestic ' levels. *Spectaculis in scenis* are the precise words of the assembled clergy. Evidently, too, these *spectacula* were formidable temptations. Canon c refers again to the importance of abstaining from " shows and spectacles," [11] while " secular shows and spectacles " are introduced once more in Canon cxlv. The good ecclesiastics were evidently much troubled by their secular appeal. At the Concilium Parisiense of 829 the backslidings of the priests are severely taken to task, and from the words of Canon xxxviii we discover that many of these had been neglecting their duties through their love of " scurrilities and foolish speeches, obscene jests of the actors, and other vanities " (*scurrilitates et stultiloquia et histrionum obscænas jocationes et cæteras vanitates*). Canon xiii of the Concilium Moguntinum (847) repeats, almost verbatim,

---

[1] Giorgio La Piana, *Le Rappresentazioni sacre nella Letteratura bizantina* (Grottoferrata, 1912), p. 59.
[2] G. La Piana, *op. cit.*, pp. 59–60.   [3] See *infra*, p. 210.   [4] *Epist.* clxxxix.
[5] *Monvmenta Germaniæ historica*, Epistolæ Karolini Aevi, ii, 541.
[6] Canon vii. J. D. Mansi, xiv, 84.
[7] The use of the word *jocorum* in connexion with *histrionum* is to be noted here.
[8] Canon xiv; Douhet, col. 21.
[9] On this word *joculatorem* see *infra*, p. 151.   [10] Canon lxxxiii. J. D. Mansi, xiv, 202.
[11] *Non spectaculis non pompis intersint.* Both words used here (*spectaculis* and *pompis*) are regularly applied to plays.

the inhibition of the jester as given in the Concilium Moguntiacum of 813, thus proving the endurance of the "obscene jests." Finally, it is interesting to notice that, in a prohibition against festival merriment, pronounced by the Concilium Nanetense in 890, there is a direct reference to *larvas dæmonum*—'devils' masks.' These masks will demand attention in a later section of this book.

Other contemporary evidence amply supports the impression given by the councils and synods —that the mimic drama was still a thing of life, was still a formidable opponent of the idea spiritual. Once more this evidence extends from east to west, touching Constantinople on the one hand and extreme France on the other. In his *Nomocanon* [1] Photius, who was Patriarch of Constantinople, pronounced a sentence of three years' penance upon any priest or bishop who should dare to attend " the theatrical spectacles," and two contemporary stories give at least an indication of the activities of the mimes who produced those shows. When the famous Liudprand, the Langobard ecclesiastic, went to the Eastern capital he witnessed an interesting appearance of the Emperor Romanus I,[2] who at that time had taken over the regency for the child Constantinus Porphyrogennetos. He had as yet no right to wear the Imperial crown, but, in making a public appearance, he decked himself up with gay-coloured garments and donned the red shoes which were a symbol of power. " It seemed to me," remarks Liudprand,

> that he appeared like an actor or a mime [*histrionum mimorumve more*]. These men, the more easily to arouse laughter in their audiences, adorn themselves with diverse colours. Consequently I as well as others laughed when he appeared as an emperor below and a commoner above. What comedy or mime could be better ?

The second contemporary picture belongs to the period of the Emperor Theophilus (829–842).[3] Apparently a certain widow had been cheated of a ship by the Prefect Nicephorus, and in her distress she went off to the mimes. In their next show, when the Emperor himself was present, they introduced a tiny ship into their play. Said one to another, " Open your mouth and swallow this ship." " How can I ? " was the answer. " What ! The Prefect has just swallowed a big ship with all its cargo, and you can't gobble up this little one ? " said the first ; whereupon the Emperor, interested in what was going on, made inquiries, learned the truth of the matter, and meted out due punishment to his erring officer. It is plain from this that, in the ninth century, the Eastern mimes were still producing plays of the older type, full of satire and expressed by means of theatrical dialogue.

Less sure evidence exists for the Western countries, but here too sufficient is extant to show the prevalence of the entertainers and their mimic playlets. The laxity of the clergy is indicated in the laws of Charlemagne (800–814). Bishops, abbots, and abbesses were forbidden by him to keep hounds or hawks or jesters (*ioculatores*),[4] while there is one particularly interesting injunction :

> If any actor has put on a garment belonging to priestly rank—or a monk's dress, a nun's dress, or a dress of any ecclesiastic—he shall be liable to corporal punishment and banishment.[5]

Now, there could only be two objects for a mime's dressing in ecclesiastical vestments ; he might wish to ridicule the clergy or he might be engaged in presenting a ' Christian ' mime—that is to say, a mimic drama with a religious subject. The consequence is that we have to assume either that the ninth-century mimes were continuing their secular ridicule of the Church or that they were

---

[1] ix, 27.   [2] See Liudprand's account in *Monvmenta Germaniæ historica*, v, 310.
[3] A. Rambaud, *De Byzantino Hippodromo* (Paris, 1870), pp. 9–10.   [4] *Cf.* Reich, i, 803.
[5] It is to be noted that this order, with the omission of reference to *mimæ*, was repeated by Roger II of Sicily in 1140; see F. Liebermann, *Schauspielerinnen fehlen dem Theater Siziliens um* 1140 (*Archiv für das Studium der neueren Sprachen und Literaturen*, cxxvii (1911), 388).

endeavouring to placate religious sentiment by the performance of ' godly ' plays. If we assume the former, then we have a direct link with those Roman mimes who presented their anti-Christian dramas ; if we assume the latter, then we have an indication of a developed ' religious ' drama at a period anterior to that usually accepted for its origin. Charlemagne was not one likely to waste time devising laws applicable to no contemporary offence, and we must give due weight to the implications of his pronouncement.

The religious writers of this time show that the mimes had considerable popularity. Alcuin,[1] the English priest, thought that they formed one of the most serious temptations for a young friend who was about to journey into Italy, and warned him that " it is better to please God than the actors ; it is better to have a care for the poor than for the mimes."[2] Alcuin often refers to these entertainers ; he advised Bishop Higbald of Lindisfarne that " it is better to feed the poor from your table than the actors,"[3] and declared to Adalhart, the Abbot of Corvey, that the actors brought only devils along with them.[4] One must believe that the clergy at this time devoted much attention to the mimic entertainers. Alcuin and Leidradus are supported by Agobard, Archbishop of Lyons (c. 836), who denounced those ecclesiastics who permitted the poor to go unfed while " they gave food and drink to actors, to the basest of mimes and to the most wretched of jesters."[5] Some kings continued the old plan of entertaining the people with " actors, jesters, and mimes,"[6] and, in spite of opposition, these entertainers seem to have enjoyed even as good a time as their ancestors had done under the Roman emperors. Before leaving the ninth century one other record must be noted. In his life of St Amandus (written about 850) Milo,[7] a pious monk, describes an encounter of his hero with an entertainer who was popularly known as Mimmus, or Mimus. " An idle, light, evilly deceitful, and proud fellow " is this one, " who whispers insulting jests basely and obscenely and rightly called by the people by the name of Mimmus."

Some of the quotations given above belong in date to the tenth century. While the survey is stopped at this point, it must not be supposed that there appears any sudden break in the record. The documents already cited seem to prove the continuance of mimic entertainment up to the year 1000, and beyond that period the Church councils continue fulminating, the Church authorities continue to utter their dismal warnings concerning the iniquities of the *histriones*, the *mimi*, and the *scurræ*. With these, however, are now named the *ioculatores*, or *jongleurs*, as well as the *Goliardi*, or *scholares vagantes*, the wandering scholars. All are grouped together in one general class, and there necessarily arises here a serious question : When religious writers of these later times use the words *histriones* and *mimi* do they really imply what we know now as ' actors,' what the Romans knew, what the Greeks knew ? Has the old mimic repertory disappeared, and are these writers merely using ancient terms to describe vagrant ballad-singers and leaders of trained animals ? Have the words *histriones* and *mimi* any serious dramatic significance ?

As we have seen, the orthodox answer to this question is that the old mimic drama, as known in the third century A.D., completely disappeared in the Dark Ages, so that no connexion may be traced between the mime of Latinus and the entertainments later given by the medieval *jongleurs*. It must, therefore, be our first endeavour to estimate how far there is evidence for the existence during the Middle Ages of a genuinely secular drama, and to form some sort of conception of what was intended when the writers of that period spoke of *histriones*, *mimi*, and *jongleurs*. In other words, we must try to find whether there are any records of a comic drama between the period

---

[1] *Epist.* cclxxxi.
[2] " Melius est Deo placere quam histrionibus, pauperum habere curam quam mimorum " (*Epist.* xxii).
[3] " Melius est pauperes edere de mensa tua quam istriones." *Cf.* Reich, i, 795.   [4] See *supra*, p. 147.
[5] " Histriones, mimos turpissimosque et vanissimos joculares " (*Opera*, Leyden, 1677, p. 301).
[6] " Themilici, scurri et mimi " (Theganus, *Vita Hludowici imperatoris*, in *Monumenta Germaniæ historica* (Hanover, 1826 f.), ii, 595).
[7] *Monumenta Germaniæ historica* ; *poetæ latini*, iii, 600.

when the Roman mime is thought to vanish and the time when the Renascence brought with it the *commedia dell' arte* and a new vernacular literary comedy.[1]

Fig. 101. Medieval Actors

Miniatures from a copy of Goffredi de Trano's *Decretalen* (early thirteenth century) in the Studien-Bibliothek, Salzburg (VI, E. 55). These may not represent actors, but the lively attitudes, together with the dress, seem to indicate a stage connexion. The phallus in the first figure seems characteristic.

(ii) THE SECULAR DRAMA OF THE MIDDLE AGES

Up to the ninth century, as has been seen, there is evidence of the continuity in the mimic tradition. In the Eastern Empire the mimes are still flourishing; in the West they are, on occasion, borrowing vestments from the cathedrals and the churches. From all sides come the records of the ' jests ' of the buffoons, who were still patronized as of old, while the faithful went in poverty. And here we must pause in order to give careful attention to the significance which is to be attached

---

[1] Obviously some of the records already cited do indicate the existence of such a secular dramatic activity, but these in themselves would not be sufficient on which to found any general theory.

to the medieval names given to these entertainers. As has been indicated, we may either believe that the *mimi* who are mentioned so frequently after the tenth century were true actors or determine that the meaning of the word *mimus* has utterly changed, the ' mime ' of later years having nothing to do with his Roman ancestor.

THE JOCULATORES OR JONGLEURS

In his *Polycraticus* (twelfth century) John of Salisbury [1] has a typical attack on the race of entertainers. Probably through his reading of classical literature rather than through his knowledge of actual amusements in this kind, he presents a formidable array of evil professions, including mimes, parasites, gladiators, wrestlers, and jugglers, describing the whole group as " the general stage of the *ioculatores* " (*tota ioculatorum scena*). Evidently for this author, and for his contemporaries, *ioculator*, whether in its Latin or in its vernacular forms, was a general term for entertainer of any kind, and consequently it is of this word first that we must study the exact significance. The word *ioculator* occurs in classical Latin, but there apparently only as an adjective. It is still used in this way by Firmicus Maternus in the middle of the fourth century—*histriones*, . . . *pantomimos, ac scænicos ioculatores,* " actors . . . pantomimes, and jesting players," [2] but some time in the course of the Dark Ages it acquired its substantive force, so that Agobard in the ninth century could speak of " basest mimes and idlest of jesters " (*mimos turpissimosque et vanissimos ioculares*).[3] In Agobard *mimus* and *ioculator* (or *iocularis*) are clearly connected, and we must proceed to inquire how far the *ioculator* was regarded by contemporaries as being theatrical. In origin the word reminds us of the familiar Greek γελωτοποιός or μῖμος γελοίων, and may well have arisen through an attempt at direct translation of these terms, and as we pass through the centuries we realize that *ioculator, histrio*, and *mimus* become almost synonymous, while the stage significance is being constantly referred to. The early glosses provide much information. *Istriones sunt ioculatores* (" Actors are jongleurs "), says definitely a gloss in a Bibliothèque Nationale manuscript,[4] and this is amply supported by other similar identifications. The word *mimi* is elsewhere translated as *ioculares*, and *scenici* is given as *histrionis ioculares*.[5] The glosses show, moreover, that the idea of the stage is regularly present. *Scenicus* and *mimus* are identified ; *histrio* is the equivalent of *mimo [sic] scenicus* ; while the explanations of *histriones* as *saltatores scenici* and as *saltatores* remind us of ancient dancing in the mimes and pantomimes. It is interesting to notice, too, that *scena* in a Vatican codex is described as a " place in the theatre or a mimic play " (*theatri locus aut ludus mimicus*). The later councils also treat the terms as practically synonymous. Thus the Concilium Lateranum of 1215 refers to " mimes, jongleurs, and actors " (*mimis, ioculatoribus, et histrionibus*) [6] together ; at the wedding of Agnes de Poitou in 1043 Henri III dismissed the entertainers, so that " an infinite multitude of actors and *jongleurs* " (*infinitam multitudinem histrionum et ioculatorum*) had to go away hungry.[7] This stage association of the word *jongleur* is to be found, too, even in vernacular

---

[1] i, 8 (J. P. Migne, *op. cit.*, Series Latina, cxcix, col. 406).

[2] *Matheseos*, viii, 22 (see Chambers, ii, 230, and Reich, i, 807).

[3] *Liber de dispensatione*, in J. P. Migne, *op. cit.*, Series Latina, civ, col. 249. On the *ioculatores* and *jongleurs* see Edmond Faral, *Les Jongleurs en France au moyen âge* (Paris, 1910; *Bibliothèque de l'école des hautes études*, clxxxvii) ; Freymond, *Jongleurs und Menestrels* (Halle, 1883) ; Chambers, ii, 230-233; Adolfo Bonilla y San Martín, *Los Bacantes o del origen del teatro* (Madrid, 1921), pp. 57-68 ; Gaetano Bonifacio, *Giullari e uomini di corte nel Dugento* (Naples, 1907); Ferdinando Gabotto, *La Epopea del buffone* (Bra, 1893 : per nozze Manzone-Ricca); V. de Bartholomæis, *Un mimo giullaresco del Dugento : il "Contrasto" di Cielo* (*Rivista d' Italia*, xxv (1922), 3, March 15) and *Le origini della poesia drammatica italiana* (Bologna, 1924); Luigi Torri, *I buffoni* (*Emporium*, xvii (1903), 362-381); F. Nick, *Die Hof- und Volks Narren* (Stuttgart, 1861); J. P. Jacobsen, *La Comédie en France au moyen-âge* (*Revue dephilologie française et de littérature*, xxiii (1909), 96-106). For comparison see Vittorio Cian, *Un Buffone del secolo XVI. Fra Mariano Fetti* (Milan, 1891) ; R. Renier, *Buffoni, nani e schiavi dei Gonzaga ai tempi d' Isabella d' Este* (*Nuova Antologia*, Ser. III, xxxiv, 618-650, and xxxv, 112-146); F. Giorgi, *Un Buffone degli Anziani di Bologna nel secolo xv* (*L' Archiginnasio*, xxiv (1929), 1-3).

[4] B.N. MS. 4883[a], f. 67[b] (see É. du Méril, *Origines latines du théâtre moderne* (Paris, 1849), p. 23).

[5] Probably intended for *histriones, ioculares*. See Reich, i, 447-448.   [6] Canon xvi.   [7] Reich, i, 798.

glosses. Thus the *Promptorium Parvolorum* of 1440 identifies the words 'bordyoure,' 'pleyere,' and *ioculator*.[1]

Now, without the possible shadow of a doubt, the majority of these *ioculatores* (with whom, as has been seen, the *mimi* and *histriones* are commonly identified) were nothing but ballad-singers and makers of romances. The *jongleur* was the popular poet of the time, and there are many who therefore believe that the *tota ioculatorum scena* was nothing but a bevy of Court and popular minstrels who had never known aught of scenic artistry. If anything different is to be proved, then we must discover some evidence which indicates activity on their part distinct from those of singing and ballad-making. That they did not all belong to one class is proved at once by an interesting description written by Thomas de Chabham, Sub-Dean of Salisbury, about the year 1213. "There are three kinds of *histriones*," he says :

> Some transform and transfigure their bodies with indecent dance and gesture, now indecently un-clothing themselves, now putting on horrible masks. . . . There are, besides, others who have no definite profession, but act as vagabonds, not having any certain domicile ; these frequent the Courts of the great and say scandalous and shameful things concerning those who are not present so as to delight the rest. . . . There is yet a third class of *histriones* who play musical instruments for the delectation of men, and of these there are two types. Some frequent public drinking-places and lascivious gatherings, and there sing stanzas to move men to lasciviousness. Besides these there are others, who are called *jongleurs*, who sing of the gestes of princes and the lives of the saints.[2]

It is clear from this that Thomas de Chabham recognizes four main groups of entertainers, whom he calls *histriones*—(1) the common ballad-singers, the 'crowders' of Elizabethan times ; (2) the makers of romances, whether secular or religious ; (3) the satirists ; and (4) those who dance, gesticulate, vary their costumes, and wear masks. Obviously it is among the last two classes, if anywhere, that we must seek for the descendants of the Roman mimic players.

In attempting to determine how far these are to be found, an investigation along the lines suggested in Thomas de Chabham's definition may not be inconvenient. If, that is to say, we are able to display evidence of action (for action is an inherent part of drama), of costuming, and of the utilization of masks on the part of the *jongleurs*, we can certainly proceed to the deduction that a regular line of 'theatrical' continuity existed throughout the whole of the medieval period.

At the start of this inquiry it is important to observe that Hugutius, in identifying *mimus* and *ioculator* in his *Liber derivationum*,[3] says that this person was "an imitator of human things," ex-plaining that when the reciter of comedy uttered his words the *mimi ioculatores* "expressed the action by bodily movement." Now, this elucidation itself depends upon a peculiar medieval misconception of the classical stage, but the very misconception helps to throw light on the question we are considering. When the idea arose we do not know, but at some period after the Roman theatres were disused in the West the opinion became prevalent that when Terence brought forward his comedies he, as poet, or a friend of his, *recited* the 'poem' while a number of actors below provided suitable accompanying mimicry. The "reciter friend" was the more popular of the two among medieval writers, and several manuscripts of the Terentian comedies have small illumina-tions which profess to show him at his task.[4] Hugutius, then, adopts the current view, but whom does he describe as *acting* the play ? None but the *mimi ioculatores*. Had he used merely the word

---

[1] 'Bordyoure' literally means 'player.' Chambers (ii, 185) takes this last reference as proving the non-dramatic character of the *ioculator*. So far as 'pleyere,' however, indicates entertainment of at least a semi-dramatic kind, it appears to indicate a connexion in the mind of the fifteenth-century compiler with the art of acting. One may note here the presence of an official 'spelar' at the Court of James IV of Scotland (J. Mill, *Medieval Plays in Scotland* (St Andrews, 1921), p. 39). 'Spelar' is evidently a variant of the German *Spieler* (L.G. *speler*).

[2] Chambers, ii, 262–263. On this passage see Helen F. Rubel, *Chabham's Penitential and its Influence in the XIII Century* (*Publications of the Modern Language Association of America*, xl (1925), 225–239).

[3] See Max Hermann, *Forschungen zur deutschen Theatergeschichte* (Berlin, 1914), pp. 287–288.

[4] On the associated idea concerning the classical stage arrangements see *infra*, pp. 153–157. On Calliopius see Abel Jenö, *Az ó-és középkori Terentiusbiographiák* (Budapest, 1887; *Kiadja a Magyar Tudomanyos Akadémia*, xiv, 1), 20–21.

mimi, we might have assumed that he was relying on his classical knowledge, but when he unites that word to *ioculatores*, to the *jongleurs* who were the entertainers of his own time, surely we must believe that he knew his readers would understand the significance of his explanation. They could not have understood had the twelfth-century *jongleurs* been only ballad-singers and poets; the interpretation presupposes the existence of a body of *ioculatores* who were " imitators of human things " in a dramatic way.

THE TERENCE CODICES

Of prime importance in connexion with this note of Hugutius is an illustration (Fig. 102) in a manuscript of Terence preserved in the Arsenal Library in Paris. The bottom portion of this picture shows the poet presenting a copy of his book to a friend. This is of no real interest. Above, however, is a picture which illustrates, or essays to illustrate, a performance of one of the comedies. In an amphitheatrical enclosure, marked *theatrum* so that there shall be no mistake, are seated a number of spectators. In the middle, with an open copy of the play before him, is seated Calliopius, the poet's " friend," reciting, and immediately in front of him are gesticulating four grotesque figures who are clearly labelled *joculatores*. Each of these characters has his own interest. To the left is seen a hunchbacked actor in a pale blue coat, yellow tights, and a green cape. He is wearing a yellow mask, the most prominent feature of which is a long hooked nose, and on his head is set a red peaked cap, the tip of which falls forward slightly. This person holds up his left hand to the central figure, who, clad mainly in yellow but with mauve tights, sports a mask with a long, straight nose and a red and mauve peaked cap of a different shape from that of his companion. His mask is green, and his costume is ornamented apparently with bells. The third actor is certainly adorned with bells; he wears a light blue mask, reminding us of nothing so much as the face of a modern circus clown. His coat is blue, girded with a brown belt, his tights are green, and his cap, also of the peaked variety, is brown with a red tip. Turned round with his back to us is the last of the quartette. His arms are naked, and he seems to be wearing a brown costume; his hat, pointed like that of the others, is bluish brown. A very similar title-page appears in another codex of Terence in the Bibliothèque Nationale (Fig. 103), where three *jongleurs* are shown. The left-hand figure here has a yellow mask and is clad in brown. He in the middle who holds both his hands on his stomach has a mauvish pink dress, with a green mask; while the right-hand actor is adorned with a blue coat, yellow-brown trousers, and a mask.[1]

At first one might suggest that these figures belonged to some conventional tradition in miniature-painting, but here other Terence manuscripts come to our aid. An examination of these points to two main models among the miniaturists. The first of these, and the earliest, is best represented in the famous Vatican Terence (Cod. lat. 3868).[2] Here the illustrations, which modern research has identified as ninth-century work by a certain Adelricus,[3] are unquestionably based on some lost original made at a time when the comedies were still being presented on the Roman stage.[4] The miniatures, therefore, while they cast important light on the typical masks used in the classic theatres, have no value in so far as the medieval stage is concerned (Fig. 104).

[1] For assistance in the description of these illustrations I have to thank M. S. Chapiro. See H. Martin, *Le Térence des Ducs* (Paris, 1907).
[2] Four MSS. come from a common early source—Vaticanus 3868, Parisinus 7899, Ambrosianus H 75 inf., and Dunelmensis Auct. F 2, 13, in the Bodleian, Oxford. The first of these in date seems to be the Vaticanus. See O. Engelhardt, *Die Illustrationen der Terenzhand-schriften* (Jena, 1905); Karl E. Weston, *The Illustrated Terence Manuscripts* (*Harvard Studies in Classical Philology*, xiv (1903), 37–54); John Calvin Watson, *The Relation of the Scene-headings to the Miniatures in Manuscripts of Terence* (*Harvard Studies in Classical Philology*, xiv (1903), 55–172); H. W. Lawton, *Térence en France au xvie siècle* (Paris, 1926). The Parisinus and Ambrosianus are reproduced in the *Album Terentianum*, edited by Iacobus van Wageningen (Groningen, 1907); the former appears in facsimile in the Bibliothèque Nationale *Comédies de Térence* (Paris, 1907).
[3] See C. R. Morey, *The Signature of the Miniaturist of the Vatican Terence* (*Philologische Wochenschrift*, xlvi (1926), No. 32, col. 879–880). He shows that the manuscript contains the signature of the artist (*Adelricus me fecit*), whom he identifies with an Aldricus who was a contemporary of the known scribe, Hrodgarius, a monk at Corvey.
[4] See C. Robert, *Die Masken der neueren attischen Komödie* (Halle, 1911), pp. 88–96.

Fig. 102. MEDIEVAL MIMES

Frontispiece to a codex of Terence in the Arsenal Library, Paris (Cod. lat. Ars. 664).

Photo Giraudon

Fig. 103. MEDIEVAL MIMES

Frontispiece to a codex of Terence in the Bibliothèque Nationale, Paris (Cod. lat. 7907 a).

Photo Giraudon

Fig. 104. A Scene from Terence

Miniature in a *Terence* (Bibliothèque Nationale, MS. Latin 7899). From the facsimile in the *Comédies de Térence*. *Réproduction du MS. latin* 7899 (Bibliothèque
Nationale, Paris), Plate XII.

Fig. 105. A Scene from Terence's "Andria" (I, v)

Miniature from Cod. Ars. 664, as reproduced in Max Hermann, *Forschungen zur
deutschen Theatergeschichte des Mittelalters und der Renaissance* (Berlin, Weidmannsche Buchhandlung, 1914), Fig. 19.

The second group of manuscripts may be regarded as entirely imaginative. In these the illuminator draws fancy pictures of characters in medieval garments and, most frequently, in medieval settings.

As illustrations here may be taken a scene from the *Andria* as represented in an Arsenal manuscript (Fig. 105) and the title-page to a manuscript of the *Hercules furens* of Seneca (Fig. 106). The latter shows the *poeta* in the middle reading the play, while the *populus expectans* watch the actions of the characters, chief of whom is a monstrous, beast-like Hercules.

So soon as we compare this last example with the Arsenal picture we realize the vast measure of difference which separates the two. In the latter is a delineation, probably realistic, of the *ioculatores* of the medieval period, indulging in their " imitation of human things."

DRAMATIC ACTIVITIES OF THE JONGLEURS

The evidence supplied by Hugutius and by this miniature may be supplemented from other sources. The class of *jongleurs* who were 'imitators' seems to have been well known. In Provence, when Guirant Riquier, the troubadour, presented a decree to King Alfonso of Castile, the *contrafazens*, or *contrafazedors*, were included as a distinct class.[1] Even if we were to doubt the authenticity (although there is no real reason to do so) of the description of fourteenth-century *histriones* who are said to have " represented the customs of English and Bretons,"[2] we possess the account, in an old French fable,[3] of how a group of *jongleurs* come to make the public merry and of how, amid the juggling and the acrobatic tricks

Fig. 106. A SCENE FROM SENECA'S " HERCULES FURENS "

Miniature from Cod. lat. Urbin 355, as reproduced in Max Hermann, *Forschungen zur deutschen Theatergeschichte des Mittelalters und der Renaissance* (Berlin, Weidmannsche Buchhandlung, 1914), Fig. 17.

---

[1] Creizenach, i, 380. For a largely sceptical judgment on these matters see Anton Glock, *Über den Zusammenhang des römischen Mimus und einer dramatischen Tätigkeit mittelalterlicher Spielleute mit dem neueren komischen Drama* (*Zeitschrift für vergleichende Litteraturgeschichte*, N.F. xvi (1906), 39–45).

[2] This reference is cited by G. Cibrario in his *Della Economia politica del medio evo* (Turin, 1839, p. 233) as from *Conti dei tresorieri generali di Savoia nel secolo xiv*. Unfortunately no other scholar has seen this document.

[3] *Du vilain au buffet*, l. 142 (in A. Montaiglon, *Recueil général et complet des fabliaux des xiiie et xive siècles* (Paris, 1872–90), iii, lxxv, 204). Cf. *Flamenca*, ll. 603 ff.

and the dancing, " some act the drunkard, and others the fool " (*l'uns fet l'ivre, l'autres le sot*). This certainly seems to imply some form of dramatic representation. The same suggestion of dramatic representation is provided in Bretel's poem *Tournois de Chauvenci*,[1] in which an account is given of after-dinner entertainments :

> After the wine they had their sports and tried who best could counterfeit the monk, the hermit, the pilgrim, the peasant, and the roysterer.

Bufoni et mimi are certainly described as giving some form of show in the *theatrum* at Milan in 1288,[2] and in the twelfth century, as we have seen, mimes were in the habit of using ecclesiastical raiment, no doubt as a kind of stage dress.[3]

This entirely agrees with a notice in the *Dolopathos* [4] which describes an entertainer " trying to imitate what he has seen and heard, indulging in representative comic gesture and modulating his voice " (*gestus comicos repræsentat, frangit verba*). It is to be noted in this connexion that no medieval authority, so far as I am aware, has drawn any distinction between the *histrio* of his classical reading and the *histrio* of his own time. Typical are the words of Johannes de Janua in his *Catholicon* under the word *persona* :

> A character [*persona*] is called an actor [*histrio*], the representator in comedy, who in diverse ways impersonates various characters through representation.

There is no suggestion here that the word *histrio*, as commonly used in that period, had any other significance. Finally, before we pass from this difficult subject of nomenclature, a word may be said concerning the accompanying term, *mimus*. Already, in the ninth century, we have encountered an actor who was named Mimmus [5] and who was so called, no doubt, because of his profession. Now, it is certainly peculiar, to say the least, to find among the medieval French farces a *Maistre Mimin*, a *Maistre Mimin le Gouteux*, and a *Testament de Maître Mimin*, together with a person of the same name in *Les trois Pélerins* (Mymin).[6] It is always dangerous to juggle with etymology, but it would certainly appear as if the word is here being used as a stage-name, just as character-titles were employed as stage-names in Roman days, and just as a Martinelli in the seventeenth century was known by no other name save that of Arlecchino. In this connexion the early Spanish drama provides some interesting parallels. Among the manifold types of *juglares* there appear those called *remedadores* or *momos*, who counterfeited the actions and words of others. These *momos* wore *falsos visajes*, or masks, and in 1513 the *momo contrahazedor* was referred back to the Latin *mimus*. Whether this derivation be correct or no, the fact remains that these men were mimes of a sort and that they recited poetry of a dramatic kind with varying inflections and appropriate gestures.[7] Spain, indeed, seems to have retained many features of the old popular drama. The clownish *bobo* of the Hispanic mysteries and farces is suspiciously like the ancient *stupidus*,[8] while in these pieces appear a braggart and a rascally knave of the true mimic nature.[9] Similar entertainments, under virtually the same name—*momarie*—were given in Italy, certainly in the early sixteenth century, probably much earlier.[10] These, in turn, are to be connected with the English ' mummings '

---

[1] L. 4341.

[2] Pio Rajna, *Il Teatro di Milano e i canti intorno ad Orlando e Ulivieri* (*Archivio storico lombardo*, Ser. II, iv (1887), 5–28).

[3] See *supra*, p. 148.   [4] See *Johannis de Alta Silva Dolopathos*, ed. H. Österley (Berlin, 1873), p. 76.

[5] See *supra*, p. 149.

[6] Reich, i, 849–859. Petit de Julleville, *Répertoire du théâtre comique en France au moyen-âge* (Paris, 1886), Nos. 129, 130, 306, 166.

[7] See A. Bonilla y San Martín, p. 60 (reference to *remedeadores* in 1275), pp. 67–68 (specimen of mimic recitation), pp. 84–85 (discussion of word *momo*).

[8] See J. P. Wickersham Crawford, *The Pastor and Bobo in the Spanish Religious Drama of the Sixteenth Century* (*Romanic Review*, ii (1911), 376–401), and A. Bonilla y San Martín, p. 43.

[9] J. P. W. Crawford, *The Braggart Soldier and the Rufián in the Spanish Drama of the Sixteenth Century* (*Romanic Review*, ii (1911), 186–208).

[10] Pompeo Molmenti, *Di un' Antica forma di rappresentazione veneziana* (Venice, 1894), and *Le origini della commedia in Venezia* (*Gazzetta musicale di Milano*, lvi (January 24, 1901), No. 4, 53–56); *Le Lettere di messer Andrea Calmo*, ed. Vittorio Rossi (Turin, 1888), p. xiii.

of which there is record from the fourteenth century.[1] The *New English Dictionary* would derive this word from the verb ' mum ' (' to murmur or keep silence '), but it may be questioned whether that is the true source.   There is a Low German word *Mumme*, meaning ' a mask,' and when we find an ancient glossary explaining *momar* as *siculus stultus, qui cito movetur ad iram* (' a Sicilian fool who is quickly roused to anger '), and quoting in support a phrase from Plautus—*Quid tu o momar sicule homo præsumis*—we may perhaps suspect the existence of another etymology.[2]   At any rate, the English mummings, the Italian *momarie*, and the Spanish *momos* are all shows in which masks were employed, and if there exists not any evidence to show that the early mummings

Fig. 107. Eastern Mimi of the Middle Ages
Fresco at St Sophia, Kiev.   From the Записки императорскаго русскаго археологическаго общества, N.S., iii, 288.

of this country were dialogue plays, dialogue of a kind was certainly present in some of the Continental examples.

All these varied references seem to show that in the West there was a group of *jongleur* entertainers who indulged in some form of mimic activity, that mimic activity involving perhaps (as the Terence illustration appears to suggest) just a touch of the exaggerated and the grotesque. In the Eastern Empire too these mimes evidently flourished.   Some time during the eleventh century a certain Michael Psellos was lamenting that his son-in-law, in spite of his marriage oath, in spite of his patrician rank, was spending all his time with the mimic actors and the players of farces.[3]   A century later Zonaras mentions both the performers and the theatres as being in regular use.[4]   In commenting on the Trullan canons he describes " the mimes, who imitate now Arabians, now Armenians, and now slaves, stirring up unseemly merriment by their slaps on the face and by their utterances."   From them he turns to the pantomime.   " The canon," he declares,

[1] Chambers, i, 393-396.
[2] P. Toldo, *Études sur le théâtre de Regnard* (*Revue d'Histoire littéraire de la France*, x (1903), 40), connects the word *momarie* with Momus, and suggests a Germanic origin, producing the German *Mummerei* and the English ' mummery.'   It is interesting to note that the Arabians had a word *mūmisa* and that *momos* appears in Hebrew, both used for mimic entertainments; see Josef Horovitz, *Spuren griechischer Mimen im Orient* (Berlin, 1905), pp. 77-90.   These seem definitely connected with μῖμος.
[3] See Reich, i, 166, referring to Sathas, Μεσαιωνικὴ Βιβλιοθήκη, v, 206, 209.
[4] See Reich, i, 134.

condemns the dancers on the stage [ἐπὶ σκηνῆς]. The stage is falsehood and hypocrisy, whence the actors are called hypocrites [ὑποκρινόμενοι]; they pretend they are slaves or masters or soldiers or magistrates. Just as the canon condemned these things through the mimes, so it condemned also the stage dancing, whether through men who behave indecently in their dancing or through women who incite the spectators to licentious thoughts.

Several hundred years after this date, when Manuel Palæologus came to the Court of Sultan Bajazet, he found there " crowds of mimes, whole bodies of instrumentalists, choirs of singers, and tribes of dancers." [1] Constantinople and the East had remained true to the mimic tradition. Pictorial evidence aids us here too. A series of eleventh-century frescoes in the cathedral of St Sophia at Kiev shows a number of scenes of a secular kind. In one the Emperor and Empress are gazing down on sports of the hippodrome; in others various *histriones* ply their trade. In Fig. 107 some of these are shown. To the right are a couple of acrobats. In the centre an orchestra (which includes one woman) is making music, while some of its members are dancing. Besides these there are five figures who might well be taking part in a play. One of them, it may be noted, has a peaked cap the tip of which falls slightly backward. If they are not taking part in an actual farce it is difficult to interpret their actions satisfactorily.

THE MEDIEVAL FOOL

What these mimes played will have to be considered in a moment; at present we must still consider the physical actors and their appearance before the spectators—and first their costume. Naturally, in any play costumes vary with the characters, but in the Roman mime we discovered one stock dress, that of the comic fool, a dress known as the *centunculus*. In the tenth century Liudprand was found commenting on a motley costume worn by a potentate in Constantinople and remarking on its likeness to a mime's dress, and the implication raised by this comment is substantiated by another made in the twelfth century by Johannes Signiensis in his *Vita s. Berardi* [2] when, after describing a dress made up of patchwork and mixed colours, he states that this costume " is rightly that of the *jongleurs*." Now, two bodies of entertainers are known to have worn dress of this kind—the Harlequins and the professional fools. The former will, of course, be dealt with in the chapters devoted to the *commedia dell' arte*; the latter, however, being medieval, belong here, and, medieval as they seem, we must consider whether they may not be descendants of ancient jesters. That the Court fool was not unknown in classic times has been amply proved,[3] and this Court fool seems to have been taken over, among other luxuries of Roman civilization, by the Germanic conquerors who broke in on the frontiers of the Empire.[4] There is, then, a direct continuity in the ' profession ' from the days of the Roman emperors down to the time when, with the hand of genius, Shakespeare gave a tragic setting to the poor jesting of the clown. How these fools were dressed is well known. Their costume of patchwork or of mixed colours is familiar to us from productions of Elizabethan dramas; it seems to have been their most noted characteristic. The fraternity of La Mère Folle at Dijon sported red, green, and yellow; [5] but the green and yellow worn by the Enfants-sans-Souci at Paris [6] appear to have been the favourite colours. Perhaps, as some writers believe, they have a symbolic significance—yellow being the colour of gaiety and green that of eternal youth. The costume into which these coloured stuffs

[1] Reich, i, 202. See also J. Horovitz, *Spuren griechischer Mimen im Orient* (Berlin, 1905).

[2] *Acta Sanctorum*, Nov., ii, Pars I, p. 128. [3] See *supra*, p. 108.

[4] The fools have a large literature to themselves. Chambers (i, 372) deals with them in general; and the French fraternities are excellently described by L. Petit de Julleville in *Les Comédiens en France au moyen âge* (Paris, 1885). See also J. Flögel, *Geschichte der Hofnarren* (Liegnitz, 1789); and Reich, i, 820. The last-mentioned draws attention to the presence of a *mimus regis* at the Court of King Miro of Galicia in the sixth century and of *mimici*, who were evidently fools, at the Court of Theodoric the Great.

[5] Petit de Julleville, pp. 195, 203. [6] *Id.*, pp. 146–148.

were made was usually distinguished by the presence of a hood, fitting round the sides of the face and adorned with large asses' ears and a peak, which is normally fashioned like a cock's comb [1] (Figs. 108, 109). Asses' ears, then, and cock's comb are its determining characteristics; but if we turn back to that terra-cotta engraved in Ficoroni's collection (Fig. 60), we find a hood of precisely the same shape, close-fitting to the head, with large, ass-like ears and a falling peak. This might well have been an illustration of a fourteenth-century type, so close is the resemblance. Comparing the two, therefore, it certainly seems probable that there is a close connexion between the one and the other—that the ass-eared hood was a traditional garment passed down from the jesters of Roman times. The peak at the top has likewise its own significance. Already it has been pointed out that the Roman stage fools often wore a pointed *pilos*.[2] Sometimes this is conical in shape and stiffened; sometimes, as in the fool-like person shown in Fig. 59, it falls down loosely over the head. Now, just such loose peaked caps are represented in the pictures of medieval entertainers shown in Figs. 102, 103, 107, and similar caps appear among the dancing entertainers depicted on the sides of the Goldene Dachel in Innsbruck.[3] This building, erected in honour of Maximilian's visit to the city in 1500, shows dancing figures in eight compartments. Some of these, such as the ones illustrated in Figs. 110, 111, are not of particularly outstanding peculiarity, although

Fig. 108. A Medieval Fool

Miniature in Cod. Heldt, fol. 168, as reproduced in Max Hermann, *Forschungen zur deutschen Theatergeschichte des Mittelalters und der Renaissance* (Berlin, Weidmannsche Buchhandlung, 1914), Fig. 14.

they depict well the vivid dances of the time; but when we come to the entertainers shown in Fig. 112 we must pause to examine them carefully. The left-hand compartment here shows a man beating a tabor, to the sound of which an hermaphrodite with long woman's hair is dancing frenziedly. The right-hand relief also depicts two figures. One is a bearded man who wears a cap, the loose peak of which falls over his forehead. The other, who bends backward in acrobatic dance, has a head which is entirely shaven. The combination of these two on this one relief is particularly interesting, for, if the medieval fool wore a hood with a peak, he also was

Fig. 109. Medieval Fools

Miniatures in *Li Romans d'Alixandre* (fourteenth century), Bodleian Library, MS. 264, f. 84 v. From Sir E. K. Chambers, *The Medieval Stage* (Oxford University Press, 1903), i, frontis.

known for his shaven head, or, to be more exact, many of his *jongleur* companions were so known. " He shaved his hair and beard," says Geoffrey of Monmouth [4] of a certain character,

---

[1] Petit de Julleville, p. 147.   [2] See *supra*, pp. 54, 57, 60, 88, and *cf.* Figs. 42, 47, 50.
[3] On the Goldene Dachel see J. Garber (in *Die Kunst in Tirol*, iv), P. M. Halm, *Der Moriskentanz* (in *Bayrischer Heimatschutz, Zeitschrift des bayrischen Landesvereins für Heimatschutz*, xxiii (1927), 138 f.).
[4] *Historia regum Britanniæ*, ix, 1.

" and took up the profession of a *jongleur* with his harp," and others testify to this custom. Cornelius Agrippa [1] speaks of a monk of early times who went about with " his head all shaved like a fool's " (*raso toto capite ut fatui*), while,

Fig. 110. DANCING ENTERTAINERS OF THE
MIDDLE AGES
Relief on the Goldene Dachel, Innsbruck.
Photo R. Müller

Fig. 111. DANCING ENTERTAINERS OF THE
MIDDLE AGES
Relief on the Goldene Dachel, Innsbruck.
Photo. R. Müller

centuries later, in the days of King Robert II of France, we are told that " sets of idle vagabonds, up to all sorts of mischief, began to flock [to the Court]—strange of manner and dress, disordered in raiment and saddlery, their heads and beards shaved in the fashion of the *histriones*." [2] " Just look at that apostle! " cries a character in a French mystery.[3] " He is shaved like a fool! " (*Mez regardez quel apostol! Il est tondu comme ung fol.*) These shaven heads, then, were a characteristic feature of the *jongleurs* and fools of the medieval period, and at Innsbruck the bald-head is set in conjunction with the peaked cap, one of the other characteristics of the Roman mimic fool. It seems hard to believe that there is not here a very definite sign of direct connexion between the one and the other.

The bald-head makes his appearance twice in the Innsbruck reliefs; for once more he is shown dancing with a companion (Fig. 113), who this time, however, wears a peakless hat. Should we wish for another illustration, we have but to go to Alexander Barclay's translation of Brant's *Narrenschiff* (1509), *The Ship of Fools*. There (Fig. 114) the fool who has thrown back his hood shows a head tonsured like that of a monk.

Fig. 112. DANCING ENTERTAINERS OF THE MIDDLE
AGES
Relief on the Goldene Dachel, Innsbruck.
Photo R. Müller

[1] *De vanitate scientiarum*, lxii.
[2] Reich, i, 817, quoting from *Glabri Radulphi Historiarum*, IV, ix (in Duchesne, *Historiæ Francorum scriptores*, iv, pp. 38c, 39a).
[3] M. L. A. Jubinal, *Mystères inédits* (Paris, 1837), i, 78.

162

Besides the peak cap and the asses' ears, which the medieval fool shared with his Roman predecessors, there is also the cock's comb. That cock's comb often takes the place of the loose top of the cowl-like hood; but, whatever shape it takes and however it is arranged, it is always associated with the fool of the Middle Ages. At once our minds revert to the cock type in the Roman mime. Again, it is strange, to say the least, to find that there is a correspondence in conception between some of the ancient mimic actors and this fool character of later times. More will have to be said of the cock type later, in discussing the *commedia dell' arte*; for the present it is sufficient to note this undoubtedly strange correspondence.

In the same connexion we may well pause for a moment to consider a series of miniatures which occur in a thirteenth-century manuscript preserved in the town library of Salzburg (Fig. 101).

These may be mere grotesques and have nothing to do with the theatre; on the other hand, their attitudes, particularly those of the pair in the bottom row, have an undoubted appearance of histrionism. It is to be observed that one of the figures is a bald-head, another has long ass's ears like the medieval fool, while several wear peaked caps recalling both the caps of the Roman mimes and those of Renascence Pulcinelli. Furthermore, one of these peaked-cap

Fig. 113. DANCING ENTERTAINERS OF THE MIDDLE AGES
Relief on the Goldene Dachel, Innsbruck.
Photo R. Müller

persons wields an instrument which is suspiciously like a wooden *batte*. By far the most important feature of these miniatures, however, is the fact that the first character represented is plainly phallephoric. Now, the Roman mimes, as we have seen, freely used the leather phallus in their performances, and when we reach pictorial illustration of the *commedia dell' arte* in the sixteenth century we find that once more the phallus is an indecent feature of the actors' attire. Hitherto no certain connecting link between the old and the new has been found, but, in view of the fact that medieval art hardly ever indicates this phallic symbol, may it not be regarded here as definitely connected with a stage type of the secular kind? These Salzburg miniatures are given in this volume in full recognition that they may not be absolutely sure evidence relating to the theatre; their inherent interest, however, seemed to demand their inclusion, seemed to demand, too, the tentative suggestion that in them we may have portraits of the *mimi* of the thirteenth century.

In a way they have taken us from that with which we were mainly concerned in this section—the medieval fool; but it is indeed difficult to make any hard and fast distinction between the fool as such and the *histrio*. It is thus by no means unfair to discuss the fool in relation to medieval secular drama, for in many ways these fools touched upon the theatre. Quite apart from their joyous association with such festivals as the Feast of the Fools and the Feast of the Ass, which have at least some bearing on the medieval stage,[1] their associations, or guilds, took a not inconsiderable part in the preservation and development of a comic spirit during the later Middle Ages. These guilds, or associations, flourished particularly in France, and many records testify to their

[1] See Chambers, i, 275–377.

163

activities.[1] Calling themselves by various names—Abbé des Foux, Abbaye Joyeuse, Enfants-sans-Souci, Connards—they provided merriment in many a Gallic town, and although it is perhaps difficult to assert that out of their efforts arose the new comic theatre of the Renascence, the statement may be hazarded that in them was retained something of the ancient secular spirit and that from them the ' new ' theatre took some of its ideas and some of its most familiar elements ; or, to express this in another way, that the classic mime tradition which seems to have had a continuity throughout the medieval period produced, among other comic forms, the activities which are associated with the *confréries des foux*. In the course of centuries a tradition may branch and spread like the branches of a tree ; one of these branches of the *moros* or *mimus calvus* tradition is to be found in the fool of the Middle Ages.

The descripcion of a wyse man.

Fig. 114. MEDIEVAL FOOLS

From *The Ship of Fools* (translated by Alexander Barclay, reprinted by William Paterson, Edinburgh, 1874), ii, 273.

RECORDS OF THE MIMI

So far we have seen (1) that there is ample evidence to prove that some of the *jongleurs* indulged in " imitation of human things," and (2) that certain features of Roman mimic stage costume are to be found reproduced in the costumes of the *jongleurs* or of their companions, the fools. On occasion these *jongleurs* also used another element of a classical stage performance—the mask. In discussing this matter it must be borne in mind that, while many of the Roman mimes undoubtedly dispensed with the use of the mask, the influence of the *fabula Atellana* and of the *pantomimus*—both mask-using forms of entertainment—can be traced up to a late period in the Dark Ages. We may take it for certain that, both on the stage and in popular celebrations of the type of the Kalendæ, the use of masks of various sorts was well known at the time when darkness begins to descend on the theatre. When we approach once more the period of light in the twelfth century we discover that just such masks were in common use. Sometimes they were employed, as the Terence miniature shows us (Fig. 102), for purposes of professional entertainment by the *jongleurs* ; sometimes they were worn during seasons of common merriment in " disguisings " or " mummings." In the middle of the thirteenth century Étienne de Bourbon in his *Anecdotes historiques* [2] speaks of *ioculatores* " who sport painted faces [*facies depictas*], which are called in French ' artifices ' (*artificia*), with which they play and delude men." [3] These masks were worn regularly at the Feasts of the Fools and were vigorously condemned ; [4] some were

---

[1] On this subject see Petit de Julleville, *op. cit.*
[3] With a pun on *ludunt* (' play ') and *deludunt* (' delude ').

[2] Ed. Lecoy de la Marche in *Société de l'histoire de France*, sec. 279.
[4] See Chambers, i, 327 and 391.

164

"bearded, horned, like devils"[1] (*larvas barbatas, cornutas, dæmonibus consimiles*), others like the heads of animals (*capita bestiarum*).[2] In the fourteenth century "viseres," both human and animal in form, were worn at the *ludi domini regis*.[3] The amateur use of masks, however, does not concern us, except in so far as that use may be traced in origin to classic pagan festival; but there is ample record besides of the employment of these *larvæ* ('masks') by the *jongleurs* and by the players of medieval mystery dramas. At the beginning of the fifteenth century Henri, Bishop of Nantes,[4] prohibited "mimes and *jongleurs*" from using "grotesque masks" (*monstra larvarum*), while Innocent III three hundred years before[5] referred to the introduction during secular spectacles of these "grotesque masks." The *jongleurs*, then, use masks of various kinds and masks are worn by the people during special times of joyous abandon; masks too, as will be seen, are worn

Fig. 115. ANIMAL MASKS IN THE MIDDLE AGES
Miniature from *Li Romans d'Alixandre* (Bodleian, 264), f. 21 v.

in the performance of the mystery plays. It may be shown also that the employment of *larvæ* is a thing strictly condemned all through the medieval period, the condemnations themselves proving a continuity of tradition. Yet another link in the chain joining the new and the old seems to have been forged.

Before passing to an examination of such relics of the secular play as are extant for our inspection, we may summarize the evidence which so far has come to our hands. A continuance of 'imitation' (the mime idea), a continuance of a fool tradition, with certain definite costume peculiarities, and the continuity in the use of masks—all of these lead us to believe that at least

Fig. 116. MEDIEVAL TUMBLERS
Miniature from J. Strutt, *The Sports and Pastimes of the People of England* (1833), p. 212.

some of the myriads of *jongleurs* with whom the Middle Ages are filled inherited part of the ancient mimic tradition. Dancing, gesticulating, they crowd in upon us, those *jongleurs* and those mimes. "The King's Court," says Peter of Blois regarding Henry II of England, "The King's Court is pestered with *histriones*, laundresses, gamesters, perfumiers, hucksters, rascals, mimes, and barbers."[6] *Histriones* and mimes attended Charles IV of France in 1356;[7] in 1324 there was a "multitude of *histriones*" (*multitudo histrionum*) at a festival held at Ariminum; when Galeazzo Visconti married the daughter of the Marchese d'Este (Beatrice) in Milan, "more than 700 good loaves were given to the *ioculatores*." Some monarchs, such as Philip August II of France, preferred to dispense their money to the poor; but laments from scholar poets on the

---

[1] L. Stoppato, p. 31.
[2] *Id.*, p. 31. These animal masks have, of course, a long ancestry; R. R. Marett, *Anthropology* (1912), suggests that the cave-drawings in Spain which show men with animal heads may represent masked dancers. See Alcade del Rio, *Las Pinturas y grabados de las cavernas prehistóricos de la provincia de Santander* (Santander, 1906), pp. 22–23.
[3] Chambers, i, 392.
[4] See E. Martène, *Thesaurus novus anecdotorum* (Paris, 1717), iv, col. 993.
[5] On this subject see Creizenach, i, 383.
[6] *Epist.*, xiv (in J. P. Migne, *op. cit.*, Series Latina, ccvii, col. 49).
[7] For this and the following references see Reich, i, 798–801.

twelfth century. In the former two lovers—a young cavalier and the wife of an old Roman merchant—are made happy; while in the latter a wife persuades her husband that a certain pear-tree is enchanted, makes him ascend it, and lets him look down on a scene of licentious embracing—a story Boccaccio later introduced into the *Decamerone*. It is a husband again who is cheated in the *Babio*,[1] interesting because of its English provenance. The other work of this kind which seems to belong to England, the *Baucis et Thraso*,[2] is certainly more Terentian, introducing the classical Baucis (a bawd), Glycerium (a prostitute), Thraso (a soldier), Davus and Byrrhia (servants), while the *Alda*[3] of Guillaume de Blois seems to go back to a lost Latin rendering of an also lost Menandrian comedy. Strangely enough, however, and in spite of the utilization by the various authors of classical themes and characters, the impression left in the mind after reading these dramatic poems is one rather of unlikeness than of likeness to the plays of Terence and Plautus. Faral is undoubtedly right in viewing these as the parents of the thirteenth-century *fabliau* in the vernacular, but it is to be questioned whether these Latin works themselves are always directly traceable to the classical comedy. *Alda, Baucis et Thraso, Geta,* and *Querolus*—these unquestionably belong in general to this tradition, but what classical comedy gave anything that resembles *Milo, Miles gloriosus, Lydia,* and *Babio?* These, and perhaps individual scenes of the others, seem to belong to another sphere of comic expression. In this connexion there is an interesting document of the early fifteenth century to which attention has recently been drawn. This is the *Comedia Bile*,[4] in dramatic dialogue, which tells how a certain Aristancus and his servant Bila are seated at their meal when they suddenly see approach a wandering *jongleur*, called Episcopus. Hurriedly they put the large fish they are engaged in eating under a footstool. The *jongleur* now enters and sits down to eat, but instead of putting the small fish set before him into his mouth, he starts talking to them. Aristancus is amazed and asks what he is doing. " Oh," says the *jongleur*, " three years ago my father was drowned, and I was just asking these fish whether they hadn't come across him." " And what did they say ? " asks Aristancus. " They couldn't give me any news of him because they are too young and small. They told me to ask their elders who are under the footstool; they might give me a more satisfactory answer." Aristancus, of course, sees that the game is up, and the *jongleur* sets to on the big fish. Now, as Beutler has shown, this is a story almost identical with one told by Athenæus,[5] and, as it seems improbable that the author could have known that Greek work,[6] the suggestion is made that this episode had been handed down by generations of wandering entertainers in their mimic repertory.[7] If this is so, then there seems some considerable justification for believing that the classical literary and the popular mimic strains are both to be traced in some at least of those *comœdiæ elegiacæ* which we have been considering.[8]

---

[1] Ed. Th. Wright, *Early Mysteries* (1838). See also F. Ermini, *Il Babio, commedia latina del secolo XII* (*Atti dell' Accademia degli Arcadi e scritti dei soci*, N.S., XI, i (1927)).

[2] Ed. H. Hagen, in *Jahrbücher für klassische Philologie* (xl (1868)).

[3] Ed. C. Lohmeyer, in *Biblioteca medii ævi teubneriana* (Leipzig, 1892). This was written probably about 1170.

[4] Ed. J. Bolte, in *Hermes* (xxi (1886), 313–318). For the association with mimic themes, and with other pieces of the same period, see Ernst Beutler, *Die Comedia Bile, ein antiker Mimus bei den Gaukiern des 15. Jahrhunderts* (*Germanisch-Romanische Monatsschrift*, xiv (1926), 3–4). Among the ' plays ' of this type note should be made also of the very popular *Liber Pamphili*.

[5] i, 6e–f.

[6] The Codex Marcianus of Athenæus was certainly known in 1423, but was not printed till Aldus brought out his *editio princeps* in 1514.

[7] It may be noted here that the mixture of narrative and dialogue in these *comœdiæ elegiacæ* no doubt depends on the medieval assumption that the Terentian drama was recited and not acted. It is possible that they were given some kind of mimetic expression by those who declaimed them in the Middle Ages. This is discussed in another connexion by Fr. Schumacher in *Les Éléments narratifs de la Passion d'Autun et les indications scéniques du drame médiéval* (*Romania*, xxxvii (1908), 570–593). Émile Roy is inclined to think that the *Comœdia sine nomine* may have been acted (*Études sur le théâtre français du xive et du xve siècle* (Dijon and Paris, 1901; from *Revue bourguignonne de l'enseignement supérieur*, xi, Nos. 3 and 4, pp. cx–cxiv).

[8] There has recently appeared a corpus of these plays, edited by G. Cohen (*La Comédie latine en France au xiie siècle*, Paris, 1931).

FARCES AND INTERLUDES

This conjunction of Terence and the mime is perhaps suggested by one of the earliest and certainly the most interesting of all the texts which throw light on the work of the medieval mimes. This text, written some time between the seventh and the tenth centuries, is called *Terentius et Delusor* (or *persona Delusoris*),[1] and takes the form of a dialogue discussion between the Latin comic dramatist and another. This other, the *Delusor*, or *persona Delusoris*, is to be identified as a player. Thus, in the fifteenth-century *Catholicon Anglicum*[2] the word 'player' is translated as *iocista* (a variant of *ioculator*) and *lusor*, while 'to play' is given as *iocari, ioculari, ludere*, or *dilusare*. The term *Delusor*, therefore, seems to be a regular medieval word for stage-player, and *persona Delusoris* simply signifies 'the character of the stage-player.' The dialogue between the two starts as an argument. Delusor says :

> If you ask who I am I reply : I am better than you. You are old and out of date, I am a strong young fellow. You are a dead trunk, I am a growing and flourishing tree. If you just keep silence, old man, you'll benefit yourself mightily.

This note of disdain, however, soon turns to one of grudging admiration, and by the end of the short piece Terence has conquered. Now, this is certainly not a play, but it looks suspiciously like a prologue for a play, and the whole thing reads as if it were an introduction to a revival of a Terentian comedy. The mime, the *persona Delusoris*, although really he is older than Terence, is the bright young flourishing spark, always up to date, always adapting himself to the needs of the moment, beside whom Terence is dull and grey and old. If this interpretation be the correct one, then we have here ample record of the power of the mimes, and at the same time we have an indication of an attempt, possibly scholarly in character, to revive one of the older Latin literary comedies. Perhaps the *Querolus* and the *Alda* were not so exclusively designed for the closet, after all.

From this prologue transition is easy to the *Interludium de clerico et puella*,[3] or *The Play of a Clerk and a Girl*, written in a Northumbrian dialect of the thirteenth century. Here a Clericus, or Clerk, woos a girl, who sends him bustling out of doors. The Clerk thereupon goes off to an old bawd, Mome Helwis, who, after protesting her religiosity and innocence, will apparently aid him in his attempt. The piece is obviously incomplete, but the story can be made out from the corresponding fables of the *Dame Siriz* type. Its importance cannot be overestimated. Here we have a true remnant of the *jongleur* dramatic tradition in English, and the subject is an 'adultery' subject similar to the lover themes of the Roman mime. Chance has preserved this fragment ; but beside it assuredly must have existed a plentiful repertory of similar pieces in the vernacular. Nor does it stand absolutely alone in extant relics. Edmond Faral has recently drawn attention to the value in this connexion of the mimed monologue.[4] Among them he singles out *Le privilège aux Bretons*,[5] where is presented a conversation between a Breton called Yvon and Le Roi, *La Paix aux Anglais*,[6] where an Englishman describes the rivalry of the French and English kings

---

[1] The text may be found in Chambers (ii, 326–328). The manuscript is in the Bibliothèque Nationale (Cod. lat. 8069). It was first noted by Charles Magnin in his *Fragment d'un comique du septième siècle* (*Bibliothèque de l'École des Chartes*, i (1839–40), 517–534).

[2] Ed. Early English Text Society, 1881.

[3] The text is also given in Chambers (ii, 324–326). It is interesting to note that this is the earliest vernacular dramatic sketch preserved in English. The earliest record of theatrical activities in Italy concerns an apparently secular *magnus Ludus de quodam homine salvatico* at Padua in 1208 (D'Ancona, i, 89).

[4] *Mimes français du xiiie siècle. Contribution à l'histoire du théâtre comique au moyen âge* (Paris, 1910). See also É. Picot, *Le Monologue dramatique* (*Romania*, xv (1886), 358–422; xvi (1887), 438–542; xvii (1888), 207–275); C. M. des Granges, *De scenico soliloquio (gallice monologue dramatique) in nostro medii ævi theatro* (Paris, 1897).

[5] Bibl. Nat. MS. fr. 837. Date between 1236 and 1252.

[6] Bibl. Nat. MS. fr. 837. Date about 1265–70.

and gives a ridiculous account of the latter's council, *Les Dits de l'herberie* and *La Goute en l'aine*,[1] by Rutebeuf and continuators, and *Les deux Bourdeurs ribauds*,[2] wherein two *jongleurs* batter one another with their tongues.

Undoubtedly the *histriones* of the Middle Ages often thus indulged in dramatic monologue, but, as the *Interludium* shows, they did not confine themselves absolutely to solitary impersonation. Of prime importance, too, in this connexion is the thirteenth-century French farce of *Le Garçon et l'aveugle*.[3] This little piece, which belongs to the district of Tournai and cannot be later in date than 1290, introduces a blind old man, who, trading on his infirmity, goes his way invoking alms in the name of God and the saints. Presently he is met by a masterless rogue, one Jeahannet by name; this fellow becomes his servant; but in the end, cheating him by means of his ventriloquial powers, betrays and beats him. The importance of this cynical but vivid playlet rests in the fact that it stands not alone, but is merely the first extant example of the treatment of a theme which carries us through two or three centuries.[4] The blind man and his servant appear during the fourteenth century in the Arras *Passion*, in the *Miracle de Sainte Geneviève*,[5] in the so-called Semur *Passion*,[6] and during the fifteenth century in the *Mystère de la Résurrection*. In one version of the last-mentioned mystery the farcical scene is elaborated by the fact that the youth, Saudret by name, imitates ventriloquially the voice of an English soldier who is guarding the tomb of Christ! Everywhere do we find traces of this story—in the *Mystère de Saint Laurent*, in the play of *Saint-Bernard de Meuthon*, in the *Mystère des Actes des Apôtres*, and in some secular or semi-secular playlets of the sixteenth century. One of these, *L'Aveugle et le boiteux* (1496),[7] is of special importance. This farce does not, it is true, introduce the familiar blind man and his guide, but evidently it belongs to a cognate tradition. The story is told here of the holy St Martin, whose body is causing miracles manifold. Among his townsfolk, however, are a blind man and a paralytic, and these, since they fare quite well on their infirmities, are terrified at the thought of being cured. A procession approaches them bearing St Martin on a litter, so up goes the paralytic on the blind man's back and off they trot—yet not fast enough to escape the train of ecclesiastics and the involuntary curing. If we seek for secularism what could be a more magnificent example?[8]

From the thirteenth century, too, come the playlets of Adam de la Halle (or Adan de le Hale). One of these is *Robin et Marion*,[9] the oldest comic opera extant. Robin and Marion are rustic lovers; a chevalier courts the latter, but is mocked at by her. Returning he beats Robin and seizes Marion, but she pleads so well that he lets her go. To this another writer has attached a kind of 'curtain-raiser' or prologue in the form of *Le Jeu du pélerin*, where the familiar cynical note of the mime is struck. Robin and Marion were stock names of rustic lovers, perhaps not without connexion with Robin Hood and Maid Marian, and this charming pastoral of Adam's is possibly only one example

[1] Bibl. Nat. MS. fr. 837, 1635, 19152.   [2] Bibl. de Berne MS. 354; Bibl. Nat. MS. fr. 837, 19152.

[3] Petit de Julleville, *Répertoire du théâtre comique en France au moyen âge* (Paris, 1886), No. 4. See ed. by Mario Roques (Paris, 1911). *Cf.* Creizenach, i, 397–398.

[4] See Gustav Cohen, *La Scène de l'Aveugle et de son Valet dans le théâtre français du moyen âge* (*Romania*, xli (1912), 346–372). In this essay Cohen favours the view that the secular farce is derived from the religious play, and not *vice versa*.

[5] Where the youth is called Hanequinet.   [6] Where the youth is called Ganimedes.

[7] P. de Julleville, *Répertoire*, No. 12.

[8] On the French farces generally, in addition to the works cited above, see P. Toldo, *La Comédie française de la Renaissance* (*Revue d'histoire littéraire de la France*, iv (1897), 366–384; v (1898), 220–245, 554–572; vi (1899), 571–608; vii (1900), 263–283); J. P. Jacobsen, *Essai sur les origines de la comédie en France au moyen âge* (Paris, 1910); E. du Méril, *Origines latines du théâtre moderne* (Paris, 1849); Eugene Lintilhac, *La Comédie: Moyen âge et Renaissance* (Paris, 1905). Charles Magnin, *Fragment d'un comique du septième siècle* (*Bibliothèque de l'École des Chartes*, i (1839–40), 517–526), supports the view that there was continuity of tradition from Roman times down to the period of the medieval farces. Interesting new material is presented by Paul Aebischer in *Fragments de moralités, farces et mystères retrouvés à Fribourg* (*Romania*, li (1925), 511–527), *Trois Farces inédites trouvées à Fribourg* (*Revue du xvie siècle*, xi (1924), 129–192), and *Quelques Textes du xvie siècle en patois fribourgeois* (*Archivium Romanicum*, iv (1920), 342–361, and vii (1923), 288–336); Ch. Samaran, *Fragments de manuscrits latins et français du moyen âge* (*Romania*, li (1925), 161–202; at pp. 200–202 is given the *Farce de Tripet*). Joachim Rolland has an *Essai bibliographique* dealing with *Le Théâtre comique en France avant le xve siècle* (Paris, 1927). An excellent general study has recently appeared—G. Cohen's *Le Théâtre profane* (Paris, 1931).

[9] P. de Julleville, *Répertoire*, pp. 21–22. See ed. by E. Langlois (Paris, 1924). *Cf.* Creizenach, i, 395–397.

of similar dramatic treatment. *Le Jeu de la feuillée* [1] is somewhat stranger in spirit, mingling, with a kind of Aristophanic abandon, the real and the fantastic. This play, which was performed at Arras in 1262, satirizes the worthy citizens of that town, introducing for the purpose both Adam and his father, Maître Henris de la Halle, and in this satire is presented an imaginative picture of a dream world, wherein figures that Hellequin who almost certainly was an ancestor of Harlequin. How far Adam's plays are representative of a *jongleur* tradition cannot be ascertained; but they certainly display a keen comic spirit existing in the midst of the thirteenth century.

The examples multiply as we move beyond the year 1300. A fragment of a Cornish interlude [2] shows us a jolly old man who, apparently, encourages a youth to woo a pretty girl and later urges the pair to forget bashfulness and kiss. In *Maître Trubert et Antroignart* [3] an advocate and his client are satirically treated. Allegorical 'moralities,' such as *Les quatres Offices de l'hôtel du roi*,[4] appear here; these, as is well known, continued to flourish in the fifteenth century; and in all comic characters of a distinctly secular type abound. From this period, too, come the many *sotties* or *farces* which are so closely associated with the fool tradition.[5] Most of these are political; practically all introduce as their chief characters a body of *sots*, or fools, who, in their folly, show up the follies of the world. Characteristic is the *Sottie nouvelle de l'astrologue*,[6] where the Prince of Sots calls his subjects together and asks them whether they should not rejoice; their reply is that lamentation is called for, and through the reply and its justification comes the inevitable political satire. Typical features, too, may be found in the *Farce nouvelle nomée la Folie des Gorriers*,[7] where two old soldiers who have lost all in the world decide to make their living by imposing on others. On their way they meet a woman, Folie, and, captivated by her, they agree to be her priests. Dressing in the latest mode of the day, they are esteemed rich men by the fools they meet and fare handsomely. The satire is now bitter and now nonsensically genial. The *nouveaux* in the *Farce nouuelle moralisee des gens nouueaulx qui mengent le monde et le logent de male en pire* [8] wish to change the world, to make doctors really cure diseases, and to make priests live holily, but the Monde ('World') only laughs at their idealistic visions; the Monde is the expression of that secularism which is smilingly wise. The secular spirit, too, is to be seen in the many *sermons joyeux* [9] which may have sprung directly out of the Feast of Fools, but which seem in spirit allied to the mythological burlesque of the earliest mime. One such, the sermon of Folie, is incorporated in Sir David Lyndsay's *Satyre of the Thrie Estaitis*.[10]

All over Europe we find similar developments in comic drama. A fifteenth-century Spanish *Dialogo entrel Amor y un Viejo* [11] introduces the popular characters of an old man, a young woman, and Love, and as has been already seen, farces of this kind are found freely developed in that country.[12] Similar pieces were being produced in Italy. Those of Giorgio Allione da Asti [13] are particularly interesting. Among them is one—*Farsa de Zoan zavatino e de Biatrix soa mogliere e del Prete ascoso sotto el grometto*—in which a wife takes revenge upon her stupid husband in a

---

[1] P. de Julleville, *Répertoire*, pp. 20–21. Ed. E. Langlois (Paris, 1911). *Cf.* Creizenach, i, 393–395.
[2] See *Revue celtique*, iv (1879–80), 258–262; article by W. S. on *The Fragments of a Drama in Add.* 19,491 *Mus. Br.*
[3] P. de Julleville, *Répertoire*, No. 5. This is by Eustache Deschamps.   [4] P. de Julleville, *Répertoire*, No. 6.
[5] See Émile Picot, *Recueil général des sotties* (*Anciens textes français*, 3 vols., Paris, 1902); A. J. V. Leroux de Lincy and F. Michel, *Recueil de farces, moralités et sermons joyeux* (Paris, 1837).
[6] É. Picot, *Recueil*, i, 195–231. Fifteenth century.   [7] *Id.*, i, 137–164. Fifteenth century.
[8] *Id.*, i, 113–136. Fifteenth century.
[9] See A. J. V. Leroux de Lincy and F. Michel, *Recueil de farces, moralités et sermons joyeux* (Paris, 1837).
[10] Ed. Early English Text Society (1869), pp. 542–543.   [11] Ed. in *Biblioteca Oropesa* (Madrid, 1907), iv.
[12] On the early Spanish drama see A. Bonilla y San Martín; Casiano Pellicer, *Tratado histórico sobre el origen y progresos de la comedia y del histrionismo en España* (Madrid, 1804). There is much interesting material in Léo Rouanet, *Coleccion de autos, farsas y coloquios del siglo XVI* (Madrid, 1901). *Cf.* J. P. W. Crawford, *A Spanish Farce of the Early XVI Century* (P.M.L.A.A., xxiv (1909), 1–31).
[13] See *Commedie e farse carnovalesche nel dialogo astigiano, milanese e francese* (Milan, 1865), and Bruno Cotronei, *Le Farse di G. G. Alione poeta astigiano della fine del secolo XV: Studio critico* (Reggio Calabria, 1889). *Cf.* also Fortunato Pintor, *Un' Antica farsa fiorentina* (Florence, 1901: per nozze Salza-Rolando and Gentile-Nudi), and Ireneo Sanesi, *La Commedia* (Milan, 1911), i, 379–430.

time-honoured manner. This theme reminds us of our own *Johan Johan*, and in reading all the interludes of Heywood we must bear in mind the close relationship existing between the English plays and the Continental.[1]

Among the most significant of these farces are those contributed by Holland. In the Hulthem manuscript five interludes have been preserved, each of prime importance for the study of the early secular drama.[2] The first tells of a foolish Lippijn whom his lewd and slovenly wife has little difficulty in cheating. So clever is she that she even succeeds in putting her husband in the wrong and in driving him to ask her forgiveness. An old peasant husband and his young wife figure in the second. A quack sells the former an elixir for restoring his youth; this is contained in a jar which he is told to blow in. The foolish old man does not observe that, as it is filled with soot, he gets as black as a Moor, so that when he comes to his wife he gets thoroughly cudgelled by her. Two women and a witch-like bawd appear in the third play. The fourth is incomplete, but sufficient remains to show us that the plot dealt with a maid who, driven off by her mistress, joins Brother Everaert on a pilgrimage. Enters the Devil in person to assert that such brothers must in the end jump into his cauldron. Most interesting of all is the fifth of this series. Rubben (Robin) has been married only three months, and is amazed at the end of that time to find that his wife has a child. Off he trots to her parents and makes his complaint. Mother-in-law and father-in-law then proceed to enlighten him. He is told that his reckoning is out. He says three months, but in reality he must count another three months of courtship, and when he adds to the six months thus postulated all the nights of his married life he will find that the period is just right—nine months in all. To end the discussion the mother-in-law swears that her daughter went to her marriage in as virgin state as she did to hers. Besides these five pieces, there are other remnants of the old Dutch farce. In one play Herr Werrenbracht has grave suspicions concerning his wife's fidelity. In order to discover the truth, he gets into a basket and causes himself to be carried to his house, where to his dismay he finds his wife closeted with a priest.

In most of these, then, old husbands, giddy young wives, and fools are made to take the principal parts; very similar are the main characters in the well-known Fastnachtsspiele of Nürnberg, the earliest of which are to be dated at the beginning of the fifteenth century.[3] Here too the married women are lewd and unruly; the husbands are doddering and stupid; the fool enters to cause his timely merriment.

Reading these, we are bound to believe that during the fourteenth and fifteenth centuries a widespread activity extended over the whole of Europe among those *menestriers et farseurs*,[4] those *joueurs de personnages*[5] who were also known as *histriones* and *jongleurs*. The majority of the texts, it is true, are of late date, but in this sphere imitation, the passing down of tradition, is what we should expect, and the early relics of twelfth- and thirteenth-century work on the same lines lead us to suppose that most of the later pieces were borrowed from, or were developed out of, originals not now extant. The interludes of John Heywood furnish a fitting example of this. It has been now conclusively demonstrated that much of his work was based on French models,[6] or (although this does not seem to have been taken into account) on English farces of a cognate character. Thus a clear connexion may be traced between the play *De Pernet qui va au vin* and *Johan Johan*, between the play *D'un Pardonneur, d'un triacleur, et d'une tavernière* and *The Four PP*, between the *Dyalogue du*

---

[1] See also Apollo Lumini, *Le Farse di carnevale in Calabria e Sicilia* (Nicastro, 1888), and Vittorio Caravelli, *Chiacchiere critiche* (Florence, 1889). The latter prints two interesting examples.

[2] These have been printed by H. E. Moltzer in *De Middelnederlandsche Dramatische Poezie* (Groningen, 1875). *Cf.* Creizenach, i, 401–404.

[3] See Creizenach, i, 406–425.

[4] See the mention of these in a *sermon joyeux* of 1480 (in Montaiglon and Rothschild, *Recueil de poésies françoises*, ii, 8).

[5] See Victor le Clerc, *Histoire littéraire de la France au quatorzième siècle* (Paris, 1865), i, 200, quoting records of 1392 and 1393.

[6] See particularly Karl Young, *The Influence of French Farce upon the Plays of John Heywood* (*Modern Philology*, ii (1904–5), 97 f.).

fol et du sage and the *Dialogue of Wit and Folly*. Imitation is here in the early sixteenth century, an imitation which gives authority for believing that that imitation had been going on for centuries, just as the presence of the English *Interludium de clerico et puella* gives authority for the belief that England too, like France, may have once upon a time possessed many of these farcical playlets.

In England, in France, in Holland, in Germany these farces have a strange similarity. The themes are commonly themes of love and adultery ; husbands are mocked at and fools are buffetted. Now, while perhaps too much may be made of it,[1] the facts that there is such correspondence in theme and that precisely such themes were the stock-in-trade of the Roman mime make us wonder whether even the subjects have not been handed down over the ages. A play of Terence generally tells how a youth falls in love with a girl of apparently low social position ; this girl, who rarely has much to say for herself, is found to be the long-lost daughter of some prosperous old man, and all ends happily. Nothing there of cheated husbands and flirting wives. Where, then, did the medieval *joueurs de personnages* get their subject-matter ? Was it reinvented independently ? It may have been so, for no period has a monopoly in cuckolds or in their makers ; but, putting these facts together with the others which have been marshalled to show the lineage of the *jongleurs* of the Middle Ages, there seems at least a possibility of direct continuity in comic plot from the times of the Phlyakes down to the arising of a new literary drama in the Renascence. That such plots were known at a very early date is indicated by an allusion in the *De arte prosaica, metrica et rhythmica*, written about the year 1260 by Johannes Anglicus.[2] In this work the author has to define comedy, and this he does in the usual medieval way by describing it as something which starts badly and ends well. He declares, moreover, that it must have five acts and introduces normally five persons, a husband, a wife, a lover, a friend, and a slave. Now, the peculiar thing is that, whereas we should have expected this writer to base his definition upon the plays of Terence and Plautus, he actually seems to model his ideas upon the plots of the mimic drama. At any rate, the fact remains that for him comedy was an affair of intrigue and adultery, with figures unlike those introduced in classical literary plays ; the implication seems to be that he is thinking of farces of his own time which resembled, on the one hand, the mimes of ancient Rome and, on the other, the farces of fourteenth- and fifteenth-century Europe.[3]

(iii) THE RELIGIOUS DRAMA OF THE MIDDLE AGES

It is at this point that we must leave, if only temporarily, and at that not altogether, the secular entertainers of the Middle Ages. Before their full activities are taken up once more in the performances of the *commedia dell' arte*, it will be necessary to consider, both in itself and in relation to the secular players, that most characteristic product of the theatre during those centuries, the mystery play and the miracle. Obviously, even a summary account of this religious drama as it

---

[1] See E. Faral, pp. 226–227.   [2] See Creizenach, i, 13, and the authorities cited there.

[3] The subject of mime influence on early German farce is briefly dealt with in W. Scherer, *Geschichte der deutschen Litteratur* (Berlin, 1891), p. 249 ; C. Reuling, *Die komische Figur in dem wichtigsten deutschen Drama bis zum Ende des XVII Jahrhunderts* (Stuttgart, 1890); and A. Glock, *Über den Zusammenhang des römischen Mimus und einer dramatischen Tätigkeit mittelalterlicher Spielleute mit dem neueren komischen Drama (Zeitschrift für vergleichende Litteraturgeschichte*, N.S., xvi (1906), 25–45, 172–193). I have not seen Weinhold's *Über das Komische im altdeutschen Schauspiel (Gosches Jahrbuch für Litteraturgeschichte*, i, 4). The opinions, of course, are various. Thus Glock, after analysing the evidence, comes definitely to the conclusion " dass das neuere komische Drama mit dem Mimus der alten Römer nicht in Verbindung stehen kann ; denn der Mimus als dramatische Kunstgattung ging bereits früher verloren ; dass das komische Drama mit einer von den Spielleuten das ganze Mittelalter hindurch getriebenen dramatischen Kunstübung ganz und gar nichts gemein haben kann " (p. 193) For the retention of old gestures in modern times (in social life as well as in the theatre) see Andrea de Joro, *La Mimica degli antichi investigata nel gestire napoletano* (Naples, 1832). This is an interesting study of the various significant signs made by the peasantry with their hands and the connexion they have with classical signs of a similar kind. It certainly indicates a continuity of tradition, and the results may be used as an analogy for the discussion of theatrical forms.

THE MYSTERY CYCLES

Naturally enough, the actual plays making up the larger cycles varied from district to district, from country to country. Our own four series of mystery dramas [1] consisted of thirty to forty independent items each; the main subjects (the Creation, Noah, the Annunciation, for example) are dealt with in all; but every cycle has its own peculiar features. Thus, the Towneley cycle has an interesting study of Cæsar Augustus, and the Ludus Coventriæ devotes a whole play to the Conception of Mary. Vaster, and consequently more comprehensive in treatment, were the French collections. The famous *Mystère du Viel Testament* deals with hundreds of separate themes: [2] episodes crowd on episodes in the many other cycles, such as those of Arnoul Greban [3] and Jean Michel, [4] such as that played at Valenciennes in 1547 [5] and that performed at Mons in 1501. [6] England and France, of course, had no monopoly in this style of drama; indeed, Germany presents an array of texts almost as rich as those which France has to offer, [7] while from Italy come many important *sacre rappresentazioni*. [8] In all countries the dramatists eagerly search for material. In time they discover that the Scriptures are insufficient for their purposes; legend comes to be freely utilized, and the power of invention serves to create scenes never referred to by the Evangelists. In almost every European country these mysteries are played, and their popularity endures down to the time when a more modern secular drama arises in Italy, in France, and in England.

Beside the mystery cycles are the miracle plays, [9] which dealt with the 'miracles' of the saints

[1] *Chester* (ed. H. Deimling, E.E.T.S., 1893); *York* (ed. Lucy Toulmin Smith, Oxford, 1885); *Coventry* (ed. K. S. Block, E.E.T.S., 1922); *Towneley* or *Wakefield* (ed. A. W. Pollard, E.E.T.S., 1897). Besides these there are *Two Coventry Corpus Christi Plays* (ed. H. Craig, E.E.T.S., 1902); *The Digby Plays* (ed. F. J. Furnivall, E.E.T.S., 1896); *The Non-Cycle Mystery Plays* (ed. O. Waterhouse, E.E.T.S., 1909); as well as a few others printed in journals. A select bibliography is provided by George R. Coffman in *A Plea for the Study of the Corpus Christi Plays as Drama* (*Studies in Philology*, xxvi (1929), 411–424).

[2] This was originally printed at Paris in 1500. The standard modern text is that edited by Baron James de Rothschild (" Anciens textes français," Paris, 1878).

[3] Ed. G. Paris and G. Raynaud (Paris, 1878). A thirteenth-century collection is printed by G. Cohen in *Mystères et moralités du manuscrit 617 de Chantilly* (Paris, 1920).

[4] For this and other French plays see Gustave Cohen, *Histoire de la mise-en-scène dans le théâtre religieux français du moyen âge* (new edition, Paris, 1926), pp. 278–280 and xiii–xiv, and G. Cohen, *Le Théâtre en France au moyen âge: (1) Le Théâtre religieux* (Paris, 1928). *Cf.* also J. Mortensen, *Le Théâtre français au moyen âge*, translated by E. Philipot (Paris, 1903); G. Cohen, *Le Théâtre au moyen âge d'après les travaux récents* (*La Civilisation française*, November 1920, pp. 495–506); É. Roy, *Le Mystère de la Passion en France du xive au xvie siècle* (*Revue Bourguignonne*, xiii (1903), 3); *id.*, *Études sur le théâtre français du xive et du xve siècle* (Dijon, 1901); A. Jeanroy, *Le Mystère de la Passion en France* (*Journal des savants*, iv (1906), 476–492); G. Hérelle, *Études sur le théâtre basque* (Paris, 1923). There are, of course, many individual collections of plays, such as the *Mystères inédits*, published by A. Jubinal (Paris, 1837), the *Mystère des Actes des Apôtres* (ed. Baron de Girardot, Paris, 1854), and *La Passion du Palatinus*, *mystère du xive siècle* (ed. Grace Frank, Paris, 1922).

[5] See N. Dupire, *Le Mystère de la Passion de Valenciennes* (*Romania*, xlviii (1922), 571–584).

[6] See the very important 'manager's book' discovered by G. Cohen—*Le Livre de conduite du Régisseur et le compte des dépenses pour le mystère de la Passion joué à Mons en 1501* (Paris, 1925).

[7] The subject of the German Passion-plays has been very fully investigated. See particularly (besides the more comprehensive works such as that of Creizenach) R. Froning, *Zur Geschichte und Beurteilung der geistlichen Spiele des Mittelalters, insonderheit der Passionsspiele* (Frankfurt, 1884); Georges Duriez, *La Théologie dans le drame religieux en Allemagne au moyen âge* (Lille, 1914); R. Froning, *Das Drama des Mittelalters* (Frankfurt, 1891); W. Köppen, *Beiträge zur Geschichte der deutschen Weihnachtsspiele* (Paderborn, 1893); F. J. Mone, *Schauspiele des Mittelalters* (Karlsruhe, 1846). A very useful compilation is M. J. Rudwin, *A Historical and Bibliographical Survey of the German Religious Drama* (University of Pittsburg, Pennsylvania, 1924). Many special studies are devoted to particular plays or districts: G. Dinges, *Untersuchungen zum Donaueschinger Passionsspiel* (Breslau, 1910); A. Pichler, *Über das Drama des Mittelalters in Tirol* (Innsbruck, 1850); Hans Rueff, *Das rheinische Osterspiel der Berliner Handschrift MS. Germ. Fol. 1219* (Berlin, 1925; from *Abhandlungen der Gesellschaft der Wissenschaften zu Göttingen*; Phil.-hist. Klasse, N.F., xviii, 1); J. Strobl, *Ein rheinisches Passionsspiel des XIV. Jahrhunderts* (Halle, 1909); J. E. Wackernell, *Die ältesten Passionsspiele in Tirol* (*Wiener Beiträge für deutsche und englische Philologie*, ii (1887), 3). *Cf.* also the many works on and editions of the *Weihnachtsspiele*, of which the following may be mentioned: August Hartmann, *Weihnachtsspiel und Weihnachtslied in Oberbayern* (Munich, 1875); Wilhelm Pailler, *Weihnachtslieder und Krippenspiele aus Oberösterreich und Tirol* (Innsbruck, 1881); C. W. Pederit, *Ein Weihnachtsspiel aus einer Handschrift des XV Jahrhunderts* (Parchim, 1869); Karl J. Schröer, *Deutsche Weihnachtsspiele aus Ungarn* (Vienna, 1858); S. Vogt, *Die Schlesischen Weihnachtsspiele* (Leipzig, 1891); C. Weinhold, *Weihnachtsspiele und Lieder aus Süddeutschland und Schlesien* (Graz, 1855).

[8] On the Italian mysteries see the careful study of D'Ancona. Colomb de Batines has a valuable *Bibliografia delle antiche rappresentazioni italiane sacre e profane stampate nei secoli XV e XVI* (Florence, 1852). In addition note may be made of F. Novati, *Il " Mistero " in Francia ed in Italia nell' età medievale* (*Natura ed arte*, xx (1910), 7–8, Marco Vattasso, *Per la storia del dramma sacro in Italia* (Rome, 1903). The most important collection is that of A. D'Ancona, *Sacre rappresentazioni dei secoli xiv, xv e xvi* (Florence, 1872).

[9] On the question of the names given to the plays see Chambers, ii, 103–105. The word 'mystery' (*mystère*) is really French, the English plays being regularly called miracles. I have retained the Continental names here, since they provide a convenient distinction between the two types of play. *Cf.* also G. R. Coffman, *The Miracle-play in England—Nomenclature* (P.M.L.A.A., xxxi (1916), 448–465).

and consequently departed from Scriptural authority. Sometimes these were related to the cult of the Virgin, as in the *Miracles de Notre-Dame*,[1] sometimes, as in the Cornish *St Meriasek* play,[2] they treated of the adventures of local saints. French literature abounds in examples of this type of miracle drama, but, strangely enough, barely anything of a kindred form is extant in England. This very fact, however, has its own interest, for it indicates surely enough how closely we have to be on our guard when discussing the medieval theatre. The lack of tangible proof in the form of manuscripts by no means indicates that the saint's play was unknown in this country. Indeed, the earliest record we have of a genuine religious drama in England is that which concerns a *St Katherine* performed in the thirteenth century.[3] From record after record come the titles of similar pieces played in all districts, from the *St Bride* and *St Helena* of Aberdeen [4] to the *St Eustace* of Braintree.[5] The list is indeed a long one, and indicates conclusively that the want of texts is naught but a freak of history—one of those oddities with which students of medieval literature are fully acquainted.

In addition to the mystery and the miracle, the medieval populace also knew the morality play, in which the characters, instead of being Scriptural or legendary figures, were abstractions of one kind or another. The morality, however, seems likely to have been a later development, and does not, in any case, concern us so much as the others. All we can say is that, while abstractions appear in early mystery dramas, the texts we possess of fully developed morality plays are all of late date.

In surveying this religious theatre it is obvious that the subject-matter forming the material of the plots could be of three kinds. First, there was the Scriptural story itself, associated with the various legends which in the course of centuries had attached themselves to the Gospels. Secondly, there was the whole field of the *Acta sanctorum*, with lives of saints who do not even figure in the Roman calendar. And, lastly, there was the invented matter. This invented matter might itself be of two kinds. An individual dramatist might recreate a Scriptural scene, as, for example, the author of *Le Mystère d'Adam* [6] recreated the story of the temptation of Adam and Eve. On the other hand, a dramatist might prefer to abandon Scripture, if even for a moment, and introduce a scene of his own making, with persons culled from his imagination or from his observation of life.

The traditional matter, clearly, does not concern us here. It may be interesting to analyse the indebtedness of the medieval playwrights to the Apocrypha and to legend, but a survey of this indebtedness would take us far from our present object, which is to see if there is any traceable connexion between the religious and the secular theatres of this period. For that purpose we must confine ourselves strictly to the invented scenes and to the invented characters.

THE COMIC SCENES

So soon as an essay is made in this direction, the peculiar fact is revealed that, for the most part, the invented material is comic in its tendency. The religious drama of the Middle Ages had, of course, a definitely moralistic and serious appeal, but it is certain that the simple-minded populace went to the play as much to laugh and be entertained as to weep and be edified. A medieval story [7] tells of two monks who went out into an open field and saw "a huge crowd of people gathered together, who now remained silent, now shouting applause, now bursting with laughter." That crowd was witnessing a miracle or mystery play. It can hardly be emphasized too much that the

---

[1] *Miracles de Notre-Dame*, ed. G. Paris and U. Robert (" Anciens textes français "). See also Émile Roy, *Études sur le théâtre français du xiv*e *et xv*e *siècle* (Dijon and Paris, 1901; from *Revue Bourguignonne de l'enseignement supérieur*, xi, Nos. 3 and 4).

[2] *Beunans Meriasek, the Life of Saint Meriasek, Bishop and Confessor : a Cornish Drama* (ed. Whitley Stokes, 1872).

[3] The play is recorded by Matthew Paris; *cf.* Chambers, ii, 64–65, 366.   [4] *Id.*, ii, 331.   [5] *Id.*, ii, 342.

[6] *Le Mystère d'Adam : An Anglo-Norman Drama of the Twelfth Century* (ed. P. Studer, Manchester University Press, 1918).

[7] See *A Selection of Latin Stories* (Percy Society, viii (1843), 100). *Cf.* Ignazio Ciampi, *Le Rappresentazioni sacre nel medio evo in Italia considerate nella parte comica* (Rome, 1865).

great cycles of the fourteenth and fifteenth centuries could not have become the popular things they were had it not been for the efforts of the comic actors to make sport and of the machinists to make wondrous entertaining shows.   This being so, it will be well worth our while to consider the nature of these items of entertainment in the midst of religious solemnity.

Some of the comic scenes tell us little.[1]   Such, for example, is the York treatment of the *Cain and Abel* playlet.   Here the treatment is realistic with a comic tinge rather than comic wholly.   Cain is the grasping, miserly peasant who will not give his tithes to God and whom his servant Brewbarrel calls " Mr Cayme."

> Ya! daunce in þe devil way, dresse þe downe,
> For I wille wyrke euen as I will,

he cries to Abel, and to the Angel :

> Take that thy self, evyn on thy crowne,

and gives him a good buffet.   Similar to this treatment of Cain is that of the women who attack the knights in the Towneley *Massacre of the Innocents*, or the other women in the Digby *Massacre* who seize on Watkyn, who is one of Herod's soldiers, and beat him soundly.   The same mood enters into many plays on the torments of Christ.   The Tortores are, in plays of all countries, represented in a spirit half fearful, half comic.   The two who appear in the Towneley *Buffetting* have some ridiculous dialogue before the scourging begins.   Comic talk appears in the York *Trial before Herod*, and laughter is bubbling over when the executioners, in the Towneley *Talents*, start to dice for Christ's gown.   Incidental elements of a comic sort are made to appear in these scenes as well.   Herod is made a wild boaster and a coward ; in the last-mentioned play he calls aloud for silence, first in English and Latin and then in French.   In the Cornish *Crucifixion* there is introduced a Faber (Smith) who will not make the nails and is goaded and jeered at by his wife.[2] In general, it may be said that any opportunity for comic treatment offered by the Scriptural story is eagerly seized on by the dramatists and that deliberate deviations from that story are made for the purpose of introducing lower-class comic characters and of indulging in popular satire.   Comic servants are invented for the Digby *Conversion of Saul*, chiefly in order to jeer at the extravagant fashions of the time.   Such, indeed, was a favourite subject.   It appears in the *Ludus Coventriæ* and in the Digby *Mary Magdalen*.   The latter presents us with a fool Coryoste (Curiosity), who boasts of his clothes :

> I haue a shert of reynnes with slevys peneawnt,
> A lase of sylke for my lady constant. . . .
> In wynter a stomachyr, In somer non att all.

Characteristic, too, is the *Tower of Babel* section in the *Viel Testament*,[3] where enter a number of ' realistic ' characters, the workmen, called Casse Tuilleau, Gaste Bois, Cul Esventé, and Pille Mortier.   The scene gives ample opportunity for the arousing of popular laughter by the use of ridiculous confusions in the dialogue, which must here be left untranslated :

> CASSE TUILLEAU. Que veulx tu dire, Gaste Bois ?
> Sçais tu rien qui soit de nouveau ?
> GASTE BOIS. Par Dieu nenny, Casse Tuilleau
> Rien de nouveau, n'est inventé.
> CASSE TUILLEAU. Pille Mortier, Cul Esventé,
> Est ja vostre tasche acomplye ?

---

[1] See Maurice Wilmotte, *Études critiques sur la tradition littéraire en France* (Paris, 1909), pp. 93–124 (" L'Élément comique dans le théâtre religieux ").   He denies influence of the secular on the religious stage.

[2] *The Ancient Cornish Drama* (ed. E. Norris (Oxford, 1859), i, 435).   It will be realized that in this summary I am taking only single examples of these scenes.   The incident of the Smith and his wife appears in many Continental mysteries.

[3] No. 12 of the series; ll. 6608–88.

Elsewl

F
on e
wor(

So poj
were
Passio
Puſter
Robin(
of cou
quack-
in the
Roma
was n(

Fir
the rel
evil p.
howev
an em
type.
physic
being
for th
procee
survey
arch-d
in ser]
Cain
presen
we ap
of the
Cheſte
exu'tir
for M
Ludus
the d(

¹ D'.
² Cre
Phil.-hiſ
³ See
Driesen,
den deuts
Medieval
Myſterien
⁴ Cf.
⁶ See

CUL ESVENTÉ. Ma bouteille n'eſt point remplie
De gourde pie, a ce matin.
PILLE MORTIER. Trois jours a que ne beuz de vin,
Par fault d'avoir ung vesseaue. . . .
CASSE TUILLEAU. Ça, du plomb pour la couverture !
PILLE MORTIER. J'ay apporté ung inſtrument
Pour commencer le fondement,
Car il n'a pas fait qui commence.
JETRAN. Vecy une grand insolence
Maçons, charpentiers, qu'esse cy ?
GASTE BOYS. *Oriolla gallaricy*
Breth gathahat mirlidonnet
Juidamag alacro brouet
Mildafaronel adaté.
NEMBROTH. Vella noſtre ouvraige gaſté.
CASSE TUILLEAU. *Quanta queso a lamyta*
La seigneurie la polita.
Volle dare le coupe toue ?
CHANAAM. Qu'esse cy ? Faut il qu'on se joue
De nous ? Mais d'ou vient ceſt erreur ?
CUL ESVENTÉ. *Bianath acaſte folleur*
Huidebref abaſtenyent.
CHUS. Bref je ne sçay d'ou cecy vient ;
Jamais ne vis tel fantasie.
PILLE MORTIER. *Rotaplaſte a la casie*
*Emy maleth a lacaſtot.*¹

Allied to these realiſtic scenes are those which deal with the shepherds, and these introduce us to what may be called the comic of the Nativity, juſt as the Tortores introduced us to the comic of the Crucifixion. Again, this realiſtic treatment is common to all lands. Alloris, Ysembart, Rifflart of the Mons *Passion*,² Gobelin and Riflart of the " Jubinal " *Myſtère* ³—these are brothers in spirit to the shepherds of the English plays. Sometimes their simplicity is ſtressed, as in the *Ludus Coventriæ Adoration*, where Maunfras, Boosras, and Moyse are their names, or as in the York play, where they remain untitled ; in these and in the Cheſter *Shepherds*, where one is called " Tud, Tibb's son," their ruſtic gifts are ſtressed—a brooch, " two cobill notis vppon a bande," and " an horne spone." Fuller development of the possibilities inherent in this scene will be found in the firſt Towneley Shepherds' play. Says the firſt shepherd (Gyb) :

When ryches is he,
Then comys pouerte,
Hors-man lak cope
Walkys then, I weyn ;

and his conversation with the second and third shepherds (John Horne and Slow-pace) is full of satire of contemporary manners. Their folly is exposed by " Iak garcio "—

Now god gyf you care foles all sam ;
Sagh I neuer ron so fare bot the foles of gotham.

When the Angel awakes them from their sleep Gyb tries to show off his knowledge :

Virgill in his poetre sayde in his verse,
Even thus by gramere as I shall reherse ;
Iam noua progenies celo demittitur alto,
Iam rediet virgo, redeunt saturnia regno ;

¹ *Le Myſtère du Viel Teſtament (ed. cit.)*, i, 259-272.   ² G. Cohen, *Le Livre de conduite*, pp. 65-69.   ³ Ed. Jubinal, ii, 1f.

the dramatists to make use of this material that they even made the Devil responsible for the dream of Pilate's wife, which ought to have been a divine dispensation. After this follows the diablerie of *The Harrowing of Hell*, of *The Coming of Antichrist*, and of *Doomsday*. Obviously the devils were dear to the medieval imagination, and dear not because of their evil, but because of their comic irresponsibility, their posturings, their extravagance.

Their names are manifold. The Old Testament had mentioned only the name of Satan, but to him became attached a whole series of subordinate figures who were called after pagan gods of the East, after classical divinities, after abstractions. Satan (Sathan, Satanus, Sathanas) is generally the chief, but often he is degraded, as in the French *Ste Geneviève*, to being the minister of another. This other is called by different names—usually Lucifer, Beelzebub (Belgibuz, Bulgibus, Belzebuth),[1] or Leviathan (Leviatam).[2] These are frequently friendly associates, and Satan can call Lucifer *mein lieber Geselle* (' my good companion '). Their subjects and fellow-conspirators include a considerable number of pagan gods who had been mentioned in the Bible—Amon,[3] Astaroth,[4] Baal,[5] Belial (Bélias, Beellath),[6] Belphegor,[7] Berith,[8] Lillis,[9] Mammon,[10] and Moloch (Milach).[11] Then come the classical divinities, a rarer group—Cerbere and Mercury. Sometimes their names are invented ones associated with Hell, as Infernus, Funkeldune, Broudly, Hellhund, Hellekrugk, Schorbrandt, Terrator. Many devils, particularly German, possessed titles which indicated their moral attributes, such as Untrew (' Untrue '), Irrtum (' Error '), Frauenzorn (' Rage of Women '), Geiz (' Greed '), Klet (probably associated with *Klette*, ' a bur '), Koltelrey (connected with *Kot*, ' dung '), Kränzlein (' Good-fellowship '), Lasterbalg (' Bag of Vice '), Leisegang (' Soft-foot '), Neid (' Envy '), Räppli (' Crazy '), Schönspiegel (' Nice Mirror '), Schoppenstugk (' A Pint '), Spiegelglanz (' Glance in the Mirror '), Unkeuscheit (' Immodesty '). To this class, no doubt, belong the Chester Ragnell and Lightbourne, the Towneley Ribald, and the Risquart and Manferas of *Ste Geneviève*. Popular jingles probably gave rise to such other names as Binkenbangk, Lykketappe, Machadantz, and Mellemäl. Many of the rest have assumed their names from their physical appearance. The Cocornifer (' Horn-bearing ') of French mysteries and the Hörnli of German refer obviously to the animal-like masks worn by these creatures. Krumnase (' Twisted Nose '), Raffenzahn (' Projecting Tooth '), Rosenkrantz (' Rosy Crown '), Snyngkenschnabel and Ziegenbart (' Goat's Beard ') are clearly of the same origin. Amid the innumerable other titles [12] a few have special significance. The German Puk suggests that folk-lore sometimes entered in to colour the depiction of the stage devils, while the Stultus (' Fool ') of the French *Ste Barbe* indicates a possible confusion with the fool tradition. Then there is the universal Tutevillus, who appears in Germany, France, and England (as Tutivillus) and who was the *notaire des enfers*, or the ' Court rollar '; and, lastly, the strange Hellequin, or Herlekin, who, with his flock of spirits, or *mesnie*, seems to have played a considerable part in the medieval imagination. Hellequin, however, carries us rather far, and a discussion of his personality on the stage may be reserved until we come to meet his namesake and descendant, Arlecchino or Harlequin.[13]

[1] See Matthew x, 25, xii, 24, 27; Mark iii, 22; Luke xi, 15, 18, 19.
[2] See Job xli, 1.
[3] See Jeremiah xlix, 6.
[4] See Judges ii, 13.
[5] See Jeremiah xix, 5; Judges vi, 25.
[6] See II Corinthians vi, 15.
[7] See Numbers xxv, 3 (Baal-Peor).
[8] See Judges viii, 33.
[9] Evidently a variant of Lilith.
[10] See Matthew vi, 24.
[11] See Leviticus xx, 2–5. On the devils' names see A. Axelsen, pp. 58–70.
[12] A few of the most interesting are as follow : Agrappart, Asmodeus, Bone, Eleatam, Federwisch, Fergalus, Kärtli, Krüttli, Länzl, Lestrer, Nichtumbsunst, Noytor, Ruffs, Schorczanage, Seltenfrum, Spränzl, Sturpans, Susemidde, Waldach, Werrebolt. The popular names of devils are, of course, innumerable. For comparative purposes the list of ancient demons given by E. Peterson in *Engel- und Dämonennamen nomina barbata* (*Rheinisches Museum*, lxxv (1926), 393–421) is useful, although this has nothing to do with stage types. The analysis of Roumanian devil names in Giorge Pascu, *Études de sémasiologie roumaine : 1. Les Noms du Diable* (*Archivium Romanicum*, v (1921), 244–251), shows that these are largely derived from physical characteristics. Thus, *mic* is ' little,' *negru* ' black,' *fleamă* ' bright eyes,' *corn* ' horned,' *cradă* ' tailed '; other titles refer to the devil's folly, cowardice, raucous voice, and even to articles of his dress. For Western theatrical devils' names see also Karl Weinhold, *Über das Komische im altdeutschen Schauspiel* (*Jahrbuch für Litteraturgeschichte*, i (1865), 18–19).
[13] With Hellequin, Herlequin, goes the Huré who appears in *Le Roi avenir* ; see Driesen, p. 58.

All these devils, for comic purposes, appeared " in orebyll a-ray " (horrible array),[1] and they entered frequently " with thunder and fyre," " cryeng and roryng."[2]   Happily, since the medieval mind was so set on them, a good deal of information, pictorial and otherwise, has been preserved concerning their appearance.   Occasionally they were clad in some birdlike costume. Archdeacon Rogers refers to " ye diuell in his fethers,"[3] and Taylor, the Water Poet, uses precisely the same phrase.[4] This feathered dress was, however, not that which was most usual.   In the *Garden of Eden* plays, of course, there was a special costume, when Satan appeared as an " Adder . . . with a maydens face."[5]   " A cote w[ith] hosen & tayle for yᵉ serpente . . . w[ith] a w[hite] heare," or mask, is recorded at Norwich in 1565,[6] while at Mons in 1501 was demanded " 1 *vies linchoel . . . pour couvrir ung serpent d'oziere allant sur son pis.*"[7]   This *serpens artificiose compositus*[8] or an actor taking the part of a " werm with an aungelys face " is to be found everywhere in medieval drama.   The ultimate source of the convention seems to lie in a passage from Petrus Comestor,[9] when, quoting from a now lost statement by Bede, he declares that the serpent in the Garden of Eden had a " maiden's face " (*virgineum vultum*).   Probably before that time either an artificial serpent, or simply Satan in his own guise, was made to tempt Eve.

The standard dress for the ordinary Devil appears to have consisted of leather, hair, or black cloth.   " Newe ledder " was required for him at Coventry in 1477,[10] while the Cornish *Creation* describes Lucifer and his companions as " apareled fowle w[ith] fyre about hem turning to hell and every degre of devylls of lether . . . runing into yᵉ playne."[11]   On the other hand, the Drapers' Guild at Coventry in 1568 needed " a payre of hose with heare [hair] " and " ij pound of heare for the demons cotts [coats] and hose,"[12] while

Fig. 123.   THE ADDER WITH A MAIDEN'S FACE

Painting by H. van der Goes, in Vienna.   From *The American Journal of Archæology*, Ser. II, xxi (1917), p. 272.

[1] Digby *Mary Magdalene, ed. cit.,* p. 91.   See Alfred Köppen, *Der Teufel und die Hölle in der darstellenden Kunst von den Anfängen bis zum Zeitalter Dante's und Giotto's* (Berlin, 1895); Bastoni, *Il Diavolo nell' arte* (Naples, 1902); A. Marenduzzo, *Il Diavolo nella leggenda e nell' arte* (*Natura ed arte,* xiii (1904), 17).   *Cf.* also F. Kuntze, *Der Mimus und die Ahnen des Mephisto* (*Kunstwart,* xxxviii (1924), 64–69).

[2] Digby *Conversion of Saul, ed. cit.,* pp. 43, 44.   [3] Digby plays, *ed. cit.,* p. xxiii.
[4] *Historical MSS. Commission, Report IV,* Appendix, p. 533.   [5] Chester *Creation, ed. cit.,* i, 28.
[6] Chambers, ii, 388.   [7] G. Cohen, *Le Livre de conduite,* pp. lviii, 527.
[8] *Mystère d'Adam,* ed. Studer, p. 15.
[9] J. P. Migne, *op. cit.,* Series Latina, cxcviii, col. 1072.   See John K. Bonnell, *The Serpent with a Human Head in Art and in Mystery Play* (*American Journal of Archæology,* Ser. II, xxi (1917), 255).
[10] Coventry plays, ed. H. Craig (E.E.T.S., p. 87).
[11] *Gwreans an Bys. The Creation of the World: A Cornish Mystery,* ed. Whitley Stokes (1864), l. 326.   [12] *Op. cit.,* p. 100.

Lucifer at Bourges was " clad in a bear skin." [1]   The black cloth dress, which seems to have been common in Germany, is yet shown in a moth-eaten costume, now in the Innsbruck Ferdinandeum, which had been used traditionally in local plays of a peasant kind.   There as elsewhere the *Tüfelscleid* [2] was a well-known garment.   Fig. 124 shows the " twisted nose " (*Krumnase*) of Belial and his hairy dress.   Scaly costumes are illustrated in the drawing of Devil Astaroth by J. Ruof (Fig. 126), while the black cloth is shown in the traditional costume from the Tyrol which, until lately in the possession of Count Dr Hans Wilczek at Schloss Seebarn, was unfortunately destroyed by fire during the War (Fig. 127.)

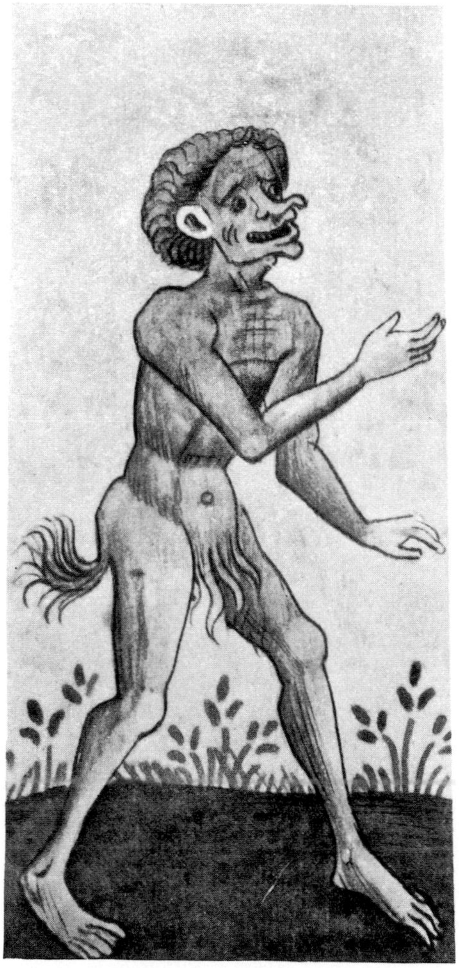

All these devils wear masks. " The devyls hede " or the " de-mones heed " is referred to often in the Coventry ac-counts.[3]   Such masks, fear-some in ap-pearance, must have varied greatly from one another. Some were animal-like [4] with, very com-monly, feline features.   One such is described for us in terrifying words :

Fig. 125.   Seilenos

Vase in the Berlin Museum.   From Max von Boehn, *Das Bühnenkostüm in Altertum, Mittelalter und Neuzeit* (Berlin, 1921), p. 21.

Now see you what a devil that was.   His head was mighty wondrous and all hairy.   His eyes were bloodshot, and a crown was on his head.   His mouth was huge and his teeth very sharp. He had the head of a cat, and a hairy animal's body.   So ugly a beast could not be found in our age.   His head was hideous and his countenance dark.[5]

Fig. 124.   Belial

Miniature by J. Stainberger v. Sprinzenstein in Jacobus da Teramo, *Ob Jesus das Recht hab gehabt, dass er die Höll unter die Teufel hat beraubt.* Studien-Bibliothek, Salzburg.

[1] Cohen, *La Mise-en-scène*, p. 95.   The medieval conception of the devil seems to have been coloured largely by the idea of the " wild man," or *uomo selvaggio*, whose masks appear as *capita de wodewose* in the 1348–49 accounts of Edward III and who is to be connected with the ancient fauns and satyrs.   On this see the interesting essay by F. Neri on *La Maschera del selvaggio* (*Giornale storico*, lix (1912), 47–68).

[2] As described for the Lucerne play in 1549.   [3] *Op. cit.*, pp. 84, 97.

[4] On these animal heads see G. G. Roskoff, *Geschichte des Teufels* (Leipzig, 1869), i, 301.

[5] Leroux de Lincy, *Livre des légendes* (Paris, 1836), p. 252 :

Plest vous oir quel déable ce fut :
Le chief ot gros merveilleus et vélu
Les yeux ot roux, et el chief embatu
La gueule ot lée et les denz mult agu
Teste ot de chat, cors de cheval crinu
Si laide beste en cest siecle ne fu . . .
Le chief hideus et oscur le visage.

Fig. 126. THE DEVIL ASTAROTH

Miniature in J. Ruof's *Weingartenspiel*, as reproduced in Max Hermann, *Forschungen*, Fig. 125.

Fig. 128. A DEVIL'S MASK

Mask from Sterzing in the Ferdinandeum, Innsbruck, as reproduced in Max Hermann, *Forschungen*, Fig. 128.

Fig. 127. AN EARLY DEVIL'S COSTUME

Original costume, now destroyed by fire, formerly in the possession of Count Dr Hans Wilczek at Schloss Seebarn, near Korneuburg, as reproduced in Max Hermann, *Forschungen*, Fig. 126.

Often, indeed, were these devils' masks ornamented with pointed animal snouts and huge horns, and noting them we recall some of the names given to the devils in the mystery plays themselves. Astaroth in Fig. 126 is wearing one kind of monster mask, and some extant examples in the Ferdinandeum at Innsbruck illustrate others. The betoothed, ram-horned example from Sterzing may be taken as typical (Fig. 130, top figure on left). Even more interesting are the 'human' masks. Belial (Fig. 124) has a long, projecting jaw, a crooked nose, and what seems to be a wart at the right-hand side of his face. A red-coloured mask with a similar wart, looking amazingly like Punch, and a dark brown mask boasting several of these warts are still preserved at Innsbruck (Fig. 130, mask beside the skull and top mask on right). Now, in noting the resemblance to Punch, it must be recalled that in the terra-cottas which in all probability give us portraits of Manducus in the Atellanæ large warts are shown on the nose and cheek ; later, in studying the figures of the *commedia dell' arte*, these warts will be found to make their reappearance on the traditional masks. This certainly is a peculiar fact, and, taken with other features which these devils share with mimic types both early and late, tends to make us believe that the demonic characters thus introduced comically in the medieval mysteries

191

were influenced by the secular entertainers who had inherited some of the traditional business of the classic mime stage.

THE ACTORS

The chief argument which can be opposed to such a supposition is that nearly all the records we possess concerning the actors who took part in the mystery cycles indicate that these were commonly either ecclesiastics or amateur laymen. Well known is the fact that in England, after the drama had passed out of the Church, the trade guilds of the various towns took over the performance of the plays. In Italy groups of youths, called *voci*, under the direction of a *Festajolo*, engaged themselves in this work.[1] In France most of the local associations which organized plays were amateur in character.[2] The majority of these actors were men, and it is only at a late date, and then sparingly, that the actress took women's *rôles*. In 1468 a girl of eighteen took the part of St Catherine,[3] and at Mons in 1501 a certain Waudru, daughter of Jorge de le Nerle, interpreted the girlhood of Mary.[4] The earliest record of an actress in Germany does not appear until the middle of the sixteenth century, when the daughter of Professor Lepusculus played in Heinrich Pantaleon's *Philargyrus* at Basel.[5] There is assuredly nothing here of the free association of men and women which is to be found in the classic mime or among the acrobatic *jongleurs* of the Middle Ages. These amateur actors, it is true, were paid and fed, but such payments seem rather to have been in lieu of time lost than in that of artistic service. In all countries books of expenses have been unearthed: " Item, payd for a pynt of wyne for Pilatt jd."; " payd for the players drynkynge at the Swanne dore ijs. viijd."; " p'd for our supper on the play day for ourselves, goodman Mawpas, the minstrull, the dresser of the pagent, and the somner and his wyfe iiijs."; [6] or " To God the Father, this day, at supper in his house, besides meat, one pot of wine vs." [7] By hundreds the *naïve* entries summon before us the social amenities of pageant preparation. Then there are the payments for service. At the smiths' play in Coventry for the year 1490 God received 2s., Cayphas 3s. 4d., Herod 3s. 4d., Pilate's wife 2s., Peter and Malkus 1s. 4d., Anna 2s. 2d., Pilate 4s., Pilate's son 4d., and a knight 2s. In 1539 the Drapers' Guild awarded God 3s. 4d., four angels 1s. 4d., three patriarchs 1s., three white souls 1s. 6d., three black souls 2s., two demons 3s., and (in 1561) two worms of conscience 1s. 4d.[8] In view of this evidence, which consistently points to payment for amateur service, how can we hope to establish the theory of a secular influence on the religious drama?

In the first place, it must be remembered that most of these records are of late date, and in the second that many of the records do not expressly deny the presence of professional players. One

FIG. 129. DEVIL BELL

Sketch for a figure in J. Ruof's *Weingartenspiel*. From Max Hermann, *Forschungen zur deutschen Theatergeschichte* (Berlin, Weidmannsche Buchhandlung, 1914), Abb. 124.

[1] D'Ancona, i, 401.

[2] P. de Julleville, *Les Comédiens en France au moyen âge* (Paris, 1885).

[3] Cohen, *La Mise-en-scène*, p. 206.

[4] G. Cohen, *Le Livre de conduite*, pp. cii and 53.

[5] Heinzel, *loc. cit.*, p. 24.

[6] Coventry expenses, *op. cit.*, pp. 85, 94.

[7] G. Cohen, *Le Livre de conduite*, p. 567: " A dieu le pere, cedit jour, au souper en sa maison, outre viande, donnét 1 pot de vin de: vs."

[8] *Op. cit.*, pp. 83, 100.

Fig. 130. MEDIEVAL DEVILS' MASKS
Collection in the Ferdinandeum, Innsbruck.
Photo Ferdinandeum

wonders, for example, whether "the minstrull" at Coventry provided only music, or in what precisely consisted his association with the play. The same problem arises at York, where in 1446 moncy was paid to minstrels at the Corpus Christi festival, and to *ludentes* at Christmas and at the

Feast of the Circumcision, and where, the following year, were present "two players Joly Wat and Malkyn."[1]   These entries can be paralleled by others.   Thus in 1427 Henry VI paid "Jakke Travail and his comrades" for "plays and interludes";[2] was Joly Wat a player of interludes like Jakke Travail, and, if so, did he take part in the actual performance of plays at York? Some indication of their activities perhaps may be provided by the record at Mons which shows that the townsfolk there, when they were preparing their play in 1501, sent to Chauny, a famous home of the *jongleur* tradition, for two men to aid them in their mechanical devices and stage tricks.[3]   This no doubt was one of their duties. Playing incidental music was another. "Here the mimes play a melody" (*Hic mimi ludent melodiam*) is a stage direction in the Cornish *St Meriasek*.[4] Perhaps dancing and acrobatics were others.   But still one suspects that their offices were not, particularly in earlier times, limited entirely to these.   When the amateur associations had gained mastery over their craft the necessity for professional assistance would decline; but it is difficult to believe that all the comic elements in the early mysteries were of amateur origin.   After all, there is that prohibition against the wearing of ecclesiastic dress by the professional *scenici*[5] which seems to point to their association with the religious play, and when it is observed that improvisation was often called for in the performance of the dramas[6] one's belief that, originally at any rate, the mimes and the *jongleurs* were called in to aid the amateur actors is strengthened.   At all events, whether the mimes aided directly in this way or not, an examination of the religious play seems to indicate fully that the comic elements were inspired by secular farce.   The boasting tyrant, the jealous husband, the shrewish wife, the comic Devil with his canvas club and his warts—all these have their prototypes in the mimic theatre.   Interesting, too, is the fact that these comic elements are connected with what must have been the very earliest Scriptural subjects to be dramatized. The Nativity (a jealous Joseph and comic midwives), the Passion (comic torturers, a quack, and a boasting Pilate), the Deluge (a shrewish Percoba), and the Devil scenes are precisely those subjects which we should expect first to be treated in this way.   One of the main implications of this must later be studied.

THE MEDIEVAL STAGES

Before we come to that matter, however, a passing glance may be devoted to the medieval stage itself, for this serves to indicate fresh methods of approach to the subject.   It were useless here to attempt such a thorough survey as is presented in Professor Gustave Cohen's *Histoire de la mise-en-scène dans le théâtre religieux français du moyen âge*, but certain aspects, at any rate, require attention here.   Once more the orthodox theory must first be considered.   This, put briefly, is that the most primitive liturgical play, such as is exemplified in the *Quem queritis*,[7] demanded originally a merely symbolic 'scene'—perhaps only a few books piled up at the altar in the church.   Then comes the establishment of a temporary or permanent sepulchre, which often was called the *monumentum*.[8]   This gave the first setting for the drama of *The Resurrection*.   Then, as other incidents were attached to this simple playlet, such as that which concerns the buying of the unguents, other localities were demanded, and these were apportioned to different parts of the church itself, so that gradually there arose that system of 'multiple setting' which places before the spectators a number of widely separated 'scenes' at one and the same time.   As the mysteries develop and are taken out

---

[1] *York Mystery Plays*, ed. L. T. Smith, p. xxxviii.   [2] Chambers, ii, 186.

[3] G. Cohen, *Le Livre de conduite*, pp. xl–xlii.   For these professionals see also G. Doutrepont, *La Littérature française à la cour des ducs de Bourgogne* (Paris, 1909), pp. 350–353.

[4] *Op. cit.*, p. 291.   [5] See *supra*, p. 148.

[6] *Cf.* Heinzel, *op. cit.*, p. 15.   [7] See *supra*, p. 177.

[8] See J. K. Bonnell, *The Easter Sepulchrum in its Relation to the Architecture of the High Altar* (P.M.L.A.A., xxxi (1916), 4); Cohen, *La Mise-en-scène*, p. vi; Chambers, ii, 16–24; Neil C. Brooks, *The Sepulchre of Christ in Art and Liturgy* ("University of Illinois Studies in Language and Literature," vii, 1921).

of the church this system is retained, with the necessary modifications demanded by the vastness of the subject-matter and the great numbers of localities required for the performance of the plays.

When the mystery cycles are being given in England and on the Continent, then, there is established a complete tradition, ultimately traceable to the symbolic ' sepulchre ' in the church. The tradition itself allows of certain variations.[1] Standard elements are the presentation before the spectator of some piece of localized scenery—called by different names in different countries and districts, the most common of which are *mansio* (' mansion '), *locus* (' place '), *castrum* (' castle '), *sedes* (' seat '), *thronus* (' throne '), *palatium* (' palace '), *tentum* (' tent '),[2] mansion, house, *hourt*, *eschauffant*, *estage*, *stat*, *burc* or *burg*, *stand*, *platz*, *sitz*, *hof*, *ort*, and *hüszlin*[3]—and an unlocalized acting space (known usually as *platea*, or place, but sometimes referred to also as *parcq*, *champ*, *terre*, and *parquet*). The variations show the localized scenery (1) arranged so as to face the spectators, (2) arranged in a circle, and (3) detached and scattered at different parts of a town, as in the English ' pageants.' These standard and varied elements we may now discuss.

The use of the *platea* is of very ancient origin. In the Anglo-Norman *Adam* " demons enter and run about the place [*per plateam*]."[4] There is no need here to quote other and later examples ; the use of this " place " was constant in the religious theatre, and, as will be seen, it was employed later by secular players both in Italy and in England. Where the scenes were set in order in one space the *platea* was a roped-in portion of the playing-ground ; where the ' pageants ' were scattered, as at Coventry, it was simply the street—" Here Erode [Herod] ragis in the pagond and in the strete also."[5] This *platea* was unlocalized in the sense that it was given no definite scenic value, but it could become, if dramatic necessity demanded, any place not indicated by a mansion or house. Stage directions demanding violent foreshortening are frequent in these plays. " Here Jacob goes from Aran to the land of his birth ";[6] " Then Isaac takes the faggots on his back and they both go to the hill ";[7] " They go down [*i.e.*, from the mansion] and walk round twice and so to their horses "[8]—these indicate the use of the *platea* (as it was employed later in the Elizabethan theatre) to convey to the audience an imaginative lapse of time and of distance.

Around or behind the *platea* were set the mansions, so many as were required for the performance of the plays. In an ordinary short episode of a mystery cycle commonly two or three were demanded, but sometimes as many as six or more appeared for one drama. *The Death of Judas* from the *Ludus Coventriæ* requires Pilate's house, Herod's house, Hell, the bedroom of Pilate's wife, and the cross ; the *Assumption of the Virgin* of the same cycle has the house of the Episcopus, three houses of the Princes, the Temple, Heaven, and Hell. When, however, an entire cycle was presented (including scores of these small plays) obviously the number was considerably increased. The Digby *Mary Magdalene* needs sixteen houses in all. Twenty-two were used at Rouen in 1474,[9] and almost certainly as many as forty were set up elsewhere at one time.

The arrangement of these mansions in a line facing the audience is shown in the well-known setting for the Valenciennes *Passion* (Fig. 131) ; this, however, does not illustrate more than eight of the mansions actually used. Sometimes, apparently, these pieces of scenery were set in a

---

[1] On medieval stagery generally see Cohen and Chambers; also Fr. Schumacher, *Les Éléments narratifs de la Passion d'Autun et les indications scéniques du drame médiéval* (Romania, xxxvii (1908), 570–593); Donald C. Stuart, *Stage Decoration in France in the Middle Ages* (New York, 1910); G. Cohen, *L'Évolution de la mise-en-scène dans le théâtre français* (Bulletin de la Société de l'histoire du théâtre, January–April, 1910, 81–99); J. Endepols, *Het decoratief en de opvoering van het middelnederlandsche Drama* (Amsterdam, 1903). Hans Rueff (pp. 43–47) divides the staging into three types: (1) as in Lucerne, illusionistic, where the mansions are regarded topographically; (2) as in Donaueschingen, chronological with the mansions arranged like the Stations of the Cross; and (3) as in Tegernsee, stylistic with the cross before the throne of Heaven as a central point. *Cf.* R. Stumpfl, *Die Bühnenmöglichkeiten im XVI. Jahrhundert* (Zeitschrift für deutsche Philologie, liv (1929), 42–80; lv (1930), 49–78).

[2] For this see E. Norris, *Cornish Drama* (Oxford, 1859), II, ll. 1578, 1618.   [3] *Cf.* Heinzel, *loc. cit.*, pp. 25–29.

[4] *Op. cit.*, p. 10. Often in this text it is referred to in the plural ; cf. *per plateas* on pp. 7, 29.

[5] Shearman and Tailors' Coventry Corpus Christi play, l. 783.   [6] Towneley *Jacob* (No. 6), p. 53.

[7] Chester *Abraham* (No. 4).   [8] Chester *Adoration of the Magi* (No. 8).   [9] Cohen, *La Mise-en-scène*, p. 90.

semicircle, as they are, for example, in the equally well-known miniature by Jean Fouquet showing the martyrdom of St Apolline (Fig. 132). Here the characters are performing in the *platea*, and the mansions, six in number, are to be seen behind them. Besides this arrangement extant plans (see Figs. 133 to 138) indicate the placing of the mansions within a rectangular space, probably suggested by the interior of a church, while the Cornish plays show the use of circular 'theatres' with the mansions arranged in order outside.

In each of these the actual position of the houses seems to have been determined largely by the symbolic association of the points of the compass, and also by the architectural features of the medieval church. Here, however, there is some slight confusion. The east is obviously the seat of hope and divinity, and in the east many plays set Heaven or Paradise; indeed, the east is almost always the

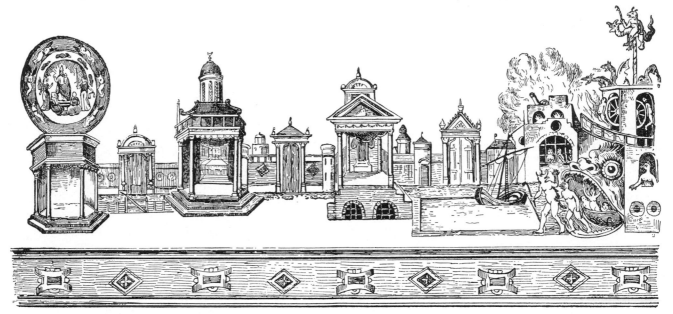

Fig. 131. THE VALENCIENNES MYSTERY PLAY
From K. Mantzius, *A History of Theatrical Art in Ancient and Modern Times* (Duckworth and Co.)

starting-point for the orientation of the mansions. The confusion is due to several facts. First, it will be obvious that if Heaven is in the east logic demands that Hell should be in the west. Logic, however, was generally made to bow to physical necessity, or to symbolic interpretation. In the medieval church, stairs to the crypt are commonly to be found to the left of the altar (from the point of view of the priest facing the congregation), and what more suitable a scene for Hell than the crypt?[1] The left of the altar is the south, but here intruded another conception. In the Old Testament it is said (with direct reference to current politics) that " evil appeareth out of the north."[2] This statement, applied generally, gave to the north a demonic significance, and as a result Hell sometimes tends to get located there. Add to these the fact that the left and right were also invested during the Middle Ages with a symbolic significance,[3] and it is realized what possibilities of confusion might appear.

An examination of extant plans and illustrations can now be undertaken. The Valenciennes set (Fig. 131) has Hell to the extreme left (which we may take as the equivalent of the south, the

[1] In all the following references left and right are the left and right of the priest or actor.   [2] Jeremiah vi, 1.
[3] See A. L. Frothingham, *Ancient Orientation Unveiled* (*American Journal of Archæology*, Ser. II, xxi (1917), 313 f. and 420 f.); R. Hertz, *La Prééminence de la main droite* (*Revue philosophique*, December 1909). Curt Fensterbusch deals with the significance of right and left in the classic theatres in *Philologus*, lxxxi (1926), 482–483. *Cf.* Matthew xxv, 34, 41.

position of the crypt stairs). Thence we proceed through Limbo, the Golden Gate, the House of Bishops, the Palace, Jerusalem, the Temple, and Nazareth to the Celestial Paradise. The same orientation appears in the Fouquet miniature (Fig. 132), where the house of God is shown to the right and a huge Hell to the left. Similar plans or descriptions of settings indicate a kindred idea at work. The prologue to the mystery of the twelfth-century *St Vincent*[1] indicates Paradise *en droit*, and *la* ('there') Hell—presumably on the left, as far from Heaven as possible. Between them are the other *lieux* or mansions—the seats of Diocletian, Maximian, and Dacian, of the Roman senators *dedan le capitolle*, in addition to *Valence la cité*, the temple, and a "vessel" with mariners. The impression one gets from the description suggests that these were set in a line facing the audience, as in the Valenciennes play (Fig. 131), although it is just possible that a series of two groups of mansions facing one another is indicated. Another description of the same period appears in the prologue to a French *Resurrection*,[2] and here almost certainly the two rows of mansions are demanded (Fig. 134).

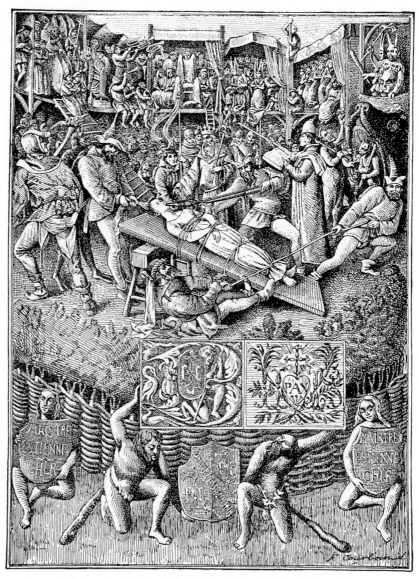

Fig. 132. THE MARTYRDOM OF ST APOLLINE
From K. Mantzius, *A History of Theatrical Art in Ancient and Modern Times* (Duckworth and Co.).

The conjectural plan made by Sir E. K. Chambers may not be precisely correct, for it is difficult to

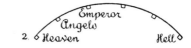

1. Paradies Nazareth Le Temple Hierusalem Le palais Maison des evesques doree [with lake] La porte Le Limbe despereo Lenfer

2. Emperor Angels Heaven Hell

3. Paradis Dioclicien Maximien Senateuro deRome Dacian Valence Le temple Chartre [Lake for the vesseau] Enfer

Fig. 133. PLANS OF THE MANSIONS IN (1) THE VALENCIENNES MYSTERY PLAY, (2) "ST APOLLINE," AND (3) "ST VINCENT"

[1] Cohen, pp. 76–77.   [2] Chambers, ii, 83; text and paraphrase also in *The Development of the Theatre*, p. 66.

make out exactly what is intended, but here again apparently Heaven is to the right and Hell to the left of the crucifix (the east). A plan of the Donaueschingen play serves to illustrate these, and at the same time introduces some interesting variants (Fig. 135). A reconstructed plan of this is given by Sir E. K. Chambers;[1] here is presented a sketch from the original manuscript. The arrangement of the mansions seems to be dominated by the three main divisions of a church—sanctuary, choir, and nave. At the top is Heaven (*Der Himmel*). Immediately below come the three crosses with four graves (*Die graben*) set round them. To the left in this section is the Holy Sepulchre (*Das heilig grab*). The middle division has two

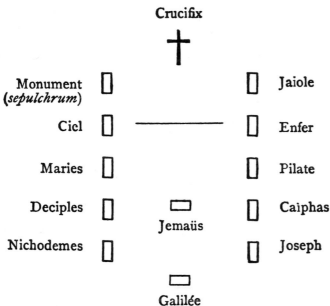

Crucifix

Monument
(*sepulchrum*)   Jaiole

Ciel   Enfer

Maries   Pilate

Deciples   Caiphas

Jemaüs

Nichodemes   Joseph

Galilée

Fig. 134. PLAN OF THE MANSIONS IN THE EARLY FRENCH "RESURRECTION"

From Sir E. K. Chambers, *The Medieval Stage* (Oxford University Press, 1903), ii, 83.

houses at the top, to the left that of Annas (*annas hus*) and to the right that of the Last Supper (*dass huss in das nachmal warc*). Below the former come the houses of Caiaphas (*kaiaf huss*) and Pilate (*pilatus huss*); below the latter the house of Herod (*herodes haus*). In the middle are two pillars, one for the cock and the other for scourging (*die sal dar an Jesus gaist*). A door leads to the last division, where Hell (*die hel*) is placed on the right and the Garden of Gethsemane, with Mount Olivet, on the left (*der gart* and *der olberg*). Now here Heaven itself is clearly in the east, and Hell, instead of being placed to the south, has been located in the north-west—that is to say, as far away from Heaven as possible. Clearly the other mansions move up from that place to the final scene on the cross and in Heaven. Especially fascinating are the two plans which accompany the Lucerne Easter play (Fig. 136).[2] This shows in the centre the square in which the performance was given, and then, round about, the setting of the houses. It is needless here to indicate fully the seats of the different characters, but a

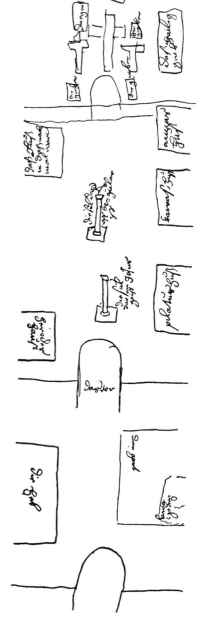

Fig. 135. PLAN OF THE DONAUESCHINGEN PLAY

Sixteenth-century sketch-plan, as reproduced in R. Froning, *Das Drama des Mittelalters* (1891), i, 276.

[1] Chambers, ii, 84. See M. B. Evans, *The Staging of the Donaueschingen Passion Play* (*Modern Language Review*, xv (1920), 65–76, 279–297).
[2] The plan for the first day is reproduced in *The Development of the Theatre*, p. 69, Fig. 58. See R. Brandstetter, *Die Luzerner Bühnenrodel* (*Germania*, xxx (1885), 205 f., 325 f., xxi (1886), 249 f.), and *Die Regenz bei den Luzerner Osterspielen* (Lucerne, 1886).

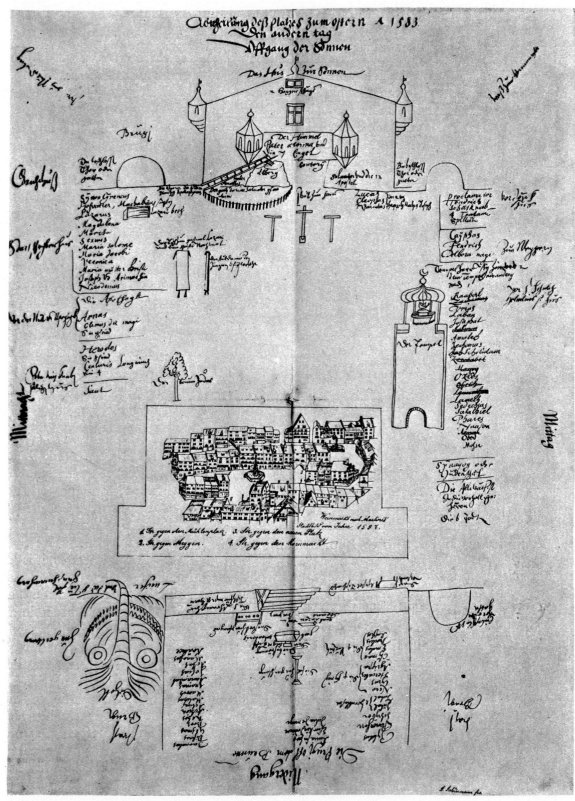

Fig. 136. Plan of the Lucerne Easter Play : Second Day

From Leibing, *Die Inscenirung des zweitätigen Luzernes Osterspiels* (1869).

few must be noted. At the top is Heaven (*Der Himmel Pater æternus vnd die 7 Engel*), with the house of the twelve apostles close by. Immediately below are the three crosses. A long line of houses moves downward both to left and to right. The former includes the seats of Caiaphas (*Caÿphas*) and other priests with the Temple (*der Tempel*). For the most part the latter is confined to New Testament characters. At the opposite end is Hell (*die Holl*), where sits Lucifer and his devils. Here too are placed a whole host of enemies to Christ, among whom, it is interesting to notice, is Hercales, who sits next to Nero, Cyrus, and Agrippa.

The arrangement of Ruof's Weingartenspiel must have been very similar, with Heaven at one end of a square and Hell immediately opposite to it (Fig. 137). The various houses, or mansions, are arranged in parallel lines at each side of these two main localities.

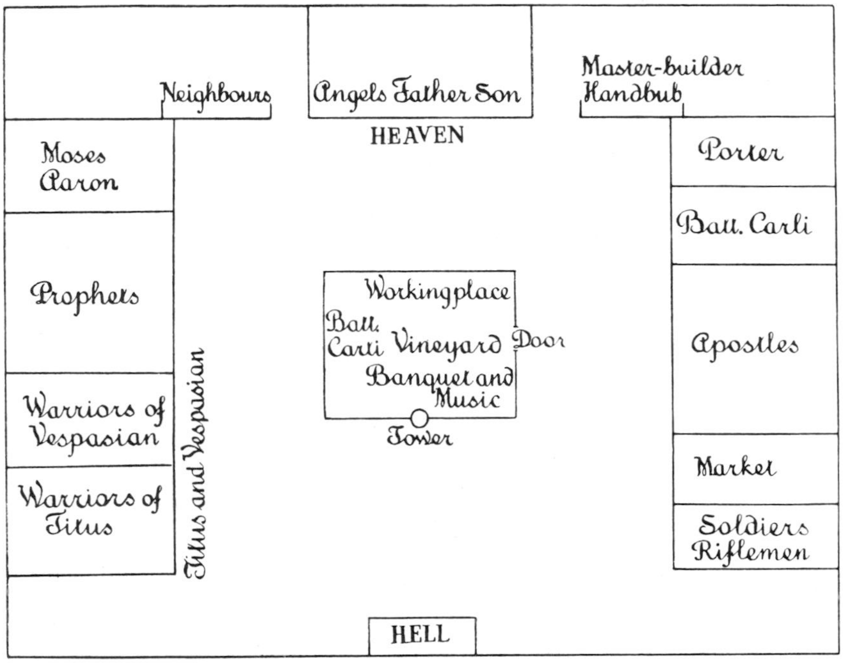

Fig. 137. RECONSTRUCTED SETTING OF RUOF'S WEINGARTENSPIEL

To complete this survey of the extant plans we may consider the two or three which are all that remain. In the Tegernsee *Antichrist* God is in the east, and the other points of the compass are granted to various nations (Fig. 138 (2)). The Alsfeld Passion-play [1] also provides a sketch-plan, which, however, is of less interest than the others (Fig. 138 (3)). Here is no Hell, and only the crosses connect it with the others. Interest, on the other hand, attaches to the Cornish rounds, but these demand a special discussion by themselves.

Amphitheatres, it is known, were used for the performances of mystery plays on the Continent.[2] In 1536 the old Roman amphitheatre was used for the *Actes des Apôtres*, while in 1541 at Paris there was made " a great theatre . . . in a round after the old Roman manner, so that the spectators could sit in a circle on tiers, one higher than the other." [3] In 1497 a German visitor to Rome noted that religious plays were being presented in the Colosseum, for performances in which Innocent III granted a special privilege to the Compagnia del Gonfalone.[4] Interestingly enough, however, the most certain records of such performances in ' rounds ' come from the manuscripts of the Cornish plays, and there are yet to be seen on Cornish land the remnants of the theatres in which these dramas once were given. One, at St Just, of stone, is now but the wall of a children's playground, but the other, at Perran, of earth, has still some of its original form intact (Fig. 139). The walls are completely circular, with two entrances, while the remains can be seen of a trench and a pit which once maybe was the grave of Adam and from which Abel's spirit cried to

[1] R. Froning, pp. 267, 860.   [2] See Cohen, *La Mise-en-scène*, pp. 65 and xiv.
[3] See N. C. Brooks, *Notes on Performances of French Mystery Plays* (Modern Language Notes, 1924); K. Christ, *Die Aufführung von Mysterien in Issoudun und Burges (1536) nach dem Bericht der Zimmerischen Chronik* (Zeitschrift für französiche Sprache und Literatur, xlvi (1923), 3).
[4] D'Ancona, i, 354–355.

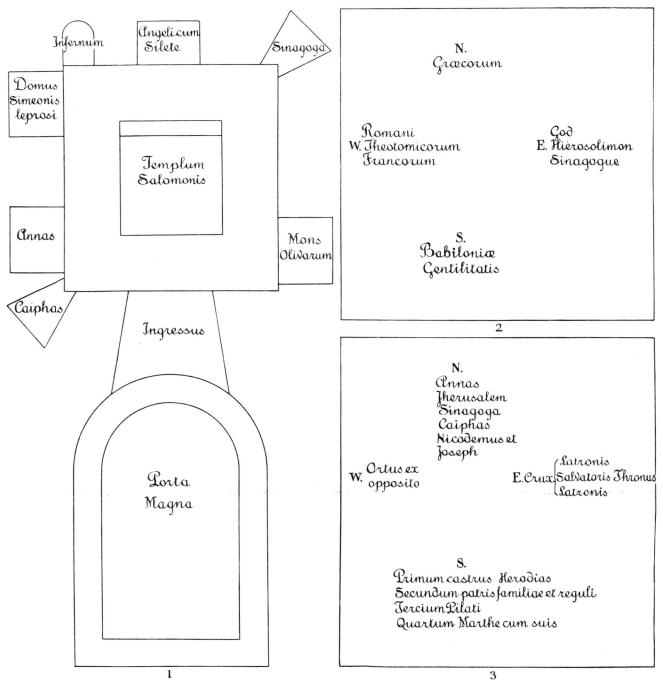

Fig. 138. Plans of the Mansions used in German Mystery Plays: (1) Vigil Raber's "Passion," 1514; (2) the Tegernsee "Antichrist"; (3) the Alsfeld "Passion"

Cain.[1] The manuscripts indicate how the mansions were arranged. The *Ordinale de Origine Mundi* [2] has thus three plans for the three parts, which show that, while some of the houses were

---

[1] See on these rounds T. C. Peter, *The Old Cornish Drama* (1906) and an article in the *Daily Telegraph* (*The Two Oldest English Theatres*, April 22, 1928).
[2] E. Norris, *ed. cit.*, i, 219, 479; ii, 201.

conception of Hell-mouth had developed somehow out of legend in the Dark Ages, and had fixed itself indelibly in the popular imagination. Already in the eleventh century the Cædmon manuscript [1] shows the damned souls miserably descending into its grinning jaws. Angels are driving down Belial into the flaming abyss in a Salzburg illumination (Fig. 145), while the dragon-head is to be seen both in the Valenciennes and Jean Fouquet miniatures (Figs. 131 and 132). Evidently this dragon-head was practicable. "Lett hell gape when ye father nameth yt," runs a stage direction in the Cornish *Creation*,[2] while in France it was described as "Hell made in the shape of a huge monster opening and closing as desired." [3] Here the machinist's aid was required, and at Mons no less than seventeen persons, under the direction of Jehan du Fayt, were required to work its marvels.[4] Attached to it was a prison which showed souls in torment, and near by was the "tower of Limbo," but clearly popular attention looked less to these than to the flaming monster's jaws from which, "with noise and clamour," devils were continually running.

SCENIC EFFECTS

That is not to say, of course, that the art of the machinist was confined to the region of Hell. Every mansion in a medieval performance had its own effects. Trap-doors were often put to various uses. The trench and pit in the Perran round (see Fig. 139) no doubt served this purpose, and this explains such a stage direction as "they put Pilate in the ground." [5] In a similar manner, and by a similar device, Christ descends in the *Appearance to Cleophas and Luke* from the *Ludus Coventriæ*.[6] These and similar effects were called *secrets* in France, and already [7] attention has been drawn to the fact that the managers of these *secrets* seem to have had a semi-professional standing; two machinists were thus summoned from Chauny to Mons in 1501. *Le Livre de conduite*, which Professor Cohen has so fortunately discovered, is full of records of the activities of these men. The devil Cerberus goes to the *secret* (here used for trap) and vomits forth fire; down goes Fergalus, his companion, and "makes a great smoke and a cannon" (*faire une grande fumée et ung canon*). At the Deluge the waters pour wildly on the stage. No conception of the medieval theatre could be falser than that which pictures it as a primitive and simple thing. *Naïveté* there may have been, as when, in the *Mystère du Viel Testament*, "a painted cloth, half white and half black," [8] is displayed to show in conventional form the dividing of light and darkness; but other records indicate a plentiful use of mechanical effects, often of a surprising nature. A flaming sword and a burning altar are called for in the *Ludus Coventriæ Fall of Man* and *Cain and Abel*; [9] sudden light gleams in the York *Bethlehem*, *Betrayal*, and *Harrowing of Hell*. In the *Actes des Apôtres* the vision of St Étienne appears, "gleaming like the sun," [10] while at Valenciennes the angels "make a great flaming splendour" (*faisant grand splendeur de flambe*).[11] The Digby *Mary Magdalene* shows a house

italien du xvᵉ siècle (*Gazette des beaux-arts*, No. 584). *Cf.* also Paul Weber, *Geistliches Schauspiel und kirchliche Kunst in ihrem Verhältnis erläutert an einer Ikonographie der Kirche und Synagoge* (Stuttgart, 1894); A. Springer, *Über die Quellen der Kunstdarstellungen im Mittelalter* (*Berichte über die Verhandlungen der königlich sächsischen Gesellschaft der Wissenschaften zu Leipzig*, Phil.-hist. Klasse, xxxi (1879), 1–40; Wilhelm Meyer, *Wie ist die Auferstehung Christi dargestellt worden?* (*Nachrichten von der königlichen Gesellschaft der Wissenschaften zu Göttingen*, Phil.-hist. Klasse (1904), 236–254; Anton Springer, *Ikonographische Studien* (*Mittheilungen der K. K. Central-Commission zur Erforschung und Erhaltung der Baudenkmale*, v (1860), 29–33, 67–75, 125–134, 309–322). In the last-mentioned pp. 125–134 deal particularly with the influence of the liturgical play. *Cf.* also A. Moore Smith, *The Iconography of the Sacrifice of Isaac in Early Christian Art* (*American Journal of Archæology*, Ser. II, xxvi (1922), 159–175).

[1] See *The Development of the Theatre*, p. 75, Fig. 66, which is reproduced from Sir Israel Gollancz' recension of the manuscript.
[2] *Ed. cit.*, l. 243.
[3] Cohen, *La Mise-en-scène*, p. 97. Part of the machinery is detailed in *Le Livre de conduite*, pp. lvi–lix.
[4] *Le Livre de conduite*, pp. lx and 544. [5] *The Ancient Cornish Drama*, ed. cit., III, 2111.
[6] For the use of traps in France see Cohen, *La Mise-en-scène*, pp. 161–162.
[7] See *supra*, p. 194; *cf.* G. Cohen, *Le Livre de conduite*, pp. xl–xli; É. Fleury, *Trompettes, jongleurs, et singes de Chauny* (Paris, 1874).
[8] *Ed. cit.*, i, 23; "Adoncques se doibt monstrer ung drap peinct, c'est assavoir, la moityé toute blanche et l'autre toute noire."
[9] *Cf.* also the *Mystère du Viel Testament*, i, 147. [10] Cohen, *La Mise-en-scène*, pp. 157–158. [11] *Id.*

and a temple on fire, and there the idols shake in an earthquake. Items of payment for the materials used in such devices are common in the accounts. "A skin of parchment and gunpowder" at Kingston,[1] "rosyn to the resurrecyon pley" at Reading,[2] "gonne poudor" at Shrewsbury,[3] refer to light effects ; "starche to make the storme" at Coventry,[4] "the baryll for the yerthequake," a link to set the world on fire, and a payment "for settyng the world of fyer" (it only amounted to 5d.) at the same town indicate the tempestuous effects which seem to have been so popular.[5]

Descents and ascents from above were freely indulged in; ropes in plenty must have been attached to the various mansions.[6] Sometimes these ropes were concealed by painted cloud-work. Fifty fathom of line was required for this at Chelmsford in 1562.[7] In the Chester *Doomsday* Jesus "descends as if in a cloud" (*quasi in nube*), and God the Father in the Cornish *Creation*[8] "must be in a clowde, and when he speakethe of heaven let ye levys open." At Mons "the cloud descends on the hill,"[9] while in the *Actes des Apôtres* there comes down "a cloud, round in shape of a crown."[10]

Various other appliances were in operation, such as the "subtil engin" of the *Mystère du Viel Testament*[11] and the *platines* on which were supported "the arms of God on the cross";[12] but we need not stay to discuss them here. Nor have the various properties special significance—the false swords, the painted animals,[13] the "Rybbe colleryd Red,"[14] even the painted scenery[15] and the title-boards.[16] It is necessary now to turn back to consider whence all this teeming life took its rise. Was it indeed only a development of the simple *sepulchrum* made of a pile of books on the cathedral altar?

Fig. 145. Belial and the Dragon's Mouth
Miniature by J. Stainberger v. Sprinzenstein in Jacobus da Teramo, *Ob Jesus das Recht hab gehabt, dass er die Höll und die Teufel hat beraubt.* Studien-Bibliothek, Salzburg.

[1] Chambers, ii, 375. [2] *Id.*, ii, 393. [3] *Id.*, ii, 394. [4] Ed. H. Craig, p. 91.
[5] Examples from all countries could be multiplied almost indefinitely. These may serve as representative.
[6] Readers of English mystery plays will be familiar with stage directions calling for such descents and ascents. For France see Cohen, *La Mise-en-scène*, p. 152, and *Le Livre de conduite*, p. 449, xciii.
[7] Chambers, ii, 346.
[8] Ed. Whitley Stokes, l. 1.
[9] *Le Livre de conduite*, p. 180. [10] Cohen, p. 153. [11] *Ed. cit.*, i, 211.
[12] G. Cohen, *Le Livre de conduite*, pp. lxiii, 501.
[13] *Omnia animalia depicta in cartis* (Chester *Noah*, No. 3). [14] Chambers, ii, 388.
[15] See G. Cohen, *Le Livre de conduite*, p. 472 (1e *autre piece de toille ayant deduit le soleille et la lune*); pp. lxii, 533 (*un petit bacquet de bois à mettre sur l'eauve . . . pour servir à la mer*).
[16] *Id.*, pp. lxiv, 536, and 565 ; and Cohen, p. 75.

MEDIEVAL IDEAS OF THE CLASSICAL STAGE

In order to answer this question, a reversion must be made to the popular idea concerning the acting of Terence's comedies. Already it has been seen [1] that these plays were supposed to have been recited either by the poet or by a friend of his, while a number of actors below provided suitable mimicry. The origin of this peculiar conception is easily traced. A classical reference to an actor who, being more skilled in gesture than in enunciation, employed a colleague to recite while he himself acted, or 'mimed,' may well have started the idea on its snowball course; but in addition to this there were the descriptions given by Isidore and others of the then puzzling word *scæna*. These grammarians and dictionary-makers, recognizing the ultimate derivation of the word, defined it as "a kind of house [*domus*]," whence there arose the idea that the *scæna* was a sort of box structure fitted up for the reciter of the play or for the poet—a theatrical pulpit, in fact. Isidore's exact words—for this is an important question—may be quoted:

> The 'scene' was the place below the theatre built in the form of a house, with a platform which was called the orchestra. On it the comic and tragic actors sang, and the *histriones* and *mimi* danced. There the comic and tragic poets ascended for their contests, while the others (the *histriones*) provided suitable gestures for the words they chanted. [2]

This interpretation of Isidore was followed by nearly all the miscellaneous writers of the following centuries. Papias in his *Vocabularium* (eleventh century) thus defines the scene as an *umbraculum*, or 'shaded place,' "in which the poets recited," as a "box which overshadowed a certain part of the theatre," and, Isidore-wise, as "a house in the theatre built with a platform." [3] More fully, in his commentary on the Senecan *Hercules furens*, Treveth [4] tried to convey the same idea. "Be it noted," says he,

> that tragedies and comedies were recited in the theatre after this fashion. The theatre was a semi-circular building in the midst of which was a small house [*parva domuncula* [5]] which was called the "scene." In it was a platform on which the poet stood to recite his poems. Outside it were the mimes, who accompanied the reciting of the poems by physical action, adapting their gestures to whatsoever character the poet was interpreting.

In their desire for embroidery other commentators went even further. Thus the author of a *Vita Terentii* explained to his readers that the scene is an *umbraculum* "which had a curtain extended before it from which the characters enter. These imitate with their gestures the words of the reciter." [6] This reference to the curtain is to be found also in the *Liber derivationum* of Hugutius (twelfth century). [7] "The scene," declares this writer,

> is an *umbraculum*, or shaded place in the theatres. It is covered with curtains. . . . In this *umbraculum* the masked characters [*personæ larvatæ*] were concealed. According to the words of the reciter, they came forth to make their accompanying gestures.

Now, there can be no question, with all this evidence before us, that the Middle Ages were woefully lacking in true knowledge of the classical theatre; it is perfectly true that this popular

---

[1] See *supra*, pp. 153–157.
[2] See also *supra*, p. 157. The Latin runs as follows: " Scena autem erat locus infra theatrum in modum domus instructa cum pulpito, qui pulpitus orchestra vocabatur; ubi cantabant comici, tragici, atque saltabant histriones et mimi. Ibi poetæ comœdi et tragœdi ad certamen conscendebant, hisque canentibus alii gestus edebant." In addition to the already-cited discussion of this question by Hermann see A. Glock, *loc. cit.*, pp. 36–37.
[3] " Scena umbraculum ubi poetæ recitabant. Scena est camera, quæ obumbrat locum in theatro. Scena domus in theatro est structa cum pulpito."—Hermann, p. 282.
[4] Hermann, pp. 280–281.
[5] An obvious elaboration of the Isidorian *domus*.
[6] Hermann, p. 287.
[7] Hermann, p. 287.

(and, in this instance, also scholarly) view of a Terentian performance was ridiculous in the extreme ; but its ridiculous character is of minor import. The significance of the Arsenal miniature (Fig. 102) for the history of the *jongleurs* has already been commented upon ; here must be considered the possible connexion between the Isidorian descriptions and the religious theatre which has been occupying our attention. It is assuredly strange to find that the word used for the ' scene '—*domus*—is precisely that which, in Latin form or vernacular, became the recognized term for a medieval religious set. This *domus* has a platform (the medieval scaffold) ; it is a " shaded place " (*umbraculum*) ; and it has curtains extended before it. All this might have been a definition of a mystery house or mansion. Noticeable, too, is the association of this *domus* by some of the commentators at least with the *personæ larvatæ*. Putting all together, it is hard for us not to find some evidence of connexion between the one and the other ; but what precisely was the nature of that connexion is harder to determine. We might assume that the ' learned ' comment on Terence and Seneca had influenced the development of the religious theatre in later years ; but, in general, there is no evidence to show that any attempt was made during the Middle Ages to differentiate the spoken word from action in the mystery play. In Cornwall, certainly, there was the curious custom whereby an ' ordinary,' holding the text of the drama, recited the words which were repeated after him by the actors. This seems suspiciously like a relic of the Isidorian idea, but no record of a similar practice elsewhere is extant. Were we to say that the religious drama influenced Isidore, we should have to postulate the existence of that religious drama in the seventh century ; but another possibility remains. The ancient mimic drama evidently employed a special technique of its own, in which were embodied certain devices of the classical literary theatre. Like the medieval religious actors, the mimes performed normally on an unlocalized *platea* behind which stretched a *siparium*, similar to " the curtains " within which " the masked characters were concealed," according to Hugutius. Is it not possible that out of this *siparium* the mimic actors evolved a kind of Punch and Judy-like structure in which they presented their shows, and which came to influence alike the grave commentaries of the scholars and the experiments of the earliest medieval religious players ? From their efforts may there not have descended through the centuries interest in those ' effects ' of which, as has been seen, the medieval drama is full ? May not the many *secrets* have been originally *secrets* of the professionals, of the *mimi*, of the *jongleurs* ? It is, at any rate, peculiar that the multiple setting seems to embody the two theatrical conditions of antiquity. The mansions arranged to face the audience represent the doors of a Roman theatre, and even the symbolic use of left and right might be traced to a similar symbolic use on the classic stage ; the *platea* represents the open place in front of the *siparium* on which the *mimi* gave their shows. Once more we seem to be in contact with a theatrical tradition connecting the ancient secular stage with the medieval religious theatre.

THE DRAMA IN BYZANTIUM

One question still remains to be asked : When and how did this religious drama arise ? Here the lack of texts prohibits the giving of a direct answer, and any theory must be put forward only tentatively. It may be suggested, however, that the orthodox conception of slow development out of a trope is not necessarily that which is true to the facts. By the middle of the twelfth century so highly developed a play as the *Mystère d'Adam* could make its appearance ; so late as the sixteenth century primitive liturgical dramas might still be given in the churches. The vast cycle and the short, few-lined Latin service-drama assuredly overlapped during the periods when available texts make the forming of definite theories possible, and, noting this fact, we may well ask ourselves whether in reality the mystery cycle evolved directly from the primitive expansion of the liturgy.

O

Only a few suggestions in this connexion may here be made. The first concerns the Byzantine theatre, or, more generally, the theatre of the East. There the mimes flourished to a late period,[1] and there are to be found several indications of a religious dramatic activity. The purely literary tradition must be largely ignored. This, of which the Χριστὸς πάσχων is the best-known example, seems to have had a long duration, the roots of which are to be found in Egypt. Already in the second century of our era[2] a certain Hellenized Jew named Ezechiel had produced a play, Ἐξαγωγή (*Exodus*), fragments of which have been preserved in later Christian writings. It included among its characters Moses, Sepphora, Chus, Raguel, God, and a Messenger, and evidently dealt with the whole subject of the departure of the Israelites. The provenance of this drama seems to be in the neighbourhood of Palestine or Syria. Perhaps the continuation of this experiment among the Christians was due to the Arian movement. The Arian Church made for a 'vulgarization' of the liturgy, and perhaps its devotees made use of the drama in the service of religion. Athanasius[3] in attacking Arius seems to refer to a Θάλεια (*Thaleia, The Comic Muse*) which he describes as κατὰ τὸν Αἰγύπτιον Σωτάδην ('fashioned according to the model of the Egyptian Sotades'— a mime writer). This work Sathas[4] calls a "liturgical drama" (λειτουργικὸν δρᾶμα), but, as La Piana[5] shows, the wording of Athanasius is decidedly ambiguous. Whether Θάλεια was or was not a play, however, the fact remains that Athanasius likens it to stage pieces[6] and connects it with the work of Sotades. Of the same period, but unfortunately equally doubtful, are the dialogues of Metodius of Byzantium (*d.* 321). Of these we have, complete or fragmentary, the Συμπόσιον ἢ περὶ ἀγνείας (*The Banquet of Chastity*), the dialogue περὶ αὐτεξουσίου (*Freewill*), and Ἀγλαοφῶν ἢ περὶ ἀναστάσεως (*Aglaophon, or The Resurrection*). These are, of course, literary exercises, and not real dramas even of the closet kind, but they do seem to betoken a living interest taken in dramatic form among fourth-century Byzantine ecclesiastics. Sathas[7] makes much of the reference in Theophylaktos Simokattes to the θεανδρικοῖς μυστηρίοις and the θεανδρικὴ πανδαισία during the time of the Emperor Maurice (A.D. 591); but these, in all probability, were merely allusions to the service of the Eucharist.[8] Out of the eighth century comes a *Susanna* (now lost) which Eustathius[9] attributes to "the Damascene" (ὁ Δαμασκηνός), whether Nicholas of Damascus (first century B.C.) or John of Damascus (eighth century A.D.) is not positively certain, although it seems probable that the allusion is to the latter. Peculiarly enough, it is declared that the earlier Nicholas also wrote tragedies and comedies, but of what kind cannot be said. The last of the series is the Χριστὸς πάσχων (*Christ's Suffering*), a play deeply influenced by the Greek tragic dramatists and written probably about the eleventh century A.D.[10] This Passion-play is not, however, a stage piece; as a literary exercise and as a document proving late interest in the Greek theatre it has interest, but it can hardly be connected, except indirectly, with the medieval religious drama.[11]

[1] See *supra*, p. 148.

[2] The date is uncertain. Some scholars would make this an ante-Christian work. See K. Philippson, Ἐζεκίηλος καὶ Φίλων (Berlin, 1830); K. Krumbacher, *Geschichte der Byzantinischen Litteratur* (527–1453) (Munich, 1891; *Handbuch der klassischen Altertumswissenschaft*, ed. I. von Müller, IX, i); and Felice Momigliano, *Il primo Dramma d'argomento sacro* (*La Nuova Rassegna* (1893), 309–314).

[3] J. P. Migne, *op. cit.*, Series Græca, xxvi, col. 705.

[4] Κρητικὸν θέατρον ἢ συλλογὴ ἀνεκδότων καὶ ἀγνώστων δραμάτων μετὰ ἱστορικῆς εἰσαγωγῆς περὶ τοῦ παρὰ βυζαντίνοις θεάτρου (Venice, 1878), p. ρμβ'.

[5] G. La Piana, *Le Rappresentazioni sacre nella letteratura bizantina dalle origini al sec. ix* (Grottaferrata, 1912), pp. 25–28.

[6] J. P. Migne, *op. cit.*, Series Græca, xxvi, col. 24. [7] P. τοη'.

[8] La Piana, pp. 29–33. [9] *Id.*, p. 59.

[10] The play is given in J. P. Migne, *op. cit.*, Series Græca, xxxviii, 131–338, and has been edited separately by J. G. Brambs (Leipzig, 1885). Various dissertations have been written on it; for earlier references see the edition of Brambs. An attempt to find an author is made by I. Hilberg in his essay *Kann Theodorus Prodromus der Verfasser des Χριστὸς πάσχων sein?* (*Wiener Studien*, viii (1886), 282–314).

[11] Much the same position is occupied by the plays of Hrotswitha in the tenth century. These may have been played, and in any case testify to the interest retained in the dramatic form; *cf.* P. von Winterfeld, *Hrotsvits literarische Stellung* (*Archiv für das Studium der neueren Sprachen und Litteraturen*, cxiv (1905), 25 f. and 293 f.).

THE RELIGIOUS DRAMA OF THE MIDDLE AGES

That Byzantium had something that resembled a true religious theatre is known from the testimony of Liudprand, Bishop of Cremona, who was in the Eastern capital during the years 949–950 and 968–969. The church of St Sophia, he declared, had been turned into a theatre, while he records that he was received by the Emperor on the day when an *Elijah* play was being performed.[1] This seems conclusive, and it indicates a form of acted religious drama existent at a period when, it is supposed, Europe was ignorant of all but the simplest trope. The plays to which Liudprand refers are connected by La Piana with the dramatic homily, a remarkable development of which can be traced from the sixth century onward. It were needless here to enter into the details of this development; sufficient is it to note that such scenes as the Annunciation, the Nativity, and the Descent into Hell were given dialogue treatment in these sermons which were almost dramas. Throughout these the influence of the secular theatre is to be traced. Joseph is made the regular ζηλότυπος, or 'jealous husband'—indeed, Mary actually calls him so: ζηλότυπος γάρ ἐστιν.[2] The Devil becomes a boaster, a *miles gloriosus*, and Orcus, the guardian of Limbo, is made the poor, trembling buffoon. How those dramatic sermons were presented is suggested by a set of miniatures in some manuscripts of sermons by James of Coccinobaphus.[3] These certainly seem theatrically inspired and belong to a popular art-form distinct from the conventional and official Byzantine miniature-painting. Their vividity, the repetition of the same scene at different moments in its

Fig. 146. A MYSTERY PLAY AT BYZANTIUM

Miniature from an early manuscript of dialogue sermons by Jacobus of Coccinobaphus as reproduced by L. Bréhier in *Monuments et mémoires publiés par l'Académie des Inscriptions et Belles-Lettres : Fondation Piot* (Paris, Librairie Ernest Leroux, xxiv (1920), p. 103).

development, the regularity of the costumes, and the settings all point to realistic depiction of stage scenes (*cf.* Fig. 146). The last show houses of the Western type, such as the Temple, the mansions of Joseph and Elizabeth, or vaguely conventional backgrounds which, as Bréhier suggests, might well be painted curtains, relics of the mimic *siparium*.

These miniatures, added to the literary investigations into the texts of the dramatic homilies, appear to prove definitely the flourishing in Byzantium of a type of religious play not over-far removed from the mystery dramas of the West, a type of play, moreover, which is deeply influenced by the mimic secular stage. La Piana, in his study of this Eastern theatre, pleads strongly for a very tangible influence exerted by it upon the Western mystery cycle. The *Vos inquam* sermon, which was the basis of many of the Prophets plays,[4] he finds to be inspired by Byzantine homilies, and he suggests that the writers of these plays often passed direct to Eastern sources, taking thence

---

[1] La Piana, pp. 60–61; Reich, i, 797. The passages appear in his *Relatio de legatione Constantinopolitana* (in *Monvmenta Germaniæ historica*, iii, 310), and in his *Antapodosis* (*id.*, iii, 354).

[2] La Piana, pp. 161–162.

[3] On these see Louis Bréhier, *Les Miniatures des " Homélies " du moine Jacques et le théâtre religieux à Byzance* (*Monuments et mémoires publiés par l'Académie des Inscriptions et Belles-Lettres : Fondation Piot*, xxiv (1920), 101 f.) and his review of La Piana's work in *Journal des Savants*, N.S., xi (1913), 357, 395.

[4] See *supra*, p. 176.

the dramatic treatment of some prophets not included in the Latin sermon.[1]   The comic treatment of Joseph and Mary, as well as the prominence given to the devils, he would associate with the same source.[2]   There is undoubtedly considerable authority for this belief, and if it be true, then we must presume a very early knowledge in the West of the activities in this kind at Byzantium.   Indeed, the question arises whether the earliest liturgical plays may not be regarded rather as simplifications of an already existing religious theatre than as the originals of that theatre.   The activities of Byzantine writers must be taken as arising out of the same ideal which inspired Arius—that of combating the secular players by providing a form of Christian entertainment.   But the West was always suspicious of the richness and artistry of the Greek ceremonial, and the simple liturgical plays may owe their primitive austerity to a desire for simplification just as, in later centuries, opponents of the mystery cycles endeavoured to counter their iniquities by less ornate, less comic, and less imaginative subject-matter.   For this view, it must be confessed, there is small extant evidence, but one truly remarkable document may be adduced.   In the Anglo-Saxon poem on *Christ* the story of Jesus' birth is told in the old style of the Teutonic epic.   The poet has been narrating the miserable patience of those who awaited in torment the coming of God's Son, when suddenly we come on a passage which, unless interpreted in one way, is wholly unintelligible.[3] The passage starts :

Eala ioseph min	iacobes bearn
mæg dauides	mæran cyninges.
nu þu freode scealt	fæste gedælan
álætan lufan mine.	Ic lungre eam
deope gedrefed	dome bereafod.

And so continues a passage of thirty lines until we reach narrative again.   Now, the only way of making sense of this section of the poem is to interpret it as a sudden breakaway from the epic manner in which reported speech is always prefaced by a " He said," and to read it as genuine dramatic dialogue, thus :

MARY. Lo, Joseph mine, child of Jacob,
Kinsman of the great King David,
Must thou forthwith renounce thy troth,
And leave my love ?
    JOSEPH.   Very deeply
Am I troubled, bereft of honour,
For because of thee I have heard, in words,
Much great grief, many sorry speeches,
Much insult, and they utter scorn against me,
And many angry words : sad in mind
I must shed tears.   God may easily
Heal the deep sorrow of my heart,
And comfort me distressed.   Alas, young damsel,
Mary maiden !
    MARY. Why mournest thou
And lamentest sorrowing ? Never found I
Fault in thee or any cause of blame
For evil done, and yet thou speakest such words,
As thou thyself wert filled with every sin
And all transgression.
    JOSEPH.   Too much bale
Have I received from this conception.

---

[1] *Op. cit.*, p. 306.   [2] *Op. cit.*, pp. 318–326.
[3] *The Exeter Book*, ed. by Sir I. Gollancz (E.E.T.S., 1893), i, 12–15.   The translation given is taken from this.

How can I escape the hateful words.
Or how can I find any answer
'Gainst my foes ?   'Tis widely known
That from the glorious temple of the Lord,
I joyfully received a maiden pure
And spotless ; and now all is changed,
Through whom I know not.   Neither availeth me,
To speak or to be silent ; speak I the truth,
Then must David's daughter die,
Slain with stones ; yet is it harder
To conceal crime, to be doomed to live hereafter
Perjured, hateful unto all the folk,
Accursed 'mong men.

At this point a return is made to epic standards with " Then the maid unravelled the true mystery, and thus she spake."   Until that, however, there is presented to us thirty lines of pure dramatic dialogue, ninth-century dramatic dialogue dealing with Joseph and Mary.   Whence has this come ? It is hardly possible to believe that it owes its origin to aught but something in the nature of a play known to the author or to his original.   At once our minds turn to the Byzantine dramas on similar themes, and we wonder whether, even before the tenth-century Saint-Gall manuscript yields us the little *Quem queritis* liturgy, there did not exist in Europe the beginnings of a religious drama based on Eastern models.   Was it for these the mimes were borrowing copes from the ecclesiastics ? What more natural than that they who wandered far and were known in many Courts should have returned from Byzantium with plots and scenes in their heads which might, because of their Scriptural character, placate the austere prelates who wished to banish all mimicry from men's eyes ? The dramatic passage in *Christ* is hard to explain on any other assumption.

IV

THE COMMEDIA DELL' ARTE

(i) INTRODUCTORY

A T first it seems a far cry from Joseph to Pantalone, from Mary to Isabella, from the Devil to Arlecchino, but if there is any validity in the thesis that the medieval religious drama owes part of its strength to the secular tradition, the chasm separating the merry comedy of the Renascence and the edifying drama of the Middle Ages may not, after all, be so great. To step from the *Christ* to a *commedia dell' arte* scenario is not entirely to move from one world into another. The two have something in common, and obviously, in endeavouring to assess what and how much they share in spirit, we must devote ourselves to the problem of the origin of the Italian Comedy itself and of the component stock types who bestow upon it its special character. This question is one to which many diverse answers have been given in the past, and perhaps it may be well, before entering upon a formal summary, to outline the three solutions which have been most commonly accepted by scholars and by critics.

THEORIES REGARDING THE ORIGIN

A regular line of descent from the Atellanæ was postulated largely in the eighteenth century, and such a line of descent forms a cardinal thesis in Maurice Sand's volumes on the Italian players. The mimic drama, naturally, with its associated *funambuli*, enters in here, but the Atellanæ, characterized by the stock figures of Pappus, Dossennus, Bucco, Maccus, and the rest, are taken as the chief inspiring force, attempts being made to identify the modern Italian figures with their Roman-Etruscan prototypes.[1]

Against this view Reich[2] has issued a caveat. The Atellanæ, in his view, perished completely in the Dark Ages ; but the pure mime persisted, both in the provinces of the Western Empire and throughout the realms of the East. In the former the mimic drama tended to decay, although it always retained its interest for the populace and eventually produced those farce-interludes which are familiar to students of fourteenth-century French literature.[3] At Constantinople, however, and in other Eastern centres, many of the primitive forms of the Roman mime were preserved unaltered. This Eastern branch of the mimic play continued its career, independently, up to modern times, the late Turkish puppet drama called Karagöz being a relic of classic days.[4] Here appears the bald-headed mime ; here the characters wear the phallus ; here is a doctor who reminds us of Dossennus ; here, even, are figures wearing ancient Greek dress, apparently dim memories of the once-popular Herakles (Fig. 147), whose name may be preserved in a comic hero called Kör-oghlu.

---

[1] This is the view taken by most writers on the *commedia dell' arte* up to recent times; but the evidence brought forward in its defence has generally been meagre in the extreme. For enunciations of this theory see Maurice Sand, *The History of the Harlequinade* (1915), i, 11–12; A. Bonilla y San Martín, p. 42; L. Stoppato, pp. 50–56; V. de Amicis, *La Commedia popolare latina e la commedia dell' arte* (Naples, 1882), p. 56 f. Mario Apollonio, *Per una Storia dei comici dell' arte* (*Rivista d'Italia*, xxx (1927), 3) stresses the importance of the medieval *jongleur* tradition.

[2] Reich, i, 679 ff.   [3] See *supra*, pp. 171–173.

[4] Reich, i, 619 f.; and see the authorities cited there. Josef Horovitz deals with this subject in *Spuren griechischer Mimen im Orient* (Berlin, 1905).

THE COMMEDIA DELL' ARTE

Besides giving this independent Oriental tradition, however, the Eastern mime, according to Reich, was responsible for the development of the *commedia dell' arte*. When Constantinople fell in 1453 many men from the East flocked into Venice. The arrival and activities of the scholars are well known; but Reich would include among the scholars bands of entertainers as well. At Venice, at Rome, and at Cyprus (under Catarina Cornaro) these mimes may have flourished, and, retaining a brighter memory of the ancient things than did their Western brethren, yet dealing with fundamentally the same style of comedy as the others did, their art was freely assimilated, bringing fresh blood to the indigenous farce and so creating the enthusiasm for the *commedia dell' arte*.

Both of these theories countenance belief in a direct tradition from classic times, but recently the opinion of the scholars has swung round to an agnostic conservatism. Here the views of Constant Mic (Constantine Miklashevsky) may be regarded as typical.[1] For him the growth of the *commedia dell' arte* is due simply to two things: first, the renewed study of the classical plays themselves, and, secondly, the satiric tendency in the Renascence movement as a whole. He believes that written imitations of classical plays preceded the improvisatorial period, pointing out that Ruzzante's early farces are fully penned, and suggests that most of the plots and characters were inspired by such literary exercises. The *commedia dell' arte* as we know it, he observes, does not make its definite appearance till the second half of the sixteenth century, whereas poets had been producing Italian plays modelled on Terence from the year 1500 onward. His whole attitude is expressed in one line: "Requiescant in pace Sanniones." [2]

Fig. 147. Herakles in Turkey
From H. Reich, *Der Mimus* (Weidmannsche Buchhandlung, Berlin, 1903), p. 628.

But are we really to put R.I.P. over Sannio's grave? Must we not first resurvey the evidence which can be brought forward on both sides before falling in with what, after all, is largely a scholarly fashion? It may be that Mic is right, in which case we must suppose the Roman mime to have vanished in the medieval period; yet such a dogmatic assertion demands careful analysis and detailed argumentation. Our task must, then, be to outline the main features of the *commedia dell' arte*, noting particularly those features in it which seem to support one or another of the views presented above.

THE MEANING OF THE TERM

Naturally, we must, as a preliminary, ask ourselves what precisely the phrase *commedia dell' arte* means. In the first place, we note that this phrase does not appear before the eighteenth century, when it seems to have been used in the sense of 'professional comedy,' as opposed to amateur or literary comedy. According to this interpretation, *arte* means 'the special art of playing these pieces,' just as the phrase 'the profession' is used in theatrical parlance to-day to signify 'the special profession of acting.' Maurice Sand, indeed, takes it in the sense of 'artistic perfection,' [3]

---

[1] Constant Mic, *La Commedia dell' arte* (Paris, 1927), pp. 208–230; *cf.* Benedetto Croce, *Saggi sulla letteratura italiana del Seicento* (Bari, 1911), p. 198, 261; G. Cortese, *Il Dramma popolare in Roma nel periodo delle origini e suoi pretesi rapporti con la commedia dell' arte* (Turin, 1897).
[2] Ireneo Sanesi, *La Commedia* (Milan, 1911), i, 437–438, ranks himself with those who attack Reich's main thesis.
[3] Sand, i, 23.

but the other view seems at once more in accordance with the facts and more favoured by students of the subject.[1]   Commonly, in earlier times, the words *commedia all' improviso* or *commedia a soggetto* were employed to designate this type of theatrical art,[2] and these perhaps have more truly the air of definitive exactitude than the vaguer term by which the Italian Comedy is known to-day. Both suggest that this special form of theatrical activity is distinguished by the fact that the actors improvise their words (*all' improviso*) and work only from a plot, theme, or subject (*a soggetto*).   This being implied by the names given to the type, it therefore behoves us first of all to consider the extent to which this improvisation was commonly to be found in the professional theatres of the sixteenth and seventeenth centuries.

"Very attractive," says Perrucci,[3]

albeit difficult and full of pitfalls, is this style of comic acting.   No one should attempt it except persons of a keen and lively disposition, such as are cognizant of grammatical rules, of figures of speech,

---

[1] *Cf.* M. Scherillo (in *The Mask*, iii (1910–11), 113).

[2] See Mic, pp. 22–25.

[3] Andrea Perrucci, *Dell' Arte rappresentativa, premeditata ed all' improvviso* (Napoli, 1699).   For convenience those passages which are cited in the interesting collection of Enzo Petraccone are referred to his anthology—*La Commedia dell' Arte : Storia, Tecnica, Scenari* (Naples, 1927), p. 69.   Besides the studies by D'Ancona, Mic, Sand, Adolfo Bartoli, *Scenari in editi della commedia dell' arte* (Florence, 1880), Duchartre, and Stoppato, and the special works cited above or later, the following may be particularly noted : Winifred Smith, *The Commedia dell' Arte: A Study in Popular Italian Comedy* (New York, 1912); Emilio del Cerro, *Nel regno delle maschere* (Naples, 1914); M. Scherillo, *La Commedia dell' arte* (Milan, 1895; in *La Vita italiana nel Seicento*); Vittorio Rossi, *Le Lettere di mess. Andrea Calmo* (Turin, 1888; with an interesting introduction); A. Neri, *Fra i comici dell' arte* (*Rivista teatrale italiana*, xi).   Articles on particular types, companies, and players will be cited later, but there must be mentioned here some dissertations on the comic figures : G. Cocchi, *Studio sulle maschere italiane* (Florence, 1891); Elvira Ferretti, *Le Maschere italiane nella commedia dell' arte e nel teatro del Goldoni* (Rome, 1904); Gordon Craig, *The Characters of the Commedia dell' Arte* (*The Mask*, iv (1912), 199–202), and *The Commedia dell' Arte Ascending* (*The Mask*, v (1912), 104–108); Giuseppe Petrai, *Lo Spirito delle maschere* (Turin, Rome, 1901); Clelia Falconi, *Le quattro Principali maschere italiane, nella commedia dell' arte e nel teatro del Goldoni* (Rome, 1896); E. Rigal, *Les Personnages conventionnels de la comédie du xvie siècle* (*Revue d'histoire littéraire de la France*, iv (1897), 161–179); Giuseppe Petrai, *Maschere e burattini* (Rome, 1885); A. Vitti, *Le Maschere nel teatro italiano* (*Nuova Antologia*, VI, lxxxiii (1916), 71–75).   To these should be added the works on the influence of the improvised comedy on various later writers (see *infra*, pp. 346–347).   Naturally, the spirit of the Italian style is discussed in many books on the fortunes of the *commedia* players abroad.   Besides Armand Baschet, *Les Comédiens italiens à la cour de France sous Charles IX, Henri III, Henri IV et Louis XIII d'après les lettres royales, la correspondance originale des comédiens, les registres de la "Trésorerie de l'Épargne" et autres documents* (Paris, 1882), and Émile Campardon, *Les Comédiens du roi de la troupe italienne pendant les deux derniers siècles* (Paris, 1880, 2 vols.), note should be made of Louis Riccoboni, *Histoire du théâtre italien* (Paris, 1727); Louis Moland, *Molière et la comédie italienne* (Paris, 1867); E. Camerini, *I Precursori del Goldoni* (Milan, 1872); G. Apollinaire, *Le Théâtre italien, avec une étude sur le théâtre italien en France* (Paris, 1910); le Baron de Fismes, *Études sur quelques comédiens, farceurs, et bouffons français et italiens au xviie siècle* (Nantes, n.d.); Gabriel Guiliemot, *Le Théâtre italien* (*Revue contemporaine*, II, li, 92–119); C. Magnin, *Les Commencements de la comédie italienne* (*Revue des deux mondes*, October–December 1847); Émile Picot, *Pierre Gringoire et les comédiens italiens* (Paris, 1878); N. M. Bernardin, *La Comédie italienne en France et les théâtres de la foire et du boulevard* (Paris, 1902); Eugenio Camerini, *La Commedia dell' arte alla Corte di Baviera nel secolo xvi* and *I Tipi comici* (in *Nuovi profili letterari*, iii, 220–224, 225–274, Milan, 1876).   Other similar studies are mentioned later.   Many important records are contained in various histories of local theatres.   Of these a bibliographical account appears in A. Ademollo, *Bibliografia della cronistoria teatrale italiana* (*Gazzetta musicale di Milano*, Nos. 35 and 36, 1888), and Guido Bustico, *Bibliografia delle storie e delle cronistorie de' teatri d'Italia* (*Rivista musicale italiana*, xxvi (1919), 36–65).   The most important modern surveys are as follows: Alessandro Ademollo, *I Teatri di Roma nel secolo decimo settimo* (Rome, 1888); A. Bertolotti, *Musici alla corte dei Gonzaga in Mantova dal sec. XV al XVIII* (Milan, n.d.); Egberto Bocchia, *La Drammatica a Parma: 1400–1900* (Parma, 1913); Bruno Brunelli, *I Teatri di Padova* (Padua, 1921); Alberto Chiappelli, *Storia del teatro in Pistoia dalle origini alla fine del secolo XVIII* (Pistoia, 1913; extracted from the *Bullettino storico pistoiese*, xii, 3 and 4); A. N. Cionini, *Teatro e arti in Sassuolo* (Modena, 1902); Giovanni Crocioni, *I Teatri di Reggio nell' Emilia* (Reggio, 1907); Federico Barbieri, *Per la Storia del teatro Lombardo nella seconda metà del secolo XVI* (*Athenæum*, Pavia, ii (1914), 105–116, 377–397); Benedetto Croce, *I Teatri di Napoli* (Bari, 1916; cited as 'Croce'); Giambattista Crovato, *La Drammatica a Vicenza nel Cinquecento* (Turin, 1895); A. Ferretto, *Il Teatro dei Duchi di Mantova a Genova nel sec. XVII* (*Il Cittadino*, October 17, 1919); Alessandro Gandini, *Cronistoria dei teatri di Modena dal 1539 al 1871* (continued by Luigi F. Valdrighi and Giorgio Ferrari-Moreni, 3 vols., Modena, 1873); P. Ghinzoni, *Trionfi e rappresentazioni in Milano* (*Archivio storico lombardo*, xiv (1887), 4); Giovanni Giannini, *Teatro popolare lucchese* (Turin, 1895); Giuseppe Radiciotti, *Teatro, musica, e musicisti in Sinigaglia* (Milan, 1893; extract from *Le Marche*, iii); Corrado Ricci, *I Teatri di Bologna nei secoli XVII e XVIII* (Bologna, 1888); Alfredo Segrè, *Il Teatro pubblico di Pisa nel seicento e nel settecento* (Pisa, 1902); Angelo Solerti, *Musica, ballo, e drammatica alla Corte Medicea dai 1600 al 1637* (Florence, 1905); A. Solerti and D. Lanza, *Il Teatro ferrarese nella seconda metà del sec. XVI* (*Giornale storico*, xviii (1891), 148–185; cited as Solerti-Lanza).   There are, of course, many other works which contain important chapters on the *commedia dell' arte*; such as Pompeo Molmenti, *La Storia di Venezia nella vita privata* (Bergamo, 1906); Ireneo Sanesi, *La Commedia* (Milan, 1906); Luigi Tonelli, *Il Teatro italiano dalle origini ai giorni nostri* (Milan, 1924); and A. Agresti, *Studii sulla commedia italiana del sec. XVI* (Naples, 1871).   *I Comici italiani* (Florence, 1897–1905), by Luigi Rasi, contains a mine of information both general and particular, and must be frequently cited; an earlier collection, Francesco Bartoli's *Notizie istoriche de' comici italiani che fiorirono intorno all' anno MDL fino a' giorni presenti* (Padua, 1780), is also important. For comparative purposes may also be mentioned G. Caminneci, *Brevi cenni storici, biografici, artistici delle maschere siciliane in Palermo* (Palermo, 1884), and F. de Maria, *La Festa dei "personaggi" a Monte San Giuliano* (*La Lettura*, x).   As this book was going through the press, there has appeared the *Storia della commedia dell' arte* (Rome, 1930), by M. Apollonio, a very important study.

of tropes and of the whole art of rhetoric ; for they are forced to express on the spur of the moment what the poet can spend time over.[1]

The dangers and difficulties are glozed over by none of the early writers on the subject. Cecchini [2] points out the care which must be taken so as to avoid awkward confusions among the characters on the stage. " The actor who is speaking a soliloquy on the stage," he warns us, " must remember to stop his discourse as soon as he is joined by another character and to pay more attention to this than to any mutilation his conceit may suffer from the breaking of his discourse." [3] " In this art," says Barbieri,[4] " there is demanded a natural talent conceded but to few men ; out of a hundred persons who come upon the stage not ten are really good." [5] " The curse of improvisation," thinks Riccoboni,[6] " is that the skill of the good actor is absolutely at the mercy of the person with whom he is conversing," [7] and the good actor is indeed rare, for

> it is not figure, memory, voice, sentiment that suffice for the improvisatorial actor ; he will fail unless he has a lively and fertile imagination, a great felicity in expression, unless he possesses all the graces of language, unless he has become fully acquainted with the requirements of all the different situations in which his *rôle* places him.[8]

Often is the weak actor forced to fall back upon monologues and the like, with the result that he introduces matter hopelessly at variance with the improvisatorial style.

On the other hand, the apologists are all full of the most glowing praise of the *commedia dell' arte* at its best. " Very attractive " (*bellissima*) Perrucci thought it, while Riccoboni, who was wide awake to its dangers, declared :

> Improvisation gives an opportunity for comic variety ; for, although a spectator may go to see the same *canevas*, or scenario, many times, it will always be a different play he witnesses. The improvisational actor performs in a more lively and natural manner than the actor who learns his part beforehand.[9]

This praise of the style when ably exercised is to be found repeated again and again throughout the course of the seventeenth and eighteenth centuries, so that we are permitted to remain in no doubt that the actors commonly re-created their parts entirely from performance to performance. That, however, improvisation was not unaccompanied by the work of memory seems equally certain, and we may suppose that a typical *commedia dell' arte* performance was not unlike an Atellan farce, where, too, written dialogue was mingled with words conjured up for the occasion. Whether there was any tradition along those lines cannot be determined. It is certainly true that Sansovino [10] declares Francesco Cherea to have been " the inventor in those parts of performing comedies *a soggetto* "—that is to say, from a scenario alone—but the phrase " in those parts " (*i.e.*, Venice)

---

[1] " Bellissima, quanto difficile e pericolosa, è l' impresa, nè vi si devono porre se non persone idonee ed intendenti, e che sappiano che vuol dire regola di lingua, figure rettoriche, tropi e tutta l' arte rettorica, avendo da far all' improviso ciò che premeditata fa il poeta."

[2] Pier Maria Cecchini, *Frutti delle moderne comedie et avisi a chi le recita* (Padova, 1628) ; Petraccone, p. 8.

[3] " Necessario ricordo è ancora a colui, che parla solo in iscena, di dover tacer subito ch' egli è sopragiunto da chi dee parlare ed aver più risguardo a questo avviso che a l' offesa del concetto ritenuto per debito di silenzio."

[4] Niccolò Barbieri, *La Supplica* (Venezia, 1634). I quote from the corrected edition published at Bologna in 1636. *Cf.* Petraccone, p. 33.

[5] " In quest' Arte è di mestiere un talento naturale, a pochi conceduto, e di cento, che si pongono a recitare, dieci non riescono buoni " (p. 70).

[6] Louis Riccoboni, *Histoire du théâtre italien* (Paris, 1727) ; Petraccone, p. 62.

[7] " Le malheur de l'impromptu est que le jeu du meilleur Acteur dépend absolument de celui avec lequel il dialogue."

[8] " La figure, la mémoire, la voix, le sentiment même ne suffisent donc pas au Comédien qui veut jouer à l'impromptu, il ne peut exceller s'il n'a une imagination vive et fertile, une grande facilité de s'exprimer, s'il ne possède toutes les délicatesses de la langue, et s'il n'a acquis toutes les connoissances nécessaires aux différentes situations où son rôle le place."

[9] Riccoboni, *Histoire*, p. 61 ; Petraccone, p. 62. " L'impromptu donne lieu à la variété du jeu, en sorte qu'en revoiant plusieures fois le même Canevas, on peut revoir chacque fois une pièce différente. L'Acteur qui joue à l'impromptu joue plus vivement et plus naturellement que celui qui joue un Rôle appris."

[10] Francesco Sansovino, *Venetia città nobilissima* (Venetia, 1604), p. 168.

seriously qualifies the general statement. Suggestions of improvisation appear in the texts of some mystery dramas, and it may have been that the secular entertainers were accustomed to eke out short texts with lively patter. But we cannot tell for certain; records are so scarce regarding the activities of earlier times that nothing may be deduced on one side or on the other.

It is necessary here to pause for a moment in order to consider how far the two styles—the improvisatorial and the memorized—might be combined. Sometimes we find play texts which present a few scenes in dialogue and others merely in summary form.[1] Such plays, however, are all of late date, and there is no evidence to show that other examples existed in the sixteenth century. Many of the comedies printed in Gherardi's *Le Théâtre italien* take this form, but these, after all, were not in the regular *commedia dell' arte* tradition; they were plays written by French authors for a troupe of mingled French and Italian performers, and may perhaps be likened to the more sophisticated Atellan farces and mimes penned by Roman authors in the days of the Empire. They preserve the cardinal features of the comic theme and characters, but they cannot be employed to throw light upon the activities of the earlier performers.[2]

Attempts, indeed, have been made to explode the so-called 'legend' of the improvisatorial comedy. Emilio del Cerro essays in caustic tone to dismiss the picturesque images which, he thinks, later historians have falsely called into being concerning the *commedia dell' arte*. That type of play, he believes, had in it hardly anything of true improvisation, or, to phrase his theory more exactly, there was not more of improvisation among the early Italian players than may be found at any period of theatrical history. 'Gagging' has always been an actor's privilege, and for del Cerro the typical *commedia dell' arte* performance consisted merely of a series of largely memorized scenes flavoured by occasional 'gagging' of this sort. Such a view, however, can in no wise be substantiated. Early records are unanimous in their testimony to the effect that the *commedia dell' arte* was improvisatorial. Among weaker performers, no doubt, memorized lines, ill fitted to the subject at hand, might wretchedly eke out a lack of talent, but for the more famous actors, who delighted Courts in Italy, in France, in England, and in Germany with the variety of their impromptu, such would be impossible. Del Cerro's arguments are those of one who wishes at all costs to maintain a theory that shall be out of the ordinary.[3]

USCITE AND CHIUSETTE

From the earliest period, on the other hand, the improvisatorial actors could not avoid storing their memories with certain stock phrases and stock speeches; and it is this admixture of improvised and memorized which now we must consider. "The actors," says Barbieri,[4]

engage in study and load their memories with a great mass of matter, such as stock sentiments, conceits, love speeches, complaints, ejaculations of despair and madness, which they keep ready for all occasions. Their studies, of course, are in accordance with the character of the stage persons whom they represent.[5]

[1] *Cf.* the interesting experiment in *commedia mista* made by G. Bartolomei in his *Didascalia, cioè la dottrina comica di Girolamo Bartolomei, già Smeducci* (Firenze, 1658–61; 3 vols.), and the examples given by A. Bartoli, pp. lxvii–lxx.

[2] Riccoboni refers to this innovation in his *Histoire du théâtre italien* (1728), i, 71–72 : " Dans ce même tems plusieurs des bonnes Comedies écrites furent metamorphosées par les Comediens; pour se servir de leurs Acteurs masqués, ils en tiroient les simples Canevas et avec quelque changement on voioit ces belles Comedies originairement écrites en Vers et en Prose, jouées par les Comediens à l'impromptu avec le Pantalon et le Docteur, à la place des deux Vieillards Bourgeois, et l'Arlequin et le Scapin, à la place des Valets." Many plays, however, were written for the Italian comedians directly; and many French plays were originally derived from earlier scenarii.

[3] For criticism of del Cerro's views see also G. Ortolani, *La Condanna d' Arlecchino ?* (*Gazzetta di Venezia*, July 10, 1914), C. Levi, *Dalla commedia dell' arte a Carlo Goldoni* (*Il Marzocco*, xix (1914), 27), E. Re, review of del Cerro's book in *Giornale storico* (lxvi (1915), 260–265).

[4] Petraccone, p. 26 ; *La Supplica*, p. 47.

[5] " I Comici studiano, e si muniscono la memoria di gran farragine di cose, come sentenze, concetti, discorsi d'amore, rimproveri, disperazioni, e deliri, per haverli pronti all' occasioni, ed i loro studij sono conformi al costume de' personaggi, che essi rappresentano."

THE COMMEDIA DELL' ARTE

Our knowledge of these studied lines is derived mainly from the essay *Dell' Arte rappresentativa*, by Andrea Perrucci, where are presented many examples of conceits and stock speeches. A jealous lover may thus fall back upon a sentence or two of fanciful despair :

> I am jealous because I am in love. O strange antithesis! Love's flame is so conjoined to the ice of jealousy that they create a mixture capable of taking my life away. Through these two horrors my passion is an infirmity. I freeze outwardly while inwardly I am consumed by a fierce-burning fever.[1]

The most useful of such speeches clearly were those which could be uttered without reference to the words of other characters. The example given above is virtually a soliloquy, and virtually soliloquies were also the so-called *uscite* (' exits ') and *chiusette* (' closures '). The former were memorized phrases, usually consisting of a passage of prose followed by a rimed couplet, which could be employed to make a fitting departure from the stage. Perrucci[2] provides specimen *uscite* for " a happy lover," for " a silent lover," for " a rejected lover," for " a scornful lover," and so on, along with miscellaneous " exits " of a philosophic cast such as one " against Love " and another " against Fortune." The *chiusette* were used for a different purpose. As the name implies, they were ' closures,' generally of the rimed couplet variety, which could be introduced to bring a discourse to a fitting end. Perrucci warns the young actor against exaggeration of their use ; but the space he devotes to the subject shows plainly their popularity among the performers.

It is to be understood, also, that the prologues to the various plays were commonly recited and not improvised.[3] Sometimes in rime and sometimes in verse, these prologues were regularly suited to the nature of the character by whom they were to be delivered, being often written in the dialects spoken by a Pulcinella, an Arlecchino, or a Graziano. The prologue, however, really is no integral part of the play itself, and accordingly this aspect of a *commedia dell' arte* performance may be dismissed immediately. So, too, can be dismissed the *intermezzi* and *duetti*, some specimens of which have been preserved. The typical *intermezzo*, as shown, for example, in the Adriani manuscript in Perugia,[4] seems to have been the equivalent of the Elizabethan ' jig,' and may indeed have had some influence on that sub-dramatic form ; the *duetto* was simply a dialogue song introduced into the midst of the action as songs had been introduced in ancient Roman mimes. Both frequently appeared between the acts, and introduced dance alongside of the music.

THE LAZZI

Besides the words improvised for the occasion and the memorized speeches, the Italian comedians had one great source of comic merriment. In the classical mime the *tricæ*,[5] or ' tricks,' of the actors had eked out the inherent dullness of many a plot, and these *tricæ*, whether through a direct line of tradition or not we cannot tell, found their counterpart in the *lazzi* of the Italian comedians. Some considerable doubt exists concerning the derivation of this word. Riccoboni[6] determined that it was a Lombard corruption of the Tuscan *lacci*, which literally means ' ties ' or ' knots,' but this derivation has been for the most part rejected in favour of the theory which makes *lazzi* a popular form of *l'azzo* or *l'azione*, meaning ' action ' or ' pieces of stage business.'[7] The latter has the merit of serving to define the word, for the *lazzi* were simply scenes of action independent of the episodes outlined in the scenario. " We give the name of *lazzi*," remarks Riccoboni, " to the actions of Harlequin or other masked characters when they interrupt a scene

---

[1] " Io son geloso perchè sono amante. O strana antiparistasi ! Il loco d' amore è così al gelo della gelosia congiunto che fanno un misto atto a tòrmi la vita, e la mia passione per questi due barbari è una infermità, che far ch' io geli nell' esterno, quando una violentissima ed ardente febre mi consuma le viscere."—Petraccone, p. 77.

[2] Petraccone, pp. 79–83.   [3] On these see Mic, pp. 99–102; Petraccone, pp. 273–277.

[4] See Petraccone, pp. 278–282. For Perrucci's remarks on the *intermedi* see Petraccone, pp. 197–198.

[5] See *supra*, p. 76.   [6] Petraccone, p. 64 ; *cf.* M. Apollonio, pp. 158–163.   [7] Mic, p. 79.

by their expressions of terror or by their fooleries. These have nothing to do with the subject on hand, and to it return must always be made." [1] This certainly seems to be the strict sense of the word, although no doubt it came to be applied to anything—dialogue as well as action—not strictly germane to the theme. " A *lazzo*," declares Perrucci, " means simply something foolish, witty, or metaphorical in word or action." [2] Various early writers have left on record descriptions of famous *lazzi* of this kind. Unfortunately, many are too vaguely narrated to be understandable at the present day, but from those that remain we can recapture some idea of the earlier style. Riccoboni chooses the following example :

> In the play of *Arlequin dévaliseur de maisons* Harlequin and Scapin are servants of Flaminia, who is a poor girl separated from her relatives and who is reduced to abject misery. Harlequin complains to his comrade about his sad predicament and of the diet which for some time he has had to put up with. Scapin consoles him, saying that he will arrange matters. He bids him make a noise in front of the house ; Flaminia, aroused by Harlequin's cries, asks him what is the matter ; Scapin explains the subject of the row, while Harlequin keeps on crying and saying he will leave her. Flaminia pleads with him to stay and recommends herself to Scapin, who makes a proposal for drawing her honourably out of the misery which afflicts her. While Scapin is explaining his plan to Flaminia, Harlequin interrupts the scene with different *lazzi* ; sometimes he pretends that his hat is full of cherries, which he feigns to eat and the stones of which he pretends to pitch at Scapin's face ; sometimes he makes show of catching a fly, of clipping off its wings in a comic manner, and of eating it ; and so on. [3]

This specimen makes clear the scope of this device, but a few others may be added from the Adriani manuscript. [4] Here is the " *lazzo* of weeping and laughing " :

> The *lazzo* of weeping and laughing is when a character goes on cheating another. For instance, when the old man weeps at the departure of his son and smiles at the thought of having free opportunity of enjoying, without any fear of jealousy, the woman he loves. The son does the same. [5]

And here the *lazzo* of Pulcinella's goodness :

> The *lazzo* of Pulcinella's goodness is that he, hearing from the Capitano or another that they wish to kill him, and not being known to them in person, praises himself, saying, " Pulcinella is a witty, straightforward, good fellow." [6]

Most of the verbal *lazzi* are of this rather crude type ; and many of the action *lazzi* deal merely with rough-and-tumble. One such is that in which Pulcinella, when being escorted to prison, tells his guards that he wishes to tie his shoelace, and, when given permission, seizes his captors by the legs, throws them over, and so escapes. [7] Others of a similar character are of frequent occurrence in the manuscript French version of Biancolelli's scenarii. There we find references

---

[1] " Nous appelons Lazzi ce que l'Arlequin ou les autres Acteurs masqués font au milieu d'une Scene qu'ils interrompent par des épouvantes, ou par des badineries étrangères au sujet de la matière que l'on traite, et à laquelle on est pourtant toujours obligé de revenir." —Riccoboni, *Histoire*, i, 65. In the Correr scenarii the word *trionfi* seems to be used as a variant of *lazzi*.

[2] " Lazzo non vuol dir altro che un certo scherzo, arguzia o metafora in parole o in fatti."—Petraccone, p. 191.

[3] " Dans la pièce d'Arlequin Dévaliseur des Maisons Arlequin et Scapin sont valets de Flaminia, qui est une pauvre fille éloignée de ses parents et qui est réduite à la dernière misère. Arlequin se plaint à son camarade de sa fâcheuse situation et de la diette qu'il fait depuis longtemps. Scapin le console et lui dit qu'il va pourvoir à tout. Il lui ordonne de faire du bruit devant la maison ; Flaminia attirée par les cris d'Arlequin, lui en demande la cause; Scapin lui explique le sujet de leur querelle; Arlequin crie toujours et dit qu'il veut l'abandonner. Flaminia le prie de ne point la quitter et se recommande à Scapin, qui lui fait une proposition pour la tirer honnêtement de la misère qui l'accable. Pendant que Scapin explique son projet à Flaminia, Arlequin par différents *lazzi* interrompe la scène: tantôt il s'imagine d'avoir dans son chapeau des cerises, qu'il fait semblant de manger et d'en jetter les noyaux au visage de Scapin; tantôt de vouloir attraper une mouche qui vole, de lui couper comiquement les ailes et de la manger, et choses pareilles."—Petraccone, p. 65.

[4] Petraccone, pp. 263–265.

[5] " Il lazzo del piangere e ridere è che uno va gabbando l' altro, come allor che il vecchio piange per la partenza del figlio e ride per aver campo aperto senza gelosia di goder l' innamorata. L'istesso fa il figlio."

[6] " Il lazzo della bontà di Pulcinella è che lui, sentendo dal Capitano o da altri dire che lo vogliono uccidere, e non essendo conosciuto, lui loda se stesso con dire, ' Pulcinella è omo faceto, semplice e buono.' "—Petraccone, pp. 264–265.

[7] Petraccone, p. 267.

to *lazzi* so well known at the time that description proved unnecessary, such as the " Catching the Flea," [1] and to others which are more fully described.   One runs thus :

> I [*i.e.*, Biancolelli as Harlequin] arrive on the stage ; there I find Trivelin stretched on the ground.   I think him dead and try to drag him to his feet ; then I let my wooden sword fall down.   He takes it and hits me on the buttocks.   I turn round without speaking, and he gives me a kick on the back so that I tumble down.   Up I get again ; I seize and carry him ; I lean him against the wings on the right-hand side of the stage.   I look round at the footlights, and meanwhile he gets up and leans against the left-hand side-wings.   This *lazzi* is repeated two or three times [2]

Many of these *lazzi* were, as may be imagined, somewhat vulgar—at least, in the modern conception ; one must always remember before passing judgment that there are scenes even in Shakespeare's plays not exactly suited to the tone of our own age.

THE MOUNTEBANKS

This question of vulgarity carries us to a familiar theme—the theme of mimic obscenity. Reading the words of an opponent such as Ottonelli, one seems to be listening once more to Chrysostom's strictures on the mime of his day :

> The Zanni, the Coviellos, the Gratianos, and their companions . . . want to draw laughter from obscenity. . . .   In the public playhouse . . . the actors introduced a licentious attempt on the part of an ardent lover to assault a woman he desired.   The woman, getting down from a window, escaped in an almost naked condition.   She tried to cover herself with a large sheet, but, in point of fact, she remained upon the stage a shameful, naked figure.[3]

An anonymous writer cited by Adolfo Bartoli declares that at Florence on one occasion was to be seen " a Europa completely naked." [4]   Now, as for the Roman mime, it must be confessed that much of this obscenity thus described by the moralists was actually apparent upon the stage, but it is not necessary to conclude, as Emilio del Cerro seems to do,[5] that the audience was inartistic and depraved, or that all the companies indulged in this pandering to vulgarity and pornographic tastes.   The audience who attended a typical *commedia dell' arte* show was a mixed audience.   " If I am not mistaken," says Barbieri—and he ought to know—

> the aims of those who go to see a play may be summed up thus : many go out of curiosity to see if the actors are good, and many because they flock to all novelties ; one man goes because he is bored, and another because he doesn't know where to spend the next hour ; many go to hear new conceits and good discourse, and others to listen to the comic parts ; one man goes in order to pick up hints, for sometimes he comes on the stage himself, and another goes for the sake of his companions' conversation and another to discover some one who will stand him a dinner ; one man goes because he does not want to spend that hour at the gambling tables, and another goes to get rid of his ill-humour.[6]

[1] *Traduction du Scenario de Joseph Dominique Biancolelli, dit Arlequin, et l'histoire du theatre italien depuis l'année 1577.   Jusqu'en 1750 et les années suivantes, par M. G.* [Gueullette], 2 vols., in the Bibliothèque de l'Opéra (Paris), i, 386.

[2] *Op. cit.*, i, 271.   " J'arriue sur La Scene J'y trouue Triuelin par terre je le crois mort, je veux Le Leuer sur ses pieds je laisse tomber ma batte, Il La prend et M'en donne sur les fesses, je me retourne sans parler Il me donne vn coup de pied dans Le dos dont je tombe, je me releue je prends et Je Le porte et appuye a droitte contre La Cantonade Je reuiens sur Le bord du theatre, pendant ce temps Il Seleue et va se placer contre La cantonnade a gauche, ce Lazzy Se repette deux ou trois fois."

[3] " I Zanni, Couielli, Gratiani e simili . . . vogliono cavare il ridicolo dalla oscenità. . . . Nel publico Theatro . . . i Comici rappresentarono un disonesto tentativo d' un ardito amante, che si sforzara di assalire una bramata donna, la quale però, calando per una finestra, sen fuggiva ignuda, e cercava coprirsi con un . . . grande lino ; ma in fatti . . . ella restava oggetto ignudo e svergognato."—*Della Christiana Moderazione* (1646), i, 29, 37.

[4] Adolfo Bartoli, p. xc, quoting from a *Trattato contro alle Commedie lascive*, MS. Cod. Riccardiano 2435.

[5] *Nel Regno delle Maschere* (1914), pp. 211–244.   *Cf.* also G. Sforza, *I Comici italiani del sec. xvi e xvii e la moralità del teatro* (*Gazzetta letteraria*, xiv, 15–19).

[6] " S' io non erro, il fine di coloro, che vanno alla Comedia, somma in questi capi : Molti vanno per la curiosità di sentir, se i Comici sono valent' huomini, e molti per l' uso di vedere tutte le novità ; chi va per passar l' ozio, e chi per non saper dove andar in quell' hora ; molti vanno per udir concetti nuovi, o bei discorsi, e altri per sentire le parti ridicole ; chi va, perchè talvolta anch' egli recita per osservar' i modi, e chi va per la conversazione de' suoi compagni, e chi per trovar chi paghi per lui ; chi va per non voler' in quell' hora giocare, e chi per passar qualche mal' humore."—*La Supplica*, p. 75.   *Cf.* Petraccone, p. 34.

populace and the profit of the charlatan. If, however, a Harlequin served a quack on occasion, at other times he was the boon companion of a king; if some performers led evil lives others were honoured for the honesty and purity of their behaviour. Barbieri has occasion to refer to various anti-theatrical pamphlets which " describe the actors as rascals and the actresses as courtesans." " The actresses," he says, speaking of those with whom he was acquainted, " are married, . . . and for my part I esteem them as excellent women." [1]   Indeed, no severer critics of the lower-class performers can be found than the apologists for the higher style of *commedia dell' arte*. " The trouble," thinks Perrucci,

> is that nowadays every one imagines that he is capable of plunging into comic improvisation; the very dregs of the populace make a try at it, esteeming it easy of accomplishment; but their failure to realize the difficulties arises from ignorance and ambition. Whence it is that the vilest rascals and acrobats take it into their heads to amuse the populace and delight them with dialogue, . . . and so propose to perform improvised plays in the public squares, mangling the plots, speaking all off the point, gesticulating like madmen, and—what is worse—indulging in countless obscenities and vulgarities.

This " vile crowd," he thinks, is " infamous and deserving of every kind of abuse." [2]   Barbieri echoes the words of Perrucci. " Those vile actors who endeavour to introduce obscenities " parallels the latter's condemnation, while the following passage emphasizes the distinction between the bad and the good:

> Comedy is an artistic and not a buffoonish entertainment, restrained and not exaggerated, witty and not vulgar; he who gives the name of comedy to every piece of clownage is condemning his own tastes. [3]

The tale is taken up by nearly all the early writers, by Garzoni in his *Piazza* and by Cecchini in his *Frutti*. [4]   The former, too, presents us with a highly entertaining picture of one of the poorer companies arriving at a town or village in the course of their strollings:

> When these companies come to a town immediately to the sound of a drum the announcement is made that my lords the players have arrived; the actress, dressed as a man, with sword in hand, goes off to beat up a muster. The citizens are asked to attend a comedy or a tragedy or a pastoral in the palace or at the Pilgrim's Inn, where the mob, naturally curious and eager for novelties, immediately hurries to secure seats, and, buying their tickets, the spectators enter the hall. Here one finds a trestle stage, scenery scrawled out with charcoal in the vilest taste; one listens to an overture of braying asses and buzzing bees; one hears a prologue fit for nothing; a stupid tune like Brother Stopino's; wearisome acts dull as ditchwater; *intermedi* bad enough to send the actors to the gallows; a Magnifico (Pantalone) not worth a farthing; a Zanni no better than a goose; a Graziano (Dottore) who mumbles his words; a Courtesan stupid and mawkish; a Lover who torments his arms at every speech; a Spaniard (Capitano) who does not know what to say except *mi vida* and *mi corazon*; a Pedant who plunges into Tuscan at every moment; a Burattino who has no other gesture but that of putting his hat on his head; a Signora with a voice like a ghost's, with the speech of the dead, the gestures of a sleep-walker, one who shows eternal enmity to the Graces and has a permanent quarrel with beauty. [5]

---

[1] The critics " descrivono i Comici per infami, e le Comiche per meretrici. . . . Le Comiche (parlo delle nostre Lombarde) sono maritate, . . . e, per me le tengo tutte per donne da bene."—Petraccone, pp. 40–41; *La Supplica*, p. 126.

[2] " Il male si è che oggi ognuno si stima abile per ingolfarsi nella comicia improvisa, e la più vile feccia della plebe vi s' impiega, stimando la cosa facile; ma il non conoscere il pericolo nasce dall' ignoranza e dall' ambizione. Ond' è che i vilissimi ciurmatori e saltinbanco, che s' hanno posto in testa d' allettare le genti e trattenerli con parole . . . vogliono rappresentare nelle pubbliche piazze commedie all' improviso, storpiando i sogetti, parlando allo sproposito, gestendo da matti e, quel ch' è peggio, facendo mille oscenità e sporchezze . . . questa gentaglia vile, infame e degna di tutti i vituperi "—Petraccone, p. 70.

[3] " La Comedia è trattenimento gustoso; e non buffonesco; convenevole, e non smoderato; faceto e non sfacciato; E chi dà nome di Comedia ad ogni frascheria, parla secondo il suo ingegno."—Petraccone, pp. 26, 37–38; *La Supplica*, p. 48.

[4] See Petraccone, pp. 6, 16; T. Garzoni, *La Piazza universale di tutte professioni* (Venezia, 1585).

[5] " Come entrano questi dentro a una città, subito col tamburo si fa sapere che i signori comici tali sono arrivati, andando la Signora vestita da uomo con la spada in mano a fare la rassegna, e s' invita il popolo a una comedia o tragedia o pastorale in palazzo o all' ostaria del Pellegrino, ove la plebe, desiosa di cose nuove e curiosa per sua natura, subito s' affretta a occupare la stanza, e si passa per mezzo di gazette dentro alla sala preparata. E qui si trova un palco postizzo, una scena dipinta col carbone senza un giudicio al mondo; s' ode un

THE SCENARIO

It will be necessary to refer later to the vulgarities and insipidities of some performances in this kind; but here for the moment we may leave the subject. It is, however, important to remember that the *commedia dell' arte* was not one single uniform art type, and that in dealing with its failings, in listening to the complaints of the Puritans, we must bear in mind the presence, in every European country during the sixteenth and seventeenth centuries, of the mountebank and his motley crew of masked entertainers.

Fig. 150. A FRENCH CHARLATAN STAGE, WITH THE FIGURES OF POLICHINELLE AND
BRIGANTIN

Seventeenth-century print. Exemplar in the Bibliothèque Nationale, Paris (Cabinet des Estampes, Tb + 1, vol. i, B. 344).
Photo Giraudon

(ii) THE SCENARIO

No true *commedia dell' arte* had a complete text. Suggestions of the dialogue might be provided by the author, but normally only the barest outline found its way into the official scenario, or *soggetto*, which took the place both of prompt-copy and of actors' parts in the performance of an ordinary play. Happily, we are able to form a good conception of the scope of these scenarii from the

concerto antecedente d' asini e galavroni; si sente un prologo da ceretano; un tono goffo come di fra Stopino; atti increscevoli come il malanno; intermedi da mille forche; un Magnifico che non vale un bezzo; un Zani che pare un' occa; un Graziano che cacca le parole; una Ruffiana insulsa e scioccarella; un innamorato che stroppia le braccia a tutti quando favella; un Spagnuolo che non sa proferire se non *mi vida* e *mi corazon*; un Pedante che scarta nelle parole toscane a ogni tratto; un Burattino che non sa far altro gésto che quello del berettino che si mette in capo; una Signora sopra tutto orca nel dire, morta nel favellare, addormentata nel gestire, c' ha perpetua inimicizia con le grazie e tiene con la bellezza differenza capitale."—Petraccone, pp. 6–7.

P

jealousy, and revenge were frequent themes in this style of comedy ; a variant example may be found in *La Forsennata prencipessa* in the Scala collection.

In general, it may be said that the aim of the 'tragic' scenarii was to thrill. Lovers' misfortunes appear in nearly all, and there are not wanting outside devices, such as the sympathetic animals and the incantations of the wizards, to capture the attention of the audience. Alongside of these 'tragic' themes, and often very similar to them, appeared the 'pastoral.' The scene of *La Nave* in the Locatelli group is Arcadia, but the action is similar to that of Scala's *L'Alvida*. Here it is Pantalone and Graziano who are lost in the wilderness ; they too suffer from hunger and thirst ; only it is Bacchus, and not a lion, who succours them. The serious loves of Elpino and Clori, as well as the comic loves of Zanni and Nespola, have their parallels in the 'tragic' plays. Nor are wizards, spirits, and incantations wanting here. These spirits, indeed, are familiar in the 'pastoral' group. One more, *Arcadia incantata*, may be mentioned in this connexion. This play reminds us of *The Tempest*. The Dottore, Tartaglia, Pollicinella, and Coviello are shipwrecked and suffer from various inconveniences. As in *The Tempest*, a " Mago " is the central figure in a drama the serious interest of which comes from a set of criss-cross love emotions.

Neither the tragic nor the pastoral, however, could vie in popularity with the purely comic plays, and to this section therefore we must devote more space than could be spared for the others. The majority of these depend mainly on two themes—that of love and that of comic intrigue. Thus, in *L'Amante interesato* we are presented with three or four groups of characters : the Magnifico, with his daughter Clarice and his servant Argentina ; the Dottore, with his son Oratio, his daughter Flavia, and Oratio's servant, Virginio ; Celio, a poor scholar, and his servant, Zanni ; Cassandro ; and Giangurgolo. The incidents and intrigues are various, until we reach a series of weddings at the close. In the beginning Cassandro had desired Clarice as his wife, but the play ends with his marrying Flavia, while Celio takes Clarice, and Giangurgolo makes a comic match with Argentina. On these lines are most of the scenarii developed. In *Non può essere* Luzio tries to put obstacles in the way of his sister Violante, who wishes to marry Orazio, and at the same time pursues his own courtship of Cinzia. Pollicinella, the Dottore, and Coviello form a merry trio in the midst of the love emotions. Disguises and tricks fill out the plot of *L'Astrologo*, where Fabio loves Eularia, Curzio loves Florinda, and Tartaglia loves Argentina. Often the emotions go in tangled wise. Thus, in *Le Disgrazie di Colafronio* Orazio loves Ardelia, who detests him ; so Zanni is detested by Colombina. In the end the knot is straightened out, Ardelia marries her adored Fabbrizio and Orazio consoles himself with Lucinda. Ottavio, in *L'Incauto ovvero l'inavvertito*, loves and is loved by Ardelia, the betrothed of Valerio. Cola is employed to further their ends, and succeeds in discovering that a slave-girl is really Lucinda, a well-born maiden ; the latter attracts Valerio, and Ottavio takes his Ardelia by the hand. In Scala's *Il Marito* it is Pantalone, the old father, who tries to prevent his son, Orazio, from marrying Graziano's daughter, Isabella. The action is complicated by the jests of the clever Pedrolino and the foolish Arlecchino, but the happiness of the lovers is secured by the devices of Franceschina, Isabella's nurse, who dresses as a young man and pretends that she is married to the girl. When the Capitano of *Il Medico volante* comes to marry Lucinda her lover, Valerio, aided by another pair of lovers, Ottavio and Leonora, as well as by Cola, uses all his wits to defeat his rival's aims, eventually proving successful. Sometimes the incidents are varied in diverse ways. *L'Onorata fuga di Lucinda* tells the story of Lucinda, who, once loved by Valerio, is deserted by him for a rival, Ardelia, who in turn is loved by and loves Ottavio. Lucinda hereupon dresses as a man, and in this guise is wounded by her beloved. Naturally everything, partly by the help of Pulcinella, is brought right in the end. Jealousy is often called in, as in Scala's *Il Ritratto*, where Isabella's indignation is aroused when she believes that Orazio has given his portrait to Vittoria. This play is complicated by Vittoria's

228

devices ; she keeps the Capitano, Pantalone, and Graziano dangling on a string, only to cheat them in the end. It is interesting to notice that this Vittoria is herself a *comica*, or actress belonging to a troupe of *commedia dell' arte* performers. To escape the attentions of the Capitano, Lucinda in *I tre Matti* pretends that she is mad, while the plot is complicated by the search of Ardelia, dressed as a man, for her beloved Orazio. More ' romantic ' even is *La Vedova costante overo Isabella soldato per vendetta*. Here Orazio and Isabella plight their troth. Ottavio, on being rejected by the latter, plans to murder Orazio, whom he leaves for dead and who is not recognized by Isabella on his recovery. He goes off to the war, and she, learning the truth, follows him dressed as a man. The action is increased by the Dottore's foolish wooing of Ardelia and by Ubaldo's equally foolish courtship of Isabella.

These old men, who appear generally as tyrannical but hoodwinked parents, often take the parts of comic lovers. In *Le Disgrazie e fortune di Pandolfo* Pandolfo, returned home after ten years of slavery, falls in love with Lucinda, but eventually discovers his real wife in the supposed widow, Costanza. Ubaldo, of *Li due Schiavi rivenduti*, loves Armellina, a supposed slave, while in *Gli Intrighi d'amore ovvero la finestra incantata* he dotes on Lucinda, but transfers his affections, in common with Pandolfo, to the servant Pasquella. Ubaldo, of *Il Padre crudele*, loves Ardelia, while Pandolfo loves Lucinda, the two women being also adored by Valerio, Pandolfo's son, and by Ottavio. In Locatelli's *Li Prigioni di Plauto* it is Pantalone who makes a fool of himself through love. This play also introduces the jealousy of Zanni, who, married to Filippa, suspects her with Burattino.

Frequently this married jealousy theme forms the centre of interest, as in *I Tappeti, ovvero Colafronio geloso*, where Colafronio or Cola is *geloso ed ignorante*, the main interest of the plot resting in Valerio's attempts on his wife, Lucinda, and in Cola's passion. Clearly, such a theme gives excellent scope for the use of disguise, and many such plays—for example, *Le Metamorfosi di Pulcinella*—exist only for this disguise element. The comedy last mentioned introduces Pulcinella as a table-stand, a laundry-boy, and a mummy, as well as the two lovers, transformed for the nonce into Chinese princes—for here we have a *Bourgeois gentilhomme* theme. Often such plots are not in the best of modern taste. In *I tre Becchi* Lucinda, the wife of Pandolfo, pretends that she is with child ; her husband, who had been the lover of Colombina, Cola's wife, has had to abandon his wicked ways because of Lucinda's jealousy. Both Lucinda and Ardelia, Ubaldo's wife, are loved respectively by two young men, Valerio and Ottavio, and these are successful in their wishes by the close of the play. The Lucinda, Ardelia, and Colombina of *Le tre Gravide* are actually with child by Orazio, Ottavio, and Zanni, and the scenes of equivoque here may be left to the imagination.

From ' romantic ' to ' realistic ' these intrigue themes pursued for the most part an even unvaried way. Occasionally, however, one comes upon novelty of treatment. Two examples will suffice here. The first is Locatelli's *La Commedia in commedia*. The usual persons people this play— Pantalone, the old father, wishes to marry his daughter, Lidia, to the old Coviello. With bad grace and after considerable promptings she accepts ; whereupon Pantalone, in his glee, commands a troupe of actors, led by Graziano, to perform at the wedding festivities. And here we enter upon something new, for the Capitano of the play within the play is none other than Pantalone's own son, Orazio, and the intrigue of the comedy is intermingled with the fictional intrigue of the little comedy to be produced in Pantalone's house. The second is *La Bellissima commedia in tre persone*, where, instead of the usual group of eight or ten characters, only three—Valerio, Lucinda, and Cola —are introduced. Lucinda and Valerio are betrothed, but Cola reveals to us that his master Ottavio is pining because he too loves the young lady, but will not wrong his friend. The servant hereupon attempts by various devices to estrange the pair of lovers. He succeeds in making Lucinda believe for a time that Valerio has fallen in love with a courtesan, although eventually his knavery is revealed. Ottavio himself never appears on the stage, and the whole action, which is cleverly developed, is sustained by the three characters alone.

THE VALUE OF THE SCENARII

It is a difficult task indeed to estimate the value of these dry bones, denuded of the living flesh which belonged to them in the seventeenth century. What, for example, can we make of this :

> *Pantalone* with *Zanni*, from the house, about the love he bears to *Flaminia*, daughter of *Coviello* ; he says he wishes to marry her ; they introduce *lazzi* ; at last they stop ; here
> *Coviello*, from the house, learns that *Pantalone* is in love with *Flaminia* and wishes to marry her ; they introduce *lazzi* ; at length they agree about the dowry.[1]

Much of the description in the scenarii is of this bare type, and even when we reach something fuller we are told little. In Locatelli's *La Commedia in commedia* the third act opens thus :

> *Capitano*, from the street (he pretends it is night), says he does not know which is *Ardelia's* house. . . .
> *Lidia*, from the house (the scene being supposed to take place in pitch blackness), thinking the *Capitano* is *Lelio*, and the *Capitano* thinking *Lidia* is *Ardelia*, they embrace and walk off by the street.

This pretended night in the scenario gives us little clue to the real merriment of the scene, yet Perrucci evidently regards these night scenes as among the best in such entertainments. " In the night scene," he declares, " is to be noted the custom among our actors of groping about, running up against each other, making grimaces, climbing up ladders, and performing other silent actions, such as cannot be surpassed either in truth to nature or in laughableness." [2] In one respect this note of Perrucci's suggests to us the power of the mimic art of the Italians, for elsewhere he indicates clearly enough that the darkness is indeed purely fictional. Giving advice to the *corago* or *concertatore*, this writer notes that the scenario must have indications of the scenes

> in which a torch is required, of those in which there is pretended moonlight, and of those in which there is supposed to be such a darkness that no person can see another. . . . The actor must not read letters by the light of the lamps which illuminate the theatre, for these are supposed not to exist.[3]

The truth is that we can never hope now to recapture fully the impression once made by these comedians and that the scenarii form the least part of the evidence which enables us to come even to a partial appreciation of their skill. From the scenarii alone we could never understand the force of the words spoken by President de Brosses :

> This way of improvised acting, which makes the style very feeble, makes the action at the same time both lively and true. . . . Gesture and inflexion of voice are harmonized always to the theme ; the actors come and go, talking and moving as though they were in their own houses.[4]

Even when an actor such as Dominique Biancolelli essays to write out his part, the living spirit cannot be captured. In *Arlecchino creato re per ventura* this performer has a comic duel :

> I come on the stage fully armed, . . . with a very long sword. Two valets in front of me carry, the one a huge piece of cheese, the other an enormous bottle of wine. When they urge me to fight I begin, in order to

[1] The opening of *Il Giuoco della primiera*. See E. del Cerro, p. 384. *Cf.* B. Croce, *Sul significato e il valore artistico della commedia dell' arte* (*Atti della Reale Accademia di Napoli*, Naples, 1929).

[2] " E nella scena di notte s' osserva così da' nostri il costume nell' andar tentoni, incontrarsi, far smorfie, salir le scale ed altri atti muti, che nulla di più può inventarsi di ridicolo e di verisimile."—Petraccone, p. 183.

[3] " Così si deve avvertire in quali scene è di mestieri il lume, in quali fingere d' esservi il lume della luna ed in quali esservi un' oscurità tale che non vi si discerna cosa alcuna. . . . Nè si serva chi recita per legger lettere o altro dei lumi posti per illuminare il teatro, perchè quelli si dànno come non vi fussero."—*Id.*, p. 196.

[4] " Cette manière de jouer à l'impromptu, qui rend le style très-faible, rend en même temps l'action très-vive et très-vraie. . . . Le geste et l'inflexion de la voix se marient toujours avec le propos au théâtre; les acteurs vont et viennent, dialoguent et agissent comme chez eux."—*Lettres sur l'Italie*, ii, 254; quoted in A. Bartoli, pp. lxxvi-lxxvii.

230

screw up my courage, to bite the cheese and to drink the wine. My opponent arrives. I am afraid and speak to him in a tremulous voice. I advise him to give in. He answers me boldly that he assuredly will not. "You don't want to give in, then?" say I. "No," he replies. "Very well, then," I say to him, "I'll give in." It is discovered that my opponent is the legitimate King of the Island and that the oracle had been falsely interpreted.[1]

That which is missing here is precisely the quality which made Biancolelli famous. We have the scenario, the plot, but we hear not his trembling voice, and the action which may have made five minutes' business on the stage is described in little more than a hundred words. Nor do the fragments of reported dialogue, even, aid us considerably. In *Il Soldato in Candia* there is a judgment scene which runs thus:

THE JUDGE. What's your name?

ARLECCHINO. Arlecchino.

THE JUDGE. Have you ever been in prison?

ARLECCHINO. Yes, sir—to carry in some dinner for one of my friends who was arrested for debt.

THE JUDGE. Have you ever done anything against . . . the Princess?

ARLECCHINO. Yes, sir. I went out of town against her orders.

THE JUDGE. What? And how did you get out?

ARLECCHINO. Four or five days ago I wanted to hang up some shirts on the wall. The wall crumbled under my feet, and I fell into the ditch along with the shirts.

THE JUDGE. Were you ever associated with anyone's death?

ARLECCHINO. Yes, sir. Last year I was at the gallows where a man was hanged.

THE JUDGE. Have you ever said anything bad about the governor?

ARLECCHINO. Yes, sir. Once he was ill. I said to every one who asked me for news, "He is very bad indeed. . . ."

THE JUDGE. Have you ever urged anyone to fight?

ARLECCHINO. Often, sir. When I see dogs quarrelling I always clap my hands together, . . . and urge them to fight it out.[2]

One can understand how effective this may have been on the stage, with the physical opposition between the old Judge and the seeming foolish Arlecchino; but as it stands it lacks vividity, lacks spirit, lacks life.

Concerning the origins of the *commedia dell' arte* these scenarii do not grant much information, but what little they do give is valuable. It is obvious that many of the plots are derived either

---

[1] " Jarriue dans cette Scene armé de pied en cap, . . . avec vne tres longue Epée, deux vallets portent devant moy, Lun vn gros morceau de fromage, Lautre, vne grosse bouteille de vin, quand on veut que je me batte, je commence pour me faire du cœur a mordre a mesme du fromage et a boire a la bouteille, mon ennemy arriue je m'effraye je luy dis Dvne voix tremblante, je le conseille de se rendre, Il me dit auec assurance qu'il n'en sera rien, tu ne veux donc pas te rendre Luy dis je non me repond Il, et bien Luy disje je me rends moy; on decouure que mon ennemy est Le roy legitime de Lisle, et quelon ausit mal jnterprete L'oracle."—*Traduction du Scenario de Joseph Dominique Biancolelli*, ii, 367.

[2] *Id.*, i, 286.

LE JUGE. Comment vous appellez vous?

ARL. Arlequin.

LE J. N'este vous jamais venu en prison?

ARL. Ouy Monsieur pour apporte a manger a vn de mes Camarades qui estoit prisonnier pour debtes.

LE J. N'auez vous jamais rien fait contre . . . La princesse?

ARL. Ouy Mr. Je suis sorty de la ville malgrez son ordre.

LE J. Comment? et par quel moyen este vous sorty?

ARL. Il y a quatre ou cinq jours je voulois etendre des chemises sur La Muraille, Elle se croulla sous moy, et je tombay dans les fossez auec mes chemises.

LE J. Ne vous este vous jamais trouué a La mort de quelquun?

ARL. Ouy Mr. Lannée derniere je me trouuay a la greue ou lon pendoit vn homme.

LE J. N'auez vous jamais dit du mal du gouuernneur?

ARL. Ouy Mr. Il y quelque temps qu'il estoit malade, a tous ceux qui me demandoient de ses nouuelles je disois, Il se porte fort mal. . . .

LE J. N'auez vous jamais excité personne a se battre.

ARL. Tres souuent Mr. Quand je vois des chens qui se querellent je ne manque jamais de battre des mains . . . et je les excite a se battre.

from classical literary sources in Terence or Plautus, or from Renascence imitations of these. Many of the themes which deal with a pair of lovers and a testy old father thus have connexions with experiments in the written drama. But these do not by any means form the whole of the subject-matter to be discovered here, and in analysing the others we note that the *commedia dell' arte* tends to repeat the old adultery and intrigue themes which have already been met with in the classic mime

Fig. 151. PANTALONE AND ZANNI
Scene from a *commedia dell' arte* show in the Bibliothèque Nationale, Paris (Cabinet des Estampes, Tb + 1, vol. i, B. 335).
Photo Giraudon

and in medieval farce. From the latter no doubt the Italian companies took this type of plot, and we are accordingly led to see in them the lineal descendants of the *mimi* of the Middle Ages. That they exploited not merely a vulgarization of literary written comedy, as some critics have imagined, seems evident after even a cursory examination of their *répertoire*. Connexions there are undoubtedly, but merely such connexions as were inevitable when in the sixteenth and seventeenth centuries two forms of theatrical art—the improvised and the 'scholarly'—met on the same stages and, vying with one another, stole freely from each other those elements which might best suit their particular media. Just as the Italian comedians took plots occasionally from the *littérateurs*, so these *littérateurs*, and even the writers of later religious drama, borrowed from the

232

commedia dell' arte.   Adolfo Bartoli has made some comparisons which involve the former,[1] while Lorenzo Stoppato has drawn attention to the fact that a highwayman in *S. Antonio* is called Scaramuccia and another in *S. Onofrio* is named Cuccodrilla.[2]

Whatever the scenarii indicate, however, it is to other sources we must go if we wish to understand the *commedia dell' arte* aright, and principally to those stock parts which, as this summary of dramatic themes has indicated, appeared in play after play of the time.

(iii) THE STOCK TYPES: (1) THE 'SERIOUS' PERSONS

In all these dramas, whether comedies, tragedies, or pastorals, it will be seen that the characters are sharply divided into two groups, which we may call the serious and the comic.   The former were played in the ordinary garments of the day and did not necessitate the use of masks. " Playing in masks," says Perrucci, " is confined to the buffoons and comic persons, caricaturing by means of dark complexion, of big or fat noses, little and blear eyes, wrinkled brows, bald heads." [3]   Such characters may be referred to generically as the ' masks.' Before dealing with their characteristics, however, a word or two must be said concerning the grouping of the figures in the plays as a whole and concerning the serious persons, who, being of least importance for our purposes, may be rapidly dismissed.

Various attempts have been made to establish the norm for the *dramatis personæ* in an Italian play of this kind, but in general such an effort is doomed to failure.   Even the carefully considered list provided by Mic,[4] although agreeing with the composition of some troupes and with the structure of some scenarii, cannot be used formally.   He finds that the essential basis consists of two old men (Pantalone and Dottor Graziano), two Zanni (Brighella and Arlecchino), a Capitano, two *innamorati*, or male lovers, two *innamorate*, and a servant-girl, or Fantesca.   We note, however, that there must be many qualifications to this ideal plan.   Often three old men make their appearance,[5] on occasion there is only one,[6] and sometimes none at all.[7]   The Zanni too present difficulty. Arlecchino and Brighella are by no means the most usual names, but, quite apart from nomenclature, we observe that sometimes there is only one Zanni,[8] sometimes there are three or even four.[9]   Often the chief of these is simply called Zanni, with a companion or companions variously named as Tartaglia, Scapino, Stupino, Trivelino, Mescolino, Scatolino, Colafronio, Pulcinella, Burattino, Gradelino.[10]   In many scenarii, even of the earliest time, no Capitano is introduced at all.   Two *innamorati*, it is true, are usual, but again there are often three,[11] sometimes only one,[12] and in a few scenarii the Capitano and the second lover are the same person.[13]   The *innamorate* necessarily correspond to the *innamorati*.   Once more, while one servant-girl occurs in many plots, almost as many have two, called variously Argentina, Rosetta, Colombina, and Pasquella.[14] Very often, too, other characters make their appearance. Pasquella is an old woman in *Le Disgrazie e fortune di Pandolfo*, and a host of an inn, distinct from the pair of Zanni, is a familiar

---

[1] *Op. cit.*, pp. xxvi–xxx.   [2] *Op. cit.*, p. 68.

[3] " Il recitar mascherato è restato alle parti de' buffoni e ridicoli, dandoli caricatura di color bruno, naso o grande o schiacciato, occhi piccoli e lipposi, fronte arrugata, capo calvo."—Petraccone, p. 139.   [4] Mic, p. 28.

[5] Magnifico, Coviello, and Casandro, in *Le due Flaminie* (Correr MS.); Magnifico, Coviello, and Michelino in *La Fida in fedeltà* (*ibid.*); Cassandro, Ubaldo, and Pandolfo in *L' Onorata fuga* (Bartoli).

[6] Ubaldo Lanterni in *Li due Schiavi* (Bartoli).   [7] *La Bellissima commedia in tre persone* (Bartoli).

[8] Scapino in *Baron Todesco* (Corret), Cola in *La Bellissima commedia* (Bartoli).

[9] *Il Castico della disonesta moglie* (Correr) has Coviello, Zanni, Tartaglia; *Il Cavalier ingrato* (*ibid.*) has Cola, Zanni, Trevelino; *La Regina d' Inghilterra* (Bartoli) has Stoppino (Cola), Zanni, Trappola (Pulcinella).

[10] See *infra*, pp. 263–298.   [11] Oratio, Fabrizio, Livio in *L' Amico infido* (Correr).

[12] Valerio in *La Bellissima commedia* (Bartoli).   [13] *La Mala lingua* (Correr).

[14] Cf. *I duoi Fratelli* (Correr), *La Finta notte* (Bartoli), *Gli Intrighi d' amore* (Bartoli), *Il Monile* (Correr).

233

figure. Indeed, almost all we can say is that the scenarii were sharply divided into two portions consisting of 'serious' and of 'comic' characters, which were bound together by ties of fictional relationship or service. With the *innamorati* of the former division we may start our survey.

THE INNAMORATO

Called by various names—Orazio, Polidoro, Flavio, Lelio, Fabrizio, Ottavio, Florindo, Silvio, Luzio, Fabio, Curzio, Valerio, Celio, Virginio, Livio, Adriano, Mario, Leandro, Fortunio—the *innamorato* or *amoroso* was always a youth of handsome appearance and pleasant manners. Generally he was the son of one of the old men, but sometimes he made his entry upon the stage independently. Usually a young man of fashion, he was reduced on occasion to being a " poor scholar," or even an " actor." His *rôle* was generally that of lover restrained by parental command, or of rival to his father, or of lover of another old man's wife. It was a " difficult part," according to Cecchini,[1] for the *innamorato* had to keep abreast of fashion and seem the educated gentleman. Cecchini advises him to read elegant books and to store his memory with " a pleasant number of noble discourses." [2] Perrucci is fuller in his advice. The *innamorati*, he says, should be handsome youths, dressed as gallants of the time.

> They must remember all the rules of behaviour in voice and action; they must acquire a perfect Italian diction with the Tuscan inflexions; . . . in this they will be aided by the reading of good Tuscan books, such as the *Onomastici*, *Crusca*, the *Memoriale della lingua*, by Pergamino, the *Fabrica del mondo*, the *Ricchezze della lingua*. . . . So little by little they will gain a habit of speech ready for every occasion, felicitous and pleasant.[3]

This young actor must keep, too, a commonplace-book ; " the conceits, prepared for use on occasion on the stage, must be collected in a volume lettered ' Commonplace-Book,' or, if desired, with subheadings such as ' Mutual Love,' ' Rejected Love,' ' Plaints,' " [4] and the like. Besides the general conceits he must also have a set of soliloquies, *uscite* and *chiusette*,[5] training himself to be able to dovetail together the memorized and the improvisatorial. In general, we must consider him as moving on stage or in street as the typical gallant of the period, handsomely dressed, elaborately perfumed, holding in his hands the Bible of all seventeenth-century lovers, the tiny duodecimo *Petrarca* or *Petrarchetto*.[6]

Many actors won fame in this *rôle*, and some carried their interpretation of the part so far as to become capable poets themselves. During the seventies of the sixteenth century several of these are known to us. Rinaldo Petignoni, called Fortunio, was a member of the famous Gelosi troupe in 1574. Porcacchi described him as excellent in arranging new subjects for the stage.[7] He was evidently *corago* as well as *primo innamorato*. Adriano Valerini, known as Aurelio, was a member of the Gelosi a few years later. He was a Veronese, and had qualified as a doctor before taking up a stage career. He is known to have been the lover of Lidia da Bagnacavallo, whom he is said to have abandoned for Vincenza Armani. A funeral oration for the latter, a tragedy called *Afrodite* (1578),

---

[1] Petraccone, pp. 8–9.

[2] " Una leggiadra quantità di nobili discorsi."

[3] " Si ricordino di tutte le regole del gestire, nelle voci, nelle azioni ; studino di sapere la lingua perfetta italiana con i vocaboli toscani, . . . a questo conferirà la lettura così de' buoni libri toscani, come gli Onomastici, Crusca, Memoriale della lingua del Pergamino, Fabrica del mondo, Ricchezze della lingua. . . . E così, pian piano, si farà la lingua pronta, facile e docile."—Petraccone, pp. 73–76.

[4] " I concetti, che si deve apparecchiare per servirsene nell' occasione, devono essere raccolti in un libro con titolo di Cibaldone repertorio, o, a suo beneplacito, con i titoli d' amor corrisposto, disprezzo, priego."

[5] See *supra*, pp. 218–219.

[6] On this *Petrarchetto* see the interesting study on *Petrarchismo ed Antipetrarchismo*, printed by Arturo Graf in his *Attraverso il Cinquecento* (Turin, 1888).

[7] See D'Ancona, ii, 468. For summaries of the careers of these actors and for references to sources of information see the Appendix, p. 359 f.

a set of *Madrigali* (1592), are among his printed works. As Flavio, Flaminio Scala acted in the late sixteenth and early seventeenth centuries. His collection of scenarii suggest that he was connected with the Gelosi, but sure records of his life start only in 1600, when he is found acting with Cecchini in the company of the Accesi. Later, in 1611, he passed into the Confidenti, among whom he was still acting in 1620. He is remembered chiefly for his *Teatro delle Favole rappresentative* (Venezia, 1611), the earliest collection of *commedia dell' arte* plots to be published. During the nineties of the sixteenth century Francesco de Pilastri won success among the Uniti under the name of Leandro. Domenico Bruni, in his *Fatiche comiche*, has left on record the pleasing impression he made upon his fellows and the wonder in which he was held for his prodigious memory.[1] Domenico Bruni himself, who was born in 1580, flourished as Fulvio in the Gelosi and Confidenti from his *début* in 1594. Some *Dialoghi scenici* of his exist in manuscript, while he published a set of *Prologhi* in 1621 (Turin) and *Fatiche comiche* in 1623 (Paris). Among the seventeenth-century exponents of this *rôle* chief in importance as well as first in time was G. B. Andreini, known as Lelio. This man, whom Barbieri praised as actor, writer, and friend of princes,[2] was born in 1576, and, after studying in Bologna, took up a stage career about the age of twenty-four. His early training he may have received in the Gelosi, but about 1604 he became head of the Fedeli, with whom he remained until his death. In 1601 he married Virginia Ramponi, and after her death in 1627 he espoused a certain Lidia Rotari. No doubt his predilection for the part of *innamorato* was a heritage from his father, Francesco Andreini, who, first playing the lover, drew more fame to himself later as the Capitano. Giovan Battista was noted in his time not merely as an actor, but also as a

Fig. 152. THE INNAMORATO
French print of the seventeenth century, published by Le Blond. Exemplar in the Bibliothèque Nationale (Cabinet des Estampes, Tb +1, vol. ii, B. 482).
Photo Giraudon

writer. From the time when in 1606 his *La Florinda* (Milano) was published, he continued to produce a series of dramas and poems, distinguished, if not by genius, at least by talent. *La Maddalena* (Firenze, 1612), *L'Olivastro* (Bologna, 1642), *Il Teatro Celeste* (Paris, 1623), *La Tecla Vergine e Martire* (Venezia, 1623), are among the more interesting of these, but none can vie in importance with *L'Adamo* (Milano, 1614), which some scholars believe to have been known to Milton. The esteem in which he was held by contemporaries is well attested by the manuscript *Poesie di diversi in lodi dei comici Gio. Battista Andreini, detto Lelio, e la moglie Virginia, nata Ramponi, detta Florinda*, preserved in the Royal Library at Brera. Like Francesco Andreini, Francesco Antonazzoni, at first known

---

[1] See D'Ancona, ii, 511.   [2] See Petraccone, p. 22; *La Supplica*, p. 40.

as Ortensio, abandoned that part later for the *rôle* of Capitano. Not much is known of him save that he had been connected both with the Gelosi and the Confidenti, and that a collection of his poems appeared in Paris about 1623. The names of various other seventeenth-century *innamorati* are preserved, but of few have we any intimate details. Francesco Allori played Valerio in the seventies and eighties of the century; and about the same period flourished Giacinto Bendinelli, also a Valerio, Pietro Cotta, known as Celio and celebrated by Riccoboni, Bernardo Narici, who played Orazio in the Modena troupe to Domenico Pannini's Florindo, Bartolomeo Ranieri, an Aurelio expelled from France in 1689, and Giovanbattista Costantini, who appeared in Paris in 1688 as Ottavio. The mere names, of course, signify nothing; but we have a record here of men famous in their day not only for their histrionic powers, but for their skill as poets and dramatists. We are bound to believe that the praise meted out to them for their refined stage performances was not undeserved.

THE INNAMORATA

" All the above speeches," says Perrucci, referring to his conceits and soliloquies for the lovers, ' can be used also by the women with the necessary changes," [1] and in many respects the *innamorate* were the pure reflections of their companion *innamorati*. Their names had a similar ring— Isabella, Flaminia, Silvia, Lidia, Ardelia, Flavia, Doralice, Lucinda, Clelia, Rosaura, Violante, Cinzia, Florinda, Eularia, Ortensia, Clarice, Angelica, Felice, Adriana, Colasia, Celia, Diana, Valeria, Olivetta, Fulvia, Rosalba, Laura—and their training was much the same, save that their manners should be more modest and their language less erudite. Perrucci gives several examples of speeches especially fitted for their lips, such as an outburst of contempt at an old man, a dialogue of disdain, and the like. Most of the dialogues read rather dully to-day; but we have to remember always that the *commedia dell' arte* was essentially the comedy of the actor, and not of the playwright. Here, for example, is a lovers' quarrel:

> WOMAN. Ropes . . .
> MAN. Chains . . .
> WOMAN. . . . which bind . . .
> MAN. . . . which fetter . . .
> WOMAN. . . . this soul . . .
> MAN. . . . my heart . . .
> WOMAN. . . . be broken !
> MAN. . . . be shattered !
> WOMAN. If faith . . .
> MAN. If love . . .
> WOMAN. . . . constrains . . .
> MAN. . . . perplexes . . .
> WOMAN. . . . may anger . . .
> MAN. . . . may hate . . .
> WOMAN. . . . destroy !
> MAN. . . . succeed ! [2]

And so on for a couple of pages. Ridiculous as this is, one could imagine its having an electrical effect in a theatre when rapidly enunciated by two performers gifted in this kind.

The *innamorate* usually appear in the scenarii as daughters of the two old men, but in several of Scala's plays, and elsewhere, the heroine is the wife of Pantalone, Graciano, or Coviello, while in others she appears as a gay young widow or as an orphan girl. Her part usually is a fairly

---

[1] " Tutte le sudette composizioni possono esser anche communi alle donne col mutarsele il genere."—Petraccone, p. 93.
[2] Petraccone, p. 100.

strenuous one, for the mute maiden of Terentian comedy was not carried over to the Renascence. It was in this *rôle*, naturally, that the actresses of the time won their greatest fame, and records of many players, gifted as well as beautiful, have come down to us. Above them all soars the figure of Isabella Andreini, *the* Isabella. Born in Padua in 1562, the daughter of a Venetian named Paolo Canali, she married Francesco Andreini in 1578. Thereafter her fortunes, in Italy and in France, were bound up with the company, the Gelosi, to which he belonged. Not a word of scandal was breathed about her. "The gracious Isabella," says Garzoni,[1]

> ornament of the stage, jewel of the theatres, superb image not less of virtue than of beauty, has herself made her profession so illustrious that, while the world endures, while time remains, . . . every voice, every tongue, every cry will re-echo the famous name of Isabella.[2]

"Signora Isabella," her husband called her, "beautiful of name, beautiful of body, and most beautiful of mind."[3] Of her seven children one was adopted by the Grand Duchess of Tuscany, another by the Duchess of Mantua, while to Giovan Battista, as we have seen, descended the genius of her line. When she died at Lyons on June 11, 1604, whole nations mourned. Gifted, like her son, with a fine style, she has left printed works by which we may judge something of her powers. *Mirtilla*, a pastoral, was printed at Verona in 1588, and saw many reprints; some fragments of her writing were collected by her husband and by Flaminio Scala, to be published as *Frammenti* (Venezia) in 1625; several years before appeared *Lettere della signora Isabella Andreini Padovana, Comica Gelosa ed Accademia Intenta, nominata l'Accesa* (Venezia, 1607); while her *Rime* were collected in one volume at Naples

Fig. 153. MEDAL STRUCK IN HONOUR OF
ISABELLA ANDREINI
Medal in the Bibliothèque Nationale, Paris.
Photo Giraudon

in 1696. It was partly for these works that she was honoured in the academies; certainly it was on their account that her statue, set alongside busts of Torquato Tasso and of Petrarca, was crowned in laurel, while she herself sat next to Tasso at a banquet given in her honour at Rome by Cardinal Aldobrandini.

Seventeenth-century literature rings with her praise. Isaac du Ryer wondered whether she were not truly divine:

> Je ne crois point qu'Isabelle
> Soit une femme mortelle,
> C'est plutôt quelqu'un des Dieux
> Qui s'est déguisé en femme
> Afin de nous ravir l'âme
> Par l'oreille et par les yeux.[4]

De la Roque was no less ecstatic in her praise, and Italian poets without number rhapsodized in her honour. Since many of these poems have not hitherto been noted, it may be worth while to make a survey of this laudatory literature. Gherardo Borgogni has many a lyric on this theme. "Actress

---

[1] *Piazza universale di tutte professioni* (Venezia, 1585); Petraccone, pp. 4–5.

[2] "La graziosa Isabella, decoro delle scene, ornamento de' teatri, spettacolo superbo non meno di virtù che di bellezza, ha illustrato ancora lei questa professione in modo che, mentre il mondo durerà, mentre staranno i secoli . . . ogni voce, ogni lingua, ogni grido risuonarà il celebre nome d' Isabella."

[3] *Bravure*, Ragionamento IV.

[4] *Le Temps perdu.*

illuſtrious and clear," he calls her,[1] and rings the changes on his admiration of her art and beauty [2]

Ah ! Phillis, Phillis mine [3] is a rather pretty set of verses in which the poet declares that " he has lived and lives and will live " for her. The same theme he repeats in *Amor, se brami ch' io.* She herſelf is the theme of a sonnet—*Filli, sotto qual Cielo, od in qual parte*—and her *Mirtilla* gives the theme for another—*Come, già ti dettar l'alme Sorelle.* There is a long lyric beginning *Filli leggiadra, e bella* and a sonnet bidding her return to the ſtage—*Riedi cara mia Filli, oue t'aspetta.* By her poems she will be made immortal :

Fig. 154. ISABELLA ANDREINI
Portrait on the verso of the title to the *Rime* (Milano, 1601) of Isabella Andreini.

Svperbe scene, Anfiteatri, e voi,
  Ch' vdiſte 'l suon de' uaghi, e dolci accenti
  Di Filli, honor del Mondo, e de' viventi,
E di gran nome, e merauiglia à noi.
Di queſte carte (hor noui pregi suoi)
  Serbate 'l grido a le future genti ;
  E sian mai sempre a riuerirla intenti,
Quanti l' udiro, e l' udiranno poi.
Si che di Filli, e di Mirtilla il grido,
  Sopra Lete s' inalzi, e sopr' Auerno,
  Onde 'l Tempo si uinca, e se ne scorni.
Oda 'l bel canto ogni ripoſto lido,
  E con felici, e fortunati giorni,
  Sia d' Isabella il chiaro nome eterno.

And his praise concludes with a fervent address to the *Sacre Miniſtre del diuin furore.*

Borgogni, however, was only one of the many poets who sang their admiration of her talents. One may perhaps put aside that exaggerated praise of her son, G. B. Andreini, who, in *La Saggia Egiziana* (Fiorenza, 1604), placed her above Arioſto, Tasso, and all the poets of her time ; but we cannot negleƈt the chorus of praise on the part of others. Some poems are conceited, such as that by Giovanmaria Guicciardi da Bagnacavallo, *To Signora Isabella Andreini, Aƈtress of the Gelosi, bitten on the Cheek by a Mosquito while she was coming on the Stage* ;[4] others, like Borgogni's, praise her beauty and her person—*To the same Lady praising her for her Loveliness, for her Hiſtrionic Art, for her Published Paſtoral, and for her Poems.*[5] Verses by della Cella on her part in a play appear in the *Parnaso de Poetici Ingegni* (Parma, 1611),[6] while Aurelio Corbellini, printing some verses addressed to her in his *Rime* (Torino, 1603), describes her in a note as " the famous aƈtress."[7] Tasso wrote a sonnet in her honour, as did Gabriello Chiabrera,[8] while Marino, besides writing a charaƈteriſtic set of verses beginning *Bella fronte serena* [9] and a charming sonnet *For the Signora Isabella Andreini, while she played in a Tragedy* :

[1] *Le Muse Toscane di diversi nobilissimi ingegni. Dal Sig. Gherardo Borgogni Nouamente raccolte, e poſte in luce* (Bergamo, 1594), p. 17. In this colleƈtion Borgogni has included (p. 29 f.) a number of her own poems.
[2] See *Rime di diversi celebri poeti dell' età noſtra* (Bergamo, 1587), pp. 257, 261, 264, 268, 271, 272, 274. Some of her own poems are included in this colleƈtion on pp. 287-289.
[3] " Deh Filli, Filli mia."
[4] " Alla Signora Isabella Andreini Comica Gelosa punta in vna guancia da vna Zanzara vscendo in iscena."—*Sonetti Cinquanta Madrigali Venticinque* (Ferrara, 1598), p. 23.
[5] " Alla medesima Signora lodandola per la beltà, per l' arte Comica, per la sua paſtorale ſtampata, e per le rime."—*Id.*, p. 24.
[6] P. 124 ; where also, on p. 44, is printed Marino's poem on her death.   [7] Pp. 146–147.   [8] Rasi, i, 91–92.
[9] *La Galeria* (fifth edition, correƈted, Venezia, 1647), p. 287.

Fig. 155. ISABELLA ANDREINI AND HER TROUPE
Painting in the Carnavalet Museum, Paris. From P. Duchartre, *The Italian Comedy* (1929), p. 265.

Tace la notte, e chiara al par del giorno
   Spiegando per lo Ciel l' ombra serena
   Già per vaghezza, oltre l' usato affrena
Di mille lumi il bruno carro adorno.
Caggia il gran velo omai, veggiasi intorno
   Dar della Donna altrui diletto e pena,
   Che in su la viva e luminosa scena
Faccia a Venere, a Palla, invidiata e scorno.
Febo le muse, Amor le grazie ancelle
   Seco accompagni, e dal' oblio profondo
   Sorga il Sonno a mirar cose si belle.
A si dolce spettacolo e giocondo,
   Dian le spere armonia, lume le stelle,
   Sia spettatore il Ciel, teatro il Mondo—

wrote a poem on her death, *Piangete orbi Teatri*.[1]   Many joined Marino in his lament.   One such
was penned by della Cella,[2] who calls her a " Real Sirena," another by Leonardo Quirini,[3] who
imitatively copies Marino's conceit on her when she was alive.   His poem may be rendered thus :

Happy ISA, you who have
On the stages of this earth—
Now with tones of love and mirth,
Now with sympathetic arts—
Pierced our souls and seized our hearts,
Now still happier tones you utter;
Through a glorious domain,
Through heaven's widely opened plain,
Your wings with gestures soft you flutter.
Your stage is now a heavenly sphere,
With earth's spectators seated here.[4]

G. P. Fabbri expresses a similar thought ; for him " Isabella is not dead, she lives in God " ;[5]
and Ottavio Rossi writes a pretty sonnet to her memory.[6]

    With all this testimony, it is clear what an enormous impression Isabella's beauty, art, and talents
made upon the poets of the time ; and, as it were, an indirect reflection is provided for us of her
histrionic powers.   She, however, by no means stood alone.   " Gracious Lidia," as Garzoni calls
her,[7] or Lidia da Bagnacavallo, was one of the earliest *innamorate* of the Gelosi troupe, and was loved
by Adriano Valerini, who seems to have abandoned her for another Lidia, Vicenza or Vincenza
Armani.   Born in Venice about 1540, the latter seems to have become a noted figure in her day.
Herself, like Isabella Andreini, a poetess, she too was sung by poets, while in 1570 appeared from the
pen of Adriano Valerini an *Oratione . . . in morte della Divina Signora Vincenza Armani, Comica*

---

[1] See *supra*, p. 238.
[2] *Rime* (Bologna, 1674), p. 64.
[3] *Vezzi d' Erato Poesie liriche di Leonardo Quirini* (Vinegia, 1649), p. 137.

      [4] ISA felice, c' hai
      Nele Scene pompose,
      Hor con voci amorose,
      Hor con teneri affetti,
      Rapiti i cori, e trasformati i petti.
      Più felice horche vai
      Per le sublimi & erte
      Del Ciel campagne aperte
      Lieue battendo e ribattendo i vanni,
      Perch' a stil sì facondo
      Sarà Scena lo Ciel, Theatro il Mondo.

[5] Rasi, i, 99.
[6] *Rime* (Brescia, 1612), p. 115.   On Isabella Andreini see the many articles cited in the Appendix.   The Carnavalet painting (Fig. 155)
is discussed by J. Cousin, *Une Scène des Gelosi.   Isabella Andreini et sa troupe* (*Bulletin des musées*, No. 2, March 15, 1890, pp. 67–70).
[7] Petraccone, p. 5.

Eccellentissima, which describes, in enthusiastic terms, her beauty, her learning, her wit, and her art. Garzoni, who may be regarded as less prejudiced, spoke too of " her wonderful beauty and her indescribable grace." [1]   Apparently, like the *archimima* of old, she had a company of her own in the years 1567 and 1568 ; this was disbanded when she was murdered on September 11, 1569.

Concerning the identity of Angelica Alberigi, or Alberghini, who flourished in the eighties of the sixteenth century, there is some doubt. Quadrio avers that she originally belonged to the Uniti and then left them for the Confidenti. It may be that she was the Angelica who in 1580 is mentioned as the wife of Drusiano Martinelli. She too was sung by poets.

During the early part of the seventeenth century Isabella's fame was like to have been handed down to her daughter-in-law, Virginia Andreini, the wife of Giovanbattista. Born in Milan on January 1, 1583, she died about the age of forty-five in or near 1628. When she went upon the stage we do not know, but at least as early as 1596 she was acting in the Gelosi troupe as Florinda. A. Bartoli avers that she first assumed this stage-name when she appeared in 1606 at Milan in her husband's tragedy, *Florinda,*[2] but, as will be evident, the play takes its title from her, and not *vice versa.* In 1603 she joined her husband in forming the company of the Fedeli. Concerning her maiden name considerable confusion has hitherto prevailed ; D'Ancona called her Virginia Maloni.[3]   Her true family name, Ramponi, was established by the set of manuscript poems addressed to her and her husband,[4] and these are corroborated by an excessively rare publication, *Rime in lode della Signora Verginia Ramponi Andreini Comica Fedele detta Florinda* (Firenze, 1604).[5] This is an 'academic' work by members of the Spensierati—Agitato, Percosso, Allettato, Svegliato, and Sollevato. It suggests that Florinda was held in much the same esteem as the still better known Isabella.

Another *innamorata* who was the wife of a famous actor was Orsola Cecchini, known as Flaminia, who must be distinct from another Flaminia who flourished in the sixties of the Cinquecento. With the Accesi, Piermaria Cecchini's company, her fortunes were intimately bound, and she too was favoured with the verses of poets. One such appears in the *Rime* (Venetia, 1608) of Cesare Rinaldi,[6] and another in the *Rime* (Bologna, 1674) of della Cella.[7] Besides these, Girolamo Graziani, when aged only fifteen, and Gian Bernardino Sessa penned sonnets for her ; [8] while in 1608 at Milan appeared a collection of verses in her praise—*Raccolta di varie rime in lode della Sig. Orsola Cecchini nella Compagnia degli Accesi detta Flaminia.*[9] Her beauty and art, like those of the others, is sufficiently lauded, and her *aurate chiome* ('golden hair') provided themes for many of her admirers.

Another 'star' of this time was Diana Ponti, who seems to have been known as Lavinia. Some confusion also attaches to her career. At times we find her with a company of her own, at times she is head of the Desiosi, at times she is with the Confidenti. It may well be that she was an unattached performer, moving from company to company. That she was a poetess is attested by a sonnet placed before a play, *Postumio,* printed at Lyon in 1601, but she seems to have called forth no special praise from the writers of her day. Already well known in 1582, the last we hear of her is as head of a company formed in 1605 under the patronage of the Prince della Mirandola. It is impossible here to enumerate even a fair percentage of those who, like her, won success in these parts, but we cannot forget the Antonia Isola, called also Lavinia, with whom Quadrio seems to have confused Diana Ponti, who flourished in the midst of the seventeenth century. Sonnets.

---

[1] " Con la beltà mirabile . . . con la grazia indicibile."—Petraccone, p. 5.   [2] *Op. cit.,* p. cxxxix.
[3] ii, 470.   [4] See *supra,* p. 235.
[5] The only copy of this booklet I have seen is in my own possession. So far as I know it has never been hitherto cited by historians of the *commedia dell' arte,* and perhaps this exemplar is unique.
[6] P. 92.   [7] P. 183. This *allude particolarmente all' andar per Italia recitando Comedie.*
[8] See D'Ancona, ii, 448.   [9] A copy is in the Biblioteca Braidense at Milan. See Rasi, ii, 639–641.

to her were written by Paolo Abriani [1] and G. A. Vestamigli.[2] Her sister Angiola was also an actress, while she herself seems to have been a bosom friend of the great Agata Calderoni, grandmother of Riccoboni's wife,[3] and famous in her day as Flaminia. The husband of Francesco Calderoni, this last-mentioned actress carried the *commedia dell' arte* tradition throughout Europe, from Bavaria to Vienna and from Vienna to Paris. Orsola Cortese, known as Eularia, and later the wife of Giovan Domenico Biancolelli, played as second *innamorata* in Paris from 1660 until the death of Brigida Bianchi, when she took the first *rôle*. To her credit remains the translation of a Spanish comedy, *La Bella brutta* (Paris, 1666). In her time she was among the most famous of the Italian company settled in the French capital. The Brigida Bianchi who acted as Aurelia and whose place she took was well known as an authoress. Born in 1613, she married Niccolò Romagnesi, and became the mother of the celebrated Marcantonio Romagnesi. Besides a play entitled *L'Inganno fortunato* (Paris, 1659), of her work there was printed a collection of poems, *Rifiuti di Pindo* (Paris, 1666). The daughter of Orsola Biancolelli also took the part of an *innamorata*, as Isabella. Nothing is known of her literary powers, but from her *début* in Paris in 1683 to her retirement in 1695 she seems to have proved herself an accomplished exponent of the *rôle*.

From this brief survey it will be realized that the more celebrated actors and actresses who assumed the characters of *innamorati* and *innamorate* were by no means without real culture or genuine artistic talents. It may be that one such as Lidia da Bagnacavallo had more love affairs than strict moralists might approve ; but against her one can place a long line of dignified figures, led by Isabella Andreini. It may be, too, that petty quarrels and jealousies have marred the memories of some. In 1616 Marina Dorotea Antonazzoni won especial success in *La Pazzia di Lavinia*, whereupon the company in which she played was torn by dissensions born of the jealousy displayed toward her by Battista and Valeria Austoni. Nearly half a century earlier Mantuan society had been fluttered by the rival charms of a Flaminia and a Vincenza ; apparently feeling ran high on both sides. But such a display of jealousy, rivalry, and ambition is no prerogative of the *commedia dell' arte* ; it is to be found in all forms of artistic endeavour and in all ages ; nor does it indicate in any respect a weakness of artistic genius. The one fact remains before us : that the exponents of the lovers in this improvised comedy were, many of them, men and women of considerable gifts, educated according to the best ideals of that time, noted occasionally for their learning, moving on equal terms in the society of *littérateurs* and poets, fit theme for those poets' rhapsodies. We are in the company here, not of rude mountebanks, but of men and women noted for their talents, often, as among the Andreini, the Cecchini, the Biancolelli, and the Locatelli, passing down a cultural tradition in their families from generation to generation. When such men and women were the performers, when dukes and princes, poets and artists, formed at least part of the audience, we can have no opportunity for dismissing as insipid, vulgar, and worthless this type of dramatic expression.

THE SERVANT-MAID, OR FANTESCA

Before passing over to the more purely comic types, it may be well here to consider the inevitable companion of the *innamorate*, the maidservant, or Fantesca, a character who varies from exponent to exponent, now appearing merely as a pert little soubrette, now sharing the qualities of a Harlequin or a Tartaglia. The names given to this person, like those given to her mistress, are many and diverse. Colombina is, of course, the most famous of them all ; but she appears as well under the guise of Argentina,[4] Corallina, Rosetta, Fioretta, Pasquella, and Ricciolina. In later times, taking the chequered dress of Harlequin, she was also introduced as Arlecchina.

---

[1] *Poesie* (Venetia, 1663), p. 16.
[3] *Histoire*, p. 59.
[2] Rasi, ii, 1060.
[4] This is the most familiar name in the Correr scenarii.

It seems probable that in the earliest plays her nature was rougher and somewhat more vulgar than that of her later representative. She appears in various *rôles*. Generally the servant of one of the *innamorate*, she is sometimes " mine hostess of the inn," sometimes she is married to a Trivellino or a Cola, sometimes she is sought in marriage by one of the two old men. She is always bright, always witty in a coarse way, always ready to assist in trick and intrigue.

Among the earliest recorded actresses who attained success in this part may be mentioned two, Angela Lucchese and Marina Antonazzoni, both known as Ricciolina, or, as Callot has it (Fig. 156), Riciulina. Concerning the former we know that in 1602 she was in a company managed by C. Fredi at Naples ; and it seems probable that the Rizzolina of the Accesi when they were at Turin in 1605 was none other than this actress. Whether the Ricciolina who was a member of the Affezionati at Bologna in 1634 was the same person we cannot tell. her career as an *innamorata*, when she

Fig. 156. RICIULINA AND METZETIN (MEZZETINO)
Etching in J. Callot's *I Balli di Sfessania*.

The other Ricciolina, Marina Antonazzoni, before played under the name of Lavinia, had apparently essayed the part of the serving-maid and seems to have won some success in the part. One of the most difficult of these stock parts to explain and analyse is that of Franceschina, the Francischina of Callot (Fig. 157). The Callot design shows her as a vivacious girl dancing with a comic figure, Gian Farina ; but, since she appears sometimes as a nurse and is sometimes impersonated by a man, we must believe that on occasion at least she was represented as older and more laughable than a typical Ricciolina.[1] Michelangiolo Buonarotti describes her in his *Fiera* [2] as *'ngelosita* (' jealous '), and pictures a little scene where the Zanni comes all sighing and moaning (*sospirando e languendo*) to press her hand, so that one might believe them a Cintio and an Ardelia. Evidently comic love was Franceschina's special *rôle*, and this comic love might include even associations with the

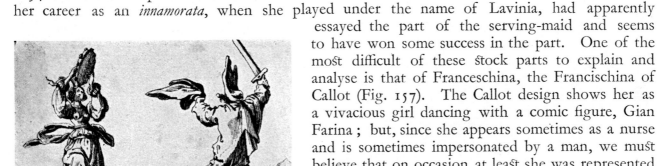

Fig. 157. FRANCISCHINA AND GIAN FARINA
Etching in J. Callot's *I Balli di Sfessania*.

innamorato. In the *Recueil Fossard* which M. Agne Beijer has lately discovered, and which has now been reproduced in facsimile,[3] Francisquine, a buxom country wench, is to be seen

[1] She often dresses as a man. In the Scala scenarii she poses as a husband (*Il Marito*) and as Mercurio (*Il Finto negromante*).
[2] Giorn. II, Atto II, Sc. 11 (1726).
[3] *Recueil de plusieurs fragments des premières comédies italiennes qui ont esté représentées en France sous le règne de Henry III. Recueil, dit de Fossard, conservé au musée national de Stockholm, présenté par Agne Beijer* (Paris, 1928). See also Agne Beijer, *Commedia dell' arte* (Ord och Bild, February 1929, pp. 71–84).

wooed by the Lover, who tells her that he will die immediately if she does not grant him her favours.

The Franceschina of the Uniti in 1584 was a man, Battista da Treviso, otherwise known as Battista degli Amorevoli. We can imagine the part as played by a male performer being wholly grotesque. During the seventeenth century it was also performed occasionally by men. An otherwise unknown Carlo, who was at Milan in 1591, connects Battista with an Ottavio Bernardini, who was the Franceschina of the Uniti in 1614. That the part was not confined to men, however,

Fig. 158. FRANCISQUINA AND SIGNOR LEANDRO

Coloured engraving in the *Recueil Fossard*. From A. Beijer and P. Duchartre, *Recueil de plusieurs fragments des premières comédies italiennes* (Paris, 1928), Plate XXXI.

is proved by the fact that in the Gelosi troupe Franceschina was taken by an actress from Bergamo, Silvia Roncagli, who was the regular stage servant to Andreini's Isabella.

The name Diamantina, taken about 1660 by a Patrizia Adami, who flourished on the French stage till 1683, seems to indicate that about the middle of the seventeenth century

MADEMOISELLE HARLEQUINE

Fig. 159. ARLECCHINA

French print of the late seventeenth century. From P. Duchartre, *The Italian Comedy* (1929), p. 282.

this part was being refined by successive generations. The refining movement was brought to a culmination when, on Patrizia Adami's retirement from the Paris troupe in 1683, Catarina Biancolelli, then aged eighteen, appeared as Colombina. This actress, the daughter of G. B.

244

Biancolelli, married in 1685 Pietro Lenoir de la Thorillière, a member of the Comédie Française and a pupil of Molière. Small, dark-haired, and with a dainty voice, she seems to have endeavoured to make of Colombina that which later generations imagined her. Under the influence of French politeness, the rather rough servant-maid of early years almost totally vanished, and, with only a little apron to indicate her profession and otherwise dressed as the *innamorate* themselves, Colombina rapidly assumed a position and an importance hitherto denied to her. This, indeed, is an essential point to remember; for the familiar Colombina does not really belong to the history of the true Italian *commedia dell' arte* at all; it is the invention of the *comédie italienne*, which is a vastly different thing. To Catarina Biancolelli, too, belongs the credit for the introduction of Arlecchina; in this guise she first appeared in *Le Retour de la foire de Bezons* in the year 1695. This Arlecchina, or, as she was sometimes known, Smeraldina, seems to have rivalled Colombina in popularity on eighteenth-century popular stages (Fig. 160).

Besides the *innamorate* and the *fantesche*, few other women characters made their appearance on the *commedia dell' arte* stage. A *cantarina*, a *ballerina*, and the like enter in only for divertisement, and hardly ever play a definite part in the development of a scenario; and, in any case, such types seem to have been more familiar in seventeenth-century France than among the original Italian companies. Courtesans, too, were of rare occurrence, although they figured so largely in Terentian comedy, and to the literary sphere also belongs the Ruffiana, or bawd. The latter, it is true, does intrude into some scenarii, but she seems to owe her position chiefly to the imitation of literary models. The true *commedia dell' arte* theatre is concerned mainly with the *innamorate* and their pert or comic servant-maids.

Fig. 160. SMERALDINA
Watercolour sketch (early nineteenth century) in the Victoria and Albert Museum.

a tight-fitting red vest, red breeches and stockings,[1] and soft slippers probably of Turkish origin. Over this is cast a black-sleeved coat, called a *zimarra*, which reaches to his ankles.[2]   On his head

is set a soft cap without a brim, reminiscent of the Turkish fez. This is the earliest Pantalone costume known ; so it appears in the *Recueil Fossard* about 1577 (Fig. 168),[3] so it is in the illustration to the *Compositions* of 1601, and so in the famous frescoes in the Schloss Trausnitz in Bavaria (Fig. 169). Callot's Pantalone of the early seventeenth century [4] is fundamentally similar. In all of these, too, the mask is the same—darkish brown in colour, marked by an outstanding hooked nose, a straggling grey beard,

Fig. 169. PANTALONE JEALOUS
Painting in the Schloss Trausnitz.   From P. Duchartre, *The Italian Comedy* (1929), p. 183.

and a few wisps of hair protruding from under the cap. In addition to these characteristic features, Pantalone was distinguished often by a phallic appendage only a little less prominent than that worn by the ancient mimes. The suggestion of this phallus, half concealed by a handkerchief, is shown in the print by Julius Goscius of 1581 (Fig. 170), which depicts Pantalone as " Le Magnifico," the person of a Venetian courtesan, and an interesting bearded Zanni playing a lute.

As times changed, naturally Pantalone's dress altered slightly, but the main features as shown in the early illus-

Fig. 170. PANTALONE, THE COURTESAN, AND ZANNI
Print by Julius Goscius (1581) in the Museo Civico, Venice.
Photo T. Filippi

[1] Later 'pantaloons,' or long trousers, were sometimes worn.
[2] But in 1568 in Bavaria the coat was " crimson-coloured " (*cremisino*).   See Troiano's *Discorsi* ; Petraccone, p. 298.
[3] See Duchartre, p. 180.   [4] *Id.*, p. 185.

254

trations were retained. The Pantalone who is shown with the Dottore and Arlecchino in one of Pietro Longhi's charming Venetian interiors (Fig. 171) might have been the same as his predecessor of a century before. Even the early nineteenth-century Pantalone of Fig. 172 has the same dress and the same type of mask as had the others. Interesting, too, for comparison is the puppet figure (Fig. 173) which is part of a set belonging to a Venetian marionette theatre now preserved in the Museo Civico at Venice. These illustrations may perhaps help to bring before us something of his personality.

Toward the gaining of this impression, also, we are served by some contemporary accounts. Of these that by Perrucci has especial value, particularly when he enumerates the qualities required for the successful performance of the part:

> The actor who takes this *rôle* must be skilled in the use of the Venetian dialect in all its varieties, proverbs, and phrases. He must give the impression of a decrepit old man who, in spite of his age, wishes to pose as a youth. He may learn by heart various speeches for special scenes, such as advice to his son, good counsel for monarchs or princes, curses, greetings to the woman he is in love with, and other similar bagatelles according to his fancy, aiming at the arousing of laughter by his obstinacy and pride at appropriate junctures, thus depicting a man ripe in years who is so far ridiculous in that, whereas he ought to be a person of authority and good example and moral behaviour for others, he is seized by love and acts like a child. . . . Even his avarice, which is common to old men, gets surmounted by this greater vice, love.[1]

Cecchini, in his turn, stresses the " seriousness " of the part, which gives it its true comic touch:

> The *rôle* of the old man . . . is always a grave part, but it gets thrust among the comic *rôles* by the language spoken and dress worn by the actor.[2]

Fig. 171. Pantalone, Dottore, and Arlecchino
Painting by Pietro Longhi in the Museo Civico, Venice.
Photo Alinari

The performer who essays it must remember always to act it in such a way that the impression is given to the audience of a dignified and important citizen; only when he speaks to his servants can this mask of dignity be thrown off. Michelangiolo Buonarotti il Giovane describes him as one who " in a rage claps his hands to his thighs, his body shaking all over; clutches his gown and draws his dagger,"[3] but this is only in certain moments, and is comic because of its contrast with the dignified gravity which sometimes is, and ought always to be, his.

---

[1] " Chi rappresenta questa parte ha da avere perfetta la lingua veneziana, con i suoi dialetti, proverbi e vocaboli, facendo la parte d' un vecchio cadente ma che voglia affettare la gioventù; può premeditarsi qualche cosa per dirla nell' occasioni, cioè persuasioni al figlio, consigli a' regnanti o prencipi, maledizioni, saluti alla donna che ama ed altre cosuccie a suo arbitrio, avertendo che cavi la risata a suo tempo, con la sodezza e gravità, rappresentando una persona matura, che tanto si fa ridicola in quanto, dovendo esser persona d' autorità e d' esempio e di avertimento agli altri, colto dall' amore, fa cose da fanciullo . . . e la sua avarizia, propria de' vecchi, viene superata da un vizio maggiore, chè l' amore."—Petraccone, p. 115.

[2] " La parte del vecchio . . . è sempre parte grave, ma vien però mescolata fra le ridicoli per la lingua e vestimento."—Petraccone, p. 12.

[3] *Fiera*, Giorn. II, Atto II, Sc. 11 : " Quel Pantalon, ch' a modo d' adirato si pon le mani a' fianchi, e la persona scuote, e 'mbraccia la toga, e 'l pistolese squadera."

The particular names by which he is known vary considerably. Il Magnifico Messer Pantalone di Bisognosi was the earliest,[1] but sometimes other titles get attached to him, and occasionally he is confused with other old men. The first we hear of him is in du Bellay's poem of 1555–56, a period when he seems to have been popular in Rome. A few years later he is found in Mantua and Venice, and by 1568 he was carrying his caricature of the Venetian merchant to Bavaria. Several actors won particular fame in this *rôle*. The first who is known to us by name is Giulio Pasquati, who was the Pantalone of the Gelosi troupe in the seventies of the sixteenth century. It may have been he who acted the Magnifico with Soldino in Austria. His career with the Gelosi certainly started by 1574, and thereafter, up to 1582, he seems to have been a tower of comic strength to his company. Praise of his acting is not wanting; Porcacchi sums up all in stressing "his grace" and "the acuteness of his fancies, uttered in such a timely and sedate manner." His portrait is to be seen, in all probability, both in the *Recueil Fossard* print (Fig. 168) and in that of 1601. Possibly his place was taken by Giacomo Braga, but

Fig. 172. PANTALONE
Watercolour sketch (early nineteenth century) in the Victoria and Albert Museum.

little is known of that actor's activities for certain until he appears at Genoa with the Uniti in 1614. Among the Fedeli from 1609 to 1620 Federigo Ricci was the Pantalone; at Paris in 1645 a Cialace Arrighi sustained the part, and there, after serving in the Modena troupe, appeared Antonio Riccoboni. This last actor has special interest for us, since it was he who was the Pantalone when the Italian players visited London in 1679.[2] The popularity of the *rôle*, of course, was not confined to Italians, and soon men of other nationality were attempting its difficulties. Thus a certain Peter Hilverding was playing Pantalone de' Bisognosi at Salzburg in 1685, and continued to interpret the *rôle* until at least the year 1720.[3]

THE DOTTORE

Pantalone's usual companion was the Dottore, although in some scenarii the latter *rôle* is displaced in favour of others, such as the popular Coviello. Nearly always, however, even when Il Dottore is not specifically mentioned, Pantalone's foil is inclined to take on doctor-like characteristics. Almost as early as the records of the one are the records of the other; a company under a Gratiano, which is simply another name for the Dottore, was playing at Mantua in 1567.[4] There is a legend that this part was 'invented' by Luzio Burchiella, who had imitated the conversation and manners of an old barber of Francolino, called Graziano delle Cetiche;[5] but such legends must be accepted with caution.

Fig. 173. A PUPPET FIGURE OF PANTALONE
Marionette in the Museo Civico, Venice.
Photo T. Filippi

[1] In 1568, in Troiano's *Discorsi*; Petraccone, p. 297.　　[2] See *infra*, p. 339.
[3] A. Kutscher, *Das Salzburger Barocktheater* (Vienna, 1924), p. 96.　　[4] D'Ancona, ii, 445–446.
[5] F. S. Quadrio, *Della Storia e della ragione d' ogni poesia* (Bologna, 1739–52), v, 219.

THE OLD MEN

The facts that comic doctors were common in all earlier mime and farce and that the charlatan and the jurist are ridiculed in scenes of early religious plays makes us cling to the theory that here is nothing but a development of an ancient type. The name Graziano may, on the other hand, have come from a living person—perhaps, as Lampertico thinks, from the famous jurist Graziano ;[1] perhaps, as D'Ancona wonders, from a popular poet, " magistro Gratiano," who published his *Frotola nova* at Lyon about 1508.[2] Much more fascinating than either of these is Rasi's tentative hypothesis. He notes in some macaronic verses a sort of prologue spoken by a Gratianus, who states that he was a native of Francolino, son of a Mser Tomas and of a certain Caterina of Ferrara, of the house of Bambagi ; his degree he had gained in Bologna.[3] Now, in a letter written by Petrarca in the fourteenth century to Pietro da Bologna in which he describes the festivals at Venice in honour of a recent victory the statement is made that Tommaso Bambasio had been summoned from Ferrara to aid in the arrangements—a man, Petrarca adds, who is regarded throughout the whole of Venice just as Roscius was once in Rome. Is it possible that here we have yet another link in the chain of evidence which goes to prove the existence of a powerful secular drama in medieval Europe ? And is it possible that in Tommaso Bambasio we have the true parent of Graziano of the *commedia dell' arte*, the macaronic verses recording vaguely the theatrical legend which had been passed down from the fourteenth to the sixteenth centuries ?[4]

Whatever the truth of this, we know that the Dottore, wherever he was born, was nearly always a doctor of Bologna, and, since Bologna was the centre of legal studies, he was usually a jurist. Occasionally he appears as a medical man, but this profession is but rarely given him before the late seventeenth century. The early Dottore is connected rather with the doctors of the Temple or with Herod's counsellors than with the quacksalvers who sold unguents to the three Marys. Like Pantalone, he has an established position in social life, appearing often as the father of the Lover or of the *innamorata*, but, unlike Pantalone, he is rarely granted so much of this world's goods. The Graziano of *Il Marito* (*The Husband*), of the Scala collection, is thus a poverty-stricken *paterfamilias*. Like Pantalone, he is sometimes a husband himself, jealous and errant, and sometimes he is a counsellor to some monarch.[5] His qualities are varied yet simple. By nature he is a hypocritical tyrant, and in treatment he is more exaggerated and more purely comic than Pantalone. His speech, of which the vernacular portion is cast usually in the Bolognese dialect, is interlarded with many Latin words and phrases, and he does not mind talking pedantically above the heads of his companions, who, however, instead of admiring him for his learning, jeer openly or behind his back at his foolish affectations and his academic excesses. " This *rôle*," says a writer in the *Calendrier historique des théâtres*,[6]

> is that of a pedant, of a perpetual babbler who cannot open his mouth without uttering a sententious saying or dragging in some Latin expressions.[7]

Once more Perrucci must be called in to give his testimony :

> The part of the Dottore has not to be so dignified [as that of Pantalone]. It serves for the secondary fathers, but, through the liveliness of spirit and the redundancy of words, it may be carried somewhat out of the serious sphere—not so much, however, as to drag it down to the level of the second Zanni. . . . His

---

[1] Fedele Lampertico, *Scritti storici e letterarii* (Florence, 1882), ii, 40.
[2] D'Ancona, ii, 446. See also Flögel, i, 55–56; Sand, ii, 30.   [3] See Rasi, i, 413–414.
[4] Ulisse Fresco, in *Una Tradizione novellistica nella commedia del secolo xvi* (Camerino, 1903), endeavours to prove, but, I think, not with success, that the Dottore derives from Boccaccio's Calandrino and Messer Simone.
[5] Very occasionally, as in *Il Finto cieco* (Correr collection), he appears as a servant; in this play, the servant of Colanio.
[6] Paris, 1751.
[7] " Ce rôle est celui d'un pédant, d'un babillard éternel et qui ne sauroit ouvrir la bouche que pour débiter une sentence ou pour proférer quelques paroles latines."

R

speech must be true Bolognese, although, when the actor is playing in Naples, Palermo, or other cities far distant from Bologna, it should be modified a little; otherwise not a word would be understood. . . . The actor playing the part must be learned enough to be able to illustrate his ideas, in fitting time and scene, with some Latin sentence, some text or pronouncement of authority, such as " Nothing is more powerful than love, *Authentict. quibus modis naturales efficiantur legitimi*, coll. 6 " or " Friends should have all their affairs open to one another—*l. Latæ § Amicos, ff. de verborum signif.*," and so on. . . . A number of years ago there was introduced a special style in the playing of the part, whereby the Dottore mutilated his words, saying, for example, " terrible urinal " for tribunal, . . . but, since it was realized that this rendered him far too stupid and clumsy, it has been abandoned. . . . That which the actor playing this part can have in his memory are various pieces of advice suitable for a counsellor, speeches urging men to devote themselves to study, condemnations of vice, and, above all, long strings of names, dates, and references. The last provide the greatest merriment, particularly when they are given in the form of recapitulations; here they serve at once to display the ostentatious show of his academic doctrine and of his memory.[1]

As is clearly suggested here, the part of the Dottore was one easily susceptible of degeneration, and even as early as 1628 Cecchini [2] was throwing scorn on those actors who could utter only meaningless vocables such as " Piantalimòn, Petulòn, Pultrunzòn," and on those who merely threw out strings of Latin sentences, without regard to the plot of the play or the situation in which they found themselves. In Cecchini's opinion the actor who wishes to interpret rightly " this so pleasant a part " must conceive a man who desires to be up to date in spite of his age, one who utters thoughts pertinent to the matter but strange in expression without being aware himself of his dialectal oddities, letting slip out-of-the-way, peculiar, or garbled terms such as *interpretare* for *impetrare*, *urore* for *errore*, *secolari* for *scolari*. It is part of his nature, too, to take for wonders the most commonplace things ; he is credulous, and, being wrapped up in his study, does not know the world.[3]

Examples abound of his typical speech. As, however, all of these are in the Bolognese dialect, or what passes as such, it is almost impossible to render them here.[4] Most are of the form of the speech on " Counsel " given by Perrucci, which may thus be paraphrased in Northern dialect :

> Ye're speirin', sirs, for coonsel, an' since *consilium est appetitus faciendi excogitata ratione*, as Zizeron says, we'll hae to bide a wee on the first reason Homer maks Ulyss gie to Achil, *neque ullus modus facti est remedium invenire : igitur multo prius consilium cape*; Menander says, *Consilio enim nil est tutius*; Vergil, *æquum est consulere*; Verin, *consilio utilius quam armis bella geruntur*; Terence, *omnia prius consilio experiri quam armis sapienter decet*. An' the Greek actor-bodies hae *sophi sophon gorgignete simboon*, which ye can tak as " Get a coonsellor that kens a'." [5]

The Dottore's dress was, like Pantalone's, a stock theatrical one, although it changed more rapidly than his in accordance with academic fashion. The earliest illustrations show a figure not over-far removed from the normal. A black dress with a white collar, a doctor's gown and cap—

---

[1] " La parte del dottore non ha da esser tanto grave, servendo per le seconde parti di padre, ma, per la vivacità dell' ingegno, per la soverchia loquela, può darsele qualche licenza d' uscire dalla gravità, ma non tanto che si abbassi al secondo Zanni. . . . Il suo linguaggio ha da esser perfetto bolognese, ma in Napoli, Palermo ed altre città lontane da Bologna non deve esser tanto strigato, perchè non se ne sentirebbe parola. . . . Ha da esser erudito per dir, a tempo e luogo, qualche sentenza latina, qualche testo o qualche autorità di dottore, verbigrazia: ' nessuna cosa è più forte dell' amor,' *Authentict. quibus modis naturales efficiantur legitimi*, coll. 6; ' l' amizi han da esser conzunti in tutti i affar,' *l. Latæ § Amicos, ff. de verborum signif.* . . . Molti anni sono s' introdusse un modo di recitar da dottore che stravolgea i vocaboli, verbigrazia: ' terribil orinal ' per tribunale, . . . ma, perchè si conobbe far il dottore da troppo semplice e balordo, si è disusato. . . . Le cose che potrà aver premeditate saranno qualche consiglio, servendo da consigliero, persuasiva allo studio, dissuasione da' vizi, ma fra tutto le tirate di memoria, che fanno il più bel gioco in questa parte, particolarmente ove vi saranno riepiloghi, perchè venirà a fare al tempo istesso pompa della dottrina e della memoria."—Petraccone, pp. 119–121.

[2] Petraccone, pp. 10–11.

[3] *Cf.* also Michelangiolo Buonarotti il Giovane, *La Fiera*, Giorn. II, Atto II, Sc. ii.

[4] See particularly the examples in Petraccone, pp. 121–129, 257–262.

[5] *Id.*, p. 121. There seems little object in giving the original, since most of the speech is in Latin. Very interesting is the late sixteenth- or early seventeenth-century document which provides speeches for a puppet Dottore, discovered and discussed by F. Picco, *Lo Scartafaccio di un burattinaio, tirate e sproloqui del dottor Balanzone* (*Bolletino storico piacentino*, i (1907), 5–6).

these were the staple features. In the *Recueil Fossard*[1] the Dottore is an ordinary Bolognese academician, and so he appears in an early seventeenth-century print (Fig. 174). Very similar is the Dottore shown in Pietro Longhi's painting (Fig. 171), and even in the early nineteenth century he retained the familiar features of his ancestors (Fig. 175).

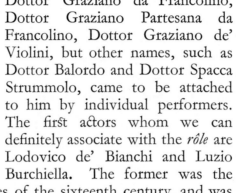

It will be noted that in the last illustration he is named " Dr Balanzoni," and this serves to remind us that his surnames were many. Graziano in early times was his regular title, and as such, indeed, without the specific addition of Dottore he was regularly known. Graziano was occasionally expanded, as in Dottor Graziano Scarpazon, Dottor Graziano da Francolino, Dottor Graziano Partesana da Francolino, Dottor Graziano de' Violini, but other names, such as Dottor Balordo and Dottor Spacca Strummolo, came to be attached to him by individual performers. The first actors whom we can definitely associate with the *rôle* are Lodovico de' Bianchi and Luzio Burchiella. The former was the Dottore of the Gelosi in the seventies of the sixteenth century, and was author of an entertaining *Cento e quindici conclusioni . . . del Plusquam perfetto Dottor Gratiano Partesana da Francolin* (1587). Concerning the latter we know that he too was connected with the Gelosi, and that he seems to have been associated with Ganassa in 1567; he was probably the Luzio Fedele of whom Quadrio speaks about 1560. He also was a *littérateur* of sorts. A poem by him, *Dal pigro sonno*, appears in Adriano Valerini's *Oratione . . . in morte della Divina Signora Vincenza Armani* (Verona, 1570). An Andreazzo Graziano was in Diana's company in 1590, and a certain Giovan Paolo Agocchi, who was in Rome three years later, carried the part to Bavaria in 1603. In 1593 the Dottore of the Uniti was Andrea Zenari, and a decade after Bartolomeo Zito, or Cito, was sustaining the *rôle* at Naples. As Dottor Spacca Strummolo, which signifies ' to chatter aimlessly,' another Neapolitan, Aniello Soldano, won special fame, eventually entering the company of the Fedeli. Soldano has special interest for us, because he is the author of *La Fondatione, & origine di Bologna* (Bologna, 1610), which, besides being an entertaining piece of Dottoresque writing, contains the actor's portrait on the title-page (Fig. 176). The Dottore of the Fedeli when they went to Paris in 1612 was Bartolomeo Bongiovanni, and about 1623 appeared among a band of Uniti, as Dottor Graziano

Fig. 174. THE DOTTORE

From the *Indice universale della Libraria* (Bologna, n.d.), attributed to G. C. Croce, but possibly written by Pietro Bagliani.

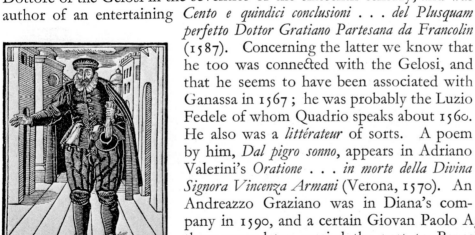

Fig. 176. ANIELLO SOL-DANO AS DOTTOR SPACCA STRUMMOLO

From the title-page to *La Fondatione, & origine di Bologna* (1610).

Fig. 175. DOTTOR BALANZONI

Watercolour sketch (early nineteenth century) in the Victoria and Albert Museum.

---

[1] Duchartre, p. 198.

Forbizone da Francolino, a Pietro Bagliani, the author of a comedy called *La Pazzia* (Bologna, 1624) and perhaps also of the *Indice universale della Libraria* (Bologna, n.d.), which presents his portrait (Fig. 174). Girolamo Chiesa, who acted in the thirties of the century, carried his art to France, and there acted Giovanni Battista Paghetti and Marc' Antonio Romagnesi. The latter, who had started his career as Cintio, a Lover, adopted the *rôle* of Dottore at the age of sixty-one on August 29, 1694, and was as famous in that as he had been in the other more gallant part. Like so many of these actors, he has left some tangible record of his literary attainments in the from of *Poesie liriche* (Paris, 1673) and of an ode " to his own genius " published in the *Livre sans nom* (Paris, 1695) of Cotolendi. Two prints preserve his likeness in the part of Dottore.[1] Other actors of this *rôle*, such as G. Paderna, G. Orlandi, G. Savorini, and G. B. A. Lolli, we may leave for the present.

Fig. 177. BRINQUENAZILLE, FRANCATRIPPE, SCAPPIN, AND PASQUARIELLE

Early seventeenth-century print in the Cabinet des Estampes, Bibliothèque Nationale. From Constant Mic, *La Commedia dell' arte* (Éditions de la Pléiade, Paris, 1927), p. 43.

PASQUARIELLO

That Pantalone and the Dottore were not the only old men of the *commedia dell' arte* is amply proved by a study of the scenarii, and, before passing to other spheres, we must consider at least the more important variants of the type. Among the ' old men ' Perrucci enumerates Pasquariello, Cola, Cassandro, and Ciccombimbo.[2]

The first of these, whom Duchartre wrongly classes as a kind of Capitano,[3] was a Neapolitan according to Cecchini.[4] He is heard of in that city, under the name of Pascariello Pettola, as early as 1588,[5] and is present in many of the Neapolitan scenarii.[6] Only two prints show his features. One, a sketch by Callot,[7] gives him a long-nosed mask, a flowing cape, and a sword. He is there named Pasquariello Truonno, which signifies ' Pasquariello the Terrible.' The other illustration, of French origin (Fig. 177), indicates a thin character, whose dress is ornamented with spots, wearing a half-mask with a prominent hooked nose and a cap ornamented with feathers. He has a wooden sword, and from his neck is suspended a box apparently containing unguents. Perhaps he is here a cross between a doctor and a Zany ; in the late *L'Avocat pour et contre*[8] he is a foolish and decrepit portrait artist ; but in most of these Italo-French plays, such as Regnard's *Les Filles errantes* (1690), he appears but as a servant. Of the actors who sustained this *rôle* we know only of Gian Gregorio d'Ariemme, in the early seventeenth century, and Giuseppe Tortoriti, who played in Paris from 1683 to 1697.[9]

---

[1] Duchartre, pp. 200, 201; Rasi, iii, 395, 397.
[2] Petraccone, p. 130.
[3] Duchartre, pp. 247–248.
[4] Petraccone, p. 16.
[5] Croce, pp. 31–32.
[6] He also appears in the scenario of *La Trapolaria*.
[7] Duchartre, p. 248.
[8] See Duchartre, pp. 248–249.
[9] He also took the parts of the Capitano and of Scaramuccia.

THE OLD MEN

COLA, CASSANDRO, AND COVIELLO

Cola, according to Cecchini,[1] was also a Neapolitan. In *Le tre Gravide* he is the foolish servant of the Capitano, and in *I Tappeti* he is the husband of Lucinda; sometimes in the nobler, sometimes in the lower, part—but always ridiculous—he figures freely in the Neapolitan scenarii. Perhaps the Colanio of the Correr *Il Finto cieco* is the same person. It seems that he was an acrobatic character,
for in 1607 he was described as "a new person who, for his tumblings and gestures, will perhaps please not less than Arlecchino."[2] It is probable that the reference is to the actor Francesco Vacantiello (evidently a type name itself), who is mentioned by Trajano Boccalini in his *De' Ragguagli di Parnaso* (Milano, 1613).[3] Cola itself is simply a contraction of Nicola.

In the Correr scenarii Cassandro appears several times alongside of Pantalone, apparently, as in *Le due Sorelle rivale* and in *Li duo Amanti furiosi*, occupying the place usually taken by the Dottore. This being so, it seems hardly correct to describe him, as Duchartre[4] does, as a "copy" of Pantalone. Nor was he always a Sienese; Perrucci, indeed, makes him definitely Florentine,[5] and calls him Cassandro d'Aretusi.

Of Ciccombimbo nothing can be said, but there are others besides him whom Perrucci does not notice. Among these Coviello, who is by no means "anonymous," "forgotten," or "little-known,"[6] is the chief. As Coviello Ciavola he appears at Naples in 1588,[7] and Cecchini lists him among Neapolitan parts.[8] In the Neapolitan scenarii he figures as a gentleman or a rich *bourgeois* citizen,[9] but elsewhere he is subject to strange transformations. As a substitute for the Dottore we find him in

Fig. 178. COVIELLO SINGING
Seventeenth-century Italian print. From P. Duchartre,
The Italian Comedy (1929), p. 44.

the Correr *L'Amante tradito*; *Le due Sorelle rivale* of the same collection makes him a merchant, playing with the Magnifico and Cassandro; he is a definite Dottore in *L'Astrologo*, but is distinct from a Dottore in *Il Sole* of the Correr collection; and as a servant, playing with Pulcinella, he appears in many other scenarii, of which may be mentioned *L'Arcadia incantata*, *Le Metamorphosi di Pulcinella*, and *Il Convitato di pietra*. It seems, from this evidence, that Rasi's conjectural placing of him among the Capitani[10] is hardly justified. In the Callot print he might be anything,[11] and the print of Bertelli's (Fig. 178) is too exaggerated to be of much service to us in establishing his personality. The only actor of importance who took this part was Gennaro Sacco, who flourished

[1] Petraccone, p. 16; *cf.* pp. 113–114.   [2] Rasi, ii, 672.   [3] i, 242; *cf.* Rasi, iii, 613.
[4] Duchartre, p. 194. He notes him as "Cassandro of Siena." A. Bartoli (p. li) rightly recognizes him as a kind of Dottore.
[5] Petraccone, pp. 114–115.   [6] Duchartre, p. 291.   [7] B. Croce, pp. 31–32.
[8] Petraccone, p. 16.   [9] B. Croce, *Saggi*, p. 245.
[10] Rasi, iii, 458. Perrucci (in Petraccone, pp. 139–140) is more correct in classing him with the Zanni. Perrucci notes that he is too apt to descend "from witticisms to stupidity." He gives an example of his speech.
[11] Duchartre, p. 291.

in the last years of the seventeenth century.   This performer was one of the *littérateurs*, too, leaving behind him a *Trionfo del merito* (Venezia, 1686) in verse and several other comic works.

Difficult of interpretation, also, is Zanobio da Piombino, or simply Piombino, a part taken by Girolamo Salimbeni among the Gelosi in the late sixteenth century.   Piombino, an actor, appears in *Il Ritratto* of the Scala collection.   Facanappa, whom Duchartre describes as a kind of Pantalone[1] and Bartoli as a kind of Dottore,[2] is equally vague.   Perhaps other old men existed on the popular stages, but those enumerated seem to have been the chief, and of them all Pantalone and the Dottore ruled as *bourgeois* kings.

[1] Duchartre (p. 195), who seems to rely mainly on Sand.   Duchartre has been misled by Sand into placing *Pangrazio il Biscegliese* among seventeenth-century types.   This was not invented till the early nineteenth century (B. Croce, *Saggi*, p. 314).

[2] A. Bartoli, p. li.

Fig. 179. EIGHTEENTH-CENTURY PUPPET-SHOW

Watercolour sketch in the *Album de Grevenbroch* (Museo Civico, Venice), No. 164. This is given in order to demonstrate the way in which the traditional " Punch and Judy " show of to-day has retained all the main features of the puppet-show of two hundred years ago.

Photo T. Filippi

(vi) THE STOCK TYPES: (4) THE ZANNI

It is at this point we reach at once the most interesting and the most puzzling of all *commedia dell' arte* types—the comic servants, or, as they were regularly known, the Zanni. These Zanni were the truly popular figures, and concerning their activities we have early record. A (probably non-dramatic) Zanni as servant is mentioned in 1514;[1] while in 1553 Girolamo Rofia, writing to Andrea degli Agli in Florence, refers to " that Zanni whom you have every evening in the piazza at your town " and connects him with Bergamo.[2] Two years later du Bellay saw the Zanni buffooning in Rome;[3] in 1559 il Lusca published among his *Canti carnascialeschi* one " On Zanni and Pantalones "; their wooden swords (*coltelli di legno*) at Abruzzo are recorded in 1566;[4] and at the same time they were playing regularly in Ferrara.[5] Their popularity spread far and wide. The " zawne " is mentioned in Edwardes' *Damon and Pithias*, which was acted in 1566;[6] he creeps into *Love's Labour's Lost*[7] and *Twelfth Night*,[8] and sports throughout English literature of the seventeenth century.

THE ORIGIN AND SIGNIFICANCE OF THE WORD 'ZANNI'

Before we proceed to consider particular forms of this stage type we must note that the word ' Zanni ' could be used both in a general and in a restricted sense. Thus, in the earliest full description of a *commedia dell' arte* performance it is simply a " Zanne " who appears,[9] and Zanni is distinct from other servants in many scenarii. In most of the Correr plays this character acts with Tartaglia, Stupino, Scapino, or Trevelino, and is often given no other name throughout the course of the play. On the other hand, under this generic title is often concealed a particular, for in some scenarii we find in the list of *dramatis personæ* a Zanni mentioned, whereas in the scenes themselves an individual name is given to the representative of the type. We must remember, then, that the word ' Zanni ' may be used either to designate a particular stage servant or else to indicate the *rôle* in general.

Concerning the name itself there has been some doubt. In former times it was customary to trace it to the classic *sannio*;[10] but against this view various objections have lately been formulated, and scholarly opinion generally, following a fashion, as scholarly opinion often does, has swung round to ridicule of the *sannio* theory. In the first place, it is pointed out that, if *sannio* were indeed the true origin, the modern word ought to have been formed from the oblique case and so appear as *sannione* or *zannione*. In the second, attention has been drawn to the fact that Zanni—or, in its

---

[1] See A. Gaspary, *Storia della letteratura italiana* (Turin, 1901), ii, 336.

[2] S. Morpurgo, *Sulla montagna pistoiese l'anno 1553* (Florence, 1896, " per nozze Biadego-Bernardinelli "), p. 8. A. Gaspary, ii, 336: " Quel zanni che havete ogni sera costì in piazza." For other early notices see *infra*, pp. 299–300.

[3] *Regrets*, sonnet cxii.   [4] Croce, p. 29.

[5] A. Solerti and A. Lanza, *Il Teatro ferrarese nella seconda metà del sec. xvi* (*Giornale storico*, xviii (1891), 156). For the Zanni in 1568 see *infra*, p. 301.

[6] Printed 1571; Sig. F2.   [7] V, ii, 463.   [8] I, v, 96.   [9] Troiano, *Discorsi* (1568), in Petraccone, p. 298.

[10] See *supra*, pp. 88–90. This, for example, was Quadrio's view (*Storia e ragione d' ogni poesia*, v, 212). It has been supported up to the last twenty years or so; *cf.* Sand, i, 27; P. C. Ferrigni, *La Storia dei burattini* (Florence, 1902), p. 120; Dieterich, p. 236. This matter of the name is, of course, connected with that of the origin of the *commedia dell' arte* as a whole. Reich supposes the Italian Comedy to have arisen largely from the influence of a Byzantine mime. More commonly older scholars pleaded for a direct descent from the Atellanæ; among these may be mentioned P. Villari (*Le Commedie di Nicolò Machiavelli*, in *Nuova Antologia*, II, xxxiii (1882), 401), and V. de Amicis, *La Commedia popolare latina e la commedia dell' arte* (Naples, 1882), pp. 21–25. This idea is a very old one. It appears in N. Rossi, *Discorso intorno alla commedia* (Vicenza, 1589), p. 34, and in B. Varchi, *Storie fiorentine* (Firenze, 1570), p. 529. For a general survey of the literature on the Zanni, albeit neglecting some important contributions, see Maria Magni, *Il Tipo dello Zanni nella commedia dell' arte in Italia nei secoli XVI e XVII* (*Bergomum*, xx (1926), 111–138, 163–184). This essay includes a good " Bibliografia facchinesca " of early popular poems. *Cf.* also Driesen, pp. 193–204, and Scherillo, pp. 48–69.

of these prints the Zanni wears a full-face mask which is heavily bearded, and such an one, made of thick hide, is preserved in the Musée du Grand Opéra at Paris (Fig. 182). For comparison with it may be taken another, but clean-shaven, mask preserved in the collection of M. Henri Lavedan (Fig. 183). One feature in both of these is of peculiar significance. On the brow of the first appears an enormous wart, and a similar wart is a prominent feature on the cheek of the other. Concerning the warts of the medieval devils something has been said already,[1] and it was then noted that such warts are to be observed on masks of the Atellan figures. Now, neither of the two Zanni masks has a devilish appearance, and one could hardly suppose that the type thus delineated had arisen out of Lucifer and his crew. It seems more probable that this stupid Zanni is a direct descendant, with a lineage through medieval secular drama, of the classic *sannio*, the *stupidus*, who, in his turn was connected with the Atellan figures and with the bald-headed mime of Greece. Whereas in Fig. 182 there is a bushy beard and moustache, and

Fig. 182. LEATHER MASK OF A ZANNI

Early mask in the Musée du Grand Opéra, Paris. From Constant Mic, *La Commedia dell' arte* (Éditions de la Pléiade, Paris, 1927), p. 119.

whereas in Fig. 183 there are enormous eyebrows, both of these masks are totally innocent of hair on the head. That feature, their peaked caps, and their warts all connect them with antique clowns.

The two Zanni who thus played clever and stupid *rôles* in the scenarii are designated by Duchartre [2] as Arlecchino and Brighella; but here we must be on our guard. Among the second Zanni Perrucci mentions Don Pasquale, Travaglini or Tabbarini, Giovanello, and Policinella, while an examination of scenarii indicates a variety of names, which often leave out altogether the Arlecchino and Brighella pair. Thus in *I Metamorphosi di Pulcinella* it is an old man, Coviello, who is first Zanni, with Pulcinella as second; in *Il Padre crudele* the first is Colafronio, and the stupid clown is Stoppino. The names here are legion, and multiply upon themselves as we move on through the seventeenth century.[3]

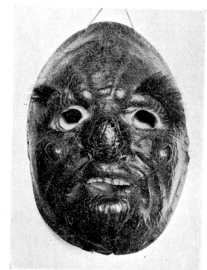

Fig. 183. LEATHER MASK OF A ZANNI

In the possession of M. Henri Lavedan.

Photo "Archives photographiques d'Art et d'histoire"

[1] See *supra*, p. 191.
[2] P. 29.
[3] For the Zanni spirit the poems of Bartolomeo Bocchini called Zan Muccina, or Muzzina, are of special interest. See *La Prima [seconda] parte della Corona Macheronica di Zan Mvccina* (fifth edition, Bologna, 1663) and *Miscvglio di pensieri Rime burlesche . . . di Bartolomeo Bocchini, detto Zan Muzzina* (Bologna, n.d.).

THE ZANNI

ARLECCHINO

This, however, is true, that of them all Arlecchino most surely captured the popular imagination. Because of this we are justified in dealing with him first. And what a pother of etymological discussion we meet so soon as we set foot on his territory! He has been the cause of almost as much academic theory as Shakespeare himself. Comes Ménage in 1650, who says the name is a variant of Harlay-quino,[1] from Hachille du Harlay, statesman and patron of actors, the fifth of his line. Comes another who says Arlecchino is but *il lecchino*, " the little glutton," [2] and a third who avers that there was a rascal of Arles who fled to Italy and became a standing name,[3] and a fourth who traces Arlecchino to the *harle*, a kind of bird, and Arlecchino himself, in the person of Dominique Biancolelli, who has a pleasant gibe, as it were, at those scholarly investigators who were to come after him. The scene is in *A fourbe, fourbe et demy*, and Cinthio

says to me that for all the time he has had me in his service it has never occurred to him to ask me my name. I answer him that my name is Arlequin Sbroufadel, and when he starts laughing at the Sbroufadel I tell him there's nothing to laugh about, that my ancestors were people of consequence, that Sbroufadel, the first of my line, was a pork-butcher by trade, but so skilled in his profession that once he presented half a dozen sausages to Nero, the Roman Emperor, who thought them so delicious that, as a reward, he created Sbroufadel a Roman senator. Sbroufadel's son was called Fregocola, a great captain who in the wars of the Carthaginians and the Romans did so many mighty deeds that the Senate made him drummajor of the Republic. This Fregocola (or Fregrocola) married Mme Chateigne, who had such liveliness that, while the other Roman ladies needed nine months to bear a child, she was hardly married when her impatience and readiness made her bear me. My father, for his part, was transported with joy, but this joy did not last long because the very day I was born a charge was laid against him on account of his excessive politeness. These were the facts. Whenever he met an honest fellow on the highroad by day, he never failed to lift his hat, and at night he lifted his hat and his cloak as well. The law (just out of sheer envy) took exception to this excess of politeness, and issued an order for his arrest. My father learned of this, took me up in my swaddling clothes, placed me in a big cauldron and the rest of his goods in a basket, dumped everything on an ass, and left the town. To hasten his progress, he beat the ass on the back, crying out at every moment, " Ar, ar," which means " Gee up " in the asinine tongue. Moving along swiftly in this way, he realized that a man was following him, and this man, seeing that my father was watching him anxiously, got behind a bush and sat down (he sits *chin*, that is to say, *chino*, or he sits down). And my father, who took him for a policeman crouching there the better to surprise him, started to beat the ass even more stoutly, crying out, " Ar-le-chin." [*Le-chino*, " he is crouching "— *i.e.*, " Gee-up, there he's crouching."] When my father arrived in town he learned that the man was only a simple peasant who had diarrhœa through having eaten too many grapes and so had been obliged to ease himself. So, as I had not yet been baptised, my father, recalling his fright over that man and the words he had so often cried to the ass—" Ar-le-chin "—called me Arlechino, Arlequin.[4]

---

[1] *Dictionnaire étymologique de la langue françoise* (Paris, 1650), *s.v.* Harlequin. [2] See Mic, p. 51.

[3] Lorenzo Mascheroni has suggested Arles as the ultimate source of the name. See Ciro Caversari, *Poesie e prose di Lorenzo Mascheroni* (Bergamo, 1903), pp. 88–90.

[4] This passage from the *Traduction du scenario de . . . Biancolelli* (ii, 31–32) is given incompletely and with several misreadings by Duchartre. The language is not *asiatique*, but *asinique*. The true text runs as follows:

" Il me dit que depuis quil m'a pris a son seruice, Il n'a pas pensé a me demander mon nom, Jeluy reponds que je me nomme Arlequin Sbroufadel, comme Il se met arire du Surnom de Sbroufadel, je luy dis quil ny apas tant de quoy rire, que mes ancestres estoient gens de Consequence que Sbroufadel premier du Nom estoit chaircuitier de son mestier, mais si Superieur Dans Saprofession quil presenta vn jour vne demy Douzaine de Saucisses a neron Empereur romain qui les trouua d'vn goust si exquis que pour L'en recompenser Il lefit senateur romain. De le Sbroufadel naquit fregocola grand Capitaine Lequel dans les guerres des Cartaginois contres Les romains fit parois tant de valleur que Le Senat Le fit tambour major de la republique Ce fregrocola epousa M^e chateigne, La quelle estoit D'vne si grande uiuacite qu'aulieu que les autres dames romaines mettoient neuf mois, a faire vn enfant Elle fut apeine Mariée que son jmpatience et Sa promptitude La firont accouchee de moy, mon pere en fu da bord transporté de joye, mais cette joye ne dura pas Longtemps parceque Le mesme jour que je Nacquis on luy chercha vne querelle fondée sur ce quil estoit trop Ciuil. Voicj dequoy Il sagissoit, Lorsque dejour sur Le grand chemin Il rencontroit quelque honneste homme, Il ne manquoit pas de luy oster son chapeau, et lorsque Cestoit de Nuit Il luy ostoit et son chapeau et son manteau Lajustice, (et cela par Enuie) trouua a reduire a cet excez de ciuilité, et ordonna a vn exempt de Larrester. Mon pere qui enfut auerty me prit dans mon maillot, me mit dans vn chaudron, et Le reste de son petit meuble dans vn panier, il chargea Letout sur

267

Unquestionably Mic is in the right when he remarks that the parlour game of searching for Arlecchino's ancestry may be continued indefinitely by the use of all the words commencing with *Arl* and *Harl* to be found in Larousse.[1] On the other hand, to say, as he does, that " the true name of Arlecchino " is " simply Zanni " is a rather weak evasion of a genuine problem. Arlecchino may associate himself with the Zanni, but even at the earliest period he can appear in the same play or print along with another actor who is described as Zanni and who is therefore a distinct character. Happily, a certain amount of the idler speculation of the past has been dissipated by recent linguistic studies, of which by far the most important is Otto Driesen's essay, *Der Ursprung des Harlekin*.[2] Put briefly, Driesen's theory is that Arlecchino, in the form of Harlequin, is truly French, and not Italian ; and that that name derives from an older form " Herlequin," which was changed to Harlequin when many words with an *er* combination were altered to *ar* in the Parisian dialect. From this he traces back the word through a fourteenth-century *Roman du Fauvel*, where " the Harlequins sang a sweet, joyous song "[3] and where " Hellequin " appears with his host, or *mesnie*, through a thirteenth-century reference to *li maisme Hierlekin* in *Renard le nouvel* and *li sires Hellequins* of *Le Jeu de la feuillée*,[4] to the *familia Herlechini* of the early eleventh century in Ordericus Vitalis. This figure, as can readily be shown, was a kind of spirit of the dead, and Driesen assumes that he entered into the religious drama as one of the devils. In proof of this can be extended the fact that the dragon's mouth which was so familiar a feature of the Hell scene in the Middle Ages was named in France *la chappe d'Hellequin*.[5] The supposition is that, after comic treatment in these religious mysteries, this Harlequin was brought on to the secular stage at the end of the sixteenth century, in all probability by Alberto Ganassa when, visiting Paris, he may have borrowed the French, once demonic and now comic, figure.

Driesen's theory, put forward with a magnificent array of well-reasoned evidence, is excellent so far as it goes ; but there are two things which must still be discussed. The one is the ultimate origin of this word Herlequin or Hellequin ; and the other is the relationship between the later stage Arlecchino of Italy and these medieval French figures. It might be suggested, as some have done,[6] that the final source of the word is to be found in the ancient myth of the Erl-könig, carried

---

vn asne et sortit de la ville, et pour aller plus viste Il frappoit dessus luy enluy disant a tous mommens *Ar Ar* qui veut dire *Marche* en Langage asinique, endoublant ainsy Le pave, Il apperceut derriere Luy vn homme qui Le suiuoit et cet homme voyant que mon pere Le regardoit auec attention se mit derriere vn buisson ou il saccroupit (se mette *Chin* pour chino, se mit abas) E mon pere qui Le prenoit pour L Exempte, et qui evoyoit quil se mettoit ainsy pour Le mieux Surprendre, commença a frapper plus fortement sur Lasne, enluy disant *Ar-le-Chin* (Lechino, Il est accroupi) cequi veut dire *Marche* Il est accroupy. Quand il fut arriué a la ville Il sçeut que cet homme N'estoit qu'un simple paŷisan qui pour auoir trop mangé de raisin, auoit vn cours de ventre qui L'auoit obligé a se mettre a son aize, de sorte que comme je n'auoir pas encore eu de nom; Mon pere se resouuenant de la peur quil auoit eu de cet homme, et des parolles quil auoit dittes alors si Souuent qui estoient Ar-le chin, me nomma Arlechino, Arlequin."

[1] P. 51.

[2] The Arlecchino literature is vast. Notes on the origin of the name will be found in A. Scheler, *Dictionnaire d'étymologie française* (Paris, 1888 ; third edition), and M. Rühlemann, *Etymologie des Wortes Harlequin und verwandter Wörter* (Halle, 1912). The latter interprets Hellekin as " little Hell," and argues for a Flemish source. The *mesnie Hellequin* is dealt with by G. Raynaud, *La Mesnie Hellequin* (*Études romanes dédiées à Gaston Paris*, Paris, 1892, p. 51) ; J. P. Jacobsen, *Harlekin og den vilde Jaeger* (*Dania*, ix (1902), 1–19) ; P. Toynbee, *La Mesnie Hellequin, Alichino, Inf. xxi*, 118 (*Academy*, No. 1170). *Cf.* also *infra*, p. 269, where are mentioned some critical essays on Driesen's theory. Alessandro Wesselofsky, in *Alichino e Aredodesa* (*Giornale storico*, xi (1888), 325–343), discusses the legend of Erodiade (Herodias), who was condemned eternally to dance in hell, and connects her with the *mesnie Hellequin*. On Harlequin generally see Cyril W. Beaumont, *The History of Harlequin* (1926) ; Lorin, *Essai sur l'origine des noms de Polichinelle et d'Arlequin* (Soissons, 1844) ; Bordelon, *Arléquin comédien aux Champs-Élysées* (Paris, 1694) ; Rapparini, *Arlichino* (Heidelberg, 1718), as quoted in Rasi ; *cf.* also M. Magni, *loc. cit.*, pp. 134–135 ; Ireneo Sanesi, *La Commedia* (Milan, 1911), i, 443–444.

[3] " Firent les herlequines
Ce descort dous et gay."
Op. cit., p. 21

[4] See *supra*, p. 173.

[5] See Cohen, pp. 95–97 ; Driesen, pp. 69–73. This figure appears in the pseudo-Chaucer (" Hurlewaynes mene," in *Tale of Beryn*, 8) and in ' Langland ' (" Hurlewaynis kynne " in *Richard the Redeless*, i, 90).

[6] Mic, p. 48. This is the view of the anonymous author of *The Evolution of Harlequin* (*Quarterly Review*, cxcvi (1902), 462–482), where an attempt is made to trace back this " Erlen-könig " to the " Erlik-Khan " of Central Asia.

to France and there acclimatized; or, as Cohen does,[1] one might suppose a Germanic origin of another kind, taking the Anglo-Saxon *helle-cinn*, which literally means 'the kin or race of hell,' and making that the origin of this strange spirit who from a devil became a joyous raiser of laughter.[2] But one path, apparently, has not yet been sought. The earliest reference to the legendary character is the phrase of Vitalis in 1100—*familia Herlechini*. Now, we have already seen that Hercules was a popular (and comic) stage figure in the days of the classic mime, and that even in the sixth century a play of *The Three Hercules* was being performed. This primitive comic Hercules was distinguished by his hunger, by the animal skin on his head, and by his wooden club. In the year 1592 a theological writer had occasion, impolitely but possibly justly, to call his opponent an ass:

> Among other things we cannot conceal from you a huge joke—that they liken you to the Cumæan ass, the pretty story of which Æsop has told in his *Fables*; that once, when this ass was immersed in his disreputable thoughts, he disguised himself as a lion and put a skin on his head, not to enter a masquerade or to play the part of Hercules or Harlequin in a Comedy, but in order, by his terrific appearance, to frighten "Oxen and sheep and other beasts of the field."[3]

This is very late evidence indeed; but may one suggest that the tuft of skin (often a rabbit's tail) which Arlecchino wore was a relic of Hercules' skin and that the wooden *batte* was a relic of Hercules' club; that the medieval Herlequinus (Herlechinus) was a corruption of Herculinus; and that Hercules as a type on the secular stage had an existence apart from the legendary leader of the *mesnie* of ghosts, who was also a dramatic devil? Such a suggestion may be hazardous, but there seems at least some justification for its proposal.

Arlecchino's wooden *batte* introduces the second matter which must be discussed. Driesen assumes that the introduction of this character into the *commedia dell' arte* did not take place until about 1572, when Ganassa's company was in Paris. That he proves the kinship of this Arlecchino with the mythical and demonic French Herlequin is certain; but one feels that he has not told all the story. It may well be that the French tradition influenced the Italian actors when they came to Paris; something of the devil may have entered into Arlecchino. But there are two points which Driesen seems to have left untouched. The one is that what may be called the spiritual essence of this character is truly Italian,[4] and perhaps Jaffei is right in saying that a new orientation will be required when Italy finds its Driesen to trace the development of the Italian tradition which is perhaps suggested by the appearance of the devil Alichino in Dante.[5] Quite apart from this, and even assuming that the name Arlecchino was of French origin, which seems doubtful, it must be remembered that Zanni with their wooden swords—the *batte* of Arlecchino—were attracting audiences in Italian towns many years before Ganassa visited Paris. That these Zanni were not individually named proves nothing; for even in the seventeenth century the word Zanni often conceals under its generic form the person of Arlecchino. It seems highly probable, then, that while Driesen's truly excellent study has cleared away much of false theorizing, still further research into this

---

[1] Cohen, *La Mise-en-scène*, p. xxv. Such is the view put forward also by Ferdinand Lot in *La Mesnie Hellequin et le comte Ernequin de Boulogne* (*Romania*, xxxii (1903), 422–441). In this essay Lot dismissed the quasi-historical Ernequin put forward by Gaston Raynaud in *La Mesnie Hellequin* (*Études romanes dédiées à Gaston Paris*, Paris, 1892), pp. 51–69. This idea had already been treated sceptically by Gaston Paris in *Romania*, xxii (1893), 139.

[2] This proposal seems to overlook the fact that *Herlechinus*, and not *Hellechinus*, is the earliest recorded form of the name.

[3] "Inter alia non possumus vobis celare unam magnam truffam, quando assimilant vos asino Cumano de quo Æsopus in Fabulis pulchram historiam recitavit, quod semel baudetus ille cum esset in suis gaillardis cogitationibus, se trauestiuit in leonem et superinduit pellem illius, non ut faceret Mascaradam vel ut luderet personam Herculis vel Harlequini in Comœdia, sed ut terreret terribili suo aspectu, 'Boues et oues et cetera pecora campi.'"—*Anti-Choppinus* (Carnuti, 1592), quoted in Driesen, p. 169.

[4] R. Renier, *Arlecchino* (*Fanfulla della Domenica*, xxvi (1904), March), and in his *Saggi critici* (Bari, 1910), pp. 465–483, emphasizes this view, which is also supported by B. Croce (*Saggi*, pp. 269–270). That the *maisne* was known in Italy is proved by Renato Serra, *Su la Pena dei dissipatori* (*Giornale storico*, xliii (1904), 291–297), where it was known as the *cazza salvarega*. For other discussions of this subject see E. Caffi, *La Questione d'Arlecchino* (*La Rassegna nazionale*, September 16, 1908), and articles by G. Nerucci and G. Rossi in the *Giornale di erudizione* (vii).

[5] G. Jaffei, *Note critiche su le maschere in genere e su Arlecchino in ispecie* (*Rivista d' Italia*, xiii (1910), 771–825). *Cf.* Flögel, i, 46.

269

question may reveal aspects of the subject which will necessitate a fresh outlook, and at the same time may indicate the direct descent of Arlecchino, not through the religious stage, but through the activities of the secular entertainers.[1]

Peculiarly enough, some of the earliest records we have of Arlecchino are of a pictorial character.

Fig. 184. COMMEDIA DELL' ARTE TYPES, 1572
Painting attributed variously to Paul and Frans Porbus, now in the Bayeux Museum.   From P. Duchartre,
The Italian Comedy (1929), p. 84.

He was a favourite subject for painters and for engravers, so that we possess ample documentary evidence from which to form an estimate of his appearance in different ages.   So far as literary records are concerned, the first, if only we were certain of his authority, would be Pellicer's statement that in 1574 Alberto Ganassa, in Madrid, introduced to Spanish audiences " the characters of Arlecchino, Pantalone, and the Dottore," [2] but possibly two years before this date was painted the canvas now preserved in the Musée de Bayeux and fortunately unearthed by Duchartre (Fig. 184).[3]

[1] That Arlecchino descended from the *mimus in centunculo* (see *supra*, pp. 90–91) is suggested by J. L. Klein, *Geschichte des italienischen Drama's* (Leipzig, 1874), i, 905; and A. W. Ward, *A History of English Dramatic Literature* (1899), i, 229.
[2] Don Casiano Pellicer, *Tratado histórico sobre el origen y progresos de la comedia y del histrionismo en España* (Madrid, 1804), p. 53.
[3] Duchartre, pp. 82–86.

This work, which must have been executed before 1574, when Charles IX died, was from the brush of Porbus—whether Paul or Frans cannot be ascertained—and apparently depicts a *commedia dell' arte* performance given by professionals with the assistance of courtly actors. To the extreme left are shown the Fantesca (possibly Francischina) and one of the Zanni (Brighella). Immediately behind this pair appears the head of a masked character who seems a kind of Arlecchino. The woman by his side cannot now be identified. In the left foreground are two men and a woman; he with the right arm thrown back is Charles IX, and the man with the right arm thrown across his breast is Henri, Duc de Guise; the woman is Marguerite de Valois. This Marguerite is kneeling before a Pantalone, who is attended by Arlecchino. Behind Pantalone stand Catherine de' Medici, the Duc d'Anjou, and the Duc d'Alençon, while to the extreme right appear Elizabeth of Spain and (standing behind her) the notorious Marie Touchet.

The significance of this picture will have to be referred to when we trace the fortunes of the Ganassa troupe; here all that concerns us is the portrait of Arlecchino. That character wears a costume of motley patches; on his face is a black half-mask, and on his head is a white skull-cap clearly simulating baldness, ornamented with a feather. Most of the other early designs correspond with this. The patches are clearly outlined in the Harlequins of the *Recueil Fossard*,[1] although in most of these, instead of being clean-shaven, as in the Porbus picture, the actors wear moustaches and pointed beards. In one (Fig. 180) Arlecchino is displayed in acrobatic posture on stilts. For comparison with these are the little engravings given in the *Compositions de rhetorique de M. Don Arleqvin* (Lyon, 1601) depicting the performer Martinelli. There he is shown by himself standing in two pictures (Fig. 185), kneeling in a third, and in a fourth standing with a basket on his shoulders while two little Harlequins sit or stand at his side. The same patchwork is to be found in the Mitelli print of the late seventeenth century,[2] proving that this early costume endured for at least a hundred years. By that time, however, a new Arlecchino costume had been evolved, in which the irregular patches had become formalized into a regular pattern sometimes lozenge-shaped, sometimes in the shape of triangles. Riccoboni sums up his appearance concisely enough :

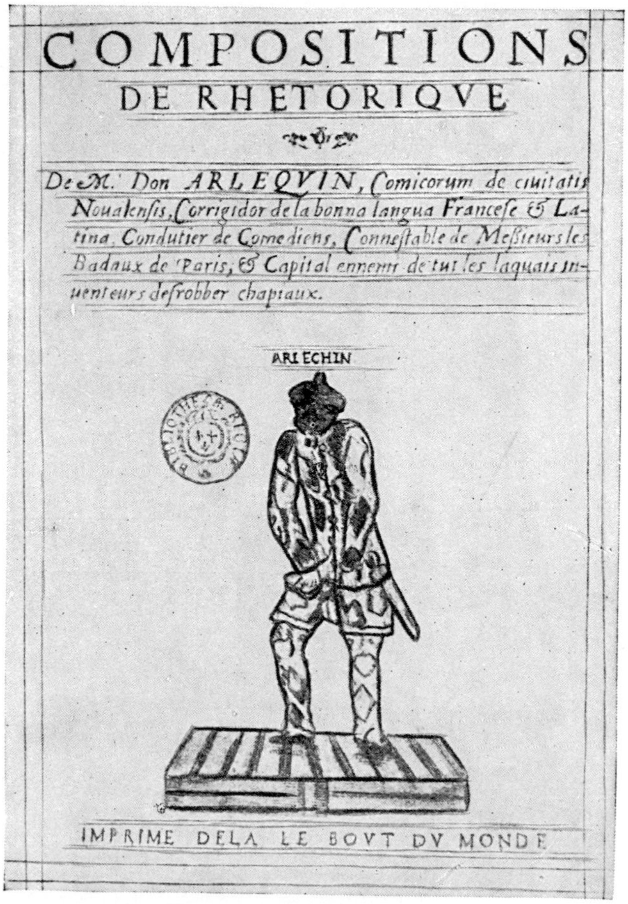

> Arlecchino's dress has never been of one style or of one nation. It consists of pieces of red, blue, and green cloth cut in triangles and arranged one above the other from top to bottom; a little hat which hardly

Fig. 185. ARLECCHINO, 1601
Title-page to the *Compositions de rhetorique* (Lyon, 1601) of Tristano Martinelli. From P. Duchartre, *The Italian Comedy* (1929), p. 127.

---

[1] See *supra*, p. 264, and *infra*, p. 272.

[2] Duchartre, p. 129.

Fig. 186. Harlequin and Horacio, or Orazio

Sixteenth-century print in the *Recueil Fossard*. From *Ord och Bild* (1929), p. 78 (also reproduced in Agne Beijer and P. Duchartre, *Recueil de plusieurs fragments des premières comédies italiennes* (Paris, 1928), p. xv).

Fig. 187. Harlequin, Zany Corneto, and Pantalon

Sixteenth-century print in the *Recueil Fossard*. From *Ord och Bild* (1929), p. 79 (also reproduced in Agne Beijer and P. Duchartre, *Recueil de plusieurs fragments des premières comédies italiennes* (Paris, 1928), p. xxii).

covers his shaven head; small heelless shoes; and a black mask with wrinkles which has no eyes but just two little holes for seeing through.[1]

A peculiar Arlecchino with spots is shown in the china figures preserved at the Musée Cluny in Paris (Fig. 188), and an equally peculiar costume, in which the pieces of coloured cloth are placed stripe-wise, is depicted in the painting by Nicholas Lancret (1690–1743) preserved in the Musée des Beaux-Arts at Strasbourg (Fig. 220).[2] More familiar are the Arlequin by an unknown French artist in the collection of Mme Pierre Decourcelle (Fig. 189) and that of an artist of the early nineteenth

Fig. 188. China Figures representing Commedia dell' Arte Characters
Seventeenth-century set in the Musée Cluny, Paris.
Photo Giraudon

century preserved at the Victoria and Albert Museum (Fig. 194). Similar to the last two is the puppet Arlecchino who is to be found among the marionette figures preserved in the Museo Civico in Venice. These puppets, indeed, tell us much concerning the *commedia dell' arte* at the end of the seventeenth century and the beginning of the eighteenth.[3] The whole of the figures in the Venice specimen are shown in Fig. 192, and among them we can easily recognize the Dottore (extreme left), with Pantalone in the centre; between them are the Lover and his *innamorata*. Arlecchino is

[1] " La forme de l'habit d'Arlequin n'a jamais été d'aucune mode, ni d'aucune nation: ce sont des morceaux de drap rouge, bleu & verd couppés en triangle, & arrangés l'un près de l'autre depuis le haut jusqu'en bas; un petit chapeau qui couvre à peine sa tête rasée; de petits Escarpins sans talons, & un Masque noir écrasé qui n'a point d'yeux, mais seulement deux trous fort petits pour voir."—L. Riccoboni, *Histoire du théâtre italien* (Paris, 1728), pp. 4–5.

[2] Another version of this picture appears in the Wallace Collection in London.

[3] On this subject see C. Ricci, *I Burattini di Bologna* (*La Lettura*, iii, 11); Pietro Toldo, *Nella baracca dei burattini* (*Giornale storico*, li (1908), 1–93); V. Malamani, *Il Teatro drammatico, le marionette e i burattini a Venezia nel sec. xviii* (*Nuova Antologia*, lxvii, 4, and lxviii, 5). A. Sorbelli has an interesting article on a nineteenth-century puppet showman, *Angelo Cuccoli e le sue commedie* (*L'Archiginnasio*, iv, 6).

S

springing in from the prompt-side wings. Another interesting puppet-show of Italian origin is now in the Victoria and Albert Museum (Fig. 193). This shows the figures of Brighella, Pantalone, the *innamorata*, the Lover, the Dottore, and a finely clad Arlecchino. The scene, as will be observed, represents the Piazza di San Marco at Venice. One could continue illustrating Arlecchino's appearance from similar sources almost without end; but this iconographic account may close with two other illustrations. The one (Fig. 190), particularly interesting for its treatment of mask, hat, and costume, comes from the late seventeenth century. The other, of eighteenth-century origin, shows how the Arlecchino dress could be on occasion supplemented by all kinds of garments (Fig. 195). In this example, Arlecchino appears with an eighteenth-century military coat, and with a classic helmet on his head. The familiar motley peers forth from below, and the eternal *batte* hangs at his side instead of a sword.

Fig. 190. ARLECCHINO
Frontispiece to C. Cotolendi, *Arliquiniana ou les bons mots, les histoires plaisantes et agréables, recueillies des conversations d'Arlequin* (Paris, 1694).

Fig. 189. ARLEQUIN
Painting by an unknown artist of the French School in the possession of Mme Pierre Decourcelle.

Fig. 191. A PUPPET
ARLECCHINO
Marionette in the Museo Civico, Venice.
Photo T. Filippi

It is peculiar that, with this array of pictorial evidence, the early records of Arlecchino's activities should be so scanty as they are. The first definite mention of his name occurs in a French document, an *Histoire plaisante des faicts et gestes de Harlequin commedien Italien contenant ses songes et visions, sa descente aux enfers pour en tirer la mère Cardine comment et avec quels hazards il en eschappa apres y auoir trompé le Roy d'Iceluy, Cerberus et tous les autres Diables* (Paris, 1585),[1] which was accompanied by a *Response di gestes de Arlequin au poëte fils de Madame Cardine, En langue Arlequine* (Paris, 1585).[2]

[1] This is printed in Driesen (pp. 248–255). The unique exemplar is in the Bibliothèque Nationale, Inv. Réserve Ye 4151.
[2] See Driesen, pp. 255–260. *Cf.* É. Picot, *Le Monologue dramatique* (*Romania*, xvi (1887), pp. 540–542).

These Driesen takes, with their infernal setting, as evidence of the devil origin of Arlecchino, and possibly they may be read in such a way. Perhaps, however, the apparently conscious choice

Fig. 192. Marionette Theatre with Figures of the Commedia dell' Arte
Eighteenth-century marionette theatre in the Museo Civico, Venice.
Photo T. Filippi

of locality and adventure is no more than a coincidence. From these verses of 1585 we have to go on to the year 1601 before we meet, in the *Compositions de rhetoriqve*,[1] another of his appearances

[1] See *supra*, p. 271.

in literature.   Strangely enough, too, he is by no means the most popular Zanni of the early scenarii. The Locatelli and Bartoli series know him not, and in the Corsiniana he appears but once.   The Scala collection, indeed, gives him a fair showing, but, taken all in all, the scenarii of the late sixteenth and early seventeenth centuries do not place him above—in fact, rather place him lower

Fig. 193. An Eighteenth-century Venetian Marionette Theatre, with Commedia dell' Arte Types

Photo Victoria and Albert Museum

than—other named comic servants.   The probability is, however, that beneath the general " Zanni " of many of the plays Arlecchino's personality is concealed.   It is always to be remembered that, while Ganassa was known only as the former, the Porbus painting of 1572 clearly delineates, among the masked actors, the patchwork-clad clown of Bergamo.

The true nature of this person is difficult to assess rightly.   Sometimes, as in *Il Marito* of the Scala collection, he appears as a stupid booby, but more commonly he mingles with his folly an element of wit, an element of liveliness, of good fun, of grotesquerie.   Most of the Harlequins, early and late, were acrobats, and they were the very spirit of the innumerable comic *lazzi*.   Dancing, tumbling, buffooning, Arlecchino carried all before him, and for many nations the *commedia dell' arte* barely existed save for him.   Even when attempts were made to father his attributes upon others,

276

he maintained his own individuality. In the Museo Civico at Venice is preserved a watercolour sketch of a person called Tracagnino (Fig. 196), who, had he not so been titled, would have been taken for an Arlecchino. This sketch must date from the early eighteenth century, for, although the *Album de Grevenbroch*, from which it is taken, is not dated, a passage in the text mentions a G. B. Garelli who was a magnificent Pantalone "in our times."[1] Garelli was already old at his spectacular retirement from the stage in 1735,[2] so that we may hazard the suggestion that these volumes of notes and sketches were prepared at some time about the twenties or thirties of the eighteenth century.[3] This Tracagnino thus depicted is described in the accompanying manuscript text as "excellently adapted" for the part of a go-between, since his mixture of cunning and stupidity makes his jests tolerated, his wit admired, and his criminal actions regarded as innocuous.[4] But concerning this Tracagnino we learn little more. He disappears, while Arlecchino lives on. At least two other cousins of Arlecchino are known to us. One is Truffaldino, sometimes called Truffaldino de' Bentruffati, which was certainly not invented by Sacchi, as Beaumont[5] states, although made famous by him. As Fig. 197 shows, Truffaldino was a genuine Arlecchino type; his name is clearly derived from *truffa*, 'deceit,' or 'trick,'

Fig. 194. ARLECCHINO

Watercolour sketch (early nineteenth century) in the Victoria and Albert Museum.

so he probably shared Arlecchino's nature as well as his garments. When exactly he was born cannot be determined, although it is interesting to notice that a "Messire Truffe," a servant, is to be found in the twelfth century,[6] a "Truffo" servant occurs in Ruzzante's *La Vaccaria*, and a "Trufactor" in the French farce of *Maître Pathelin*. Among the *commedia dell' arte* troupes he is first found played by Francesco Mozzana in the mid-seventeenth century, but the records given above seem to suggest that his ancestry, like that of Arlecchino, is a long one. Mozzana is remembered chiefly for his *Curioso capriccio di bellissimi giuochi non più veduti*, published at Milan about 1650. At the same time (1658–75) Carlo Palma was playing the part in Rome, Venice, and Mantua, while a few years later Marc' Antonio Zanetti was sustaining the *rôle* in the Modena troupe. A kindred spirit was Trivellino, whose name seems to mean 'little gimlet' rather than 'tatterdemalion,' as it is interpreted in Duchartre.[7] Concerning him we know less than about Truffaldino. As a servant or a host of an inn he appears in various scenarii, particularly of the Biancolelli set,[8] and then frequently as a

Fig. 195. ARLEQUIN

From the frontispiece to *La bonne Mère* in *Le Théâtre de M. de Florian* (Paris, 1786), vol. ii.

---

[1] *Album de Grevenbroch*, under No. 82; vol. iii (Cod. Correr, 1040).   [2] Rasi, ii, 988.

[3] For other pictures of Arlecchino mostly of late date see Cyril Beaumont, *The History of Harlequin* (1926).

[4] "La mascara di Tracagnino era la più addattata per questa facenda, come quella, che avvalorata da goffagine, ed astuzia, vengono tolerati gli scherzi, ammirata la sagacità, e convertiti gli casi criminali in civili."

[5] *Op. cit.*, p. 63.   [6] *Cf.* M. Magni, *loc. cit.*, p. 175.   [7] P. 157. *Cf.* M. Magni, *loc. cit.*, pp. 178–179.

[8] Also in *Le due Sorelle rivale* (Correr collection) and in *Il Dottor Bacchettone* (Bartoli collection).

companion or rival of Arlecchino.[1] The earliest-known Trivellino was Andrea Frajacomi in a company of Uniti (in 1614), the most famous, Domenico Locatelli, who seems to have varied the *rôle* with that of Arlecchino both in France and in Italy. The portrait preserved of him in this part [2] gives him Arlecchino's earliest patchwork costume and a mask not unlike that worn by the more famous character.[3] A third Trivellino is to be found in Carlo Sangiorgi, who was acting in the Modena troupe between 1681 and 1686.

There yet remain to be noted those performers who acted the Arlecchino type proper during the sixteenth and seventeenth centuries. Very probably Alberto Ganassa took this *rôle*, although only Zanni is recorded, and it seems likely that Simone da Bologna was the Arlecchino of the Gelosi, although he too is mentioned solely as Zanni.[4] When, however, we hear that he was " most excellent in interpreting the character of a Bergamask peasant," [5] we are fully justified in seeing him as Arlecchino. The first genuine named Arlecchino was Tristano Martinelli, one of the strangest characters whom the *commedia dell' arte* companies produced. Born about 1557, Martinelli is found acting with Pedrolino's and Diana's troupes at Cremona in 1595, and thereafter we can follow his career with some exactitude. By 1599 he was in the Accesi, and the following year he set off for France. There, at Lyon, appeared the strange *Compositions de Rhetoriqve* (1601), written apparently in order to beg a gift of the King, Henri IV. Heaping honour on honour, the rest of his life was spent in acting, both in Italy and in France, until he died, at the age of about seventy-five, in 1630. This man, who signed himself " Dominus Arlechinorum," as though there were many Harlequins in his time, has left an impression both of his personality and of his social and artistic position in the form of letters

Fig. 196. TRACAGNINO
Watercolour sketch in the *Album de Grevenbroch*, Museo
Civico, Venice, iii, No. 83.

sent by him to those reigning monarchs who, delighted by his skill in performance, begged for his services. Most of these have been unearthed from the Mantuan archives by Armand Baschet and " Jarro," and pretty reading do they make. The Queen Mother, Marie de' Medici, in 1611 sends him a friendly note :

HARLEQUIN,
    It was with great pleasure that I received the news you send me, that your wife, besides the son which God has given you, is now about to present you with another. Concerning this, I am writing to say that I have very gladly accepted your proposal that I should act as godmother for the child which she is to bear. . . .

So it runs on, and then, that the bait might not be lost :

If I am not sending you just now the present which it is my pleasant duty to give the child when it

---

[1] *Cf.* A. Bartoli, p. lvi. *Cf.* A. Momigliano, *Truffaldino e Smeraldina nel " Servitore di due padroni "* (*L' Italia moderna*, IV, ii, 18).
[2] See Rasi, ii, 577.
[3] The Biancolelli MS. (ii, 52) records him only in *Le Rosle d'arlequin*.
[4] See Driesen, pp. 274–275.
[5] Tomaso Porcacchi, *Le Attioni d' Arrigo terzo* (Vinetia, 1574).

278

is baptised, I am delaying only in order to give it into your own hands ; and therefore I beg you and pray you to gather a good company of Italian players as quickly as you can, and I shall issue an order in the meantime to have money given you for your journey. . . .

MARIE [1]

The correspondence goes on for long, dragging into its folds as well the stately figure of the Cardinal Gonzaga. To him Arlecchino writes in a free and easy style, remarking off-handedly that he has received letters " from his Gaulish Gossip the Queen of the Gauls over the mountains " [2] and signing himself " Your Very Christian Gossip." Among the letters sent by him to Marie de' Medici not the least interesting is that addressed " To his Most Christian Gossip," which is reproduced by Luigi Rasi in facsimile.[3] " Sacred Majesty and Most Dear Gossip," it starts, and continues in the same strain, telling how a company has been gathered together which includes " a good Zanni and my Harlequinesque person." [4] All this correspondence, which would occupy too much space to reproduce here, throws a brilliant light on the position occupied by the comedians in the seventeenth century. The freedoms which Martinelli took with the King, Queen, and Cardinal seem unbelievable now ; but there they are preserved amid serious political records, proving what a position a good Arlecchino held in the later Renascence.

It is pleasing to imagine that Martinelli, whose brother Drusiano had certainly been in England in 1578,[5] was the " Harlaken " whom our own clown, William Kemp, met in Rome. Late in 1600 the latter seems to have left England for a tour abroad. On September 2, 1601, is found an entry in a diary kept by a certain William Smith, of Abingdon, saying that

Fig. 197. Trufaldino de' Bentruffati

Seventeenth-century Italian print. Exemplar in the Bibliothèque Nationale, Paris (Cabinet des Estampes, Tb + 1, vol. ii, B. 493).

Photo Giraudon

Kemp, a mime, who went on a tour in Germany and Italy, has . . . returned ; he has much to say of Anthony Sherley, . . . whom he met . . . at Rome.[6]

Now, in John Day's chronicle play, *The Travailes of the Three English Brothers*, published in 1607,

---

[1] The French text is given in Baschet (pp. 202–203).

[2] Baschet, p. 220. " Della Comadre Galina Regina di Galli oltramontani," with a pun on *Galina-Galli*, which may mean " Gauls " or " hens."

[3] Rasi, iii, opposite 100.   [4] " Un bon Zane, et la mia Arlechinesca p[er]sona."

[5] See *infra*, p. 308.

[6] " Kemp, mimus quidam, qui peregrinationem quandam in Germaniam et Italiam instituerat . . . reversus ; multa refert de Anthonio Sherley . . . quem Romæ . . . convenerat."—E. K. Chambers, *Elizabethan Stage*, ii, 326. The passage had been noted by Halliwell and by Furnivall.

Sir Anthony Sherley is shown talking to Zariph the Jew, when a servant announces that an Englishman, one Kemp, desires to speak with him. Kemp enters, and immediately after comes in "an *Italian Harlaken*"; at this Sherley asks Kemp "to play a part" with him, whereupon the following scene ensues:

KEMP. I am somewhat hard of study, and like your honor; but if they will inuent any extemporall merriment ile put out the small sacke of witte I ha' left, in venture with them.

SIR ANT. They shall not deny't: Signior *Harlaken* he is content: I pray thee question him.   [*Whisper.*

KEMP. Now, Signior, how many are you in companie?

HARL. None but my wife and my selfe, sir.

KEMP. Your wife! Why, hearke you, wil your wife do tricks in publique?

HARL. My wife can play.

KEMP. The honest woman, I make no question. . . . But the proiect; come, and then to casting of the parts.

HARL. Marry, sir, first we will haue an old Pantaloune.

KEMP. Some iealous Coxcombe.

HARL. Right, and that part will I play.

KEMP. The iealous Cox-combe?

HARL. I ha plaid that part euer since——

KEMP. Your wife plaid the Curtizan.

HARL. True, and a great while afore; then I must have a peasant to my man, and he must keepe my wife.

KEMP. Your man, and a peasant, keepe your wife? I haue knowne a Gentleman keepe a peasant's wife, but 'tis not vsuall for a peasant to keepe his maister's wife.

HARL. Oh, 'tis common in our countrey.

KEMP. And ile maintaine the custome of the country.   [*Offer to kisse his wife.*

HARL. What do you meane, sir?

KEMP. Why, to rehearse my part on your wiues lips: we are fellowes, and amongst friends and fellowes, you knowe, all things are common.

HARL. But shee shall bee no common thing, if I can keepe her seuerall.—Then, sir, we must haue an *Amorado* that must make me Cornuto.

KEMP. Oh for loue sake let me play that part.

HARL. No, yee must play my mans part, and keepe my wife.

KEMP. Right; and who so fit to make a man a Cuckold as hee that keepes his wife.

HARL. You shall not play that part.

KEMP. What say you to my boy?

HARL. I, he may play it and you will.

KEMP. But he cannot make you iealous enough.

HARL. Tush, I warrant you, I can be iealous for nothing.

KEMP. You should not be a true Italian else.

HARL. Then we must have a Magnifico that must take vp the matter betwixt me and my wife.

KEMP. Any thing of yours, but Ile take vp nothing of your wives.

HARL. I wish not you should: but come, now am I your Maister.

KEMP. Right, and I your seruant.

HARL. Lead the way then.[1]

There is a genuine confusion here between the parts of Arlecchino and Pantalone; but the impression is given of a real scene—such a scene as Kemp might have reported on his return to England. No authority exists for identifying the "Harlaken" here with Martinelli, although it is interesting to note that Martinelli may have been "that famous Francatrip Harlicken" who, some time before 1590, was inquiring about Kemp at Venice.[2] It is interesting here to notice that

---

[1] *The Plays of John Day*, Part V, ed. A. H. Bullen, pp. 56–59. *Cf.* L. B. Wright, *Will Kemp and the Commedia dell' Arte* (*Modern Language Notes*, December 1926).

[2] *The Works of Thomas Nashe*, ed. R. B. McKerrow, iv, 462; *cf.* Chambers, *Elizabethan Stage*, ii, 263. The use of the word 'Francatrip' may not be exact; that part and Harlequin's were, of course, distinct.

the English comedians, apart from their international tours, were well known to Italians. Barbieri had thus occasion to observe that " England has most excellent companies of actors, and the King takes great pleasure in their shows, and the members of his troupe are both distinguished and rich." [1] The Italians and the English must have looked on each other as fellow-princes in the realm of their art.

After Martinelli we need dwell on but few of the famous actors of this *rôle* during the seventeenth century. Of these Giuseppe Domenico Biancolelli, called Dominique, is of special interest to us because of that manuscript collection of scenarii and notes which preserve some dim relics of his art. Born between 1637 and 1646, Biancolelli seems to have gained his early training in Vienna; but by 1661 he had come to Paris and there settled down for the rest of his life. On his death, in 1688, artistic France went into mourning, and the Comédie Italienne shut its doors for a whole month. Even the *Mercure de France* [2] broke into rime:

> Les plaisirs le suivoient sans cesse,
> Il répandoit partout la joie et l'allégresse.
> Les jeux avec les ris naissoient dessous ses pas:
> On ne pouvoit parer les traits de sa satire;
>   Loin d'offenser elle avoit des appas.
> Cependant il est mort, tout le monde en soupire.
> Qui l'eût jamais pensé sans se désespérer
> Que l'aimable Arlequin qui nous a fait tant rire
>   Dût sitôt nous faire pleurer?

After Biancolelli came Evaristo Gherardi, an actor who, born at Prato in 1663, appeared first in Regnard's *Le Divorce forcé* one year after the former's death. He himself acted the Arlecchino *rôle* until the closure of the Comédie Italienne in 1697. He too was mourned at his death, and many verses in his honour were collected together in *La Pompa funebre di Arlecchino* (Paris, 1701). Apart from his acting, in which he seems to have excelled, Gherardi has remained famous for his *Le Théâtre italien, ou le recueil de toutes les scènes françaises qui ont été jouées sur le théâtre italien de l'Hôtel de Bourgogne* (Paris, 1700).[3] Perhaps his companions were not over-well pleased with his action, and perhaps, too, his association with them was not always of the best. Campardon presents the documents relating to an affair wherein " Octave " (Giovanni Battista Costantini) gave Gherardi a blow on the nose—the results were described as *une contusion sur le haut du nez* [4]—after a wild battle of words at which most of the company were present. But, testy though he may have been by nature, and just a trifle careless of authority, he passed through Parisian life of the late seventeenth century in a blaze of glory. What though a dull *commissaire*, one Lefrançois, complained to the Lieutenant of Police that in *Le Retour de la foire de Bezons* Gherardi, in collaboration seemingly with Brugière de Barante,[5] had ridiculed officialdom " in the most shameless manner " by making

Mezzetin come on the stage panting and crying, " I want an honest man or a rascal." Arlequin replies, " I'm a rascal," and comes in a *commissaire's* robe to receive the complaint of the bailiff and inhabitants of Bezon. Entering, he says, " Has the complaint of that woman who beat her husband been drawn up? One must arrange that the blows remain in the husband's hands and that he pays damages with interest for them." After receiving the complaint of the bailiff and the inhabitants he gets it signed, and it is found that in reality it is a marriage contract between the bailiff's daughter and Octave.[6]

---

[1] " L' Inghilterra ha superbissime Compagnie, e quel Re se ne compiace molto, e i suoi Comici sono virtuosi, e ricchi."—*La Supplica*, p. 106.

[2] August 1688.

[3] This was several times reprinted. The fifth edition appeared at Amsterdam in 1721. An earlier edition had appeared in 1694.

[4] Campardon, i, 242-244.   [5] See Campardon, i, 247-248.

[6] " Mezzetin vient tout hors d'haleine et dit: ' Je cherche un honnête homme ou un fripon.' Arlequin fait réponse; ' Je suis le fripon,' et vient en robe, faisant le commissaire, pour recevoir la plainte du bailli de Bessons et des habitans et, en entrant, dit: ' A-t-on dressé la plainte de cette femme qui a battu son mari? Il faut faire les choses d'une manière que les coups restent au mari et qu'il en paye les dommages et intérêts.' Reçoit la plainte du bailli et des habitans, la fait signer et il se trouve que c'est un contrat de mariage de la fille du bailli avec Octave."

As the poor *commissaire* says, "If you allow the *commissaires* to be thus ridiculed [*ainsi turlupinés*] by the French and Italian players, what will happen to their offices, so important both for the service of the King and for that of the public?"

So does Arlecchino jest, and so do dull-witted folks take offence.

Fig. 198. MEZETIN

Seventeenth-century French print by I. Bonnart. Exemplar in the Bibliothèque Nationale, Paris (Cabinet des Estampes, Tb 34b).

Photo Giraudon

(vii) THE STOCK TYPES: (5) BRIGHELLA, SCAPINO, MEZZETINO, AND SCARAMUCCIA

BRIGHELLA

Arlecchino is sometimes second Zanni in his foolishness, sometimes first Zanni in his wit. His companions, for the one *rôle* or the other, vary in name, but two out of the extraordinary array of comic servants have won special popularity—Brighella and Pulcinella. The former, however, has a peculiar history.[1] Among the characters of the *commedia dell' arte* he is well known, and

---

[1] The origin of the name is unknown, although Parmenio Bettòli suggests it came from the actor Burchiella (*I "Gelosi" e la commedia dell' arte*, in *Emporium*, xiv (1901), 212).

yet we find it exceedingly hard to track him down before the eighteenth century. In the extant scenarii his part is excessively rare, and the only actor of the period who can definitely be said to have taken it is a shadowy Domenico Bononcini, most of whose activities seem to have been connected with performances in Austria. As Briguelle, however, Brighella was famous in France during the latter part of the seventeenth century, and his portrait is presented to us in a print which depicts him standing beside a " Trivelin " Arlecchino (Fig. 199). The verse below his name indicates

his love of witty laughter, his prevailing satirical tendency, and his cynical contempt for both " wise men and fools " (*les scavans et les sots*). The costume shown in this print is composed of trousers and jacket rather fully cut, ornamented by strips of green braid. That this was his dress in the sixteenth century is asserted by M. Sand,[1] but there seems no authority for this statement or for the picture of the sixteenth-century Brighella in his book. All that can be said is that the Zanni of the Porbus painting (Fig. 184) has a stock dress not unsimilar to that of a century later, and that the somewhat hard-featured mask of the one resembles the mask of the other. This mask, with its close beard and moustache, its hooked nose and licentious eyes, gives an impression far different from that of Trivelin or Arlecchino, for no doubt this seventeenth-century Brighella was in spirit akin to his eighteenth-century follower— cruel, libidinous, cynically witty, and self-seeking. In describing his characteristics, however, so far as the period before 1700 is concerned, we are treading on dangerous ground, and it must always be remembered that there is barely a shadow of evidence to prove his existence as Brighella in the sixteenth century and that all the early scenarii are chary of allowing him to enter in.

Fig. 199. BRIGUELLE (BRIGHELLA) AND TRIVELIN
Engraving published in Paris by Mariette (*c.* 1647).

As Rasi[2] has shown, on the other hand, a print by Stefano della Bella delineating the actor Carlo Cantù as Buffett or Buffetto (Fig. 200) makes us believe that the *rôle* of Brighella may perhaps have been played under different names ; this Buffett is almost identical with the other Briguelle—the same dress, the same braid, and the same mask. Moreover, there is some reason for believing that Cantù was playing as Brighella in the year 1651. Born in 1609, this actor came on the stage in 1632, and thereafter, until the middle of the century, he pursued a prosperous career. Associated with the Locatelli he went to France in 1645, where he seems to have gained for himself special favour. Among the archives of Modena and elsewhere a number of his letters have

---

[1] Sand, ii, 166. On Brighella see M. Magni, *loc. cit.*, 133–135, 178; and Cesare Levi, *Il signor Brighella* (*The Mask*, v (July 1912), 20–27, translated from *Natura ed arte*).
[2] Rasi, ii, 574–578.

simply hens introduced for comparative purposes. " This noble bird," says the poet allegorically, " was driven out of every place, just as the kite will drive off chickens " (*Quest' alta uccella . . . per tucto era scacciata co' nibio perseguendo i pulcinelli*).

These *pulcinelli*, on the other hand, may indeed truly be the ancestors of Pulcinella ; the majority of commentators, indeed, favour the assumption that the word *pulcino*, ' chicken,' taking an original form of *pullicino*, was adopted at some time unknown by the comic stage figure.

But here we must pause. Accepting *pullicino* as the origin of the name, we find that two or three problems present themselves. Why, in the first place, is the form of the word apparently feminine (Pulcinella, and not Pulcinello) ?[1] And, secondly, has this Pulcinella any connexion with the ' cock type ' which we have met with in classic mime ? The answer to the second of these questions is usually that given by Croce,[2] who denies all relationship between the one and the other, but this

Fig. 209. RAZULLO AND CUCURUCU
Etching in J. Callot's *I Balli di Sfessania*.

requires not to be dismissed so rapidly. The name of Pulcinella dalle Carceri is not by any means unique, and Fainelli need not have gone to Verona for his example. An Oddo, or Odone, di Policeno, nephew to Pope Martin IV, appears at Naples in 1290 ; a Ioan Polcinella in 1484 ; and a Lucio Pulcinella in 1572.[3] The name is one, therefore, which is borne by a number of real persons, not connected with the stage, from the thirteenth century to the sixteenth. But this name is a peculiar one, and, moreover, takes the feminine form in three of the examples. One might therefore expect it to be in the nature of a nickname. On the one hand, we might suppose that a real Pulcinella gave his own surname to the type ; but, on the other—and this seems more probable—we might assume that a stock type, Pulcinella, gave rise to a family called after him. Most of the argument

can be read in Dieterich's masterly account,[4] where attention is drawn to the likely association of Pulcinella's name with *pulcino* or with the late Latin *pullicenus*, to the cock-like mask of the stage character, and to the use made of cock's feathers in the Callot sketch. Peculiarly enough, however, Dieterich has failed to make one important point. It is he who discovered the Atellan mime figure called Cicirrus,[5] one who, in spite of Croce's scepticism,[6] seems to have been a genuine companion of Maccus and Bucco. Now, as we have seen, Cicirrus is an onomatopœic name for a cock, and therefore we are justified in seeing in the stage character a ' cock type.' What Dieterich has not noticed is that, besides the design showing Pulcinella, Callot has another depicting a person whom he calls Cucurucu (Fig. 209). This Cucurucu has a large stomach, a hump-back, a long-nosed mask, and a hat with two long cock's feathers. He is, in other words, a true Pulcinella in all but name ; whence comes that name if not from Cicirrus, and what does it mean if not ' cock ' ?

In many ways can Pulcinella be connected with the ancient mimes. Those statuettes reproduced in Figs. 68 and 69 might have stood for the Neapolitan character. It is true that Mic, noting the

---

[1] Besides the other articles cited here note should be made of the important essay by B. Croce, *Pulcinella e le relazioni della commedia dell' arte con la commedia popolare romana* (originally printed in the *Archivio storico per le provincie napoletane*, xxiii (1898), 3, and reprinted in *Saggi sulla letteratura italiana del seicento*, Bari, 1911, pp. 195 f.). Croce denies continuity in the stage type. See also H. Lyonnet, *Pulcinella et le théâtre napolitain* (Paris, 1901); Ireneo Sanesi, i, 441–442 ; M. Apollonio, pp. 197–202.

[2] *Saggi*, pp. 219–220.   [3] *Cf.* Dieterich, pp. 251–252.

[4] *Cf.* also G. Racioppi, *Per la Storia di Pulcinella* (*Archivio storico per le provincie napoletane*, xv (1890), 18 ff.), where it is argued that, though the name may be modern, the mask is ancient.

[5] See *supra*, pp. 74–75.   [6] *Saggi*, p. 219.

resemblance, perversely takes it to prove non-identity, for, says he, " the primitive type would have assuredly changed in the course of the centuries if it really had endured, . . . because life means change." [1] Perhaps ; but it is dangerous to apply evolutionary laws to stage types. Punch of the puppets in a London street is fundamentally the same in appearance as the Pulcinella who dances upon the stage of the Comédie Italienne in 1688, and we know that a direct line of tradition connects the one with the other. So with the peaked cap. It too, visible on the puppet figure, is to be found in the seventeenth century, and already we have seen reason to believe that the peak-capped mime was carried through the course of the Middle Ages from a remote antiquity.[2]

Having thus summoned together a certain portion of the evidence concerning Pulcinella's name and origin, we may now turn to inquire whether Silvio Fiorillo were really the theatrical founder of this type in what we know as the *commedia dell' arte*. A rival appears in the person of Andrea Calcese, or Ciuccio.[3] Not much is known of this person, who is said to have been a lawyer who turned to the stage, and died, nearly a century old, in 1656. Unfortunately, we have no means either of proving or disproving Pacichelli's statement. We note, however, a Zan Polo of Venice who was recorded by Sanudo in 1515 and 1522 ; could Zan or Zanni Polo have anything to do with Policinella or Pulcinella ? Apart from this, Croce [4] observes that already in Fiorillo's time a Neapolitan, Francesco, was playing Pulcinella's part. This may have been Francesco Baldi called Ciccio, who is said to have been the pupil of Calcese and to have passed on his tradition to Mattia Barra and Michelangelo Fracanzani. It is at least possible, and seems to me highly probable, that the tradition thus indicated is of far greater antiquity than is suggested by the use of Calcese's name.

The puzzle concerning the early exponents of Pulcinella's *rôle* is that all are associated also with differently named characters. Ciuccio and Ciccio we have met with, and Silvio Fiorillo, who is also credited with Pulcinella's genesis, was famous as Capitan Matamoros. All the records of his life, from 1584, when he is found at Naples, to the third decade of the seventeenth century, refer to him as Capitano, and yet both Cecchini and Perrucci assert positively that he was the ' inventor ' of Pulcinella. When it was that he changed his *rôle*, or whether he alternated the two while playing with the various companies—the Affezionati, the Risoluti, and the Accesi—cannot now be ascertained. All that can be said is that, according to the testimony of his companions in 1612, he had then passed his best in the part of the Capitano. " There is no need to engage Matamoros," they write to the Duke of Mantua ; " he is no longer what he was." [5] It is just possible that his adoption of the *rôle* of Pulcinella may have been due to his failing powers in his original part.

The other exponents of Pulcinella's part do not seem to have won especial glory. An Antonio Tonti who took this *rôle* died at Rome in 1694, but otherwise nothing is known of him. Little, too, is known of Michelangelo Fracanzani, brother of the painter Cesare, who played in France from 1685 to 1697. That he was in the direct line of tradition seems certain,[6] and his portrait it is which appears in the Comédie Italienne scene reproduced in Fig. 203: It is important to remember that this illustration shows a Pulcinella who is, in all essentials, identical with the puppet Punch of to-day. There can therefore be no doubt about the ancestry of that still living representative of the *commedia dell' arte*.

---

[1] Mic, p. 211.

[2] See *infra*, p. 365. It is interesting to note that, according to V. Caravelli (*Chiacchiere critiche*, Florence, 1889, pp. 78–79), these hats are sometimes called *muriuni*. Now, *muriuni* may come from the military *morione*, or ' helmet,' as Croce believes (*Saggi*, p. 220), but it may also be derived from *moriones*, the name of the fool being given to that which the fool wears.

[3] Averred by Giovan Battista Pacichelli (*Schediasma iuridico-philologicum de larvis capillamentis chirothecis, vulgo mascheris perruchis guantis*, Naples, 1693, p. 70) to have been the creator of the character.

[4] *Saggi*, p. 244.   [5] See Baschet, p. 225.   [6] See *supra*.

PEDROLINO

Closely connected with Pulcinella, yet developing an independent tradition of his own, Pedrolino is another character difficult to analyse.[1] Perhaps even he is not one character, but several; so that we must think, not of a single type, but of a Pedrolino, a Pagliaccio, a Pierrot, constantly changing in kaleidoscopic variations, with the merry figure of Pulcinella sometimes standing aside and applauding, sometimes entering into the merry game. The credit of creating the French Pierot is regularly given to Giuseppe Giaratone, or Geratoni. According to a manuscript note in the Biancolelli scenarii, this actor took the part of a valet, and, after playing various small *rôles*,

Fig. 210. PIEROT

Painting by an unknown artist of the French School in the possession of Mme Pierre Decourcelle.

was eventually received into the company under the name and in the costume of Pierot. The nature of the *rôle* is that of a Neapolitan Pulcinella a little altered. In point of fact, the Neapolitan scenarii, in place of Arlecchino and Scapino, admit two Pulcinellas, the one an intriguing rogue and the other a stupid fool. The latter is Pierot's *rôle*.[2]

It is impossible to trace back this Pierot into Italy itself, although a character Piero appears in one or two literary comedies. Duchartre asserts that " Pedrolino and Pierro often appear as valets in the scenarii of several authors between 1547 and 1604," [3] but this, quite apart from the fact that there is no scenario so old as 1547, seems to be a statement without any foundation in fact. It seems true, however, that Pedrolino is, if not the same, at least closely connected with the Pierot type, and probably from it the French Pierot developed. This Pedrolino does figure in the scenarii of the Scala collection (1611), appearing sometimes as a servant of Pantalone (*Il Marito*, *Il Ritratto*) and as a lover of Franceschina (*Li Tappeti Alessandrini*), sometimes as a husband foolish and kindly (*L'Alvida*), sometimes as a servant of a serious character (*La Forsennata prencipessa*). That he was at this period a person of considerable importance is proved by the records which outline the career of Giovanni Pellesini. Pellesini seems to have been born about the year 1526. As an actor he first appears in 1576, playing in Florence and apparently directing his own company. From

[1] See M. Magni, *loc. cit.*, 131–134.

[2] " Il fut enfin recu comedien sous le nom et dans L habit de Pierot. Le Caractere dele rosle, est celuy du polichinelle Napolitain vn peu deguisé Effectiuement dans les comedies Napolitaines, au lieu D'arlequin et de Scapin, on admet deux polichinelles Luy fourbe jntrigant, et L autre Stupide et jmbecille, le dernier est Le rosle de Pierot."—*Op. cit.*, i, 113.

[3] Duchartre, p. 252.

that time on he is frequently heard of. In 1580 his troupe was fused with that of the Confidenti, and a few years later (1583) the Gelosi-Uniti claimed his services. As late as 1612, when he must have been eighty-six years of age, he was performing with the G. B. Andreini troupe (the Fedeli) in Tuscany. No doubt can exist that he was a noted and important actor of his time, and probably he was responsible for the carrying on of much of both the Pierot and Pulcinella tradition. Unfortunately, his costume cannot be even guessed at. When we reach the time of Giaratone we find the typical loose white garments and the wide, frilly ruff, the pale white face, and the ' bald-head ' wig which were familiar features of the eighteenth-century Pierot—but whether these derived from Pellesini we cannot say. In France he was sentimentalized, without doubt (Fig. 210), but possibly in this dress we should look for the main features of the typical early Zanni's costume.

Pedrolino, however, does not stand absolutely alone. There is also that Pagliaccio who has come down to us in living form through Leoncavallo's opera. Unfortunately, he too has not been recorded in early illustration. The picture of " Pagliaccio (1600) " in Sand, reproduced by Duchartre,[1] does not seem to have any original, nor does there seem to be any authority for Sand's statement that a Pagliaccio appeared in the Ganassa company of 1570. One thing about him, however, is interesting. Already we have seen how, in an ancient mime, one character beats another with " a bundle of straw." [2] Pagliaccio really means ' chopped straw,' and perhaps here we may be once more in the presence of an ancient tradition which has carried the tricks of the Atellan players down to the seventeenth century.

OTHER ZANNI

It is not necessary here to say much more concerning the many Zanni who made merry many a comic intrigue or serious plot, but there are a few who seemed to win more popularity than the others and of whom something can be averred that is definite. Among these is Giangurgolo, " a Calabrian actor," according to the Biancolelli manuscript, " whose *rôle* it is to mimic the Capitano." [3]

Fig. 211. TARTAGLIA

Watercolour sketch (early nineteenth century) in the Victoria and Albert Museum.

Counterfeiting or mimicking the Capitano, however, does not mean that he was one, as some writers have asserted. His part, indeed, was various in kind. Sometimes, as Perrucci points out, he is to be classed among the old men, and several times does he appear as the father in the Neapolitan scenarii. More commonly, on the other hand, he is a servant, a gaoler, or a host of an inn.[4] Often is he, as in the Correr *L'Amante interesato*, the lover of Argentina or of another Fantesca. His chief forte— so his name implies—was gluttony, and we can imagine him speeding on those traditions in farcical guzzling scenes which are of such hoary antiquity. According to the illustration of his person given by Riccoboni,[5] he was dressed like a comic captain with a strange half-mask characterized by an enormous and ill-shapen nose.

Another character popular in Naples was Tartaglia, ' The Stammerer,' who is certainly among the earliest of the *commedia dell' arte* types. Usually he too is a servant, sometimes a host of an inn,[6]

---

[1] Duchartre, p. 258. This statement of Sand is repeated in M. Magni, *loc. cit.*, 177. [2] See *supra*, p. 77.
[3] " Giangurgolo est vn acteur calabrois dont Le rosle est de contre faire Le capitan."—*Op. cit.*, i, 366. *Cf.*, however, p. 252.
[4] See Rasi, i, 79–81; B. Croce, *Saggi*, pp. 245–246, 311–312; Croce, p. 33. [5] *Cf.* Rasi, i, 79; Duchartre, p. 235.
[6] As in the Correr *Mastro di Terentio.*

For some years after this we lose sight of him, but he reappears once more in Rome in 1564, when, on October 10, he entered into an agreement (evidently forming a fresh company) with Gian Carlo Guarnera, Alfonso Castaldo, Michelangelo Coletti, Domenico de' Rossi of Forlì, Claudio Orsino, and Lucrezia Senese—"all vulgarly called Comedians." [1] Here he is named Marco Antonio de Gabiati. With his companions he agrees to adhere to the troupe, to bring in any good actor who he thinks may benefit the company, to share in the takings, and to forfeit that share should he miss a performance. And, last of all, unless the identification suggested below be accepted, we meet him at Genoa on February 1, 1567,[2] entering into another contract with Guglielmo Perillo, of Naples, and Angelo Michele, of Bologna. In this he is named " Marcus Antonius venetus," and the designation recalls the " Venetians " of whom he possibly formed a part seventeen years before.

Soldino and Anton Maria

Of another troupe operating in the sixties of the Cinquecento notice is given in an unhappily not verified document which concerns Soldino, Tarasso Vicentio, Scevola Senese, and *Pantalone* in Rome during the course of the year 1565.[3] Whether this document is or is not a fabrication, we know something about the activities of the first member of the group. It may have been his company which was in Lyon on December 29, 1571 ; [4] at any rate, payment was made by the royal treasurer on March 2, 1572, to " Soldini and other Italian players," [5] on account of their expenses in journeying from Paris to Blois in order to provide his Majesty Charles IX with some amusement. From a later warrant (dated March 25, 1572), we learn that " Soldino of Florence " had with him eleven actors and acrobats ; this payment was made " in consideration of plays and acrobatic shows which they performed daily before his Majesty." [6] Complications arise, however, when, in a further order, a sum of money is made payable (on March 27, 1572) " to Anthoine Marie, Italian comedian," for himself and nine companions [7] and when, in a warrant of April 11, 1572, another payment is granted " to Soldini of Florence and Anthoine Marie of Venice, comedians of Italy." The implication seems to be that these two men were working together. It is certainly true that in the one record Soldino had eleven actors, and in the other Anthoine Marie had nine, but this could readily be explained by the particular circumstances of performance on two separate occasions.[8] If it be that these men were acting in one company at Paris in 1572 there is some reason for believing that one of their companions was Giulio Pasquati, the *Pantalone* of 1565. Immediately

---

[1] " Omnes ut vulgo dicitur Commedianti." (See E. Re, *loc. cit.*, pp. 297–299.)

[2] E. Re, *loc. cit.*, p. 297, where the date is mistakenly given as 1667; D'Ancona, ii, 477–478.

[3] This seems to have been first cited by Bertolotti in his *Artisti veneti in Roma nei secoli xv, xvi, e xvii* (Venice, 1884, p. 54), and has been copied since in many later works, including D'Ancona (ii, 457). E. Re (*loc. cit.*, pp. 296–297) indicates that a careful search of the Roman archives has failed to reveal this document. Soldino may have had something to do with the *comedie de Zani* at Bologna in 1568 mentioned by Angelo Solerti in *Due documenti dei primordj della commedia dell' arte* (*Rassegna bibliografica della letteratura italiana*, ii (1894), 194–195). *Cf.* A. Ademollo, p. 36.

[4] Baschet (p. 25) suggests that this may have been the Ganassa company. See *infra*, p. 301.

[5] Baschet, pp. 34–35.

[6] *Id.*, pp. 35–36. " En considération des commedies et saults qu'ils font journellement devant Sa Majesté."

[7] *Id.*, pp. 36–37.

[8] One possibility, not hitherto suggested, enters in here. Baschet has noted that a document belonging to the reign of Henry VIII, and hence earlier than 1547 (printed by J. P. Collier in his *History of English Dramatic Poetry* (1831), i, 83), records the presence in England among the " King's minstrels " of a Nicholas Andria and an Anthony Maria, and he wondered whether these might not be André and Anthoine Marie. This document, however, mentions as well a Marcus Antonius. Since there seems reason to believe that André and Marcantonio were associated with the company playing at Rome in 1551, it may well be that these two men were none other than the Nicholas Andria and Marcus Antonius referred to in the English list. If this be so, then we may with some assurance identify Anthoine Maria with the Anthoine Marie (Anton Maria) who was in France in 1572. The conjunction of the three names would otherwise certainly be a most strange coincidence. The chief interest of this supposition lies in the fact that thus we have here the earliest record of the presence of Italian actors in England. With the three mentioned above may have been a regular company, for, besides a number of apparently English ' minstrels,' appear the names of Ihon de Bassani, Antony de Bassani, Jasper de Bassani, John Baptiste de Bassani, Nicholas de Forrewell (possibly a corruption of an Italian name), Pellegrine Symon, and Antony Symon. Ten players seems to have been about the normal strength of an early *commedia dell' arte* company.

before and after journeying to Paris Soldino, whom we now meet as Antonio Soldino, seems to have spent some time in northern parts. In 1570, 1571, and 1574 he is to be found, at times with Julio (probably Pasquati), in Munich and Linz.[1] Through his efforts, without a doubt, the spirit of the *commedia dell' arte* was spread widely in strange lands and the way prepared for the visits of still more famous companies.

THE TROUPE OF ALBERTO GANASSA

Many Italian actors, of course, tried their fortunes abroad. Giovanni *Taberino* was at Linz on December 12, 1568;[2] there he stayed during the following year, moving on to Vienna in 1570. It may be that he was connected with the Soldino company; for he too is found in France in 1571.[3] None, however, won quite the same fame as was earned by Alberto Ganassa and his companions. The early history of Ganassa's troupe is wrapped in mystery. He himself first appears in historical record when, on April 26, 1568, Baldassare de Preti wrote to the Castellano of Mantua that "his Excellency has got plays acted by two companies, one belonging to *Pantalone* and the other to Ganaza."[4] Apparently to the first belonged a *Flaminia* and to the second a *Vicenza*, who is probably Vicenza, or Vincenza, Armani. These two ladies had been causing much flutter in Mantuan hearts at least a year before. Luigi Rogna, the ducal secretary, mentions their conflicting charms in a number of letters. On July 1, 1567, he tells us,

> there were performed two plays at the same time, one in the accustomed place by Signora *Flaminia* and *Pantalone*, who were accompanied by Signora *Angela*; . . . the other at Purgo, in Lanzino's house, by that Signora *Vincenza* who is loved by Signor Federigo da Gazuolo.[5]

These concurrent shows evidently caused much discussion, which Rogna duly notes in his next bulletin on July 6;[6] by the 9th of that month Don Antonio Ceruto, *littérateur* and theatre-lover, could declare that "one hears nothing else but the words, 'I am of *Flaminia*'s party,' and 'I am of *Vincenza*'s.'"[7] The rivalry was stopped by *Vincenza*'s departing for Ferrara, although *Flaminia* still remained in Mantua.[8] Unhappily, the former's race had not long to run. Playing, as we have seen, with Ganassa on April 26, 1568, at Mantua, she moved on to Montalta in August of the same year,[9] and thence in September to Cremona. On September 15, 1568, a correspondent, writing to the Castellano of Mantua, laconically noted that "*Vicenza* the actress has been stabbed to death in Cremona."[10]

Where Vicenza Armani was there too was Adriano Valerini *Aurelio*.[11] So, too, we may suppose as a member of the company Luzio Burchiella *Dottore Graziano*. A sonnet of his appears prefaced to Valerini's oration, while there is reason to believe that he formed part of Ganassa's troupe when it visited France in 1572. Also, only a few months before *Vincenza*'s charms aroused Mantuan Society, Rogna informs us that "his Excellency has got a comedy performed to-day by the Gratiani."[12] Another "comedy of the Gratiani" is mentioned by him on May 18, and is

---

[1] Karl Trautmann, *Italienische Schauspieler am Bayrischen Hofe* (*Jahrbuch für Münchener Geschichte*, i (1887), 193–312). Agne Beijer suggests that it is Pasquati's portrait which appears in some of the early prints of the "Recueil Fossard" (*Recueil de plusieurs fragments des premières comédies italiennes qui ont esté représentées en France sous le règne de Henry III*, edited by Agne Beijer and P. L. Duchartre, Paris, 1928, p. 10). This collection provides some of the most important iconographical material we possess relating to the early Italian troupes.

[2] J. Meissner, *Die englischen Comödianten zur Zeit Shakespeares in Österreich* (Vienna, 1884), p. 21; see also D'Ancona, ii, 458.

[3] D'Ancona, ii, 458; Sir E. K. Chambers, *Elizabethan Stage*, ii, 262.

[4] D'Ancona, ii, 455–456.

[5] "Hoggi si sono fatte due comedie a concorrenza: una nel luogo solito, per la sig.ra Flaminia et Pantalone, che si sono accompagnati colla sig.ra Angela . . . l' altra dal Purgo, in casa del Lanzino, per quella sig.ra Vincenza che ama il sig. Federigo da Gazuolo."—D'Ancona, ii, 449.

[6] *Id.*, ii, 451.   [7] *Id.*, ii, 452–453.

[8] *Id.*, ii, 453. Letter dated July 15 when Vincenza had already left Mantua.

[9] *Id.*, ii, 461.   [10] *Id.*, ii, 461.   [11] See *supra*, p. 234.

[12] Letter of May 11, 1567; D'Ancona, ii, 445; "S.E. ha fatto recitare hoggi una comedia dai Gratiani."

separately referred to as a comedy " of Gratiano " by Ettore Micoglio.[1]   It seems reasonable, therefore, to identify these Gratiani with *Vincenza* and with Ganassa.

In January 1570 Ganassa was in Ferrara, contributing to the festivities associated with the marriage of Lucrezia d' Este,[2] and already perhaps he had merged his identity in a group to be more famous than his own personal company, for it seems almost certain that out of the Ganassa group allied to that of *Flaminia* and *Pantalone* grew the illustrious company known as the Gelosi.[3]

[1] D'Ancona, ii, 445.
[2] Rasi, ii, 979; Solerti-Lanza, p. 159.   He was accompanied on this occasion by " a certain Spaniard Ernandicco," evidently a *Capitano*.
[3] The whole question of the early troupes is, of course, very obscure, and it may be that I have erred in identifying quite distinct companies.   Thus, it is possible that in the documents cited above not two, but four or even five companies are referred to : (1) Pantalone, (2) Ganassa, (3) Flaminia, (4) Vicenza, (5) Graziano.   It seems, however, that one may be allowed to conjecture the association of the players mentioned on the lines suggested on p. 301.   Similarly, in the documents given at p. 303 three separate companies might conceivably be recorded ; personally I believe that the same troupe (the Gelosi-Ganassa troupe) was in Paris during the spring and autumn of the year 1571.   Admittedly, however, there can be no certainty concerning this unless other documentary evidence is forthcoming.

Arlequin

Fig. 214.   ARLEQUIN

Seventeenth-century French print by Dolivar. Exemplar in the Bibliothèque Nationale, Paris (Cabinet des Estampes, Tb + 1 vol. ii, B. 474).

Photo Giraudon

(x) THE COMPANIES: (2) THE GELOSI AND GELOSI-UNITI

The Gelosi, or ' the Zealous,' mentioned by Garzoni with the Confidenti as the chief of " honoured companies," [1] are first referred to vaguely as playing at Milan in 1569,[2] but the earliest true records we have of their activities are those in France when the company appeared at Paris alongside of Ganassa. It may be well to take the evidence in chronological order. On March 4, 1571, Lord Buckhurst, then English Ambassador to France, wrote to London saying that he had that day witnessed " a comedie of Italians that for good mirth and handling thereof deserved singular comendacion." [3] These were no doubt " les Galozi " mentioned in a contemporary French document,[4] which at any rate proves that the Gelosi were then in Paris. No more do we hear of them until a violent *arrêt* of Parlement descended on their heads on September 15, 1571.[5] Apparently, having secured *lettres patentes* from the King, the Italians had imagined that they could perform in a public theatre. All their preparations made, they announced that the prices of admission would be from three to six sols. This, however, the worthy city authorities decided was " a kind of exaction on the poor people," and they commanded the players not to attempt any performances " on pain of prison and corporal punishment." Apparently the poor actors made an appeal, with the result that a second *arrêt* was issued on October 15, addressed this time to " Alberto Ganassa and his Italian companions." [6] What happened to them after this second rebuff we do not know ; but of their presence in France for the succeeding months there is no evidence. Sufficient proof, on the other hand, seems to be given to show that Ganassa by this time had become part of the Gelosi. Unfortunately, we cannot tell exactly the composition of the troupe. It is, however, probable that three of its members were Adriano Valerini *Aurelio*, Lidia da Bagnacavallo, and Orazio Nobili.[7] To these may be added Luzio Burchiella *Dottore*, and, if we are right in conjecturing that the Gelosi grew out of a fusion of the Ganassa and the Flaminia groups, then we can suggest still further the presence in the company of Giulio Pasquati *Pantalone*, who was certainly a member in 1574,[8] and who at this time may have been acting both with Soldino and with the Gelosi.

What Ganassa did between October 1571 and the summer of 1572 cannot be ascertained, but it was evidently his company which was seen in June of the latter year by the Earl of Lincoln. He describes " an Italian playe, and dyvers vauters and leapers of dyvers sortes verie excellent," as well as a " pastyme showed him by Italian players." [9] In July " Albert Ganasse " was paid by the treasurer for comedies acted before the King, and an additional payment was given warrant on October 10.[10] The only difficulty that faces us is that on March 21, 1572, the Gelosi petitioned for permission to play in Milan,[11] and that in October of the same year " the poor Gelosi actors " [12] sent another petition to the authorities of Genoa, requesting leave to act there, permission being granted

---

[1] Petraccone, p. 5. On the fortunes of this company see, besides the major authorities such as D'Ancona and Solerti-Lanza, Parmenio Bettòli, *I "Gelosi" e la commedia dell' arte (Emporium*, xiv (1901), 197–214); E. Picot, *I "Gelosi" in Francia (Rassegna bibliografica*, iv (1896), 98–99); A. Neri, *I Comici Uniti nel 1593 (Fanfulla della Domenica*, viii (1886), No. 14). All the studies of Isabella Andreini essay to record the activities of the troupe.

[2] D'Ancona, ii, 468.
[3] *Calendar of State Papers: Foreign Series* (1569–71), p. 413.
[4] Baschet, p. 18: document dated May 1.
[5] *Id.*, pp. 19–21.
[6] *Id.*, pp. 23–25.
[7] Rasi, iii, 23.

[8] A peculiar difficulty arises from the fact that on December 7 the Ferrara Ambassador mentioned in Paris a *Pantalone* and Zanni " who were worth naught," and on December 22 spoke of a company in which only the Zanni was good (Solerti-Lanza, pp. 163–164). The players of the spring of 1571 and those of the autumn may, of course, not have been the same, but in all probability were so (cf. *supra*, p. 302).

[9] Nichols, *Progresses of Queen Elizabeth*, i, 302–303. Cf. Sir E. K. Chambers, *Elizabethan Stage*, ii, 261–263; Baschet, p. 41.
[10] Baschet, p. 42.
[11] Solerti-Lanza, p. 160.
[12] *I poveri Comici Gelosi* (D'Ancona, ii, 499); noted first by A. Neri, *Una Supplica dei comici gelosi (Gazzetta letteraria*, ix (1885), No. 30).

them on the 13th of the month.   From these records it would seem that the Ganassa-Gelosi group of 1571 had split at the end of the year, Ganassa himself remaining in Paris and others returning to Italy.

At this point arises an interesting speculation regarding the English stage.   On September 1, 1573, five shillings was given by the Town Council of Nottingham " to the Italyans for serteyne pastymes that they shewed before Maister Meare and his brethren." [1]   This company evidently stayed in England for a considerable time.   In July 1574 it accompanied Elizabeth on her progress in Windsor and Reading, the Office of the Revels expending money both for players' fees and for various dresses and properties, including " iij devells cotes and heades & one olde mannes fries cote. . . . Golde lether for coronetes, Thred & sheperdes hookes, Lamskynnes for Shepperds, Horstayles for the wylde mannes garment, Arrowes for Nymphes." [2]   Probably they played publicly in London ; at any rate, the preacher Thomas Norton attacked " the unchaste, shamelesse and unnaturall tomblinge of the Italian weomen." [3]   Perhaps these were the actors led by Ganassa.   Undoubtedly the main Gelosi troupe was at Ferrara during the late summer [4] and at Venice during the winter of 1573. [5]   The affairs of the Ganassa group, however, cannot be reliably traced until we meet this exponent of the Zanni acting at Madrid in 1575. [6]   Sir E. K. Chambers declares that " during the summer of 1574 he seems to have been in Madrid," [7] but, in view of recently gathered facts, this statement requires modification.   These facts now seem to indicate that it was Ganassa who visited London in the summer of 1574, his tour terminating in the autumn for a visit to Spain.

Before continuing with the history of the Gelosi it may be well to follow this Zanni to Spanish territory. In 1575 he was acting at Seville, and there he appeared again in 1578. [8]   The likelihood is that he had returned to Italy between those years, but in 1578 he seemed determined to make a lengthy sojourn.   An interesting diary presents records of continuous performances given by him at Madrid and Toledo

Fig. 215. SPANISH COMIC TYPES

Seventeenth-century Spanish print. Exemplar in the Bibliothèque Nationale, Paris (Cabinet des Estampes, Tb 34b).

Photo Giraudon

---

[1] T. Murray, *English Dramatic Companies* (1910), ii, 374; Sir E. K. Chambers, *Elizabethan Stage*, ii, 262.

[2] A. Feuillerat, *Documents relating to the Office of the Revels in the Time of Queen Elizabeth* (Louvain, 1908), pp. 227–228.

[3] E. K. Chambers, *Elizabethan Stage*, ii, 262.   [4] Solerti-Lanza, p. 164.

[5] D'Ancona, ii, 463, 466.

[6] Emilo Cotarelo y Mori, *Noticias biográficas de Alberto Ganasa, cómico famoso del siglo XVI* (*Revista de archivos, bibliotecas y museos*, III, xii (1908), 42–61), p. 45.   Casiano Pellicer in his *Tratado histórico sobre el origen y progresos de la comedia y del histrionismo en España* (Madrid, 1804, p. 53) says Ganassa was at Madrid in 1574 with " a company of Italian comedians, introducing the persons of Arlequino, Pantalone, and the Dottore," but his survey is notoriously inaccurate, and it seems likely that 1574 is an error for 1575.   June 1575 is the date given from a record in Jóse S. Arjona, *El Teatro en Sevilla* (Madrid, 1887), p. 83.   Ottonelli in 1644 met a Florentine who, in 1610, heard it said that Ganassa had introduced the Italian style into that country (*Cristiana Moderazione*, ii, 37).

[7] *Elizabethan Stage*, ii, 263.

[8] E. Cotarelo y Mori, *loc. cit.*, p. 45.

from June 1579 to February 1580.[1] In March 1581 he was at Madrid, engaging a number of Spanish musicians,[2] and in December of the same year he was performing at La Cruz.[3] At La Cruz he remained until the first week of January; on the 20th it was noted that Ganassa was no longer giving his performances there, " he being at Guadalajara at the bidding of Rodrigo de Mendoza." [4] February found him back at La Cruz, but on the 27th a significant note declared that " Ganassa did not act to-day because of his imprisonment." [5] The last records of his activities come with the following year. Adam Hochreiter on December 27, 1583, witnessed one of his performances at some town in Spain; after that there is silence.[6]

Something, however, can be said of his company. Ganassa himself played the Zanni, under what name is not known, and two of his companions at least may be named. One was an actor whose stage-name was *Trastullo*.[7] The other was Vicentio Botanelli, who evidently played the lover as *Curzio*.[8] Perhaps these two, with Ganassa himself, may be depicted in what is by far the most important record of this company—a painting, mentioned by several early historians of the *commedia dell' arte*, which remained a complete enigma until M. Duchartre rediscovered it in the Musée de Bayeux (Fig. 184). As we have seen, this canvas represents a group of French courtiers and royalty amid a number of figures of a *commedia dell' arte* company, in all probability that of the Ganassa-Gelosi. The Court persons themselves interest us little, but prime value attaches to the various ' masks ' represented.[9]

From this time on Ganassa disappears; and we must now turn to survey the activities of the other Gelosi group in their wanderings. Spending the spring of 1572 in Milan, they came to Genoa in the autumn; and certainly played at Ferrara and Venice during the year 1573.[10] Apparently their chief in February 1574 was Rinaldo Petignoni *Fortunio*; in a letter to Mantua he writes of a disturbance in which some members of the company were involved during the progress of the Carnival.[11] Meantime Henri III, who had been on a visit to Poland and was now returning, heard that the players who had so pleased him in Paris were performing in the lovely city of the Adriatic, and on July 7, 1574, sent word ahead that he " desired extremely to see . . . the comedians." [12] Arrangements were immediately made to meet the wishes of his Majesty. The Gelosi were, however, not in Venice, but in Milan,[13] whence they were hurriedly summoned to present at least two plays before the King. The whole affair created some stir, and a certain Tomaso Porcacchi saw fit to issue a pamphlet entitled *Le Attioni d'Arrigo terzo Re di Francia et quarto di Polonia* (Vinetia, 1574) in which are described, among other matters, the shows of the comedians. This provides us luckily with some names. Ganassa was no longer with the company, so the part of *Arlecchino* was enacted by Simone da Bologna. Giulio Pasquati was the *Magnifico* or *Pantalone*, Rinaldo Petignoni took the *amoroso*, while Vittoria Piissimi sustained the *amorosa*. The whole passage is worthy of citation in Porcacchi's words, for we are here permitted a more intimate glimpse of the excellence of this company than has hitherto been given us :

You know, in general, how rarely this troupe performs tragedies, comedies, and other theatrical

---

[1] Cristóbal Pérez Pastor, *Nuevos datos acerca del histrionismo español en los siglos XVI y XVII; segunda série* (*Bulletin hispañique*, viii (1906), 71–78, 148–153, 363–373), in particular pp. 72–76.

[2] E. Cotarelo y Mori, *loc. cit.*, p. 52.

[3] C. Pérez Pastor, *loc. cit.*, pp. 148–149.

[4] *Id.*, p. 149.

[5] *Id.*, p. 150; *cf.* E. Cotarelo y Mori, *loc. cit.*, p. 55.

[6] See Arturo Farinelli, review of Alfred Morel-Fatio's edition of Lope de Vega, *Arte nuevo de hazer comedias en este tiempo* (*Archiv für das Studium der neueren Sprachen und Litteraturen*, cix (1902), 458–474), in particular p. 471.

[7] He is known from Lope's reference in *Filomena* to " donaires de Ganasa y de Trastulo " (*cf.* A. Farinelli, *loc. cit.*, p. 471, and E. Cotarelo y Mori, *loc. cit.*, p. 58).

[8] Named in a document of March 31, 1581, printed in E. Cotarelo y Mori, *loc. cit.*, p. 52.

[9] See *supra*, pp. 270–271.

[10] See Rasi, iii, 230, and *supra*, p. 303.

[11] D'Ancona, ii, 463–464.

[12] Baschet, p. 56; Solerti-Lanza, p. 164; P. de Nolhac and A. Solerti, *Il Viaggio di Enrico III in Italia* (Turin, 1890).

[13] *Cf.* Federico Barbieri, *Per la storia del teatro lombardo nella seconda metà del secolo XVI* (*Athenæum*, Pavia, ii (1914), 382).

U

shows. Simone of Bologna is the most excellent for interpreting the character of a Bergamask peasant, but more excellent still in flashes of wit and fiery epigram, . . . Giulio Pasquati is skilled in playing the person they call " Il Magnifico." I don't know which to admire most in him—his acting grace or the acuteness of his sayings, of both an improvisatorial and a memorized kind. And here too is Rinaldo, who is mightily clever in arranging new plots and in producing tragedies and comedies with [suitable] costumes, gestures, and magnificent settings. I could go on thus analysing the virtues of them all, one by one, paying special attention to that actress who is truly unique [*Vittoria*].[1]

The following year (1575) on May 28 the Gelosi received permission to play at Milan,[2] while on December 3 " the company of *Vittoria* " was acting at Florence.[3] Throughout the next twelve months they were continuing their usual tour of Italian towns, but had evidently now split into two portions. On February 13 some of the company were at Ferrara, but " the lady and the best characters," who had lately been acting in Florence, were now gone to Venice.[4] Apparently the latter were summoned to the Este Court, for four days later a correspondent was announcing that *Vittoria* and *Ottavio* were journeying to join the others.[5] At Ferrara they remained until at least the beginning of March.[6] Meanwhile, Henri III, who had enjoyed so much those Venetian festivities to which the Gelosi had contributed in 1574, dispatched a letter to his Ambassador saying that he wished the company with *Magnifico* to pay a new visit to the French capital. The Ambassador's reply, dated June 22, indicates that the *Magnifico* is out of Italy attending the Court of the Emperor ;[7] probably he had gone north from Venice when *Vittoria* moved westward to Ferrara. The other group seems to have been at Florence in November, for on the 6th of the month Lodovico de' Bianchi *Dottore Graziano*, describing himself as *Comico Geloso*, was writing from that city to a correspondent.[8]

Arrangements were now being actively made for a fresh visit to France, and the Gelosi set off some weeks before the Christmas of 1576. They did not reach Blois, however, until January 25, 1577.[9] Travelling in the sixteenth century was by no means without its discomforts and dangers, and of these the Gelosi encountered at least one. This was the time when the Huguenots were arming in the South of France ; about Christmas the Italians blundered into their hands and were held at ransom for some time before the King sent them relief. Compensation, however, was given to them by the obvious pleasure with which the Court viewed their arrival. Staying at Blois from the end of January until the early summer, they moved to Paris, came to a satisfactory financial arrangement with the Confrérie de la Passion (the French players) and started performances on May 19 at the Hôtel de Bourbon.[10] " They charged," says the Sieur de l'Estoile,

> four sols to every Frenchman who desired to see their performances ; there was such a concourse and crowd of spectators that the four best preachers in Paris, all together, did not gather so many people when they gave their sermons.[11]

The authorities, it is true, tried to make trouble, but, fortified with *lettres patentes* granted on July 27, the Gelosi continued to act in France until the late autumn of 1577. Unfortunately, nothing

---

[1] " La quale schiera, sapete quanto suole esser rara nel recitar tragedie, comedie ed altri componimenti scenici, essendovi Simon Bolognese rarissimo in rappresentar la persona d' un facchino Bergamasco ma piu raro nell' argutie et nell' inventioni spiritose. . . . Giulio Vinitiano [sa] incontrafar quella che domandono ' Il Magnifico ' nella qual rappresentatione sto in dubio qual sia maggiore in lui o la gratia o l' acutezza de' capricci spiegati a tempo et sententiosamente. Evvi anche Rinaldo che vale infinitamente nell' accomodar nuovi argomenti ed in sapergli ridurre alla scena tragica e comica con habiti, con fogge e con rappresentationi nobili. Cosi vi potrei discorrer di tutti a un per uno et massimamente della donna che è unica." (P. 27 *verso*.)

[2] Solerti-Lanza, p. 160.   [3] *Id.*, p. 160.   [4] *Id.*, p. 165.   [5] *Id.*, p. 165.   [6] *Id.*, p. 165.

[7] Baschet, pp. 63–64.   [8] A. Bartoli, p. cxxxiii.   [9] Baschet, pp. 69–71 ; D'Ancona, ii, 468–469.

[10] Baschet, pp. 73–74. A record of this journey is preserved in a poem by " Battista Amorevoli da Triviso, *comico geloso detto la Francischina*," printed at Paris on April 26, 1578 ; see Emilio Picot, I " *Gelosi* " in Francia (*Rassegna bibliografica della letteratura italiana*, iv (1896), 98–99).

[11] " Ils prenoient de salaire quatre sols par teste de tous les François qui les vouloient aller voir jouer, ou il y avoit tel concours et afluence de peuple que les quatre meilleurs prédicateurs de Paris n'en avoient pas tretous ensemble autant quant ils preschoient."—Baschet, p. 74.

whatsoever is known for certain regarding the composition of this troupe, although it may be presumed that it included at least some of the actors who are mentioned in Andreini's *Bravure* [1] as playing at Florence the following year.   At that time the two lovers were Orazio Padovano (Orazio Nobili) and Adriano Valerini of Verona, and their partners Isabella Andreini and Prudentia, or Prudenza, of Verona.   Francesco Andreini took the captain's part, Lodovico da Bologna was the Dottore, Giulio Pasquati was Pantalone, and Silvia Roncagli was Franceschina.   The two Zanni were played by Simone da Bologna and Gabriele da Bologna, while Girolamo Salimbeni of Florence was described as " the old Florentine," Zanobio da Piombino.   The whole question of the composition of the Italian troupe is complicated by the presence in England during 1577 and 1578 of still another company.   Some suggest that these were the Gelosi, but detailed analysis of the evidence would suggest that such a theory cannot be substantiated.[2]

At any rate, the main Gelosi company appears to have been in Florence early in 1578.[3]   One of those puzzles which are ever confronting the student of these actors, however, faces us when we learn of the presence of a band of " uniti comici " at Ferrara on February 8, 1578.[4]   From the fact that after this date Vittoria Piissimi seems to have abandoned the Gelosi and allied herself with the Confidenti, it seems that Solerti's explanation is the correct one ; the " uniti comici " are the " united comedians," consisting of the old Confidenti joined now to *Vittoria* and perhaps some of her companions.   The Gelosi themselves, at the end of this year, were performing at Venice,[5] where they appear to have remained until the spring of 1579.   They were certainly there on January 9,[6] and were preparing to leave for Mantua in March.[7]   At Mantua misfortune came upon them.   In some way they must have offended the Duke, who, on May 5, issued an order of banishment, naming especially " Simone [da Bologna], who takes the part of the Bergamask, and Signor Orazio [Nobili] and Signor Adriano [Valerini], who take the parts of the *amorosi*, and Gabriele called *dalle Haste*, their friend." [8]   On the 13th of the following month they were granted leave to play at Milan,[9] and in July the company sought similar permission at Genoa.[10]   Probably they stayed there throughout the summer, moving to Ferrara on November 15, 1579,[11] whence they probably went to Venice.[12]   Their wanderings in 1580 can be traced at Milan, where they performed throughout the summer,[13] Pisa, Venice, and Bergamo.[14]   At the last-mentioned town, as a 'madriale' by Cristoforo Corbelli [15] informs us, they played with a company of Uniti of whom the chief star was *Angelica*.   This is the second time we have met with a body of actors calling themselves Uniti, and here they are distinctly associated with an *Angelica* who is almost certainly Angelica Alberghini, the wife of Drusiano Martinelli.   Since references to the Uniti appear frequently in later years, it may be well here to stay this account of the Gelosi in order to consider the implications raised by the mention of *Angelica*.

The story starts probably with a certain Massimiano Milanino, of whom we first hear in 1578.

[1] Venezia, 1607, Ragion. XIV.

[2] See *infra*, p. 309.   The list given above cannot be exactly true of the troupe of 1577.   The engravings in the *Recueil Fossard* indicate Orazio, Francatrippa, Franceschina, Isabella, Pantalone, and Dottore.   But the other lover is Leandro (probably Francesco Pilastri) ; Isabella has companions in Lucretia and Lucia, and Franceschina has a fellow-servant named Licetta.   The Zany is called Zany Corneto, and there is a Harlequin, who might be Martinelli or Ganassa.   Finally it is to be noted that the Capitano is styled Cocodrillo, which points to the actor Fabrizio de Fornariis (see Agne Beijer, pp. 17–19).

[3] Rasi, iii, 230; Baschet, p. 82; D'Ancona, ii, 469–470.   [4] Solerti-Lanza, pp. 166–167.

[5] D'Ancona, ii, 470.   [6] Solerti-Lanza, p. 171.   [7] D'Ancona, ii, 470.

[8] " Simone, che recita la parte di Bergamasco, e il sigr. Orazio, e il signᵣ. Adriano, che recitano la parte amantiorum, e Gabriele detto dalle Haste, loro amico."—D'Ancona, ii, 464, 470–472.

[9] Solerti-Lanza, p. 161.

[10] D'Ancona, ii, 470; quoting from Belgrano, *La Commedia nel cinquecento* (*Caffaro*, December 1882, No. 361).

[11] Solerti-Lanza, p. 171.   [12] Rasi, iii, 230.

[13] Solerti-Lanza, p. 161.   They were granted leave to play on May 2, and an extension until September was given them on August 20.

[14] Rasi, iii, 230.

[15] *Rime di diversi Celebri poeti dell' età nostra* (Bergamo, 1587).   Cf. D'Ancona, ii, 465; Rasi, i, 15–16.

In the December of that year a band of Italian players then serving the King of Navarre had given performances at Nérac in honour of the arrival there of Catherine de' Medici. The two chief players were named as Massimiano and Antonio Scotivelli.[1] As payments were made about the same time to a *Paul de Padoue chef d'une troupe de Comédiens*,[2] it seems likely that we have here another name to add to the list of the company, while from the facts that an unknown Italian company was in

Fig. 216. L'Amour au Théâtre Italien
Painting by Watteau in the Kaiser Friedrich Museum, Berlin.
Photo J. E. Bulloz

France from January to December 1576,[3] and that an Italian play was presented before the Council at Durham Place in April of the following year,[4] we may suggest that the same group of players had been for some time touring outside of Italy. Here, however, there enters in one of those particular problems of peculiar interest for the English reader. On January 13, 1578, " one Drousiano, an Italian, a commediante, and his companye " were in London, where they were recommended to the Lord Mayor by the Privy Council ; the Chamber accounts of the same year mention likewise " the Italian Tumblers." [5] Now, there is not the slightest doubt that " Drousiano " was the famous Drusiano Martinelli *Arlecchino*. The question is : to which company did he belong

[1] Baschet, pp. 86–87.   [2] *Id.*, p. 87.
[3] *Id.*, pp. 71–72.   [4] E. K. Chambers, *Elizabethan Stage*, ii, 262.
[5] *Id.*, ii, 262–263. *Cf.* Winifred Smith, *Italian Actors in England (Modern Language Notes*, xliv (1929), 375–377).

308

in 1578? Sir E. K. Chambers suggests that this was the Gelosi, but such a theory is a mere supposition, as no record indicates that Martinelli was then in their troupe. We do know, however, of an association between this player and Massimiano. On October 27, 1591, he wrote a letter from Milan to a Captain Alessandro Catrani, of the Court at Mantua, complaining that a certain Gasparo in Milan was " resolved to slash *Angelica's* face at the bidding of the actress *Malgarita.*" Various players had been called in to this quarrel, including *Leandro*, " Carlo, who acts *Franceschina*," and " Masimigliano," the last almost certainly the Massimiano of 1578.[1] *Angelica* was certainly Drusiano's wife, perhaps Angelica Alberghini ; *Malgarita* was in all probability Margarita Pavoli. Considering the connexion here between the two men in 1591, and the fact that Massimiano was in France a few months later than we find Drusiano in England, we are allowed at least to suggest that the Massimiano troupe, with Drusiano as *Arlecchino*, paid this visit to England. It is, however, possible that these men formed merely a part of the larger Gelosi group ; at any rate, it is important to notice that, while the Gelosi were mentioned as playing at Florence early in 1578, Battista da Treviso, who had been in their company in Paris, did not leave that city till May 10, 1579.[2] May it be that he, too, accompanied Martinelli to England?

It seems highly probable that Martinelli, with his wife Angelica, perhaps, accompanied by Fabrizio de' Fornariis, *Capitano Coccodrillo* of the Confidenti, revisited England toward the end of the century. No formal evidence of this is available, but it is peculiar at least that Marston should refer to a " nimble, tumbling Angelica " in 1597 or 1598,[3] while in 1593 John Eliot introduces a " Crocodill " as a boaster in his *Ortho-epia.*[4] It may be, of course, that the latter is drawing on his knowledge of the Continent. He was probably in Paris during the year 1584, when Fornariis was performing there.

Little more is known of the fortunes of this troupe. In 1580, as we have seen, it appeared as Uniti at Bergamo, and on July 4 of the same year it was at Ferrara, being described then as *comici nuovi* (' new actors '),[5] so that we must believe that Martinelli had then reconstituted the company. *Angelica* was directing her own company in 1583.[6] In 1588 Drusiano was with his brother in Spain,[7] while on November 9, 1591, he is found at Caravaggio, still grumbling about *Angelica* and *Margarita*[8] and on June 10, 1592, at Florence. If " Malgarita " is Margarita Pavoli, then there is the additional information that on January 6, 1589, she and *Pantalone* were in dire straits,[9] and that on October 11, 1592, the Duke of Mantua saw fit to recommend her to the Uniti.[10] This, however, was a later set of Uniti, and to explain their presence we must turn back to the year 1581 and the wanderings of the Gelosi.

After their recorded activities in various cities during the course of the year 1580 the fortunes of this company are hard to trace for a number of months. They were at the Carnival at Venice in 1581,[11] and in July they returned to Milan.[12] Before July 28, 1582, they were playing at Mantua, but there once more disaster overtook them. A news-letter of that date lucidly illuminates the difficulties which even the most favoured players were likely to encounter in the course of their dealings with the princes of the Renascence. The Duke, we are told, had a desire

to see a comedy presented by the Gelosi ; he wanted it all ridiculous and amusing. The actors obeyed him by presenting a most ingenious and laughable play in which all the characters were hunchbacks. At this his Highness laughed so much and took so much pleasure in it that nothing would satisfy him at the end but that he should summon the chief players and inquire of them who was the author of the comedy. The *Zanni* answered " Me, me " ; the *Magnifico* said that he had been responsible ; and *Gratiano* desired the praise—each one imagining that he would get a nice present out of it. The Duke

[1] D'Ancona, ii, 504–506.   [2] Rasi, i, 307.   [3] *The Scourge of Villainy*, xi, 101 ; *cf.* Chambers, *id.*, ii, 263.
[4] See *supra*, p. 250.   [5] Solerti-Lanza, p. 169. *Cf.* D'Ancona, ii, 478–479.   [6] D'Ancona, ii, 479.
[7] A. Bartoli, p. cxxx.   [8] D'Ancona, ii, 506–507.   [9] *Id.*, ii, 493–494.
[10] *Id.*, ii, 494.   [11] *Id.*, ii, 479.   [12] Solerti-Lanza, p. 161.

ordered all three to be arrested and condemned to the gallows; the ladies gathered there all begged him for mercy. They were refused; only they succeeded in supplying the halters, which were made, by their device, of so fragile a rope that the three actors fell to the ground, and the populace cried, "Mercy! Mercy!" and though the poor wretches were led back half dead to their cells, and there stripped and tortured, the Duke remained fixed in his desire to see them strung up again.[1]

His Highness the Duke was a patron of literature and art; the three players were the chief of their company—*Zanni* probably Gabrielo Panzanini, the *Magnifico* Giulio Pasquati, and the *Dottore* Lodovico de' Bianchi.

We can imagine a rather hurried retreat from Gonzaga's anger on their release, but we do not encounter the company again until the following year (1583). In the spring they were in Genoa,[2] and a letter from Francesco Andreini *Capitano* indicates that the troupe was acting contemporaneously at the Venetian Carnival with the newly formed group of Confidenti.[3] It seems that at this time the Duke of Mantua had been responsible for forming a new company, and his letter to which Andreini's is a reply suggests that the latter should aid in establishing one united troupe. When precisely Francesco Andreini became a *Comico geloso* we do not know; but the fortunes of the company hereafter were to be intimately related to those of him and of his wife Isabella.

Here, however, we enter a tangle of difficulties raised by the many records relating to a company of Uniti, certainly not those who were so called in earlier times. In endeavouring to explain the progress of events we must note that these Uniti are always spoken of in the plural. Individual actors of other troupes might sign themselves *Comico geloso* or *acceso* or *desioso* or *fedele*; but nowhere do we find the phrase *Comico unito*. The word Uniti, therefore, seems to be used rather as an adjective than as a genuine title such as Gelosi and Confidenti, and is to be interpreted as indicating, not a new company, but the union of elements from various companies. The first definite mention of the new group is to be found in a document of April 3, 1584, when the Uniti, then at Ferrara, wrote to ask permission to play at Mantua. This letter is subscribed by *Pedrolino, Bertolino, Magnifico, Gratiano, Lutio, Capitan Cardone, Flaminio,* Battista da Treviso *Franceschina,* Giulia Brolo, *Isabella,* Gio. Donato, and *Grillo.*[4] On the following day the Duchess of Ferrara wrote to Mantua praising them highly and noting that "the company of *Pedrolino*" was one constituent of the union.[5] Here once more we get confused with other companies, and the full record of *Pedrolino's* activities must be considered before we can move on further. The earliest record of the *Pedrolino* troupe is dated July 28, 1576, when we learn that it has been wintering at Florence, Pisa, and Lucca.[6] In April 1580 this *Pedrolino* was at Ferrara, where, in addition to performing plays, he and his *Pantalone* acted as domestic clowns. G. B. Rossetti thus tells us how at a great dinner given by Signor Gaspare di Monte a central table was set with

a hole in the middle big enough for a man to get through; it was covered by a large, empty pie which had a hole at the bottom to correspond with the hole in the table. A cover was set on the pie, but this

---

[1] "Anchora che da Mantoua non habbia hauuto tal auiso nondimeno qua si dice ch' essendo uenuto capriccio al Duca di uedere una Comedia dai Gelosi che fosse tutta redicolosa et faceta, i recitanti lo seruirno con farne una ingieniosissima et ridicolosissima solo che tutti i recitanti erano gobbi della qual cosa Sua Altezza rise tanto, et tanto piacere se ne prese che niente più, finito il spasso, chiamo quei Principali comedianti et disse qual di loro era stato l' inuentore. Il Zani, diceua mi mi, Il Magnifico diceua esser stato lui, et Gratiano uoleua la palma, pensando ogn' uno d' hauerne un grasso premio. Il Duca li fece pigliar tutti 3 et furno condannati alla forca, le gentildonne radunate insiemme tutte di Mantoua suplicaro per la gratia, et non fù possibile mai d' hauerli, solo che ottenero di farli i lacci, a lor modo i quali furno di fune così fragida che tutti 3 cadero in terra, et la città gridò gracia gracia, et benche i meschini fossero condotti alle prigioni semiuiui et che fossero tosati et salassati nondimeno il Duca staua anchor risoluto di uolere che fossero impiccati di nouo."—Rasi, iii, 228.

[2] Belgrano, in *Coffaro*, December 28, 1882; D'Ancona, ii, 470.

[3] Baschet, pp. 90–91; D'Ancona, ii, 484–485. They were also in Milan this year (Federico Barbieri, *loc. cit.*, p. 113).

[4] D'Ancona, ii, 486.

[5] Baschet, p. 91. *Pedrolino* was Giovanni Pellesini; see A. Valeri, *Chi era Pedrolino?* (*Rassegna bibliografica della letteratura italiana,* iv (1896), 94–98).

[6] D'Ancona, ii, 476.

could be raised. *Pedrolino* the actor was concealed under the table; no one knew he was there except her Highness the Duchess. When they had all taken their seats . . . *Pantalone* came into the room, indicating that he was looking for *Pedrolino*, since he was a greedy fellow, in the dining-hall, and called out for him. *Pedrolino* then raised only his head out of the pie, so that none of his body was seen, and replied that by misfortune his greed had driven him to the kitchen, where the cooks had made him into a pie.[1]

At the same period (1580) Vittoria Piissimi, with the Confidenti, was acting in the same Italian towns which formed *Pedrolino's* circuit, and in June we find the Duke of Mantua endeavouring to join together these two companies.[2] Evidently he succeeded not only in joining the companies, but in making *Pedrolino* and *Vittoria* man and wife.[3] By September 17 they were undoubtedly performing together, almost certainly under the title of the Confidenti. Perhaps in later years they added some other members to their cast, for in 1583 we find mention both of the Uniti Confidenti and of a group including *Pedrolino*, Giacomo Braga, and the actors calling themselves Uniti.[4] The fortunes of *Pedrolino* and of *Vittoria*, then, between 1580 and 1583 are identical with those of the Confidenti.

The group of Uniti in 1584, however, are not by any means all Confidenti actors. *Bertolino*, *Grillo*, and *Gratiano* are unfortunately untraceable. The *Magnifico* may be Giacomo Braga, who was with *Pedrolino* in 1583, or Giulio Pasquati. *Lutio* is possibly Lucio Fedele, *Flaminio* is G. P. Fabbri, Giulio Brolo is probably the Giulio Bolico whom the Confidenti asked for in 1583.[5] Now of these, as well as the named actors Battista da Treviso [6] and Gio. Donato, there were several who were, early or late, associated with the Gelosi, and it is perhaps not too hazardous a suggestion to say that *Isabella* was Isabella Andreini and that *Capitan Cardone* was an early name for her husband Francesco. If this be so, then we find Andreini accepting that post proposed for him by the Duke of Mantua, and we recognize in the Uniti, not a separate company, but an expansion of the Gelosi, the remnants of the Confidenti going their own way.

These Uniti were at Reggio on their way to Mantua on June 27, 1584,[7] and in May 1585 were granted permission to act at Mantua,[8] but it is not absolutely certain that they went there at that particular date. In July the Duke of Mantua was proposing that the "company of Diana," along with *Gratiano*, should come to his Court, but he is told that *Gratiano* (Lodovico de' Bianchi) will not act unless Giulio Pasquati *Pantalone* comes as well. This may refer to the Gelosi, of whom perhaps *Diana* (Diana Ponti) had become temporarily a member. A few months later, on January 1, 1586, the Gelosi were writing from Bologna to say they were ready to come to Mantua,[9] and on May 31 they were granted a licence to act in Milan.[10] Perhaps they later went to Turin.[11]

In the spring of 1587 the Gelosi are to be found again at Florence,[12] and in the early summer of 1588 at Mantua and Milan.[13] The following year special festivities were arranged at Florence for the marriage of Ferdinando de' Medici and Cristina of Lorraine, and the Gelosi were immediately summoned to contribute their activities. We know of the presence in the city in May 1589 of *Pantalone* (Giulio Pasquati), *Gratiano* (Lodovico da Bologna), *Zanni*, *Pedrolino*, *Francatrippe* (Panzanini) *Burattino*, *Capitan Cardone* (? Francesco Andreini), *Franceschina* (Battista da Treviso), *Diana* (D. Ponti), *Isabella* (I. Andreini), and *Vittoria* (V. Piissimi).[14] From Florence the

---

[1] G. B. Rossetti, *Dello scalco* (Ferrara, 1584), pp. 171, 306. [2] D'Ancona, ii, 475.

[3] See *infra*, p. 315. [4] See *infra*, p. 316. [5] See *infra*, p. 316.

[6] In 1584 this actor published a *Canzone* at Turin, calling himself *Comico confidente*. See V. Cian, *Galanterie torinesi del secolo xvi* (*Gazzetta letteraria*, xvi, 4).

[7] D'Ancona, ii, 488. For an unfortunate visit of the Gelosi to Milan at this period see G. B. Castiglione, *Sentimenti di S. Carlo Borromeo intorno agli spettacoli* (Bergamo, 1759), p. 140.

[8] D'Ancona, ii, 488. [9] *Id.*, ii, 490. [10] Solerti-Lanza, p. 162.

[11] *Id.*, p. 162. [12] D'Ancona, ii, 490–491, 493. [13] *Id.*, ii, 493.

[14] *Id.*, ii, 467–468; Rasi, iii, 243.

Gelosi then moved to Milan in September, having with them their *Dottore* (Lodovico da Bologna).[1] On October 21 this *Dottore* was at Pistoia,[2] and the rest of the actors, including Isabella and Gio. Donato, were at Parma.[3] During December they seem to have been in Mantua.[4]

March 1590 found *Vittoria* by herself in Rome,[5] the rest of the company being apparently at Mantua and Milan in April[6] and at Milan again in November and December.[7]

During 1592 we hear that the Uniti (March 19) wished to go from Mantua to Verona, but were refused permission (March 23),[8] and that about November the Gelosi were at Florence.[9] On October 11 the Duke of Mantua recommended Margarita to the Uniti, who were then at Florence,[10] but otherwise no documents exist to show their course of wandering. The following year, however, is rich in record. A certain *Aurelia* wished to join the "company of Vittoria" on March 27;[11] on July 4 a reimbursement was made to Francesco Pilastri for expenses incurred by him in sending the Uniti from Ferrara to Mantua in 1592;[12] while in a petition of October 1593 a list of some members of the Uniti who wished to play at Genoa has been preserved.[13] These include Francesco Pilastri *Leandro*, Vittoria Piissimi, Andrea Zenari *Graziano* (evidently Michel Zanardi), Giovanni Pellesini *Pedrolino*, *Capitan Cardone*, Giovanni Balestri, G. P. Fabbri, Girolamo Salimbeni *Piombino*, and Gabriello Panzanini *Francatrippe*. It will be noted that of these Panzanini, Salimbeni, and Fabbri are all elsewhere noted as belonging to the Gelosi. On November 1, 1592, a news-letter from Ferrara mentions that both *Diana* and *Insabelina* (presumably Isabella Andreini) were proposing to journey soon to that city.[14]

Some time in 1594 they were at Florence, when Domenico Bruni *Fulvio* was in the company.[15] In October 1594, too, the Uniti are recorded as having taken part in the sumptuous entertainments presented in honour of the Conte di Haro, son of the Constable of Castile, Juan Fernandez de Velasco, then Governor of Lombardy.[16] A special theatre was constructed for the company by Giuseppe Meda. Nunzio Galiti was called in as inventor of the *intermedi*, while Francesco Pilastri produced the show in settings painted by Valerio Profondavalle. The names of the players included *Vittoria* (V. Piissimi), *Leandro* (F. Pilastri), *Ottavio, Franceschina* (possibly Battista da Treviso), *Lucilla, Virginia, Angelica, Emilia, Fortunio*, and *Silvio* (evidently Silvio Gambi). Two months later, in December 1594, the troupe was playing in Florence.[17]

On March 2 of the following year Silvio Gambi was being recommended to the Cardinal di S. Clemente by the Duke of Mantua, so that there is the probability that the company had been playing in the New Year at the ducal town. A month later (April 10) a letter was sent by the Ducal Counsellor Cheppio addressed to the Mantuan Ambassador in Milan recommending to his care "the company of his Highness the Duke of Mantua," evidently the Gelosi-Uniti, of whom, we are told, Drusiano Martinelli was now the chief.[18] This was followed up by a petition of the players to be allowed to perform in Milan,[19] this being favourably received by the authorities on June 7.[20] Toward the end of this year comes a puzzling document which takes the form of a letter from Tristano Martinelli to one of the Mantuan household. In this the *Dominus Harlequinorum* makes announcement of the fact that he has left the company of *Pedrolino* and joined *Diana's* company (the Desiosi).[21] Now, it is possible to assume either that Tristano, along with his brother, had been

---

[1] A. Bartoli, p. cxxxiv.   [2] *Id.*, p. l.

[3] D'Ancona, ii, 476. That there was much confusion among the companies at this time is shown by the fact that in October 1589 *Pedrolino* and *Isabella* were styled *comici confidenti* (Antonio Valeri, *loc. cit.*, p. 96).

[4] D'Ancona, ii, 495.   [5] Rasi, iii, 290.   [6] D'Ancona, ii, 501-502.   [7] A. Bartoli, p. cxxxiv.

[8] D'Ancona, ii, 503.   [9] Solerti-Lanza, p. 162.   [10] D'Ancona, ii, 494.   [11] *Id.*, ii, 511-512.

[12] *Id.*, ii, 510-511.   [13] *Id.*, ii, 511. See A. Neri, *I Comici Uniti nel 1593* (*Fanfulla della Domenica*, viii (1886), No. 14).

[14] Solerti-Lanza, p. 183.   [15] F. Bartoli, i, 136; A. Bartoli, p. cxxxiv.   [16] D'Ancona, ii, 514-516.

[17] *Id.*, ii, 511.   [18] *Id.*, ii, 517-518.   [19] *Id.*, ii, 518.

[20] *Id.*, ii, 518. Permission was granted them on the same terms as were *già concessa a Diana Desiosa.*

[21] *Id.*, ii, 519.

for a time in the troupe of the Gelosi-Uniti, or that about the late eighties of the century *Pedrolino* abandoned that company in favour of the Confidenti, with whom he is later found in 1599.

In 1596 a special licence was granted to the Uniti for performances at Milan,[1] while the Gelosi are found acting at Genoa[2] and at Bologna;[3] from the latter town Isabella Andreini wrote (November 27) to the Duke of Mantua in such terms as showed that she had fallen temporarily into disgrace at Court. If Drusiano Martinelli continued his association with the company, then we catch sight of these players again two years later, in 1598. On March 11 Drusiano was writing to Cheppio in Mantua,[4] and this note, which is of no particular importance, is followed by another, penned by Capitano Catrani and addressed to the same Mantuan official.[5] This casts a lurid light on the actor's character, and provides again one of those intimate pictures which make these performers live for us. "All the time," Catrani writes,

> that Drusiano has been lately in this city—about five months in all—he has lived on the money which I sent to his wife. He was content to use this and to enjoy it, although he knew well whence it derived; he arranged that his wife should come to my house, and troubled his head about nothing save sleeping and eating. . . . Concerning this I shall get testimony made before his Highness by many men worthy of being believed.

The letter goes on to say that now Drusiano is threatening to have recourse to the Duke, only because he finds this source of income stopped. The picture is not a pretty one; but it is likely to be true. What happened over this affair is not known; but the Duke's hands at this period seem to have been pretty full with the pair of Zanni brothers. On May 2, at any rate, Tristano is found writing to the Duke from Modena.[6] From this it seems that he had been requested to join the Uniti. Vaguely he refuses, proffering many excuses—he must go to Florence by contract with the company he is in, he fears enemies in Mantua, and so on. It seems probable that, possibly owing to the Catrani affair, Drusiano left the Mantuan company about this time and joined the Accesi.

Again there comes a break in the history of the company. It seems that the Duke's patronage in the succeeding years was extended to the Accesi, and one might imagine that this latter troupe inherited some of the traditions of the Uniti. The Uniti, however, still retained an independent existence.[7] On June 12, 1601, a letter of the Comici Uniti was sent from Pavia begging permission to play in Milan. The letter mentions an *Isabella* and *Pedrolini*, evidently leaders of the company, and informs us that they had lately been both in Mantua and in Milan.[8] The following year a French correspondent wrote from Turin saying that attempts were being made to form a company for Paris, but that *Pedrolino* was causing difficulties.[9] This company was actually formed, with Francesco and Isabella Andreini as its leaders, and through the records concerning its progress the Gelosi once more spring back into the limelight of history. On September 28, 1602, the arrangements were being made, and by August 26 of the following year Isabella was addressing a letter from Paris.[10] Acting at Fontainebleau during November,[11] they later proceeded to give public performances in the Hôtel de Bourgogne.[12] From a receipt preserved in the Paris archives it is known that G. P. Fabbri *Flaminio* and G. Pellesini *Pedrolino* were in the troupe.[13] The King gave them formal permission to return to Italy on April 13, 1604,[14] and at the same time the Queen sent a letter of recommendation on Isabella's behalf to the Duchess of Mantua.[15] This

---

[1] D'Ancona, ii, 518. [2] *Id.*, ii, 470. [3] *Id.*, ii, 521.

[4] *Id.*, ii, 523. [5] *Id.*, ii, 523–525; Rasi, iii, 105. [6] D'Ancona, ii, 526.

[7] It seems probable that Isabella Andreini and the Gelosi were at Padua in April 1600; *cf.* Bruno Brunelli, p. 02, and C. Ruelens, *Erycius Puteanus et Isabelle Andreini* (Anvers, 1889), p. 10.

[8] Rasi, iii, 244. Presumably these were *Pedrolino* and Isabella Andreini, although *Pedrolino* was certainly with the Confidenti in 1599.

[9] Baschet, pp. 126–127, letter dated September 28, 1602. [10] Rasi, i, 95–96.

[11] See a letter of Isabella written on December 7, 1603, given in Baschet (p. 137) and Rasi (i, 94–95). *Cf.* A. Bartoli, p. cxxxvii.

[12] Baschet, p. 143. [13] *Id.*, p. 137. [14] *Id.*, pp. 144–145.

[15] *Id.*, p. 145.

recommendation was never required.　When the troupe reached Lyon Isabella suddenly was taken ill and died there on June 11, 1604.　Her death deprived the stage of one of its greatest ornaments, and the news was received with universal grief.[1]　Francesco, her husband, immediately retired from his profession, and the Gelosi, who had become the most famous of Italian troupes, were disbanded, its members scattering among the other companies then playing in Mantua and the North of Italy.

　That the Gelosi and the Uniti were fundamentally the same company seems proved not only by the presence in both of the same actors, but by the fact that the two troupes disappear together. The Uniti mentioned in a document of 1614 [2] cannot be the same, and no documentary proof exists to substantiate Adolfo Bartoli's assertion that Pietro Bagliani was of the Uniti in 1623.[3]　In any case, temporary unions might easily create bands of Comici Uniti, and it seems that we are bound to dismiss entirely the vague Uniti of the sixteenth century as merely an expansion of the original Gelosi troupe.　With Isabella's death both vanished.

[1] Baschet, pp. 146–148.　　　　　[2] Rasi, i, 359.　　　　　[3] A. Bartoli, p. clxvi; cf. Rasi, i, 248–249.

TVRLVPIN

Turlupin d'une humeur plaisante.
Par Les choses qu'il represente
Se fait Louer des Escoutans.

Et S'accommodant à l'vsage
Sçait iouer son personnage
Aussi bien qu'homme de son temps

Fig. 217. TURLUPIN

Seventeenth-century French print by H. I. Rouselet.　Exemplar in
the Bibliothèque Nationale, Paris (Cabinet des Estampes, Tb + 1,
vol. ii, B. 464).

Photo Giraudon

314

(xi) THE COMPANIES: (3) THE CONFIDENTI

The Confidenti, 'the Confident,' mentioned by Garzoni[1] along with the Gelosi as a troupe of "honoured" performers, had, as we have seen, many points of connexion with the latter; sometimes, indeed, it is difficult to disentangle the records of the one from the records of the other. Apparently the Confidenti were formed in a troupe in the early seventies of the sixteenth century, but the evidence concerning their first activities is generally inconclusive. That they were in Paris in 1571 or 1572 is often stated,[2] but there seems no direct proof of this, and we must remain at least suspicious of the assertion. The first sure information we have regarding them appears in a petition dated June 25, 1574, which informs us that the Confidenti had that year been in Cremona, Pavia, and Milan, and that their *Zanni* was Giovanni Battista Vannini,[3] otherwise known as Battista da Rimini. Thereafter for some years we lose sight of them until they reappear on May 30, 1580, at Mantua,[4] when the Duke recommended them to the Podestà of Verona, informing him that the company wished to perform there.

By this time possibly they were in process of being reconstituted. The earlier history of *Pedrolino* and *Vittoria* has already been told;[5] we must now catch up that history when *Vittoria* has left the Gelosi and *Pedrolino* is guiding a company of his own. Both were in Mantua in June 1580, and throughout the summer toured in Padua, Verona, and Bologna.[6] At length the Duke's endeavours bore fruit; by September 19 she and *Pedrolino* had joined forces.[7] On October 28 the pair were at Ferrara,[8] whence they moved to Bologna.[9] On December 25 the Duke of Mantua ordered *Pedrolino* to repair to his Court for his marriage to Margherita Farnese.[10] Apparently, however, he did not choose to go there; Italian actors were at Mantua from January to April 1581,[11] but *Vittoria* and *Pedrolino*, definitely named now as Confidenti, remained at Venice.[12] The consternation which *Vittoria* felt when she feared that her companion might be taken from her is fully revealed in her letters at this time. On January 1 of that year she wrote an anxious, ill-spelled, and unpunctuated letter to that "Most Serene Lord":

> I have seen what your Highness has got written to *Pedrolino*, and, though as your humble servant I ought to acquiesce in what I know to be your will, none the less constrained by that compassion which every one feels for himself seeing so great disaster and dishonour so near to me again I beg you by the Bowels of Jesus Christ not to be the cause of my ruin and believe that if so it were not I should rather die than cease to obey you do me the favour of getting some one who knows this matter to give you information . . . from them you'll learn what I refrain from saying in order not to weary you asking your pardon for my troubling you with which I remain your humble servant begging you again to grant to me and *Pedrolino* the life of my honour and of body which consists in the remaining of *Pedrolino* yea grace my Lord grace for the love of God this I beg of you on my bended knees and with my heart's tears Our Lord preserve you and may He grant grace to me to be able to serve you.[13]

This was followed two months later by another in penitent strain:

[1] See *supra*, p. 303.

[2] A. Bartoli, p. cxxx; Croce, p. 33. The original statement was made by Magnin in his article *Teatro celeste: Les commencements de la comédie italienne en France* (*Revue des deux mondes*, iv (1847), 1099), but no documentary proof is cited.

[3] Paglicci-Brozzi in *Scena illustrata*, October 15, 1890; Rasi, iii, 622–623. For their activities in Milan see Gentile Pagani, *Del Teatro in Milano avanti il 1598* (Milan, 1884), p. 21. They were in Milan again in 1575 (*id.*, p. 36).

[4] D'Ancona, ii, 474–475.   [5] See *supra*, pp. 310–311.

[6] D'Ancona, ii, 475. *Pedrolino* was in Ferrara during April; *Vittoria* departed in July for Padua, having been at Mantua on June 22. The recommendation to Padua is dated August 27 (Solerti-Lanza, p. 168; B. Brunelli, p. 63).

[7] D'Ancona, ii, 478–479.   [8] Solerti-Lanza, p. 174.

[9] A letter of recommendation is dated November 2 (*id.*, pp. 168, 174).   [10] D'Ancona, ii, 479–480.

[11] *Id.*, ii, 480.   [12] Solerti-Lanza, pp. 174–175.   [13] Rasi, iii, 289.

(xii) THE COMPANIES: (4) THE DESIOSI AND THE ACCESI

THE DESIOSI

There were, of course, many troupes operating in the last decades of the sixteenth century. Concerning many, such as that of the Intronati, who applied for permission to act at Milan in 1578,[1] nothing can be said, but there remain two about which some tangible record has come down to us. One of these is the Desiosi, 'the Desirous,' or 'those who desire to give pleasure.' On November 11, 1580, Montaigne saw the Desiosi acting at Bologna, and on July 3 of the following year found them at Pisa, where a certain *Fargnoccola* was in the company. Later on, in 1588, they were allowed to act in the Pope's palace in Rome, but without women (whether women actors or women spectators cannot be determined).[2] In 1593 they were at Mantua, in the spring of 1595 at Milan,[3] in January 1596 at Mantua [4] and preparing to go to Ferrara, in February of the same year at Bologna,[5] and in May 1597 at Genoa. Among these records, unfortunately, only one actor's name emerges, that of Giuseppe Scarpetta in 1596. Ill-luck, however, meets us here, for the only other record concerning him tells us that, in 1613, he was " formerly an actor " (*già comico*) and then a vendor of some patent oil. Besides this actor only one other performer of this troupe is known. Quadrio [6] states that Diana Ponti *Lavinia* was a *comica desiosa*, and although he makes a wild error in her date, there is no real reason to doubt his words, particularly as some of the documentary records of her life seem to fit in with what is known of the Desiosi. The first that is heard of her is when the Confidenti, preparing to go to Mantua in 1582 for some festivities, write to say that they are waiting only for Diana and Graziano.[7] Perhaps the two companies were being temporarily united for this special occasion. With Cesare de' Nobili she was at Genoa in 1586,[8] but otherwise her companion is unknown to us. Four years later she is said to be with a certain Andreazzo *Graziano* and then preparing to go to Rome.[9] Tristano Martinelli joined her company in December 1595, after leaving the *Pedrolino* troupe. She was then acting at Cremona along with a Giambattista Lazaro.[10] The last-mentioned might possibly be Battista da Rimino *Franceschina*. After that she vanishes until, in 1605, we find her gathering a new " good and numerous " troupe for the Principe della Mirandola.

The difficulties of interpretation are here obviously many. We cannot be absolutely certain that the *Diana* of these records was Quadrio's Diana Ponti, and even if we do assure ourselves of their identity there remains the problem of establishing with certainty the fact that the company of *Diana* was also the company of the Desiosi. All that can be said with assurance, indeed, is that from 1580 to 1595 the Desiosi were performing their plays and that from 1582 to 1605 a *Diana*, who may be Diana Ponti and who seems to have some connexion with their activities, was also treading the boards, at one time in association with the redoutable Tristano Martinelli.

THE ACCESI

The Accesi, the 'flashing' or 'inspired' actors, are first recorded on January 8, 1590, when we learn that, with letters of recommendation from the Duke of Mantua, they have received per-

---

[1] D'Ancona, ii, 478. [2] *Id.*, ii, 500–501. [3] Rasi, iii, 304–305.
[4] D'Ancona, ii, 520. [5] *Id.*, ii, 520.
[6] The information comes from a sonnet, *Della signora Diana Ponti detta Lavinia, Comica Desiosa*, printed with Scala's *Il Postumio* (Lyon, 1601).
[7] Rasi, iii, 305; D'Ancona, ii, 481. [8] Belgrano (*Caffaro*, December 29, 1882); Rasi, iii, 305; ii, 758.
[9] D'Ancona, ii, 496–497. [10] *Id.*, ii, 519.

mission to play at Brescia.[1] The next certain documentary evidence of their activities comes nine years later, when, on March 13, 1599, the Duke of Mantua, writing to the Cardinal di San Clemente at Ferrara, announced that the Accesi desired to go to Ferrara after Easter,[2] to which the Cardinal replied that he had already licensed the Confidenti for that date and proposed that the Accesi should come after the former had left. In the following year, on April 19, the Duke of Mantua was recommending the company of the Accesi to the Duc d'Aiguillon and the Duc de Nevers; the troupe was then about to set out for France.[3] Here at last we come on records of a definite kind in so far as the composition of the company was concerned, for it is known that the leaders of the actors in this Parisian journey were Tristano Martinelli and Pier Maria Cecchini *Fritellino*. Having established these, we may return for a moment to see if perchance some other activities of the Accesi may be determined through an analysis of the fortunes of the two Zanni. The first that is heard of Cecchini is a record of his name (as Pietro Maria Chezzini) in 1590–91 at Mantua, when he was there with Gabriele Canovaro, G. B. Austoni, Giacomo Braga, and G. Paolo de Righetti.[4] Of Canovaro no other mention is elsewhere made, but G. B. Austoni *Battistino* in 1608 was certainly with the Accesi in France, and one might hazard the suggestion that all these men were in 1591 of this troupe. If this is so, then the Accesi were at Bologna on June 7, 1590, when Cecchini was described as a servant of the Duke of Sabioneta,[5] and at Florence on September 14, 1595, when Cecchini wrote to the Ducal secretary at Modena.[6] He and Tristano, no doubt with the Accesi, were at Bologna in May 1599, according to two letters dated May 8 and May 28.[7] The question now arises, For how long was Tristano associated with this company? We cannot go too far back. In 1600 the two brothers Tristano and Drusiano were acting together, just as they had been in 1588.[8] Now, Drusiano in 1590 was the chief of *Pedrolino's* company,[9] and in 1595 Tristano had moved from that group to the company managed by *Diana*. It seems highly probable, however, that shortly after this date both brothers joined the Accesi. In 1598 Drusiano may still have been of the Gelosi-Uniti,[10] but thereafter he and the more famous *Arlecchino* must be counted of the other troupe. On May 8, 1599, Tristano was at Bologna with Cecchini, as we have seen, and no doubt the description of *comico scriso* given him by himself in a letter to Mantua on August 7 cannot be taken seriously.[11] He was then assuredly an Acceso, and the company was at Verona. By December they had moved on to Florence,[12] whither Henri IV sent a letter begging Martinelli to come to him in Paris, but by March 1600 Martinelli, at any rate, was stationed in Mantua.[13]

This record of the activities of Cecchini and Martinelli has considerably expanded our knowledge of the Accesi company, which was now officially recommended to the Parisian Court. With true Harlequinesque contempt of royalty, however, Martinelli does not seem to have hastened his departure for France. When Henri IV, travelling through France, arrived on July 9 at Lyon he found there only Drusiano Martinelli, the rest of the company being still at Turin. Hurriedly the actor-ambassador was dispatched to fetch them, evidently with an imperative command, for by August 8 French majesty was being diverted with their plays.[14] With this troupe was Flaminio Scala, who was responsible for getting published at Lyon *Il Postumio, comedia del signor I.S.* (1601).[15] During the latter part of the year the Accesi journeyed to Paris, and here started one of those quarrels between the chief actors which seem to have been inevitable in all companies. Cecchini bombarded the Duke of Mantua with complaints, going so far as to declare that Tristano was

[1] D'Ancona, ii, 495–496. For some records of the Accesi see A. Valeri (" Carletta "), *Un Palcoscenico del seicento* (*La Nuova Rassegna* (1893), 797–800). Some letters were first printed by A. D'Ancona in *Lettere di comici italiani* (Pisa, 1893; per nozze Martini-Benzoni).

[2] *Id.*, ii, 531. [3] Baschet, p. 108. [4] D'Ancona, ii, 502.

[5] Solerti-Lanza, p. 182. [6] Rasi, ii, 627. [7] A. Bartoli, p. cxxxvi; D'Ancona, ii, 532.

[8] See *supra*, p. 309. [9] See *supra*, p. 309. [10] See *supra*, p. 313.

[11] D'Ancona, ii, 527–528. It may be a misreading for *comico acceso*.

[12] Baschet, p. 106; A. Bartoli, p. cxxxv. [13] Baschet, p. 107; A. Bartoli, p. cxxxiv.

[14] Baschet, pp. 109–110. [15] Rasi, ii, 513; Baschet, p. 120.

end it all comes to this—that he doesn't want to go." [1]   So off goes the irascible *Fritellino* back to Naples, where he appeared in 1621, " after a long tour," with Silvio Fiorillo *Capitano*. [2]   From this time onward little is known of the fortunes of the Cecchini troupe.   In the spring of 1622 these actors were at Venice, [3] and toward the end of the following year they are to be found at Florence.   On October 23 performances were there given by the *comedianti di Zanni della compagnia di Fritellino e della Flaminia* ; these were continued throughout November and December, the players on the 9th of the former month being distinctly named as Accesi. [4]   From these records we learn that one of the plays presented was *La Pazzia di Flaminia* and that *Cinthio* was a member of the troupe.

Nothing more seems to be heard of them until in 1626 some extant letters show that Cecchini was once more in association with the Fedeli and was causing the usual tumult of recriminations. [5]   Whatever temporary union may have been effected was soon broken, and off went the testy *Fritellino* once more on his wanderings.   How long his company continued active there is no means of ascertaining, although the fact that Fiorillo, when he published his *Lucilla costante* in 1632, still called himself *Comico Acceso* may indicate its endurance into the early thirties of the century.

Just one other record may bear witness to their activities.   In June 1614 Cecchini was certainly in Bavaria, and that same year Silvio Fiorillo published at Milan his *La Cortesia di Leone e di Ruggero*, therein describing himself as *Comico Acceso*.   Now, a company of players, calling themselves Uniti, petitioned to play at Genoa on August 4, 1614, [6] and these included —besides Silvio Fiorillo *Capitan Mattamoros*

Fig. 219. POLICHINELLE AND PANTALON

Seventeenth-century French print published by Mariette.   Exemplar in the Bibliothèque Nationale, Paris (Cabinet des Estampes, Tb + 1, vol. ii, B. 460).

Photo Giraudon

and Gio. Batta Fiorillo *Scaramuzza* his son—Jacomo Braga *Pantalone*, Domenico de' Negri *Curzio*, Andrea Frajacomi *Trivellino*, Hippolito Monteni *Cortelazzo*, Andrea Mangini *Adriano*, Michel Zanardi *Graziano*, Ottavio Bernardini *Franceschina*, Gio. Paolo Fabbri *Flaminio*, together with nine *portinari* and *servitori*.   As few of these actors are recorded elsewhere, it may be suggested that this was a ' scratch ' second company gathered together by Fiorillo to play in Italy until Cecchini's return.   If so, information is given us concerning some at least of those who were associated with his activities.

---

[1] " L' à cominciato a strepitare, a biastemare Idio, giurando ch' el non vol venire, et minaciandomi . . . et molte altre parolazze impertinenti ma dette con gran rabia, et in conclusione ch' el non vol venire."—A. Bartoli, p. cxlii.
[2] Croce, p. 65.   They had stopped at Milan in October; see Rasi, ii, 628.
[3] Solerti-Lanza (p. 182) shows that the earlier Accesi were under the patronage of the Duke of Sabbioneta.
[4] Angelo Solerti, *Musica, ballo e drammatica alla Corte Medicea dal 1600 al 1637* (Florence, 1905), pp. 170–171.
[5] See *infra*, p. 332.   [6] Rasi, ii, 359.

326

THE FEDELI

(xiii) THE COMPANIES: (5) THE FEDELI

Above it has been seen how, when Cecchini returned from France in 1609, he joined with the Andreini and others of the Fedeli troupe. These Fedeli, the 'Faithful,' must have been in existence as early as 1598, for Miss Winifred Smith has discovered a *Dialogo amoroso* written by a *Fedele comico* and dedicated on November 1 of that year.[1] All early record of the company, however, has perished, and perhaps we may be justified in believing that at that period it was of small account. Quite possibly it was formed by Giovan Battista Andreini, who, born in 1576,[2] seems to have started acting in the last years of the sixteenth century. Whether that be so or not, certain record of his activities comes with the date 1603, when he produced his first play, *Florinda*, at Florence, and when his wife, Virginia Ramponi, won poetic praise from the members of the Accademi degli Spensierati on account of her acting in the title-*rôle*.[3] The following year the Fedeli, with G. B. Andreini, were formally admitted to the service of Mantua; from the facts that a number of the old Gelosi troupe joined it after the death of Isabella and that Andreini in his *Saggia Egiziana* (Firenze, 1604) connects the Gelosi and the Fedeli, we may believe that there was a conscious emulation of the former by the new company.[4]

For two years the activities of these actors cannot be traced, but in 1606 they reappear, in close association with P. M. Cecchini, of the Accesi, with whom they seem to have been temporarily merged. During September both the Cecchini and the Andreini were at Milan, and thence Pier Maria wrote to Mantua bitterly complaining of the various members of the troupe. "As for *Lelio* and *Florinda*," he ends, "may God guard me and my like from being associated with them!"—from which it appears that no formal fusion of the two companies had yet been made.[5] The main cause of trouble is outlined by him in an enclosed letter intended for the eyes of the Duke:

> The stratagems and persecutions woven round me by *Florinda* and her husband, and the ill-treatment I have received from them, are so great that they have brought me to ruin and disaster. They tell me to stay this winter at Milan, and since that doesn't seem to me to be fair, and since I refuse to stay here, the said husband of *Florinda* has stopped making a question of it; this would have been successful had not God interfered.[6]

Nine days later Cecchini was again writing to Mantua. He had by that time received letters from the Duke, and complains once more of the action of the Andreini:

> I wished to let all the company see these letters, and in order to get them all together, I spoke to them behind the scenes after the play, and then I went into the dressing-room; but *Lelio*, the husband, and *Florinda* would not come, and although I begged them and sent a public servant twice to tell them that I wanted to speak to them by order of his Highness—in spite of all, the said *Lelio* laughed and turned away and wouldn't listen.[7]

By September 20 Cecchini had evidently got his own way, and it was Andreini's turn to make complaint. The Duke's goodwill had gone to Cecchini, and *Lelio* was ordered to obey or leave the company.[8]

---

[1] W. Smith, *Aurelio, comico* (*Giornale storico*, xcii (1928), 208–211). This manuscript is in the Biblioteca Estense, Modena. A. Bartoli (p. cxxxvii) thought the Fedeli first arose in 1605. By far the most complete study of their activities is that given by Enrico Bevilacqua, *Giambattista Andreini e la compagnia dei " Fedeli "* (*Giornale storico*, xxiii (1894), 76–155; xxiv (1895), 82–165).

[2] This is usually given as 1579, but see Antonio Valeri, *Un Palcoscenico del seicento* (*La Nuova Rassegna* (1893), 799) and Rasi, i, 117, 138.

[3] Bevilacqua, xxiii, 101–109. The first edition of *Florinda* was printed at Florence in this year, but was burned by the author. The volume of *Rime*, of which the dedication was dated February 22, 1603, forms a record of the performance. As noted above (p. 241), this volume has hitherto never been cited by historians of the *commedia dell' arte*.

[4] Bevilacqua, xxiii, 110–111.   [5] *Id.*, xxiii, 114–115.   [6] *Id.*, xxiii, 115–116.
[7] *Id.*, xxiii, 116–117.   [8] *Id.*, xxiii, 117–118.

Apparently the two companies, temporarily united, now split, for in February 1608 Cecchini was in France, acting in his own band of Accesi, while in May and June of the same year the Fedeli were participating in the festivities arranged for the marriage of Francesco Gonzaga and Marguerite de Savoy. In October the Accesi set off once more for Italy, and seemingly trial was made again of a joint company. At any rate, we find the Andreini and the Cecchini together, and quarrelling as usual, in the late summer of 1609. On August 4 *Florinda* was forced through her raised temper to apply directly to Cardinal Ferdinando Gonzaga. Signora *Flaminia* (Orsola Cecchini), she declared,

> is hated by the whole of Turin on account of her pride and her passion for *Cintio*—nay, she is thoroughly despised. . . . All the actors are grumbling at her boldness and at that of *Fritellino*. . . . For my part, I do what I can to bear their ill-humours, but truly things cannot go on in this way.[1]

Ten days later G. B. Andreini was writing on the same theme to the Duke :

> The whole of this company was in arms, but they hurt one another much more with sharp words than with swords. . . . Praise be to God, I settled the whole affair ; but what then ? I acted just like a man who temporarily stays a great rush of water which in a little will break every restraint and more impetuously than ever will sweep out and flood everything.[2]

This letter he signs in the name of himself and of his companions—Hieronimo, Federico, Carlo, Aniello, and Bartolomeo.[3] These two letters thus provide ten names of members of the company. *Fritellino* and *Flaminia* are Pier Maria and Orsola Cecchini. Giovan Battista Andreini *Lelio* and Virginia Andreini *Florinda* are the correspondents. *Cintio* is unknown, but Hieronimo is Girolamo Garavini *Capitan Rinoceronte*, Federico is Federico Ricci *Pantalone*, Carlo is Carlo Ricci, his son, Aniello is Aniello Soldano *Dottor Spacca Strummolo*, and Bartolomeo is probably Bartolomeo Bongiovanni *Dottor Graziano*.[4]

These, we must assume, were actors of two troupes, the Accesi and the old Fedeli, and the mixing of the companies no doubt largely explains the animosities then taxing the nerves of all. Apparently the union was vaguely maintained for a couple of years, but it is difficult to trace accurately the fortunes of the players. On August 21, 1610, Virginia Andreini was at Venice,[5] and P. M. Cecchini was at Mantua on January 15 following.[6] On March 21, 1611, *Florinda*, in a " discontented " state—apparently because of Cecchini—was at Mantua,[7] and in December at Bologna.[8] By this time the long rancour between the Cecchini and the Andreini had reached a head, and in January 1612 the former were ignominiously dismissed from Mantuan service.[9]

Meanwhile arrangements were going ahead for another visit to France. On September 3, 1611, Marie de' Medici wrote to " Harlequin " (Tristano Martinelli) asking him to collect " a good company," [10] and on the 30th of the same month Martinelli replied, asking for an official letter to be sent to him for this purpose.[11] Negotiations dragged on for some months ; on December 3 Martinelli, writing from Mantua, was still making general and vague recommendations and promising to send on a letter to *Florinda*, who was then at Bologna.[12] It seems, then, that Martinelli was at this period not in the Fedeli troupe, and *Florinda* (December 14, 1611) addressed a strong letter to the Cardinal Gonzaga pointing out that it was she and her husband who ought to be given the leadership of the French company.[13] Cardinal Gonzaga found himself incapable

---

[1] Bevilacqua, xxiii, 123–124; A. Bartoli, p. cxxxviii. [2] Bevilacqua, xxiii, 124-126. [3] Rasi, i, 141, 164.

[4] This gives two *Dottori* to the troupe, but certainly Bartolomeo cannot be B. Ranieri, as Rasi (i, 164) suggests. He was born about 1640. Bongiovanni was in the Fedeli in 1612. *Cf.* Antonio Valeri, *loc. cit.*, p. 798.

[5] Bevilacqua, xxiii, 126. [6] Rasi, ii, 637. [7] Bevilacqua, xxiii, 129.

[8] *Id.*, xxiii, 129, and xxiv, 83. [9] See *supra*, p. 325. [10] Baschet, pp. 202–203.

[11] A. Bartoli, p. cxl. [12] Baschet, pp. 203–204; *cf.* A. Bartoli, p. cxl ; and *supra*.

[13] Baschet, pp. 206–207. She was then still at Bologna. *Cf.* also A. Bartoli, pp. cxl–cxli; Bevilacqua, xxiv, 84.

of reconciling these opposites, and on December 24 wrote off to his father, the Duke of Mantua, in despairing and pleading terms.[1] To this the Duke replied that, since he had banished the Cecchini, he did not dare to send the troupe to France, since "only two or three of the actors are good."[2] No doubt a similar letter was dispatched to Paris, for on June 28, 1612, Marie de' Medici sent a

Fig. 220. A Scene at the Théâtre Italien
Painting by Nicolas Lancret in the Musée des Beaux-Arts, Strasbourg.
Photo J. E. Bu loz

note to "Harlequin" requesting him to see that *Fritellino* should be in the proposed company,[3] and this request, in a succeeding letter dated July 21, became almost a demand.[4] Martinelli, it seems, in spite of the impertinent and bantering tone of his letters, really tried to do his best. On August 15 he was writing about the company to the new Duke[5] and complaining of his troubles. *Florinda* (V. Andreini) and *Flavia* had quarrelled; neither *Flavia* nor her husband, the *Capitano*, would hear of the journey to France. Besides, other good actors would have to be engaged, either

[1] Baschet, pp. 207–208. [2] *Id.*, pp. 208–209.
[3] *Id.*, pp. 210–211. Martinelli on January 4, 1612, was at Bologna (Rasi, iii, 102). [4] *Id.*, pp. 211–212.
[5] *Id.*, pp. 212–214. Duke Vincenzo I had died on February 1612. The new Duke was Francesco Gonzaga, who also died shortly after (December 22, 1612).

Zan Farina or *Scapino* as a Zanni, and *Fulvio*, who took both the parts of the *amoroso* and of the *Dottore*;[1] *Scapino* at that time was with Andreini, who had no special need of him, since he had lately taken *Mezzetino* into his company and these parts were fundamentally similar.[2] He informs us that *Flavia*, the *Capitano*, *Zan Farina*, and *Fulvio* were at Venice; we know from a letter of Virginia Andreini's of the same day[3] that her company (the Fedeli) were then in Milan, where, too, Martinelli was staying. The long delays now began to irritate French royalty, and on September 4 Marie de' Medici wrote a somewhat sharp note to Martinelli and another to her nephew, the Duke of Mantua.[4] During the course of the next month Martinelli was still in the throes of gathering the actors together and pleading that " to unite a good company demands more than a Harlequinesque authority."[5] Having received a reply from Cardinal Gonzaga, he set himself down again on October 26 at Florence to pen a long epistle about the whole matter. Characteristic indeed is this document :

> I have opened your letter, by which I understand in very nice terms that you love me, that you wish to help me, and other nice little words pleasant to swallow down with a pinch of salt. . . . But I should have been better pleased if you had written to me, as my dear gossip the French hen [*i.e.*, *galina*, Marie de' Medici] does ; she always ends her royal letters with phrases such as, " Come, Signior Arlecchino, come to us, and we shall be your godmother." Those are nice words ! And in all her letters she never forgets to put in some pleasant paragraph that pleases us infinitely, which charms our person infinitely. It is she, our hen gossip, who understands our letters ! But you, sir, you don't seem to understand them too well, or, at any rate, don't wish to understand them.

Here follows a list of complaints, and then :

> The Queen has written to the Duke and to you to get you both to collect a fine and perfect company of actors in which will figure Signora *Florinda* and her husband, *Flaminia*, *Fritellino*, Signora *Flavia*, *Capitano Rinoceronte*, and myself, besides two other good characters—namely, a *Graciano* and a good *Pantalone*. These are the persons the Queen desires in France, and it is up to you, my gossip sirs, to gather these together—Arlecchino's power is not sufficient for that.[6]

On November 26 Martinelli was still in Florence, whence he, with nine other actors, wrote a strong letter to the Duke of Mantua, who seems to have been thinking of replacing *Capitan Mattamoros* (Silvio Fiorillo) for *Capitan Rinoceronte*. The players are up in arms at this proposal, declaring that the former is by no means what he once was. They subscribe themselves Tristano *Arlecchino*, Federigo (Ricci) *Pantalone*, (Benedetto) Rizzi *Leandro*, Giovanni Pellerini (evidently *Pedrolino*), Baldo Rotari,[7] Giovan Battista Andreini (*Lelio*),[8] (G. Garavini) *Rinoceronte*, and *Nicolina* and Bartolomio Bon Giovani *Graciano*.[9] A few days before this G. B. Andreini had written from Florence (November 16) to the Duke, showing that his company had been asked to go to Rome, and on the same day he and his wife sent a reply to that city.[10] On December 13 they were still at Florence. It is likely that the proposed trip to Rome was deferred, for by this time the difficulties which met those who were trying to form a company for France were being overcome. On May 27, 1613, Marie de' Medici was thanking Martinelli for his services and assuring him that *toute l'Harlequinerie* would return well pleased with their visit.[11] On August 26 of that year the company were in Lyon,

---

[1] This may be Domenico Bruni *Fulvio*, although it is not recorded that he acted the *Dottore*.

[2] Baschet, p. 215.

[3] *Id.*, pp. 216–217; *cf.* also Bevilacqua, xxiii, 130; xxiv, 86–87. A letter of G. B. Andreini dated August 28, 1612, also written from Milan is extant (*id.*, xxiv, 87).

[4] A. Bartoli, p. cxli; Baschet, pp. 217–219.

[5] Baschet, pp. 219–221; letter dated from Bologna October 16. Evidently at this time Martinelli was acting with the Fedeli.

[6] Baschet, pp. 222–224.

[7] On behalf of his wife, *Lidia*.

[8] For himself and his wife.

[9] Baschet, pp. 225–226.

[10] Bevilacqua, xxiii, 131.

[11] Baschet, p. 230.

where four performances had been given,[1] and on September 6 the Italians arrived in Paris, active preparations being made for a show in the Louvre.[2] Martinelli wrote from Fontainebleau on October 4,[3] and there he stayed with his company until November 24, when they all returned to Paris and opened a public theatre in the Hôtel de Bourgogne.[4] Here and at Court they played until July 1614, when, it seems, the troupe split, Martinelli returning one way, and the Andreini, with Virginia Rotari *Lidia*, another.[5]

Few records of the company are extant for the following few years. Martinelli was at Mantua on June 30, 1615,[6] but whether he was with the Fedeli is uncertain. In the summer of 1616 Andreini is found in the service of the Prince della Mirandola. During this and the following year he is also traceable at Mantua and Venice.[7] He was at Venice, too, in 1619,[8] and this year he toured likewise in Brescia and Verona. From Brescia on May 21, 1619, he wrote a letter to Mantua from which we learn that *Gallotta* was the second Zanni; among the other actors are mentioned *Cola*, *Farina*, and *Fabrizio*.

Meanwhile, renewed efforts were being made to gather a fresh company for another visit to France. In the spring of 1618 Don Giovanni de' Medici was resisting a proposal of the Andreini to engage some of the Confidenti, including Ottavio Onorati *Mezzetino*, Francesco Gabbrielli *Scapino*, and Flaminio Scala *Flavio*.[9] Nothing seems to have come of these negotiations, although they were pursued up to the end of the year.[10] Throughout 1619 rumours are heard of this French visit, and at last in May 1620 the Duke of Mantua was able to write to the new King, Louis XIII, saying that he was about to send his actors to Paris.[11] This announcement, however, was somewhat premature. G. B. Andreini had something to say,[12] and by August P. M. Cecchini *Fritellino*, who had been approached on the subject, had still more to object. In place of *Scapino* he would suggest Pavolino Zanotti, who was a brilliant actor owning only one fault—that he was enslaved by the charms of his *Fantesca*. As for *Pantalone*, he was not much good; *Fritellino* himself could take his place. But the real trouble was *La Baldina* (apparently Virginia Rotari *Lidia*, wife of Baldo Rotari). She truly causes the company real torments, and because of her *Florinda* (Virginia Andreini) has lately run off in tears to a convent.[13] There was, of course, a second side to the question, and this Martinelli provided in his letter to the Duke of Mantua from Due Castelli, dated September 28, 1620.[14] From it we learn that the Fedeli included then, besides Martinelli and the Andreini, Virginia Rotari *Lidia*, G. Rivani, and Girolamo Garavini *Capitano*. A month later, on October 16, the *Dominus Arlechinorum* wrote once more to the Duke from Milan, by which time they had shaken off *Fritellino*. At this period some special trouble seems to have arisen over a certain *Aurelio* [15] who is probably Marcello di Secchi. Judging from a letter of Cecchini's of December 5, this actor does not seem to have belonged definitely to the Fedeli, but he may have been temporarily drafted from the Confidenti with the idea of engaging him for France.

On November 6 Martinelli was penning once more a long epistle to the Duke,[16] mentioning in its course the success of the chief players, who included himself, the Andreini, Giovanni Rivani,

[1] Baschet, p. 232; Bevilacqua, xxiv, 89.
[2] Baschet, p. 242.
[3] *Id.*, pp. 234–235; D'Ancona, ii, 529–530.
[4] Baschet, p. 246.
[5] *Id.*, pp. 253–254. D'Ancona (ii, 530) seems to give as members of the troupe, besides the Andreini, Virginia Rotari and Tristano Martinelli, G. Garavini *Rinoceronte*, L. Nettuni *Fichetto*, F. Ricci *Pantalone*, and U. Liberati *Bernetta*. Rasi (i, 265) adds N. Barbieri *Beltrame*. With the troupe certainly was *Lidia* (Bevilacqua, xxiv, 90).
[6] See the letter reproduced by Rasi (iii, 100) in facsimile.
[7] Bevilacqua, xxiv, 91–92.
[8] *Id.*, xxiv, 101. He was there also in December 1619 (*id.*, xxiv, 104).
[9] Rasi, iii, 515–516.
[10] Baschet, p. 260.
[11] *Id.*, pp. 270–271.
[12] *Id.*, p. 271; Bevilacqua, xxiv, 105; letter dated from Milan, July 18, 1620.
[13] *Id.*, pp. 273–274; Rasi, i, 153; Bevilacqua, xxiv, 107.
[14] A. Bartoli, p. cxlii; Bevilacqua, xxiv, 107. See *supra*, p. 325.
[15] *Cf.* W. Smith, *Aurelio, comico* (*Giornale storico*, xcii (1928), 208–211); Jarro, *L' epistolario d' Arlecchino* (Florence, 1895), p. 38.
[16] From Turin; Baschet, pp. 277–279; Bevilacqua, xxiv, 108–109.

G. Garaccini (or Garavini) *Capitano*, L. Nettuni *Fichetto*, F. Ricci *Pantalone*, V. Rotari *Lidia*, and U. Liberati *Bernetta*. To these must be added B. Ricci *Leandro*, who died shortly after at Chambéry. From Turin the long-delayed journey to France was started, and by January 12, 1621, the Italians had settled down in Paris.[1] Staying there till April,[2] they then moved to Fontainebleau, where they remained until the end of the month.[3] Meanwhile *Arlecchino* had got tired of France, and on April 21 he wrote a note to the King asking for his release.[4] Royalty, however, was by no means willing to rid itself of his services, even although he pressed his point verbally and by further letters.[5] The company too were concerned, and on May 12 sent a request that Martinelli be forced to remain.[6] A Harlequin's wish, however, is not to be stayed, and on June 27 he set off home,[7] the company writing to explain to majesty all his errors.[8] On July 14, 1621, the testy *Arlecchino* had reached Lyon.[9]

Meanwhile the Fedeli continued to perform at Paris until at least March 1622, Louis XIII writing to the Duke of Mantua on February 3 to explain that they are being kept at his Court only because he takes such pleasure in their histrionic skill.[10] In all probability they departed thence in the early summer, and, so deep had been the impression made by them, on October 10 Louis was writing once more to the Duke of Mantua begging for their return.[11] To this the Duke replied by sending a letter by the person of a *Dottore*, and by arranging for a new expedition to France. Before December 6 the company, under G. B. Andreini, had arrived at Lyon, and there Louis witnessed their first performances.[12] In January 1623 they arrived at Paris, where they gave performances publicly and before the Court. How long they stayed is unknown, but in Easter they were already back at Turin[13] and were at the Venetian Carnival the same year,[14] along with Tristano Martinelli. Later on they journeyed to Padua and Verona. By August 6 Louis was again clamouring for his " *Lelio, Florinda*, cappitano *Rinoceronte*, and Federic *Pantalon*,"[15] and the Queen a week later was adding her entreaties.[16] The Duke once more bowed himself to the task of organization, and on November 12 G. B. Andreini was writing from Turin to say that all was going well for the start. Whenever *Rinoceronte* (G. Garavini) arrived, they would set off. It would be a good company, and they had got a good *innamorato*, a young actor called *Cintio*.[17] Just when they arrived at Paris cannot be determined, but on December 17 payment was ordered to G. B. Andreini, F. Gabbrielli, and N. Barbieri.[18] Gabbrielli *Scapino* and Barbieri *Beltrame* were evidently then of this company. Little can be said concerning their activities in Paris, but it is probable that the sojourn was of long duration.[19]

On September 20, 1626, however, they were back in Italy, and once again Cecchini is discovered in conflict with the Andreini. On that day Giovan Battista wrote to Mantua, complaining of *Fritellino's* tricks and of the actions of " that harpy *Flaminia*," his wife.[20] It is difficult to make

---

[1] Baschet, pp. 281–282.
[2] See the letter of G. B. Andreini of March 3 mentioned by Baschet (pp. 282–283); Bevilacqua, xxiv, 109.
[3] Baschet, pp. 284–285.   [4] *Id.*, pp. 286–7.   [5] *Id.*, pp. 287–290.
[6] *Id.*, pp. 291–292. The names of the signatories are G. B. Andreini, U. Liberati, G. Rivani, G. Gharaceni, V. Rotari, L. Nettuni, and F. de Ricci.
[7] *Id.*, pp. 298–299.
[8] *Id.*, pp. 295–297. The names here were G. B. Andreini, G. Garacini, G. Rivani, F. Rizzi, L. Nettuni, U. Liberati, L. Rotari, and *Florinda* (V. Andreini). Three letters of Andreini's to Mantua are cited in Bevilacqua (xxiv, 111–112).
[9] Baschet, p. 299.
[10] *Id.*, p. 304. For a letter on July 23, 1621, see Bevilacqua, xxiv, 112.   [11] Baschet, p. 313.
[12] *Id.*, pp. 315–316. Bevilacqua (xxiv, 116–117) tends to doubt whether this Italian company was truly that of the Fedeli. It seems highly probable, however, that Baschet is right in thus identifying them.
[13] Rasi, i, 123; F. Bartoli, i, 18.   [14] Baschet, p. 301; F. Bartoli, i, 18.
[15] Baschet, p. 321.   [16] *Id.*, p. 322.
[17] *Id.*, p. 323. Bevilacqua (xxiv, 119) shows that Baschet was wrong in reading *Cintia* for *Cintio*.
[18] Baschet, pp. 332–333. It is noticeable that both *Scapino* and *Beltrame* had been of the Confidenti company. Possibly they joined the Fedeli after the breaking up of their troupe about the year 1621.
[19] It certainly extended to 1625.   [20] Bevilacqua, xxiv, 124–125.

out exactly what this letter imports.   Certainly a reorganization of the companies must have taken place, for F. Gabbrielli and Maria Malloni *Celia* were at Florence from September 26 to October 31, 1626,[1] thus separated from the Andreini group.   *Lelio's* letter seems to imply that Cecchini had once more joined the Mantuan company, but that he was refusing to go to Mantua, preferring a visit to Rome.   From the reference to " the company of *Cintio* " it seems that that youth was also playing apart from the Fedeli.   On October 2 Andreini wrote to Mantua telling of an invitation he had received to visit Venice during the Carnival, and mentioning the breaking up of the company.   Some had gone to Naples, some to Rome and some, including *Moschetta, Cintio,* and *Scappino,* to Modena.[2]

This last-mentioned group was at Ferrara on January 6, 1627, and they, like Andreini, had their bitter things to say about Cecchini.   Francesco Gabbrielli is here writing to the secretary of the Duke of Mantua, and from his words it seems likely that the Andreini, the Cecchini, and the *Scappino* troupes were all bidding for the favour of that potentate.   Thus *Scappino* begins his epistle : [3]

On Sunday at 4 o'clock while I was playing his Highness the Marchese Nicolò Tassone handed me a letter of yours which conveyed your goodwill toward me in such terms as brought the tears to my eyes with joy.   I am glad that you are disposing of me, my wife (*Spinetta*), the *Dottore,* the *Capitano* (actor unidentified), *Citrullo,* and *Flavia* (Margherita Garavini), but I am sorry that *Fritellino* (P. M. Cecchini), his wife (O. Cecchini), *Cintio* (J. A. Fidenzi), *Lavinia* (M. Antonazzoni), *Ortensio* (F. Antonazzoni), the *Pantalone della Podagra* (F. Ricci), and lastly *Mezzetino* (O. Onorati) should be submitted to the Duke.   The reason I shall explain as briefly as I may ; you can show it to his Highness, since I shall not put down a word that is not true.   Let us start with Signora *Lavinia.*   I say that you will have difficulty in getting her without *Beltrame* (N. Barbieri), since she is his companion and owes him 500 scudi. . . . And then, O Signor Antonio, *Lavinia* is no good at improvising, so that the company can make no use of her except in memorized parts.   Her husband once took the *rôle* of second *innamorato,* but, because he hated study, changed that for the *rôle* of an Italian captain, and in this he fails lamentably.   For his own reasons *Cintio* will not leave *Franceschina* and her husband, . . . and when there's another *Fantesca* there's no opportunity for my wife. . . . *Mezzetino* . . . will not be separated from *Olivetta,* and that would be a third *Fantesca.*   *Fritellino* is fit to be hated not only by actors, but by everybody, . . . and as for his wife— she is old now, and it does not suit her to pretend she is a mere girl ; at this time the stage wants youth. The *Pantalone* has been so ravaged by the disease which afflicted us last year in Venice that he cannot put on his clothes or tie on his mask, and it certainly seems to me a bad thing to put on the stage a mere wooden stock which can move nothing but its tongue. . . . You will see you can't get *Cintio* without a big bribe, or *Lavinia* and *Ortensio* without paying their debts and giving them presents, or *Mezzetino* without *Olivetta.*   He who wishes *Fritellino* will have to pay the piper and control the same confusion in the company as we had before, and he who wishes *Pantalone* will get a mere natural ninny. . . . But *Celia* (M. Malloni) is the best actress on the stage whether for improvised or memorized parts ; if the company . . . puts on new operas or plays she acts them at once, which neither *Lavinia* nor the other actress will do unless they spend a month in studying the *scenario.*   Concerning *Flavia* I say nothing save that she is the best second *innamorata,* both in improvisation and memorized *rôles.*   You would find our *Pantalone* good both for his sound speech and for his knowledge of old and new scenarii.   *Bagattino,* our second *Zanni,* . . . you would find a second *Arlecchino.*   I shall say nothing of myself, my wife, the *Dottore,* the *Capitano,* and *Citrullo,* since his Highness graciously esteems our work.   True it is that the *innamorato* is not such as *Cintio* or as the late *Aurelio,* but you could easily find some young students who have graduated high in the Florentine school of Tuscan speech, with the confidence that they may succeed, thanks to their study, as well as some who put their feet on the boards, and, what is of greater importance, without too much pay.

As for Andreini, beyond the fact that he did go to Venice for the Carnival,[4] nothing is known of his movements until, on January 29, 1628, he suddenly makes his appearance at Prague, where

---

[1] Rasi, ii, 964–965.

[2] Bevilacqua, xxiv, 125–126.

[3] Rasi, ii, 964–966.

[4] Bevilacqua, xxiv, 127.

he had been apparently for some months.[1]   A few months later, on November 16, *Lidia* (V. Rotari), describing herself as a " widowed mother, with the care of seven children," and as " a servant of twenty-five years' standing " of the Mantuan household, addressed a letter to the Archduchess of Tuscany from Vienna,[2] and from the same city G. B. Andreini wrote to Mantua a few days later.[3]

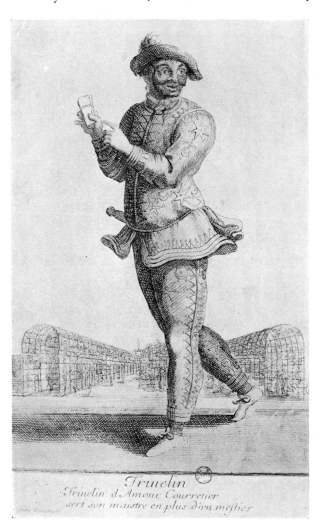

Fig. 221. TRIVELIN

Seventeenth-century French print published by Le Blond. Exemplar in the Bibliothèque Nationale, Paris (Cabinet des Estampes, Tb +1, vol. ii, B. 481).

Photo Giraudon

There is no evidence to show the composition of this troupe, or the duration of its stay.   Italy was ravaged with pestilence during the years 1629 and 1630, and it is probable that it was then that *Florinda* died.[4]   That Giovan Battista was at Bologna late in 1630 seems certain,[5] but for this period of disaster he could not have been engaged in his usual profession.   By May 24, 1633, he was back at his trade, acting at Verona, and apparently married now to that *Lidia* who, years before, had made *Florinda* fly in a jealous passion to a convent.[6]   At Verona he remained till at least June 20, when he penned a humble letter to the Duke of Mantua.[7]   By September 27 he had gone to Vicenza,[8] and in the winter was at Venice. Things were now beginning to change.   Instead of summoning his own comedians to Mantua for the Carnival, the Duke had asked the *Scappino* group to go there, and, finding he could not have them, had extended a similar invitation to the Carpiano troupe.   Even they could not come, and the old Fedeli were summoned eventually. From Andreini's letters of November 29 and December 17, however, it is plain that the Duke preferred companies other than his.   Like *Lelio* himself, the Fedeli were getting old.[9]   Within a few years all connexions between Mantua and his actors were to be broken.[10]

After the Carnival of 1634 at Mantua Andreini went to Bologna [11] in June, and later, in 1635, to Milan.[12]   After that he vanishes until 1638, when he was at Pavia, and 1639, when he was evidently at Bologna.[13]   Two years later he seems to have been at Perugia, and in 1642 at Bologna.[14]

Once more in his old age he set out for Paris, arriving there some time in 1643.[15]   It has generally been thought that this visit was of short duration, but it seems probable that there he joined the famous company of 1644 and

[1] Bevilacqua, xxiv, 130–131. *Cf.* Rasi, i, 124.   [2] Bevilacqua, xxiv, 132.   [3] *Id.*, xxiv, 132–133.
[4] A. Bartoli says he was still at Prague in 1630 (p. cxliii), but gives no proof.
[5] F. Bartoli, i, 23; Bevilacqua, xxiv, 136.   [6] Bevilacqua, xxiv, 137.
[7] *Id.*, xxiv, 138.   [8] *Id.*, xxiv, 139.   [9] *Id.*, xxiv, 140–141.
[10] *Id.*, xxiv, 141–142.   [11] *Id.*, xxiv, 142–143. *Cf.* Rasi, i, 124; A. Bartoli, p. cxliii.
[12] Rasi, i, 124.   [13] Bevilacqua, xxiv, 143.   [14] *Id.*, xxiv, 146.
[15] Baschet, p. 320.

remained at the French capital for three or four years.[1] There, at any rate, he published various books—*Le Lagrime : diuoto componimento* (1643), *L'Ossequio alla Maestà Clementissima, e Realissima della Regina Anna* (1643), *Il Vincente* (1644), *Le Vittorie, prodigo felice* (1644)—besides leaving behind him a manuscript, *La Ferinda*, dated March 28, 1647.

No doubt he now left the stage. Nothing is heard of him until March 19, 1652, when he wrote a rather pathetic letter to Mantua, describing himself as a " servant grown old in Mantuan service." [2] It was two years later he died.

With him vanished the famous company of the Fedeli. That troupe had certainly done its best work in the first quarter of the seventeenth century, and no doubt drifted, like its master, slowly into a vague decrepitude.

(xiv) THE COMPANIES: (6) THE LATER MANTUAN TROUPES AND THE TROUPES OF PARMA AND MODENA

The Dukes of Mantua continued throughout the whole of this period to patronize the players, and from 1648 onward we have records of unnamed companies (or of an unnamed company) supported by them. On December 1, 1648, a certain Francesco Zbrazin *Gabinetto* was writing from Florence to Niccolò Zecca, or Zecco *Bertolino*, at Piacenza, from which it appears that both were in the Ducal company.[3] The latter is said by Adolfo Bartoli [4] to have been in the Fedeli about 1605, but this seems exceedingly doubtful. He was a " young man " when Barbieri published his *Supplica* in 1634 ; nearly all the documents which deal with him are later than 1640 ; and he was still acting in April 1670.[5]

A few years later, on July 28, 1674, Francesco Allori *Valerio* is found at the head of a company, then at Padua, but apparently belonging to Mantua. He seems then to have been intending to go to the latter city by way of Vicenza.[6] On March 16 of the following year Allori was at Venice, and he stayed there till April 20 with Carlo Palma *Truffaldino*, Federico Beretta *Capitano*, and Giovan Battista Turri *Pantalone*.[7] The chief point of interest about this troupe seems to be its harmonious unity. In a letter of Palma's Beretta is said to be " an actor verily good in the *Capitano s* part," while *Ortensia* (Allori's wife) is described as " a good actress." The same month Allori himself drew the Duke's attention to the fact that there was " the very best harmony " among his players.[8]

After 1682 Allori too disappears, and nothing is heard of the Mantuan company until the nineties of the century, when Bartolomeo Falconi *Trapolino* is recorded as a " servant " of the Duke [9] in 1690 and 1694.

Of much greater importance during these years were the troupes belonging to Parma and Modena. The first that is heard of the former is a document which tells of the worries incident upon one of those eternal quarrels which were ever breaking out among the actors. In February 1638 Iacopo Antonio Fidenzi *Cintio*, evidently the captain of the company, sent a piteous appeal from Rome,[10] explaining how *Brighella, Leandro,*[11] *Pantalone* (Orazio Carpiani), and *Leandro's* wife have formed a group within the company and are demanding special privileges. Poor *Cintio* is greeted by *Brighella* with such " insults and threats " that he is " forced to reply "—but, he

[1] E. Picot, *Gli ultimi anni di G. B. Andreini in Francia* (*Rassegna bibliografica della letteratura italiana*, ix (1901), 61–67).
[2] Bevilacqua, xxiv, 149–150.   [3] Rasi, iii, 750–751.   [4] A. Bartoli, p. cxxxix.
[5] For visits of the Mantuan company to Padua in 1662 and 1670 see B. Brunelli, p. 106.
[6] Rasi, i, 32.   [7] *Id.*, i, 33–34; iii, 210.
[8] It is interesting to note that in this letter he states that he will keep his company " far from Milan, for that city is the ruin of actors."
[9] Rasi, ii, 858.   [10] *Id.*, ii, 880–881.
[11] Who cannot be B. Ricci, as Rasi suggests; Ricci died in 1620.

hastens to add, " not in an insulting manner." The two opponents are rapidly losing their tempers, when *Beltrame* (N. Barbieri) hurries up and cries, " Be quiet, *Cintio*; it is enough that *Brighella* has so miserably lost his sense of decency." *Aurelia* (Brigida Bianchi), *Leonora* (L. Castiglioni), *Trappolino* (G. B. Fiorillo), *Buffetto* (C. Cantù), *Bagolino*, and *Beatrice* (wife of Fiorillo) are all dragged into the *mêlée*, and soon Fidenzi hardly knows where he stands.

How this was settled is not told us, and for the next record of the Parmesan actors we have to go on to April 29, 1646, when we find N. Zecca *Bertolino* in this company, and then waiting for C. Cantù.[1] As Cantù had married Isabella Franchini-Biancolelli *Colombina* in 1645, it is probable that she too was in Parmesan service. It seems that, immediately after this date, part of the company, including Cantù and his wife, joined or formed a troupe serving the Duke of Modena. At any rate, five months later, on September 3, 1646, O. Carpiani is writing to tell of the disasters which have befallen his companions, but does not mention Cantù, who, in January 1647, is found among the Modenese actors. In this letter Carpiani tells that the *Capitano* is dead, *Armellina* has just had a child, and *Trappolino* (G. B. Fiorillo) is ill; the other actors he mentions are G. Chiesa *Violone*, *Aurelia* (B. Bianchi), *Beatrice* (Fiorillo's wife), and G. A. Fidenzi *Cintio*.[2] It is no wonder that the Duke wished to see some changes in the composition of the troupe. Little, however, is known of its fortunes. In 1655 we find a certain Capellino acting *Pantalone*,[3] and possibly the *Dottore* of that year was a certain Giarattoni.[4] Agostino Grisanti took the *amoroso* as *Mario* when the company was at Livorno in 1659,[5] but who his companions were cannot be ascertained; and two years later G. A. Lolli is found as the *Dottore*.[6]

During the next decade it seems that there was a tentative fusion of the old Parma and the Modena companies. In 1664 a certain Fabrizio of Naples proposed to bring his company under the *ægis* of the former. This company included *Angiola*, *Flaminia* (M. Fiala) or *Lucinda*, *Auretta* (daughter of *Angiola*), *Colombina* (probably I. Franchini), *Leandro* (G. Caccia), *Capitano* (G. Fiala), *Lucindo* (D'Odoardo), *Leonardo*, *Pantalone*, *Dottore* (G. Milanta), *Bagolino* (possibly C. Cantù under another name), and *Volpino* (G. C. Barbieri).[7] Not all these were then in one group; but, we are informed, all were ready to enter the Parmesan service. Whether any temporary alteration in allegiance took place cannot be ascertained; all other records show the Fialas faithful to Modena, although A. Grisanti was certainly acting with Marzia Fiala in August 1664.[8]

Few other records remain of the Parmesan company. In 1677 Antonia Isola *Lavinia* was *prima donna*,[9] and the following year the Duke refused to allow her and her husband *Lelio* (A. Torri) to join the actors who were going to London.[10] Some years later, in 1682, F. Calderoni *Silvio* and his wife *Flaminia* belonged to Parma,[11] but Calderoni's fortunes were later to be associated with other lands than Italy. From 1687 to 1691 he, with a troupe consisting of D. Bononcini *Brighella*, B. Bonifaci, A. Bonifaci, A. Broglia *Bertolino*, A. Calderoni, F. Balletti, G. Balletti, V. D'Orsi, T. D'Orsi, and D. Orsatti, played with some considerable success in the neighbourhood of Munich.[12]

Clearly, the troupes of Parma and of Modena were closely united, and for some years their activities can hardly be dissociated. The first we hear of the latter is in a letter of Giulio Cesare Torri *Zacagnino*, dated from Rome on January 16, 1647, in which he refers to *Buffetto* (C. Cantù), *Flaminio* (Marco Napolioni), *Dottore*, *Pantalone* (possibly Albani), and *Ottavio* (G. A. Zanotti).[13]

---

[1] E. Bocchia, *La Drammatica in Parma* (Parma, 1913), p. 113.
[2] *Id.*, p. 117.
[3] Rasi, ii, 585.
[4] *Id.*, ii, 1020.
[5] *Id.*, ii, 1042. He had been acting with C. Cantù at Venice already in 1651 (see *infra*, p. 370).
[6] *Id.*, iii, 30. He was then asking to join the Modena troupe.
[7] Rasi, ii, 854–855; Bocchia, p. 121.
[8] Rasi, ii, 1042.
[9] *Id.*, ii, 1061.
[10] *Id.*, ii, 1061.
[11] Bocchia, p. 123.
[12] Rasi, ii, 544–545. They returned in 1691 to Mantua, toured through Italy (1692–93 Naples and Livorno), went thence to Brussels, and by the end of the century were at Vienna.
[13] *Id.*, iii, 587.

On February 22 Cantù wrote a letter from that city,[1] and on the 27th a joint note was penned by Zanotti, Cantù, and Napolioni.[2] By April the usual storms were agitating the troupe. Cantù, still in Rome, was complaining then that *Flaminio* had " suborned " *Pantalone* and *Zacagnino*, and had gone off to play with *Delia*, *Policinella*, *Giangurgolo*, " and other Neapolitan actors." [3] Apparently a *Dottore*, *Beatrice*, and *Angiolina* [4] then belonged to the company. Napolioni was back in Rome by 1648,[5] but the Modenese actors are not found again until 1650–51. The Marchese Obizzi of Padua was then endeavouring to get a company under his patronage, and had commissioned Bernardino Coris *Silvio* to collect the actors, among whom figured one, E. Lolli *Fichetto*, who belonged to the Modena troupe and about whom various letters were written.[6] By August 10, 1651, this company consisted of G. A. Zanotti *Ottavio*, G. Bendinelli *Valerio*, E. Lolli *Fichetto*, B. Coris *Silvio*, his wife *Florinda*, G. Albani *Pantalone*, D. Locatelli *Trivellino*, G. A. Fiala *Capitano*, I. Biancolelli-Franchini *Colombina*, E. Nelli *Dottore*, and his wife *Angiola*. An interesting series of letters concerns these players in the spring of 1651. At the end of March they were at Bologna and had been invited to pay a visit to Padua, but Angiola Nelli, evidently because of the fact that a rival *Armellina* was in the latter city, would not go. Her husband backed her up in a letter of April 14, declaring that " the town was divided into two factions." The Paduan authorities now started to bombard the actors with commands and entreaties,[7] to which came a strange answer in the shape of a testament signed by six of the actors.[8] This document runs as follows :

IN THE NAME OF GOD
on the 15th day of April, 1651, in Bologna.

We, the undersigned actors, testify that three letters addressed to our companion *Fichetto* [Eustacio Lolli] have arrived from Padua. These were written by gentlemen of that city and incited us not to go to play there, otherwise we should encounter grave dangers, since the city is divided in its praise of our company and of *Armellina's*. So they advise us not to go there, so as not to risk the life of one of our players. These three letters have been taken back by a Bolognese gentleman who has ordered us not to reveal either his name or those of the letter-writers. In testimony of which we have all subscribed to affirm that this is the truth, and not a fiction either of Signora *Angiolina* or of the *Dottore*, her husband, etc.

> I ISABELLA FRANCHINI called *Colombina* affirm as above
> I BERNARDO CORIS called *Silvio* actor affirm as above
> I EUSTACHIO LOLLI *Fichetto* affirm as above
> I GIO. ANDREA ZANOTTI called *Ottavio* affirm, etc.
> I GIUSEPPE ALBANI called *Pantalone* affirm
> I GIACINTO BENDINELLI called *Val°* affirm, etc.

The Duke of Modena, however, did not listen to their prayers ; and on April 30 ordered the actors to be in Padua within the next few weeks. No doubt they went there, and in May moved on to Milan.[9] At the beginning of August a petition addressed to Verona [10] adds to those who signed the earlier " testimony " the names of D. Locatelli *Trivellino*, G. B. Fiala *Capitano*, and E. Nelli, who was both a *Zanni* and a *Dottore*. The last-mentioned was still at Verona on September 8, when he wrote to the Modena Court saying that he must take his wife *Angiolina* to Venice and that he had much of which to complain about in the Parma troupe under Carlo Cantù (*Brighella*) and Agostino Grisanti (*Mario*), who, " not content with having worn out the towns we had to go to,

---

[1] Rasi, ii, 571. See some quotations from it *supra*, p. 284. The company included *Colombina* (I. Franchini), *Zacagnino*, *Flaminio*, *Dottore*, *Olimpia*, and *Angela*. See also the letters of March 6, 1647 (*id.*, ii, 581), March 9 (*id.*, ii, 582), and March 29 (*id.*, ii, 582–583).
[2] *Id.*, iii, 742.   [3] *Id.*, ii, letter reproduced in facsimile opposite p. 578.
[4] The last two evidently came with Cantù from the Parmesan troupe.
[5] *Id.*, iii, 175.   [6] See B. Brunelli, pp. 88–90.
[7] For all this correspondence (letters of Zanotti, March 23, April 10 and 17; of Angiola Nelli, April 12; of Ercole Nelli, April 12 and 17; of the Paduan authorities, April 12, 13, 14, and 30) see B. Brunelli, pp. 91–93, 95.
[8] Rasi, iii, 743, 29; B. Brunelli, p. 94.   [9] Rasi, iii, 744.   [10] *Id.*, ii, 876.

are trying now to prevent us playing our own works (which are mine) at Venice." [1]   At the beginning of February the company had returned to Modena, and a correspondent was giving some entertaining news of them :

> Last night the actors, in the concluding act of their comedy, came a little to blows.   Off stage *Trivellino* and *Ottavio* quarrelled, and they say that *Trivellino* punched *Ottavio*.   Immediately afterwards *Trivellino* came on the stage without his mask and asked pardon of his Highness, who was among the spectators. [2]

For his fault *Trivellino* was bound with ropes in the Piazza, but was soon released.   As for *Ottavio*, he

> has gone into the Carmine in hiding, for fear of worse happening ; but his Highness is angry with him. Above all, a noble Venetian who was here is in a rage at him.   This Venetian had followed *Lucilla*, wife of *Trivellino*, with whom he is passionately enamoured.   He has left Modena suddenly with very bad feelings toward *Ottavio*.

So *Trivellino's* blow seems to have been justified.   *Lucilla* and *Ottavio* had been carrying their love affairs out of the comedy.

For some years we lose sight of these players.   Nelli is vaguely heard of in April 1654, [3] and there are documents which note the appearance of this or that actor at various towns during this decade.   On March 6, 1655, Battista Ventura was being engaged as *Pantalone*, [4] and in April 1658 an amateur, none other than Giovanni Raparelli, who had been Criminal Chancellor at Perugia, joined the company as *Orazio*. [5]   Apparently this gentleman had fallen in love with an actress *Angiola* and married her in January 1658.   Three months later he found his wife unfaithful to him ; whereupon there started scenes of recrimination and threats.   *Angiola* and her mother now determined to get rid of this encumbrance and got the company to perform a play called *Gli Infelici amori della Regina d' Inghilterra* (*The Unhappy Loves of the Queen of England*), in which *Orazio* had to appear with firearms.   The two women then complained to the police that *Orazio* was threatening their lives and got the wretched man arrested with the pistol upon him.   A pretty story of play, passion, and intrigue.

A few years later Zanotti appeared in Paris, and probably many changes were being made in the Modena troupe, old actors leaving and new actors joining.   In 1670 a union, perhaps temporary, fused these players with the troupe of Niccolò Zecca at Mantua ; [6] and in 1674 G. A. Fiala is to be found at Naples, impoverished and praying the Duke to send him the means whereby he may bring back the company to Modena. [7]   A document of the following year gives a partial list of the company. [8]   This includes, besides G. A. Fiala and his wife Marta Fiala *Flaminia*, Costantino Costantini *Gradelino*, Domenica Costantini *Corallina*, Teodora Areliari *Vittoria*, L. Areliari *Mario*, Antonio Riccoboni *Pantalone*, Giuseppe Orlandi *Dottore*, G. A. Cimadori *Finocchio*, Bernardo Narisi *Orazio*, and Domenico Pannini, or Parrino, *Florindo*. [9]   By 1677, possibly before, Teresa, wife of G. B. Costantini, known on the stage as *Diana*, was in the troupe, [10] which was at Genoa in June [11] and at Mantua in August. [12]   At this time there seems to have arisen trouble over some trunks belonging to *Florindo* (Parrini), who was writing distractedly to Modena on October 21, 1678 :

> My bitter fate brings me to extremity ; after such a long series of misfortunes and ill-haps it is more bitter than can ever be expressed.   On Wednesday at night, accompanied by five armed men—three of the civic guard and two of my host's house—I was suddenly led out of Mantua, where I was forced to leave the rest of my few belongings.

[1] Rasi, iii, 181–182.   [2] *Id.*, iii, 28.   [3] *Id.*, iii, 182.   [4] *Id.*, iii, 628.
[5] *Id.*, iii, 325.   [6] *Id.*, iii, 752.   [7] *Id.*, ii, 876.
[8] A. Gandini, *Cronistoria de' teatri di Modena* (Modena, 1873).   *Cf.* Rasi, i, 199–200; A. Bartoli, p. cl.
[9] This actor was lent to Mantua in 1676 and was sent back in March 1677 (Rasi, iii, 220).
[10] Rasi, ii, 723.   [11] *Id.*, iii, 220.   [12] *Id.*, iii, 221.

If G. A. Lolli *Dottore* is to be believed, *Florindo* deserved the ill-treatment of which he complained.[1] It was in this year that the Duke of Modena was aiding in the arrangements for dispatching a company of Italian players to England. These were captained by Tiberio Fiorilli *Scaramuccia*, who had already been in London in 1673 and 1675,[2] but included members of the Ducal troupe. In November 1678 they arrived, their goods comprising six portmanteaus, two great baskets, and twenty-two trunks;[3] they left in February 1679. Apparently little success met their efforts, if we are to judge by a letter sent from London on February 17, 1679, by G. A. Lolli:

> The supreme goodness of her Royal Highness the Duchess of York . . . has secured for us the licence we so much desired. After having been for three months unprofitably at this Royal Court this is of the greateſt import for us, since we have been able to present only about six plays, with very little success— that is not much use. It is certainly true that, through recourse had to our Moſt Serene Proteĉtress and Patron, we had twice 150 pieces and once 30 pieces; a draught that served not to assuage, but to excite ſtill more the thirſt of this dropsical body of a company. Hardly had the branches of the old debt been lopped off than they ſtarted to grow once more in such profusion that, moved again by pity, the magic hand of her Royal Highness has found the means of rooting up this unprofitable plant. Hence, sowing in quantity sufficient silver salt on the fertile ground of our poverty, she has now made it barren. We are, then, rich, for the company has no debts—an infirmity that would have reduced us almoſt to extremities if it had not been cured by golden syrups, an illness so terrible that to treat it but once requires the use of 800 pieces. Convalescent, then, without other doĉtor's licence, we wish, so please God, to change the air, and, if the troubles which I have had from this ill-regulated crowd of aĉtors don't cause a relapse in me, I hope to return in good health to see the Panaro once more, when I shall have finished looking at the horrid Thames. I await then a favouring south wind to take me off as quickly as may be from these shores. Meanwhile I pray you anew not to forget me and what I wrote you in my laſt letter. My patience is gone, and I cannot go on further—either a change in the company or liberty.[4]

The south wind came, and on May 15, 1679, Lolli was writing from Lyon, evidently on his way back to Italy, declaring that he "would not wish an enemy" of his "in this company, because of the continual dissensions that surge in it."[5] We may presume that nearly the whole of the Modena company was with Lolli. Riccoboni *Pantalone* was certainly there,[6] although a number of the others remained in Italy. In Oĉtober 1678, as we have seen, D. A. Parrino *Florindo* was in trouble, and he was probably the "Antonio" of whom Anna Maria Millita *Cintia* was writing to the Duke from Mantua on December 16 of that year. "I beg you," she says,

> I beg you to pardon my boldness in writing to your Highness. The reason I do so is the imprisonment of Signor *Antonio*; he is kept secretly in much danger of his life. While he was ill I pawned everything I had, and now while he is in prison I have sold everything. I don't know what to do to keep him alive there, and on that account I am informing your Highness of the labyrinth in which we both ſtand.[7]

Evidently those who ſtayed behind had even worse times than poor Lolli, far from Italian skies by the shores of the "horrid Thames."

Parrino, however, escaped. In June 1680 he left Modena, so probably the Duke had secured his release, and thence travelled to Naples, where he seems to have remained for some years.[8] About this time the company was ſtrengthened by the entry of Carlo Schiavi *Cintio*[9] in 1679 and of Giuseppe Tortoriti *Pasquariello*, or *Scaramuccia*, in 1681.[10] A document of this year gives a full liſt of the company, which included D. A. Parrino *Florindo*, B. Narici *Orazio*, G. Fiala *Capitano*, G. Caccia (?) *Leandro*, G. B. Coſtantini *Cintio*, Marzia Fiala *Flaminia*, Teresa Coſtantini *Diana*, Isabella Servilli (?) *Eulalia*, Domenica Coſtantini *Corallina*, A. Riccoboni *Pantalone*, G. Orlandi *Dottore*,

---

[1] Rasi, iii, 220–221. [2] See *infra*, p. 344.
[3] *Calendar of State Papers: Treasury Books (1676–79)*, pp. 1160, 1230. [4] Rasi, iii, 31.
[5] *Id.*, ii, 752. [6] *Id.*, iii, 347. [7] *Id.*, iii, 126.
[8] *Id.*, iii, 222–223. [9] *Id.*, iii, 530. [10] *Id.*, iii, 592.

G. A. Cimador *Finocchio*, C. Costantini *Gradelino*, and G. Tortoriti *Scaramuccia*.[1] Apparently not too much goodwill was to be found among its members, for when the troupe went to Padua in April 1681 the Duke of Modena saw fit to dispatch to the authorities at that city a set of rules which were to be strictly observed by the players.[2]

It appears probable that in 1683 the Modena company was temporarily disbanded. In March of that year the Duke of Mantua asked for T. Costantini *Diana* and C. Costantini *Gradelino*,[3] and from the terms of his request the Modena troupe seems to have been breaking up. It was certainly still in existence in 1684, when Bernardo Narici *Orazio* wrote to the Duke detailing the misfortunes of himself and his companions. *Corallina* (D. Costantini) was ill at Verona, and her daughter would not leave her. *Diana* (T. Costantini) has not put in an appearance, and *Cintio* (G. B. Costantini) would not act without her.[4] But we hear no more of these players until 1686, when possibly they were reconstituted. Here a full list is provided from two independent sources. The first of these is given in a document which shows the Modena company at Sassuolo.[5] Fiala and his wife—*Capitano* and *Flaminia*—are here, as well as Bernardo Narici *Orazio*, A. Riccoboni *Pantalone*, G. A. Lolli *Dottore*, Gaetano Caccia *Leandro*, Domenico Bononcini *Campana*, Anna Marcucci *Angiola*, Maddalena Francesca Paruti *Prinpinella*, and Giovan Battista Paruti *Finocchio*.[6] The second list, which is provided in a letter of Martia Fiala, supplements this considerably.[7] From it we learn that *Angiola* was the daughter of Martia Fiala, and that Lolli had a companion doctor, who was Giovan Battista Paghetti. *Trivellino* seems to be the *Arlecchino* of the second list, but, even allowing for that, we find three additions, *Colombina*, *Cintio*, and *Buffetto*, while *Campana* does not appear at all. Since, however, Bononcini is elsewhere noted as a *Brighella*, and as *Brighella* and *Buffetto* are one, we may assume that he took these parts. Other lists of the company when at Sassuolo from 1687 to 1689 are also preserved,[8] and from them we may guess that either changes were being made in the composition of the troupe or that that troupe was playing in two detachments. The first included two *amorose*, *Flaminia* (M. Fiala) and *Angiola* (A. Marcucci); two *amorosi*, *Silvio* and *Mario* (L. Archiari, or Rechiari); *Pantalone* (A. Riccoboni); two Zanni, *Trappola* and *Bertolino*; as well as three persons whose identity is doubtful—Isabella Berza, *Spinetta*, and Celio Becho. Later in the year *Truffaldino* (M. A. Zanetti), *Capitan Sbrana Leoni* (G. Fiala), and *Orazio* (B. Narici) joined the others. The following year not only were the Fialas absent when the company was at Sassuolo, but many new characters made their appearance. *Lavinia* (Antonia Torri) and *Vittoria* (Teodora Archiari, or Rechiari) were then playing *prima amorosa* in turns, with Lucinda Nadasti as *seconda amorosa*. Similarly *Leandro* (Gaetano Caccia) and Lucca Archiari, or Rechiari (*Mario*), were sharing the part of *primo amoroso*, with *Lelio* (A. Torri) as second Lover. The Fantesca was *Argentina* (G. Gardellini), and the male servant Giorgio Archiari. The *Pantalone* was A. Riccoboni, and the *Dottore* was A. A. Muzio. The first Zanni was *Guaretto*, or *Guazetto*, and the second *Truffaldino* (M. A. Zanetti). Finally we reach the list of 1689 where *Lavinia* (A. Torri) and *Leonora* (Angiola Isola) are found as *prima donna* and *Aurelia* (Colomba Coppa) as second, with *Virginio* (Giuseppe Coppa) and *Lelio* (A. Torri) as the men Lovers. *Argentina* (G. Gardellini) and *Armellina* (Maddalena Sacchi) were evidently servants; *Coviello* (Gennaro Sacchi), *Pantalone* (A. Riccoboni), and *Dottore* (Francesco Matterazzi) were the old men, and *Finocchio* (Carlo Zagnoli) and *Pasquino* (Gio. Battista Trezzi) were the Zanni.[9]

These Sassuolan lists may be supplemented by information from a variety of other sources. A petition to Modena dated 1686 and signed by *Truffaldino* is recorded by Rasi,[10] and the company's

[1] B. Brunelli, *op. cit.*, p. 110. [2] *Id.*, pp. 108–109. [3] Rasi, ii, 723. [4] *Id.*, iii, 179.
[5] N. Cionini, *Teatro e arti in Sassuolo* (Modena, 1902), pp. 38–40. They were also at Padua this year; *cf.* B. Brunelli, p. 110.
[6] The last two joined the company on July 18, 1686. [7] Rasi, ii, 879. [8] N. Cionini, p. 40.
[9] *Id.*, p. 42. [10] Rasi, iii, 730.

wanderings in that year through Padua, Venice, and Turin can be easily traced.[1] In 1687 C. Costantini left for Paris, and the rearrangements made necessary by his departure are obvious in the lists. On May 19, 1687, the Fialas, G. Caccia, and B. Narici were given special awards at Modena, and on the 23rd some money was handed over to Martia Fiala to be granted to *Gabionetto*, his wife, and *Florindo*.[2] The following month the company was at Cremona, and in October and December at Lodi.[3] At this time Fiala left the troupe, and shortly after Coppa took control,[4] when, too, Antonia, or Angiola, Isola (*Lavinia*) joined the Modenese actors.[5]

During the summer of 1689 the company was at Finale and Modena,[6] whence in the autumn they set out on a tour which seems to have been peculiarly disastrous. On August 10, 1690, we find the whole group writing to " his most Serene Highness " :

> Already twenty days have passed since the company of actors, most humble servants of your most Serene Highness, arrived at Brescia. So little luck has it had that one may speak rather of disaster ; it is sinking into a deplorable misery, while our receipts are not sufficient to pay for our lodgings. Our present position (and what is worse the hopelessness of bettering it at this time of the year) after a costly journey from Genoa to this town, with a very heavy debt owed by the company for the escort, forces us to put our miseries before your Highness, certain as we are that you will look upon us with the eyes of your most benign compassion, and that you will not leave us without that succour, lacking which it will be impossible for us to leave this city without pawning our properties. . . . Humbly do we beg you to display at so urgent need those acts of your generosity with which you have ever aided your servants, assuring you that your Highness would not have been troubled with our supplications had not necessity forced us.[7]

This letter is signed by, or on behalf of, Anna Arcagiati *Rosaura*, Gaetano Caccia *Leandro*, Giuseppe Coppa *Virginio*, Coppa *Aurelia*, Gennaro Sacchi *Coviello Cardocchia*, M. Sacchi *Armellina*, Galeazzo Savorini *Dottore*, Marco Antonio Zanetti *Truffaldino*, Carlo Zagnoli *Finocchio*, and Antonio Riccoboni *Pantalone*. From another document it is known that the disastrous tour embraced the cities of Pescia, Camajore, Lucca, Livorno, and Florence.[8]

Whether aid came to them we do not know, but three months later, on November 20, Gennaro Sacchi was writing to the Duke from Reggio complaining that the company was in the hands of the inhabitants of the Ghetto and praying " to be released from the clutches of Hebraism." [9]

On April 9, 1691, M. A. Zanetti *Truffaldino* was writing to the Duke from Bologna, making it plain that the company had been summoned to Vicenza and Verona after Easter.[10] September 3 found the Coppas at Sassuolo,[11] and December 5 similarly found Lucca Rechiari, or Archiari, now signing himself *Leandro*, at Arezzo.[12] In April 1692 Rechiari was at Rome, preparing evidently to go to Naples ; in June 1693 at Perugia, in October at Fermo, in December at Chieti, and during the Carnival of 1694 at Rome again.[13] Before January 1693 Gennaro Sacchi, or Sacco, had abandoned the troupe,[14] and before October 1694, when the actors were at Orvieto, M. A. Zanetti seems to have become their chief.[15] From this time on the records grow scarcer. Many changes, evidently, had been made by 1697, when, in April, an order was made to arrest Rinaldo Rosa *Pantalone* and Giuseppe Sontra or Sondra *Flaminio*—both belonging to Modena.[16] The following year the latter was lent to the Prince of Tuscany by the Duke.[17] Save for a vague reference to a Diana Averara who was sent to join the company in March 1698 [18] and a piteous letter from Galeazzo

---

[1] *Cf.* Rasi, iii, 334.   [2] *Id.*, ii, 877-878.   [3] *Id.*, ii, 878.
[4] The lists of 1688 and 1689 may be compared with those given in Rasi, iii, 588-589.   [5] *Id.*, ii, 1061.
[6] *Id.*, iii, 348.   [7] *Id.*, ii, 694.   [8] *Id.*, iii, 508. This was by February 18, 1690.
[9] *Id.*, iii, 455.   [10] *Id.*, iii, 731.
[11] *Id.*, ii, 694. On July 20 of this year the old *Pantalone* of the troupe (G. Gabbrielli) wrote to the Duke asking for some assistance "in memory of his part " (*id.*, ii, 967). A list of the company is provided when they went to Padua in 1691. It then included A. Arcagiati *Rosaura*, G. Caccia *Leandro*, G. Coppa *Virginio*, C. Coppa *Aurelia*, G. Sacchi *Coviello*, M. Sacchi *Armellina*, G. Savorini *Dottore*, M. A. Zanetti *Truffaldino*, C. Zagnoli *Finocchio*, A. Riccoboni *Pantalone* (see B. Brunelli, p. 111).
[12] Rasi, iii, 334.   [13] *Id.*, iii, 334-335.   [14] *Id.*, iii, 456.   [15] *Id.*, iii, 731.
[16] *Id.*, iii, 408, 544.   [17] *Id.*, iii, 544.   [18] *Id.*, ii, 762.

Savorini *Dottore* dated from Bologna on October 1, 1699, there is little more to record of their activities. Perhaps it is not unfitting to take leave of them with this last appeal to the " munificence " of the Ducal house.

Fig. 222. GANDOLIN

Seventeenth-century French print by J. Falck, published by Le Blond. Exemplar in the Bibliothèque Nationale, Paris (Cabinet des Estampes, Tb 34b).

Photo Giraudon

(xv) THE COMPANIES: (7) THE ITALIAN COMEDIANS IN FRANCE

This survey of the chief companies of Italian actors from the mid-sixteenth century to the end of the seventeenth would not be complete without a record of the activities of those players who found their way to Paris and beyond in the later years. The first visits of the Italians have already been chronicled ; now must be taken up the tale from 1639 onward.

In 1639 a troupe including Margherita Bartolazzi, Brigida Bianchi *Aurelia*, Giuseppe Bianchi *Capitano Spezzaferro* (*Aurelia's* father), and Giulia Gabbrielli *Diana* were in Paris, leaving that city in 1641.[1] The chief members of this group were also in the " Mazarin company " which returned

---

[1] A. Bartoli, p. cxliii; Rasi, under the various actors.

342

to France in 1644–45. Giuseppe and Brigida Bianchi were there, the latter perhaps already the wife of N. Romagnesi *Orazio* ; so, too, were Margherita Bartolazzi, one Bonnetti, and probably Carlo Cantù *Buffetto*, Giulia Gabbrielli *Diana*, Luisa Gabbrielli-Locatelli *Lucilla*, and Domenico Locatelli *Trivellino*,[1] her husband. Evidently at this time also Tiberio Fiorilli *Scaramuccia* was in Paris, no doubt in this very company.[2] To these may be added Giovan Battista Andreini *Lelio*, Giovan Battista Turi *Pantalone*,[3] and A. Agostino Lolli *Dottore*.[4] Some of these, no doubt, remained for several years in the French capital ; the most famous of them all, Fiorilli, was a continual bird of passage, flying, as the swallow does, lightly to the south and back again. Fiorilli, indeed, may have been with the company of 1639–41. On the authority of Gueullette, translator of the Biancolelli manuscript, it is said that once this actor and Brigida Bianchi entered the room of the Dauphin (later Louis XIV) when that Prince was two years old. The child was in a vexatious mood and yelled lustily, as even princes do when they are at that objectionable stage of their career. Fiorilli thereupon asked the Queen to let him take the wailing infant in his arms. This he was allowed to do, and, grimacing with such ingenuity that the child was surprised into silence, he succeeded at length in changing the tears to laughter. The laughter, however, brought with it its own discomforts, which left their material tracks on *Scaramuccia's* hands and clothes. Whereupon the Queen and her ladies laughed heartily, as even queens are known to do.[5]

Of the visit of 1645 certain tangible records exist in the text of *La Finta pazza*, by Giulio Strozzi, which was performed at the Petit-Bourbon with all the splendour of Giacomo Torelli's scenes on November 14, 1645.[6] Two years later most of the Italians, including Fiorilli, left Paris, but some, again including Fiorilli, returned in 1653 and opened their season on August 1 at the Petit-Bourbon.[7] Back again in Italy in 1655,[8] Fiorilli revisited France in 1658, sharing the Petit-Bourbon with no less a person than Molière until the summer of 1659.[9] This was followed by the famous expedition of 1660–61, which finally established the Théâtre Italien at Paris. Its organization seems to have been due to Cardinal Mazarin, who sent an invitation to the company which was then acting at Pavia. Among the actors whom he desired was G. B. Biancolelli *Arlecchino*, and, Biancolelli being then at Vienna under Tabarino, he was ordered to join the rest in Italy.[10] In 1661 the troupe arrived at Paris, and from various sources we can build up a list of its members. G. D. Biancolelli *Arlecchino* has already been mentioned. In addition to him, there were two other Zanni —D. Locatelli *Trivellino* and Tiberio Fiorilli *Scaramuccia*. The *Pantalone* was G. B. Turri and the *Dottore* A. A. Lolli. The latter's wife, Patrizia Adami, played the servant *Diamantina*, and the former's son, Virginio, was for a time the second lover. The first Lover, under the name of *Octavio*, was A. Zanotti, called " le vieux Octave " to distinguish him from another of that name. Other Lovers, *Cintio* and *Valerio*, appeared in the persons of M. A. Romagnesi and Bendinelli. Brigida Bianchi, the widow of N. Romagnesi, was an *amorosa* under the name of *Aurelia*, playing with *Eularia*, Ursula Cortese, who married G. D. Biancolelli in 1662.[11] From this time on the Italians, with, of course, changes in their personnel, remained continuously in Paris. In 1662 Alessandro Chiavarelli *Scapino* and Collalto *Pantalone* made their appearance ;[12] continually new

---

[1] A. Bartoli, p. cxliii; Rasi, ii, 575.   [2] Rasi, ii, 892.

[3] Who seems to have appeared at Paris on August 10, 1653 (*id.*, iii, 605).

[4] Turi and Lolli are cited in the list of the 1645 company given in the Biancolelli manuscript at Paris (i, 52). For Andreini see *supra*, p. 335.

[5] *Cf.* Rasi, ii, 893–894. On the Italian comedians in France see A. Bragaglia, *La Maschera mobile* (Foligno, 1926).

[6] *Explication des decorations du theatre, et les arguments de la piece, qui a pour tiltre, la Folle Supposée, ouurage du Seigneur Giulio Strozzi* (Parigi, 1645). In this " Marguerite Bertolotti " spoke the prologue, and " Louyse Gabrielli Locatelli *Lucille* " took the part of Flora.

[7] Rasi, ii, 894.   [8] *Id.*, ii, 895.

[9] *Id.*, ii, 897. In this time was performed *La Rosavre Imperatrice de Constantinople*, the *Argument* of which was published at Paris in 1658. This was the work of Domenico Locatelli.

[10] Biancolelli manuscript, i, 80.

[11] This list is based mainly on the Biancolelli manuscript, i, 80. See also Campardon, i, xvi, and Rasi, ii, 898.

[12] At least, according to A. Bartoli (p. cxlvii).

actors were making their *débuts*; and continually men like Fiorilli were going and returning. By 1664 Fiorilli's wife, *Mariette*, had joined them; in 1673, on February 4, appeared Giuseppe Geratoni as *Pierrot*,[1] and in 1675 Giovanni Gherardi as *Flautino*.[2]

Interesting to us is the visit made by some of these actors to London in 1673. On April 21 a warrant to admit their properties was made by order of King Charles.[3] Evidently they acted all through the summer. On September 4 and 6 gifts of medals, chains of gold, and silver plate were made to " Scaramouchi and Harlekin," with others of their company.[4] This reference proves that one of the actors was Fiorilli and the other Biancolelli. Apparently the silver plate was weighty enough, for two years later they returned, when they were permitted to use the Great Hall at Court as a public theatre. Marvell on July 24, 1675, was speaking of " Scaramuccio acting daily in . . . Whitehall, and all sorts of people flocking thither, and paying their money as at a common playhouse." [5] One of their shows was seen by Evelyn on September 29 of the same year.[6] One companion of Fiorilli's on this occasion can be traced. This is M. A. Romagnesi *Valerio*, or *Cintio*, whose wife, Elisabetta Giulia della Chiesa, died while the company was in London.[7]

Fig. 223. COMEDIANS ON AN OPEN-AIR STAGE

Watercolour by an unknown artist of the seventeenth century in the Staatliche Bibliothek, Bamberg. The Zanni wears a large red hat, and has a black mask.

Photo Rudolf Hatzold, Magdeburg

In 1685 the composition of the Parisian troupe was as follows: *Dottore*, A. A. Lolli; *Eularia*, U. Cortese; *Aurelia*, B. Bianchi; *Diamantina*, P. Adami-Lolli; *Cintio*, M. A. Romagnesi; *Aurelio*, B. Ranieri; *Scaramuccia*, T. Fiorilli; *Pasquariello*, G. Tortoriti; *Pierrot*, G. Geratoni, and *Mezzetino*, A. Costantini.[8] On October 11, 1683, at a performance of *Arlequin Protée* Catarina Biancolelli made a first appearance as *Colombina* and Francesca Maria Apollina Biancolelli as *Isabella*.[9] Five years later, on August 2, 1688, a

---

[1] Campardon, i, 245.   [2] *Id.*, i, 240.   [3] *Calendar of State Papers: Treasury Books* (1672-75), p. 119.
[4] Public Record Office, L.C. 5/140, pp. 328, 329. They left England later in September (see *A History of Restoration Drama*, p. 238).
[5] Grosart's edition, ii, 467.   [6] *Diary*, under that date.
[7] Biancolelli manuscript, i, 99. This is evidently the source of Rasi's statement at iii, 394.
[8] Biancolelli manuscript, i, 122.
[9] *Ibid.*, i, 123. Cf. Rasi, i, 437. These took the place of *Diamantina* and *Aurelia*. In 1685 M. Fracanzani *Pulcinella* joined the company (*id.*, ii, 939).

terrible blow befell the Italian theatre. "Dominique," Domenico Biancolelli *Arlecchino*, died. For one whole month the doors of the Théâtre Italien were dismally closed. When they reopened there were many changes, and changes followed in succeeding years. The new *Arlecchino* was Evaristo Gherardi,[1] *Ottavio* was G. B. Costantini, *Marinetta* was Angelica Toscano, the wife of Tortoriti, *Leandro* was C. V. Romagnesi,[2] while M. A. Romagnesi abandoned the *amorosi* and assumed the guise of the *Dottore*. Many records of their activities will be found in Campardon's

Fig. 224. A COMMEDIA DELL' ARTE SCENE

Painting attributed to F. Porbus (sixteenth century) in the possession of Mme Wenner Gren, Stockholm. This is one of the earliest pictorial representations, if not the earliest, of the *commedia dell' arte*.

collection of documents, but these need not concern us here. The end of an epoch came in 1697. For some years the Italians had been complained of because of their "indecencies," their scurrilities, and their satire, but so far they had escaped. In May 1697, however, they went a step too far. There was much talk in Paris of a book called *La fausse Prude*, published in Holland, which, it was said, was an attack on Mme de Maintenon. Now the Italian actors had then in preparation a play by de Fatouville entitled in Italian *La Finta matrigna*, and boldly they announced it as *La fausse Prude*. Retribution came swiftly. On May 13 an order came to the police:

> The King has dismissed his Italian actors; his Majesty commands me to write to you, ordering you to shut up their theatre to-morrow for good.

On the following day, accordingly, seals were set on all the doors of the playhouse, and the

[1] *Début*, October 1, 1689.   [2] *Début*, August 24, 1694.

players [1] departed sorrowfully with their belongings.[2] For years Paris knew not the merry laughter which once arose from *Arlecchino's* posturing and the *Dottore's* blundering accents.

(xvi) CONCLUSION

These studies in the popular drama have carried us far—carried us almost from ancient Egypt down to the time when a great and wonderful literary drama was, through the inspiration of the Renascence, being born in Western Europe. To that literary drama the popular improvised comedy contributed not a little. Tiberio Fiorilli was assuredly the "master of Molière," and concerning the influence generally of the *commedia dell' arte* upon the author of *Tartuffe* there can remain not the slightest doubt.[3] Molière's companions, too, mingled freely with the Italians, and were not averse from collaborating with them in their efforts. The account of those half-improvised, half-written comedies which figure in Gherardi's *Le Théâtre italien* forms a not unimportant chapter in the history of French dramatic activities.[4] Regnard, Noland de Fatouville, Dufresny, Brugière de Barante, Palaprat—they all were closely associated with the Italian comedians, and, in collaborating with them, drew inspiration from their stock characters, themes, and treatment.[5]

To England also the Italians came. Drusiano Martinelli and his wife Angelica were certainly known at London and Nottingham, and there is reason to believe that others [6] at a later period paid their touring visits to English shores. And what travelled Londoner was ignorant of their plays on the Continent? Did not most of them find something on the Italian stage which appealed to them because of its essential polish and charm? Perhaps, if we were to seek a little deeper into this sphere of comparative theatre study, we should find that the Elizabethan stage owed much more than we now suspect to those professional comedians of the Continent. Zanni appeared as an English "Zawne" in 1566, only a few years after the type is definitely recorded in Italy. Soon, too, Pantalone, as Pantaloun or Pantalowne, was being familiarly introduced on the London stage—and introduced by no less a person than William Shakespeare. No one who has studied the prints representing the early Venetian type can turn to the "Seven Ages of Man" and deny that Shakespeare had seen a real Pantalone. His leanness, his spectacles, his pouch—all are there to testify to the exactitude of the dramatist's knowledge. Perhaps it may even be true that, in this famous speech, Shakespeare's imagination had been fired by witnessing the Italian *amoroso* (lover), Capitano (soldier), Dottore (justice), and Pantalone whom he has thus introduced at their

---

[1] A. Costantini *Mezzetino*, G. B. Costantini *Ottavio*, M. A. Fracanzani *Pulcinella*, E. Gherardi *Arlecchino*, G. Geratoni *Pierrot*, M. A. Romagnesi *Cintio*, C. V. Romagnesi *Leandro*, G. Tortoriti *Pasquariello*, C. Biancolelli *Colombina*, A. Toscano *Marinetta*, D'Orsi *Spinetta*, and E. Daneret *Babet-la-chanteuse*. [2] See Campardon, i, xxiii–xxv.

[3] The most important study on this question is that of Louis Moland, *Molière et la comédie italienne* (twelfth edition, Paris, 1867). In addition, besides innumerable references in critical works on Molière, W. Vollhardt, *Die Quelle von Molières Tartuffe* (*Archiv für das Studium der neueren Sprachen und Literaturen*, xci (1893), 55–68), which discusses Scala's *Il Pedante*; P. Toldo, *Di Alcuni scenari inediti della commedia dell' arte e delle loro relazioni col teatro del Molière* (*Atti della R. Accademia delle Scienze di Torino*, xlii (1907), 460–482); T. Matic, *Molières Tartuffe und die italienische Steigreifkomödie* (*Studien für vergleichende Literaturgeschichte*, i (1900), 1); Theodor Schröder, *Die dramatischen Bearbeitungen der Don Juan-Sage in Spanien, Italien und Frankreich bis auf Molière einschliesslich* (*Beihefte zur Zeitschrift für romanische Philologie*, xxxvi (1912), 117–130); August Kugel, *Untersuchungen zu Molières Médecin malgré lui* (*Zeitschrift für französiche Sprache und Literatur*, xx (1898), 1–71).

[4] On this see O. Klingler, *Die Comédie Italienne nach der Sammlung von Gherardi* (Strassburg, 1902); P. Toldo, *Études sur le théâtre de Regnard* (*Revue d'histoire littéraire de la France*, x (1903), 1), and *Il Teatro d' Evaristo Gherardi a Parigi* (*La Rassegna nazionale*, xciv (1897), 603–629); and, in general, Eugène Lintilhac, *La Comédie: Dix-huitième siècle* (Paris, 1909), pp. 33–90. It is needless here to cite the many early works on the *comédiens italiens*.

[5] No reference, of course, is made here to the later course of the *commedia dell' arte* in Italy and to its influence on Goldoni. On this subject the following works may be mentioned: Olga Marchini-Capasso, *Goldoni e la commedia dell' arte* (Naples, 1912); E. del Cerro, *op. cit.*; Elvira Ferretti, *Le Maschere italiane nella commedia dell' arte e nel teatro di Goldoni* (Rome, 1904); C. Falconi, *La quattro Principali maschere italiane, nella commedia dell' arte e nel teatro di Goldoni* (Rome, 1896); Maria Ortiz, *Goldoni e la commedia dell' arte* (*La Cultura*, xxxi (1912), 641–651); Giuseppe Gallico, *Il " Bugiardo " di Carlo Goldoni e la commedia dell' arte* (Bergamo, 1907); E. Grillo, *Studies in Modern Italian Literature* (Glasgow, 1930).

[6] On Scoto of Mantua, mentioned by Jonson in *Volpone* and by James I in his *Dæmonologie*, who seems to have been a leader of a company, see Winifred Smith, *Italian Actors in England* (*Modern Language Notes*, xliv (1929), 376–377).

appropriate cues.[1] Shakespeare, indeed, leaves no doubt in our minds that such performances had impressed him deeply. In stage direction and dialogue of *The Taming of the Shrew* Gremio is distinctly referred to as a " pantalowne," and elsewhere the zany is for ever peeping through the dress of his Elizabethan clowns. Hamlet's " law of writ " and law " of liberty " may well be an allusion to the literary and improvised styles, indicating Shakespeare's appreciation of the two main forms of theatrical art in his own day. How far he borrowed from the Italians will never be known, but that he did borrow seems to be undeniable from his own references to the *commedia dell' arte*, and from his apparent use of *lazzi*, which might have developed independently, but which more probably were based on Italian example. Ferdinando Neri has shown good reason to believe that *The Tempest* owed its being to the shipwrecked clowns of *L'Arcadia incantata*, or of another similar scenario ; [2] while other scenarii can be shown to have close connexions with various Shakespearian plots. Several deal with the *Measure for Measure* story,[3] and seem to treat that independently of Cinthio's novel or play.[4] Another reproduces the subject-matter of *Romeo and Juliet*,[5] while still others present scenes not dissimilar from Shakespeare's comic episodes. One such may suffice here as an example. In the Locatelli *Il Giuoco della primiera* Flaminia is about to be married to Pantalone, and the latter's servant, called Zanni, comes running joyously from the house with

> money to spend. He learns of the love of Lelio and Flaminia, tells them of the approaching marriage, is asked to upset his master's plans. Zanni says Pantalone has to go and get 4000 scudi for the dowry, he will get another sent instead of him and so trick him. Lelio says he will wait for him at the broker's and goes out. Zanni [speaks] of the shopping he has to do, making *lazzi* with the counting of the money. Here enters a Thief, from the street, with a pack of playing-cards. He makes *lazzi* with Zanni on playing at *primiera*. He teaches Zanni the game, making *lazzi*. He wins Zanni's money and clothes, leaving him in his shirt.

Now, no scene in Shakespeare precisely reproduces this, but when we think of that episode in *The Winter's Tale* in which Autolycus steals the clown's purse after he had been ' making *lazzi* ' of the shopping he has to do, we realize that often Shakespeare approached very close to the comic style of the Italians, and we wonder whether those Elizabethan scenes may not have been inspired, indirectly at least, by this professional comedy of the Continent. Acting, in Shakespeare's time, was still an integral part of drama, and the Elizabethan actors were international in their outlook. They toured abroad themselves, and individuals, such as Kemp, were prepared to take a part in some improvised Harlequinade.[6] Inevitably there must have been influence exerted upon them by those Continental players with whom they came in contact, and the reflections of that influence are to be found in the quartos of the sixteenth and seventeenth centuries.[7]

It is not from such influence on the literary drama, however, that the popular comedy can gain

---

[1] See J. Isaacs, *Shakespeare as Man of the Theatre* (in *A Series of Papers on Shakespeare and the Theatre* (1927), p. 115).

[2] F. Neri, *Scenari delle maschere in Arcadia* (Città di Castello, 1913). On this suggestion see H. D. Gray, *The Sources of " The Tempest "* (*Modern Language Notes*, xxxv (1920), 6, June), W. J. Lawrence, in *The Times Literary Supplement* (November 11, 1920), and *cf. Le Lettere* (ii (1921), 1, January 15; *Shakespeare avrebbe tratto il soggetto di " La Tempesta " da scenari italiani ?*), and E. Carrara, *Le Maschere in Arcadia* (*Fanfulla della Domenica*, xxxvii, 2). The latter seems to ignore the fact that in this case the use of the shipwreck-wizard theme can be carried far back—into the sixteenth century. On the possible influence in general of the improvised comedy see M. J. Wolff, *Shakespeare und die Commedia dell' arte* (*Shakespeare-Jahrbuch*, xlvi (1910), 1–20).

[3] See Winifred Smith, *Two Commedie dell' Arte on the " Measure for Measure " Story* (*Romanic Review*, xiii (1922), 3, July).

[4] W. Smith asserts that the Locatelli and Casamarciano texts are taken from Cinthio, but it seems more probable that these texts derive from others made when the historical episode was fresh in men's minds.

[5] Max J. Wolff, *Flaminio Scala und sein Szenarium " Li tragici successi": Ein Beitrag zur Geschichte des Stoffes von " Romeo und Julia "* (*Archiv für das Studium der neueren Sprachen und Litteraturen*, cxxviii (1912), 380–388); A. L. Stiefel, *Bemerkungen zu den Dramatisierungen der Romeo-und-Julia-Fabel* (ibid., cxxvii (1911), 392–399); W. Smith, *A Comic Version of " Romeo and Juliet "* (*Modern Philology*, vii (1910), 217–220).

[6] See *supra*, pp. 279–280. *Cf.* W. Marschall, *Das " Sir Thomas Moore "—Manuskript und die englische Commedie dell' Arte* (*Anglia*, lii (1928), 193–241).

[7] See G. S. Gargàno, *La Commedia dell' arte e l' antico teatro inglese* (*Il Marzocco*, xxxiii, 3, January 15, 1928); Piero Rébora, *L' Italia nel dramma inglese* (Milan, 1925), pp. 103–132; W. Smith, *Italian and Elizabethan Comedy* (*Modern Philology*, v (1908), 555–567). Kathleen M. Lea has an essay (*Modern Language Review*, xxiii (1928), 47–51) showing that Sir Aston Cokayne's *Trappolin suppos'd a Prince* (1662) is based directly on an Italian *scenario*.

its right to be considered by historians. Perhaps hereby some *apologia* may be entered against Winifred Smith's judgment :

> The *commedia dell' arte* will be seen to belong to the class of drama that has contributed nothing to the spiritual advance of mankind.[1]

But, after all, what, one may ask, is " spiritual advance " doing in this galley at all ? If, of course, we adopt the typical Anglo-Saxon critical standard wherein morality is the sure and only foundation for all literary judgments, then the *commedia dell' arte* and all its gay supporters must pass like beaten curs into the darkest kennels of history ; but if, on the other hand, we regard the theatre as the theatre, if we forget for a moment the claims of the *littérateur*, and if we accept, light-heartedly, laughter for what it is worth in itself, then the whole of this popular comedy assumes an importance vast and significant. Here truly is the theatre—the theatre vivid in its appeal, guiltless of literary distinction, depending, as a true theatre ought to do, chiefly on the talents of the performers. Here is an art, amoral in its scope, pleading from the earliest days to the latest for a frank acceptance of life. Here is secularism incarnate and, in spite of the evanescence of its art form, imperishable.

Down through the ages the entertainers and the mountebanks have travelled—wearily sometimes, but often with gaiety, for

> A merry heart goes all the day,
> Your sad tires in a mile-a.

Occasionally they are feasted by Roman emperors or Renascence dukes ; but their true companions are the people. In ancient times the *mimi* did not hesitate to ridicule the highest, even Imperial majesty itself, when the popular mind found something there detestable, despicable, or tyrannous.[2] In the Eastern Empire it was the mimes who took up the cause of a poor widow when her goods were being seized upon and squandered by a corrupt official.[3] And in the times of the *commedia dell' arte* at Naples, when the popular mood was aroused against the tax known as the *terzi*, the actors behaved just as their ancestors had done centuries before. Coviello and Pulcinella are speaking, and the former proposes to call in a third. " A third ? " says Pulcinella. " You can't call in a third." " Why not ? " queries Coviello. " Because," answers Pulcinella, " all the ' thirds ' have been taken by his Excellency." His Excellency in question—the Viceroy Monterey—was in the theatre when this scene was improvised, and, being a good-humoured man, he merely laughed, and suspended the odious exaction.[4]

Perhaps we shall say that this is a mere coincidence ; but all the innumerable points of contact between the old mime and the new cannot be coincidence only, nor can we dismiss as of no account the many links which even the sparsely documented Middle Ages present to us, joining classic mime with Italian actor by means of the *ioculatores*. We may, of course, go too far. It is thus unnecessary and futile to see, as Reich does, elements of the *mimus* in every work of literature which exhibits a tendency toward realism.[5] This merely confuses the issue. Influence in this direction there may have been, but it is an influence impossible to trace. So long as we keep within the field of drama, however, we may justifiably postulate the continuance of a largely improvisatorial comic tradition, utilizing stock types as its means of expression, and usually having laughter only as its end—a tradition which depended on the art of the actor and on his ability to see clearly, frankly, and unashamedly the life of his day. By the end of the seventeenth century the *commedia dell' arte* was beginning to fade back into that darkness which overwhelmed it in the Middle Ages, and the reasons for that reversion are to be discovered in the penitential and pious poems of some of its exponents. There are many who say that it was killed by Goldoni in the eighteenth century,

---

[1] *Op. cit.*, p. 238.   [2] See *supra*, p. 125.   [3] See *supra*, p. 148.   [4] Croce, p. 75.
[5] Reich, *passim*; see also his essay, *Antike Romane, Novellenkränze und Schwankbücher, ihre Entwicklungsgeschichte und Beziehung zum Mimus* (*Deutsche Literaturzeitung*, xxxvi (1916), 10–12). For a criticism of this view consult Allen, *op. cit.*

CONCLUSION

but there are two errors in that statement. Goldoni only completed a process which had been developing since 1650, and he did not kill the *commedia dell' arte*, for the *commedia dell' arte*, the *mimus*, is, like a dream, like a god, immortal. Goldoni has long been dead; but Pulcinella still sows his wild oats and lives his unholy life, still Arlecchino remains a being instinct with vitality. Pulcinella, it is true, is now only a thing of wood, and Arlecchino is merely a pantomimic shadow of his former self, but perhaps the real Pulcinella, the real Arlecchino, and all their true companions have only been sleeping awhile behind the wings, just as they slept during the Middle Ages, leaving their higher art to be carried on by mountebanks and *jongleurs* and puppet-showmen, just waiting for a new cue which will call them once more to their scenario and the swift traffic of the boards. Who knows?

DEPART DES COMEDIENS ITALIENS EN 1697   ITALORUM COMŒDORUM DISCESSUS ANNO MDCXCVII

Fig. 225. The Departure of the Italian Comedians, 1697
Engraving by L. Jacob after A. Watteau, 1697. Exemplar in the Bibliothèque Nationale, Paris (Cabinet des Estampes, Tb + 1, vol. i, B. 392).
Photo Giraudon

349

APPENDIX

THE COMMEDIA DELL' ARTE

THE following appendix is not intended to be exhaustive, but rather to be a guide toward an understanding of the scope of the *commedia dell' arte*. In the first section is presented a list of the chief character-parts up to the beginning of the eighteenth century, in which is included a number of names taken from 'Zannesque' poems of the period. Many of these must have been used by minor companies of entertainers. In the second appears an alphabetical list of the principal actors, with bibliographical references where these seemed required. Not all the facts concerning their careers are here enumerated, but merely such as serve to put them in their historical position. The third section contains an alphabetical list of the chief scenarii. No notice is taken here of eighteenth-century examples, but an effort has been made to include at least the chief collections of the earlier period. Among these the Correr and Biancolelli series do not appear to have been hitherto described in detail. In preparing this appendix the main object has been to collect the facts conveniently together, and, incidentally, to relieve some of the notes in the text.

I. THE PARTS

[References to Callot indicate the *Balli di Sfessania*, published about 1622; to Bocchini the *Corona Macheronica* (two parts, Bologna, 1663); and to Rapparini *Arlichino* (Heidelberg, 1718), as quoted by Rasi. Most of the Zanni names mentioned under M. Magni are derived from popular manuscript poems.]

ADRIANO. Lover. Andrea Mangini (*fl.* 1614).

AMOROSO. Or *moroso, innamorato*; generic name of the stage lover. The various names adopted by individual actors are separately listed. Niccolò Biancolelli (*fl.* 1650–68) and Francesco delli Angioli (*fl.* 1679, Modena) acted this part under unknown titles.

ANDREA AGRESTINI. The Pedant in *L'Amici infidi*.

ANGELICA. Lover. Angelica Alberigi, or Alberghini (*fl.* 1580–91, Uniti, Confidenti).

ANGIOLA. Or *Angela, Angiolina*. Lover. It is almost impossible to identify the various actresses who took this part in the late seventeenth century. Anna Marcucci (*fl.* 1686, Modena) was the daughter of Marzia Fiala; but, besides her, there was an *Angiola*, wife of Fabrizio, another who was the wife of E. Nelli, and a third, wife of G. Raparelli.

ANSELMO. Old Man. Occurs in several scenarii for *Pantalone*.

ARGENTINA. Servant. Gabbriella Gardellini (*fl.* 1688–89, Modena).

ARLECCHINA. Servant. Such a type appears in France toward the end of the seventeenth century; it was probably originated in Paris.

ARLECCHINO. Or *Arlichino, Arlechino*. Zanni. Although not named as such until the late sixteenth century, some of the early Zanni were probably *Arlecchini*. Tristano Martinelli (*b.* 1555 or 1557, *d.* 1630); Drusiano Martinelli (*fl.* 1578–98, Accesi, Gelosi-Uniti; probably an *Arlecchino*); Giuseppe-Domenico Biancolelli (*b.* 1640, *d.* 1688, France); Evaristo Gherardi (*b.* 1663, *d.* 1700).

ARMELLINA. Servant. First mentioned 1641. A sonnet to *Signora Armellina Comica celebre* appears in *Poesie di Paolo Abriani* (Venetia, 1663), p. 184; this probably refers to the *Armellina* who was in the Parma troupe in 1647. Maddalena Sacco (*fl.* 1689, Modena).

AURELIA. Lover. An *Aurelia* wished to join the Uniti in 1593; and to her probably belongs the manuscript sonnet printed in Rasi (i, 235). This name is particularly common in the Biancolelli scenarii.[1] Brigida Bianchi (*b.* 1613, *d.* 1703); Colomba Coppa (*fl.* 1689, Modena).

AURELIO. Lover. One of the earliest of the Lover names. Adriano Valerini (*fl.* 1570–84, Gelosi-Uniti; possibly in Ganassa troupe 1567–68); Marcello di Secchi (*fl.* 1618, Costanti; probably the *Aurelio* whose activities can be traced during 1610–40); —— Testa (*d.* 1630); Bartolomeo Ranieri (*b. c.* 1640, *fl.* till 1689).

---

[1] A list of the collections of scenarii is given at pp. 377–379.

AURETTA. Servant. *Auretta* d'Orsi (*fl.* 1664–78).

BACCALARO. Zanni. Rasi, i, 458.

BADIL. Zanni. See *Contraſto di bravura tra il capitano Deluvio e Zan Badil* (Ferrara, 1613).

BAGATINO. Or *Bagattino*. Callot; Bocchini. Appears in Casanatense scenarii.

BAGOLINO. Or *Bagulino*. A *Bagolino* was in the Parma troupe in 1638, and this may have been the name used by Carlo Cantù in 1664 (see under *Buffetto*). The type appears in Bocchini, and in the Biancolelli scenario of *Arlequin soldat et bagage* (printed La Haye, 1698). *Bagolin* is a subſtitute for *Arlequin*.

BALZARMA. Servant or Lover. See the sixteenth-century print in Duchartre (p. 68).

BARESE. Or *Calabrese*. Old Man. Cited by Perrucci in 1699 (Petraccone, p. 130).

BARILLE. Zanni. Occurs in the Casanatense scenarii.

BARZELLETTA. Servant. Mentioned in 1620.

BATTISTINO. Zanni. G. B. Auſtoni (*fl.* 1591–1615, Accesi, Confidenti).

BATTOCCHIO. Zanni. See *Versi di Veggio Alanio, detto Zan Battocchio* (Venezia, 1620).

BEATRICE. Servant. Beatrice Fiorillo (*fl.* 1639–54, Parma, France). A Beatrice was at Verona in 1663, and another at Bologna in 1695–96.

BELFONTE. A type which appeared in several of the loſt Eſte scenarii.

BELLO SGUARDO. Zanni. Callot.

BELTRAME. Zanni. Niccolò Barbieri (*fl.* 1600–40, Gelosi, Fedeli, Confidenti, Parma).

BENOUALLA. Zanni. Callot.

BERLNEA. "La zia." See M. Magni, *loc. cit.*, p. 167.

BERLOC. Zanni. See M. Magni, *loc. cit.*, p. 167.

BERNETTA. Servant. U. Liberati (*fl.* 1615–20).

BERTA. Servant. See M. Magni, *loc. cit.*, p. 167.

BERTOLINA. Servant (?). See M. Magni, *loc. cit.*, p. 170.

BERTOLINO. Zanni. The earlieſt mention of the part occurs in 1584 concerning the Uniti. It was probably a variant of *Pulcinella* (see the scenario of *L' Ateiſta fulminato*, where *Bertolino* takes *Pulcinella's* place). Niccolò Zecca (*fl.* 1646–87, Parma, Modena); Ambrogio Broglia (*fl.* 1672–87).

BITONTINO. Zanni. Gio. Donato (*fl.* 1589–1618, Uniti).

BOCCALINO. Zanni. Rasi, i, 458.

BRIGHELLA. Zanni. A *Brighella* was at Parma in 1638. Domenico Bononcini (*fl.* 1687–98). *Buffetto* was a variant of this type.

BRINQUENAZILLE. Zanni. For this see Fig. 177.

BRUNETTINA. Servant (?). See under *Tabarì*.

BUFFETTO. Zanni. A type of *Brighella*. Carlo Cantù (*b.* 1609, *fl.* till 1647, Parma, Modena). D. Bononcini may also have used this name in 1686 in the Modena troupe.

BURATTINO. Zanni. Mentioned in 1585 by Garzoni (Petraccone, p. 5). Appears in many scenarii of the Scala and Locatelli collections. See the sixteenth-century prints in Duchartre, pp. 67, 271, 301. A poem quoted by M. Magni (*loc. cit.*, p. 167) mentions *Burati*.

CACONE. Zanni (?). Occurs in Corsiniana scenarii.

CALABRESE. See *Barese*.

CAMILLA. See *Cortegiana*.

CAMOSZA. Zanni. See M. Magni, *loc. cit.*, p. 167.

CANDELOTT. Zanni. Bocchini.

CAPELLINO. Zanni. Occurs in the Casanatense scenarii.

CAPELLO. Zanni. Bocchini. See *Genealogia di Zan Capella*, printed in Rasi, i, 462.

CAPITANO. Usually a Spanish type, sometimes played without a special cognomen, sometimes expanded with names of a grandiloquent sort: *Cap. Coccodrillo* (Fabrizio de' Fornariis, *fl.* 1571–1637, Confidenti); *Cap. Spavente della Valle Inferna* (Francesco Andreini, *b.* 1548, retired 1604, Gelosi-Uniti); *Cap. Matamoros* (Silvio Fiorillo, *fl.* 1584–1634, Accesi, Risoluti, Affezionati); *Cap. Rinoceronte* (Girolamo Garavini, *fl.* 1605–24, Accesi, Fedeli); *Cap. Spezzaferro* (Giuseppe Bianchi, *fl.* 1640–80, France); *Cap. Sbranaleoni* (Giuseppe Antonio Fiala, *fl.* 1651–1687, Modena); *Cap. Terremoto* (Francesco Manzani, *fl.* 1661); *Cap. Sangue e Fuoco* (Diego Ancatoni, *fl.* 1658); *Capitano* (Federico Beretta, *fl.* 1675). In addition to these names we find *Cap. Tremante* (in an early Eſte scenario), *Cap. Zerbino, Cap. Spessa Monti, Cap. Bonbardon, Cap. Grillo, Cap. Mala Gamba, Cap. Bellauata, Cap. Sgangarato, Cap. Babeo, Cap. Cardoni, Cap. Cerimonia* (all in Callot), *Cap. Terremoto Spaccamondi* (in *L' Amici infidi*), *Cap. Sprofonda* (in *Flaminio disperato*), *Cap. Deluvio* (see under *Badil*).

APPENDIX

CAPOCCHIA. Zanni. Rasi, i, 458.

CARDOCCHIA. Zanni. A variant name for, or addition to, *Coviello*, used by Gennaro Sacco (*fl.* 1689–1715).

CASSANDRO. Old Man. Cited by Perrucci (Petraccone, p. 130). From his appearance in the Correr scenarii, *Cassandro* seems to have been a variant of *Pantalone*; in the Casanatense series he is, however, a kind of *Dottore*.

CASSANDRO D' ARTEUSI. Cited by Perrucci (Petraccone, pp. 114–115) as a Florentine comic part.

CAVICCHIO. M. Magni (*loc. cit.*, p. 179) asserts that this type appeared among the Gelosi.

CAZAMOLETA. Zanni. See the *Nuova scelta di Villanelle . . . raccolte da Zan Cazamoleta* (Turin, n.d.).

CELIA. Lover. Maria Malloni (*b.* 1599, *fl.* till 1627, Fedeli, Confidenti).

CELIO. Lover. First mentioned 1641. Pietro Cotta (*fl.* 1679–97).

CHECCA. Servant (?). See M. Magni, *loc. cit.*, p. 167.

CHIARA. Servant (?). See M. Magni, *loc. cit.*, p. 167.

CIAMBELLOTTO. Probably a character-name; mentioned in 1546.

CICALINO. Zanni. Occurs in the Casanatense scenarii.

CICCOMBIMBO. Old Man. Cited by Perrucci (Petraccone, p. 130).

CICHO SGARRA. Zanni. Callot.

CINTIA. Lover. In 1654 a sonnet by Carlo d' Aquino, *In Lode di Cintia, comica famosa*, was published in *Rugiade di Parnaso* (Cosenza, 1654). Anna Maria Millita (*fl.* 1678, Modena).

CINTIO. Lover. Iacop' Antonio Fidenzi (*fl.* 1627–50, Fedeli, Modena); Marc' Antonio Romagnesi (*b. c.* 1633, acted Lover till 1694, France); Carlo Schiavi (*fl.* 1679, Modena).

CITRULLO. Zanni. Mentioned in Fedeli 1627. Occurs in the Casanatense scenarii.

CIURLO. Zanni. Callot.

CLAUDIO. Lover. Appears in some of the Scala scenarii.

CLAUDIONE. In Confidenti 1615. This type appears in three of the Scala scenarii.

COCCALINO. Zanni or Old Man. Occurs in the Casanatense scenarii.

COLA. Zanni. A *Cola* was proposed for a French company in place of *Arlecchino* in 1607, and appeared at Paris in 1608. This may be Francesco Vacantiello, but Vacantiello itself may be a type name. *Cola* is listed by Perrucci (Petraccone, p. 130) as an old man, while Cecchini gives it as a Neapolitan part (*id.*, p. 16). It is of frequent occurrence in the Naples scenarii.

COLANIO. Old Man. Probably a variant of *Cola* ; appears in the Correr scenarii.

COLLO FRANCISCO. Zanni. Callot.

COLOMBINA. Servant. Isabella Franchini-Biancolelli-Cantù (*fl.* 1640–51, Modena); Catarina Biancolelli (*fl.* 1683–1716, France).

CORALLINA. Servant. Domenica Costantini (*fl.* 1675, Modena).

CORBELIA. Servant. See M. Magni, *loc. cit.*, p. 167.

CORNELIA. Lover. See the sixteenth-century print in *Recueil Fossard*.

CORNETO. Or *Zani Corneto*. Zanni. Cited as early as 1585 (Driesen, p. 267). In *Recueil Fossard* (*c.* 1577).

CORTEGIANA. A figure of rare occurrence, although one such, called *Camilla*, appeared in the 1568 Bavarian performance. Another, called *Marsila*, appears in the scenario of *La Schiava*.

CORTELLACCIO. Zanni. Ippolito Monteni, or Montini (*fl.* 1614, Uniti, Costanti).

COVIELLO. Old Man or Zanni. This Neapolitan part is of various character; he appears as servant, courtier, and Old Man. A *Coviello Ciavola* is mentioned as early as 1588 at Naples, and the *rôle* is prominent in many scenarii. Ambrogio Buonomo (*fl. c.* 1590); Gennaro Sacco (*fl.* 1689–1715). The latter also called himself *Coviello Cardocchia*.

CUCORONGNA. Zanni. Callot.

CUCUBA. Zanni. Callot.

CUCURUCU. Zanni. Callot.

CURZIO. Lover. Vicenzio Botanelli (*fl.* 1581); Domenico de Negri (*fl.* 1614).

DELIA. Lover. Besides Camilla Nobili-Rocca (*d.* 1613, Confidenti), there was a *Delia* at Naples in 1647.

DESÁVEDO. Or *Desévedo*. Zanni. This seems to be a peculiarly Parmesan type. It occurs in three of the Modena scenarii, and is referred to as *Dessevedo di Malalbergo* by Quadrio (*cf.* A. Bartoli, pp. clxxxii–clxxxiii, who points out that Dsevad = *desapidus* = *insipido*, 'stupid').

DIAMANTINA. Servant. Patrizia Adami (*b.* 1635, retired 1683, France).

DIANA. Lover or Servant. Giulia Gabbrielli (*fl.* 1645, France); Teresa Costantini (*fl.* 1677–86, Modena).

DOTTORE. Old Man. This was one of the most popular parts in the sixteenth and seventeenth centuries, and many actors gave special cognomens to the type. The commonest of these was *Graziano*. Of actors who are known

Z

only as *Dottore* or as *Dottor Graziano* the following are of most note: Bernardino de Lombardi (*fl.* 1575-83, Confidenti); Andreazzo (*fl.* 1590); Luzio Burchiella (*fl.* 1572-78, Gelosi ; probably in Ganassa troupe, 1567-68); Bartolomeo Zito (*fl.* 1602-28); Andrea Zenari (*fl.* 1593, Uniti); Giovan Paolo Agocchi (*fl.* 1593-1603); Bartolomeo Bongiovanni (*fl.* 1609-12, Fedeli); Michel Zanardi (*fl.* 1614); —— Giarattoni (*fl.* 1655); Giovanni Paderna (*fl. c.* 1660); Giuseppe Orlandi (*fl.* 1675, Modena); Gio. Battista Paghetti (*fl.* 1686, Modena); Francesco Materazzi (*b. c.* 1652, *fl.* till 1689, Modena); Angelo Antonio Muzio (*fl.* 1688-89, Modena); Galeazzo Savorini (*fl.* 1689-99, Modena); Giovanni Nanini (*fl.* 1689, Austria); Marc' Antonio Romagnesi (took part 1694, retired 1697, France).   Others with special titles were *Dottor Graziano Forbizone da Francolino* (Pietro Bagliani (*fl.* 1623); *Dottor Gratiano Partesana da Francolino* (Lodovico de' Bianchi, *fl.* 1575-89, Gelosi); *Dottor Graziano de' Violoni* (Girolamo Chiesa, *fl.* 1630-47, Affezionati, Parma); *Dottor Spacca Strummolo* (Aniello Soldano, *fl.* 1609-10, Fedeli); *Dottor Brentino* (Giovan Antonio Lolli, *fl.* 1661-92, Parma, Modena); *Dottor Graziano Baloardo* (Giovanni Battista Angelo Lolli, *fl.* 1683-94, France); *Dottor Lanternone* (Giuseppe Milanta, *fl.* 1655-87, Modena).

DURINO. Zanni. Occurs in the scenario of *L'Alvida* in the Scala collection.

EMILIA. Lover. An *Emilia* was in the Uniti 1594.

EULARIA. Lover. Eularia (perhaps Orsola) Coris (*fl.* 1652-58, Fedeli); Orsola Biancolelli (*fl.* 1660-91, France); Isabella Servilli (*fl.* 1697-1700).

FABIO. Zanni or Lover. An actor *Fabio* was mentioned by Garzoni in 1585 (Petraccone, p. 4); this was no doubt the *Fabio* who was in the Confidenti 1584.

FAGINOLINO. Zanni. Rapparini.

FAGOTTINO. Zanni. Rapparini.

FALSETTO. Zanni. In *L'Amici infidi*.

FANTESCA. The generic name for the maid-servant. These might be either young or old, and are cited here under their special names.

FARGNOCCOLA. Zanni. A Fargnoccola was in the Desiosi 1581. See also *Frognocola*.

FARINA. Or *Gian Farina*. Zanni. This type was mentioned in 1612, and appears in Callot.

FEDELINDO. Lover. Appears in the scenario of *La Trapolaria*.

FEDERICO. Lover. Luigi Riccoboni (*fl.* 1690-96, Modena).

FELIPPA. Or *Felipetta, Felippotta*. Servant (?). See M. Magni, *loc. cit.*, p. 167.

FENOCCHIO. Zanni. Bocchini.

FIAMETTA. Servant. An actress of this name was in the Affezionati in 1634.

FICHETTO. Zanni. Lorenzo Nettuni (*fl.* 1610-21, Confidenti, Fedeli); Eustachio Lolli (*fl.* 1650-51, Modena).

FIDELIN. This part is noted at Modena in 1673.

FIDETTO. Zanni. Appears in several of the Correr scenarii.

FILIPPA. Servant. Appears in the scenario of *Li Prigioni* in the Locatelli collection.

FILIPPO ZOPPO. Zanni. Filippo Angeloni (*fl.* 1525-80).

FILONO. Zanni. See the sixteenth-century print in Duchartre, p. 67.

FINOCCHIO. Zanni. Cited by Bocchini as *Fenocchio*. His *rôle* was described by Pier Iacopo Martello in the early eighteenth century (*cf.* Scherillo, p. 16) as " a deceiver, ever ready to catch even at straws to save himself from drowning; . . . his dialect—that of a Bergamask mountaineer—is not among the most beautiful of Italian dialects; he boasts a white and green dress, a flat hat, and a marmot-like mask." Gio. Andrea Cimadori (*fl.* 1675-76, Modena); Giovan Battista Paruti (*fl.* 1686, Modena); Carlo Zagnoli (*fl.* 1689, Modena).

FIORE. Servant. In *L'Amici infidi*.

FIORETTA. Servant. This part, as well as *Vittoria*, seems to have been taken by Vittoria Piissimi (*fl.* 1575-90).   It occurs frequently in the Correr scenarii.

FLAMINIA. Lover. A Flaminia was acting from 1567 to 1569, but cannot now be identified. Orsola Cecchini (*fl.* 1605-12, Accesi); Marzia Fiala (*fl.* 1664-86, Modena); Agata Calderoni (*fl.* 1664-82).

FLAMINIO. Lover. Giovan Paolo Fabbri (*fl.* 1584-1614, Gelosi-Uniti); Marco Napolioni, (*fl.* 1647-59, Parma); Giuseppe Sondra (*fl.* 1698-99, Modena).

FLAUTINO. Zanni. Giovanni Gherardi (*fl.* 1675, France).

FLAVIA. Lover. Margherita Garavini (*fl.* 1605-25, Accesi).

FLAVIO. Lover. Flaminio Scala (*fl.* 1577-1620, Gelosi, Accesi, Confidenti).

FLORINDA. Lover. Virginia Ramponi-Andreini (*b.* 1583, *d. c.* 1628); —— Coris (*fl.* 1658).

FLORINDO. Lover. Domenico Pannini, or Parrino (*fl.* 1675, Modena).

FORTUNIO. Lover. Rinaldo Petignoni (*fl.* 1574, Gelosi); Gio. Maria Bachino (*fl.* 1620).

APPENDIX

FRACASSO. Zanni. Callot. A *Fracasso* is mentioned in 1519.

FRANCATRIPPA. Or *Francatrippe*. Zanni. One of the earliest Zanni. Gabriello Panzanini or Francesco Gabriello (*fl.* 1578–93, Gelosi-Uniti).

FRANCESCHINA. Servant. Called *Francischina* by Callot; originally played by men. Battista da Treviso (*fl.* 1579–87, Gelosi-Uniti); Carlo —— (*fl.* 1591); Silvia Roncagli (*fl.* 1600 ?); Ottavio Bernardini (*fl.* 1614).

FRAVOLETTA. Servant. Appears in many of the Naples scenarii.

FREGNOCOLA. Zanni. See M. Magni, *loc. cit.*, p. 167.

FRICASSO. Zanni. Callot.

FRITELLINO. Zanni. This and *Gian Fritello* both appear in Callot. A Court buffoon called *Fritella* lived at the Este Court in 1479. Pier Maria Cecchini (*b.* 1563, *fl.* till 1622).

FRITTADA. Zanni (?). See M. Magni, *loc. cit.*, p. 170. There exists a popular versified *Viaggio di zan Fritada* (*id.*, 102).

FROGNOCOLA. Zanni. Rasi, ii, 957. See *Fargnoccola* and *Fregnocola*. There is a *Maridazzo di M. Zan Frognocola* (1618).

FULVIO. Lover. Domenico Bruni (*b.* 1580, *fl.* till 1621, Gelosi, Confidenti).

GABINETTO. Zanni. Francesco Zbrazin (*fl.* 1648, Mantua); G. Bonazzo (*fl.* 1658, Mantua).

GALLOTTA. Zanni. In Fedeli, 1619.

GARIGLIA LO ZOPPO. Zanni. Orazio Graziullo (*fl.* 1626).

GENTILE. Servant. In *L' Amici infidi*.

GIANGURGOLO. Zanni, Old Man, or Captain. This Calabrian type had many forms. It evidently is derived from *Zan* (Zanni) *Gurgolo*, and as Zan Gurgolo it appears in Bocchini. The earliest mention of the part is in 1647, but it appears in many scenarii—Naples, Correr, Bartoli, Casanatense, and Biancolelli.

GIOVANELLO. Zanni. Mentioned by Perrucci.

GIRACÒ. Zanni. In *L' Amici infidi*.

GNIGNIOCOLA. Servant (?). A comic Bergamask type, 1618. See M. Magni, *loc. cit.*, p. 172 ; Rasi, ii, 956.

GONELLA. Zanni. A kind of bravo or servant, frequent in the Correr scenarii. *Cf.* Rasi, i, 458.

GRADELINO. Zanni. Costantino Costantini (*fl.* 1668–96, Modena, France).

GRADELLA, ZAN. Zanni. Bocchini.

GRAMUSTINO. Zanni (?). Appears in several of the lost Este scenarii and in other collections.

GUAZZETTO. Or *Guatsetto* (Callot), *Guaretto*. Zanni. An actor of this name was playing *c.* 1630, and another was in the Modena troupe 1688. The part is mentioned in Bocchini.

GURGOLA, ZAN. See *Giangurgolo*.

ISABELLA. Lover. Isabella Andreini (*b.* 1562, *d.* 1604, Gelosi-Uniti); Vittoria degli Amorevoli (*fl. c.* 1614); Francesca Biancolelli (*b.* 1664, *d.* 1747, France).

ISOTTA. Servant (?). See M. Magni, *loc. cit.*, p. 167.

LAURA. Servant. A *Laura* appears as *Pedrolino's* wife in the scenario of *L' Alvida*.

LAVINIA. Lover. Diana Ponti (*fl.* 1582–1605, Desiosi); Marina Antonazzoni (*b.* 1593, *d.* 1639, Confidenti); Antonia Isola (*fl.* 1672–91, Parma, Modena). Callot.

LAVINIO. Lover. A *Lavinio* was in the Affezionati in 1634, and he or another was still acting under this name in 1641.

LEANDRO. Lover. Francesco Pilastri (*fl.* 1590–94, Gelosi-Uniti); Benedetto Ricci (*fl.* 1612–20, Confidenti, Fedeli); Luca Rechiari, or Archiari (*fl.* 1675–93, Modena); Gaetano Coppa (*fl.* 1690); Carlo Virgilio Romagnesi (*fl.* 1694–97, France). A *Leandro* was in the Parma troupe 1638.

LELIO. Lover. Giovan Battista Andreini (*b.* 1576, *d.* 1654, Fedeli); Stefano Marchetti (*fl.* 1673–79); Antonio Torri (*fl.* 1678–89, Parma, Modena); Luigi Riccoboni (*fl.* 1696–1700, Modena).

LEONARDO. Lover. Mentioned in 1664.

LEONORA. Lover. Leonora Castiglioni (*fl.* 1630–38, Parma).

LEPIDO. Lover (?). Mario di Tommaso (*fl.* 1575).

LESSANDRO. Lover. An actor taking this name was in the Confidenti in 1584.

LICETTA. Servant. In *Recueil Fossard* (*c.* 1577).

LIDIA. Lover. Vincenza Armani (*fl.* 1567–69); Lidia da Bagnacavallo (*fl. c.* 1571, Gelosi). There was another *Lidia* in the Confidenti 1584.

LUCIA. Lover. In *Recueil Fossard* (*c.* 1577). Callot.

LUCILLA. Lover. A *Lucilla* was in the Uniti in 1594. Luisa Gabbrielli-Locatelli (*fl.* 1640–52, France, Modena).

LUCINDA. Lover. Lucinda Nadasti (*fl.* 1664–88, Parma, Modena).

LUCINDO. Lover. —— d'Odoardo (*fl.* 1664). *Lucido* occurs in *L' Amici infidi*.

LUCIO. Or *Lutio*. Lover. A *Lutio* was in the Uniti 1584; this may be Lucio Fedele. Apparently *Lutio* is a stage name.

LUCRETIA. Lover. In *Recueil Fossard* (*c.* 1577).

LUPINO. Zanni. Rasi, i, 458.

MAGNANINO. Old Man (?). Giacomo di Ventura (*fl.* 1562–69).

MAGNIFICO. See *Pantalone*.

MAMBRE. Zanni. See M. Magni, *loc. cit.*, p. 167.

MARAMAO. Zanni (?). On this Neapolitan type see Croce, p. 32. It has been assumed that Callot's Maramao represents a real Fabrizio Maramao or Maramaldo; but *cf.* F. de Gubernatis in *Rivista delle tradizioni popolari italiane* (i (1893), 371, 445, 641, 723).

MARCANTONIO. Lover. In *L'Amici infidi*.

MARINETTA. Servant. Isabella Fiorilli (*fl.* 1660–88); Angelica Tortoriti (*fl.* 1688, France).

MARIO. Lover. Agostino Grisanti (*fl.* 1651–64, Parma); Luca Rechiari or Archiari (*fl.* 1675–93, Modena).

MARSILA. See under *Cortegiana*.

MASSARA. Servant. See M. Magni, *loc. cit.*, p. 167.

MASSIMO PIGOLI. Old Man. In *L'Amici infidi*.

MASTELLARA. Servant. See M. Magni, *loc. cit.*, p. 167.

MASTELLETTA. Servant (?). See M. Magni, *loc. cit.*, p. 167.

MEDICO. The figure of the medical Doctor is not a common one, and can exist independently of the *Dottore*. A *medico* called Tofano occurs in the Locatelli scenario of *La Commedia in commedia*.

MELOSINA. Servant (?). See M. Magni, *loc. cit.*, p. 170.

MENATO. A peasant type interpreted by Marco Aurelio Alvarotto in the company of Angelo Beolco.

MENGONE. On this later mask see G. Branca, *La Maschera marchegiana e il suo teatro* (*Picenum*, xi, 6).

MEO-PATACCA. A Roman carnival type; it is not certain whether it entered the *commedia dell' arte* before 1700. See A. Baldini, *Cronache di Roma antica e moderna: Meo Patacca ovvero Roma in festa* (*L'Illustrazione italiana*, xlvi, 29, July 20, 1919).

MEO SQUAQUARA. Zanni. Callot. On this see Croce, p. 32.

MERLINO PULPETTONE. Old Man. In *Flaminio disperato* takes part of *Dottore*.

MESCOLINO. Zanni. This is evidently the *Mestolino* of Callot. It occurs often in the Correr scenarii. Pietro di Re (*fl. c.* 1625).

MEZZETINO. Zanni. The earliest-recorded *Mezzetino* is one who was in the Accesi in 1612. The part is illustrated, as *Metzetin*, by Callot, and is mentioned by Bocchini. Ottavio Onorati (*fl.* 1615–18, Accesi, Confidenti); Angelo Costantini (*fl.* 1683–1729, France).

MICHELINO. Old Man. Under this name the *Dottore* figures in some of the Correr scenarii.

MOSCHETTA. Zanni (?). Mentioned in 1626.

MOSCHINO. Zanni. Mentioned in 1545.

MUCCINA. Or *Zan Muzzina*. The name adopted by Bocchini.

NACCHERINO. Zanni. Rapparini.

NESPOLA. Servant. —— di Secchi (*fl.* 1618, Confidenti). The type is shown in a sixteenth-century print (Duchartre, p. 68).

NESPOLINO. Zanni. Rapparini. This character appears as a " page " in *L'Amici infidi*.

NICOLINA. Servant. Mentioned among the Fedeli in 1612.

NORCINO. Zanni. Apparently a Roman stage type, mentioned in 1551.

ODOARDO. Lover (?). Francesco Servillo (*fl.* 1660).

OLIMPIA. Lover (?). Appeared in Modena troupe 1647.

OLIVETTA. Servant. An *Olivetta* appears in several of the Scala scenarii, and is referred to in a poem by Gio. Battista Miamiano (*Rime*, 1620) and in another by Bocchini. There was also an *Olivetta* acting in 1627.

ORAZIO. Lover. Bartolomeo Rossi (*fl.* 1584, Confidenti); Orazio Nobili, or Mobili (*fl.* probably 1570–79, Gelosi); Giovanni Raparelli (*fl.* 1684, Modena); N. Romagnesi (*fl.* 1660, France); Bernardo Narici (*fl.* 1675–84, Modena).

ORTENSIA. Lover. An *Ortensia* was acting in 1641; this may have been Francesca Allori (*fl.* 1668).

ORTENSIO. Lover. Francesco Antonazzoni (*fl.* 1618–23, Confidenti).

OTTAVIO. Lover. An *Ottavio* was in the Gelosi and Gelosi-Uniti in 1575 and 1594. Giovan Andrea Zanotti (*b.* 1622, *fl.* till 1693, Modena, France); Giovanbattista Costantini (*fl.* 1688–1720, France).

PADELLA, ZAN. Zanni. Bocchini. See the early print in Mic, p. 179.

APPENDIX

PAGLIACCIO. Zanni. No certain record exists concerning this type before the end of the seventeenth century. There is absolutely no authority for the statement in Sand (i, 192) that a *Pagliaccio* appeared in Ganassa's troupe. The part, however, may be an old one.

PALETTA. Zanni. See M. Magni, *loc. cit.*, p. 167.

PANDOLFO. Old Man. Occurs in many of the Correr scenarii; evidently a variant of Pantalone. In *L'Amici infidi* he is called *Pandolfo Berlinghieri*.

PANTALONCINO. Occurs in Corsiniana I scenarii.

PANTALONE. Or *Il Magnifico*. Old Man. This Venetian type, with the *Dottore*, was one of the earliest and most popular characters in the *commedia dell' arte*. It was certainly in existence in 1551. The *Pantalone* was often called *Pantalone de' Bisgognosi*. Giulio Pasquati (*fl.* 1567–75, Gelosi); Giacomo Braga (*fl.* 1583–1614, Uniti); Marc' Antonio Romagnesi (*fl.* 1612–34, Confidenti); Federigo Ricci (*fl.* 1612–20, Fedeli); Orazio Carpiani (*fl.* 1638, Parma); Cialace Arrighi (*fl.* 1645, France); —— Capellino (*fl.* 1655, Parma); Giuseppe Albani (*fl.* 1647–51, Modena); Giovan Battista Turri (*fl.* 1653–75, France, Modena); Battista Ventura (*fl.* 1655, Modena); Tiberio Fortunati (*fl.* 1655); Carlo Malossi (*fl.* 1658); G. Gaggi (*fl.* 1660); —— Collalto (*fl.* 1662, France); Antonio Riccoboni (*fl.* 1670–95, Modena, France); Girolamo Gabbrielli (*fl.* 1687–91, Modena); Rinaldo Rosa (*fl.* 1697, Modena).

PANZETTA. Zanni. See M. Magni, *loc. cit.*, p. 167.

PASQUALE, DON. Zanni. Mentioned by Perrucci.

PASQUARIELLO. Zanni or Old Man. This Neapolitan character was already in existence at Naples in 1588. It occurs in many of the Naples scenarii, and is illustrated by Callot. Gian Gregorio d' Ariemme (*fl.* before 1628); Giuseppe Tortoriti (*fl.* 1681–97, Modena, France).

PASQUELLA. Servant. Occurs in some of the Correr and Bartoli scenarii.

PASQUINO. Zanni. Giovan Battista Trezzi (*fl.* 1689, Modena).

PASSERINO. Zanni. Rapparini.

PEDROLINO. Zanni. This seems to have been the original of the Franco-Italian *Pierrot*. The *rôle* appears frequently in the Scala scenarii. Giovanni Pellesini (*fl.* 1576–1612, Uniti, Confidenti, Fedeli). See M. Magni, *loc. cit.*, pp. 131–132.

PEDRULÌ. See M. Magni, *loc. cit.*, p. 167.

PERNOUALLA. Zanni. Callot.

PETTOLA. Or *Pettolino*. Zanni. Of frequent occurrence in the Corsiniana I scenarii.

PIATELLO. Old Man. Probably an eighteenth-century character.

PIDURLINO. Zanni. Rasi, i, 458. Possibly the same as *Pedrolino*.

PIERROT. Zanni. This type, called also *Piero*, seems to have been evolved out of Pedrolino, by Giuseppe Giaratone or Geratoni (*fl.* 1673–97, France).

PIMPINELLA. Or *Prinpinella*. Servant. Probably a Neapolitan type. Maddalena Francesca Paruti (*fl.* 1686, Modena).

PIOMBINO. Old Man. Also called *Zanobio da Piombino*. Girolamo Salimbeni (*fl.* 1578–94, Gelosi-Uniti).

PIPE FIORENTINO. Zanni. Mentioned in 1620.

PODETT. Zanni. See M. Magni, *loc. cit.*, p. 167.

POLO, ZAN. Zanni. Mentioned at Venice in 1515 and 1522.

POLONIA. Lover (?). A *Polonia* was in the Confidenti in 1584.

POLPETTA. Zanni. Mentioned by Bocchini. Carlo Gabbrielli (dates not known) is said to have taken this part.

POLPETTINO. Zanni. Rapparini.

PRUDENZA. Lover. A Prudenza da Verona was *seconda donna* in the Gelosi in 1576, and a Prudenza was *prima donna* of the Affezionati in 1634.

PULCINELLA. See *supra*, pp. 290–293.

RATSA DI BOIO. Zanni. Callot.

RAZULLO. Zanni. Callot.

RICCIOLINA. Servant. Illustrated as *Riciulina* by Callot. Angela Luccese (*fl.* 1602–5, Accesi); Marina Antonazzoni (*b.* 1593, *d.* 1639, Confidenti).

RODELINO. Zanni. Occurs in the Correr and Casanatense scenarii.

ROMAGNUOLO. A *Romagnuolo* was a part occasionally taken by D. Bruni in 1615.

ROSALBA. Servant (?). Lucilla Trenta (*fl.* 1636).

ROSAURA. Servant or Lover. Anna Arcagiati (*fl.* 1690, Modena).

ROSETTA. Servant. Of common occurrence in the Scala scenarii.

ROTALINDA. Old Woman. Virginia Clarini (*fl. c.* 1665).

RUFFIANA. Old Woman. This type of bawd is of rare occurrence. See the print in Duchartre, p. 285.

SABADINA. Servant (?). See M. Magni, *loc. cit.*, pp. 167, 169.

SANDRA. Servant (?). See M. Magni, *loc. cit.*, p. 167.

SARDELLINO. Zanni. Of frequent occurrence in the Corsiniana I scenarii.

SCALOGNA. Zanni. Rasi, i, 458.

SCAPINO. Zanni. Illustrated twice by Callot. Pavolino Zanotti (*fl.* 1620); Francesco Gabbrielli (*fl.* 1611–35, Accesi, Confidenti); Alessandro Chiavarelli (*fl.* 1622, France); Giovanni Bissoni (*b.* 1666, *d.* 1723, France).

SCARAMUCCIA. Zanni. Apparently a kind of cross between the Zanni and the Captain. The type is illustrated by Callot. Giovan Battista Fiorillo (*fl.* 1614–47, Parma, Affezionati); Tiberio Fiorilli (*b.* 1608, *fl.* till 1692).

SCARNECCHIA. Zanni (?). Apparently a character-name; mentioned in 1673.

SCARPINO. Zanni. A *Scarpino* was at Florence in 1626.

SCATOLINO. Zanni. Appears in some of the Correr scenarii.

SCATOZZA. Zanni. For this Neapolitan type see Croce, p. 64.

SCATTALONE. Old Man. Evidently a kind of *Pantalone* ; mentioned in 1622.

SCATTARELLO. Zanni. Bocchini. Cf. *Commedia piacevolissima . . . de un bravo chiamato Rovinazzo* (in Stoppato, p. 117) and *Dialogo in versi . . . fra Scatorello e Campagnolo* (Modena, 1665).

SGARUGLIA. Zanni (?). A wool-carder in *L'Amici infidi*.

SIGNORA. Lover (?). Apparently a generic name for *amorosa* ; mentioned by Garzoni in 1585 (Petraccone, p. 6).

SILVIO. Lover. Silvio Gambi (*fl.* 1594–95, Gelosi-Uniti; probably playing as *Silvio*); Bernardino Coris (*fl.* 1651–1658, Modena); Francesco Calderoni (*fl.* 1664–1703).

SIMONA, LA. Old Woman. See the sixteenth-century print in Duchartre, p. 67.

SIVELLI. Old Man (?). Giovanni Gabbrielli (*fl.* 1611–18).

SMARAOLO CORNUTO. Zanni. Callot.

SPAZZA. Zanni. In *Flaminio disperato*.

SPINETTA. Servant. A *Spinetta* is mentioned in 1627, and another was in the Modena troupe in 1687.

STENTERELLO. On this later mask see G. Piccini (Jarro), *L'Origine della maschera di Stenterello* (Florence, 1898).

STOPPINO. Or *Stupino*. Zanni. Occurs in several scenarii, particularly those of the Correr series. A *Stoppino* is mentioned in 1641.

STUPPOLINO. Zanni. Occurs in the Casanatense scenarii.

TABACCHINO. Zanni. Rapparini.

TABARÌ. Zanni. See D'Ancona, ii, 458, 468; M. Magni, *loc. cit.*, p. 167. See *Opera nuova nella quale si contiene il Maridazzo della bella Brunettina, sorella di Zan Tabarì Canaja de Val Pelosa* (Brescia, 1582).

TABARINO. Zanni. Giovanni Tabarino (*fl.* 1568–74).

TARTAGLIA. Old Man and Zanni. A Neapolitan type; occurs in many of the Naples, Biancolelli and Correr scenarii. Ottaviano Ferrarese (*fl.* 1602).

TEMELLINO. Zanni. Rapparini.

TESTONE. Zanni. Of frequent occurrence in the Corsiniana I scenarii.

TOFANO. See *Medico*.

TOGNIN. Zanni. See M. Magni, *loc. cit.*, p. 167.

TORTELLINO. Zanni. Rapparini.

TORTORINA. Servant (?). Francesca Broglia (*fl.* 1672).

TRACAGNINO. Zanni. A type of *Arlecchino*, probably originated in the eighteenth century.

TRAPPOLA. Zanni. This *rôle* appeared in the Modena troupe in 1686.

TRAPPOLINO. Zanni. A *Trappolino* was acting in 1613, and he or another died in 1634. Giovan Battista Fiorillo (*fl.* 1614–50, Parma, Affezionati); Bartolomeo Falconi (*fl.* 1690–94, Mantua).

TRASTULLO. Zanni. Callot. A *Trastullo* was with Ganassa in Spain in 1581.

TRAVAGLINI. Zanni. Mentioned by Perrucci. See also *Tabarino*.

TRIPPONE. Zanni. Rasi, i, 458.

TRIPPU. Zanni. Mentioned in 1598. See *Francatrippa*. Cf. the print in Duchartre, p. 68. (This is not Tripuando, as Duchartre says: the title reads *Cvcina per il pasto de Zan Trippu qvando prese moglie*.) See *Vita e custùm de Messir Zan Tripù* (in Ambrosiana, M. Magni, *loc. cit.*, pp. 182 and 167).

TRIVELLINO. Zanni. Andrea Frajacomi (*fl.* 1614); Domenico Locatelli (*fl.* 1640–71, France); Carlo Sangiorgi (*fl.* 1681–86, Modena); Domenico Bononcini (*fl.* 1686–98, Modena).

TRUFFALDINO. Zanni. Evidently originated in the medieval period (see *supra*, p. 277). Francesco Mozzana (*fl. c.* 1650–51); Carlo Palma (*fl.* 1658–75, Mantua); Marc' Antonio Zanetti (*fl.* 1686–94, Modena).

APPENDIX

TURLUPIN.   Zanni.   Probably developed in France in the seventeenth century.

UBALDO LANTERNI.   Old Man.   Occurs frequently in the Correr scenarii.

VALERIA.   Lover.   Valeria Antonazzoni-Auſtoni (*fl.* 1618, Confidenti).

VALERIO.   Lover.   Giacinto Bendinelli (*fl.* 1651–68, France); Francesco Allori (*fl.* 1674–82)

VASPA.   Servant (?).   See M. Magni, *loc. cit.*, p. 167.

VERTOLINO.   Zanni (?).   Natale Consalvo (*fl.* 1602).   See Croce, p. 37.

VINCENZA or VICENZA.   Lover.   Vincenza Armani (*fl.* 1567–69).

VIRGINIA.   Lover.   A *Virginia* was in the Uniti 1594.

VIRGINIO.   Lover.   Virginio Turri (*fl.* 1653); Giuseppe Coppa (*fl.* 1689–91, Modena).

VITTORIA.   Lover.   There was a *Vittoria* in the Gelosi in 1575; possibly this was Vittoria Piissimi (*fl.* 1575–90). Antonella Bajardi (*fl.* 1600–20); Isabella Fanegotti (*fl.* 1660); Teodora Areliari or Archiari (*fl.* 1675–88, Modena).

VOLPINO.   Zanni.   Giulio Cesare Barbieri (*fl.* 1664).

ZACCAGNINO.   Zanni.   This name is already found in 1496.   In the sixteenth century an actor Francesco Ruino essayed the *rôle*.   Giulio Cesare Torri (*fl.* 1647–62, Modena).   The type appears in the Casanatense scenarii; *cf.* the print of Zan Zaccagni in Duchartre, p. 68.

ZACHAGNA.   Zanni.   See M. Magni, *loc. cit.*, p. 167.

ZAMPETTO or ZAMPET.   Mentioned in a manuscript poem at Bergamo (M. Magni, *loc. cit.*, pp. 167, 170).

ZANEL, ZAN.   Zanni.   *Zanel, Zanül,* and *Zanott* occur in a manuscript poem at Bergamo (M. Magni, *loc. cit.*, p. 167).

ZANNI.   The generic name for the comic servant (see *supra*, pp. 263–266, where the actors who took this *rôle* are enumerated).

ZANOBIO DA PIOMBINO.   See *Piombino*.

ZORG.   Zanni.   See M. Magni, *loc. cit.*, p. 167.

ZUCCARINO.   Zanni.   Occurs in the Casanatense scenarii.

II. THE ACTORS

[Since, in dealing with the movements of the actors of the *commedia dell' arte*, it is the year that it is important to bring to the reader's notice, dates have usually been arranged through this section of the Appendix with that detail first.   Thus, 1593, 13/11, indicates November 13, 1593.]

ADAMI, PATRIZIA.   *Diamantina.*   Wife of an actor Adami, and later married G. B. Lolli.   She came to Paris about 1660, and was there naturalized with her husband in June 1683.   She seems to have retired then, when Caterina Biancolelli made her *début* as *Colombina.*   Died September 5, 1693.   (Rasi, i, 3–4; Campardon, i, 295; Sand, i, 162; Biancolelli MS., i, 52, 80.)

AGOCCHI, GIOVAN PAOLO.   *Dottor Graziano Scarpazon.*   Also called Gioanpaolo dalli Agochij.   1593, 13/11: in Rome, after having acted at Mantua.   1603: in Bavaria.   (Rasi, i, 11–12.)

ALBANI, GIUSEPPE.   *Pantalone.*   1651: in Modena troupe; possibly there also in 1647.   (B. Brunelli, p. 90.)

ALBERGINA, LODOVICO.   At Mantua in 1590, 1591, and 1592.   (Bertolotti, p. 70; Rasi, i, 16.)

ALBERIGI, or ALBERGHINI, ANGELICA.   *Angelica.*   Apparently the *Angelica* who was wife of Drusiano Martinelli and this actress were the same.   1580, 17/9: head of Uniti.   1583, 15/1: at Bologna, directing a company. 1587: in Spain.   1591, /10: in Confidenti.   1594: evidently in Uniti.   When she was at Bergamo in 1580 Criſtoforo Corbelli wrote a poem in her praise; another poem was written to her by Jeronimo Cassone (*Rime,* Genova, 1591).   (Rasi, i, 15–16; Quadrio, iii, 2; A. Bartoli, p. cxxv; E. Cotarelo y Mori, *op. cit.,* p. 61.)

ALLORI, FRANCESCA.   *Ortensia.*   Wife of Francesco Allori.   1668, 20/3: at Bologna.   It is not known for how long she shared the fortunes of her husband.   (Rasi, i, 29–35.)

ALLORI, FRANCESCO.   *Valerio.*   1674, 28/7: at Padua, preparing to go to Venice.   1675, 16/3–20/4: at Venice. 1682, 4/3: at Bologna.   He evidently belonged to the Mantuan company (Rasi, i, 29–35).

ALVAROTTO, MARCO AURELIO.   *Menato.*   An actor of the Angelo Beolco, *Ruzzante,* troupe.   (Rasi, i, 37.)

AMOREVOLI, BATTISTA DEGLI.   *Franceschina.*   Otherwise known as Battiſta da Treviso.   1579, 1/5: at Paris, which he left on 10/5; he was then probably with Massimiano and Martinelli.   1584, 3/4: at Ferrara in Uniti. 1587, 24/11: at Vicenza.   It seems almoſt certain that " degli Amorevoli " here is a cognomen and does not refer to a company of the Amorevoli, as has been conjectured.   Battiſta's wife was probably V. degli Amorevoli.   He wrote a *Canzone in laude dell' illuſtrissima Quadriglia delle dodese Dame di Torino* (Torino, 1584), in which he called himself *Comico Confidente.*   (É. Picot, *Una Lettera del comico Battiſta degli Amorevoli da Treviso, detto la Franceschina* (*Rassegna bibliografica della letteratura italiana*, vi (1898), 30–32); Rasi, i, 307–309; D'Ancona, ii, 486; V. Cian, *Galanterie torinesi del sec. XVI* (*Gazzetta letteraria*, xvi, 4).)

AMOREVOLI, VITTORIA DEGLI. *Isabella.* Probably the wife of Battista degli Amorevoli. She may be the *Isabella* who was in the Uniti in 1584. Her name appears in the undated list of the Costanti (early seventeenth century). (Rasi, ii, 743.)

ANCATONI, DIEGO. *Capitan Sangue e Fuoco.* 1658: at Rome. (Bertolotti, p. 109; Rasi, i, 39.)

ANDRÉ, or ANDREA. Probably identical. André was at Paris in 1530. Andrea was at Rome on January 23, 1551. (É. Picot, *Pierre Gringoire et les comédiens italiens* (Paris, 1878); Baschet, p. 4; Rasi, i, 51–52; E. Re, in *Giornale storico*, lxiii (1914), 295–296).)

ANDREA DA CATHARO. 1549: at Padua. (E. Cocco, *loc. cit.*, p. 68.)

ANDREAZZO. *Dottor Graziano.* 1590, 13/1 and 24/1: in company of Diana. (D'Ancona, ii, 496; Rasi, i, 52–53.)

ANDREINI, FRANCESCO. *Innamorato* and later *Capitan Spavento.* Born at Pistoia in 1548, his father's name being Cerracchi or dal Gallo. In his youth he was taken prisoner by the Turks, and was kept by them for eight years. On his return he started playing, and married Isabella Canali in 1578. Possibly the *Franncischo Ysabella* noted at Luiz in 1568 was this pair, but only so if there has been some error in the dating of the document in which the record appears. 1583: at Venice with Isabella in Gelosi. With this company he went to France in the winter of 1603, and retired from the stage when Isabella died in April 1604. Died at Mantua August 20, 1624. For his portrait see *supra*, p. 252. Works: (1) *Le Bravure del Capitan Spavento* (Venezia, 1607; Venetia, 1624; of these an abridged French translation was published at Paris in 1608); (2) *L'Ingannata Proserpina* (Venezia, 1611); (3) *L'Alterezza di Narciso* (Venezia, 1611); (4) *Ragionamenti fantastici posti in forma di dialoghi rappresentativi* (Venezia, 1612); (5) *Alcune rime* (Venezia, 1613); (6) editions of the *Lettere* and *Frammenti* of Isabella. By some a *Prologo di un ragazzo* contained in Bruni's *Fatiche comiche* (Paris, 1623) is also attributed to him. In 1889 Domenico Lanza published from a Turin manuscript a poem entitled *Il Felicissimo arrivo del Serenissimo Don Vittorio Prencipe di Savoja . . . nella famosa città di Torino, descritto in verso sdrucciolo da Francesco Andreini* (published " per le nozze Solerti-Saggini," Pinerolo, 1889). (Baschet, p. 127; Rasi, i, 54–87; Bevilacqua, xxiii, 82–89; F. Bartoli, i, 8–13; Sand, i, 149–150.)

ANDREINI, GIOVAN BATTISTA. *Lelio.* Son of Francesco and Isabella Andreini, born at Florence on February 9, 1576.[1] He studied first at the University of Bologna, and then joined the company of Flaminio Scala (apparently the Fedeli). In 1601 he married Virginia Ramponi at Milan. 1603: at Florence. 1604: entered service of the Gonzagas of Mantua. 1609, 8/8 and 14/8: at Turin with Fedeli. 1611, 3/12: at Bologna. 1612, 26/11: at Florence with Fedeli. 1613–14: in France. 1619: at Brescia and Venice. 1620, 28/9: near Mantua, 6/11: at Turin with Martinelli. 1621, 12/1 and 3/3: at Paris. 1623: at Turin. 1628, 23/11: at Vienna. 1634–35: at Mantua. 1638: Pavia. 1639 and 1642: at Bologna. His career was throughout associated with the Fedeli, among whom he won great fame. Barbieri (Petraccone, p. 22) says he was a member of the Accademia degli Spensierati, a friend of princes, and at Mantua held the post of *Capitano di caccia*. In 1633, after the death of his first wife, he married *Lidia* (V. Rotari). He died at Reggio on June 7 or 8, 1654, in a common inn. There are many accounts of his skill in comedy, and many poems written in his praise. Especially important are the *Poesie di diversi in lodi dei comici Gio. Battista Andreini, detto Lelio, e la moglie Virginia, nata Ramponi, detta Florinda*, preserved in manuscript at Brera; some of these are printed by Bevilacqua (xxiv, 157–165), and others by Rasi. Andreini's own works are numerous: (1) *La Florinda*, a tragedy (acted at Florence 1603; Milano 1606); (2) *La Saggia Egiziana*, a poetic dialogue (Fiorenza, 1604); (3) *La Divina visione in soggetto del Beato Carlo Borromeo*, a poem (Firenze, 1605; Venezia, 1610); (4) *Lo Sfortunato poeta* and *Il Pianto d'Apollo* (Milano, 1606); (5) *La Maddalena*, a poem (Venezia, 1610; Firenza, 1612; Prague, 1628); (6) *Lo Schiavetto*, a comedy (Milano, 1612; Venezia, 1620); (7) *L'Adamo*, a *sacra rappresentazione* (Milano, 1613; Milano, 1617; Perugia, 1641); (8) *La Turca*, a play (Venezia, 1616 (?); Venezia, 1620; (9) *La Maddalena*, a *sacra rappresentazione* (Mantova, 1617; Milano, 1620); (10) *La Venetiana*, a comedy (Venezia, 1619); (11) *Intermedio* (Mantova, 1620); (12) *Lelio bandito*, a tragi-comedy (Milano, 1620); (13) *La Sultana*, a play (Paris, 1622); (14) *La Ferinda*, a play (Paris, 1622); (15) *L'Amor nello specchio*, a play (Paris, 1622); (16) *Li duo Lelii simili*, a play (Paris, 1622); (17) *La Centaura*, a play (Paris, 1622); (18) *Un Prologo* (Torino, 1623); (18) *Le due Commedie in commedia*, a play (Venezia, 1623); (19) *La Tecla vergine e martire*, a poem (Venezia, 1623); (20) *L'Inchino per la novella servitù, della nuova compagnia de' comici*, a prologue (Paris, 1623); (21) *Lo Specchio*, a poem (Paris, 1625); (22) *La Ferza contro le accuse date alla commedia ed a' professori di lei* (Paris, 1625); (23) *Il Teatro celeste* (Paris, 1625); (24) *La Campanaccia*, a comedy (Venezia, 1627; Milano, 1627); (25) *Il Pentimento alla SS Vergine del Rosario*, a poem (Bologna, 1631); (26) *La Rosella*, a tragi-comedy (Bologna, 1632);

[1] The date of birth is doubtful. The horoscope gives 1576, but this is two years before Isabella's marriage.

APPENDIX

(27) *I due Baci*, a play (Bologna, 1634); (28) *La Rosa*, a play (Pavia, 1638); (29) *L'Ismenia*, an opera (Bologna, 1639); (30) *L'Olivastro, ovvero Il poeta sfortunato*, a poem (Bologna, 1642); (31) *L'Ossequio alla Maestà Cristianissima e Realissima della Regina Anna* (Paris, 1643); (32) *Cristo sofferente, meditationi in versi divotissimi sopra i punti principali della Passione di Cristo* (Firenze, 1651; Roma, 1651). (Baschet, pp. 317–318; A. Bartoli, pp. cxiv–cxviii; Bevilacqua; Rasi, i, 117–139; F. Bartoli, i, 13–30; Winifred Smith, *G. B. Andreini* (*Modern Language Review*, xvii (1922), 31–41); Antonio Valeri, *Un Palcoscenico del seicento* (Rome, 1893); Virginio Mazzelli, *Un Famoso comico e autore drammatico del seicento morto in Reggio nell' Emilia* (Reggio, 1915); Maria Ortiz, *Filodrammatici e comici di professione in una commedia di G. B. Andreini* (*Rivista teatrale italiana*, xiii, 5); É. Picot, *Gli Ultimi anni di G. B. Andreini in Francia* (*Rassegna bibliografica della letteratura italiana*, ix, 3–4); Lodovico Frati, *I codici Morbio della R. Biblioteca di Brera* (Forlì, 1897), pp. 10–12.)

ANDREINI, ISABELLA. *Isabella.* One of the most famous actresses of her time. She was the daughter of Paolo Canali, a Venetian, and was born at Padua in 1562. She married Francesco Andreini in 1578. Besides Giovan Battista she had seven children, four of whom were girls. The eldest of the daughters was taken into her Court by the Grand Duchess of Tuscany, while the second was adopted by the Duchess of Mantua. Little is recorded of her activities until the visit to France when she met her death, but we must assume that she acted regularly with the Gelosi, which was captained by her husband (see *supra*, pp. 310–314). In 1589 there is recorded the performance at Florence of *La Pazzia, commedia d' Isabella*, but this is probably *La Pazzia d' Isabella*, of the Scala collection. In 1603 she went with the Gelosi to France and died on the return to Lyon. Garzoni called her *la graziosa Isabella, decoro delle scene* in 1585 (Petraccone, pp. 4–5), and Barbieri similarly sang her praise (*id.*, pp. 21–22). The latter tells us that she was a laureate of the Accademia de' Intenti. More poetic laudation was accorded to her than to any other actress (see *supra*, pp. 237, 239–240, where the various poems are cited). Her own works included: (1) *La Mirtilla, favola pastorale* (Verona, 1588; and reprinted frequently); (2) *Sonetti, canzoni* (Milano, 1601; Paris, 1603); (3) *Lettere* (Venezia, 1607; Venetia, 1625); (4) *Fragmenti di alcune scritture* (Venetia, 1625); (5) *Rime* (Napoli, 1696). Some of her poems are included in *Rime di diversi celebri poeti dell' età nostra* (Bergamo, 1587) and in *Componimenti Poetici delle più illustri Rimatrici d' ogni secolo, raccolti da Luisa Bergalli* (Venezia, 1726). (Baschet, pp. 130–134; Bevilacqua, xxiii, 89–94; D'Ancona, ii, 482; A. Bartoli, pp. cix–cxii; Rasi, i, 87–117; F. Bartoli, i, 31–37; G. C. Molineri, *Un' Attrice del sec. XVI, Isabella Andreini* (*Strenna della Gazzetta Piemontese per l' anno* 1888); E. del Cerro, *Un' Attrice di tre secoli fa, Isabella Andreini* (*Natura ed arte*, xvii, 7–8); Ugo Falena, *Isabella Andreini* (*La Rassegna nazionale*, cxliii (May 16, 1905), 267–279); C. Ruelens, *Erycius Puteanus et Isabelle Andreini* (Anvers, 1889); A. Bruno, *Gabriello Bruno e Isabella Andreini* (*Bullettino della Società storica savonese*, i, 1); V. A. Arullani, *Relazioni di Gherardo Borgogni con Isabella Andreini* (*Alba Pompeia*, ii, 5–6).)

ANDREINI, LIDIA. See *Rotari, Virginia.*

ANDREINI, VIRGINIA. *Florinda.* This actress, *née* Virginia Ramponi, a native of Milan, was born on January 1, 1583. She married Giovan Battista Andreini in 1601, and acted with him in the Fedeli. She may have been acting as early as 1596, but reliable records of her activities do not start till the seventeenth century. 1609, 4/8: at Turin with Fedeli. 1611, 3/12: at Bologna. 1612, 15/8: at Milan; 26/11: at Florence with Fedeli. 1621: in France. She seems to have died about 1627–30. From extant documents she appears to have had a prominent artistic rival in Orsola Cecchini, and a domestic one in a certain Lidia, whom G. B. Andreini apparently married after her death. Her praise was also sung by many (see *supra*, p. 241). Apart from the manuscript poems cited under *Andreini, Giovan Battista*, there are Marino's verses (*La Galeria*, eighth edition, Venezia, 1647, p. 288); those of G. B. Bidelli (in *Idillij di diversi ingegni*, Milano, 1618); and the excessively rare *Rime in lode della Signora Verginia Ramponi Andreini Comica Fedele detta Florinda* (Firenze, 1604), for which see *supra*, p. 241. (D'Ancona, ii, 470; A. Bartoli, p. cxxxviii; E. Bevilacqua; F. Bartoli, i, 38–42; Rasi, i, 139–151.)

ANELLI, FRANCESCO. A native of Florence who was at Mantua in 1590. (Bertolotti, *op. cit.*, p. 70; Rasi, i, 158.)

ANGELA. An actress of this name was performing with Flaminia and Pantalone in 1567. She may be Angela, daughter of Maffeo dei Re. (D'Ancona, ii, 449; Rasi, i, 158; E. Cocco, in *Giornale storico*, lxv (1915), 63–64.)

ANGELICA. See *Alberigi, Angelica.*

ANGELO. See *Michele, Angelo.*

ANGELONI, FILIPPO. *Filippo Zoppo.* A native of Mantua who presented a comedy in 1525. In 1580 he was made director of the charlatans at Mantua. (Rasi, i, 162.)

ANGIOLA. It is almost impossible to identify the actresses who took this part. In 1647 there was an *Angela* in the Modena company; she seems to have been the wife of E. Nelli (*q.v.*), who was in Modenese service in 1651. In 1650 an *Angiolina* who was the wife of Fabrizio is noted, and an *Angiola* is mentioned in 1664 along with

Fabrizio; this may be A. D'Orsi. In 1658 an *Angiola* married G. Rapparelli, and in 1686 an Anna Marcucci (*q.v.*), daughter of Marzia Fiala, was an *Angiola* or *Angela*.

ANGIOLI, FRANCESCO DELLI. *Amoroso*. This actor was apparently in the Modena troupe on May 15, 1679. (Rasi, ii, 751–752.)

ANTON MARIA. Or *Anthonie Marie*. This actor was in France in 1572, probably working with Soldino. Collier in his *History of English Dramatic Poetry* (1831, i, 83) quotes from a document which he says is of the reign of Henry VIII, mentioning among the " King's Minstrels " Nicholas Andria and Anthony Maria. These sound as if they were André and Anton Maria. (Rasi, i, 185; and references *supra*, pp. 299–300.)

ANTONAZZONI, FRANCESCO. *Ortensio* and later *Capitano*. Very little is known of this actor, who was the husband of Marina Dorotea. On March 4, 1618, he was in the Confidenti. Still acting in 1627. (Rasi, i, 169.)

ANTONAZZONI, GIOMARIA. This actor was in the Costanti in the early seventeenth century. (Rasi, ii, 743.)

ANTONAZZONI, MARINA DOROTEA. *Lavinia* and *Ricciolina*. The family name of *Lavinia*, who was born at Venice on February 5, 1593, is not known. She married at the age of thirteen and took Francesco Antonazzoni as her second husband when she was eighteen (1611). It seems impossible, as Neri states, that she should have acted in the Gelosi, which was disbanded in 1604. By 1615 she was in the Confidenti. In March 1618 she was at Ferrara, writing to Don Giovanni de' Medici concerning her husband's flirtations with Nespola. Strangely enough in a letter sent from Milan on July 18, 1622, she signs herself *Marina dorotea antonaconni deta Lauinia comicha gielossa*, from which it might be argued that there was a resuscitation of the name Gelosi in the second decade of the seventeenth century. A poem was written in praise of her acting in *La Pazzia di Lavinia*, by Ridolfo Conte Campeggi, another by B. G. Mamiani (*Rime*, Venetia, 1620, pp. 83–84), and on her death in 1639 other poets, such as Pietro Michiele, burst into rime. A pastoral by her, *Arianna*, is discussed by Rasi. (Achille Neri, *La " Lavinia " dei Confidenti* (*Gazzetta letteraria*, xiii (1889), Nos. 19–20, May 11 and 18); Rasi, i, 169–184; F. Bartoli, i, 43–45.)

ANTONIO PIETRO. 1549: at Padua. (E. Cocco, *loc. cit.*, p. 68.)

ARCAGIATI, or ARCAGNATI, ANNA. *Rosaura*. Wife of Galeazzo Savorini. 1689, 15/2: passport from Modena, in whose service she and her husband were, for touring in Italy. 1690, 10/8: at Brescia in Modena troupe. 1691: in Modena troupe. (Rasi, ii, 694, iii, 508–509; B. Brunelli, p. 111.)

ARCHIARI, or ARELIARI, or RECHIARI, GIORGIO. Son of Luca Archiari. He is put down as a *servo* in the Modena list of 1688, but Rasi says he played the *terzo amoroso* under the name of *Ottavio*. (Cionini, p. 40; Rasi, iii, 335.)

ARCHIARI, or ARELIARI, or RECHIARI, LUCA. *Mario* and *Leandro*. Father of Giorgio Archiari and husband of Teodora. He was a native of Trento, and seems to have remained constantly in the service of Modena. 1675: in Modena troupe. 1686: at Turin, in Modena troupe. 1688: at Milan and Sassuolo in Modena troupe. 1690, 25/2: at Rome. 1691, 5/12: at Arezzo. 1692, 2/4: at Rome, then going to Naples. 1693, /6: at Perugia; /10: at Fermo; /12: at Chieti, going to Rome for the Carnival. (Cionini, p. 40; Rasi, i, 199–200; iii, 334–335. Rasi seems to confuse the facts by treating " Areliari " and " Rechiari " as separate persons and saying that the first took the part of *Lucca*.)

ARCHIARI, or ARELIARI, or RECHIARI, TEODORA. *Vittoria*. Wife of Luca Archiari, also in the service of Modena. 1675: in Modena troupe. 1688: *prima donna* in Modena troupe acting in turns with *Lavinia*. (Cionini, pp. 40–41; Rasi, i, 199–200; iii, 335.)

ARIEMME, GIAN GREGORIO D'. *Pascariello*. Mentioned by B. Zito in his commentary on Cortese (1628, p. 94). (Croce, p. 38.)

ARMANI, VINCENZA, or VICENZA. *Lidia* (?). A native of Venice, and one of the most famous of the early *innamorate*. 1567–68: acting at Mantua (see *supra*, p. 301). 1569, 11/9: murdered at Cremona. On her death Adriano Valerini, who seems to have been her lover, published an *Oratione* (Verona, 1570) in which he included many poems in praise of her and also *alquante leggiadre e belle Compositioni di detta Signora Vincenza*. (D'Ancona, ii, 450, 461; Rasi, i, 202–211; Garzoni in Petraccone, p. 5; A. Bartoli, p. cxix; F. Bartoli, i, 50–64.)

ARMANO, PIETRO D'. Mentioned in 1561. (Rasi, i, 211; D'Ancona, ii, 450.)

ARMANO, TIBERIO D'. Probably son of Tiberio. He acted Ascanio in Dolce's *Didone*, and published the printed text of this play. It is highly probable that neither of these two actors belonged to the professional troupes. (D'Ancona, ii, 450; Rasi, i, 211.)

ARRIGHI, CIALACE. *Pantalone*. Was in the company summoned to France by Cardinal Mazarin in 1645. (A. Bartoli, p. clxi; Rasi, i, 212.)

AURELIA. An actress taking this part wanted to join the Uniti on March 27, 1593. It may be to her that the sonnet quoted from manuscript by Rasi is addressed. Another *Aurelia* was in the Modena troupe in 1690; this could hardly be Brigida Bianchi, who was then seventy-seven years of age. (D'Ancona, ii, 512; Rasi, i, 235.)

APPENDIX

AURELIO. The various documents concerning *Aurelio* are gathered under Marcello di Secchi on the assumption that they all refer to him.

AUSTONI, GIOVAN BATTISTA. *Battistino*. A native of Ferrara. 1591, 6/2 and 5/5: at Mantua. 1608: with Accesi in France. 1615–1618 : with Confidenti. (Baschet, pp. 167, 169; Bertolotti, p. 71; Rasi, i, 237.)

AUSTONI, VALERIA. *Valeria*. Sister of Francesco Antonazzoni and wife of G. B. Austoni. She belonged in 1618 to the Confidenti, and seems to have been a jealous rival of Lavinia. Apparently Domenico Bruni was then her lover. (Achille Neri, in *Gazzetta Letteraria*, May 11 and 18, 1889; Rasi, i, 170–175, 237.)

AVERARA, DIANA. *Diana* (?). 1698, 22/3: called to serve in Modena troupe. (Rasi, ii, 762.)

BACHINO, GIO. MARIA. *Fortunio*. The only record concerning this actor comes from a letter of 1620 written by P. M. Cecchini. Bachino was then acting in a poor company with G. P. Fabbri, and Cecchini proposed that he should join his troupe. (D'Ancona, *Lettere di comici italiani*; Rasi, i, 247–248.)

BACHINO, ——. *Silvia*. Wife of G. M. Bachino.

BAGLIANI, PIETRO. *Dottor Graziano Forbizone da Francolino*. A native of Bologna. He is said to have been in a company of Uniti about 1623. Of his work there is extant a comedy, *La Pazzia* (Bologna, 1624), and Rasi has suggested that the *Indice universale della Libraria o Studio del celebratiss. Arcidottore Gratian Furbson de Frâculin* (Bologna, n.d.), usually attributed to G. C. Croce, is really by him. (A. Bartoli, p. clxvi; Rasi, i, 248–249; F. Bartoli, i, 67.)

BAGNACAVALLO, LIDIA DA. *Lidia*. Little for certain is known of this actress, who, however, seems to have won considerable fame in her time. Garzoni (Petraccone, p. 5) praises her, and she seems to have been connected with the Gelosi in 1571. There was a current story that Adriano Valerini abandoned her for Vincenza Armani. (D'Ancona, ii, 461; Rasi, iii, 23–25.)

BAJARDI, ANTONELLA. *Vittoria*. Practically nothing is known of A. Bajardi except the record given by F. Bartoli. He says she acted about 1620, and notes a special performance of *La Vittoria migliorata*, by A. M. Prati, at Parma. This play she got printed, and dedicated it on February 18, 1623, to a princess of the Farnese family. (F. Bartoli, i, 70; Rasi, i, 249–250.)

BALDI, FRANCESCO. *Pulcinella*. Often called Baldo Ciccio. He is said to have been acting at Naples about 1660 and to have inherited the Pulcinella tradition from Andrea Calcese " Ciuccio," passing that on to Mattia Barra and Michelangelo Fracanzani. (A. Bartoli, pp. clxxx–clxxxi; Rasi, i, 251.)

BALDUINO, EMILIO. A native of Parma who was at Mantua in 1592. (Bertolotti, p. 71; Rasi, i, 251–252.)

BALESTRI, GIOVANNI. 1593, /10: one of the Uniti begging leave to play at Genoa. (A. Neri, in *Fanfulla della Domenica*, April 4, 1886; D'Ancona, ii, 511; Rasi, i, 252.)

BALLETTI, FRANCESCO. 1687: one of the Calderoni troupe at Munich.

BALLETTI, GIOVANNA. Probably the wife of Francesco Balletti. 1687: in the Calderoni troupe at Munich.

BARBARIZZA, CONCORDIA. A native of Venice. 1590, /12: at Mantua. (Bertolotti, p. 70; Rasi, i, 265.)

BARBIERI, GIULIO CESARE. *Volpino*. Acting in 1664. (Rasi, ii, 855.)

BARBIERI, NICCOLÒ. *Beltrame*. A native of Milan. 1600–4: at Paris with Gelosi. Probably entered Fedeli *c.* 1604. 1613: at Paris with Fedeli. 1615: in Confidenti. 1624: in France with Fedeli. 1638: at Parma. Died *c.* 1640. Works: (1) *L' Inavvertito, ovvero Scappino disturbato, e Mezzetino travagliato*, a comedy (Torino, 1629; Venezia, 1630); (2) *La Svpplica Discorso Famigliare . . . diretta à quelli che scriuédo ò parlando trattano de Comici trascurando i meriti delle azzioni uirtuose* (Venezia, 1634). (A. Bartoli, pp. cxxxix, cxliii; F. Bartoli, i, 69–72; Rasi, i, 265–272; Baschet, pp. 334–335; Eugenio Treves, *Niccolò Barbieri detto il Beltrame, comico del secolo XVII* (*Archivio della Società vercellese di storia e d'arte*, v, 3).)

BARRA, MATTIA. *Policinella*. Said by Perrucci to have inherited the traditions of Francesco Baldi. (Rasi, i, 277; F. Bartoli, i, 73.)

BARTOLAZZI, MARGHERITA. 1640 and 1645: at Paris in Bianchi troupe. (A. Bartoli, p. cxliii.)

BATALLIA, TOMASO. In troupe of G. Nanini (*q.v.*).

BATTISTA DA RIMINO. See *Vannini, Gio. Battista*.

BEATRICE. For the Beatrice who won fame in France see *Fiorillo, Beatrice*. She is hardly likely, however, to be the Beatrice who acted in *La Pazzia* at Verona in 1663, and must be distinct from another Beatrice who was in the Mantua company at Bologna in 1695 and 1696. (Rasi, i, 6–7 ; *cf.* F. Bartoli, i, 117–118.)

BECCARINA. It is not certain that this was an actress. She was at Piacenza in 1688. (Bertolotti, p. 109; Rasi, i, 315.)

BECHO, CELIO. 1687: in the Modena troupe.

BENDINELLI, GIACINTO. *Valerio*. A native of Modena; son of Luca Bendinelli and Francesca Sennasoni or Scavasoni. 1651: in the Modena troupe. 1658: at Rome. 1660: at Paris. 1665, 1/9: married Jeanne-Marie Poulain. 1667: retired. 1668, 15/3: died. (Campardon, i, 33–34; Rasi, i, 342–343; Bertolotti, p. 108.)

BENOTTI, LUIGI. *Pantalone.* A native of Vicenza. Sand declares he was in the Fedeli in 1630; but no proof seems forthcoming. (Rasi, i, 348.)

BEOLCO, ANGELO. *Ruzzante.* Born at Padua in 1502. 1520, 13/2: played a *comedia a la vilanesca* at the Palazzo Foscari, Venice. Records of his activities at Venice are found in 1522, 1526, and 1527. 1542, 17/3: died. Scardeone (*De Antiquitate urbis Patorii* (Padova, 1560), p. 583) called him the Plautus and Roscius of his age. Many of his comedies are extant. (A. Mortier, *Essai sur les manuscrits et la bibliographie de Ruzzante* (Paris, 1913), and *Ruzzante* (Paris, 1925–26); A. Bartoli, p. cxxvii; Gaspary, *Storia della Letteratura italiana*, ii, 281–284; Rasi, i, 350–353; B. Brunelli, pp. 30–34.)

BERETTA, FEDERICO. *Capitano.* 1675: F. Allori and C. Palma of Mantua ask the Duke to get him in the company. (Rasi, i, 354.)

BERETTARO, FRANCESCO. Mentioned by Quadrio on the authority of Sansovino. (Quadrio; Rasi, i, 354.)

BERNARDINI, OTTAVIO. *Franceschina.* 1614, 4/8: at Genoa in a company of Uniti. (A. Neri, in *Fanfulla della Domenica*, July 16, 1882; Rasi, i, 359.)

BERTANI, LAURO. 1680, 3/4: at Mantua. Died before 1683. (Bertolotti, pp. 112–113; Rasi, i, 362.)

BERTOLINO. The Bertolino who was in the Uniti in 1584 is unidentifiable. The Bertolino who was in the Modena company in 1687 may be A. Broglia. (D'Ancona, ii, 486–487.)

BERZA, ISABELLA. 1687: in the Modena troupe. (Cionini, p. 40.)

BIANCHI, BRIGIDA. *Aurelia.* Daughter of Giuseppe Bianchi, and wife of N. Romagnesi; mother of M. A. Romagnesi. Born 1613. 1638: in Parma troupe. 1640–41: at Paris. 1645: returned to Paris. 1647: in Parma troupe. 1669–83: at Paris. 1683: retired. 1703, /11: died. Works: (1) *L'Inganno fortunato, ovvero L'amata aborrita* (Parigi, 1659) (this contains also some of her poems); (2) *Rifiuti di Pindo* (Parigi, 1666). This last work is printed as by "Aurelia Fedeli"; some believe that this means 'of the Fedeli'; others that it indicates that she was married a second time, to some one called Fedeli. It is difficult to judge; as the Fedeli acted on to 1642, she may well have been a member of that troupe. No record of a husband Fedeli is extant. (D'Ancona, ii, 512; A. Bartoli, p. cxliii; F. Bartoli, i, 123–124; Rasi, i, 419–423; Biancolelli manuscript, i, 52; Giuseppe Marcucci, in *Rassegna nazionale*, March 1, 1888.)

BIANCHI, GIUSEPPE. *Capitan Spezzaferro.* 1640 and 1645: at Paris. Evidently returned to Paris in 1668, and retired or died about 1682. His daughter was Brigida Bianchi. (Rasi, i, 415–419; A. Bartoli, pp. cxliii, clxx.)

BIANCHI, LODOVICO DE. *Dottor Gratiano Partesana da Francolino.* The *Dottore* of the Gelosi troupe. 1576, 6/11: at Florence. 1587, 11/7: at Venice. 1589, 6/9: at Milan. 1589, 21/10: at Pistoia. He has left a work entitled *Cento e quindici conclusioni in ottava rima del Plusquam perfetto Dottor Gratiano Partesana da Francolino Comico Geloso* (probably Bologna, 1587). (D'Ancona, ii, 469; Rasi, i, 404–415.)

BIANCOLELLI, CATERINA. *Colombina.* Daughter of Domenico and Orsola Biancolelli, born in 1665. 1683, 11/10: début as *Colombina* in *Arlequino Proteo.* Acted in Paris till 1697. 1685, /11: married Pierre Lenoir de la Thorillière, of the Comédie Française. Died at Paris, February 22, 1716. (Sand, i, 164–173; A. Bartoli, p. cxliv; Rasi, i, 437–443; Biancolelli manuscript, i, 96.)

BIANCOLELLI, FRANCESCA MARIA APOLLINE. *Isabella.* Sister of Caterina, born in 1664. 1683, 11/10: début as Isabella in *Arlequino Proteo.* Acted at Paris till 1695. 1691: married Constantino di Turgis, an officer of the Guard; he died by April 29, 1706. Died September 3, 1747. (A. Bartoli, p. cxliv; Rasi, i, 437; Biancolelli manuscript, i, 122.)

BIANCOLELLI, GIUSEPPE DOMENICO. *Arlecchino* or *Dominique.* Born at Bologna *c.* 1640. Entered company of Tabarini about 1657. Summoned to Paris 1661, where he acted all his life. 1663, 2/4: married Orsola Cortesi, by whom he had eight children. 1680: naturalized in France. Died August 2, 1688. There is extant much praise of his skill in acting. (Campardon, i, 61–70; Rasi, i, 430–435; A. Bartoli, p. clxxv; F. Bartoli, i, 124; Sand, i, 65–69; Biancolelli manuscript, i, 89–95. The *Arlequiniana* (Paris, 1694) of Carlo Cotolendi is apocryphal. *Cf.* also *Domenico Biancolelli, A Biographical Note* (*The Mask*, iv (1912), 340–341).)

BIANCOLELLI, ISABELLA. *Colombina.* Mother of G. D. Biancolelli; *née* I. Franchini, the daughter of Francesco Franchini. Biancolelli, her husband, died in 1640, and on April 15, 1645, she married Carlo Cantù, the young "Dominique" being then only a few years old. She acted thereafter with Cantù, and is found in the 1651 list of the Modena troupe. (Rasi, i, 425–430, ii, 582–583, ii, 876.))

BIANCOLELLI, NICCOLÒ. *Innamorato.* Said to have flourished about 1650, but nothing certain is known of him. He may have been the uncle of "Dominique." Works: (1) *Il Carnefice de sè stesso* (Napoli, n.d.); (2) *Il Nerone* (Bologna, 1664); (3) *La Regina statista d'Inghilterra, et il Conte di Essex* (Bologna, 1689); (4) *Il Principe tra gl' infortunij fortunato* (Bologna, 1668). (Rasi, i, 446–447; F. Bartoli, i, 124–125.)

BIANCOLELLI, ORSOLA. *Eularia.* Wife of G. B. Biancolelli, daughter of Antonio Cortesi and Barbara Minuti.

APPENDIX

She came to Paris as *seconda donna* in 1660, aged 24 or 25, and there married " Dominique " on April 2, 1663. She became *prima donna* on the death of Brigida Bianchi, and acted till 1691. Entering a convent in 1704, she died on January 11, 1718. She translated a Spanish comedy as *La Bella brutta* (Paris, 1666). (Campardon, i, 61; Rasi, i, 435–437; F. Bartoli, i, 126; Biancolelli manuscript, i, 80.)

BIANCOLELLI, PIETRO FRANCESCO. *Arlecchino* and *Pierrot*. Son of G. D. and O. Biancolelli, born at Paris on September 20, 1680. When Tortoriti organized a provincial company in 1697 after the closing of the Théâtre Italien, he made his *début* at Toulouse. Most of his career belongs to the eighteenth century. Died at Paris on April 18, 1734. (Sand, i, 68, 98; Rasi, i, 443–445.)

BISSONI, GIOVANNI. *Scapino*. Born at Bologna in 1666, and at age of fifteen joined a charlatan troupe under a certain Girolamo. Little is known of his activities until the eighteenth century. Died May 9, 1723. (Rasi, i, 450–452.)

BOCCHINI, BARTOLOMEO. *Zan Muzzina della Valle Retirada*. Author of several comic works: (1) *Le Pazzie dei Savj, ovvero il Lambertaccio* (Venezia, 1641); (2) *Il Trionfo di Scapino* (Bologna, 1663); (3) *La Prima (seconda) parte della corona macheronica* (Bologna, 1663); (4) *Miscvglio di pensieri rime bvrlesche* (Bologna, 1663). It is probable that he was an actor. (Antonio Orlandi, *Notizie degli scrittori bolognesi* (Bologna, 1714), p. 67; Rasi, i, 453–457.)

BOLICO, GIULIA. This actress was wanted by the Confidenti in 1583. She is probably the Giulia Brolo who was in the Uniti in 1584. (D'Ancona, ii, 485; Rasi, i, 470–471.)

BONAZZO, GIACOMO. *Gabinetto*. In Mantuan company 1658. (Bertolotti, p. 112; Rasi, i, 485. Bertolotti's *Gabucetto* is evidently *Gabinetto*.)

BONGIOVANNI, BARTOLOMEO. *Dottor Graziano*. 1612, 26/11: at Florence with Fedeli. (Rasi, i, 486–487.)

BONIFACI, ANGELA. In Calderoni troupe 1687.

BONIFACI, BERNARDO. In Calderoni troupe 1687. (Rasi, i, 487.)

BONONCINI, DOMENICO. *Brighella* and *Trivellino*. 1686: in Modena troupe. 1687: in Calderoni troupe. 1698, 22/6: at Rimini. (Cionini, p. 40; Rasi, i, 488–489.)

BOTANELLI, VICENZIO. *Curzio*. With Ganassa in Spain in 1581. (E. Cotarelo y Mori, p. 52.)

BOTTARGA, STEPHANEL. Little is known of this actor, save that he took a kind of *Pantalone* part in the late sixteenth century. To him was addressed a *Lamento sulla morte d'un pidocchio* by Ganassa.

BRAGA, GIACOMO. *Pantalone*. A native of Ferrara. 1583: in Gelosi-Uniti. 1591: at Mantua with G. B. Austoni. 1614, 4/8: in company of Uniti at Genoa. (Bertolotti, p. 71; Rasi, i, 503, 359; A. Bartoli, p. clxi.)

BRAMBILLA, GIACOMO. A native of Milan. 1590: at Vienna. (Rasi, i, 503.)

BRANCACCIO, FLAMINIO. *Fl. c.* 1636. (F. Bartoli, i, 131.)

BROGLIA, AMBROGIO. *Bertolino*. 1672: at Bologna. 1687: Modena and later in Calderoni troupe. (Rasi, i, 515.)

BROGLIA, FRANCESCA. *Tortorina*. Wife of A. Broglia. 1672: at Bologna. (Rasi, i, 515.)

BROLO, GIULIA. See *Bolico, Giulia*.

BRUNI, DOMENICO. *Fulvio* (and also occasionally *Romagnuolo* and *Graziano*). A native of Bologna. Born 1580, and entered Gelosi in 1594. On the death of Isabella Andreini, entered Confidenti, with whom he was acting in 1615 and 1621. Works: (1) *Dialoghi scenici . . . fatti da lui in diverse occasioni ad istanza delle sue compagne* (manuscript, see Rasi); (2) *Prologhi* (Torino, 1621); (3) *Fatiche comiche* (Parigi, 1623). (A. Bartoli, pp. cxxvii–cxxxix; Rasi, i, 518–525; F. Bartoli, i, 136–138.)

BUONOMO, AMBROGIO. *Coviello*. Acted at Naples in early seventeenth century. (Croce, p. 37; Rasi, i, 532–533.)

BURCHIELLA, LUZIO. *Dottor Graziano*. This actor may have been in the Ganassa troupe at Mantua in 1567. 1569: contributed poem on the death of Vincenza Armani. 1572: with Gelosi in France. His place seems later to have been taken by Lodovico de' Bianchi. (D'Ancona, ii, 446; Rasi, i, 534–535; F. Bartoli, i, 140–142.)

CACCAMESI, CESARE. *Innamorato*. Acted in Sicily in the mid-seventeenth century. (F. Bartoli, i, 143.)

CACCIA, GAETANO. *Leandro*. In Modena troupe 1686, 1688, 1690, and 1691. (Cionini, p. 40; B. Brunelli, p. 111.)

CALCESE, ANDREA " CIUCCIO." *Pulcinella*. A native of Naples. He is said to have ' invented ' the part of *Pulcinella*. He died in 1656, aged ninety-nine years. (A. Bartoli, p. clxxx; Croce, p. 63; Rasi, ii, 542; F. Bartoli, i, 143–144.)

CALDERONI, AGATA. *Flaminia*. Wife of Francesco Calderoni, and grandmother of L. Riccoboni's wife, Elena Balletti. She shared the fortunes of her husband in Germany and Austria. (L. Riccoboni, *Histoire du théâtre italien* (Paris, 1728), i, 59; F. Bartoli, i, 144; D'Ancona, in *Giornale storico*, vi (1885), 12; A. Ademollo, *Una Famiglia di comici* (Firenze, 1885); Rasi, i, 547.)

CALDERONI, FRANCESCO. *Silvio*. In 1664 Calderoni was acting in Italy, and was in the Parma troupe in 1682. His chief activities, however, were in Germany. 1687–91: in Bavaria. 1692, 5/8: at Naples, where he is found also on March 3 and 17, 1693. 1693, 4/9: at Livorno. 1694: recalled to Germany. 1699: at Vienna. When he died is not known, but he was still at Vienna in 1703. (Rasi, ii, 542; L. Riccoboni, i, 75; Bocchia, p. 82; F. Bartoli, i, 144–145.)

CALEGARO, GIOVANNI. Acting 1549. (E. Cocco, in *Giornale storico*, lxv (1915), p. 68.)

CALMO, ANDREA. A native of Venice, actor of old men's parts and dramatist. Born 1509; died 1570. Works: (1) *La Lettere* (Venezia, 1547, 1548, and 1552); (2) *Las Spagnolas* (Venezia, 1549); (3) *Il saltuzza* (Venezia, 1551); (4) *La Potione* (Venezia, 1552); (5) *La Fiorina* (Venezia, 1552); (6) *L' Egloghe pastorali* (Venezia, 1553); (7) *Le Rime pescatorie* (Venezia, 1553); (8) *La Rodiana* (Venezia, 1553); (9) *Il travaglia* (Venezia, 1556). (Vittorio Rossi, *La Lettere di Andrea Calmo* (Turin, 1888); Rasi, ii, 549–553; F. Bartoli, i, 146–147.)

CAMIA, GIULIA. A native of Piacenza. 1590, /12: at Mantua. (Bertolotti, p. 70.)

CAMPO, ISABELLA DEL. See *Fiorilli, Isabella*.

CANALI, ISABELLA. See *Andreini, Isabella*.

CANOVARO, GABRIELE. 1591, /2: at Mantua with P. M. Cecchini and G. B. Austoni. (Bertolotti, p. 70.)

CANTINELLA. An early actor apparently of improvised comedy. 1538, 30/4: already acting in Rome. 1546, 10/3: paid for comedies at Rome. Before 1566 Antonfrancesco Grazzini il Lasca referred to him, and from the reference it would seem that he took the part of the *Magnifico*. (E. Re, in *Giornale storico*, lxiii (1914), 292–298; Rasi, ii, 569–570; Bertolotti, *Speserie segrete e pubbliche di Papa Paolo III (Atti e memorie delle Regie Deputazioni di storia patria per le provincie dell' Emilia*, iii (1878), 1 ; Quadrio, v, 236; F. Bartoli, i, 151–153.)

CANTÙ, CARLO. *Buffetto*. Born 1609 and started acting 1632. 1638: in Parma troupe. 1645: at Paris. 1646, 30/11: at Florence; married about this time Isabella Franchini-Biancolelli. 1647: in service of Modena. 1647, 22/2, 6/3, 9/3, and 29/3: at Rome. Died about 1676. He wrote *Il Cicalamento*. (Rasi, ii, 571–583.)

CANTÙ, ISABELLA. See *Biancolelli, Isabella*.

CAPELLINO. *Pantalone*. 1655, /5: in Parmesan troupe at Mantua. 1655, 4/6: at Modena. (Rasi, ii, 585–586.)

CARLO. *Franceschina*. 1591, 27/10: at Milan.

CARPIANI, CARPIONI, or CARPIARI, ORAZIO. *Pantalone*. 1633, 20/12: mentioned in letter of Enzo Trenti. 1638: in Parma troupe. 1641: at Parma, invited to go to Ferrara. 1647: in Parma troupe. (Rasi, ii, 593–595, 880–882.)

CASTALDO, ALFONSO. 1564, 10/10: at Rome.

CASTIGLIONI, LEONORA. 1630, 13/2: at Rome. 1634, 15/2: at Ferrara. 1638: in Parma troupe. In her letters she mentions her husband. (Rasi, ii, 606–607, 880–882.)

CECCHINI, ORSOLA. *Flaminia*. Wife of P. M. Cecchini, and with him associated from 1605 with the Accesi; she may have been the daughter of Flaminio Scala. Her many quarrels with *Florinda* (V. Andreini) have been indicated above (pp. 327–329). Much poetic praise was accorded her: cf. *Raccolta di varie rime in lode della Sig. Orsola Cecchini* (Milano, 1608); *Rime del Sig. Cesare Rinaldi Bolognese* (Venetia, 1608), p. 92; *Rime di Scipione de' Signori della Cella* (Bologna, 1674), p. 183. The last two have not apparently been cited before, but D'Ancona mentions two sonnets, one by G. B. Sessa and another by G. Graziani. (F. Bartoli, i, 227; ii, 293; Rasi, ii, 638–643; D'Ancona, ii, 448; Croce, p. 61. A. Valeri, *Un Palcoscenico del Seicento* (Rome, 1893) suggests she was a daughter of Flaminio Scala.)

CECCHINI, PIER MARIA. *Fritellino*. Born at Ferrara on May 14, 1563; married apparently in 1594. His first appearance on the stage, as an amateur, was in 1583 at Mantua. Eight years later (1591) he was a professional actor at Mantua, and is found at various Italian cities 1595–1601. In 1601 he went to France, returning in 1602. In 1606 the Accesi, his company, seems to have joined the Fedeli, but in 1608 he broke off to go to France. In 1612 he was dismissed from Mantuan service, and in 1614 is found in Bavaria. During 1616–18 he made his headquarters at Naples, but came to the north of Italy in 1619. He continued acting until the thirties of the century. Died c. 1645. Works: (1) *La Flaminia schiava*, a play (Milano, 1610); (2) *I Brevi discorsi intorno alle comedie, comedianti et spettatori* (Venetia, 1621); (3) *Lettere facete e morali* (Venetia, 1622); (4) *Frutti delle moderne comedie et avisi a chi le recita* (Padova, 1628); (5) *L'Amico tradito*, a play (Venetia, 1633). Besides these there is a manuscript *Discorso sopra l'arte comica*. (Rasi, ii, 626-638; F. Bartoli, i, 166–168; Baschet, pp. 176–190; D'Ancona, ii, 532; Bertolotti, p. 70; F. Anaretti, *Un Artista e scrittore drammatico italiano del sec. XVII (Filotecnico*, ii (1886), 1–2).)

CHECO. Taking women's parts 1549. (E. Cocco, in *Giornale storico*, lxv (1915), 62.)

CHEREA, FRANCESCO. Pseudonym of Francesco de' Nobili, a native of Lucca. He was a particular favourite of Pope Leo X, and is said at Venice to have " invented in those parts " the improvisatorial style of acting. The records of his activities extend from 1508 to 1532. (Rasi, ii, 651–652.)

CHIAVARELLI, ALESSANDRO. *Scapino*. At the Opéra Comique in Paris in 1662. (A. Bartoli, p. cxlvii.)

CHIESA, GIROLAMO. *Dottor Graziano de' Violini*. Considerable doubt remains concerning this actor. He lived

APPENDIX

about 1630–50, and is found in the Parma troupe in 1647. (Rasi, ii, 655; Croce, p. 62; A. Bartoli, pp. cl and clxvi.)

CHIESA, ISABELLA. Wife of G. Chiesa. With her husband she was in the Affezionati in 1634. Poetic praise to her was written by G. F. M. Materdonna (*Rime*, Venezia, 1629), Paolo Cersonti, and T. Gradivello (*La Scena illustrata*, Bologna, 1634). (F. Bartoli, i, 169–171; Rasi, ii, 655–657.)

CIMADOR. Son of *Zan Polo*, acted at Venice in 1527. (Rasi, ii, 663.)

CIMADORI, GIO. ANDREA. *Finocchio*. A native of Ferrara. 1675–81: in Modena troupe. Died at Lyon after 1684. (A. Bartoli, p. cl; Rasi, ii, 663–664; B. Brunelli, p. 110.)

CINTIA. It seems impossible to identify the Cintia, *comica famosa*, who was sonnet-praised by Carlo d'Aquino (*Rugiade di Parnaso*, Cosenza, 1654). Rasi thought she might be the Cintia mentioned by G. B. Andreini in 1623, but Bevilacqua has shown that the reading Cintia is an error for Cintio (Rasi, ii, 665; Bevilacqua).

CLARINI, VIRGINIA. *Rotalinda*. Acted about 1665. A poem to her was written by G. Ugolani (*Rime*, Milano, 1667). (Rasi, ii, 671.)

COLETTI, MICHELANGELO. 1564, 10/10: acting at Rome.

COLLALTO. *Pantalone*. 1662: at Opéra Comique. (A. Bartoli, p. cxlvii.)

CONCEVOLI, FLORINDA. 1612: given leave to act at Milan. (Rasi, ii, 691.)

CONSALVO, NATALE. *Madamma Diana* and *Vertolino*. Acted in the beginning of the seventeenth century. (Croce, p. 37.)

COPPA, COLOMBA. *Aurelia*. Wife of G. Coppa. 1689: *seconda donna* in Modena troupe. 1691: in Modena troupe. (Cionini, p. 42; B. Brunelli, p. 111.)

COPPA, GIUSEPPE. *Virginio*. 1683–91: head of Modena troupe. (Rasi, ii, 693–694.)

CORIS, ALESSANDRINA. Probably a sister of Eularia Coris; *fl.* 1658. (Rasi, ii, 701.)

CORIS, BERNARDO, or BERNARDINO. *Silvio*. 1643–51: in Modena troupe. 1658: at Rome. (Rasi, ii, 701–702.)

CORIS, ORSOLA. *Eularia*. Apparently the daughter of B. Coris; almost certainly Eularia Coris and Orsola Coris are one and the same person. 1652: took chief part in G. B. Andreini's *La Maddalena*, in the printed edition of which are given some poems in her praise. A stupid sonnet to her and a parody by P. Abriani (not Adriani, as F. Bartoli and Rasi give it) appear in *Poesie di Paolo Abriani* (Venetia, 1663), pp. 181–182. Some letters of O. Coris dated in 1658 are given by Rasi; she seems then to have been in the Parma troupe. (A. Bartoli, p. cxxxix; F. Bartoli, i, 180–183; Rasi, ii, 696–702; Bertolotti, p. 109.)

CORIS, ——. *Florinda*. Wife of B. Coris. (Rasi, ii, 701.)

CORTESE, ALFONSO. A native of Naples. 1575, 5/7: acting at Naples.

CORTESE, ORSOLA. See *Biancolelli, Orsola*.

COSTANTINI, ANGELO. *Mezzetino*. Son of C. and D. Costantini. Born at Verona, *c.* 1655. 1678: probably in Parma troupe. 1683, 11/10: took part of Mezzetino in *Arlequino Proteo* at Paris, where he continued till 1697. In 1688 he assumed the *rôle* of Arlecchino, left vacant by the death of Biancolelli, but retained the name of Mezzetino. In 1697 he went to Brunswick, where he was given titles of nobility in 1699, but, rivalling the Elector of Saxony in an *amour*, he was cast into prison for twenty years. In 1729 he returned to Paris, but soon left for Verona, where he died the same year. He wrote *La Vita di Scaramuccia* (Parigi, 1695). (A. Bartoli, pp. cxliv, cxlviii; Rasi, ii, 710–720; Biancolelli manuscript, ii, 478.)

COSTANTINI, COSTANTINO. *Gradelino*. Born at Verona. 1668–87: in Modena troupe. 1687: appeared at Paris as *Gradelino*, but apparently returned soon to Italy. He must have gone back to France, where he was acting certainly in 1696. (Campardon, i, 136–139; A. Bartoli, p. cl; Rasi, ii, 708–710.)

COSTANTINI, DOMENICA. *Corallina*. Wife of Costantino Costantini. 1675–81: in Modena troupe. She published a revised version of *Il Natale de' fiori*, by Andrea Salvadori (1669). (Rasi, ii, 710; B. Brunelli, p. 110; F. Bartoli, i, 189.)

COSTANTINI, GIOVAN BATTISTA. *Cintio* and *Ottavio*. Son of C. and D. Costantini. Originally in the Modena troupe (1681), he appeared as *Ottavio* or *Octave* at Paris on November 2, 1688. When B. Ranieri was exiled the following year Costantini succeeded him, playing the *secondo amoroso* till 1694, when he became *primo amoroso* after M. A. Romagnesi abandoned the Lover for the Doctor. Died at La Rochelle May 16, 1720. (Campardon, i, 139–142; Rasi, ii, 721–723; A. Bartoli, p. cxliv; B. Brunelli, p. 110.)

COSTANTINI, TERESA. *Diana*. Wife of G. B. Costantini. She seems to be the Teresa Corona Sabolini who signed a document in 1677. 1677–88: in Modena troupe. (Rasi, ii, 723–724.)

COSTANTINI, ——. *Auretta*. Apparently a daughter of Angela D'Orsi, and wife of A. Costantini. 1664: in Parma troupe. 1678, 1/4: with Costantini in Parma troupe. She went with her husband to France, but did not win much fame there. (Rasi, ii, 716; 794–795.)

COTTA, PIETRO. *Celio*. An actor praised by Riccoboni. Works: (1) *Il Romolo, opera scenica* (Bologna, 1679); (2) *Le Peripezie di Aleramo e di Adelasia* (Bologna and Venezia, 1697). (L. Riccoboni, i, 75–76; F. Bartoli, i, 190–191; Rasi, ii, 727–730; A. Bartoli, p. cxxvii.)

DANNERET, ELISABETTA. See *Gherardi, Elisabetta*.

DONATO, GIO. See *Lombardi, Bernardino de*.

D'ORSI, or D'ORSO, ANGELA. Little for certain is known of this actress; she may have been the wife of Fabrizio. She was acting by 1650. 1664: mentioned with her daughter Auretta. 1672: in Parma troupe. A poem was written to her by the Marchese Giovanni Malaspina (*Rime*, Verona, 1653). Works: (1) *Di Bene in meglio*, a comedy translated from the Spanish (Venezia, 1656); (2) *Con chi vengo, vengo*, also from the Spanish (Ferrara, 1666); (3) *Il Ruffiano in Venezia, e medico in Napoli* (Roma, 1672). (Rasi, ii, 792–794.)

D'ORSI, TERESA. 1687: in Calderoni troupe at Munich.

D'ORSI, VITTORINO. 1687: in Calderoni troupe at Munich.

D'ORSI, ——. *Auretta*. See *Costantini, ——*.

FABA, PIETRO. Acting 1546. (E. Cocco, *loc. cit.*, lxv, 60–61.)

FABBRI, GIOVAN PAOLO. *Flaminio*. Born at Cividal del Friuli in 1567 (?). 1584, 3/4: in Uniti. 1603: in Gelosi at Paris. The latest record of his activities is that of 1614, when he was in a band of Uniti. Works: (1) *Due Suppliche e duo ringraziamenti alla Bernesca* (Trento, 1608); (2) *Quattro Capitoli alla Carlona* (Trento, 1608); (3) *Quattro Sonetti spirituali* (Perugia, 1610); (4) *Rime varie* (Milano, 1613). Other sonnets and prologues by him are cited by Rasi. (F. Bartoli, i, 202–205; A. Bartoli, p. cxxi; Baschet, p. 136; Rasi, ii, 840–846.)

FABIO. The *Fabio* praised by Garzoni in 1585 is not known. (Petraccone, p. 4; Rasi, ii, 854; *cf*. F. Bartoli, i, 201–202.)

FABRIZIO. A native of Naples, where he was directing a company *c*. 1650. 1664: desired to join the Parma service. His wife was named Angiolina; perhaps this is Angela D'Orsi with whom he appeared in 1664. (Rasi, ii, 854–855; F. Bartoli, i, 205.)

FALCONI, BARTOLOMEO. *Trapolino*. 1690 and 1694: in Mantua troupe. (Bertolotti, p. 116; Rasi, ii, 858.)

FANEGOTTI, ISABELLA. *Vittoria*. An undated letter (*c*. 1660) of hers is printed by Rasi. (Rasi, ii, 861.)

FARGNOCCOLA, or FRIGNOCOLA. A character type; the actor's name cannot now be ascertained. (Rasi, ii, 862.)

FARINO, or FARINA, GIULIO CESARE. 1575, 5/7: at Naples. See *Farina*. (Rasi, ii, 862–863.)

FAVELLA, GERONIMO. *Innamorato*. Flourished in the early seventeenth century at Naples, but abandoned the stage to become *gazzettiere* to the Viceroy. (Croce, p. 75; Rasi, ii, 863–864.)

FERARIIS, IACOPO ANTONIO DE. 1575, 5/7: at Naples. (Croce, p. 27.)

FIALA, ANGIOLA. Daughter of Marzia Fiala. See *Marcucci, Anna*.

FIALA, GIUSEPPE ANTONIO. *Capitan Sbranaleoni*. A native of Naples. For most of his life he seems to have been associated with the Modena troupe. 1651, 10/8: at Verona. 1664: acting at Modena. 1674, 14/8: at Naples. 1675: in list of Modena company. 1677, 1/11: at Venice. 1682: company disbanded, but reunited 1686. 1687, 19/5: at Modena. Probably died *c*. 1688. (A. Bartoli, p. cl; Rasi, ii, 876–878.)

FIALA, MARZIA. *Flaminia*. Probably a sister of Bernardo Narici and wife of G. A. Fiala; a native of Modena. She acted with her husband in the Modena troupe 1664–86. (A. Bartoli, p. cl; Rasi, ii, 878–879.)

FIAMETTA. The name of the Fiametta who was in the Affezionati in 1634 is not known. (A. Bartoli, p. cl; Rasi, ii, 881; F. Bartoli, i, 211.)

FIDENZI, IACOP' ANTONIO. *Cintio*. A native of Florence. Barbieri called him *onor delle scene e amico delle muse*. He seems to have been with P. M. Cecchini in 1607, but it is not certain that the Cintio of this date was in reality Fidenzi. At any rate, the Cintio of 1623 was described as a " youth," and he appears to have been Fidenzi. In 1627 he broke off from the Fedeli, forming a company of his own. This company was playing in 1633, and had become the Parma troupe by 1638. Fidenzi was still acting in 1650. Works: (1) *Un Effeto di diuozione* (Venezia, 1628); (2) *Poetici capricci* (Piacenza, 1652); (3) verses in the *Raccolta funebre* (Venezia, 1613) written on the death of Maria Nobili. (Bevilacqua, xxiv, 119; A. Bartoli, pp. cxxiv–cxxv; Rasi, ii, 880–884; F. Bartoli, i, 211–213.)

FIORILLI, ISABELLA. *Marinetta*. A native of Palermo, *née* Del Campo, wife of T. Fiorilli. Rasi prints a broadsheet poem to her in which she is called *Comica Confederata*. (Rasi, ii, 912–913; Bertolotti, p. 106.)

FIORILLI, TIBERIO. *Scaramuccia*. Born at Naples November 9, 1608. He is said by Angelo Costantini to have been a son of S. Fiorillo, but this is doubtful. His early training was in a poor touring company, but he soon made a name for himself at Mantua and Florence. At Palermo he married Isabella del Campo. He was in Paris apparently in 1640–47, and returned thither in 1653. Successive visits to Paris were made in 1658 (when he acted with Molière), 1661, 1665, 1666, 1670, 1685, 1686, 1688, 1692. He journeyed to England in 1673, 1675, and 1678. In 1688 he married Maria Roberta Duval, who had lived with him from 1680 to 1682, had fled from him to England, and then returned to him. He was by far the greatest actor of his time, and praise of his acting abounds. He died in 1694. (Campardon, i, 222–225; A. Bartoli, pp. cxliii, clxx–clxxii; Rasi, ii, 888–912; Biancolelli manuscript, i, 52; A. Costantini, *La Vie de Scaramouche* (Paris, 1695); preface by Paul Lacroix to *Les Caravanes de Scaramouche* (Paris, 1881).)

FIORILLO, BEATRICE. *Beatrice.* The wife of G. B. Fiorillo, *née* Vitelli. She was already married to him in 1639, when she was outraged by Conte Bonaparte Ghisleri when journeying from Rome to Ferrara. 1638: in Parma troupe. In 1650 she appears at Bologna, in 1651 at Rome, in 1653–54 at Paris. (A. Ademollo, *I Teatri di Roma del secolo decimo settimo* (Roma, 1888), p. 137; Rasi, ii, 928–930; A. Bartoli, p. cxliii; Biancolelli manuscript, i, 52, 80.)

FIORILLO, GIOVAN BATTISTA. *Trappolino* and *Scaramuccia.* Son of S. Fiorillo. He took the part of *Scaramuzzia* in a company of Uniti in 1614. 1634: in Affezionati. 1638: in Parma troupe. 1647: seeks to join Mantuan service. He was still acting in 1651. (A. Bartoli, p. cl; Rasi, ii, 927–928; F. Bartoli, i, 222–223; Bertolotti, p. 107.)

FIORILLO, SILVIO. *Capitan Matamoros.* Born at Naples, where he had a company in 1584 and 1599. 1600: came to Mantua. 1614: in a company of Uniti. 1621: acting with Cecchini (in Accesi). 1632: in Accesi. 1634: describes himself as of Affezionati. He is said to have been the 'inventor' of *Pulcinella*, and possibly he assumed this part in his early years, or alternated it with that of the Capitano. Works: (1) *L'Amor giusto*, an eclogue (Milano, 1605); (2) *La Ghirlanda*, an eclogue (Napoli, 1609); (3) *La Cortesia di Leone e di Ruggero con la morte di Rodomonte*, a play (Milano, 1614); (4) *I tre Capitani vanagloriosi*, a play (Napoli, 1621); (5) *Il Mondo conquistato*, a poem (Bologna and Milano, 1627); (6) *L'Ariodante tradito, e morte di Polinesso da Rinaldo Paladino* (Pavia, 1629); (7) *La Lucilla costante con le ridicolose disfide e prodezze di Policinella*, a play (Milano, 1632). (Croce, p. 65; A. Bartoli, pp. cxxviii, clxix–clxx, clxxx; Rasi, ii, 921–927; F. Bartoli, i, 223–229.)

FLAMINIA. The *Flaminia* who flourished in 1566–67 is unknown. (D'Ancona, ii, 447.)

FORNARIIS, FABRIZIO DE. *Capitan Cocodrillo.* Born at Naples. He may have been *lo spagnuolo* mentioned in 1566. 1571 (?) and 1584: in France, in Confidenti. He is said to have died in 1637. In Paris he caused to be printed *La Fiamella* (Paris, 1584), by B. Rossi, and in 1585 published *L'Angelica* (Paris). (A. Bartoli, pp. cxxiii, cxxx; F. Bartoli, i, 230–232; D'Ancona, ii, 444; Rasi, ii, 741–743; Croce, p. 33; A. L. Stiefel, *Tristan l' Hermite, Le Parasite und seine Quelle* (*Archiv für das Studium der neueren Sprachen und Litteraturen*, lxxxvi (1891), 1).)

FORTUNATI, TIBERIO. *Pantalone.* 1655: at Genoa and praised for his art. (Rasi, ii, 935.)

FRACANZANI, MICHELANGELO. *Pulcinella.* Brother of the painter Cesare Fracanzani, born at Naples c. 1638. 1685, /4: *début* at Théâtre Italien, where he played till 1697. (Campardon, i, 235–236; Rasi, ii, 939–940; Croce, p. 99; F. Bartoli, i, 236–238.)

FRAJACOMI, ANDREA. *Trivellino.* 1614, 4/8: in a company of Uniti. (Rasi, i, 359.)

FRANCESCO. *Il Giechino.* 1591, /12: at Mantua. (Bertolotti, p. 71.)

FRANCESCO. *Moschino.* Acting 1545–53. (E. Cocco, in *Giornale storico*, lxv (1915), 57–68.)

FRANCESCO DE LA LIRA. Acting 1545–46. (E. Cocco, in *Giornale storico*, lxv (1915), 57–60.)

FRANCHINI, FRANCESCO. *Pantalone.* 1647: at Bologna, when he seems to have been in a bad way. (Rasi, ii, 582.)

FRANCHINI, ISABELLA. See *Biancolelli, Isabella.*

FRANCIOTTO. See Rasi, i, 354.

FREDI, CARLO. 1602: acted as impresario at a Naples carnival. (Croce, p. 36.)

FROSIA. 1551, 23/1: acting at Rome. (E. Re, in *Giornale storico*, lxiii (1914), p. 296.)

GABBRIELLI, CARLO. *Polpetta.* Younger brother of F. Gabbrielli. (Rasi, ii, 966.)

GABBRIELLI, FRANCESCO. *Scapino.* A native of Florence, son of G. Gabbrielli. 1611, 12/4: seeks to join Mantua troupe. 1612: in Accesi. 1615: in Confidenti. 1624–25: at Paris with Fedeli. 1626, 26/9: apparently rejoined Accesi. 1636, /5: at Bologna. F. Bartoli says he died in 1654. (Rasi, ii, 957–966; Baschet, p. 333; F. Bartoli, i, 245–246; A. Bartoli, p. clxxix; A. Saviotti, *loc. cit.*, p. 68; *L'Infermità, testamento e Morte di Francesco Gabrielli detto Scapino* (Verona, Padoa, and Parma, 1638).)

GABBRIELLI, GIOVANNI. *Sivelli.* Born 1588. 1611, 12/4: mentioned. Author of a *Maridazzo di M. Zan Frognocola con Madonna Gnigniocola alla Bergamasca* (Venetia, 1618). (A. Bartoli, p. clxxx; Rasi, ii, 953–957.)

GABBRIELLI, GIROLAMO. *Pantalone.* Possibly a son of F. Gabbrielli. 1687: in Modena company. Sent petition to Modena in 1691. (Rasi, ii, 966–967.)

GABBRIELLI, GIULIA. *Diana.* Daughter of F. Gabbrielli. 1639 and 1645: in Paris. (A. Bartoli, p. cxliii; Rasi, ii, 966 Biancolelli manuscript, i, 52.)

GABBRIELLI, IPPOLITA. *Amorosa*, probably *Ippolita.* 1655: going to join Modena company. 1663: granted leave to play at Modena. (Rasi, ii, 967.)

GABBRIELLI, LUISA. See *Locatelli, Luisa.*

GABIATI, MARCO ANTONIO DE. See *Marc' Antonio.*

GABRIELLO DA BOLOGNA. See *Panzanini, Gabriele.*

GAGGI, G. *Pantalone.* 1660: at Livorno. (Rasi, iii, 536.)

GAMBI, SILVIO. *Innamorato,* probably *Silvio.* 1594, 13/10: probably *Silvio* in Uniti. 1595, 2/3: letter of recommendation. (D'Ancona, ii, 517.)

GANASSA, GIOVANNI ALBERTO. *Zanni,* perhaps *Arlecchino.* 1568: at Mantua. 1570: at Ferrara. 1571–72: at Paris, possibly visited London. 1574–75, 1578, 1580–83: in Spain. During the French tour he seems to have been associated with the Gelosi. He is credited also with inventing the part of the *Baron de Guenesche.* In Spanish documents he is often cited as Nazeri, Naseli, or Anaseli de Ganaça, or alias Ganasa. (A. Bartoli, p. cxxx; F. Bartoli, i, 248–251; Baschet, pp. 44–46; Solerti-Lanza; Rasi, ii, 979–981; E. Cotarelo y Mori, *Noticias biográficas de Alberto Ganasa, cómico famoso del siglo XVI* (*Revista de archivos, bibliotecas y museos* (III, xii (1908), 42–61); Cristóbal Pérez Pastor, *Nuevos datos acerca del histrionismo español en los siglos XVI y XVII; segunda série* (*Bulletin hispanique,* viii (1906), 71–78, 148–153, 363–373).)

GARAVINI, GIROLAMO. *Capitan Rinoceronte.* A native of Ferrara. 1605: in Accesi. 1609–20: in Fedeli. 1620: in Fedeli at Paris. Died October 2, 1624. He was much praised for his art. (A. Bartoli, pp. cxxxix and clxx; F. Bartoli, i, 252–253; Rasi, ii, 984–986.)

GARAVINI, MARGHERITA. *Flavia.* A native of Bologna, *née* Luciani, wife of G. Garavini. 1605: in Accesi, later joined the Fedeli. She was still acting in 1625. (Rasi, ii, 986–987; F. Bartoli, i, 253–254.)

GARDELLINI, GABBRIELLA. *Argentina.* 1688–89: in Modena troupe. (Rasi, ii, 987.)

GEROLAMI, GIACOMO. 1641: sends petition with E. Nelli to Milan. He apparently belonged to the Mantuan troupe. (Rasi, ii, 1006.)

GHERARDI, ELISABETTA. *Babet la chanteuse.* Née Danneret, wife of E. Gherardi. 1694, 24/8: *début* at Paris. (Rasi, ii, 1013.)

GHERARDI, EVARISTO. *Arlecchino.* Son of G. Gherardi, born at Prato, November 11, 1663. 1689, 1/10: *début* at Paris in Regnard's *Le Divorce forcé.* Acted there till 1697. Died August 31, 1700. His death was celebrated in *La Pompa funebre di Arlecchino* (Paris, 1701). To-day he is most remembered for his *Théâtre italien.* (A. Bartoli, p. clxxvi; F. Bartoli, i, 262–263; Campardon, i, 242; Rasi, ii, 1008–13; Sand, i, 76–78; *A Biographical Note on Evaristo Gherardi* (*The Mask,* 1910–11).)

GHERARDI, GIOVANNI. *Flautino.* 1675: appeared at Paris, from which later he was expelled. (Rasi, ii, 1006–8; Campardon, i, 240.)

GIARATONE or GERATONI, GIUSEPPE. *Pierrot.* A native of Ferrara, born *c.* 1639. 1673, 4/2: *début* at Paris in the *Suite du festin de Pierre.* Acted in Paris till 1697. (Sand, i, 207–211; Rasi, ii, 1021–22; Biancolelli manuscript, i, 113.)

GIARATTONI, ——. *Dottore.* 1655: apparently in Parma troupe. (Rasi, ii, 1020.)

GIOVAN MARIA ROMANO. 1574: at Trausnitz, and took part in the festivities there. (Rasi, ii, 1023–24.)

GIOVANNI PIETRO. *Ciambellotto.* 1546: at Padua. Probably the same as Zuane or Giovanni da Treviso mentioned in 1545. (E. Cocco, *loc. cit.,* pp. 57, 60.)

GRAZIULLO, ORAZIO. *Gariglia lo zoppo.* 1626: at Naples. (Croce, p. 41.)

GRISANTI, AGOSTINO. *Mario.* 1651–64: apparently in Parma and Modena troupes. (Rasi, ii, 1042–43.)

GUARNERA, GIAN CARLO. 1564, 10/10: acting at Rome.

GUAZZETTO. It is almost impossible to identify the Guazzetto who was in the Affezionati in 1634. (F. Bartoli, i, 276–277; Rasi, ii, 1045–46.)

HILVERDING, PETER. *Pantalone de' Bisognosi.* 1685–1720: acting in Austria. (Kutscher, p. 96.)

ISOLA, ANGIOLA. *Angiola.* 1689–91: in Modena company. (Rasi, ii, 1061; Cionini, p. 42.)

ISOLA, ANTONIA. See *Torri, Antonia.*

JULIO. 1570, 8/4: at Linz. This was no doubt a character-name, but may refer to Giulio Pasquati. A Julio was also at Mantua on December 29, 1591. (Bertolotti, p. 71.)

LAVINIO. It is impossible to identify the Lavinio who was in the Affezionati in 1634, and who was later acting in 1641. (Rasi, iii, 15; F. Bartoli, i, 289.)

LAZARO, BATTISTA. *Zanni* (?). 1583: at Paris. 1595, 4/12: Giambattista Lazaro in Desiosi at Cremona. (Rasi, iii, 15.)

LIBERATI, URANIA. *Bernetta.* 1620–21: went to France with Fedeli. (Rasi, ii, 23; Baschet, p. 280; D'Ancona, ii, 530.)

LIDIA. See *Bagnacavallo, Lidia da.*

LOCATELLI, DOMENICO. *Trivellino.* Born in 1613, Locatelli came to France about 1644, his son, Carlo Francesco, being baptized there on January 9, 1645. In 1651 he returned to Italy and joined the Modena troupe, but settled in France again in 1653, where he acted until his death on April 26, 1671. His first wife was Luisa Gabbrielli; his second (married June 9, 1665) was Maria di Creil. In 1648 he composed a French *argument* for an Italian comedy *Rosaura*. (A. Bartoli, p. cxliii; Rasi, iii, 27–29; Biancolelli manuscript, i, 52; B. Brunelli, p. 90.)

LOCATELLI, LUISA. *Lucilla*. *Née* L. Gabbrielli. Went to France in 1644 and was acting in the Modena troupe in 1651–52. She probably died in 1653. (A. Bartoli, p. cxliii; Rasi, iii, 28; Biancolelli manuscript, i, 52.)

LODOVICO DA BOLOGNA. See *Bianchi, Lodovico de*.

LOLLI, BEATRICE. See *Adami, Patrizia*.

LOLLI, EUSTACHIO. *Fichetto*. 1651: in Modena troupe. (Rasi, iii, 29; B. Brunelli, pp. 88–94.)

LOLLI, GIOVAN ANTONIO. *Dottor Brentino*. 1661: in Parma troupe, asked to join that of Modena. 1676: in France, returned to Italy within a year. 1679: in London. 1683–92: in Modena troupe. (Cionini, p. 40; Bertolotti, p. 108; Rasi, iii, 30–32.)

LOLLI, GIOVANNI BATTISTA ANGELO AGOSTINO. *Dottor Grazian Baloardo*. A native of Bologna, born c. 1628. Married Patrizia Adami; both he and his wife were naturalized French on June 16, 1683. He went to France in 1645 and acted there till 1694. Died November 4, 1702. (A. Bartoli, p. clxvi; Campardon, i, 294; Rasi, iii, 32–34; Biancolelli manuscript, i, 61.)

LOMBARDI, BERNARDINO DE. *Dottor Graziano*. Three men, if they be three, get confused in the last years of the sixteenth century: (1) B. de Lombardi, who was in the Confidenti in 1583, and published that year at Ferrara *L'Alchimista*; (2) Gio. Donato Lombardo, author of *Nuovo prato di prologhi di Gio. Donato Lombardo da Bitonto, detto il Bitontino* (Venezia, 1618) and of *Il Fortunato amante* (Messina, 1589); (3) Gio. Donato, who was in the Uniti in 1584 and in 1589 signed with Isabella Andreini a joint petition of the Uniti and Confidenti. (Croce, pp. 33–34; D'Ancona, ii, 476, 487; A. Bartoli, p. cxxii; Rasi, iii, 36, 44–45; F. Bartoli, i, 295–296 and 301–304.)

LOMBARDO, GIO. DONATO. See under *Lombardi, Bernardino de*.

LONGAVILLA, FRANCESCO. 1626 : at Naples. (Croce, p. 41.)

LUCCHESE, ANGELA. *Ricciolina*. 1602: at Naples. 1605: in Accesi. A *Ricciolina* was in the Affezionati in 1634. (Croce, p. 36.)

LUCIANI, MARGHERITA. See *Garavini, Margherita*.

LUCREZIA. A native of Siena. 1564, 10/10: at Rome. (E. Re, *loc. cit.*, lxiii, 298.)

LUTIANI, GIULIO and FRANCESCO. 1591, 29/12: at Mantua. (Bertolotti, p. 71.)

LUTIO. It is impossible to identify this actor who was in the Uniti in 1584. He may be the same as a certain Lucio Fedele mentioned elsewhere. (D'Ancona, ii, 487; Rasi, iii, 46.)

MALDOTTI, ——. A child acting Amorino in the Affezionati in 1634. (A. Bartoli, p. cl; F. Bartoli, ii, 11.)

MALLONI, MARIA. *Celia*. Born at Ferrara in 1599. 1611: *Corona di lodi alla signora M. M. detta Celia Comica* (Venezia, 1611). 1618: joined Confidenti. 1622: left Confidenti. 1626: in Fedeli. 1627, 6/1: praised for her art. Many poems were written in her praise; Marino placed her as the Fourth Grace in his *Adone*. (A. Bartoli, pp. cxxx–cxxxi, cl; Rasi, iii, 61–67, ii, 963; F. Bartoli, ii, 11–18; A. Saviotti, in *Giornale storico*, lxi (1903), 62.)

MALOSSI, CARLO. *Pantalone*. 1658: at Rome. (Bertolotti, p. 109; Rasi, iii, 67.)

MANGINI, ANDREA. *Adriano*. 1614: in a company of Uniti.

MANI, TOMASA DE. 1590, 10/12: at Mantua. (Rasi, ii, 752; Bertolotti, p. 70.)

MANZANI, FRANCESCO. *Capitan Terremoto*. Little is known of this actor. In 1661 he published at Torino a translation of a Spanish play as *A Gran danno gran rimedio*. (A. Bartoli, p. clxx; Rasi, iii, 68; F. Bartoli, ii, 19-20.)

MARC' ANTONIO. Probably the same as Marco Antonio de Gabiati, who was at Rome in 1564. 1550–53: at Rome. 1567: at Genoa. (E. Re, *loc. cit.*, lxiii, 296; D'Ancona, ii, 477–478.)

MARCHETTI, STEFANO. *Lelio*. Acting 1673–79. (Rasi, iii, 72.)

MARCUCCI, ANNA. *Angiola*. Daughter of Marzia Fiala. 1686: in Modena troupe. (Cionini, p. 40.)

MARIO DI TOMMASO. *Lepido*. A native of Siena. Acting in 1575. Is this Tomasa de Mani (*supra*)?

MARTINELLI, ANGELICA. See *Alberigi, Angelica*.

MARTINELLI, DRUSIANO. *Zanni*. Brother of T. Martinelli. 1578, 13/1: in England. 1580, 17/9: at Florence. 1588: in Spain. 1591–93: acting in various Italian towns, evidently in Mantuan service. 1594–95: at head of Uniti. 1598: at Mantua. 1600: with Accesi in France. Died between 1606 and 1608. (D'Ancona, ii, *passim*; Rasi, iii, 104-106 ; Winifred Smith, *Italian Actors in England* (*Modern Language Notes*, xliv (1929), 375–377).)

MARTINELLI, TRISTANO. *Arlecchino*. Born *c.* 1557, son of a Francesco Martinelli of Mantua. 1588: in Spain. 1595: abandons Pedrolino's troupe and joins Desiosi. 1597: at Mantua. 1599–1601: in Accesi at Paris. 1612–21: in Fedeli. 1613 and 1621: in France. Still acting at Mantua in 1626. Died 1630. Wrote *Compositions de Rhetoriqve* (Paris, 1600). (Baschet, pp. 118–119, 194–196, 244; Rasi, iii, 95–104; G. Jarro, *L' Epistolario d' Arlecchino* (Florence, 1895).)

MASSIMIANO, MILANINO. 1578, /12: in France. Possibly the same as the Masimigliano who was at Milan in 1591. (D'Ancona, ii, 504–506; Baschet, pp. 86–87.)

MATERAZZI, FRANCESCO. *Dottore*. Born at Milan *c.* 1652. 1686–1689: in Modena troupe. His chief career was in the eighteenth century. Died November 29, 1738. (Rasi, iii, 112–113; Cionini, p. 42.)

MATTEO. 1551: at Rome. (E. Re, *loc. cit.*, lxiii, 296.)

MICHELE, ANGELO. A native of Bologna. 1567: at Genoa. (D'Ancona, ii, 477.)

MILANTA, GIUSEPPE. *Dottor Lanternone*. 1655–87: apparently in Modena troupe. In 1664 he was among the actors whom Fabrizio wanted to bring to the service of Parma. (Rasi, iii, 125–126.)

MILLITA, ANNA MARIA. *Cintia*. 1678: in Modena troupe. (Rasi, iii, 126.)

MINUTI, BARBARA. *Florinda*. Mother of Orsola Cortesi-Biancolelli. (Rasi, i, 435.)

MONTINI, or MONTENI, IPPOLITO. *Cortellaccio*. A native of Mirandola. 1614, 4/8: in a company of Uniti. In Costanti at an unknown date. Works: (1) *Segreti maravigliosi di natura* (Bologna, 1611); (2) *Contesa di precedenza* (Bologna, 1624). (Rasi, iii, 152–153, i, 359, ii, 743.)

MOZZANA, FRANCESCO. *Truffaldino*. This actor may have been the Truffaldino who was in the Modena troupe in 1650–51. Author of *Un Curioso capriccio di bellissimi giuochi non più veduti* (Milano, n.d.). (Rasi, iii, 168–169.)

MUSI, MARIA MADDALENA. 1690, 31/3: apparently in Mantuan troupe. (Rasi, iii, 169.)

MUTIO. An Italian player of this name was in Spain in 1538. (Jóse S. Arjona, *El Teatro en Sevilla* (Madrid, 1887), p. 43.)

MUZIO, ANGELO ANTONIO. *Dottore*. 1688–89: in Modena troupe. (Rasi, iii, 169.)

NADASTI, LUCINDA. *Lucinda*. 1664: in Parma troupe (?). 1688: in Modena troupe. (Rasi, iii, 173.)

NANINI, GIOVANNI. *Dottore*. 1689: directing company in Bavaria. (Rasi, iii, 173–174.)

NAPOLIONI, MARCO. *Flaminio*. A native of Naples. Called Flaminione to distinguish him from other Flaminios. 1647–59: in Modena troupe. (Rasi, iii, 174–175 (Rasi makes him a member of the Parma troupe and quotes from Allacci a long list of his works); Biancolelli manuscript, i, 56; Bertolotti, p. 109; F. Bartoli, ii, 57–58.)

NARICI, BERNARDO. *Orazio*. A native of Genoa. 1675–87: in Modena troupe. (A. Bartoli, p. cl; Rasi, iii, 179.)

NARICI, MARZIA. See *Fiala, Marzia*.

NEGRI, DOMENICO DE. *Curzio*. 1614, 4/8: in a company of Uniti. (Rasi, iii, 758; i, 359.)

NELLI, ANGELA. *Amorosa*. 1650–51: in Modena troupe. She was the wife of E. Nelli. (Rasi, iii, 182–183; see the poem to her in *Poesie di Paolo Abriani* (Venetia, 1663), p. 13; F. Bartoli, ii, 61–62.)

NELLI, ERCOLE. *Zanni* and *Dottore*. 1650–54: in Modena troupe. (Rasi, iii, 181–182.)

NETTUNI, LORENZO. *Fichetto*. A native of Bologna. 1610: in Confidenti. 1620–21: in Fedeli. (Baschet, p. 280; Rasi, iii, 183.)

NOBILI, CAMILLA. *Delia*. Daughter of C. de Nobili, wife of —— Rocca. See *Le Funebri rime, di diversi eccell. autori, in morte della signora Camilla Rocha Nobili comica confidente detta Delia* (Venetia, 1613), and L. Quirini, *Versi d' Erato Poesie liriche di Lorenzo Quirino* (Vinegia, 1649). (Rasi, iii, 386–388; F. Bartoli, ii, 292–293.)

NOBILI, CESARE DE. A native of Florence. 1586: in Desiosi. (Rasi, ii, 755.)

NOBILI, NOBILE DE. 1590, 12/9: at Mantua. (Bertolotti, p. 70.)

NOBILI, ORAZIO. *Orazio*. 1570: probably the *Orazio* who was at Linz. 1571–79: probably in Gelosi. The *Orazio* of 1570 is described as a native of Florence; Bruni says he of the Gelosi was a native of Padua. (D'Ancona, ii, 469, 471; Rasi, iii, 184; F. Bartoli, ii, 63–64.)

NOLFI, GUIDO. A native of Fano. 1590, 1/12: at Mantua. (Bertolotti, p. 70.)

ODOARDO, —— D'. *Lucindo*. 1664: one of the actors whom Fabrizio wanted to bring into Mantuan service. (See *supra*, p. 336.)

OLIVETTA. The name of this actress cannot be traced. F. Bartoli notes a poem to her by G. B. Miamiano (*Rime*, 1620). From the Scala *scenari* she seems to have been in the Scala company. (F. Bartoli, ii, 65–66; Rasi, iii, 194–196.)

ONORATI, OTTAVIO. *Mezzetino*. 1615–18: in the Confidenti. (Rasi, iii, 196; Saviotti, pp. 60–62.)

ORLANDI, GIUSEPPE. *Dottore*. A native of Ferrara. 1675–81: in Modena troupe. (A. Bartoli, p. cl; Rasi, iii, 196; B. Brunelli, p. 110.)

ORSATTI, DOMENICO. 1687: in Calderoni troupe at Munich. (See *supra*, p. 336.)

APPENDIX

ORSINO, CLAUDIO. 1564, 10/10: at Rome. (E. Re. *loc. cit.*, lxiii, 298.)

OTTAVIO, or OTTAVIANO. *Tartaglia.* A native of Ferrara. 1602: at Naples. (Croce, pp. 33–36; Rasi, ii, 867.)

PADERNA, GIOVANNI. *Dottore.* A native of Bologna; flourished in the mid-seventeenth century. (A. Bartoli, p. clxvi; F. Bartoli, ii, 69–70.)

PAGHETTI, GIO. BATTISTA. *Dottore.* 1686: in Modena troupe. *C.* 1690: praised by Riccoboni. (L. Riccoboni, i, 73; Rasi, iii, 203; F. Bartoli, ii, 76.)

PAGHETTI, PIETRO. Born at Brescia in 1674. His main career falls in the eighteenth century. (Rasi, iii, 203–204.)

PALMA, CARLO. *Truffaldino.* 1658: at Rome with Lolli. 1675: in Mantuan company. (Rasi, iii, 210.)

PANZANINI, GABRIELE. *Francatrippe.* Evidently the same as Gabriello da Bologna. 1582: probably in Gelosi. 1585: in Gelosi. 1593: in Uniti. Later he was in the Costanti. (A. Bartoli, p. cxxxiii; Rasi, iii, 212–213, ii, 743.)

PAOLO. A native of Padua. 1579: in France, probably with Massimiano and Martinelli. (Baschet, p. 87; Rasi, iii, 213.)

PARRINO, or PANNINI, DOMENICO ANTONIO. *Florindo.* A native of Naples. 1675–86: in Modena troupe. He was the author of *Teatro eroico e politico del governo de' Vicerè del Regno di Napoli dal tempo del Re Ferdinando il Cattolico fino al presente* (Napoli, 1692). (A. Bartoli, p. cl; Rasi, iii, 219–224; F. Bartoli, ii, 79–80.)

PARUTI, GIOVAN BATTISTA. *Finocchio.* 1686: in Modena troupe. (Rasi, iii, 224; Cionini, p. 40.)

PARUTI, MADDALENA FRANCESCA. *Pimpinella.* 1686: in Modena troupe. (Rasi, iii, 224.)

PASQUATI, GIULIO. *Pantalone.* 1567: possibly *Pantalone* at Mantua. 1570–74: possibly *Pantalone* in Soldino troupe. 1574–85: in Gelosi. 1575: in Vienna. Pasquati was famous in his own day and received praise from F. Andreini and Garzoni. (A. Bartoli, p. clxi; Rasi, iii, 226–235; Baschet, p. 61; D'Ancona, ii, 468; F. Bartoli, ii, 80.)

PAUL DE PADOUE. See *Paolo.*

PAVOLI, MARGHERITA. 1589: at Mantua. 1591: at Milan. 1592, 11/10: recommended by Duke of Mantua to Uniti. (D'Ancona, ii, 494.)

PELLESINI, GIOVANNI. *Pedrolino.* Born *c.* 1526. 1576: evidently directing a company of his own. 1580: joined Confidenti with Vittoria, who seems to have been his wife. 1583–1602: in Uniti-Gelosi. 1610: at Florence. 1612: in Fedeli. (Rasi, iii, 241–244; D'Ancona, ii, 511; A. Valeri, *Chi era Pedrolino?* in *Rassegna bibliografica,* iv (1896), 2.)

PERILLO, GUGLIELMO. 1567: forms a company at Genoa with Michele and Marcantonio. (D'Ancona, ii, 477–478; Croce, p. 34.)

PETIGNONI, RINALDO. *Fortunio.* 1574: in Gelosi. He was praised by Porcacchi. (D'Ancona, ii, 468; Baschet, p. 61.)

PIETRO, PAOLO. 1640, 4/3: mentioned in a letter addressed to Modena. (Rasi, iii, 286.)

PIISSIMI, VITTORIA. *Vittoria* and perhaps also *Fioretta.* A native of Ferrara. 1575: in Gelosi. 1578 or 1580: in Confidenti. 1582: evidently married to G. Pellesini. 1585–94: in Gelosi-Uniti. It is possible that she was an unattached 'star' moving from company to company. (D'Ancona, ii, 466: F. Bartoli, ii, 273–275; Rasi, iii, 287–292.)

PILASTRI, FRANCESCO DE. *Leandro.* 1590–94: in Uniti. He was especially praised by D. Bruni. (D'Ancona, ii, 511; Rasi, iii, 292–293; F. Bartoli, ii, 89–90.)

PILASTRI, IMILIA. Wife of F. de Pilastri. 1591, 5/12: at Mantua, apparently in Gelosi-Uniti. (Bertolotti, p. 71.)

POLO, ZAN. 1515, 1522: acting at Venice. (Rasi, iii, 748.)

PONTI, DIANA. *Lavinia* and possibly also *Diana.* 1582, 8/7: evidently in Confidenti. 1585, 20/7: acting with Gratiano, possibly in Gelosi. 1586–90: possibly in Gelosi. 1595, 7/6: mentioned as belonging to Desiosi. 1601: probably in France with Accesi; in the same year a sonnet was published as by " signora Diana Ponti detta Lavinia, Comica Desiosa." 1605, 26/3: has a company of her own at Ferrara; 8/5: her company leaves Mirandola. It seems probable that Diana was another 'star' who temporarily joined various major companies. (A. Bartoli, p. cxxxix; D'Ancona, ii, 481; Rasi, iii, 304–306.)

PRUDENZA. *Innamorata.* 1634: in Affezionati. (Rasi, iii, 313–315; F. Bartoli, ii, 99–101.)

PRUDENZA, or PRUDENTIA. *Innamorata.* A native of Verona. *C.* 1576: in Gelosi. (D'Ancona, ii, 469; Rasi, iii, 312–313; F. Bartoli, ii, 101.)

RAMPONI, VIRGINIA. See *Andreini, Virginia.*

RANIERI, BARTOLOMEO. *Aurelio.* A native of Piedmont, born *c.* 1640. He is probably the *Aurelio* who was in Mantuan service in 1676. 1685, /4: appeared in Paris, whence he was expelled in 1689. He returned to Piedmont and became a priest. (D'Ancona, ii, 471; Rasi, iii, 323–324.)

RANUZZI, GIOVAN BATTISTA. 1626: at Naples. (Croce, p. 41.)

RAPARELLI, GIOVANNI. *Orazio.* A native of Viterbo, who was in official service at Perugia. In 1658 he married Angiola, but was cheated by her. (Rasi, iii, 324–325.)

RE, MAFFEO DEI. *Zanni.* 1545, 25/2: head of a company at Padua. He acted till 1553, when he was slain in a brawl at Rome. (E. Cocco, *loc. cit.*, 57–68.)

RE, PIETRO DI. *Mescolino.* Acted apparently about 1625. (F. Bartoli, ii, 103; Rasi, iii, 333.)

RECHIARI, G., L., and T. See *Archiari, Giorgio*; *Archiari, Luca*; and *Archiari, Teodora.*

RICCI, or RIZZI, BENEDETTO. *Leandro.* A native of Venice, nephew of F. Ricci, born May 9, 1592. 1612, 26/11: in Fedeli. 1618: at Naples, summoned to Confidenti. Died at Chambéry 1620. From his horoscope it appears he married in 1614 and killed a man in 1616. (Rasi, iii, 341–342.)

RICCI, or RIZZI, FEDERIGO. *Pantalone.* 1609–20: in Fedeli. (Rasi, iii, 341; Baschet, p. 280.)

RICCIOLINA. A Ricciolina was in the Affezionati in 1634. The Rizzolina of the Accesi in 1605 may be Angela Lucchese. (Rasi, iii, 34–35; F. Bartoli, ii, 110.)

RICCOBONI, ANTONIO. *Pantalone.* A native of Venice. 1675–91: in Modena troupe, but paid visits to France and England (in 1679). He was still acting in 1695. (A. Bartoli, pp. cl, clxii; Rasi, iii, 346–348; B. Brunelli, p. 111.)

RICCOBONI, BARBARA. A *cantatrice*, at Mantua in 1693. (Rasi, iii, 345–346.)

RICCOBONI, LUIGI. *Federico* and *Lelio.* Son of A. Riccoboni, born at Modena in 1675 or 1677. About 1692 joined the Modena troupe, but, moved by religious aspirations, wished to leave the stage and become a monk. The Duke prevented him, and he remained an actor, winning great fame in later years. (Rasi, iii, 348–355; Cionini, p. 43; F. Bartoli, ii, 111–119.)

RIGETTI, GIAN PAOLO DE. A native of Bologna or of Friuli. 1590–91: at Mantua, possibly in Accesi. (Rasi, iii, 356–357.)

RIVANI, GIOVANNI. 1620, 28/9: in Fedeli. (Baschet, p. 280.)

RIZZI, B. and F. See *Ricci, Benedetto*, and *Ricci, Federigo.*

ROCCA, CAMILLA. See *Nobili, Camilla.*

ROLENZINO. 1691, 14/8: mentioned in a letter addressed to Modena. (Rasi, iii, 393.)

ROMAGNESI, BRIGIDA. See *Bianchi, Brigida.*

ROMAGNESI, CARLO VIRGILIO, DI BELMONT. *Leandro.* Son of M. A. Romagnesi, born at Paris May 7, 1670. 1694, 24/8: *début* at Théâtre Italien. Acted there till closing of theatre in 1697, then joined Tortoriti on tour. He won considerable fame before his death in 1708. (Rasi, iii, 399–403; Biancolelli manuscript, i, 82, 99.)

ROMAGNESI, GÆTANO. Son of M. A. Romagnesi. Acted first in Holland and later in France. Died October 26, 1700. (Rasi, iii, 399.)

ROMAGNESI, MARC' ANTONIO. *Cintio* and, later, *Dottore.* A son of Brigida Bianchi, born *c.* 1633. 1653, 31/3: married Elisabetta Giulia della Chiesa, who died at London in 1675. 1655–59: in Mantuan service. 1660: in France. At first he took the part of the *secondo amoroso*, then in 1688 he assumed the *rôle* of the first. 1694, 29/8: first essayed part of *Dottore*. Retired 1697; died October 29, 1706. His *Poesie liriche* was published at Paris in 1673. (Rasi, iii, 394–399; A. Bartoli, pp. cxxv–cxxvi; L. Riccoboni, *Histoire*, i, 73; Biancolelli manuscript, i, 99; F. Bartoli, ii, 124–127.)

ROMAGNESI, MARC' ANTONIO. *Pantalone.* A native of Ferrara. 1612–16: associated with Cecchini. His *Dichiaratione del Re Christianissimo* was published at Venice in 1634. (Rasi, iii, 393–394.)

ROMAGNESI, N. *Orazio.* Husband of Brigida Bianchi. He died during the visit of the company to Paris in 1660. (Rasi, iii, 394; Biancolelli manuscript, i, 82.)

RONCAGLI, SILVIA. *Franceschina.* A native of Bergamo. She seems to have been in the Gelosi in 1576–78. (D'Ancona, ii, 469; Rasi, iii, 407.)

ROSA, RINALDO. *Pantalone.* 1697: in Modena troupe. (Rasi, iii, 408.)

ROSSI, BARTOLOMEO. *Orazio.* A native of Verona. 1584: in Paris, where his *Fiamella* was published. (Rasi, iii, 413–417.)

ROSSI, DOMENICO DE'. A native of Forlì. 1564, 10/10: acting at Rome with Marc' Antonio.

ROTARI, VIRGINIA. *Lidia.* Originally the wife of Baldo Rotari, and so called La Baldina. *C.* 1603: commenced acting at Mantua. From 1612 she was associated with the Fedeli. 1614 and 1621: in France. 1628: at Vienna, when she said she was a widow with seven children. She later married G. B. Andreini. (Rasi, i, 151–157; F. Bartoli, i, 37–38.)

SACCO, or SACCHI, GENNARO. *Coviello* and *Cardocchia.* A native of Naples. 1689–93: in Modena troupe. Died *c.* 1715. He published several works: (1) *Sempre vince la ragione* (Genova, 1686); (2) *Il Trionfo del merito* (Venezia, 1686); (3) *La Luna ecclissata dalla fede trionfante di Duba, regina dell' Ungheria* (Verona, 1687);

(4) *La Commedia smascherata, ovvero i Comici esaminati* (Varsavia, 1699). (Rasi, iii, 455–457; Cionini, p. 42; F. Bartoli, ii, 149–151.)

SACCO, or SACCHI, MADDALENA. *Armellina.* Wife of G. Sacco. 1689–91: in Modena troupe. (Rasi, iii, 456; Cionini, p. 42; B. Brunelli, p. 111.)

SALAMONA, ANGELA. *Angela* (?). In Confidenti, 1587. (E. Cotarelo y Mori, p. 61.)

SALIMBENI, GIROLAMO. *Zanobio,* or *Piombino,* or *Zanobio da Piombino.* 1578: in the Gelosi. 1593–94: in Uniti. (D'Ancona, ii, 469; Rasi, iii, 476–477; F. Bartoli, ii, 153–154.)

SANGIORGI, CARLO. *Trivellino.* 1681, 28/12: at Venice. 1686, 28/6: in Modena troupe. (Rasi, iii, 502–503.)

SAVORINI, ANNA. See *Arcagiati, Anna.*

SAVORINI, GALEAZZO. *Dottore.* A native of Bologna. 1689–99: in Modena troupe. (Rasi, iii, 507–509; L. Riccoboni, *Histoire,* i, 73.)

SCALA, FLAMINIO. *Flavio.* Scala was certainly associated at one period with the Gelosi, but no record exists to prove this. 1600: at Lyons with Cecchini in Accesi. 1610: at Ravenna. 1611–20: in Confidenti. He published *Il Teatro delle favole rappresentative* (Venezia, 1611). (A. Bartoli, p. cxviii; Rasi, iii, 512–520; F. Bartoli, ii, 155–159.)

SCARNECCHIA. 1673: acting with Fidelin at Modena. (Rasi, iii, 521.)

SCARPETTA, GIUSEPPE. 1596, 15/2: in Desiosi. He had retired by 1613. (Rasi, iii, 521–522.)

SCATTOLONE. 1622, 15/11: mentioned. (Rasi, iii, 525.)

SCEVOLA. 1565: said to have been acting at Rome; cited as Scevola Senese.

SCHIAVI, CARLO. *Cintio.* 1679, 19/4: agrees to join Modena troupe. (Rasi, iii, 530.)

SCOTIVELLI, MARCANTONIO. 1578, /12: in France with Massimiano. (Rasi, iii, 531–532.)

SECCHI, MARCELLO DI. *Aurelio.* This is apparently the same as the *Aurelio* mentioned *c.* 1620, although the latter may be *Aurelio* Testa. 1618: M. di Secchi and his wife in Confidenti. 1620, 16/10: mentioned by Martinelli. 1620, 5/12: mentioned by Cecchini. 1621, 11/5: with S. Fiorillo at Naples, described as *giovane di tanto honore e de così buone qualità, com' è noto a tutti;* 1/6: letter from Naples, promising to join Cecchini's company, signed *Aurelio fedele;* 7/7: still at Naples. It is probable that this is the *Aurelio* who was at Genova in 1610, and who was mentioned by Ottonelli as at Florence in 1640. *Aurelio* di Secchi also appears in the undated list of the Costanti. (D'Ancona, ii, 471; Rasi, i, 236, ii, 743, iii, 773; Baschet, p. 276; F. Bartoli, i, 66; W. Smith, *Aurelio, comico* (*Giornale storico,* xcii (1928), 208–211).)

SECCHI, —— DI. *Nespola.* Wife of M. di Secchi.

SERIO, GIOVANNI. *Contrallo* (a type name?). (Rasi, i, 247.)

SERVILLI, ISABELLA. *Eularia,* or *Eulalia.* 1681: in Modena troupe. 1697: apparently in Mantuan service. (Rasi, iii, 532–535.)

SERVILLO, FRANCESCO. *Odoardo.* 1660, 26/6: at Livorno. (Rasi, iii, 536.)

SIMONE DA BOLOGNA. *Zanni.* 1574, 18/7: in Gelosi. He was praised by contemporaries such as Porcacchi and Rossi. (Baschet, p. 61; Driesen, pp. 274–275; Rasi, iii, 539–540; *Un Capitolo in morte di Simone da Bologna, comico geloso* (1585), ed. L. Bonfigli (Arezzo, 1907); F. Bartoli, ii, 240.)

SOLDANO, ANIELLO. *Dottor Spacca Strummolo.* A native of Naples. 1609: in Fedeli. Works: (1) *Fantastiche e ridicolose etimologie* (Bologna, 1610); (2) *La Fondatione, & origine di Bologna* (Bologna, 1610). (A. Bartoli, p. cxxvi; F. Bartoli, ii, 242–245; Rasi, i, 164–166; Croce, p. 33; G. Martucci, *Un comico dell' arte* (*Aniello Soldano*) (*Nuova Antologia,* Ser. II, xlviii (1884), 618–628).)

SOLDINO, ANTONIO. 1565: at Rome according to an unverified document. 1570–71: in Bavaria. 1572: in France. 1574: in Bavaria. (Rasi, iii, 541.)

SONDRA, GIUSEPPE. *Flaminio.* 1697–99: in Modena troupe. (Rasi, iii, 544.)

SPADACIN, SIMON. 1549: at Padua. Spadacin may be a character name. (E. Cocco, *loc. cit.,* p. 68.)

SPERINDI. A native of Venice. 1567: in Bavaria. (Rasi, iii, 545.)

STOPPINO. An unidentifiable *Stoppino* was acting in 1641.

TABARINO, GIOVANNI. *Tabarino.* A native of Venice. 1568–70: in Bavaria. 1571–72: in France. 1574: in Austria. (D'Ancona, ii, 458; Rasi, iii, 555–560; G. Mazzoni, *Per la Maschera di Tabarrino* (*Miscellanea di studi critici edita in onore di Arturo Graf,* Bergamo, 1903), pp. 195–200.)

TABÒ, FRANCESCA. In Costanti troupe. (Rasi, iii, 560.)

TEDESCHI, MARIA. Wife of V. Tedeschi. 1665: in Modena troupe. (A. Bartoli, p. cl.)

TEDESCHI, VINCENZO. 1665: in Modena troupe. (A. Bartoli, p. cl.)

TESTA, ——. *Aurelio.* Killed at Naples in 1630. It is possible that he is the *Aurelio* of 1620 cited under Marcello di Secchi. (Croce, p. 40; Rasi, iii, 583–584.)

THOFANO DE BASTIAN. 1545: at Padua. (E. Cocco, *loc. cit.*, p. 57.)

TOMMASO, MARIO DI. *Lepido.* A native of Siena. 1575, 5/7: at Naples.

TONTI, ANTONIO. *Pulcinella.* 1694, /6: died at Rome. (Rasi, iii, 586.)

TORRI, ANNA MARIA. Perhaps a sister of Antonio Torri. She may have been a singer, and not an actress. 1683, 2/6: at Modena. 1684, 7/4: going to Reggio. (Rasi, iii, 589–590; E. Re, in *Giornale storico*, lv (1910), 326.)

TORRI, ANTONIA. *Lavinia.* This is apparently Antonia Isola, who had married A. or G. C. Torri by June 1658. 1663: poem to her as A. Isola *in età fanciullesca* by P. Abriani (*Poesie*, Venetia, 1663, p. 16). 1672 : at Bologna. 1677–78: in Parma troupe. 1689–91: in Modena troupe. (Rasi, ii, 700, 1059–61, iii, 588–589; F. Bartoli, i, 279–281; Cionini, p. 42.)

TORRI, ANTONIO. *Lelio.* 1678: in Parma troupe. 1689: in Modena troupe. (Cionini, p. 42.)

TORRI, GIULIO CESARE. *Zaccagnino.* 1647–62: in Modena troupe. (Rasi, iii, 587–588, ii, 700.)

TORTORITI, ANGELICA. *Marinetta.* Wife of G. Tortoriti, *née* Toscano. Came to France after the death of D. Biancolelli in 1688. (Rasi, iii, 594–595; Biancolelli manuscript, i, 122.)

TORTORITI, GIUSEPPE. *Pasquariello.* 1680–82: in Modena troupe. 1685: appeared at Paris as a *Capitano*, later playing *Pasquariello* and *Scaramuccia* (in 1694). In 1697 he formed a company for provincial tours, but died soon after its formation. (Rasi, iii, 591–594.)

TOSCANO, ANGELICA. See *Tortoriti, Angelica.*

TOSCANO, ——. 1579: head of an unnamed company. (Rasi, iii, 596.)

TOSCHI, FRANCESCO. Acted about 1670. (Rasi, iii, 596–597.)

TRAPPOLINO. It seems impossible to identify the Trappolino who, according to Barbieri, died *c.* 1634. (Petraccone, p. 49; Rasi, iii, 600–601.)

TRENTA, LUCILLA. Mentioned in 1636. (Rasi, iii, 602–603.)

TREZZI, GIOVAN BATTISTA. *Pasquino.* 1689: in Modena troupe. (Rasi, iii, 604; Cionini, p. 42.)

TURRI, GIOVAN BATTISTA. *Pantalone.* A native of Modena. 1653: in Paris. 1671, 30/3: in Venice. 1675: in Mantuan troupe. (A. Bartoli, p. clxii; Rasi, iii, 605–606; Biancolelli manuscript, i, 52.)

TURRI, VIRGINIO. *Virginio.* Son of G. B. Turri. 1653: in France. Returned to Modena and became a Carmelite. (Rasi, iii, 606; Biancolelli manuscript, i, 80.)

VACANTIELLO, FRANCESCO. *Cola.* Probably the *Cola* who was to substitute Martinelli in 1607 and who went to France in 1608. (Rasi, ii, 672, iii, 613.)

VALERINI, ADRIANO. *Aurelio.* A native of Verona. 1567–68: possibly a member of Ganassa troupe. *C.* 1576–83: in Gelosi-Uniti. He was praised by Garzoni and Barbieri. Works: (1) *Oratione in morte della Divina Signora Vincenza Armani* (Verona, 1570); (2) *Afrodite*, a tragedy (Verona, 1578); (3) *Le Bellezze di Verona* (Verona, 1586); (4) *Cento madrigali* (Verona, 1592). (D'Ancona, ii, 461, 469, 471; F. Bartoli, ii, 259–261; A. Bartoli, p. cxxxvii, cxx; Rasi, iii, 616–622; Petraccone, pp. 5, 48–49.)

VALLE, ANDREA. 1626: at Naples. (Croce, p. 41.)

VANNINI, GIO. BATTISTA. *Zanni.* Also called Battista da Rimino (?). 1574, 25/6: in Confidenti. 1584: praised in B. Rossi, *La Fiamella.* (Rasi, iii, 622–623.)

VENTURA, BATTISTA. *Pantalone.* 1655, 6/3: engaged for Modena troupe. (Rasi, iii, 628.)

VENTURA, GIACOMO DI. *Magnanino.* 1562 and 1568: at Mantua. Died November 1569, aged 50. (Rasi, ii, 773.)

VICENTIO. A Vicentio of Venice was at Padua in 1545. Elsewhere he is called Vicentio Scuffionario, or Scuffion, and so may be the Scuffion Cantarin mentioned by Calmo. (E. Cocco, *loc. cit.*, pp. 57, 60; Calmo, *Lettere*, ed. V. Rossi, p. 151.)

VICENTIO, TARASSO. 1565: at Rome according to an unverified document.

VIGLIANI, ORETTA. A poem to her was printed at Naples in 1651. (Rasi, iii, 666–667.)

VITELLI, BEATRICE. See *Fiorillo, Beatrice.*

VIZIANI, FRANCESCO. A native of Lucca. 1575, 5/7: at Naples. (Croce, pp. 29–31.)

ZACCAGNINO. 1496: mentioned in a letter from Ferrara. (Rasi, iii, 703.)

ZAGNOLI, CARLO. *Finocchio.* 1689–91: in Modena troupe. (Cionini, p. 42; Rasi, iii, 716; B. Brunelli, p. 111.)

ZANARDI, MICHEL. *Graziano.* 1614, 4/8: in a troupe of Uniti going to Genoa.

ZANETTI, MARC' ANTONIO. *Truffaldino.* 1686–94: in Modena troupe. (Rasi, iii, 730–731; Cionini, p. 40.)

ZANOTTI, PAVOLINO. *Scapino.* A native of Bologna. 1620, 28/8: mentioned by Cecchini. (Baschet, p. 272.)

ZANOTTI-CAVAZZONI, GIOVAN ANDREA. *Ottavio.* Born at Caselle, near Bologna, in 1622. 1647–59: evidently in Modena troupe. 1660: at Paris. 1668, 11/1: his first wife, Teodora Blaise, died; he had remarried before 1674. 1684: returned to Italy. 1688–89: in Modena troupe. Still acting in 1693. Died September 13,

APPENDIX

1695. Works : (1) *Relatione dell' udienza data dal Sig. di Lione a Soliman Mustaferraga inviato al Rè Christianissimo dall' Imperatore de Turchi à Surena. Tratto dal Francese da Gio. Andr. Zanotto* (Venetia, 1670); (2) *L'Eraclio Imperatore d' Oriente*, a tragedy translated from the French of Corneille (Bologna, 1691); (3) *Honore contro amore*, a translation of *Le Cid* (Bologna, 1691). (Rasi, iii, 742–748; Biancolelli manuscript, i, 52, 82; F. Bartoli, ii, 286–287.)

ZBRAZIN, FRANCESCO. *Gabinetto.* 1648, 1/12: in Mantuan troupe. (Rasi, iii, 750–751.)

ZECCA, NICCOLÒ. *Bertolino.* 1646: in Parma troupe. 1648: evidently in Mantuan troupe, whence he possibly seceded later. Recorded at Piacenza 1648, at Reggio 1659, at Parma 1660. 1670, /4: joined the Mantuan troupe. He cannot be the Bertolino of the Fedeli in 1603, as Bartoli thinks. (Rasi, iii, 751–752; A. Bartoli, p. cxxxix; F. Bartoli, ii, 289–290.)

ZENARI, ANDREA. *Graciano.* 1593, /10: in Uniti. It may be that he and Michel Zanardi are one and the same. (Rasi, iii, 753.)

ZITO, or CITO, BARTOLOMEO. *Gratiano.* 1602: at Naples. He has left numerous works. (Croce, pp. 36–37.)

ZUANDOMENEGO. *Rizo.* 1545: at Padua. (E. Cocco, p. 57.)

ZUCCATO, POLONIA. Wife of V. Zuccato. Tabarino had a child by her in Paris in 1572. (Rasi, iii, 768; and references below.)

ZUCCATO, VALERIO. Acted with his wife in the company of Tabarino. (Rasi, iii, 768; F. Sansovino, *Venetia descritta* (Venetia, 1581), p. 168; M. Apollonio, *Per una Storia dei comici dell' arte* (*Rivista d' Italia*, xxx, 3; March 1927).)

III. THE SCENARII

The obvious basis of all work on the *commedia dell' arte* is the series of scenarii, of which many collections have been unearthed in Italian libraries within the last thirty or forty years. Besides a number which are known only by their titles, no less than 800 plays of this type belonging to the sixteenth, seventeenth, and early eighteenth centuries have been preserved, and of these about 150 have been printed either in series or separately. I have given here (1) a list of the various collections, with references to critical sources, and (2) an alphabetical list of the known scenarii. In citing the titles of the plays the original spelling is normally retained, save that *u* for *v* is rendered *v*. The first title given to each of the collections in the list below is that by which the collection is referred to in the second list. The figure in brackets indicates the number of plays included in each collection.[1]

COLLECTIONS OF SCENARII

1. (1.) An unnamed scenario is described by Massimo Troiano da Napoli in *Discorsi delli triomfi, giostri, apparati e delle cose più notabili, fatte nelle sontuose nozze dell' Illustrissimo et Eccellentissimo signor duca Guglielmo, primo genito del generosissimo Alberto Quinto, conte palatino del Reno e duca della Baviera alta e bassa, nell' anno 1568, a' 22 di febraro* (Monaco, 1568). Printed by Petraccone, pp. 297–301, Eugenio Camerini, *La commedia dell' arte alla Corte di Baviera nel secolo XVI* (*Nuovi profili letterari*, Milano, 1876, iii, 220–224), and elsewhere.

2. ESTE (2). Biblioteca Estense, Parma, I, 740 (α. S. 8, 14). Sixteenth century. Names in E. Re, *Scenarii modenesi* (*Giornale storico*, lv (1910), 325–338). *La Schiava* printed there.

3. SCALA (50). *Il Teatro delle favole rappresentative overo la ricreatione comica, boscareccia e tragica* (Venezia, 1611), edited by Flaminio Scala. These belong to the late sixteenth or early seventeenth century. The following have been reprinted: *Il Marito, Il Ritratto, Li Tappeti Alessandrini, L'Alvida, La Forsennata Prencipessa* (all in Petraccone, pp. 302–349).

4. LOCATELLI (103). Biblioteca Casanatense, Rome, F. IV, 12–13 (1211–12); two volumes. The first is inscribed *Della Scena de soggetti comici . . . In Roma M.D.C.XVIII*; the second is dated 1622. They were prepared for Basilio Locatelli, and no doubt contain much work earlier than the dates on the manuscript. The list of plays is given by " Carletta " (A. Valeri) in *Gli Scenari di Basilio Locatelli* (*Nuova Rassegna*, ii (1894), pp. 441–456, 523–537) who prints *L'Acconcia serve*. An incomplete list appears in L. Allacci, *Drammaturgia*, reproduced in A. Bartoli, pp. xxv–xxvii. The following have been printed: *La Comedia in comedia, Li Prigioni di Plauto, La Nave*, and *La Pazzia di Doralice* (Petraccone, pp. 350–373), *La Pazzia di Filandro, La Pazzia di Dorindo, Il Gran Mago, La Nave*, and *Li tre Satiri* (F. Neri, *Scenari delle maschere in Arcadia* (Città di Castello, 1913), pp. 46–86), *Il Giuoco della primiera* and *La Comedia in comedia* (Emilio del Cerro, *Nel Regno delle maschere* (Naples, 1914), pp. 381–400),

---

[1] Since this list was prepared Kathleen M. Lea has published an article on *The Bibliography of the Commedia dell' Arte : The Miscellanies of the Comici and Virtuosi* in *The Library*, N.S., xi (1930), 1–38. Two entries have been added here from that article.

Il Giusto principe (Winifred Smith, *Two Commedie dell' Arte on the "Measure for Measure" Story*, in *The Romanic Review*, xiii (1922)), *Il Vecchio avaro* (Rosario Bonfanti, *Uno Scenario di Basilio Locatelli* (Noto, 1901)).

5. CORSINIANA I (100). Biblioteca Corsiniana, Rome, 45 G. 5 and 45 G. 6; two volumes, the first of which is inscribed *Raccolta di Scenari più scelti d' Istrioni*. For the greater part this presents abbreviated versions of the Locatelli collection. It is distinguished by the fact that it contains many illustrations; fifteen of these are reproduced by Mic and eight by Kathleen M. Lea, *loc. cit.* The list of plays is given in A. Zenatti, *Una Raccolta di scenari della Commedia dell' arte* (*Rivista critica della letteratura italiana*, ii (1885), 156–159). *Cf.* also F. de Simone Brouwer, *Due Scenari inediti del secolo XVII* (*Giornale storico*, xviii (1891), 277–290), who prints there *Li due Fratelli rivali* and *La Trappolaria*. *L'Acconcia serve* is given by A. Valeri, *loc. cit.*

6 and 7. BARTOLI (22). Two codices: (1) Biblioteca Nazionale, Florence, Cod. Magliabechiana, II, i, 90; (2) Biblioteca Riccardiana, Florence, Cod. Riccardiano 2800. Both are of the seventeenth century, but many of the plays seem to be of an early date. Codex I was printed entire in Adolfo Bartoli, *Scenari inediti della commedia dell' arte* (Florence, 1880). The following have been reprinted: *Le tre Gravide* and *Il Dottor bacchettone* (Petraccone, pp. 390–405).

8. (1.) A single scenario, *L'Amici infidi*, is preserved in a letter of Bernardino Bernardini, dated October 25, 1632 (Cod. Magliabechiana, II, i, 190). It is printed in A. Bartoli, pp. lix–lxviii.

9. CASANATENSE II (48). Biblioteca Casanatense, Rome, 4186. Mid-seventeenth century. A list of the plays is given in F. de Simone Brouwer, *Ancora una raccolta di scenari* (*Rendiconti della Reale Accademia dei Lincei*, "Classe di scienze morali, storiche e filologiche," Ser. V, x (1901), 391–407, 430–435), where two plays, *L'Ateista fulminato* and *Convitato di pietra*, are printed. The former is also given in Petraccone, pp. 374–382. Winifred Smith prints *La Regina d' Inghilterra* in her article on *The Earl of Essex on the Stage* (*P.M.L.A.A.*, xxxix (1924), 147–173), and the *Marescial di Biron* in *The Maréchal de Biron on the Stage* (*Modern Philology*, xx (1922–23), 301–308).

10. MODENA (10). Archivio di Stato, Modena. Early seventeenth century. A list of the plays is given in E. Re, *Scenarii modenesi* (*loc. cit.*). E. Re has also printed *Truffaldino balordo* in *La Tradizione comica dell' imprudente* (*Rivista teatrale italiana*, ix, 2), and A. Paglicci-Brozzi has printed *Le Bizzarrie d' Argentina* in *Uno Scenario inedito di una commedia dell' arte* (*Rivista teatrale italiana*, xiii, 2).

11. CORSINIANA II (2). Biblioteca Corsiniana, Rome, 45 F. 1. Seventeenth century. This contains two untitled scenarii. See A. Valeri, *loc. cit.*, p. 443, and F. de S. Brouwer in *Rendiconti della R. Accademia dei Lincei*, Ser. V, x (1901), 393.

12. CORRER (51). Museo Correr, Venice, 1040. Seventeenth century. This collection has been less examined than most of the others. The following plays have been printed: *I Suppositi* (S. C. V. Rossi, "per le nozze Flamini-Fanelli," Bergamo, 1895), *L'Astrologo* (S. C. V. Rossi, *Una Commedia di Giambattista della Porta ed un nuovo scenario*, in *Rendiconti del Reale Istituto lombardo di scienze e lettere*, Ser. II, xxix (1896), 881–895; also in Petraccone, pp. 383–389).

13. (1.) A single untitled scenario is preserved in the Museo Correr, Venice, Cod. Miscell., 998–2546. This was printed by L. Stoppato in *La Commedia popolare in Italia*, pp. 221–234.

14. (1.) One scenario in narrative form, *Le Gemelle*, is in the Biblioteca Vaticana, fondo Ottoboni, 2418, Part ii. See A. Valeri, *loc. cit.*, p. 443.

15. BARBERINIANO (9). Biblioteca Vaticana, fondo Barberiniano, 3895. Seventeenth century. A list of the plays is given in A. Valeri, *loc. cit.*, p. 443, and in F. de S. Brouwer, *loc. cit.*, p. 394.

16. (1.) One scenario, *Gli Sdegni amorosi*, is preserved in the Bibliothèque de Rouen, fond Coquebert de Montbret; it is dated November 25, 1651. Printed in P. Toldo, *Gli Sdegni amorosi di Frandaglia di Val di Sturla, da un MS. della Biblioteca di Rouen* (*Giornale storico*, lxiv (1914), 372–385).

17. NAPLES (183). (1) Biblioteca Nazionale, Naples, XI, AA. 41, containing 93 scenarii; (2) Biblioteca Nazionale, Naples, XI, AA. 40, containing 90 scenarii. The first is inscribed *Gibaldone de soggetti da recitarsi all' Impronto. Alcuni proprij, e gl' altri da diversi. Raccolti di D. Annibale Sersale Conte di Casamarciano*; the second *Gibaldone comico di varij suggetti di Comedie, ed Opere Bellissime copiate da me Antonino Passanti detto Oratio il Calabrese per comando dell' Ecc.mo sig. Conte di Casamarciano. 1700.* As the MSS. include a burlesque letter of Pulcinella dated 1676, the plays probably belong to the latter half of the seventeenth century. A list of the titles is given in Benedetto Croce, *Una Nuova raccolta di scenarii* (*Giornale storico*, xxix (1897), 211–215). The following plays have been printed: *Arcadia incantata*, *Nerone imperadore*, *Non può essere*, *Convitato di pietra*, and *Barliario* (Petraccone, pp. 406–444), *L'Amante geloso*, *Le Disgrazie di Pulcinella*, and *Nerone imperadore* (Del Cerro, pp. 401–443), *Arcadia incantata* (F. Neri, pp. 87–93), *Ingiusto rettore* (W. Smith, *Two Commedie dell' Arte on the "Measure for Measure" Story*, in *The Romanic Review*, xiii (1922)), *Il Tradito* (C. Levi, *Uno Scenario inedito della commedia dell' arte*, in *Rivista teatrale italiana*, x, 1), *Malizie di Coviello* (C. Levi, *Malizie di Coviello, scenario inedito*, in *Rivista*

teatrale italiana, xi, 1); *Medico volante* (Pietro Toldo, *Di Alcuni scenari inediti della commedia dell' arte e delle loro relazioni col teatro del Molière*, in *Atti della R. Accademia delle Scienze di Torino*, xlii (1907), 460–482); *Ricco Epulone* (F. Neri, in *Giornale storico*, lxv (1915), 39–44).

18. (1.) Biblioteca Vittorio Emanuele, Rome, 1641, Fondo Sant' Andrea della Valle, contains a scenario, *Flaminio disperato*. Printed in G. Martucci, *Uno Scenario inedito della commedia dell' arte* (*Nuova Antologia*, Ser. II, li (1885), 219–233).

19. (1.) A single scenario, *La Trappoleria*, is printed by Perrucci, and reprinted by A. Bartoli, pp. xxxi–xxxiv.

20. (1.) A single scenario, *Il Principe Sidonio*, is preserved in the Biblioteca Vaticana, Cod. Barberiniana 3737. *Cf.* Kathleen M. Lea, *loc. cit.*, p. 17.

21. BIANCOLELLI I (80). Bibliothèque du Grand Opéra, Paris, two volumes, inscribed *Traduction du Scenario de Joseph Dominique Biancolelli; dit Arlequin. Et L'histoire du Theatre Italien depuis l'année 1577, Jusqu'en 1750 Et Les Années Suivantes.* Par M. G[ueulette]. This contains translations of the scenarii in which Biancolelli appeared; his own Arlecchino parts are fully given, but often the other portions of the plays are contracted. Some of these were printed in part in early collections or separate editions.

22. BIANCOLELLI II (72). Bibliothèque Nationale, Paris, fonds français 9328 (3358), described as a *Copie de la traduction du Scenario de Dominique, faite par Gueulette.* This follows the same order as No. 21, but omits eight pieces. The collection of which it forms a part contains much matter of value for the later history of the Italian comedians; see particularly MS. 9308, *Pièces de théâtre inédites, représentées sur le Théâtre Italien*; 9309, same title; 9310, *Canevas et compliments inédits de pièces italiennes-françaises, représentées sur le Théâtre Italien*; 9329, *Sujets de comédies italiennes non imprimées dans le recueil de Gherardi* (reproducing some of the Biancolelli themes); 9331, *Théâtre inédit de Dominique Biancolelli*; 9334, *Théâtre inédit de Romagnesi*.

23. (1.) A single scenario, *Diarbech*, dated 1692, is preserved in the Biblioteca Casanatense, Rome, Misc. Fol. 152 (2) and 172 (1), according to Kathleen M. Lea, *loc. cit.*, p. 17.

24. (1.) The same authority records another scenario, *Plauto alla moderna*, dated 1693, in the same library, Misc. Fol. 172 (3).

25. (1.) Biblioteca Palatina, Vienna, 10124 (Rec. 1491), contains one eighteenth-century scenario, *Un Pazzo guarisce l'altro*. Printed in E. Maddalena, *Uno Scenario inedito*, in *Sitzungsberichte der kaiserlichen Akademie der Wissenschaften, Wien*, Phil.-hist Klasse, cxliii (1901), Abhandlung xvi, pp. 1–22.

26. (1.) Archivio di Stato, Parma, contains one unnamed scenario of the seventeenth century. Printed in P. Toldo, *Uno Scenario inedito della commedia dell' arte* (*Giornale storico*, xlvi (1905), 128–135)

27. ADRIANI (22). Biblioteca Communale, Perugia, A. 20. Early eighteenth century, but contains plays of the preceding century; compiled by D. Placido Adriano, or Adriani, of Lucca. A list of the scenarii is given in Benedetto Croce, *Un Repertorio della commedia dell' arte* (*Giornale storico*, xxxi (1898), 458–460). The manuscript is inscribed *Selva overo Zibaldone di concetti comici raccolti dal P. D. Placido Adriani di Lucca. MDCCXXXIV.* The following plays have been printed: *Le Metamorfosi di Pulcinella* (Petraccone, pp. 445–453, and Del Cerro, *op. cit.*, pp. 445–464), *Non può essere ovvero la donna può ciò che vuole* (E. Del Cerro, *Un Commediografo dimenticato*, in *Rivista d' Italia*, xiv (1911), 8).

28. (1.) Arsenal, Paris, 6099, contains one scenario, *Giovanna d'Arco*, presumably of the early eighteenth century. See A. Valeri, *loc. cit.*, p. 443.

29. (12.) Vatican Library, Cod. lat. 10244. Late seventeenth or early eighteenth century. A list of the contents is given by M. Vattasso and H. Carusi in *Codices Vaticani Latini. Codices 9852–10300* (Rome, 1914), pp. 578–579. One of these, *La Donna demonio*, has been printed by G. M. Monti in *Rivista abruzzese di scienze, lettere ed arti*, xxxiv (1919), 5–6, May–June.

Of the series of scenarii which are known now only by their titles the most important are the following:

1. ESTE. List given in E. Re, *Scenarii modenesi* (*loc. cit.*). These include 17 titles.

2. MODENA I. List given in B. Brunelli, *op. cit.*, p. 109, where many of the plays are divided between two rival *amorose* (*Diana* and *Eulalia*). These include 31 titles, and belong to the year 1681.

3. MODENA II. List given in Cionini (p. 41) of plays given by the Modena company when they played at Sassuolo in 1688. This includes a selection of those in the preceding list.

Notices of and extracts from later scenarii appear in such publications as the *Dictionnaire des théâtres de Paris* (Paris, 1756), but no note is made of these here, although a list is appended of the pieces included in the Russian collection of 1733–35 (see *infra*, pp. 389–390). As this book was going through the press an important article by T. Beltrame, *Gli scenari del museo Correr*, appeared in the *Giornale storico* (xlix (1931), 1–48). Here are printed *Li duo Amanti furiosi* and *Il Mastro di Terentio*.

LIST OF SCENARII

Many of the scenarii listed here are duplicates, in the sense that in several instances the same themes have been treated similarly, the individual examples sometimes following one another scene by scene, sometimes agreeing merely in the general outlines of the plot. In a few cases, but in a few cases only, I have indicated such correspondences. An asterisk is prefixed to those scenarii which are to be found in print; a dagger marks those which appear to have perished.

1. Unnamed (Archivio di Stato, Parma).
*2. Unnamed (description in Troiano, *Discorsi* (1568)).
3. Unnamed (Este).
4. Unnamed (Modena).
5. Unnamed (Modena).
*6. Unnamed (Museo Correr, Venice, Cod. Miscell., 998–2546).
7. *L'Abbattimento d'Isabella* (Corsiniana I, ii, 96; similar to *La Fantasma*, No. 264).
8. *L'Abbattimento di Zanni* (Locatelli, i, 11).
*9. *L'Acconcia serve* (Corsiniana I, ii, 100).
*10. *La Acconcia serve* (Locatelli, i, 16).
11. *Accordie e scordie ovvero guerra e pace* (Naples, i, 1).
12. *Li Adelfi di Terentio* (Corsiniana I, ii, 88; similar to *Il Formento*, No. 321, and to *Il Fromento*, No. 337).
13. *L'Adrasto* (Corsiniana I, i, 37).
14. *Advocato criminale, cioè il Rosildo* (Casanatense II, 47).
15. *A Fourbe, fourbe et demi* (Biancolelli I, 62; Biancolelli II, 59; written by Cinthio, produced in Paris October 1674).
16. *L'Albergo d'Arliechino, giudice, parte, advocato e testimonio* (Biancolelli I, 75; Biancolelli II, 72).
17. *Albergo nobile* (Naples, i, 9).
†18. *Altro basilisco di Bernagasso* (Lost Este, 12. See *Basilisco del Bernagasso*, Nos. 92–94).
†19. *L'Alvarado* (Lost Modena I (25) and II).
*20. *L'Alvida* (Scala, 43).
21. *L'Amante astuto* (Vatican, 8).
*22. *L'Amante geloso* (Naples, i, 2).
23. *Amante inavertito* (Naples, i, 4).
24. *Lo Amante ingrato* (Locatelli, i, 23).
25. *Amante ingrato* (Naples, i, 5).
26. *L'Amante interesato* (Correr, 1).
27. *Amante lunatico* (Naples, i, 3).
28. *Amante tradito* (Correr, 50).
29. *L'Amante volubile* (Vatican, 7).
30. *L'Amanti ingrati* (Corsiniana I, i, 22).
31. *Amanti licenziati* (Naples, ii, 7).
32. *Amanti senza vedersi* (Naples, i, 6).
33. *Amanti volubili* (Naples, ii, 2).
†34. *Amare e fingere* (Lost Modena I (11) and II).

35. *Amar per fama* (Naples, ii, 3).
*36. *L'Amici infidi* (Cod. Magliab. II, i, 190, printed in A. Bartoli, pp. lix–lxviii; date about 1632).
37. *L'Amico infido* (Correr, 2).
38. *L'Amico tradito* (Correr, 12).
39. *L'Amore constante* (Locatelli, ii, 24).
40. *L'Amore costante* (Corsiniana I, ii, 60).
41. *Amore et onore di Ramidoro* (Naples, i, 10).
†42. *Amore non vuol rivali* (Lost Modena II).
43. *L'Amore sopra l'odio e la raggione* (Barberiniano, 4).
44. *Amore tra nemici* (Naples, i, 7).
45. *L'Amorosi incauti* (Corsiniana I, i, 12; similar to *Gli Incauti amorosi*, No. 391).
46. *Amphitrioni di Plauto* (Correr, 38).
47. *Li Anfitrioni* (Corsiniana I, ii, 68; similar to *La Tramutatione*, No. 693).
48. *Aquidotto* (Naples, ii, 5).
*49. *L'Arbore incanto* (Scala, 49).
*50. *Arcadia incantata* (Adriani, 6).
*51. *Arcadia incantata* (Naples, ii, 1).
52. *L'Arcadia travagliata per l'ira di Diana contro Enea* (Casanatense II, 13).
53. *Arlechino creato re per ventura* (Biancolelli I, 59; Biancolelli II, 56; produced in Paris November 1672).
54. *Arlechino creduto principe* (Biancolelli I, 25; Biancolelli II, 25; produced before 1668).
55. *Arlechino ladro, sbiro e giudice* (Biancolelli I, 31; Biancolelli II, 31; produced before 1668).
56. *Arlechino medico d'aqua dolce* (Biancolelli I, 52; Biancolelli II, 50).
57. *Arlechino porco per amore* (Biancolelli I, 65; Biancolelli II, 62).
58. *Arlechino servo incanto* (Biancolelli I, 53; Biancolelli II, 51).
59. *Arlechino suri* (Biancolelli I, 51; Biancolelli II, 49).
60. *Arlequin berger de Lemnos* (Biancolelli I, 63; Biancolelli II, 60; produced in Paris November 1674; written by Cinthio).
61. *Arlequin, dogue d'Angleterre et medecin du temps* (Biancolelli I, 74; Biancolelli II, 71; produced in Paris June 1679).
62. *Arlequino, hotte et masson* (Biancolelli I, 73; Biancolelli II, 70).

APPENDIX

*63. *Arlequin soldat et bagage ou hoste et hostellerie* (Biancolelli I, 79; produced in Paris July 1673).

64. *Additions a la comedie d'Arlequin soldat et bagage* (Biancolelli I, 37; Biancolelli II, 37; a separate rendering).

65. *Arlichino poeta e putino* (Biancolelli I, 49; Biancolelli II, 47).

66. *Arlichino spirito foletto* (Biancolelli I, 48; Biancolelli II, 46; written by Cinthio, produced in Paris March 1670).

67. *Arliechino e Scaramuza hebrei erranti di Babilonia* (Biancolelli I, 68; Biancolelli II, 65; produced in Paris January 1677; the same as *Les Juifs de Babylone*).

68. *L'Arme mutate* (Corsiniana I, i, 23).

69. *L'Arme mutate* (Locatelli, i, 48).

70. *L'Arme mutate* (Naples, ii, 4).

*71. *L'Astrologo del Porta* (Correr, 13).

72. *Astute semplicità di Angiola* (Naples, i, 11).

73. *Le Astutie di Zanni* (Corsiniana I, ii, 59).

74. *L'Astuzia di Mariolo* (Naples, i, 8).

75. *Le Astuzie di Zanni* (Locatelli, ii, 12).

*76. *L'Ateista fulminato* (Casanatense II, 4).

77. *Ausa* (or *Ansa*) (Correr, 20).

78. *Avaritia* (Naples, ii, 6).

*79. *Gli Avvenimenti comici, pastorali e tragici* (Scala, 42).

80. *Baldoino e Carlotto* (Casanatense II, 16).

81. *Balia grande* (Naples, ii, 8).

82. *Il Banchetto* (Locatelli, ii, 43).

83. *Li Banditi* (Locatelli, ii, 33).

84. *La Barbaria del dottore* (Biancolelli I, 26; Biancolelli II, 26).

*85. *Barliario* (Naples, ii, 12).

86. *Le Baron de fœneste* (Biancolelli I, 60; Biancolelli II, 57; produced in Paris January 1674).

87. *Baron Tedesco* (Naples, i, 12).

88. *Baron Todesco* (Correr, 48).

89. *Il Baron Todesco* (Biancolelli I, 10; Biancolelli II, 10; produced before 1668).

90. *Il Basilisco* (Adriani, 14).

91. *Il Basilisco* (Vatican, 10).

92. *Basilisco del Barnagasso* (Naples, i, 13).

93. *Basilisco del Barnagasso (d'altro modo)* (Naples, i, 14).

†94. *Il Basilisco del Bernagasso* (Lost Este, 11).

95. *Il Basilisco di Bernagasso ou le dragon de Moscovie* (Biancolelli I, 5; Biancolelli II, 5).

96. *Bastarda impertinente* (Naples, ii, 9).

97. *La Battagliola* (Corsiniana I, i, 41).

98. *La Battagliola* (Locatelli, ii, 42).

†99. *Belfonte inavvertito* (Lost Este, 3).

100. *Belisario* (Naples, ii, 11).

101. *Bellisario (scenario nell' opera di)* (Casanatense II, 29).

*102. *La Bellissima commedia in tre persone* (Bartoli, pp. 29-39).

103. *Bernardo del Carpio* (Naples, ii, 10).

*104. *Le Bizzarrie d'Argentina cavaliere e gentildonna, Ippolito e Boffetto creduti Turchi con Zaccagnino amante disperato* (Modena; dated 1643).

†105. *Bugia verità* (Lost Modena, I (10)).

106. *Le Burle di Fedele* (Corsiniana I, i, 38; similar to *Le Burle di Filandro*, No. 107).

107. *Le Burle di Filandro* (Locatelli, ii, 13. See No. 106).

*108. *Le Burle d'Isabella* (Scala, 4).

109. *Il Cabalista, o il cavalier del industria* (Biancolelli I, 47; Biancolelli II, 45).

*110. *La Caccia* (Scala, 37).

†111. *Il Calamaro prigioniero* (Lost Este, 16).

†112. *Il Calamaro ruffiano onorato* (Lost Este, 14).

113. *La Cameriera* (Naples, ii, 15).

†114. *La Cameriera* (Lost Modena, I (22) and II).

115. *La Cameriera* (Adriani, 12).

†116. *Can dell' ortolano* (Lost Modena I (27) and II).

†117. *Canuto* (Lost Modena I (20) and II).

*118. *Il Capitano* (Scala, 11).

119. *Il Capitano burlato* (Naples, i, 15).

120. *Li Carcerati* (Corsiniana I, i, 19).

121. *Il Carnovale* (Locatelli, ii, 38; similar to *Il Torneo*, No. 685).

122. *Casa con due porte* (Naples, ii, 16).

†123. *Casa con due porte* (Lost Modena I (29) and II).

124. *Case svaliggiate* (Naples, i, 16).

125. *Le Case svaligiate* (Biancolelli I, 22; Biancolelli II, 22; produced before 1668).

126. *La Casta e costante Ipsicratea con i trionfi di Pompeo nel regno di Ponto nella Farsaglia* (Casanatense II, 5).

127. *Il Castico della disonesta moglie* (Correr, 15).

128. *Castigo dell' infedeltà* (Naples, ii, 17).

*129. *Il Cavadente* (Scala, 12).

130. *Cavadenti* (Naples, i, 25).

131. *Il Cavalier discreto* (Correr, 6).

132. *Cavaliere errante* (Naples, ii, 19).

133. *Cavaliere favorito dal suo nemico, obligato con aggravio* (Naples, i, 24).

134. *Il Cavaliere pazzo o sia il giuoco di fortuna* (Vatican, 2).

*135. *Il Cavaliere perseguitato* (Bartoli, pp. 213-223; "opera di N. N.").

136. *Cavalier ingrato* (Correr, 17).

137. *Il Cavaliero da i tre gigli d'oro* (Casanatense II, 23).

138. *Il Cavalier Pignataro co 'l Prencipe dissoluto, e Buffetto fornaciaro di pignatte e boccali* (Casanatense II, 43).

139. *Chi la fa l' aspetti* (Naples, i, 17).

140. *Chi opera inganni se stesso offende* (Naples, i, 18).

141. *Chi vuole ammogliar resta ammogliato, overo il matrimonio per convenienza* (Naples, i, 19).

142. *Le Cieca* (Corsiniana I, ii, 50).

143. *Cintio giuocatore* (Vatican, 6).
144. *Cintio infedele e Flaminia costante* (Correr, 33).
†145. *Cit de l'Espagne* (Lost Modena I (8)).
146. *Clarinda perseguitata* (Casanatense II, 15).
147. *Claudione fallito* (Corsiniana I, i, 30; similar to *Il Gratiano fallito*, No. 372).
*148. *Le Collier de perles et sa harangue* (Biancolelli I, 57; Biancolelli II, 55; written by Girardin, produced in Paris July 1672).
149. *Colonnello indiano* (Naples, ii, 21).
*150. *La Comedia in comedia* (Locatelli, i, 43).
151. *Comedia in comedia* (Naples, ii, 18).
152. *La Cometa* (Locatelli, ii, 40; similar to *La Spada mortale*, No. 658).
153. *La Commedia in commedia* (Corsiniana I, i, 34).
154. *Li Consigli di Pantalone* (Corsiniana I, i, 36).
155. *Li Consigli di Pantalone* (Locatelli, i, 40).
156. *Conte di Essex* (Naples, ii, 13. See Nos. 378, 586, 587, and 588).
†157. *Convitato, Dona Isabella* (Lost Modena I (17)).
158. *Convitato di pietra* (Biancolelli I, 23; Biancolelli II, 23; produced in Paris November 1669).
*159. *Convitato di pietra* (Casanatense II, 24).
*160. *Convitato di pietra* (Naples, ii, 14).
161. *Convitato di pietra, Agiunta al* (Biancolelli I, 24; Biancolelli II, 24; produced in Paris February 1673).
162. *Corriero balordo* (Naples, ii, 20).
163. *La Cortigiana onesta* (Correr, 34).
†164. *La Cortigiana onesta* (Lost Este, 9).
165. *La Costanza di Flaminia con le furbarie di Stoppino* (Correr, 28).
166. *Covello barbiero ruffiano ladro e finto diavolo col Dottore furbo malpratico* (Naples, i, 20).
167. *Covello cornuto* (Naples, i, 21).
168. *Covello e Policinella amanti delle proprie padrone* (Naples, i, 23).
169. *Covello traditore del padrone* (Naples, i, 22).
*170. *La Creduta morta* (Scala, 7).
*171. *Il Creduto morto* (Scala, 22).
172. *Il Creduto prencipe* (Casanatense, II, 20).
173. *Il Crispo* (Casanatense II, 6).
174. *Dal Disordine il buon ordine ne nasco* (Corsiniana II).
175. *Dama creduta spirito folletto* (Naples, i, 26).
†176. *La Dama demonio* (Lost Este, 10. See also *La Donna demonio*, No. 196).
177. *Demonii sono le donne, overo la donna sfarzosa chiarita* (Naples, i, 27).
178. *Il Descienzo de Coviello* (Adriani, 1).
†179. *Diana e Colombina finte dive* (Lost Este, 8).
180. *Diarbech* (Biblioteca Casanatense, Misc. 152 (2) and 172 (1); dated 1692).
181. *Diavolo predicatore* (Naples, ii, 28).
182. *Discenso* (Naples, i, 28).
*183. *Le Disgratie di Flavio* (Scala, 35).

*184. *Disgratie di Pollicinella* (Naples, ii, 25).
*185. *Le Disgrazie di Colafronio* (Bartoli, pp. 249–260; " commedia di N. N.").
*186. *Le Disgrazie e fortune di Pandolfo* (Bartoli, pp. 261–273).
187. *Li Dispetti* (Corsiniana I, ii, 85).
188. *Li Dispetti* (Locatelli, i, 7).
189. *Disprezzare chi s' ama* (Naples, ii, 23).
190. *Don Bernardo di Cabrera* (Casanatense II, 39).
†191. *Don Gaston* (Lost Modena I (4), and II).
192. *D. Gile schiavo del diavolo* (Naples, ii, 27).
193. *D. Giovan d' Alvarado* (Naples, ii, 22).
†194. *Don[na] Anna* (Lost Modena I (7)).
195. *Donna Caterina d'Aragona* (Casanatense, II, 22).
*196. *La Donna demonio* (Vatican, 1. See also *La Dama demonio*, No. 176).
197. *Donna Zanni* (Naples, ii, 26).
198. *Donzella di lavoro* (Naples, i, 32).
199. *Le Dopie gielosie* (Biancolelli I, 1; Biancolelli II, 1; produced before 1668).
200. *Dorina serva nobile* (Naples, i, 31).
201. *Dotte per la metempsicose* (Biancolelli I, 71; Biancolelli II, 68).
*202. *Il Dottor Bacchettone* (Bartoli, pp. 287–303).
*203. *Il Dottor disperato* (Scala, 13).
204. *Dottore bacchettone* (Naples, i, 30).
205. *Dottore burlato* (Naples, i, 29).
†206. *Il Dottore disgraziato in amore con Belfonte e Gramustino impazziti per accidente* (Lost Este, 2).
207. *Li Dubij* (Corsiniana I, ii, 67).
208. *Li Dubii* (Locatelli, ii, 34).
†209. *Duchessa di Sassonia* (Lost Modena I (16) and II).
210. *Due Anelli incantati* (Naples, i, 34).
211. *Due Capitani ladri* (Naples, i, 33).
212. *Due Flaminie simili* (Correr, 11).
213. *Le due Fonti incantate, la principessa muta, e Buffetto governatore* (Casanatense II, 44).
*214. *Li due Fratelli rivali* (Corsiniana I, i, 15).
†215. *I due Mezzetini* (lost; acted by Confidenti in 1615).
216. *Due Pulcinelli simili* (Adriani, 11).
217. *[I due Rivali]* (Barberiano, 9; title given by Valeri).
218. *Le due Schiave* (Corsiniana, i, 16; similar to *Le due Sorelle schiave*, No. 228).
219. *Le due Schiave* (Locatelli, i, 28; similar to *La Schiava*, No. 614).
*220. *Li due Schiavi rivenduti* (Bartoli, pp. 41–52).
221. *Li due Simili* (Adriani, 9).
222. *Le due Simile* (Locatelli, i, 24).
223. *Li due Simili* (Locatelli, i, 25).
224. *Li due Simili, colla pazzia d' amore* (Corsiniana I, i, 39; similar to *Li dui Fratelli simili*, No. 235).
225. *Due Simili d' Andriini* (Naples, ii, 24).

APPENDIX

226. *Li due Simili di Plauto* (Locatelli, i, 26. See No. 246).
227. *Due Sorelle rivale* (Correr, 23).
228. *Le due Sorelle schiave* (Locatelli, ii, 9. See No. 218).
229. *Li due Trappolini* (Corsiniana I, i, 32. See No. 24).
230. *Li due Venetiani* (Locatelli, ii, 6).
231. *Li dui Arlechini* (Biancolelli I, 19; Biancolelli II, 19; produced before 1668).
232. *Li dui Capitani* (Locatelli, ii, 7).
233. *Li dui Finti pazzi* (Corsiniana I, ii, 91).
234. *Li dui Fratelli rivali* (Locatelli, ii, 10).
235. *Li dui Fratelli simili* (Locatelli, ii, 8. See No. 224).
236. *Li dui Pantaloni* (Corsiniana I, i, 4).
237. *Li dui Scolari* (Corsiniana I, ii, 56; similar to *La Gelosia*, No. 345, and to *La Lite*, No. 423).
*238. *Li duo Amanti furiosi* (Correr, 5).
*239. *Li duo Capitani simili* (Scala, 17).
*240. *Li duo Fidi notari* (Scala, 20).
*241. *Li duo Finti zingani* (Scala, 32).
242. *I duoi Fratelli avelenati* (Correr, 43).
243. *Li duoi Scolari* (Correr, 25).
†244. *Li duoi Simili Belfonte e Gramustino* (Lost Este, 7).
245. *Duo Simili con le lettere mutate* (Correr, 29).
246. *Li duo Simili di Plauto* (Corsiniana I, i, 11. See No. 226).
247. *Li duo Trappolini* (Locatelli, i, 13. See No. 231).
*248. *Li duo Vecchi gemelli* (Scala, 1).
249. *Elisa Ali Bassa* (Corsiniana I, ii, 53).
250. *Elisa Alii Bassà* (Locatelli, i, 38).
251. *Emilia* (Naples, ii, 29).
†252. *Gli Equivoci* (Lost Modena I (1) and II).
253. *Equivoci d'una notte* (Naples, i, 35).
254. *L'Ermafrodito* (Casanatense II, 35).
255. *L'Ermafrodito* (Corsiniana I, i, 10).
256. *Eularia balorda* (Naples, ii, 30).
257. *La Fabbrica* (Corsiniana I, ii, 70).
258. *La Fabrica* (Locatelli, ii, 45).
259. *Fabriche* (Naples, i, 36).
260. *Le Fabriche* (Biancolelli I, 29; Biancolelli II, 29).
261. *Il Falso indovino* (Corsiniana I, ii, 62).
262. *Il Falso indovino* (Locatelli, i, 37).
263. *Il Famoso triumvirato, con lo spartimento del mondo tra Ottaviano, Lepedo e Marc' Antonio* (Casanatense, II, 11).
264. *La Fantasma* (Locatelli, i, 19; similar to *L'Abbattimento d'Isabella*, No. 7).
265. *La Fantesca* (Locatelli, i, 17; similar to *Il Furbo*, No. 340).
266. *Il Fate voi* (Locatelli, ii, 27).
267. *Additions au faux prince ou Arlequin roy par hazard* (Biancolelli I, 76).
268. *La Suite du festin de pierre* (Biancolelli I, 58).

269. *Festivo amoroso colle cinque lettere cambiate* (Naples, ii, 40).
270. *La Fida infedelta* (Correr, 10).
271. *Il Fido amico* (Correr, 22).
*272. *Il Fido amico* (Scala, 29).
273. *Figlia disubidiente* (Naples, ii, 33).
274. *La Figlia disubidiente* (Biancolelli I, 4; Biancolelli II, 4; produced in Paris October 1667).
275. *Figlio della morte, overo Cardellino cornuto volontario* (Naples, ii, 39).
276. *Figliol prodigo* (Naples, ii, 32).
277. *Il Figliuol prodigo* (Corsiniana I, ii, 78).
278. *Finta madrigna* (Naples, i, 39).
279. *La Finta madrigna* (Vatican, 3).
*280. *La Finta notte di Colafronio* (Bartoli, pp. 15–27).
281. *La Finta pazza* (Locatelli, ii, 3).
*282. *La Finta pazza* (Scala, 8).
283. *La Finta prigione* (Locatelli, ii, 23).
284. *La Finta sorella* (Correr, 8).
285. *Finte morte* (Naples, ii, 31).
286. *Le Finte morte* (Corsiniana I, ii, 66).
287. *Le Finte morte* (Locatelli, i, 35).
288. *Li Finti amici* (Corsiniana I, ii, 80).
289. *Li Finti amici* (Locatelli, i, 34).
290. *Li Finti mariti* (Corsiniana I, ii, 76).
291. *Li Finti pazzi* (Locatelli, i, 33).
*292. *Li Finti servi* (Scala, 30).
293. *Finti spiritati* (Naples, i, 38).
294. *Li Finti Turchi* (Locatelli, i, 31; similar to *Li tre Turchi*, No. 723).
295. *Finti Turchi* (Naples, i, 38).
†296. *I Finti Turchi* (Lost Este, 13).
297. *Il Finto astrologo* (Locatelli, ii, 22; similar to *La Zengara*, No. 757).
298. *Finto astrologo* (Naples, ii, 35).
299. *Finto bravo* (Naples, i, 40).
300. *Finto cieco* (Correr, 39).
301. *Finto cieco* (Naples, ii, 36).
*302. *Finto cieco* (Scala, 34).
303. *Finto Gioannicco* (Naples, ii, 34).
304. *Il Finto marito* (Locatelli, i, 32; similar to *Li tre Becchi*, No. 706).
*305. *Il Finto negromante* (Scala, 21).
306. *Finto prencipe* (Naples, i, 41).
*307. *Il Finto principe* (Bartoli, pp. 179–189).
308. *Finto re* (Naples, i, 42).
309. *Il Finto schiavo* (Locatelli, i, 30).
310. *Il Finto servo* (Locatelli, i, 36).
311. *Il Finto servo di Cicognino* (Correr, 26).
*312. *Il Finto Tofano* (Scala, 24).
313. *Flagello del padrone* (Naples, i, 43).
*314. *Flaminio disperato* (MS. Emanuele, Rome).
*315. *Flavio finto negromante* (Scala, 28).
*316. *Flavio tradito* (Scala, 5).
317. *La Flora* (Casanatense II, 30).

318. *Il Fonte incantato* (Corsiniana I, ii, 77).
319. *Il Fonte incantato* (Locatelli, i, 44).
320. *La Forestiera* (Locatelli, ii, 17; similar to *La Pellegrina*, No. 527).
321. *Il Formento* (Corsiniana I, ii, 63; similar to *Li Adelfi di Terentio*, No. 12, and *Il Fromento*, No. 337).
322. *Fornaro geloso* (Naples, ii, 38).
*323. *La Forsennata prencipessa* (Scala, 41).
*324. *La Fortuna di Flavio* (Scala, 2).
*325. *La Fortuna di Foresta principessa di Moscou* (Scala, 50).
326. *Fortuna non conosciuta* (Naples, i, 44).
*327. *La Fortunata Isabella* (Scala, 3).
328. *La Forza d' Astimosa* (Casanatense II, 40).
†329. *La Forza del fato* (Lost Modena I (13) and II).
330. *La Forza dell' amicizia* (Vatican 9).
331. *Forza del maggia* (Naples, i, 45).
332. *Forza della maggia* (Barberiniano, 1).
333. *La Forza di amore con la Turca costante* (Casanatense II, 46).
334. *Fratelli avelenati* (Naples, ii, 37).
335. *Il Fratricida crudele, le finte caccie, con Bertolino impiccato* (Casanatense II, 32).
336. *Les Fripiers* (Biancolelli I, 77; produced in Paris December 1672).
337. *Il Fromento* (Locatelli, i, 39; similar to *Il Formento*, No. 321, and *Li Adelfi di Terentio*, No. 12).
338. *Le Furberie di Coviello* (Adriani, 21).
339. *Il Furbo* (Corsiniana I, i, 8; similar to *La Fantesca*, No. 265).
340. *Li Furti* (Locatelli, ii, 32).
341. *La Gageure* (Biancolelli, I, 70; Biancolelli II, 67).
342. *Gare della gelosia* (Naples, ii, 42).
343. *La Gelosa guerriera* (Corsiniana I, i, 49).
*344. *La Gelosa Isabella* (Scala, 25).
345. *La Gelosia* (Locatelli, i, 47; similar to *La Lite*, No. 423, and *Li dui Scolari*, No. 237).
346. *Gelosia e fedeltà di Rosalba* (Barberiniano, 2).
347. *Geloso non amante, e l' amante non geloso* (Naples, i, 46).
348. *Le Gemelle* (Vatican Ottoboni).
349. *Il Gentilhommo campagnano* (Biancolelli I, 46; Biancolelli II, 44; written by Angelo Lolli, produced in Paris 1670).
350. *Il Giardino* (Corsiniana I, i, 29).
351. *Il Giardino* (Locatelli, ii, 46).
352. *Giardino metaforico* (Naples, ii, 44).
353. *La Giostra* (Locatelli, ii, 41).
354. *Giostra amorosa* (Naples, ii, 46).
354A *Giovanna d' Arco* (Arsenal.)
355. *Giudicii del cielo* (Naples, ii, 47).
356. *I Giudici del duca d' Ossuna* (Biancolelli I, 54; Biancolelli II, 52).
*357. *Il Giuoco della primiera* (Locatelli, i, 1; similar to *Sententia in favore*, No. 635).

358. *La Giustitia catalana* (Casanatense II, 17).
*359. *Il Giusto castigo* (Scala, 40).
360. *Il Giusto prencipe* (Corsiniana I, i, 24).
*361. *Il Giusto principe* (Locatelli, ii, 53).
362. *Le Glorie di Scanderbech con la libertà della patria sotto Amurat imperatore di Constantinopoli* (Casanatense II, 45).
†363. *Gramustino medico volante* (Lost Este, 5).
†364. *Gramustino servo sciocco, flagello del suo padrone* (Lost Este, 6).
365. *Il Granchio* (Corsiniana I, ii, 79).
366. *Il Granchio* (Locatelli, i, 46).
367. *Grancio* (Naples, ii, 41).
368. *Le Grandezze di Zanni* (Locatelli, i, 10; similar to *La Nobiltà*, No. 480, and *La Nobiltà di Bertolino*, No. 481).
369. *Il Gran mago* (Corsiniana I, i, 5).
*370. *Il Gran mago* (Locatelli, ii, 21).
371. *La Gran pazzia d' Orlando* (Corsiniana I, i, 1).
372. *Il Gratiano fallito* (Locatelli, ii, 25; similar to *Claudione fallito*, No. 147).
373. *Il Gratiano innamorato* (Corsiniana I, ii, 90).
374. *Grotta di Mescolino* (Naples, ii, 45).
375. *La Grotta nuova* (Biancolelli I, 30; Biancolelli II, 30).
376. *Grotta vechia* (Biancolelli I, 28; Biancolelli II, 28).
377. *Guardia di se stesso* (Naples, ii, 43).
378. *Gli Honesti amori della Regina d' Inghilterra con la morte del conte di Sessa* (Casanatense II, 48. See No. 156).
379. *L' Honorate povertà di Rinaldo, con i tradimenti di Florante e codardi di Gano Maganzese* (Casanatense II, 36).
380. *Horatio burlato* (Corsiniana I, i, 44).
381. *Horatio burlato* (Locatelli, i, 21).
382. *Hospedale de pazzi* (Naples i, 47. See *L'Ospital de pazzi*, No. 505).
383. *Huomo da bene* (Naples, i, 49).
384. *Huomo povero tutti pensieri, overo chi tutto vuole tutto perde* (Naples, i, 48. See *L'Omo povero tutto cabala*, No. 496).
385. *Gl' Imbrogli* (Adriani, 18).
386. *L' Imbrolgliti intrighi* (Correr, 35).
†387. *Gl' Impegni* (Lost Modena I (15) and II).
388. *L' Impegno d' un acaso* (Biancolelli I, 33; Biancolelli II, 33).
†389. *Improprio carnefice* (Lost Modena I (2)).
390. *La Incamisciata* (Corsiniana I, ii, 55).
391. *Gli Incauti amorosi* (Locatelli ii, 20; similar to *L'Amorosi incauti*, No. 45).
*392. *L' Incauto ovvero l'inavvertito* (Bartoli, pp. 89–101).
393. *L' Incoronato cieco* (Casanatense II, 3).
394. *Ingani di Flaminia* (Correr, 40).
395. *Inganni* (Naples, ii, 49).
*396. *Ingiusto rettore* (Naples, ii, 48).

397. *Inimicie de i vecchi* (Correr, 41).
398. *L' Inimicitia* (Locatelli, i, 49).
399. *L' Innamorata scaltra* (Adriani, 22).
400. *L' Innocente inganata coi duplicati sponsalitii* (Modena).
*401. *L' Innocente Persiana* (Scala, 45).
402. *L' Innocente rivenduta* (Corsiniana, ii, 61).
403. *Innocente venduta e rivenduta* (Naples, i, 50).
404. *L' Innocentia rivenduta* (Locatelli, i, 4).
405. *Innocenza felice ed il tradimento fortunato* (Naples, i, 51).
406. *L' Jnocente travagliata* (Biancolelli I, 20; Biancolelli II, 20; produced before 1668).
407. *Insalata* (Naples, i, 54).
408. *L' Insalata* (Adriani, 4).
409. *Intrichi della notte ben riusciti* (Naples, i, 52).
410. *Intrichi di Covello per la moglie* (Naples, i, 53).
411. *L' Intrighi amorosi* (Corsiniana I, i, 48).
*412. *Gli Intrighi d' amore ovvero la finestra incantata* (Bartoli, pp. 117–131).
413. *Intronati* (Correr, 51).
414. *L' Intronati* (Corsiniana I, ii, 64).
415. *L' Intronati* (Locatelli, i, 50).
416. *Invenzioni di Covello* (Naples, i, 55).
417. *L' Ipocrita* (Biancolelli I, 55; Biancolelli II, 53).
*418. *Isabella astrologa* (Scala, 36).
419. *Isole* (Naples, ii, 50).
420. *Ladrarie accidentali* (Naples, i, 56).
421. *Ladro amoroso* (Naples, i, 57).
†422. *Ladro, sbiro e giudice* (Lost Modena I (23) and II. See No. 54).
423. *La Lite* (Locatelli, ii, 48).
†424. *Lucretia* (Lost Modena I (9) and II).
425. *Lucretia Romana* (Naples, ii, 51).
426. *Il Lunatico* (Biancolelli I, 8; Biancolelli II, 8; produced before 1668).
427. *La Maga* (Corsiniana I, ii, 57).
428. *La Maggia naturalle* (Biancolelli I, 72; Biancolelli II, 69).
429. *Maggior gloria* (Naples, ii, 54).
430. *La Maggior gloria d' un grande è il vincere se stesso* (Vatican, 11).
†431. *La Maggior gloria d' un grande è vincer se stesso* (Lost Modena I (28) and II).
432. *La Maggior gloria d' un grande è vincer se stesso, con Rastellino spia muta, buffone attaccato alla corda* (Modena).
433. *La Magia d' amore con Bertolino creduto gentilhuomo di corte, senza la pazzia* (Casanatense II, 7).
434. *Magia d' amore con la pazzia di Leonora, pazza furente* (Casanatense II, 10).
435. *La Magica di Pantalone* (Corsiniana I, ii, 93).
436. *Il Mago* (Corsiniana I, i, 13).
437. *La Maladia di Scaramuza* (Biancolelli I, 67; Biancolelli II, 64).

438. *Mala lingua* (Correr, 19).
*439. *Malizie di Coviello* (Naples, i, 58).
440. *Ma Maitresse est preferable a tout autre chose* (Biancolelli I, 35; Biancolelli II, 35).
*441. *La Mancata fede* (Scala, 27).
*442. *Marescial di Biron* (Casanatense II, 14).
†443. *Il Maritarsi per vendeta* (Lost Modena I (21) and II).
444. *Marito* (Naples, i, 59).
445. *Il Marito* (Biancolelli I, 56; Biancolelli II, 54).
*446. *Il Marito* (Scala 9).
447. *Marito più onorato, cornuto in sua opinione* (Naples, i, 60).
448. *Mascarata nova* (Correr, 24).
*449. *Il Mastro di Terentio* (Correr, 31).
450. *Il Matrimonio eguale* (Modena).
451. *Matrimonio per furto* (Naples, i, 61).
452. *Medaglia* (Naples, ii, 52).
453. *Il Medico di suo honore* (Casanatense II, 1; produced in Florence October 1642).
†454. *Medico volante* (Lost Modena I (24) and II).
455. *Medico volante* (Biancolelli I, 13; Biancolelli II, 13; produced before 1668).
*456. *Medico volante* (Naples, ii, 53).
*457. *Il Medico volante* (Bartoli, pp. 103–115).
458. *Metamorfosi d' Arliechino* (Biancolelli I, 41; Biancolelli II, 41; written by Cinthio, produced in Paris March 1669).
*459. *Le Metamorfosi di Pulcinella* (Adriani, 5).
460. *Moglie di sette mariti* (Naples, ii, 55).
461. *Le Moglie superbe* (Corsiniana, i, 31).
462. *Le Moglie superbe* (Locatelli, ii, 29).
463. *Il Mondo a la roversa* (Biancolelli I, 45; Biancolelli II, 43; produced in Paris July 1669).
464. *Il Monile* (Correr, 32).
465. *Montagnese* (Casanatense II, 42).
466. *La Morte di Leonello e Brisseida* (Casanatense II, 26).
467. *I Morti vivi* (Biancolelli I, 2; Biancolelli II, 2; produced before 1668).
468. *La Mula* (Locatelli, ii, 44; similar to *La Mula grande*, No. 469).
469. *La Mula grande* (Corsiniana I, i, 20. See No. 468).
470. *Naufraggio di lieto fine* (Naples, ii, 57).
471. *La Nave* (Corsiniana I, i, 33).
*472. *La Nave* (Locatelli, ii, 26).
473. *Ne la Damma, ne la spada non si fida al amico* (Biancolelli I, 44).
†474. *Nella bugia si trova la verità* (Lost Modena II).
475. *Nel servitore da palco* (Biancolelli I, 27; Biancolelli II, 27).
†476. *Nerone* (Lost Modena I (6) and II).
*477. *Nerone Imperadore* (Naples, ii, 60).
478. *La Ninfa del cielo tradita nell' honore con la forza del pentimento* (Casanatense II, 38).

2 B

479. *Nobile plebeo* (Naples, ii, 59).
480. *La Nobiltà* (Corsiniana I, ii, 84. See No. 481).
481. *La Nobiltà di Bertolino* (Corsiniana I, ii, 54; similar to *Le Grandezze di Zanni*, No. 368, and *La Nobiltà*, No. 480).
482. *Non amando amare* (Naples, ii, 61).
*483. *Non può essere* (Naples, ii, 58).
*484. *Non può essere ovvero la donna può ciò che vuole* (Adriani, 3).
485. *Non vol rivali amore* (Biancolelli I, 17; Biancolelli II, 17; produced before 1668).
†486. *Non vol viver (rivali) l'amore* (Lost Modena I (30). See No. 485).
487. *Nozze degli Ebrei* (Correr, 7).
488. *Nozze interrotte* (Naples, i, 62).
489. *La Nuova pazzia* (Casanatense II, 12).
490. *Nuovo finto principe* (Naples, ii, 56).
491. *Obligo più ch' amore, overo il Moro* (Naples, i, 63).
492. *Oggetto odiato* (Naples, i, 64).
†493. *L' Oggetto odiato sempre davanti agli occhi* (Lost Este, 17).
494. *Ohime il cuore* (Biancolelli I, 9; Biancolelli II, 9; produced before 1668. See No. 495).
†495. *Oimè il core* (Lost Modena I (26) and II).
†496. *L' Omo povero tutto cabala* (Lost Modena I (31) and II. See *Huomo povero tutti pensieri*, No. 384).
*497. *L' Onorata fuga di Lucinda* (Bartoli, pp. 133–147; "di P. C.").
498. *Oratio inavertito* (Correr, 46).
499. *Orlando Furioso* (Locatelli, ii, 1).
500. *Ormondo de Poni* (Casanatense II, 34).
501. *Orologio* (Correr, 37).
*502-4. *Orseida, Dell'* (three parts; Scala, 46, 47, and 48).
505. *L' Ospital de pazzi* (Biancolelli I, 3; Biancolelli II, 3. See *Hospedale de pazzi*, No. 382).
506. *L' Ospite amoroso* (Corsiniana I, i, 35).
507. *Oste geloso* (Naples, ii, 62).
*508. *Il Padre crudele* (Bartoli, pp. 71–87).
509. *Padri ingannati* (Naples, ii, 70).
510. *Padrone e servo* (Naples, ii, 64).
511. *Pantaloncino* (Corsiniana I, ii, 69; similar to *Il Pantaloncino*, No. 513).
512. *Il Pantaloncino* (Corsiniana I, ii, 65).
513. *Il Pantaloncino* (Locatelli, ii, 50; similar to *Pantaloncino*, No. 511).
514. *Pazzia d' Aurelio (soggetto primo)* (Casanatense II, 41).
†515. *Pazzia del Dotor* (Lost Modena I (5) and II).
516. *La Pazzia d' Eularia* (Biancolelli I, 50; Biancolelli II, 48).
517. *Pazzia di Cintio* (Naples, i, 66).
518. *La Pazzia di Doralice* (Corsiniana I, i, 43).
*519. *La Pazzia di Doralice* (Locatelli, i, 19).

*520. *La Pazzia di Dorindo* (Locatelli, ii, 5; similar to *La Pazzia di Filandro*, No. 521).
*521. *La Pazzia di Filandro* (Locatelli, ii, 4. See No. 520).
522. *La Pazzia di Lavinia* (acted by the Confidenti in 1618).
*523. *La Pazzia d' Isabella* (Scala, 38).
524. *Il Pazzo (or Il Pozzo) del Pasquati* (Correr, 27).
*525. *Un Pazzo guarisce l' altro* (Bibl. Palatina, Vienna).
*526. *Il Pedante* (Scala, 31).
527. *La Pellegrina* (Corsiniana I, i, 26; similar to *La Forestiera*, No. 320).
528. *La Pellegrina* (Naples, i, 65).
*529. *Il Pellegrino fido amante* (Scala, 14).
530. *Pensieri vani* (Correr, 36).
531. *La Peregrina* (Modena).
532. *Peregrino amante* (Naples, i, 68).
533. *Pericco spagnolo* (Naples, i, 67).
534. *La Perna* (Corsiniana I, ii, 75).
535. *Per Ogni scampo mille intoppi* (Naples, i, 75).
536. *La Pietra incantata* (Adriani, 13).
537. *Pittor fortunato* (Naples, ii, 66).
538. *Pittori ladri* (Naples, i, 69).
539. *Plauto alla moderna* (Biblioteca Casanatense, Misc. 172 (3)).
540. *Policinella burlato* (Naples, i, 72).
541. *Policinella dama golosa* (Naples, i, 73).
542. *Policinella finto regente* (Naples, i, 70).
543. *Policinella inamorato* (Naples, i, 71).
544. *Policinella ladro, spia, sbirro, giudice e boia* (Naples, i, 74. See No. 422).
545. *Policinella pazzo per forza* (Naples, i, 76).
546. *Pollicinella finto prencipe* (Adriani, 16).
547. *Pollicinella marchese* (Adriani, 7).
548. *Pollicinella medico a forza* (Adriani, 15).
549. *Pollicinella pittore* (Naples, ii, 67).
550. *Pollicinella sposo e sposa* (Naples, ii, 69).
551. *Il Ponte nuovo* (Biancolelli I, 40; Biancolelli II, 40).
552. *Li Porci* (Corsiniana I, ii, 83).
553. *Li Porci overo specchio de' giovani* (Locatelli, i, 42).
*554. *Il Porta lettere* (Scala, 23).
555. *Povertà di Rinaldo* (Biancolelli I, 16; Biancolelli II, 16. See No. 379).
556. *Il Pozzo* (Corsiniana I, i, 25).
557. *Il Pozzo* (Locatelli, ii, 47).
558. *Pozzo incantato* (Naples, ii, 65).
559. *Il Prencipe d' Altavilla* (Corsiniana I, ii, 81. See No. 565).
560. *La Prencipessa tiranna* (Vatican, 12).
561. *La Presa di Gerusalemme* (Casanatense II, 18).
562. *Prigioner vendicativo* (Naples, ii, 63).
563. *Prigioner vindicativo* (Biancolelli I, 32; Biancolelli II, 32).
*564. *Li Prigioni di Plauto* (Locatelli, ii, 31).

565. *Il Principe d' Altavilla* (Locatelli, i, 6. See No. 559).
566. *Principe pollacco* (Naples, ii, 68).
567. *Il Principe severo* (Locatelli, ii, 52).
568. *Il Principe Sidonio* (Biblioteca Vaticana, Cod. Barb. Lat. 3737).
569. *Le Prodezze di Roderigo* (Casanatense II, 27).
570. *La Proprietà, o Arlequin roy de Tripoli* (Biancolelli I, 69; Biancolelli II, 66; produced in Paris June 1677).
571. *Proteo* (Corsiniana I, i, 45).
572. *Proteo* (Locatelli, i, 41).
573. *Pulcinella disammogliato* (Vatican, 5).
574. *Li quatro Arlechini* (Biancolelli I, 11; Biancolelli II, 11; produced before 1668).
575. *Quatro finti Spiritati* (Correr, 3).
*576. *Li quattro finti Spiritati* (Scala, 33).
577. *Quattro Medici, quattro astrologi e tre vammane* (Naples, ii, 72).
*578. *I quattro Pazzi* (Bartoli, pp. 201–211).
579. *Li quattro Pazzi* (Casanatense II, 37).
580. *Quattro Pollicinelli simili* (Naples, ii, 71).
581. *Quattro simili di Plauto* (Naples, i, 77).
†582. *Li quattro Simili* (Lost Este, 3).
583. *Il Ragazzo delle littere* (Corsiniana I, ii, 87; similar to *Il Zanni beccho*, No. 753).
584. *Ragazzo per le lettere* (Naples, i, 78).
585. *Il Regallo delle damme* (Biancolelli I, 36; Biancolelli II, 36; produced in Paris May 1668).
*586. *La Regina d' Inghilterra* (Bartoli, pp. 53–70. See Nos. 156, 378, 587, 588).
†587. *La Regina d' Inghilterra* (Lost Modena I (3) and II).
*588. *La Regina statista regnante* (Casanatense II, 2).
589. *Le Remede anglois ou arlequin prince du quinquina* (Biancolelli I, 78; produced in Paris September 1680).
590. *La Ricca superba* (Correr, 16).
591. *Il Ricco con Lazzaro povero* (Casanatense II, 33).
*592. *Ricco epulone* (Naples, ii, 75).
593. *Il Rimedio a tutti malli* (Biancolelli I, 39; Biancolelli II, 39; produced in Paris August 1668; by Cinthio).
594. *Rinegato per amore* (Naples, ii, 73).
595. *Ritrato amoroso* (Biancolelli I, 14; Biancolelli II, 14).
596. *Li Ritratti* (Corsiniana I, i, 17).
597. *Li Ritratti (tragicommedia pastorale)* (Locatelli, i, 3).
598. *Li Ritratti (tragicommedia pescatoria)* (Locatelli, ii, 51).
*599. *Il Ritratto* (Scala, 39).
600. *Rivalità di Policinella e Covello* (Naples, i, 79).
601. *Rosalba bizzarra* (Naples, ii, 77).
*602. *Rosalba incantatrice* (Scala, 44).
603. *Rubella per amore* (Naples, ii, 76).

604. *Ruberto del diavolo* (Naples, ii, 74).
605. *La Ruffiana* (Locatelli, ii, 18).
606. *Ruota di fortuna* (Casanatense II, 31).
607. *Saccaria* (Naples, ii, 83).
608. *Salernitana* (Naples, ii, 86).
609. *Sansone* (Naples, ii, 87).
610. *Sapera apporta danno* (Naples, ii, 80).
611. *Sardellino invisibile* (Corsiniana I, i, 40; similar to *Trappolino invisibile*, No. 703).
612. *Li Scambi* (Corsiniana I, i, 7).
613. *Li Scambi* (Locatelli, ii, 30).
614. *La Schiava* (Corsiniana I, i, 2; similar to *Le due Schiave*, No. 219).
*615. *La Schiava* (Este).
616. *La Schiava* (Locatelli, i, 27).
617. *Schiava di Messina* (Naples, i, 80).
618. *Schiava padrona* (Naples, i, 81).
619. *La Schiavetta* (Corsiniana I, ii, 98; similar to *La Turchetta*, No. 728).
620. *Lo Schiavo de demonio* (Casanatense II, 28).
621. *Scipione trionfante de Cartagine con gli amori di Siface e Massinissa con Sofonisba* (Casanatense II, 19).
622. *Scola di Terenzio, overo il Dottore mastro di scola* (Naples, i, 82).
623. *Li Sdegni* (Biancolelli I, 18; Biancolelli II, 18).
*624. *Gli Sdegni amorosi* (Rouen).
625. *Sdegni amorosi* (Naples, ii, 81).
626. *Sdegni amorosi* (Correr, 42).
627. *Li sei Contenti* (Corsiniana I, ii, 51).
628. *Li sei Contenti* (Locatelli, i, 2).
629. *Li sei Simili* (Corsiniana I, i, 47).
630. *Li sei Simili* (Locatelli, ii, 11).
631. *La Semiramide* (Casanatense II, 8).
632. *La Senese* (Corsiniana I, i, 52).
633. *La Senese* (Locatelli, ii, 16).
634. *Sensale di matrimonii* (Naples, ii, 78).
635. *Sententia in favore* (Corsiniana I, ii, 58; similar to *Il Giuoco alla primiera*, No. 357).
636. *La Sepoltura* (Corsiniana I, i, 14).
637. *La Sepoltura* (Locatelli, i, 20).
638. *Il Serpe fatale* (Locatelli, ii, 39; similar to *Il Serpe incantato*, No. 639).
639. *Il Serpe incantato* (Corsiniana I, ii, 73. See No. 638).
640. *Servi innamorati* (Naples, ii, 82).
641. *Il Servo fidele* (Corsiniana I, i, 46).
642. *Il Servo padrone* (Adriani, 2).
643. *Servo padrone* (Biancolelli I, 34; Biancolelli II, 34; produced before 1668).
644. *Il Servo ritornato* (Locatelli, i, 15; similar to *Il Servo scacciato*, No. 645).
645. *Il Servo scacciato* (Locatelli, ii, 35. See No. 644).
646. *Il Servo sciocco* (Vatican, 4).
647. *Sette Infanti di Lara* (Naples, ii, 85).

†648. *Siviglia* (Lost Modena I (18)).

649. *Il Sogno fatale con li tre finti ciechi* (Casanatense II, 21).

650. *Soldato per vendetta* (Naples, ii, 84).

651. *Il Soldato per vendetta o Arlichino soldato in Candia* (Biancolelli I, 42; Biancolelli II, 42; written by Cinthio, produced in Paris May 1669).

652. *Agiunta al soldato in Candia* (Biancolelli I, 43).

653. *Sole* (Correr, 4).

654. *La Sorella* (Adriani, 10).

655. *Sorella picciola* (Naples, ii, 79).

656. *La Soverchia bonta di Virginio* (Correr, 14).

*657. *La Spada fatale* (Bartoli, pp. 225–233; "commedia del Bricci").

658. *La Spada mortale* (Corsiniana I, ii, 95; similar to *La Cometa*, No. 152).

*659. *Lo Specchio* (Scala, 16).

660. *Lo Specchio con la Turca constante* (Casanatense II, 25).

661. *Li Spiriti* (Corsiniana I, i, 6).

662. *Li Spiriti* (Locatelli, i, 18).

†663. *Lo Spirito foletto* (Lost Este, 1).

664. *Spirito folletto* (Modena, dated 1682, no title and incomplete).

665. *Spirito folletto* (Modena; similar to No. 664, dated Genua, 1683).

666. *Spirito folletto nuovo* (Modena; dated Ferrara, May 6, 1675).

*667. *La Sposa* (Scala, 10).

668. *Gli Straccioni* (Adriani, 19).

669. *Stravaganze d' amore* (Naples, i, 83).

670. *Li Stroppiati* (Corsiniana I, i, 27; similar to *La Travestita*, No. 705).

671. [*Gli studenti*] (Barberiniano, 7; title given by Valeri).

672. [*Gli studenti*] (Barberiniano, 8; title given by Valeri).

*673. *Suppositi dell' Ariosto* (Correr, 30).

674. *La Tabernaria* (Adriani, 8).

675. *Li Tapeti* (Biancolelli I, 21; Biancolelli II, 21; produced before 1668).

*676. *I Tappeti, ovvero Colafronio geloso* (Bartoli, pp. 275–285).

677. *Tappetti Alessandrini* (Naples, i, 84).

*678. *Li Tappetti Alessandrini* (Scala, 26).

679. *Terza del tempo* (Corsiniana I, ii, 99).

680. *Il Tesoro* (Corsiniana I, ii, 71. See No. 684).

681. *Le Teste incantate* (Corsiniana I, ii, 97).

682. *Le Teste incantate* (Locatelli, i, 8).

683. *Il Theatro senza comedie* (Biancolelli I, 38; Biancolelli II, 38; written by Cinthio, produced in Paris July 1668).

684. *Il Thesoro* (Locatelli, ii, 49. See No. 680).

685. *Il Torneo* (Corsiniana I, i, 42; similar to *Il Carnovale*, No. 121).

686. [*La Tradita*] (Barberiniano, 6; title given by Valeri).

687. *Il Tradito* (Corsiniana I, ii, 74; in 5 acts).

688. *Il Tradito* (Corsiniana I, i, 3; in 3 acts).

689. *Il Tradito* (Locatelli, i, 22).

*690. *Il Tradito* (Naples, i, 85).

691. *Traditor fortunato* (Naples, i, 86).

*692. *Li Tragici successi* (Scala, 18).

693. *La Tramutatione* (Locatelli, ii, 36; similar to *Li Anfitrioni*, No. 47).

694. *Trapola* (Naples, i, 87).

695. *Trapolaria* (Correr, 47).

696. *Trapolaria* (Naples, i, 88).

697. *Trapole di Covello* (Naples, i, 89).

698. *Trapole di Covello, overo il finto pazzo* (Naples, i, 90).

699. *La Trappolaria* (Adriani, 17).

*700. *La Trappolaria* (Corsiniana I, i, 28).

701. *La Trappolaria* (Locatelli, ii, 14).

702. *La Trappoleria* (Bartoli, pp. xxxi–xxxv, from Perrucci).

703. *Trappolino invisibile* (Locatelli, i, 14; similar to *Sardellino invisibile*, No. 611).

*704. *La Travagliata Isabella* (Scala, 15).

705. *La Travestita* (Locatelli, ii, 37; similar to *Li Stroppiati*, No. 670).

706. *Li tre Becchi* (Corsiniana I, ii, 92; similar to *Il Finto marito*, No. 304).

*707. *Li tre Becchi* (Bartoli, pp. 163–177; "commedia di N. N.").

708. *Tre Capitani* (Correr, 44).

*709. *Li tre Fidi amici* (Scala, 19).

710. *Tre Finti Turchi* (Biancolelli I, 15; Biancolelli II, 15; produced before 1668).

*711. *Le tre Gravide* (Bartoli, pp. 149–161; "commedia di Francesco Ricciolini").

712. *Tre Ladri scoperti* (Biancolelli I, 6; Biancolelli II, 6; produced before 1668).

713. *Li tre Matti* (Corsiniana I, ii, 82).

714. *Li tre Matti* (Locatelli, ii, 2).

*715. *I tre Matti* (Bartoli, pp. 235–247).

716. *Tre Orbi* (Naples, ii, 88).

717. *Tre Prencipe di Salerno* (Naples, i, 91).

*718. *I tre Principi di Salerno* (Bartoli, pp. 191–199).

719. *Li tre Satiri* (Corsiniana I, i, 9).

*720. *Li tre Satiri* (Locatelli, ii, 28).

721. *Li tre Schiavi* (Corsiniana I, ii, 94).

722. *Li tre Schiavi* (Locatelli, i, 29).

723. *Li tre Turchi* (Corsiniana I, i, 18; similar to *Li Finti Turchi*, No. 294).

724. *Triomphe de la médecine* (*addition au*) (Biancolelli I, 61; Biancolelli II, 58).

725. *Il Triumvirato dell' amicizia* (Biancolelli I, 7; Biancolelli II, 7).

726. *Les Trompeurs trompés* (Biancolelli I, 66; Biancolelli II, 63).

388

*727. *Truffaldino balordo, flagello alle fortune del suo padrone* (Modena; dated Milan, 1680. See No. 313).

728. *La Turchetta* (Locatelli, ii, 15; similar to *La Schiavetta*, No. 619).

729. *Il Tutore* (Barberiniano, 3).

†730. *I Vecchi burlati* (Lost Este, 15).

731. *Il Vecchio avaro* (Adriani, 20).

732. *Il Vecchio avaro* (Corsiniana I, ii, 72).

*733. *Il Vecchio avaro ovvero li scritti* (Locatelli, i, 45).

*734. *Il Vecchio geloso* (Scala, 6).

735. *Vecchio ingannato* (Naples, i, 92).

736. *Li Vecchi scherniti per l' amore* (Biancolelli I, 80).

737. *Vedova con due mariti* (Naples, i, 93).

*738. *La Vedova costante overo Isabella soldato per vendetta* (Bartoli, pp. 1–14).

739. *Il Veleno* (Corsiniana I, ii, 89).

740. [*La Vendetta per marito*] (Corsiniana II; title given by Valeri).

741. *Il Veneno* (Locatelli, i, 5).

742. *Vengane quel che si voglia, overo il fischietto* (Naples, ii, 90).

743. *Veste* (Naples, ii, 89).

*744. *Il Viaggio di Scaramuccia e Arlechino all' Indie* (Biancolelli I, 64; Biancolelli II, 61).

†745. *Le Vicende [d'] amore e fortuna* (Lost Modena I (19) and II).

746. *Il Villano creduto principe, il principe creduto villano; il valore premiato, le dame concorrenti* (Modena).

†747. *Vita è sogno* (Lost Modena I (12) and II).

748. *Vittoria cacciatrice, lo scherno delli favolosi Dei antichi con le metamorfosi amorose e Zaccagnino creduto Apollo, e Spinetta Diana* (Casanatense II, 9).

749. [*Il volubile in amore*] (Barberiniano, 5; title given by Valeri).

750. *Volubilità di Flaminia* (Correr, 9).

751. *Il Zanni astuto* (Corsiniana I, ii, 86).

752. *Zanni barbiero* (Correr, 49).

753. *Il Zanni becco* (Locatelli, i, 12; similar to *Il Ragazzo delle littere*, No. 583).

754. *Zanni finto morto* (Correr, 45).

755. *Zanni incredibile con quattro simili* (Correr, 21).

756. *Zanni vendicativo* (Correr, 18).

757. *La Zengara* (Corsiniana I, i, 21; similar to *Il Finto astrologo*, No. 297).

†758. *La Zenobia* (Lost Modena I (14) and II).

759. *La Zerla* (Biancolelli I, 12; Biancolelli II, 12; produced before 1668).

760. *La Zinghera* (Locatelli, ii, 19).

While I have omitted here all reference to the scenarii given in various eighteenth-century French collections, these being easily obtainable, I append a list of the forty odd pieces printed in St Petersburg between 1733 and 1735, because most of the originals are unique and because the volume in which they are reprinted, V. N. Peretz' Италіанскія комедіи и интермедіи представленныя при дворѣ Императрицы Анны Іоанновны въ 1733–1735 гг. (Petrograd, 1917), seems to be unknown in this country. Among works on the *commedia dell' arte* it is referred to only by Constant Mic and, from his allusion to it, by Kathleen M. Lea. Since, however, the original Italian titles have not been preserved, it was impossible to include the various items in the main list. I present here literal English translations of the Russian titles, with indication of the alternative German in the few instances where these occur. The order is that of Peretz.

1. *The Honest Courtesan* (cf. Nos. 163, 164, *La Cortigiana onesta*).

2. *Smeraldina in a Rage.*

3. *Smeraldina believed a Phantom* (*Smeraldina als ein umherschweiffender Geist*).

4. *Crossing a Fence* (*Die Bestürmung*).

5. *The Newspaper, or The News* (*Die Zeitung*).

6. *Arlequin and Smeraldina, the Quarrelling Lovers.*

7. *The Birth of Arlequin.*

8. *The Disguises of Arlequin* (*Die Verwandelung des Arlequins, oder Misch-Masch*).

9. *The Four Arlequins* (cf. Nos. 580, *Quattro Pollicinelli simili*; 581, *Quattro simili di Plauto*; and 582, *Li quattro Simili*).

10. *Arlequin a Statue.*

11. *The Manager of an Opera in the Canary Islands* (*Der Opern-Meister auf den Canarischen Inseln*).

12. *The Old Miser* (*Der alte Geitzhalsz*) (cf. Nos. 731–733, *Il Vecchio avaro*).

13. *The Great Basilisk of Bernagasso* (cf. Nos. 90, 91, *Il Basilisco*, 92–94, *Il Basilisco del Bernagasso*).

14. *Brighella, Soldier and Baggage* (cf. No. 63, *Arlequin soldat et bagage*).

15. *The Frenchman in Venice* (*Der Frantzose in Venedig*).

16. *The Metamorphoses, or The Disguises of Arlequin* (*Die Verwandelung des Arlequin*) (cf. Nos. 458, *Metamorfosi d' Arliechino*, and 459, *Le Metamorfosi di Pulcinella*).

17. *The Gamester* (*Der Spieler*) (cf. No. 357, *Il Giuoco della primiera*).

18. *The Nobleman.*

19. *More Haste less Speed.*

20. *The Jealous Husband.*

21. *The Successful Lie* (*Der glückliche Betrug*).

22. *The Charwoman turned Gentlewoman.*

23. *A Clever Cure for a Disease.*

24. *The Pretended German Woman.*

25. *Narcissus, or He who fell in love with Himself.*

26. *The Lucky Mishaps of Arlequin* (cf. the various " Disgrazie " plays, Nos. 183–186).

27. *The Entertainments on Water and Land.*

28. *The Perjury* (*Die Untreue*).

389

29. *The Ridiculous Marquis (Der lächerliche und affectirte Marquis).*

30. *The Witchcraft of Peter Daban and Smeraldina the Queen of Spirits.*

31. *The Misfortunes of Pantalone, and Arlequin a Pretended Courier, and later a Fashionable Barber (cf. No. 186, Le Disgrazie e fortune di Pandolfo).*

32. *The Two-faced Doctor.*

33. *The Fulfilment of Apollo's Oracle, or the Innocent Slave Redeemed (Die Erfüllung des Oraculs oder Die verkauffte und wieder gekauffte Unschuldige) (cf. No. 403, Innocente venduta e rivenduta).*

34. *The Lovers their own Rivals, with Arlequin a Pre-tended Pasha (Die Nebenbuhlerey der Liebhaber oder Arlequin der verstellete Basza).*

35. *The Dispute regarding Nobility between Eularia, the Doting Widow, and Pantalone, the quarrelsome merchant, or The Marquis d' Alta Polvere (cf. No. 559, Il Prencipe d' Altavilla).*

36. *The Honest Poverty of Rinaldo, the Ancient Cavalier of Gaul in the Time of Charlemagne (cf. Nos. 379, L'Honorate povertà di Rinaldo, and 555, Povertà di Rinaldo).*

37. *The Secret Place.*

38. *Samson.*

39. *The Greatest Glory of a King is to conquer Himself (cf. Nos. 430–432, La Maggior gloria d' un grande è vincer se stesso).*

The names of the characters vary in the several pieces of this Russian collection. Pantalone and the Dottore appear in almost all, and the zanni are normally Arlequin and Brighella, although a Tabarin also occurs. The women servants are named Smeraldina or Colombina. Odoardo and Silvio are the usual lovers, with counterparts in Cornelia, Diana, Silvia, Aurelia, Vittoria, Celia, and Isabella. Coviello, a " Neapolitan captain," appears but rarely, as do two other figures—Momol, described once as a " gondolier " and once as a " host," and Sabadin, described as an " old man."

INDEX

[*It has not been thought necessary to include in the Index entries from the Appendix, since the lists there are arranged in alphabetical order.*]

A fourbe, fourbe et demy, 267
A Gran danno gran rimedio, 252
Abbaye Joyeuse, 164
Abbé des Foux, 164
Aberdeen, medieval plays at, 179
Abriani, P., 242
Accesi, troupe of Italian actors, 235, 241, 243, 251, 278, 293, 297, 313, 322–326, 327, 328
Accius, 111, 125
Acharnians, 30
Acrobats, and the ancient mime, 35–37, 81, 83, 84–85, 109–110; in medieval times, 166–167
Acta Sanctorum, 18, 121, 160, 179
Actes des Apôtres, 200, 206, 207
Actresses, in the mime, 36–37, 49–50, 85, 87, 92–93; in medieval mysteries, 192
Adalhart, Abbot of Corvey, 149
Adam de la Halle, 172–173
Adami, P., 'Diamantina,' 244, 343, 344
Adamo, L', 235
Adelphæ, 169
Adelricus, 153
Ademollo, A., 216, 299, 300, 365
Admetos, 45
Adoniazousai (*The Women at the Adonis Festival*), 39, 44
Adultery themes, in the mimes, 119–120; in medieval drama, 169–175, 184; in *commedia dell' arte*, 226–231
Aebischer, P., 172
Ælius Lampridius, 123, 129, 130, 134
Ælius Spartianus, 77, 98
Æmilius Severianus, 110
Æschylus, 35, 39, 42, 68
Æsopus, writer of mimes, 110
Affezionati, troupe of Italian actors, 243, 251, 293
Agamemnon suppositus, 68
Agape, 136
Agathocles, entertainer, 36
Agde, Council of, 142
Agesilaus, 26
Agobard, Archbishop of Lyons, 149, 151
Agocchi, G. P., 'Dottore,' 259
Agresti, A., 216
Agricola, 69
Agrippa, 75
Agrippus Memphius, Apolaustus, mimic actor, 94
Agrostinos, 38
Agyia, 26
Aiguillon, Duc d', 323
Aix-la-Chapelle, Council of, 147
Akko, 28
Alazon, comic type, 43, 246
Albani, G., 'Pantalone,' 337
Alberigi, A., 'Angelica,' 241, 307, 316
Alcuin, 147, 149
Alda, 170, 171
Aldobrandini, Cardinal, 237

Alexander the Great, 35
Alexander Severus, Emperor, 130
Alexandrea, 112
Alexandria, actors in, 19, 44, 45, 47, 50, 81, 90, 137
Alexis, writer of comedies, 53
Aliturus, mimic actor, 94
Alkinoos, 45
Alkyoneus, 39
Allacci, L., 377
Allen, P. S., 135, 348
Allione da Asti, Giorgio, 173–174
Allori, F., 'Valerio,' 236, 335
All's Well that ends Well, 39
Alphito, 28
Alsfeld mystery play, 200, 201
Alt, H., 136
Alvida, L', 227, 228, 294
Amante interesato, L', 228, 253, 295
Amante tradito, L', 261
Amateur performances, of Atellan farce, 77; of medieval mysteries, 192
Amicis, V. de, 48, 214, 263
Amico infido, L', 233
Ammianus Marcellinus, 110, 113, 138
Amorevoli, B.—*see* Battista da Treviso
Amphitheatres, performances of mimes in, 107–108; performances of mystery plays in, 200–201
Amphitruo, 51
Amphitryon, 169
Amykos, 39
Anastasia, mimic actress, 98
Anastasius, 143
Ancatoni, D., 'Capitan Sangue e Fuoco,' 252
André (Andrea), 299, 300
Andreazzo, 'Dottor Graziano,' 259, 322
Andreiev, L., 88
Andreini, F., 'Capitan Spavento,' 235, 237, 246, 249, 252, 307, 310–314
Andreini, G. B., 'Lelio,' 235, 237, 238, 321, 325, 326–335, 343
Andreini, I., 'Isabella,' 237–240, 307, 310–314, 316, 317
Andreini, V., 'Florinda,' 235, 241, 325, 327–334
Andria, 157
Andromache, 69
Angelica, L', 251, 316
Animal characters, in the mime, 31–32, 45, 74–75; in medieval entertainments, 165–166, 188–189, 190–191
Anthoine Marie, 300
Anthologia Palatina, 51
Antinoe, 17–18
Antioch, 97, 115, 130, 138
Antiochus II, interest of, in mimes, 35, 46, 94
Antiochus IV, interest of, in mimes, 94
Antiochus, Bishop, 121
Antiodemis, mimic actress, 96
Antipater of Sidon, 96
Anton Maria, 300

Antonazzoni, F., ' Ortensio,' 235–236, 246, 252, 317–320, 333
Antonazzoni, M. D., ' Lavinia ' and ' Ricciolina,' 242, 243, 317–320, 333
Antonio da Treviso, P., 299
Ants, The, 31
Anz, H., 176
Apollinaire, G., 216
Apollo ephebus, 123
Apollodorus of Karystus, writer of comedies, 47
Apollonio, M., 214, 216, 219, 292, 377
Apollonius of Tyre, 90
Aprissius, writer of Atellan farces, 68, 69
Apuleius, 37, 72, 73, 91, 126
Aquæ caldæ, 112
Aquileia, 96
Arbuscula, mimic actress, 96
Arcadia incantata, L', 228, 261, 347
Arcagiati, A., ' Rosaura,' 341
Archelaus, tragic actor, 94
Archiari, L., ' Mario,' 338, 340, 341
Archimima, 87, 241
Archimimus, 85–86
Archippus, writer of comedies, 31
Ardalio, character in the mime, 90
Ardalio, mimic actor, 90, 94, 121, 130
Areliari, T., ' Vittoria,' 338, 340
Arete, *archimima*, 87
Arezzo, 341
Ariadne, 68
Arianism and the mime, 139, 210
Arianus, prefect of Antinoe, 17
Ariemme, G. G. d', ' Pasquariello,' 260
Aries, 112
Ariminum, 165
Aristophanes, 19, 24, 25, 26, 27, 31, 38, 39, 45, 50, 72, 78, 141
Aristophanes of Byzantium, 28
Aristotle, 20, 33, 36, 37, 38, 80, 81, 99
Arjona, J. S., 304
Arlecchino, stock type in *commedia dell' arte*, 70, 77, 88, 114, 158, 160, 173, 188, 214, 255, 267–282, 321
Arlecchino creato re per ventura, 230–231
Arlequin dévaliseur des maisons, 220
Arlequin Protée, 344
Arles, 267; Council of, 136
Armani, V., ' Lidia,' 234, 240–241, 301
Armorum iudicium, 68
Arnobius, 80, 91, 122
Arras, Council of, 140; *Passion* played at, 172
Arrighi, C., ' Pantalone,' 256
Artemidorus, 36
Arullani, V. A., 361
Aruspex, 69
Asina, 68, 74
Asinus, 74
Assteas, 51, 55, 58
Astrologo, L', 228, 261
Atalanta, 68
Atalantai, 39
Ateista fulminato, L', 227
Atella, 65, 66, 67
Atellan farce, 48, 65–79, 85, 88, 89, 99, 106, 112, 138, 164, 191, 214–216, 217, 263, 266, 295
Athanasius, 139, 210
Athenæus, 25, 26, 27, 28, 34, 35, 36, 37, 41, 46, 50, 53, 69, 84, 94, 129, 133, 170, 253
Athens, actors in, 19, 20, 23, 24, 46–47
Atta, writer of comedies, 84

Attalus, writer of mimes, 110
Aucassin and Nicolette, 168
Auctoratus, 68, 77
Augur, 112
Augustine, St, 95, 122, 133, 140, 141
Augustus, Emperor, 82, 108, 109, 125, 129, 133, 134
Auleum, curtain used in Roman theatres, 99, 100
Aulularia, 112, 169
Aurelian, Emperor, 130
Ausonius, 137
Austoni, G. B., ' Battistino,' 242, 317–320, 323, 324–325
Austoni, V. D., ' Valeria,' 242, 317–320
Autokabdaloi, 26, 27
Automata, in Greece, 37
Averara, D., Italian actress, 341
Aversa, 65
Aveugle et le boiteux, L', 172
Avocat pour et contre, L', 260
Axelsen, A., 187, 188

Babylas, mimic actor, 94, 141
Bacchæ, 39
Bacchides, 69
Back to Methuselah, 54
Bagattino, stock type in *commedia dell' arte*, 333
Bagliani, P., ' Dottore,' 260, 314
Bagnacavallo, Lidia da, 234, 240, 303
Bagolino, stock type in *commedia dell' arte*, 336
Bajazet, Sultan, 160
Bald-headed mimic clown, 47–49, 61, 82, 87–88, 114, 144, 161–162, 266
Baldi, F., 293
Balestri, G., 312
Balletti, F., 336
Balletti, G., 336
Balsamon, 146
Bambasio, T., entertainer, 257
Bamberg, Staatliche Bibliothek, 344
Barante, Brugière de, 346
Barbieri, F., 216, 305, 310
Barbieri, G. C., ' Volpino,' 336
Barbieri, N., ' Beltrame,' 217, 218, 221, 224, 235, 281, 297, 317–320, 332, 333, 335, 336
Barclay, Alexander, 162, 164
Bari, 24, 25, 55
Baron Todesco, 233, 265
Barra, M., 293
Bartholomaeis, V. de, 151
Bartolazzi, M., 342
Bartoli, A., 216, 218, 221, 223, 226, 230, 233, 241, 261, 262, 278, 296, 297, 306, 309, 312, 313, 314, 315, 316, 323, 327, 328, 330, 331, 334, 335, 338, 343
Bartoli, F., 216, 312, 334
Bartoli, P. S., 79
Bartolomei, G., 218
Baschet, A., 216, 278, 279, 293, 299, 300, 303, 305, 306, 307, 308, 310, 313–314, 323, 324, 325, 328, 329, 330, 331, 332, 334
Bastian, T. de, 299
Bastoni, 189
Bathyllus, pantomimic actor, 97, 133
Batines, C. de, 178
' Batte,' Arlequin's, 77, 163, 263, 269
Battista da Treviso, ' Franceschina,' 244, 310, 311, 312, 322
Baucis et Thraso, 170
Baumeister, F., 59
Bavaria, Italian actors in, 226, 256, 259, 297, 300, 325
Beaumont and Fletcher, romantic style of, 115, 227

INDEX

Becho, C., 340
Bede, the Venerable, 189
Beijer, A., 243, 301, 307
Bekker, I., 80, 129
Bella, G., 222, 223
Bella, S. della, 283
Bella brutta, La, 242
Bellay, J. du, 256, 263, 299
Bellissima commedia in tre persone, La, 229–230, 233
Belonistria, 123
Beltrame, N., 379
Bendinelli, G., 'Valerio,' 236, 337, 343
Bergamo, actors in, 263, 265, 307, 309
Berlin Museum, 29, 31, 57, 59, 190, 300
Bernardakis, G. N., 120
Bernardin, N. M., 216
Bernardini, O., 'Franceschina,' 244, 326
Bertolotti, A., 216, 300
Berza, I., 340
Bethe, E., 20, 26, 50, 72, 110
Bettòli, P., 282, 303
Beutler, E., 170
Bevilacqua, E., 327, 328, 329, 330, 331, 332, 333, 334, 335
Bianchi, B., 'Aurelia,' 242, 336, 342, 343, 344
Bianchi, G., 'Capitan Spezzaferro,' 247, 252, 342, 343
Bianchi, L. de', 'Dottor Graziano,' 259, 305, 307, 310, 312
Biancolelli, C., 'Colombina,' 244 245, 344, 346
Biancolelli, F. M. A., 'Isabella,' 344
Biancolelli, G. B., 'Arlecchino,' 220, 226, 230–231, 242, 245, 267, 281, 343, 344, 345
Biancolelli, I. Franchini-, 'Colombina,' 336, 337
Bieber, M., 23, 25, 29, 47, 48, 50, 52, 53, 54, 55, 56, 59, 61, 62, 70, 105, 132
Birds, The, 31
Bitonto, 24
Block, K. S., 178
Blois, 306
Blümner, H., 35, 84
Boccaccio, G., 73, 170
Boccalini, T., 261
Bocchia, E., 216, 336
Bocchini, B., 266, 286, 351
Boehn, M. von, 23, 167, 190, 205
Böhme, M., 176
Boisacq, É., 41
Boissevain, U. P., 57
Bologna, actors in, 257, 311, 313, 315, 316, 317, 322, 323, 328, 329, 334, 337, 341
Bolte, J., 170
Bonfanti, R., 378
Bongiovanni, B., 'Dottore,' 259, 328, 330
Bonifaci, A., 336
Bonifaci, B., 336
Bonifacio, G., 151
Bonilla y San Martín, A., 151, 158, 169, 170, 173, 183, 214, 316
Bonnell, J. K., 189, 194
Bononcini, D., 'Brighella,' 283, 336, 340
Bordelon, J., 268
Borgogni, G., 237–238
Borlase, W., 202
Bossu, Comtesse Marie de, 324
Boston Museum of Fine Arts, 31
Bota, feasts in honour of Pan, 145
Botanelli, V., 'Curzio,' 305
Botzon, J., 45
Boulanger de Rivery, 80

Bourgeois gentilhomme, Le, 229
Bourges, 189
Braga, G., 'Pantalone,' 256, 311, 323, 326
Bragato, G., 299
Braintree, medieval plays at, 179
Brambs, J. G., 210
Brandstetter, R., 198
Brandt, S., 162
Bréhier, L., 211
Brera, 235
Brescia, 323, 331
Bretel, J., 158
Brigantin, 225
Brighella, stock type in *commedia dell' arte*, 282–284
Brinkmann, H., 176
Brinquenazille, comic type, 260
Brizio, E., 88, 91
Broglia, A., 'Bertolino,' 336
Brolo, G., 310, 311, 316
Brooks, N. C., 194, 200
Brosses, President de, 230
Brouwer, F. de S., 250, 378
Brumalia, feasts in honour of Bacchus, 145
Brunelli, B., 216, 299, 313, 315, 325, 335, 337, 340, 341
Bruni, D., 'Fulvio,' 235, 312, 317–321, 330
Bruni, S., 'Spinetta,' 317–320
Bruno, A., 361
Bucco, stock type in Atellan farce, 69–70, 74, 76, 80, 214
Bucco adoptatus, 69
Bucco auctoratus, 69
Buckhurst, Lord, 303
Bulengerius, J. C., 35
Bullen, A. H., 280
Buonarotti il Giovane, M., 243, 248, 255, 258, 297
Burattino, stock type in *commedia dell' arte*, 297
Burchiella, L., 'Dottore,' 256, 259, 301, 303
Burlesque, in Dorian comedy, 25, 27; in *hilarodia*, 34; in the mimes of Epicharmus, 40; in Greek mime, 47; in the Phlyax, 51, 54, 61, 62; in the Atellan farce, 67–68, 78; in the mime, 113, 121–123
Busiris, 39
Bustico, G., 216
Butler, H. E., 72
Byzantium, theatrical activities in, 97, 121, 126; religious drama in, 210–212

Caccia, G., 'Leandro,' 336, 337, 340, 341
Caffi, E., 269
Calcese, A., 'Cuiccio,' 293
Calderoni, A., 'Flaminia,' 242, 336
Calderoni, F., 'Silvio,' 242, 336
Calendrier historique des théâtres, 257
Caligula, Emperor, 76, 90, 129, 134
Calliopius, 152–154
Callot, Jacques, 78, 243, 247, 251, 252, 260, 285, 286, 290, 292, 297, 351
Calmo, A., 299
Cambridge, Fitzwilliam Museum, 62
Camerini, E., 216, 377
Caminucci, G., 216
Campani, 71
Campardon, É., 216, 281, 282, 284, 343–345
Canali, P., 237
Cancer, 112
Candium, 74
Canovaro, G., Italian actor, 323
Cantù, C., 'Buffetto,' 283, 336–340, 343
Capella, 68

Capellino, ' Pantalone,' 336
Capitan Cocodrillo, stock type in *commedia dell' arte*, 250, 251
Capitan Fracasso, stock type in *commedia dell' arte*, 249
Capitano, stock type in *commedia dell' arte*, 186, 224, 246–252
Capua, 74
Caravaggio, 309
Caravan, The, 121
Caravelli, V., 174, 293
Carcer, 112
Carceri, Pulcinella dalle, 291, 292
Cardamas, mimic actor, 94, 141
Carinus, Emperor, 85, 130
Carlo, ' Franceschina,' 244
Carpi, 317
Carpiani, O., ' Pantalone,' 335, 336
Carrara, E., 347
Carthage, 98 ; Councils of, 136, 140
Carus, mimic actor, 95
Casnar, variant name of Pappus, 73
Cassandro, stock type in *commedia dell' arte*, 260, 261
Cassiodorus, 113, 131, 132, 142
Cassius, mimic actor, 95
Cassius Severus, 115
Castaldo, A., 300
Castico della disonesta moglie, Il, 233
Castiglione, G. B., 311
Castiglioni, L., ' Leonora,' 336
Castle of Perseverance, The, 202, 204
Catalano, M., 297
Catholicon Anglicum, 171
Catinenses, 112
Cato, 107
Catrani, A., 309, 313
Catullus, writer of mimes, 110–111, 118
Cavalier ingrato, Il, 233
Cavaliere perseguitato, Il, 227
Caversari, C., 267
Cecchini, O., ' Flaminia,' 241, 298, 324, 325, 327, 328
Cecchini, P. M., ' Fritellino,' 217, 224, 234, 235, 241, 248, 255, 257, 261, 265, 290, 293, 297, 323–326, 327–334
Cella, della, 238, 240, 241
Centunculus, patchwork costume of mimic actors, 91
Cerro, E. del, 216, 218, 221, 230, 264, 346, 361, 377, 378
Chambers, Sir E. K., 98, 136, 145, 151, 152, 159, 160, 161, 163, 164, 165, 166, 168, 171, 176, 178, 179, 189, 194, 195, 197, 198, 203, 204, 207, 279, 280, 301, 304, 308, 309
Charlatans, 221–224
Charlemagne, Emperor, 148–149
Charles IV of France, 165
Charles IX of France, 271
Chaucer, G., 268
Chauny, 194, 206
Chelmsford, 207
Cherea, F., actor, 217
Chester cycle of mystery plays, 178, 181, 182, 184, 185, 186, 187, 189, 195, 203, 204, 207
Chiabrera, G., 238
Chiappelli, A., 216
Chiavarelli, A., ' Scapino,' 343
Chiesa, G., ' Dottore,' 260, 336
Chieti, 341
Chionides, author of comedies, 20, 38
Chiusette used in *commedia dell' arte*, 218–219, 234
Choricius, 99, 107, 113, 120, 123, 124, 126, 142
Christ, 212–213, 214
Christ, K., 200
Christ, W., 27, 45

Christianity and the mimic drama, 17–21, 25, 85, 120–123, 131, 135–150
Christ's Suffering, 147, 210
Chrysostom, Dio, 126, 138
Chrysostom, Johannes, 87, 88, 92, 93, 99, 108, 121, 123, 127, 138, 139, 140, 221
Ciampi, I., 179
Cian, V., 151, 311, 360
Cibrario, G., 157
Ciccombimbo, stock type in *commedia dell' arte*, 260, 261
Cicero, 36, 66, 77, 81, 83, 87, 89, 94, 95, 96, 97, 99, 106, 110 115, 125, 126, 127, 128, 129
Cicirrus, stock type in Atellan farce, 74–75, 292
Cimadori, G. A., ' Finocchio,' 338, 340
Cinthio, Giraldi, 347
Cionini, A. N., 216, 340
Circus clown, 87
Citrullo, stock type in *commedia dell' arte*, 333
Clark, R. T., 41
Claudia Hermione, *archimima*, 87
Claudian, 85, 93
Claudius, Emperor, 75, 105, 110
Clemens Romanus, 137
Cleopatra, juggler, 35
Clerc, Victor le, 174
Cloetta, W., 169, 177
Clouds, The, 31, 39, 44
Cloveshow, Council of, 146
Cocceius, 74
Cocchi, G., 216
Cocco, E., 264, 299
Cock type, in mimic drama, 32 ; in the Phlyax, 62, 63 ; in Atellan farce, 74 ; in medieval drama, 161, 163 ; in *commedia dell' arte*, 292
Coffman, G. R., 176, 178
Cohen, G., 169, 170, 172, 176, 178, 181, 185, 187, 189, 190, 192, 194, 195, 197, 203, 204, 205, 206, 207, 268
Cokayne, Sir Aston, 347
Cola, stock type in *commedia dell' arte*, 260, 261
Coletti, M. A., 300
Collalto, ' Pantalone,' 343
Collier, Jeremy, 123
Collier, J. P., 300
Collignon, M., and Couve, L., 23
Cologne, 70
Colombina, 290
Colombina, stock type in *commedia dell' arte*, 242–244
Colosseum used for performances of mystery plays, 200
Comedia Bile, 170
Comédie Française, 245
Comestor, Petrus, 189
Comic elements in mystery plays, 179–183
Comito, mimic actress, 97
Commedia dell' arte, 19, 27, 43, 79, 106, 128, 163, 166, 175, 214–349
Commedia in commedia, La, 229, 230
Commodus, Emperor, 94, 125, 129
Compitalia, 112
Concertatore in *commedia dell' arte*, 226–227, 230
Concilium Trullanum, 145
Confidenti, troupe of Italian actors, 235, 236, 241, 285, 295, 307, 309, 310, 311, 312, 315–321, 323, 331, 332
Confrérie de la Passion, the, 306
Conjurers in Greece, 35
Connards, the, 164
Constantine II, Emperor, 139
Constantinople, actors in, 95, 108, 138, 142, 159–160 ; Museum, 61
Constantinus Porphyrogennetos, 148

INDEX

Contrafazeus, entertainers in Spain, 158
Conversione della Maddalena, 186
Convitato di pietra, Il, 261, 296
Cook, A. B., 31
Coppa, C., ' Aurelia,' 340, 341
Coppa, G., ' Virginio,' 340, 341
Coranus, C. Manneius, mimic actor, 95
Corbelli, C., 307
Corbellini, A., 238
Corinthian vases, theatrical scenes on, 20–22, 23, 24, 25
Corinthus, mimic actor, 95, 119
Coris, B., ' Silvio,' 337
Cornaro, Catarina, 215
Cornelius Agrippa, 162
Corneto, 33, 88
Cornish interlude, 173; mystery plays, 179, 180, 189, 196, 200, 204, 206, 207, 209
Cortese, A., 98
Cortese, G., 215
Cortese, O., ' Eularia,' 242, 343, 344
Costantini, A., ' Mezzetino,' 286, 289, 344, 345, 346
Costantini, C., ' Gradelino,' 338, 340, 341
Costantini, D., ' Corallina,' 338, 339, 340
Costantini, G. B., ' Ottavio,' ' Cintio,' 236, 281, 339, 340, 345, 346
Costantini, T., ' Diana,' 338, 339, 340
Costume, of early comic figures, 21–24; of actors in Phlyax, 62–63; of actors in the mime, 88–89, 90–91, 148; of medieval fools, 160–161; of medieval devils, 189–190
Cotarelo y Mori, E., 304, 305, 316, 370
Cotolendi, C., 260, 271
Cotronei, B., 173
Cotta, P., ' Celio,' 236
Court fools in classic times, 108–109
Courtesans introduced into *commedia dell' arte*, 245
Cousin, J., 240
Coventry cycle of mystery plays, 178, 180, 181, 182, 184, 185, 186, 187, 189, 190, 192, 193, 195, 203, 204, 205, 206, 207
Coviello, stock type in *commedia dell' arte*, 256, 261–262
Craig, E. G., 216
Craig, H., 176
Crassitius, writer of mimes, 110
Crawford, J. P. W., 158, 173
Creizenach, W., 136, 157, 165, 167, 172, 173, 174, 175, 178, 184, 187
Cremona, 315, 322, 341
Crete, 70
Cretensis, 112
Crimea, the, 23
Croce, B., 215, 216, 223, 230, 251, 261, 262, 263, 264, 269, 291, 292, 293, 295, 298, 315, 325, 326, 348, 378
Croce, G. C., 250
Crocioni, G., 216
Crovato, G. B., 216
Crusius, O., 41, 46, 51
Cucurucu, stock type in *I Balli di Sfessania* (Callot), 292
Cunningham, P., 265
Cyclops, 39
Cymbeline, 227
Cyprian, St, 122, 123, 137, 138
Cyprus, 215
Cytheris, mimic actress, 96–97

DALMEYDA, G., 41
Dame Siriz, 171
Damon and Pithias, 263
Dance, association of, with the mimic drama, 32–33
Dancers, The, 40

D'Ancona, A., 136, 145, 171, 178, 186, 192, 200, 216, 223, 234, 235, 241, 256, 257, 297, 300, 302, 303, 305, 306, 307, 309, 310, 311, 312, 313, 315, 316, 317, 322, 323, 331
Dante Alighieri, 177
Dati, C., 264
Datus, writer or actor of Atellan farces, 68, 69, 75, 76
Day, J., 279, 280
De mercatore, 169
De Pernet qui va au vin, 174
Death of Christ, The, 147
Debate type of drama, 41, 69
Decius Mundus, 113
Decourcelle, Mme Pierre, 273, 274, 288, 294
Deikeliftai, mimic entertainers, 25, 26, 43, 50
Deikterias, name given to mimes, 50
Deimling, H., 178
Deinolochus, writer of mimes, 45
Deipnosophiftai, 25
Delbrueck, R., 143
Delos, 35
Demetrius, 45
Demosthenes, 37
Deschamps, E., 173
Desiosi, troupe of Italian actors, 241, 312, 322
Deucalion and Pyrrha, 113
Deukalion, 40
Deux bourdeurs ribauds, Les, 172
Devils in mystery plays, 187–192
Dialogo entrel Amor y un Viejo, 173
Dialogue of Wit and Folly, 175
Diamantina, stock type in *commedia dell' arte*, 244
Diels, H., 41, 46
Dierks, H., 23
Dieterich, A., 23, 34, 40, 65, 66, 68, 69, 72, 73, 74, 76, 88, 89, 246, 263, 292
Digby plays, 178, 180, 189, 195, 203, 206
Dijon, 160
Dindorf, L., 130
Dinges, G., 178
Dio Cassius, 57
Diocletian, Emperor, 17
Diodorus, 35, 36, 89
Diogenes, 38, 129
Diogenes, mimic actor, 95
Diomedes, 66, 67, 69, 72, 81, 84, 106, 131
Dionysia, mimic actress, 97, 99
Dionysius, mimic actor, 95
Dionysius, tyrant of Syracuse, 45
Dionysus, 21, 23, 34, 39, 56, 57, 67, 68, 145
Diopeithes, entertainer, 35
Dioxorus, Bishop of Alexandria, 137
Disgrazie di Colafronio, Le, 228
Disgrazie e fortune di Pandolfo, Le, 229, 233
Disguise tricks in *commedia dell' arte*, 229
Dits de l'herberie et la goute en l'aine, Les, 172
Dittenberger, W., 45
Diversi linguaggi, Li, 264
Divorce forcé, Le, 281
Doctor, comic figure of, in Greek mime, 26, 27, 43, 114; in medieval drama, 186–187, 257; in the Karagöz shadow-play, 214; in the *commedia dell' arte*, 257
Doctus, *archimimus*, 86
Dog acting in mime, 120
Domitian, Emperor, 95, 111, 122, 129, 133, 134
Domitius, 98
Donato, G., 310, 311, 316
Donatus, 84, 99, 106, 123

Donaueschingen mystery play, 195, 198
Dorian drama, 20–37, 60
Dossennus, stock type in Atellan farce—*see* Manducus, stock type in Atellan farce
Dotalis, 68
Dottor Bacchettone, Il, 277
Dottore, stock type in *commedia dell' arte*, 114, 187, 253, 255, 256–260
Douhet, J. de, 136, 140, 142, 146
Doutrepont, G., 194
Dream, The, 42, 43
Driesen, O., 187, 188, 263, 268–269, 274, 278
Duchartre, P. L., 71, 107, 135, 216, 239, 243, 244, 246, 247, 253, 254, 259, 260, 261, 262, 264, 266, 267, 271, 272, 285, 286, 287, 290, 291, 294, 295, 297, 301, 305
Duchesne, L., 137
Due Flaminie, Le, 233
Due Mezzettini, I, 317
Due Schiavi rivenduti, Li, 229, 233
Due Sorelle rivale, Le, 261, 277
Duetti in *commedia dell' arte*, 219
Dufresny, J., 346
Dugdale, W., 203
Dugga, 104
Duo Amanti furiosi, Li, 261
Duo Dossenni, 70
Duoi Fratelli, I, 233
Duoi Scolari, Li, 265
Dupire, N., 178
Duriez, G., 178
Dürre, K., 176, 186
Dyalogue du fol et du sage, 175

Earth and Sea, 39, 41
Ecphantides, 27
Edmonds, J. M., 41
Edward III, accounts of, 190
Edwardes, R., 263
Egypt, mimes in, 17–18
Elegiac comedies, 169–170
Eliot, J., 250, 309
Elvira, Council of, 136
Endepols, J., 195
Enfants-sans-Souci, 160, 164
Engelhardt, O., 153
Ephebus, 112
Epicharmus, 20, 25, 27, 37, 38–41, 42, 43, 44, 45, 58, 61, 67, 70, 76, 77, 113
Epinikios, 39
Epiphanius, 95, 113
Ergastilus, 68
Eriau, J. B., 136, 137, 139
Ermini, F., 170
" Erotic Fragment," the, 45–46
Eski-Zaghra, 45
Este, Beatrice d', 165
Este, Lucrezia d', 302
Ethelontai, 26, 27
Ethelwold, St, 176, 177
Étienne de Bourbon, 164
Étienne, St, 144
Euanthius, 81, 124
Eucharis, mimic actress, 97
Eudicus, clown, 36
Eunous, Dionysiac demon, 21
Eupolis, writer of comedies, 27, 31
Euripides, 68, 126
Eurykleides, mimic entertainer, 35

Eusebius, Bishop of Barcelona, 145
Eusebius, Pope, 136
Eustathius, 26, 89, 210
Eutyches, Aurelius, a mimic actor, 87
Eutyches, L. A. P., *archimimus*, 85–86
Evans, M. B., 198
Evelyn, J., 344
Exodium, in Roman theatres, 67, 99
Exodus, 210
Ezechiel, 210

Faba, P., 299
Fabbri, G. P., 'Flaminio,' 240, 310, 311, 312, 313, 326
Fabrizio, 336
Fabula Atellana—*see* Atellan farce
Fabula prætexta, 68
Fabula togata, 68
Fainelli, V., 29
Falconi, B., ' Trappolino,' 297, 335
Falconi, C., 216, 346
Falena, V., 361
Fantesca, stock type in the *commedia dell' arte*, 242–244, 271
Faral, E., 151, 166, 167, 169, 170, 171, 175
Farce de Tripet, 172
Farce nouuelle moralisee des gens nouueaulx qui mengent le monde et le logent de male en pire, 173
Farces, medieval, 171–175
Fargnoccola, stock type in *commedia dell' arte*, 322
Farinelli, A., 305
Farino, G. C., 298
Farnell, L. R., 25
Farsa satyra morale, 246
Farsa de Zoan zavatino, 173
Fatouville, N. de, 345, 346
Favor, *archimimus*, 86
Feast of the Boy Bishop, the, 19
Feast of Fools, the, 19, 163, 173
Fedele, L., 259, 311
Fedeli, troupe of Italian actors, 235, 241, 251, 252, 256, 259, 295, 325, 327–335
Fensterbusch, C., 196
Fermo, 341
Ferrara, actors in, 263, 301, 304, 305, 306, 307, 309, 310, 312, 315, 317, 322, 323, 333
Ferrari, S., 285
Ferrariis, J. A. de, 298
Ferretti E., 216, 346
Ferrigni, P. C., 263
Festus, 29, 34, 83, 99, 106
Feuillerat, A., 304
Fiala, G. A., ' Capitan Sbranaleoni,' 252, 336, 337, 338, 339, 340, 341
Fiala, M., ' Lucinda,' 336, 338, 339, 340, 341
Fiamella, La, 316
Ficoroni, F., 19, 48, 49, 62, 63, 69, 70, 72, 73, 77, 82, 109, 128, 133, 134, 161
Fida in fedeltà, La, 233
Fidenzi, J. A., ' Cinthio,' 333, 335, 336
Filles errantes, Les, 260
Finta notte, La, 233
Finta pazza, La, 343
Finto cieco, Il, 257, 261
Finto negromante, Il, 243
Fiorilli, T., ' Scaramuccia,' 287, 288, 339, 343, 344, 346
Fiorillo, G. B., ' Trappolino ' and ' Scaramuccia,' 287, 297, 326, 336
Fiorillo, S., ' Capitan Matamoros,' 251, 290, 291, 293, 326, 330
Firmicus Maternus, 151
Fish, The, 31

INDEX

Fismes, Baron de, 216
Flamenca, 157, 167
Flautino, stock type in *commedia dell' arte*, 284
Flavius Vopiscus, 85, 130
Fleres, U., 250
Fleury, É., 206
Flickinger, R. C., 31
Flögel, K. F., 20, 72, 87, 108, 160, 269, 287
Floralia, 92, 107
Florence, actors in, 221, 252, 294, 306, 307, 310, 311, 312, 313, 317, 323, 325, 326, 330, 333, 335, 341
Florez, H., 145
Florinda, 241, 327
Folengo, Theofilo, 72
Fontainebleau, 313, 331, 332
Fools, Court, in classic times, 108–109, 160; medieval, 160–163, 173, 188
Formichi, C., 80
Formigé, J., 106
Fornariis, F. de, 'Capitan Coccodrillo,' 250, 251, 307, 309, 316
Forsennata prencipessa, La, 228, 294
Fouquet, J., 196, 197, 206
Four PP, The, 174
Fracanzani, M., 'Pulcinella,' 293, 344, 346
Frajacomi, A., 'Trivellino,' 278, 326
Francatrippa, stock type in *commedia dell' arte*, 260, 296, 297
Franceschina, stock type in *commedia dell' arte*, 243–244
Francesco, 'Moschino,' 299
Francesco de la lira, 299
Franchini-Biancolelli, I., 'Columbina,' 336, 337
Frank, G., 178
Frati, L., 361
Fredi, C., 243
Fresco, U., 257
Freymond, 151
Fritella, Court fool, 297
Fritellino, stock type in *commedia dell' arte*, 297
Frogs, The, 31
Froning, R., 178, 198
Frons scænæ, 64, 100, 103, 105
Fronto, M. C., 67, 76, 77, 111, 124, 126
Frosia, 299
Frothingham, A. L., 196
Führ, J. A., 20
Fulgens, Bishop, 142
Fullo, 112
Fullones, 69
Furnivall, F. J., 178
Furtwängler, A., 26, 50

Gabbrielli, F., 'Scapino,' 285, 298, 317–320, 325, 331, 332, 333
Gabbrielli, G., 'Pantalone,' 341
Gabbrielli, G., 'Diana,' 342, 343
Gabiati, M. A., 299, 300
Gabotto, F., 151
Gabrici, E., 55
Gabriele da Bologna, 'Zanni,' 307
Gabrielli, 'Spinetta,' 333
Gabrielli-Locatelli, G., 'Lucillia,' 343
Galba, 76, 84
Galiti, N., 312
Galli, 112
Galli transalpini, 68
Gallico, G., 346
Gallienus, Emperor, 138
Gallotta, stock type in *commedia dell' arte*, 331
Gambi, S., 'Silvio,' 312

Ganassa, A., 'Zanni,' 268, 269, 270, 271, 278, 295, 300, 301–306
Gandini, A., 216, 338
Gandolin, stock comic type, 342
Garavini, G., 'Capitan Rinoceronte,' 252, 324, 328, 330, 331, 332, 333
Garavini, M., 'Flavia,' 324, 333
Garber, J., 161
Garçon et l'aveugle, Le, 172
Gardellini, G., 'Argentina,' 340, 341
Gardthausen, V., 138
Gargàno, G. S., 347
Garzoni, T., 224, 237, 240, 265, 297, 303, 315
Gaspary, A., 263
Gaultier Garguille, French comic type, 249
Geiserich, King of the Vandals, 86, 141
Gelasinus, mimic actor, 95, 121, 130
Gellius, 84, 111, 112, 127
Gelo, tyrant of Syracuse, 20, 38, 45
Gelosi, troupe of Italian actors, 234, 235, 236, 237, 241, 244, 256, 259, 278, 295, 302–314, 315, 316, 317
Gelotopoios, comic character, 36
Gemelli, 112
Genesius, mimic actor, 87, 95, 121
Genoa, actors in, 256, 300, 303, 305, 307, 310, 312, 313, 316, 322, 326, 338
Geoffrey of Monmouth, 161
Georgios Monachos, 113
Georgius, H., 123
Gercke, A., 90
Geta, 169, 170
Gherardi, E., 'Arlecchino,' 218, 281, 345, 346
Gherardi, G., 'Flautino,' 284, 344
Ghinzoni, P., 216
Gian Farina, stock type in *commedia dell' arte*, 243
Giangurgolo, stock type in *commedia dell' arte*, 252, 295
Giannini, G., 216
Giaratone, G., 'Pierot,' 294, 344, 346
Giarattoni, 'Dottore,' 336
Giorgi, F., 151
Giovanni, 'Taberino,' 301
Girardot, Baron de, 178
Giuoco della primiera, Il, 347
Globe Theatre, 222
Glock, A., 157, 175
Goats, The, 31
Goes, H. van der, 189
Goldoni, C., 223, 346, 350
Goliardi, 166
Gollancz, Sir I., 185, 206, 212–213
Gonzaga, Cardinal, 328, 329
Gonzaga, Francesco, Duke of Mantua, 329
Gonzaga, Vincenzo I, Duke of Mantua, 306, 329
Gordian the Elder, Emperor, 130
Gori, A. F., 95
Goscius, J., 254
Gospel of the Twelve Apostles, 184
Gossips, The, 42–43
Graf, A., 234
Granges, C. M. des, 171
Graux, C., 142
Gray, H. D., 347
Graziani, F., 66, 69, 72
Graziani, G., 241
Graziano—*see* Dottore, stock type in *commedia dell' arte*
Greban, A., 178
Greek romance, 115
Gregory of Nazianzus, 87, 88, 121, 140, 141

Grenfell, B. P., 46, 115, 116
Grillo, E., 346
Grimm, J., 166
Grisanti, A., ' Mario,' 336, 337
Gros Guillaume, French comic type, 249
Grysar, K. J., 20, 35, 36, 67, 83, 85, 87, 91–92, 94, 95, 96, 98, 110, 111, 112, 113, 115, 122, 124, 125, 127, 128, 131, 132, 133
Guadalajara, 305
Guappo, stock type in *commedia dell' arte*, 252
Guarnera, G. C., Italian actor, 300
Gueullette, G., 221, 343
Guicciardi, G., 238
Guillaume de Blois, 170
Guillemot, G., 216

Haase, F., 87
Hadrian, Emperor, 77, 98
Hag type, in Greek mime, 28; in the Phlyax, 55; in the mime, 93
Hagen, H., 170
Halm, P. M., 161
Hanswurst, comic type in German farce, 40, 264
Harlay, Hachille du, 267
Harlequin—*see* Arlecchino, stock type in *commedia dell' arte*
Harpagai, 39
Hartmann, A., 178
Hartmann, J. J., 66
Hartwig, P., 50
Hauler, E., 126
Haupt, M., 169
Hauvette-Besnault, 35
Havet, L., 169
Hawthorne, Nathaniel, 124
He Who Gets Slapped, 88
Headlam, W., 41
Hecyra, 46
Hefele, C. J., 136, 137
Heinzel, R. L., 187, 192, 194, 195
Helbig, W., 88
Helinopolis, 95
Heliogabalus, Emperor, 123, 130, 134
Hell, mansion of, 205–207
Hellequin, 173, 188, 268–269
Helvidius Priscus, writer of mimes, 110, 111, 122
Henri III of France, 151, 305, 306
Henri IV of France, 278, 323, 324
Henri, Bishop of Nantes, 165
Henri, Duc de Guise, 271
Henry VI of England, 194
Henry VIII of England, 300
Hense, O., 41
Hephæstus, as a comic figure, 22, 39, 56
Hera, 22
Herakleides, mimic actor, 95, 96
Herakleitus of Mitylene, entertainer, 35
Herakles (Hercules), comic figure in Greek mime, 27, 30, 39; in the Phlyax, 51–53, 65, 75, 78; in the mime, 113; in the Karagöz shadow-play, 214; possible connexion with Arlecchino, 269
Herakles before Pholos, 39, 40, 58
Herakles upon the Girdle, 39
Hercules coactor, 69
Hercules furens, 157, 208
Hérelle, G., 178
Hermann, M., 152, 191, 192, 208
Hermes, E., 120, 124
Hero of Alexandria, 37
Herod, comic treatment of, 185

Herodas, writer of mimes, 39, 41–44, 45, 46, 67, 76, 82, 85, 97, 118, 119, 127, 135
Herodian, 80, 129
Herodotus, mimic actor, 46, 94
Héron de Villefosse, A., 104
Herrmann, M., 152, 156, 157, 161
Hertling, C., 20, 41
Hertz, R., 196
Herzog, R., 41, 46, 80
Hesiod, 114
Hestiæa, 35
Hesychius, 26, 28, 74, 89
Hetæra, 112
Heydemann, H., 50, 51, 56, 57, 58, 59, 63, 64
Heywood, J., 174
Hiero, tyrant of Syracuse, 38
Hieronymus, 68, 113
Hilarodia, 34
Hilarotragodia, 51, 63
Hilary, St, 138
Hilberg, I., 66, 76, 126, 210
Hildesheim, 47
Hiller, E., 34
Hilverding, P., ' Pantalone,' 256
Hippias, mimic actor, 95
Hirnea Pappi, 73
Hirschfeld, O., 82
Histoire anecdotique du théâtre italien, 226
Histrio, significance of, 80, 83, 136, 140, 145–146, 151–152
Hochreiter, A., 305
Hoffmann, E., 112
Holland, medieval farces in, 174
Homer, 26
Honorius d'Autun, 168
Hope, 39
Horace, 68, 71, 74, 84, 87, 96, 97, 105, 111, 129
Horovitz, J., 114, 143, 159, 214
Hörschelmann, W., 20
Horse, The, 45
Hostilius, writer of mimes, 112, 113
Hrodgarius, 153
Hrotswitha, 210
Hübner, E., 110
Hübner, H. G., 38
Hugutius, 152, 157, 208
Hümer, A., 127
Hump-back, used for comic purposes, 70, 94
Hunt, A. S., 115, 116
Hylas, pantomimic actor, 131, 133, 134
' Hypothesis,' used for mime, 46, 128

Iacobitz, C., 133
Iambistai, 26, 27
Ignatius, deacon in Constantinople, 147
Improvisation, in Greek mime, 26–27; in the Phlyax, 50–51; in Atellan farce, 75, 78; in the *commedia dell' arte*, 216–218, 225–229
Incanto, L', 228
Infelici amori della Regina d' Inghilterra, Gli, 338
Inganno fortunato, L', 242
Innamorata, stock type in *commedia dell' arte*, 236–242
Innamorato, stock type in *commedia dell' arte*, 233–236
Innocent III, Pope, 165
Innsbruck, Goldene Dachel, 161, 162, 163; Ferdinandeum, 190, 191, 193
Insects, The, 31
Interludes, medieval, 171–175
Interludium de clerico et puella, 42, 171, 175

Intermezzi in *commedia dell' arte*, 219
Intrighi d'amore, Gli, 229, 233
Intrigue episodes, in the Phlyax, 59; in the *commedia dell' arte*, 228–230. *See also* Obscenity
Intronati, troupe of Italian actors, 322
Iphigenia in Tauris, 116
Isaacs, J., 347
Isabella, stock type in *commedia dell' arte*, 214
Isidore of Seville, 81, 127, 145–146, 208
Isidorus, mimic actor, 95, 97, 129
Islands, The, 39
Isola, A., 'Lavinia,' 241–242, 336
Isola, 'Angiola,' 242, 341
Italy, medieval interludes in, 173–174
Ithuphalloi, 26, 27
Ivanoushka-Douratschok, Russian comic type, 264

Jacobsen, J. P., 95, 151, 169, 172, 268
Jacobus of Coccinobaphus, 211
Jaffei, G., 264, 269
Jahn, O., 50
James I of England, 346
James, M. R., 108
Jarro, 216, 331, 372
Jeanroy, A., 176, 178
Jenö, A., 152
Jerome, St, 113, 126, 138
Jeu de la feuillée, Le, 173, 268
Jeu du pèlerin, Le, 172
Jig in Elizabethan theatres, 219
Johan Johan, 174
Johannes, Bishop of Ephesus, 143
Johannes Anglicus, 175
Johannes de Janua, 158
Johannes Signiensis, 160
John, St, of Damascus, 92, 146, 210
John of Salisbury, 151, 167
Jones, I., 265
Jongleurs, activities of, 135, 149–156, 160–172 ; association of, with mystery plays, 192–194
Jonson, B., 346
Joro, Andrea de, 175
Joseph and Mary, comic treatment of, 182–183
Josephus Flavius, 94, 111, 113, 122
Jubinal, M. L. A., 162, 178, 181, 185, 187
Jugglers and the ancient mime, 35–37, 81, 84–85, 109–110
Julia Bassilla, mimic actress, 96, 98, 107, 223
Julian, Emperor, 130
Julianus, Bishop of Eclanum, 141
Julius Cæsar, 112, 127, 129
Julius Capitolinus, 83, 94, 113, 125, 129, 130
Julius Victor, 76, 94
Julleville, Petit de, 158, 160, 161, 164, 172, 173, 192
Justinian, Emperor, 92, 98, 143, 146
Justinus, Emperor, 92
Juvenal, 67, 70, 87, 91, 95, 97, 98, 99, 106, 107, 110, 119, 133

Kabeiroi vases, 23–24, 27
Kaibel, G., 25, 39, 41, 45, 51
Kalendæ, 164
Kallipides, tragic actor, 26
Kapp, J., 92, 123
Karagöz, Turkish shadow-play, 214–215
Keil, H., 83, 106, 131
Kemp, W., English actor, 279, 280
Kenyon, Sir Frederick, 41
Kepheus, 45

Kephisodorus, clown, 36
Kiev, 159
Kinaidos, name applied to mimes, 50
King and No King, A, 227
Kingfishers, The, 45
Kingston, 207
Kinyras and Myrrha, 122
Kissos, 26
Klapper, J., 176
Klein, J. L., 20, 270
Kleon, actor of Phlyakes, 50
Klingler, O., 346
Knights, The, 72
Knox, A. D., 41
Kock, T., 27
Köppen, A., 189
Köppen, W., 178
Kordax, Greek dance, 33
Körte, A., 20, 23, 41, 46, 80
Kos, 38, 42, 44
Kratinus, 89
Kratisthenes, 35
Krausius, J. C. K., 77
Kretzmann, P. E., 176
Krumbacher, L., 210
Kugel, A., 346
Kuntze, F., 189
Künzelsauer Fronleichnamspiel, 187
Kutscher, A., 256
Kybisteter, acrobatic dancer, 35

La Cruz, 305
Labbé, P., 136
Laberius, writer of mimes, 80, 110, 111-112, 115, 123, 124, 126, 127, 129
Lacedæmon, comedy in, 25, 27
Lacroix, P., 369
Lactantius, 92, 123, 139
Lacus Avernus, 112
Lampertico, F., 257
Lampridius, 94
Lancret, N., 273
Landsberg, Herrad von, 167
Langland, W., 268
Langlois, E., 172, 173
Lanza, D., 216, 263
Lar familiaris, 68
Lasca, il, 263
Late loquentes, 112
Latinus, mimic actor, 89, 95, 107, 119
Lattes, E., 66
Laureolus, 110-111, 112, 115, 118, 120
Lautier, R., 106
Lavedan, H., 266
Lawrence, W. J., 347
Lawton, H. W., 153
Lazaro, G., 322
Lazzi in *commedia dell' arte*, 76, 219–221, 347
Lea, K. M., 347, 377, 378, 379, 389
'Leading Slave,' the, 29
Leda and the Swan, 122, 133
Leendertz, P., 203
Leibing, 199
Leidradus, 147
Leningrad, 23 ; Hermitage, 23, 52, 53, 60, 62
Lenoir de la Thorillière, P., French actor, 245
Lentini, 52

Lentulus, mimic actor, 110
Lentulus, writer of mimes, 110, 112–113, 141
Leo, F., 46
Leoncavallo, R., 295
Leontius, Bishop, 146
Leroux de Lincy, A. J. V., 173
Levi, C., 218, 283
Liber Pamphili, 161, 170
Liberati, U., 'Bernetta,' 331, 332
Liebermann, F., 148
Lincoln, Earl of, 303
Lincy, Leroux de, 190
Lindsay, J., 44, 250
Lindsay, W. M., 83, 87
Linos, 53
Lintilhac, E., 346
Linz, 300, 301
Liturgical drama, 175–177
Liudprand, Bishop of Cremona, 148, 160, 211
Livorno, 336, 341
Livy, 66, 67, 77
Locatelli, D., 'Trivellino,' 278, 337, 343
Locatelli, G. Gabrielli-, 'Lucilla,' 343
Lodi, 341
Loeschcke, G., 20
Lohmeyer, C., 170
Lolli, E., 'Fichetto,' 337
Lolli, G. A., 'Dottore,' 336, 339, 340
Lolli, G. B. A., 'Dottore,' 260, 343, 344
Lombardi, B. de', 'Dottor Graziano,' 316
London, British Museum, 30, 33, 35, 45, 48, 49, 51, 54, 57, 58, 60, 64, 66, 74; Victoria and Albert Museum, 144, 245, 256, 273, 274, 276, 277, 284, 295; Italian actors in, 256, 279, 300, 304, 309, 339, 344
Longhi, P., 255, 259
Loo, P. van, 287
Lorenz, T., 38
Lorin, J., 268, 291
Lot, F., 269
Louis XIII of France, 331, 332
Love's Labour's Lost, 263
Lucca, 310, 341
Lucchese, A., 'Ricciolina,' 243, 324
Lucerne, 190, 195, 198, 199
Lucian, 133
Lucilius, 112, 125
Lucrezia Senese, Italian actress, 300
Lugli, G., 109
Lumini, A., 174
Luria, mimic actress, 97
Lydia, 169, 170
Lydus, Johannes, 67, 78, 84
Lyndsay, Sir David, 173
Lyon, 300, 314, 323, 332, 339
Lyonnet, H., 292
Lysiodia, 34
Lysios, 34
Lysis, 34

McKerrow, R. B., 280
Macaronic poetry, 72
Macchioro, V., 50
Macci gemini, 73
Macci priores, 73
Maccus, 68
Maccus copo, 73
Maccus exul, 72

Maccus miles, 72
Maccus sequester, 73
Maccus virgo, 73
Maccus, stock type in Atellan farce, 66, 67, 72–73, 74, 76, 90, 214
Machines, on Roman stage, 105; in mystery plays, 204–207
Macrobius, 68, 69, 111, 112, 123, 131, 133
Maddalena, E., 250, 379
Maddalena, La, 235
Madrid, 270, 304, 305
Mæcenas, 133
Mæterlinck, L., 187
Maffei, R., 66
Magnes, writer of comedies, 31, 38
Magni, M., 263, 265, 268, 277, 283, 284, 285, 294, 295
Magnin, C., 20, 36, 111, 124, 131, 136, 167, 171, 172, 216, 315
Magodia, 34
Mai, Angelo, 123
Maison, comic character, 28–29, 70, 78
Maître Patelin, 277
Maître Trubert et Antroignart, 173
Mala lingua, La, 233
Malagoli, G., 111, 112
Malalas, Johannes, 142
Malamani, V., 273
Mâle, É., 205
Malkyn, actor, 194
Malloni, M., 'Celia,' 320, 333
Manducus, stock type in Atellan farce, 70–72, 74, 76, 77, 90, 214
Mangini, A., 'Adriano,' 326
Manitius, M., 115
Mansi, J. D., 136, 140, 145
Mansions, use of, in medieval religious drama, 195–212
Mantua, 223, 256, 297, 301, 307, 309, 311, 312, 313, 315, 316, 322, 323, 325, 327, 328, 330, 331, 332, 333, 334, 335, 336, 338
Mantzius, K., 196, 197
Manzani, F., 'Capitan Terremoto,' 252
Marche, Lecoy de la, 164
Marchini-Capasso, O., 346
Marco, 299
Marco Antonio—*see* Gabiati, M. A.
Marcucci, A., 'Angiola,' 340
Marcus Aurelius, 82, 113, 125, 129
Marcus Diaconus, 114
Marenduzzo, A., 189
Marett, R. R., 165
Maria, F. de, 216
Maricas (Marikas), 28
Marino, 238, 240
Marito, Il, 228, 243, 257, 276, 294
Marius Mercator, 141
Mark Antony, 96–97, 129
Marliani, E., 321
Marlowe, C., 223
Mars and Venus, 122
Marsæus, 97
Marston, J., 309
Marsya, 68
Martène, E., 165
Martial, 88, 90, 93, 95, 97, 108, 110, 111, 113, 123, 133
Martin, H., 153
Martinelli, D., 'Arlecchino,' 241, 279, 307–309, 312, 313, 323, 346
Martinelli, T., 'Arlecchino,' 158, 271, 278–279, 312, 313, 322, 323–325, 328–330
Martucci, G., 375, 379
Marullus, writer of mimes, 110, 113, 125, 141
Marvell, A., 344

Marx, F., 66
Mascheroni, L., 267
Masculas, *archimimus*, 86, 141
Masculine and Feminine Reason, 39, 41
Masks, in Atellan farce, 75; in mime, 91; in pantomime, 131–132; in medieval plays, 153, 158, 164–165, 190–191; in *commedia dell' arte*, 233, 266
Massimiano Milanino, 307, 308, 309
Mathieu de Vendôme, 169
Matic, T., 346
Matius, writer of mimes, 110
Matreas, clown, 35
Matteo, 299
Matterazzi, F., 'Dottore,' 340
Maurice, Emperor, 146, 210
Maximilian, Emperor, 161
Maximinus the Elder, Emperor, 125
Maximus, 113
Maximus, Bishop, 121
Mayor, J. E. B., 95, 99, 110
Mazzetti, V., 361
Mazzoni, G., 375
Measure for Measure, 347
Meda, G., 312
Medici, Catherine de', 271, 308
Medici, Ferdinando de', 311
Medici, Giovanni de', 317–320, 324, 331
Medici, Marie de', 278, 279, 324, 328, 329, 330
Medico volante, Il, 228
Medicus, 68
Megara Hyblæa, 20
Megarean drama, 20–38, 50
Megarean Woman, The, 39
Meissner, J., 301, 325
Mekler, S., 41
Mélida, J. R., 106
Memphis, mimic dancer, 36
Menagio, E., 264, 267
Menander, 50, 60, 113, 114, 126, 170
Merida, 106
Méril, E. du, 20, 151, 169, 172
Merlini, D., 264
Messala, L., 129
Messalina, 95
Metamorfosi di Pulcinella, Le, 229, 261, 266
Metodius of Byzantium, 210
Meyer, P., 167
Meyer, W., 115, 206
Mezzetino, stock type in *commedia dell' arte*, 243, 282, 285–287
Mic, C., 89, 215, 216, 219, 233, 253, 260, 264, 266, 267, 268, 293
Michaut, G., 66
Michel, F., 173
Michel, J., 178
Michele, A., 300
Middle Comedy, the, 53
Mierlo, J. van, 176
Migne, J. P., 87, 91, 92, 106, 110, 113, 121, 122, 123, 126, 127, 130, 133, 136, 138, 139, 140, 141, 146, 151, 165, 167, 168, 189, 210
Milan, actors in, 158, 303, 305, 306, 307, 309, 310, 311, 312, 313, 315, 316, 318, 322, 325, 326, 327, 330, 331, 335
Milanta, G., 'Dottore,' 336
Miles gloriosus, 169, 170, 246
Mill, J., 152
Millita, A. M., 'Cintia,' 339
Milne, H. J. M., 46
Milo, 149
Milo, 169, 170

Milton, J., 235
'Mime,' the word and its cognates, 36, 80–82, 83–84, 145–146
Mimiambos, 127
Mimin, apparently name of a stock type, 158
Mimmus, entertainer, 149, 158
Mimodos, 34
Mimus calvus, 47. *See also under* Bald-headed mimic clown
Minucius Felix, 123, 126
Miracle plays, 178–179
Miracle de Sainte Geneviève, 172
Miracles de Notre-Dame, 179
Mirandola, Principe della, 241, 322, 331
Miro, King of Galicia, 160
Mirtilla, 237
Modena, 226, 256, 317, 321, 323, 333, 336, 338, 339, 340, 341
Moland, L., 216, 346
Molière, 245, 289, 343, 346
Molineri, G. C., 361
Molmenti, P., 158, 216
Molpeinos, 42
Moltzer, H. E., 174
Momar, 28
Momarie, entertainments in Italy, 158
Mome Helwis, 28, 42
Momigliano, A., 278
Momigliano, F., 210
Mommsen, T., 67
Momos, entertainers in Spain, 158
Mone, F. J., 178
Monile, Il, 233
Mons, mystery play at, 178, 181, 185, 187, 189, 192, 194, 205, 206, 207
Montaiglon, A. de, 169
Montaiglon, J., 157
Montaigne, F., 322
Monteni, H., 'Cortelazzo,' 326
Months, The, 39
Monti, G. M., 379
Morality plays, 173
Morey, C. R., 153
Moriones, 108–109
Mormo, 28
Moros, generic name of mimic fool, 28, 47–48, 87, 88, 114
Morpurgo, S., 263
Mortensen, J., 178
Mortier, A., 299, 364
Mortis et vitæ iudicium, 69
Morychos, 28
Moschetta, stock type in *commedia dell' arte*, 333
Mozzana, F., 'Truffaldino,' 277
Müllenbach, E., 169
Müller, H. F., 176
Müller, L., 91
Mumming, 158–159, 164
Mummius, writer of Atellan farces, 68, 69
Munich, 48
Munk, E., 66
Murmurcones, 115
Murray, J. T., 304
Murtilos, writer of comedies, 27
Musæ, 39
Music, and the mime, 34, 127; and Atellan farce, 75
Muzio, A. A., 'Dottore,' 340
Myrina, 43
Myrtion, mimic actress, 49
Mystère des Actes des Apôtres, 172
Mystère d'Adam, Le, 179, 198, 195, 205, 209

Mystère de la Résurrection, 172
Mystère de Saint Laurent, 172
Mystère du Viel Testament, 178, 180, 184, 185, 186, 205, 206, 207
Mystery cycles, 177, 178

NABER, S. A., 124, 126
Nadasti, L., 340
Nævius, 111
Nairn, J. A., 41, 44, 45
Naples, 57, 293, 298, 325, 326, 333, 336, 338, 339; Museo Nazionale, 29, 30, 63, 104
Napolioni, M., ' Flaminio,' 336–337
Narici, B., ' Orazio,' 236, 338, 339, 340, 341
Natal, 112
Nauck, A., 115
Nave, La, 228
Necyomantia, 112
Negri, D. de', ' Curzio,' 326
Neikias, writer of mimes, 45
Neilos, 140
Nelli, E., ' Dottore,' 337, 338, 339
Nérac, 308
Neri, A., 216, 250, 303, 312, 317, 318, 362
Neri, F., 190, 347, 377, 378
Nero, Emperor, 75, 76, 94, 95, 99, 110, 129, 132, 133, 134
Nero Imperadore, 227, 296
Nerucci, G., 269
Nettuni, L., ' Fichetto,' 317, 331, 332
Nevers, Duc de, 323
New Comedy, the, 25, 28, 81
New York, Metropolitan Museum of Art, 48
Nicæa, Synod of, 146
Nicephorus, Prefect, 148
Nicholas, St, cult of, 176
Nichols, J., 303
Nick, F., 151
Nicolaus, 69
Nicolina, stock type in *commedia dell' arte*, 330
Nicomachean Ethics, 20, 27
Night scenes in *commedia dell' arte*, 230
Nikotychos, 141
Noah, comic treatment of, 185
Nobili, C. de', 322
Nobili, C. R., ' Delia,' 317
Nobili, O., ' Orazio,' 303, 307
Noemon, an ' ethologue,' 36
Nola, 59
Nöldechen, E., 80
Nolhac, P. de, 305
Non può essere, 228
Nonius Marcellus, 87, 88, 91
Nonnus, Bishop of Antioch, 97
Norris, E., 180, 195, 201
Norton, T., 304
Norwich, 189, 203
Nottingham, 304
Novati, F., 178
Novius, writer of Atellan farce, 68, 69, 70, 73, 89
Nucula, writer of mimes, 110
Nuptiæ, 68
Nymphodorus, entertainer, 35, 50

OBSCENITY, accusation of, in Atellan farce, 76 ; in mime, 92–93, 107, 123–124 ; in *commedia dell' arte*, 221–222
Odoardo, D', ' Lucindo,' 336
Odysseus, comic hero in Greek mime, 40, 41; in the Phlyax, 51, 54, 88; in Atellan farce, 68

Odysseus on his Own, 39
Odysseus Shipwrecked, 40
Œdipus, character in Greek mime, 40
Old Comedy in Athens, 22, 23, 24, 25, 43, 78
Olivastro, L', 235
Omrikos, name given to Dionysus, 21, 23
Onorata fuga di Lucinda, L', 228, 233
Onorati, O., ' Mezzetino,' 286, 317–320, 325, 331, 33
Ophelandros, Dionysiac demon, 21, 23
Orange, 106
Orcus, 35
Orelli, I. C., 87, 95, 131, 132
Origen, 113
Origo, mimic actress, 97, 129
Orlandi, A., 365
Orlandi, G., ' Dottore,' 260, 338, 339
Orsatti, D., 336
Orsi, d', ' Spinetta,' 346
Orsi, T. d', 336
Orsi, V. d', 336
Orsino, C., 300
Ortiz, M., 361
Ortolani, G., 218
Ortygia, 61
Orvieto, 341
Osterley, H., 158
Ottaviano, ' Tartaglia,' 296
Ottonelli, D., 221, 252, 304
Ovid, 80, 107, 123
Owen, A. S., 72
Oxford, Bodleian Library, 161, 165, 166
Oxyrhynchus mimes, 85, 90, 109, 115–119, 124, 227

PACICHELLI, G. B., 293
Paderna, G., ' Dottore,' 260
Padre crudele, Il, 229, 266
Padua, 299, 313, 315, 325, 332, 335, 337, 340, 341
Pæstum, 50, 63
Pagani, G., 315
Pageants used for mystery plays, 203–204
Paghetti, G. B., ' Dottore,' 260, 340
Pagliaccio, stock type in *comédie italienne*, 77, 294, 295
Paglicci-Brozzi, A., 378
Paignion, 128
Pailler, W., 178
Paix aux Anglais, La, 171
Palæologus, Manuel, 160
Palaprat, J., 346
Palma, C., ' Truffaldino,' 277, 335
Pandar, The, 42
Pannini, D., ' Florindo,' 236, 338
Pantaleon, Greek clown, 36, 253
Pantalone, stock type in *commedia dell' arte*, 214, 232, 233, 253–256, 326
Pantomime, 131–134
Panzanini, G., ' Francatrippa,' 297, 310, 312
Paolo, G., ' Trappolino,' 297
Papias, 208
Pappus, stock type in Atellan farce, 73–74, 76, 214
Pappus agricola, 73
Pappus præteritus, 73
Paradise, mansion of, 204–205
Pardi, A., 250
Pardonneur, d'un triacleur, et d'un tavernier, D'un, 174
Paris, Louvre, 21, 23, 33, 43, 71; Bibliothèque Nationale, 33, 36, 88, 143, 153, 155, 156, 225, 232, 235, 237, 248, 249, 252, 260, 274, 279, 282, 284, 286, 288, 289, 302, 304, 314, 321, 327, 334, 342, 349;

Arsenal, 153, 154, 156, 157; Carnavalet Museum, 239; Italian actors in, 236, 252, 256, 259, 260, 297, 299, 300, 301, 303, 306, 309, 313-314, 315, 316, 323, 324, 331, 332, 334, 338, 341, 342-345; Musée du Grand Opéra, 266; Musée Cluny, 273; Comédie Française, 287; Bibliothèque Sainte Geneviève, 316

Paris, mimic actor, 94

Paris, pantomimic actor, 133, 134

Paris, G., 178, 269

Paris, L., 205

Paris, M., 179

Paris and Œnone, 111, 122

Parma, actors in, 312, 335-340

Paruti, G. B., ' Finocchio,' 340

Paruti, M. F., ' Prinpinella,' 340

Pascu, G., 188

Pasquariello, stock type in *commedia dell' arte*, 260, 289

Pasquati, G., ' Pantalone,' 256, 300, 301, 303, 305, 307, 310

Pasqui, 75

Pastor, C. P., 305, 370

Pastor Fido, Il, 325

Pastoral themes in *commedia dell' arte*, 228

Patroni, G., 50

Patrono, C. M., 111

Paul de Padoue, 308

Paulinus of Nola, 95

Pavia, 313, 315, 334

Pavoli, M., ' Margarita,' 309

Paz y Mélia, A., 183

Pazzia di Flaminia, La, 326

Pazzia di Lavinia, La, 242, 318

Peaked cap worn by clowns—see *Pilos*

Pederit, C. W., 178

Pedrolino, stock type in *commedia dell' arte*, 294-295

Pelagia, mimic actress, 97, 107

Pellesini, G., ' Pedrolino,' 294, 310-313, 315-316, 330

Pellicer, C., 173, 270, 304

Peloponnesus, 25, 50

Peretz, V. N., 389

Periallos, 40

Perillo, G., 300

Perran, 200, 202, 206

Perrucci, A., 216, 217, 219, 220, 224, 226, 230, 233, 234, 236, 247, 248, 255, 257, 258, 260, 261, 265, 266, 293, 295

Perseus, 45

Persians, The, 40

Perugia, 219, 338, 341

Peter of Blois, 165

Peter, T. C., 201

Peterson, E., 188

Petignoni, R., ' Fortunio,' 234, 305

Petraccone, E., 216, 217, 218, 219, 220, 221, 224, 225, 226, 230, 233, 234, 235, 236, 237, 240, 241, 247, 248, 254, 255, 256, 258, 260, 261, 263, 265, 290, 295, 297, 303

Petrai, G., 216, 253

Petrarca, 234, 237, 257

Petronius, 84, 106, 115, 127, 131

Phædrus, mimic actor, 95

Phallophoroi, 26, 27

Phallus as a comic symbol, in Greece, 21, 23, 24, 26, 38, 41, 48, 49, 76; in Rome, 91, 121, 141-142; in medieval times, 150, 163; in the Karagöz shadow-play, 214

Phasma, 110

Pherecrates, writer of comedies, 39

Philadelpheus, A., 20

Philargyrus, 192

Philemon, mimic actor, 17-18, 76, 95, 98

Philip August II of France, 165

Philippson, K., 210

Philistides of Syracuse, entertainer, 35

Philistion, writer of mimes, 90, 110, 113-115, 141

Philo, 90

Philogelos, 114

Philoktetas, 40

Philosophia, 71

Phlyakes, the, 20, 24, 25, 26, 27, 29, 39, 43, 50-65, 66, 67, 68, 69, 70, 74, 75, 76, 77, 88

Phœbus, mimic actor, 95

Phœnissæ, 69, 77

Phormus, writer of mimes, 45

Photius, 148

Piacenza, 335

Piana, G. la, 176, 210, 211

Picard, C., 50

Picco, F., 258

Pichler, A., 178, 202

Pichon, R., 66, 75

Pickard-Cambridge, A. W., 20, 23, 26, 27, 28, 38, 45, 51

Picot, É., 171, 173, 216, 274, 303, 306, 335, 360, 361

Pierrot, stock type in *comédie italienne*, 294-295

Piissimi, V., ' Vittoria,' 305, 306, 307, 311-312, 315-316

Pilastri, F. de, ' Leandro,' 235, 307, 311, 312, 320

Pilos, or peaked cap, 54, 57, 60, 88, 161, 293

Pintor, F., 173

Pisa, actors in, 307, 310, 322

Piscator, 112

Piscatores, 68

Pistoia, actors in, 312

Pithon, 8, 40

Platea, significance of, in medieval staging, 195

Plato, 37

Plato, writer of comedies, 25, 31

Plautus, 25, 29, 51, 69, 70, 111, 112, 169, 170, 175, 232

Plutarch, 25, 26, 34, 86, 97, 120, 122, 128, 129

Poccetti, B., 252

Polichinelle—*see* Pulcinella, stock type in *commedia dell' arte*

Political satire, in Atellan farce, 75-76; in mime, 124-126, 148; in *commedia dell' arte*, 348

Pollard, A. W., 178, 182

Pollux, 28, 29

Pompeii, 77, 100, 109

Pomponius, 66, 68-69, 71, 73, 77

Ponti, D., ' Lavinia,' 241-242, 311, 322, 324

Poppelreuter, J., 20

Porbus, F. and P., 270, 271, 345

Porcacchi, T., 256, 278, 305

Porphyrius, mimic actor, 95, 121, 122, 130

Postumio, Il, 241, 322

Potheinos, Greek puppet-showman, 37

Pots of Pulse, The, 40

Præfectus morum, 68

Præsepe in Catholic churches, 176

Prague, 334

Preston, K., 131

Préville, French actor, 286, 287

Prigioni, Li, 229

Private theatres in classical times, 77, 108-109

Privilège aux Bretons, Le, 171

Procopius, 98, 142

Prodromus, 99, 166

Professionalism and the mime, 36

Profondavalle, V., 312

Prologues in *commedia dell' arte*, 219

Promptorium Parvolorum, 152

Prophets sermon, influence of, on liturgical drama, 177, 211

Protevangelium of James, 184
Protogenes, mimic actor, 95
Prou, V., 37
Proverbs in early drama, 41
Prudentius, 122
Prudenza, 307
Prynne, J., 136, 139
Psellos, Michael, 159
Pseudolus, 29
Ptolemæus Philadelphus, 49
Publilius Syrus, writer of mimes, 83, 110, 111, 112, 115, 126
Pulcinella, stock type in *commedia dell' arte*, 70, 88, 163, 219, 220, 225, 251, 290–295, 326
Punch—*see* Pulcinella
Punch and Judy shows, 167, 262, 293
Puns, in Epicharmus, 77; in Atellan farce, 77; in Roman mime, 112, 125, 126
Puppets, in ancient Greece, 37; in medieval times, 165–166, 167; representing *commedia dell' arte* types, 255, 256, 258, 262
Putatores, 115
Pylades, pantomimic actor, 132, 133, 134
Pyrra, 40
Pythagoras, 126
Python, 51

QUADRIO, F. S., 241, 256, 259, 263, 322
Quatres offices de l'hôtel du roi, Les, 173
Quem queritis, 176
Querolus, 169, 170, 171
Quillard, P., 41
Quintilian, 80, 83, 85, 126, 127, 128
Quirini, L., 240

RABER, V., 201
Racioppi, G., 292
Radiciotti, G., 216
Rajna, P., 158
Rambaud, A., 148
Ramponi, V.—*see* Andreini, V.
Ranieri, B., 'Aurelio,' 236, 328, 344
Raparelli, G., 'Orazio,' 338
Rapparini, 268, 290
Rasi, L., 216, 238, 240, 241, 242, 250, 251, 252, 257, 260, 261, 264, 268, 277, 278, 279, 283, 284, 285, 286, 287, 289, 290, 295, 298, 301, 303, 305, 307, 309, 310, 311, 312, 313, 314, 315, 316, 317, 318, 319, 320, 321, 322, 323, 326, 328, 329, 331, 332, 333, 334, 335, 336, 337, 338, 339, 340, 341, 343, 344, 351
Räuber, Die, 111, 121
Raynaud, G., 178, 268, 269
Re, E., 218, 226, 299, 300, 377, 378, 379
Re, M. dei, 'Zanini,' 264, 299
Rè, P. del, 'Mescolino,' 286
Reading, 207, 304
Realism, in classical mime, 58, 59, 81; in comic scenes of the mystery plays, 179–182; in *commedia dell' arte*, 229–230
Rébora, P., 347
Recueil Fossard, 243, 244, 253, 254, 256, 259, 264, 271, 272, 296, 297, 300, 307
Reggio, 311, 317, 341
Regina d'Inghilterra, La, 227, 233, 296
Regnard, 260, 281, 346
Reich, Hermann, 18, 25, 26, 27, 28, 31, 34, 35, 36, 37, 45, 46, 47, 66, 75, 76, 80, 83, 84, 87, 88, 90, 91, 92, 93, 94, 95, 96, 97, 99, 108, 112, 113, 114, 115, 120, 121, 123, 124, 126, 128, 129, 130, 131, 137, 138, 139, 140, 141, 142, 146, 148, 149, 151, 159, 160, 162, 165, 167, 177, 214–215, 263, 348
Reichold, C., 50

Reinach, A., 56
Remedadores, entertainers in Spain, 158
Renier, R., 151, 269
Representaçion del Naçimiento de Nueſtro Señor, 183
Reſtio, 112
Resurrection, The, 194, 197
Retour de la foire de Bezons, Le, 245, 281
Reuling, C., 175
Reveillont, 184
Revellers, The, 39
Reynolds, Frederick, 121
Reyval, A., 136
Rhinthon of Tarentum, writer of mimes, 51, 89
Ribbeck, O., 44, 84, 111
Ricci, B., 'Leandro,' 330, 332, 335
Ricci, C., 216, 273
Ricci, F., 'Pantalone,' 256, 328, 330, 331, 332, 333
Ricciolina, stock type in *commedia dell' arte*, 242–243
Riccoboni, A., 'Pantalone,' 256, 338, 339, 340, 341
Riccoboni, L., 'Federico' and 'Lelio,' 216, 217, 218, 219, 220, 236, 271, 287, 295
Richter, G. M. A., 48
Ricinium, garment used by mimic actors, 91
Rigal, E., 216
Righetti, G. P. de, 323
Rinaldi, C., 241
Rio, Alcade del, 165
Risoluti, troupe of Italian actors, 251, 293
Riſtelhuber, P., 41
Ritratto, Il, 228, 262, 294
Rivani, G., 331
Robert, C., 28, 29, 153
Robert, U., 179
Robert II of Sicily, 162
Robin et Marion, 172
Rofia, G., 263
Rogantino, stock type in *commedia dell' arte*, 252
Roger II of Sicily, 148
Rogers, Archdeacon, 189
Rohde, E., 46
Roi avenir, Le, 188
Rolland, J., 172
Romagnesi, C. V., 'Leandro,' 345, 346
Romagnesi, M., 'Cintio' and 'Dottore,' 242, 260, 343, 344, 345, 346
Romagnesi, M. A., 'Pantalone,' 317–320
Romagnesi, N., 'Orazio,' 242, 343
Romagnoli, E., 115
Romanus I, Emperor, 148
Rome, actors in, 19, 67, 77, 263, 299, 300, 312, 322, 324, 325, 330, 333, 335, 336, 341; Museo Nazionale, 105
Romeo and Juliet, 347
Roncagli, S., 'Franceschina,' 244, 307
Rope-walkers in classical Rome, 84
Roque, J. de la, 237
Roques, M., 172
Rosa, R., 'Pantalone,' 341
Rose, H. J., 41
Rosenthal, V., 89
Roskoff, G. G., 190
Rossetti, G. B., 310
Rossi, B., 'Orazio,' 316
Rossi, D. de', 300
Rossi, G., 269
Rossi, G. P. dei, 'Ciambellotto,' 299
Rossi, N., 263
Rossi, O., 240
Rossi, S. C. V., 378

Rossi, V., 158, 216, 299
Rotari, B., 330
Rotari, V., ' Lidia,' 235, 325, 330, 331-334
Rothschild, Baron James de, 178
Rouanet, L., 173
Rouen, 184, 195
Roy, É., 170, 178, 179
Rubel, H. F., 152
Rudens, 70, 115
Rudwin, M. J., 178, 187
Rueff, H., 178, 186, 195
Ruelens, C., 313, 361
Rühlemann, M., 268
Ruof, J., 190, 191, 192, 200
Rustic, comic figure of, in Epicharmus, 39; in Phlyax, 61; in Atellan farce, 72, 77; in *commedia dell' arte*, 265
Rusticellius, pantomimic actor, 131
Rutebeuf, 172
Ruvo, 52, 59, 60
Ruzzante, 215, 277, 298, 299
Ryer, I. du, 237

SABIANUS, 138
Sacchi, M., ' Armellina,' 341
Sacco, G., ' Coviello,' 261, 340, 341
Sachier, H., 168
Sack of Troy, The, 45
Saint-Bernard de Meuthon, 172
St Bride, 179
St Eustace, 179
St George plays, 26
St Helena, 179
St Just, 200
St Katherine, 179
St Meriasek, 179, 186, 194, 202
St Vincent, 197
Ste Geneviève, 188
Saisset, L. and F., 246, 250
Salamona, A., 316
Salimbeni, G., ' Zanobio,' 262, 307, 312
Salinator, 112
Salvianus, 138, 141
Salzburg, 256; Studien-Bibliothek, 150, 163, 190, 206, 207
Samaran, C., 172
S. Antonio, 233
S. Onofrio, 233
S. Tommaso, 187
Sand, M., 214, 215, 216, 262, 263, 283, 295
Sanesi, I., 173, 215, 216, 264, 268, 291, 292
Sangiorgi, C., ' Trivellino,' 278
Sannio, mimic fool type, 88-89, 141, 215, 263-264
Sanniones, 89
Sansovino, F., 217
Santia, variant of Xanthias, 65
Sarmentus, Roman entertainer, 74
Sassuolo, 340
Sathas, 159, 210
Saturnalia, 19
Saturnalia (Laberius), 112
Saturnus senex, 123
Satyre of the Thrie Estaitis, Ane, 173
Satyric drama, 66
Satyrs, attendant on Dionysus, 22
Sausage, The, 40
Saviotti, A., 317, 320, 325
Savorini, G., ' Dottore,' 260, 341
Saxo Grammaticus, 168

Scala, F., ' Flavio,' 235, 237, 317-320, 322, 331, 377
Scapino, stock type in *commedia dell' arte*, 260, 285
Scaramuccia, stock type in *commedia dell' arte*, 252, 287-280
Scarpetta, G., 322
Scenarii of the *commedia dell' arte*, 225-229
Scevola, Senese, 300
Schanz, M., 66, 68, 69, 111, 112
Scherer, W., 175
Scherillo, M., 72, 216, 263, 290, 291
Schiavi, C., ' Cintio,' 339
Schiller, F., 111, 120
Schippke, A., 66
Schmidt, L., 38
Schmidt, W., 37
Schnabel, H., 20, 33, 34
Schönemann, O., 176
Schoolmaster, The, 42, 43
Schröder, T., 346
Schröer, K. J., 178
Schultz, A., 167
Schumacher, F., 170, 195
Schwietering, J., 176
Scop, 135
Scotivelli, A., 308
Scoto of Mantua, 346
Scurra, name of buffoon, 94
Sea Voyage, The, 118, 120, 124
Secchi, M. de, ' Aurelio,' 318, 331
Secchi, N. de, ' Nespola,' 317-320
Secondary parts in the mime, 87, 121
Secrets, medieval scenic effects, 206-207
Sedulius, 169
Segesta, 101
Segrè, A., 216
Semur, *Passion* of, 172
Seneca, 71, 82, 83, 87, 90, 91, 105, 115, 120, 124, 126, 127, 157, 208
Senigaglia, G., 246, 250
Septet, M., 176, 177
Sepulchre, use of, in liturgical drama, 194
Serdon, entertainer, 35
Sermons joyeux, 173
Serra, R., 269
Servilli, I., Italian actress, 339
Servus fugitivus, 110
Sessa, G. B., 241
Setti, G., 41
Severianus, Bishop, 121
Sforza, G., 221
Shakespeare, W., 38-39, 121, 160, 221, 223, 253, 289, 346-347
Sherley, Sir Anthony, 279, 280
Shoemaker, The, 42, 43
Sicily, 38
Sicyon, comic entertainments in, 26
Sidonius Apollinaris, 36
Simodia, 34
Simone da Bologna, ' Zanni,' 278, 305, 307
Simus of Magnesia, 34
Simus, satyr, 34
Siparium, curtain used in mimes, 99, 100, 105-106, 107, 108, 209, 211
Sirens, The, 40
Sisebuto, King of Spain, 145
Sisyphus, 68
Sisyphus Fugitive, 68
Sisyphus Roller of Rocks, 68
Sittl, K., 66, 69, 70, 72, 73
Skiron, 40
Skymnus of Tarentum, entertainer, 35

Smeraldina, stock type in *comédie italienne*, 245
Smith, A. M., 206
Smith, C., 31
Smith, L. T., 178
Smith, W., 216, 308, 327, 331, 346, 347, 348, 361, 371, 375, 378
Soldino, Aniello, 'Dottor Spacca Strummolo,' 259, 328
Soldato in Candia, Il, 231
Soldino, 300
Sole, Il, 261
Solerti, A., 216, 263, 300, 302, 303, 304, 305, 306, 307, 309, 311, 312, 315, 316, 323, 325, 326
Sommerbrodt, J., 33, 50
Sondheimer, I., 176
Sontra, G., 'Flaminio,' 341
Sophistai, 26, 27
Sophocles, 68
Sophron, writer of mimes, 37, 39, 42, 45, 76, 80, 140
Sorbelli, A., 273
Sorix, *archimimus*, 85
Sorredus Valerianus, pantomimic actor, 132
Sosibius, 25
Sotades, writer of mimes, 50, 76, 139, 210
Sottie nouvelle nomée la Folie des Gorriers, 173
Sotties, medieval, 173
Spain, performances in, 158; medieval interludes in, 173
Spanish features in Capitano, 246–247
Sparta, comedy in, 26, 28
Spengel, M. A., 115
Sphinx, The, 40
Sponsa Pappi, 73
Spooner, W. A., 95
Springer, A., 206
Staging, for mimes of Herodas, 44; for Phlyax mimes, 63–64; for Atellan farces, 77; for Roman mimes, 99–109; for medieval religious plays, 194–212
Stecher, J. A., 203
Stefano, 299
Stephanos the Sabbaite, 147
Sterzing, 191
Stiefel, A. L., 347, 369
Stock types, in Herodas, 43–44; in Phlyax, 60–62; in Atellan farce, 69–72; in medieval drama, 179–187; in *commedia dell' arte*, 233 ff.
Stokes, W., 179, 189, 207
Stoppato, L., 72, 73, 92, 165, 186, 214, 216, 233, 246
Strabo, 67
Strasbourg, Musée des Beaux-Arts, 273, 329
Stratonicea, 62
Strobl, J., 178
Strozzi, G., 343
Strutt, J., 165
Stuart, D. C., 195, 205
Studer, P., 179
Stumpfl, R., 115, 195
Stupidus, name of a fool in the mime, 87, 158
Sudhaus, S., 46, 80, 118
Suetonius, 66, 75, 76, 77, 82, 84, 98, 105, 106, 108, 110, 111, 122, 125, 129, 132, 133, 134
Suidas, 45, 50, 113, 114
Sulla, L. Cornelius, 69, 86
Susanna, 210
Susarion of Icara, reputed author of mimes, 45
Symeon Metaphrastes, 97
Synesius, 47, 87
Syracuse, comic entertainments in, 26, 38, 44, 45, 50, 51; Museum, 61
Syri, 68
Syria, centre of mimic activity, 83, 94

TABARINO, 343
Tacitus, 76, 95, 134
Taming of the Shrew, The, 347
Taormina, 96, 102–104
Tappeti, I, 229, 294
Tarantinos, 89
Taras, 56
Tarentum, home of the Phlyax, 24, 50, 51, 56, 57, 70
Tarraco, 110
Tarragona, Council of, 167
Tartaglia, stock type in *commedia dell' arte*, 295–296
Tasso, T., 237, 239
Taurus, 112
Taylor, G. C., 176
Taylor, J., 189
Teatro celeste, Il, 235
Tecla, La, 235
Tegernsee mystery play, 195, 200, 201
Tempest, The, 121, 228, 347
Terence, 25, 47, 50, 60, 126, 171, 215; medieval conceptions of performances of his plays, 152–158, 169, 170, 175, 208; influence of, 232
Terentius et Delusor, 171
Tertia, mimic actress, 95, 97, 129
Tertullian, 106, 110, 112, 122, 137, 138, 167
Terzaghi, N., 41
Teuber, P. V., 176
Teuffel, W., 51
Thalassia, mimic actress, 97
Thaleia, 210
Thaumatopoios, generic name for juggling entertainer, 35, 36
Theagenes, tyrant of Megara, 20
Thearoi (The Visitors to the Temple), 39
Thebes in Bœotia, comic entertainments in, 23, 26
Theocritus, 39, 42, 44–45, 46, 76, 82
Theodora, Empress, 85, 92, 98, 142, 223
Theodoric, Emperor, 98, 141, 142, 160
Theodorus, juggler, 35
Theodosius, Emperor, 92, 141, 143
Theophilus, Emperor, 148
Theophrastus, 81
Theophylaktos Simokattes, 210
Theopompos, writer of comedies, 27
Theoroi (The Spectators), 39
Thiele, G., 21, 27, 50
Thirties, The, 40
Thomas, P., 51
Thomas Aquinas, 168
Thomas de Chabham, 152, 168
Thymele, mimic actress, 95, 97, 119, 133
Tiberius, Emperor, 76, 110, 113, 129, 134
Tiepolo, D., 89
Timgad, 106
Tischbein, W., 74
Toldo, P., 159, 172, 273, 346, 378, 379
Tommaso, M. di, 'Lepido,' 298
Tonelli, L., 216
Tonti, A., 'Pulcinella,' 293
Torelli, G., 343
Torre, A. della, 264
Torri, A., 'Lavinia,' 340
Torri, A., 'Lelio,' 336, 340
Torri, G. C., 'Zaccagnino,' 336
Torri, L., 151
Tortoriti, A., 'Marinetta,' 345, 346
Tortoriti, G., 'Pasquariello,' 339, 340, 344, 346
Tournai, 172

INDEX

Tournois de Chauvenci, 158
Tours, Synod of, 147
Tower of Danaë, The, 122
Towneley cycle of mystery plays, 178, 180, 181, 182, 185, 188, 195, 203
Toynbee, P., 268
Tracagnino, stock type in *commedia dell' arte*, 277, 278
Tragedy, significance of word in the Middle Ages, 177
Trajan, Emperor, 134
Tralles, 61
Trapolaria, La, 260
Trappola, stock type in *commedia dell' arte*, 249–250, 296
Trappolin suppos'd a Prince, 347
Trappolino, stock type in *commedia dell' arte*, 296
Trastullo, stock type in *commedia dell' arte*, 305
Trausnitz, Schloss, 254
Trautmann, K., 301
Travail, Jakke, actor, 194
Travailes of the Three English Brothers, The, 279–280
Tre Becchi, I, 229
Tre Gravide, Le, 229, 261
Tre Matti, I, 229
Tre Principi di Salerno, I, 227
Trebellius, 83
Tretise of Miraclis Pleyinge, A, 168
Treves, E., 363
Treveth, 208
Trezzi, G. B., 'Pasquino,' 340
Tribunus voluptatum, 98, 141
Tricæ in Atellan farce, 76
Trivellino, stock type in *commedia dell' arte*, 277–278, 283
Troades, 133
Troiano, Massimo, 226, 254, 256, 263, 377
Trojans, The, 40
Tropes, 176
Troy, F. de, 286
Truffaldino, stock type in *commedia dell' arte*, 277, 279
Turin, actors in, 311, 313, 321, 324, 331, 332, 341
Turlupin, stock type in *commedia dell' arte*, 249, 314
Turri, G. B., 'Pantalone,' 335, 343
Tutor, mimic actor, 95
Twelfth Night, 263
Tzetzes, 113

UNITI, troupe of Italian actors, 235, 241, 244, 251, 256, 259, 278, 297, 307, 309, 310–314, 316, 320, 326
Urbicus, actor in Atellan farce, 67
Uscite used in *commedia dell' arte*, 218–219, 234
Utrecht, 70

VACANTIELLO, F., 'Cola,' 261, 324
Vaccaria, La, 277
Vahlen, J., 51
Valenciennes, mystery play at, 178, 195, 196, 205, 206
Valens, mimic actor, 95
Valeri, A., 310, 312, 323, 326, 328, 361, 366, 377, 378
Valerini, A., 'Aurelio,' 234–235, 240, 259, 301, 303, 307
Valerius, writer of Atellan farce, 69
Valerius Maximus, 92, 107, 123
Valois, Marguerite de, 271
Vannini, G. B., 'Zanni,' 315
Vannozzo, Francesco di, 291
Varchi, B., 263
Varro, 70, 73, 77, 133
Vattasso, M., 178
Vedova costante, La, 229
Vega, Lope de, 305

Velleius Paterculus, 68, 77
Venice, actors in, 217, 299, 304, 305, 306, 307, 309, 310, 315, 320, 321, 326, 328, 331, 332, 333, 335, 337, 338, 341; Pinacoteca Querini, 222, 223; Museo Civico, 254, 255, 256, 262, 274, 275, 277
Ventura, B., 'Pantalone,' 338
Venturini, V., 246
Venus and Adonis, 122
Vergil, 74, 123, 133
Verona, 108, 291, 292, 312, 315, 323, 331, 332, 334, 337, 341
Verres, 129
Verucci, V., 290
Verus, Emperor, 83, 94, 125
Vespasian, Emperor, 86
Vestamigli, G. A., 242
Vicentio, Tarasso, 300
Vicenza, 334, 335, 341
Victor, Bishop, 86
Vienna, 297, 334; Kunsthistorisches Museum, 247
Villari, P., 263
Vincentio, 299
Visconti, Galeazzo, 165
Vitalis, mimic actor, 95, 119
Vitalis of Blois, 169
Vitalis, Ordericus, 268, 269
Vitti, A., 216
Vittorello de l'hosta, 299
Viziani, F., 298
Voelker, C., 136
Vogt, S., 178
Vollhardt, W., 346
Volumnius Eutrapelus, 96
Vows and Sacrifices of the Women to Asklepius, The, 42, 43

WACE, A. J. B. 26, 47
Wackernell, J. E., 178
Waddell, H., 166
Wageningen, I. van, 153
Walters H. B., 50
Ward, A. W., 270
Warnecke, B., 115
Wasps, 27, 31
Wat, Joly, actor, 194
Waterhouse, O., 178
Watson, J. C., 153
Watteau, J., 286, 308, 350
Wattenbach, W., 169
Watzinger, C., 46
Weaver, J., 80
Weaver, R. T., 71
Weber, P., 206
Wechssler, E., 176
Wedding of Hebe, The, 39
Weege, F., 33
Weihnachtsspiele 178
Weil, H., 41, 46
Weinhold, C., 175, 178
Weinhold, K., 188
Wennergren, Mme, 345
Wesselofsky, A., 268
Wessely, J. E., 187
Wessner, P., 84, 99
Weston, K. E., 153
Wickham, E. C., 68
Wieck, H., 187
Wiener, L., 28
Wilamowitz-Moellendorff, U. von, 20, 45, 82
Wilczck, Count Dr Hans, 190

Wilmotte, M., 176, 180
Wilthemius, A., 144
Windows used in Phlyax stage, 64
Windsor, 304
Winter's Tale, The, 347
Winterfeld, P. von, 210
Withington, R., 203
Witkowski, J., 26, 92
Wolff, M. J., 347
Wölfflin, E., 115
Women at Breakfast, The, 42
Women Confederates, The, 42
Worms, 70
Wright, T., 170
Wünsch, R., 67
Würzburg University, 22

Xanthias, name of comic slave, 27, 51, 57, 61
Xanthippe and Polyxena, 108
Xenarchus, writer of mimes, 45
Xenophon, 37, 167
Xenophon, entertainer, 35

Yeames, A. H. S., 47
York cycle of mystery plays, 178, 180, 183, 185, 186, 193, 194, 206
Young, K., 174, 176

Zachary, Pope, 146
Zagnoli, C., 'Finocchio,' 340, 341
Zan Polo, 293
Zanardi, M., 'Dottor Graziano,' 326
Zanetti, M. A., 'Truffaldino,' 277, 340, 341
Zanni, stock type in *commedia dell' arte,* 224, 232, 254, 263–297
Zanobio da Piombino, stock type in *commedia dell' arte,* 262
Zanotti, G. A., 'Ottavio,' 336, 337, 338, 343
Zanotti, P., 331
Zbrazin, F., 'Gabinetto,' 335
Zecca, N., 'Bertolino,' 335, 336, 338
Zelotypos, 42
Zelotypos, comic type, 42, 43, 97, 118; reproduced in Byzantine drama, 211
Zenari, A., 'Dottore,' 259, 312
Zenatti, A., 378
Zerbini, E., 264
Zeus as a comic figure, 51, 54, 55, 122
Ziegler, 110
Zieliński, T., 20, 66
Zito, B., 'Dottore,' 259
Zonaras, 146, 159
Zuandomengo, 299
Zuane da Treviso, 299
Zuccaro F., 324